W9-ANF-560

Financial and Accounting Guide for Not-for-Profit Organizations

NONPROFIT LAW, FINANCE, AND MANAGEMENT SERIES

Financial and Accounting Guide for Not-for-Profit Organizations

Fifth Edition

Malvern J. Gross, Jr., CPA
Retired Partner, Price Waterhouse LLP

Richard F. Larkin, CPA
Director, Price Waterhouse LLP

Roger S. Bruttomesso, CPA
Chairman, Price Waterhouse LLP

John J. McNally, CPA
Vice-Chairman, Price Waterhouse LLP

John Wiley & Sons, Inc.

New York • Chichester • Brisbane • Toronto • Singapore

This text is printed on acid-free paper.

Copyright © 1995 by John Wiley & Sons, Inc.

All rights reserved. Published simultaneously in Canada.

Reproduction or translation of any part of this work beyond
that permitted by Section 107 or 108 of the 1976 United
States Copyright Act without the permission of the copyright
owner is unlawful. Requests for permission or further
information should be addressed to the Permissions Department,
John Wiley & Sons, Inc., 605 Third Avenue, New York, NY
10158-0012.

This publication is designed to provide accurate and
authoritative information in regard to the subject
matter covered. It is sold with the understanding that
the publisher is not engaged in rendering legal, accounting,
or other professional services. If legal advice or other
expert assistance is required, the services of a competent
professional person should be sought.

Library of Congress Cataloging in Publication Data:

Gross, Malvern J.
    Financial and accounting guide for not-for-profit organizations /
Malvern J. Gross, Richard F. Larkin. — 5th ed.
        p.   cm. — (Nonprofit law, finance, and management series)
    Includes bibliographical references and index.
    ISBN 0-471-10474-4 (alk. paper)
    1. Nonprofit organizations—Accounting.   I. Larkin, Richard F.
II. Title.   III. Series.
HF5686.N56G76   1995
657'.98—dc20   94-33767

Printed in the United States of America

10 9 8 7 6 5 4 3 2

To the millions of volunteers
who make the not-for-profit sector
and all of its achievements possible

SUBSCRIPTION NOTICE

This Wiley product is updated on a periodic basis with supplements to reflect important changes in the subject matter. If you purchased this product directly from John Wiley & Sons, Inc., we have already recorded your subscription for this update service.

If, however, you purchased this product from a bookstore and wish to receive (1) the current update at no additional charge, and (2) future updates and revised or related volumes billed separately with a 30-day examination review, please send your name, company name (if applicable), address, and the title of the product to:

Supplement Department
John Wiley & Sons, Inc.
One Wiley Drive
Somerset, NJ 08875
1-800-225-5945

For customers outside the United States, please contact the Wiley office nearest you:

Professional & Reference Division
John Wiley & Sons Canada, Ltd.
22 Worcester Road
Rexdale, Ontario M9W 1L1
(416) 675-3580
1-800-567-4797
FAX (416) 675-6599

John Wiley & Sons, Ltd.
Baffins Lane
Chichester
West Sussex, PO19 1UD
UNITED KINGDOM
(44) (243) 779777

Jacaranda Wiley Ltd.
PRT Division
P.O. Box 174
North Ryde, NSW 2113
AUSTRALIA
(02) 805-1100
FAX (02) 805-1597

John Wiley & Sons (SEA) Pte. Ltd.
37 Jalan Pemimpin
Block B # 05-04
Union Industrial Building
SINGAPORE 2057
(65) 258-1157

About the Authors

Malvern J. Gross, Jr. is a retired partner of Price Waterhouse and a nationally recognized authority on accounting and financial reporting for not-for-profit organizations. He was chairman of the AICPA Subcommittee on Nonprofit Organizations that wrote the 1978 landmark Statement of Position for Certain Nonprofit Organizations, and of the Accounting Advisory Committee to the Commission on Private Philanthropy and Public Needs. He was a member of the committee that wrote the second edition of *Standards of Accounting and Financial Reporting for Voluntary Health and Welfare Organizations,* and a co-author of the *Museum Accounting Handbook.* He served as an advisor to the Financial Accounting Standards Board in the early phases of its work on setting accounting standards for not-for-profit organizations, and to the New York State Charities Registration Office, as well as an adjunct professor of accounting at Lehigh University, his alma mater. After retirement from Price Waterhouse, he was president of a not-for-profit organization, the National Aeronautics Association. He now lives in the San Juan Islands off of the state of Washington.

Richard F. Larkin is technical director of the Not-for-Profit Industry Services Group in the national office of Price Waterhouse. He is a certified public accountant with over twenty-five years of experience serving not-for-profit organizations as independent accountant, board member, treasurer, and consultant. He teaches, speaks, and writes extensively on not-for-profit industry matters and is active in many professional and industry organizations. He is a member of the Financial Accounting Standards Board Not-for-Profit Advisory Task Force, and chaired the AICPA Not-for-Profit Audit Guide Task Force. He participated in writing both the third and fourth editions of *Standards of Accounting and Financial Reporting for Voluntary Health and Welfare Organizations* and in the chapter on Not-for-Profit Organizations in the seventh edition of the *Accountants' Handbook.* He graduated from Harvard College and has an MBA from Harvard Business School.

Roger S. Bruttomesso is chairman of the Price Waterhouse LLP Not-for-Profit Industry Services Group and also serves as engagement partner on many of the firm's not-for-profit clients in the Metro New York region. He has over thirty years of experience serving the industry both professionally and as a volunteer. He is presently a member of the AICPA Not-for-Profit Organizations Committee and is on the Board of the Nonprofit Coordinating Committee of New York City. He has spoken extensively on governance and accountability issues confronting not-for-profit organization boards. He is a certified public accountant and a graduate of Dartmouth College, with an MBA from its Amos Tuck School of Business Administration.

John J. McNally is vice-chairman of the Not-for-Profit Industry Services Group and is located in the Washington, DC office of Price Waterhouse LLP. He has extensive experience in serving not-for-profit organizations as an auditor, consultant, and as a board member. He has represented Price Waterhouse in the business and not-for-profit communities for over thirty years. He currently serves as a member of a number of not-for-profit boards including the Hugh O'Brian Youth Foundation. He is also a member of the President's Advisory Board of LaSalle University, his alma mater.

Preface

This book, like its predecessors, has many objectives. Two major objectives are to help the not-for-profit organization better communicate its financial activities and financial condition to its members and to the public, and to better manage its financial resources. The book is also intended to aid those in leadership positions in such organizations in fully understanding the annual financial reports issued by their organization, thereby assisting them in making more informed judgments. For the treasurer and chief executive of the eleemosynary institution, as well as for the professional accountant, this book provides a wide range of practical and professional guidance.

The most significant change in the Fifth Edition is complete coverage of the two recently issued accounting and reporting standards for not-for-profit organizations: Statements of Financial Accounting Standards No. 116, *Accounting for Contributions Received and Contributions Made,* and No. 117, *Financial Statements of Not-for-Profit Organizations.* These two statements reflect the most significant changes in accounting and financial reporting standards which have ever been, and probably ever will be, issued affecting not-for-profit organizations. Almost every organization will find its accounting methods and reporting formats changed, at least somewhat, by these standards. As a member of the Not-for-Profit Advisory Task Force of the Financial Accounting Standards Board, which issued the new standards, one of the authors brings to this book his firsthand knowledge and intimate familiarity with both the language of these standards and their implications for affected organizations.

This edition also contains a comprehensive discussion of the AICPA Statement of Position applicable to all not-for-profit organizations not covered by one of the earlier-issued AICPA Audit Guides. As chairman of the committee that conceived and drafted this document, one of the authors was privileged to directly participate in this endeavor, which facilitated establishment of generally accepted accounting principles and reporting practices for the not-for-profit sector. The accounting principles and reporting practices presented in the Statement of Position are carefully analyzed and annotated with meaningful interpretive commentary. This discussion will be of particular value to the professional accountant.

The AICPA Statement of Position, in concert with AICPA Audit Guides for colleges and universities, health care providers, and voluntary health and welfare organizations, and the two FASB standards noted earlier, prescribe accounting principles and reporting practices applicable to virtually every type of not-for-profit organization. We take particular satisfaction in the knowledge that earlier editions of this book suggested many of the accounting principles and reporting practices that appear in these AICPA and FASB pronouncements on not-for-profit accounting.

Throughout the text, based on the extensive experience of the authors with the operations of not-for-profit organizations, innovative suggestions are offered. For example, we have long recommended that all legally unrestricted funds be reported as a single fund rather than as a series of separate funds, as an aid to the unsophisticated reader or constituent in comprehending the entire financial picture of an organization. A distinction is made between recording unrestricted board-designated endowment funds separately for bookkeeping purposes, and reporting them in a single unrestricted fund, now, class, in public statements.

The book continues to provide detailed help on tax form preparation, and systematically presents compliance requirements for each state, as well as a description of reporting rules applicable to recipients of government grants. In addition, it offers several chapters of procedural advice for the smaller organization that includes guidelines for setting up and keeping the books, maintaining proper internal controls, developing and presenting a meaningful budget, and dealing with the mechanics of pooled investments.

Grateful acknowledgment is due to many people for their assistance in the preparation of this Fifth Edition. While responsibility for the opinions and conclusions expressed are solely the authors', sincere thanks are expressed for the generous help of their Price Waterhouse associates, particularly Edward Chait, Stanley Corfman, Karen Dingfelder, Carl Duyck, Martha Garner, Joyce Nugent, and Charles Valadez.

MALVERN J. GROSS, JR.
RICHARD F. LARKIN
ROGER S. BRUTTOMESSO
JOHN J. MCNALLY

Washington, DC
November, 1994

Contents

Responsibilities of Treasurers and Chief Executive Officers

Not-for-profit organizations are among the most influential and powerful institutions in our free society. They range in size from small, local organizations to large national and international ones. Their scope covers almost every activity imaginable—health and welfare, research, education, religion, social organizations, and professional associations. They include foundations, membership societies, churches, hospitals, colleges, and political organizations. A 1990 study of the not-for-profit sector by Independent Sector, a support and advocacy organization for not-for-profits, estimated that there were, at that time, 1.4 million not-for-profit organizations in the United States, that their share of national income was 6.8 percent ($289 billion), and that they employed 10.4 percent of the national workforce (14.4 million paid and volunteer workers).

Typically, these organizations are controlled by boards of directors composed of leading citizens who volunteer their time. Where the organization is large enough, or complex enough in operation to require it, the board may delegate limited or broad operating responsibility to a part-time or full-time paid executive, who may be given any one of many alternative titles—executive secretary, administrator, manager, etc. Regardless of size, the board will usually appoint one of its own part-time volunteer members as treasurer; in most cases, the treasurer is second in importance only to the chairperson of the board because the organization's programs revolve around finances. While not always responsible for raising contributions, the treasurer is charged with stewardship of these resources and with the responsibility of anticipating problems and difficulties.

The treasurer is usually a businessperson who is extremely active in both professional and community affairs and so has only a limited amount of time to devote to the organization. Where there is a paid executive, many of the operating duties and responsibilities of the treasurer can be delegated to this executive and, in large organizations, through this executive to a chief accountant or business manager. However, in small organizations there may be no chief executive to delegate to, and in the following pages this will be assumed to be the case, both because small not-for-profit organizations predominate, and because it simplifies the presentation. It will further be assumed that the treasurer is not an accountant and doesn't want to become one, but at the same time recognizes the need to understand something about the principles of not-for-profit accounting and, more important, financial reporting.

The treasurer has significant responsibilities, including the following:

1. Keeping financial records.
2. Preparing accurate and meaningful financial statements.
3. Budgeting and anticipating financial problems.
4. Safeguarding and managing the organization's financial assets.
5. Complying with federal and state reporting requirements.

While this list certainly is not all-inclusive, most of the financial problems the treasurer will face are associated with these five major areas.

1.1   KEEPING FINANCIAL RECORDS

The treasurer is charged with seeing that the organization's financial records are maintained in an appropriate manner. If the organization is very small, the treasurer will keep the records, probably in a very simple and straightforward manner. If the organization is somewhat larger, a part-time employee—perhaps a secretary—may, among other duties, keep simple records. If the organization is still larger, there may be a full-time bookkeeper, or perhaps even a full-time accounting staff reporting to the chief executive and responsible for keeping the records of the organization. Regardless of size, the ultimate responsibility for seeing that adequate and complete financial records are kept is clearly that of the treasurer. This means that to some extent the treasurer must know what is involved in elementary bookkeeping and accounting, although not at the level of a bookkeeper or a CPA. Bookkeeping and accounting are largely matters of common sense and with the guidance provided in this book there should be no difficulty in understanding basic procedures and requirements.

The important thing to emphasize is that the treasurer is responsible for seeing that reliable records are kept. The detailed procedures to be followed may be delegated to others but it is up to the treasurer to see that the procedures are being followed and that the records are reasonably accurate. This is emphasized because frequently in large organizations the treasurer feels somewhat at a disadvantage being a volunteer with relatively few hours to spend and not an experienced accountant. The bookkeeping staff on the other hand is full-time and presumably competent. There is a natural reluctance for the treasurer to ask questions and to look at the detailed records, to be satisfied that sound bookkeeping procedures are being followed. Yet the responsibility is the treasurer's, and questioning and probing are necessary to ensure that the record-keeping function is being competently performed.

1.2 PREPARING ACCURATE AND MEANINGFUL FINANCIAL STATEMENTS

One of the most important responsibilities of the treasurer is to see that complete and straightforward financial reports are prepared for the board and membership, to tell clearly what has happened during the period. To be meaningful, these statements should have the following characteristics:

1. They should be easily comprehensible so that any person taking the time to study them will understand the financial picture. This characteristic is the one most frequently absent.
2. They should be concise so that the person studying them will not get lost in detail.
3. They should be all-inclusive in scope and should embrace all activities of the organization. If there are two or three funds, the statements should clearly show the relationship between the funds without a lot of confusing detail involving transfers and appropriations.

4. They should have a focal point for comparison so that the person reading them will have some basis for making a judgment. In most instances, this will be a comparison with a budget, or figures from the corresponding period of the previous year.

5. They should be prepared on a timely basis. The longer the delay after the end of the period, the longer the period before any necessary corrective action can be taken.

These statements must represent straightforward and candid reporting—that is, the statements must show exactly what has happened. This means that income or assets should not be arbitrarily buried in some subsidiary fund or activity in such a way that the reader is not likely to be aware that the income or assets have been received. It means that if the organization has a number of "funds," the total income and expenses of all funds should be shown in the financial statements in such a manner that no one has to wonder whether all of the activities for the period are included. In short, the statements have to communicate accurately and clearly what has happened. If the statement format is confusing and the reader doesn't understand what it is trying to communicate, then it is not accomplishing its principal objective.

The characteristics just listed would apply equally to the statements of almost any type of organization, including a business. Unfortunately, financial statements for not-for-profit organizations frequently fail to meet these characteristics. There are a number of reasons for this. Probably the most important is that the treasurer is doing the job on a part-time basis and does not have the time to develop a new format or set of statements. It is easier to continue with what has been done in the past. Also there is a marked reluctance on the part of non-accountants to make changes in statement format because they lack confidence in their abilities to tinker with the "mysteries" of accounting. Furthermore, at just about the time that the treasurer is really becoming conversant with the statements and could start to make meaningful changes, his or her term may expire.

(a) "Non-Accountant Test"

Since the purpose of any set of financial statements is to communicate to the reader, a good test of whether they accomplish this objective is the "non-accountant test." Can these statements be clearly understood by any interested non-accountant of average intelligence who is willing to take some time to study them? After studying them, will he or she have a good understanding of the overall financial activities for the year? If not, then the statements are not serving their purpose and should be revised and simplified until they do meet this test.

There are illustrations of all types of financial statements throughout this book, as well as suggestions on how to simplify financial statements to make them more readable. If these suggestions are followed, the statements should meet the "non-accountant test."

1.3 BUDGETING AND ANTICIPATING FINANCIAL PROBLEMS

Another major responsibility of the treasurer is to ensure that financial problems of the organization are anticipated so that the board or membership can take steps to solve these problems on a timely basis. A budget carefully prepared by management and the board is the principal tool that should be used. Budgets can take many different forms, from the very simple to the fairly complex, and all have as their primary objective the avoidance of the "unexpected." Budgets and budgeting techniques are discussed in some detail in Chapter 20.

But there is more to budgeting than merely anticipating the activities of the coming year. Budgeting in a very real sense represents planning ahead for several years in an effort to foresee social and economic trends and their influence on the organization's program. This means that the treasurer must be a forecaster of the future as well as a planner. In many organizations this is done in a very informal, almost intuitive manner; in others, this function is more formalized.

1.4 SAFEGUARDING AND MANAGING FINANCIAL ASSETS

Unless the organization is very small there will be a number of assets requiring safeguarding and, again, it is the responsibility of the treasurer to be sure that there are both adequate physical controls and accounting controls over these assets.

Physical controls involve making sure that the assets are protected against unauthorized use or theft, and seeing that adequate insurance is provided. Internal accounting controls involve division of duties and recordkeeping functions that will ensure control over these assets and adequate reporting of deviations from authorized procedures. Another function of internal control is to provide controls that will help remove undue temptation from the employees and volunteers of the organization. Chapters 23 and 24 offer guidance on these matters.

Another responsibility of the treasurer is to see that the organization's excess cash is properly invested to insure maximum financial return. One of the accounting techniques often followed by not-for-profit organizations is to combine cash from several funds and to make investments on a pooled basis. Chapter 25 discusses the technique of pooling of investments and discusses some of the physical safeguards that should be established.

1.5 COMPLYING WITH FEDERAL AND STATE REPORTING REQUIREMENTS

The treasurer and chief executive officer are also charged with complying with the various federal and state reporting requirements. Most larger tax-exempt organizations, other than churches, are required to file annual information returns with the Internal Revenue Service (IRS), and some are even required to pay federal taxes. In addition, certain organizations must register and file information returns with certain of the state governments even though they are not resident in the state. All of these requirements taken together pose a serious problem for a treasurer, who is usually not familiar with either the laws involved or the reporting forms used. Chapters 26, 27, and 28 discuss these requirements in some detail.

1.6 CONCLUSION

Few positions have more opportunity to influence institutions that affect society than that of the volunteer treasurer of a not-for-profit organization. In the past, many treasurers have struggled to perform their duties but have become mired in detail or lost in the intricacies of the apparently different accounting and financial principles applicable to not-for-profit organizations. One of the principal objectives of this book is to help the treasurers and chief executive officers of such organizations discharge their responsibilities in an effective manner with the least expenditure of time.

Key Financial Concepts

Accounting Distinctions between Not-for-Profit and Commercial Organizations

Many businesspersons, as well as many accountants, approach not-for-profit accounting with a certain amount of trepidation because of a lack of familiarity with such accounting. There is no real reason for this uneasiness because, except for a few troublesome areas, not-for-profit accounting follows many of the same principles followed by commercial enterprises. This chapter explores the principal differences and pinpoints the few troublesome areas.

2.1   STEWARDSHIP VERSUS PROFITABILITY

One of the principal differences between not-for-profit and commercial organizations is that they have different reasons for their existence. In oversimplified terms, it might be said that the ultimate objective of a commercial organization is to realize net profit for its owners through the provision of some product or performance of some service wanted by other people, whereas the ultimate objective of a not-for-profit organization is to meet some socially desirable need of the community or its members.

Like any organization (or individual), a not-for-profit organization should have sufficient resources to carry out its objectives. However there is no real need or justification for "making a profit" (having an excess of income over expenses for a year) or having an excess of assets over liabilities at the end of a year beyond that which is needed to provide a reasonable cushion or reserve against a rainy day or to be able to take advantage of an unexpected opportunity, should one of these situations occur. While a prudent board should plan to provide for the future, the principal objective of the board is to ensure fulfillment of the functions for which the organization was founded. A surplus or profit per se is only incidental.

Instead of profit, many not-for-profit organizations are concerned with the size of their cash balance. They can continue to exist only so long as they have sufficient cash to provide for their program. Thus the financial statements of not-for-profit organizations often emphasize the cash position. Commercial organizations are also very much concerned with cash, but if they are profitable they will probably be able to finance their cash needs through loans or from investors. Their principal concern is profitability and this means that commercial accounting emphasizes the matching of revenues and costs.

Not-for-profit organizations have a responsibility to account for funds that they have received. This responsibility includes accounting for certain specific funds that have been given for use in a particular project, as well as a general obligation to employ the organization's resources effectively. Emphasis, thus, is placed on accountability and stewardship. To the extent that the organization has received gifts restricted for a specific purpose, it may segregate those resources and report separately on their receipt and disposition. This separate accounting for restricted resources is called *fund accounting,* and is discussed in Chapter 4. As a result, the financial statements of not-for-profit organizations can often be voluminous and complex because each restricted fund grouping, as well as the unrestricted fund, may have its own set of financial statements.

The volume and intricacy of the statements often produce problems in terms of both meaningful disclosure, and comparability with the financial statements of commercial enterprises. The financial statements of commercial organizations are generally easy to understand, relative to those of not-for-profit organizations, because there is only a single set of statements, the terminology and format are usually standardized and familiar, and accounting principles are more clearly defined.

2.2 PRINCIPAL AREAS OF ACCOUNTING DIFFERENCES

There are five areas where the accounting principles followed by not-for-profit organizations often differ from the accounting principles followed by commercial organizations. While the accounting significance of these five areas should not be minimized, it is also important to note that once the significance of each is understood, the reader will have a good understanding of the major accounting principles followed by not-for-profit organizations. The principal remaining difficulty will then be designing financial statements that reflect these accounting distinctions and are straightforward and easy to understand. The five areas are discussed next.

(a)   Cash versus Accrual Accounting

In commercial organizations the records are almost always recorded on an accrual basis. The accrual basis simply means keeping your records so that in addition to recording transactions resulting from the receipt and disbursement of cash, you also record the amounts you owe others, and others owe you. In not-for-profit organizations, the cash basis of accounting is frequently used instead. Cash basis accounting means reflecting only transactions where cash has been involved. No attempt is made to record unpaid bills owed by you or amounts due you. Most small not-for-profit organizations use the cash basis, although many of the medium and larger organizations are now using the accrual basis.

The accrual basis usually gives a more accurate picture of an organization's financial condition than the cash basis. Why, then, is the cash basis frequently used by not-for-profit organizations? Principally because it is simpler to keep records on a cash basis than on an accrual basis. Everyone has had experience keeping a checkbook. This is cash basis accounting. A non-accountant can learn to keep a checkbook but is not likely to comprehend readily how to keep a double-entry set of books on the accrual basis. Furthermore, the cash basis is often used when the nature of the organization's activities is such that there are no material amounts owed to others, or vice versa, and so there is little significant difference between the cash and accrual basis.

Sometimes not-for-profit organizations follow a modified form of cash basis accounting where certain items are recorded on an accrual basis and certain items on a cash basis. Other organizations keep their records during the year on a cash basis, but at the end of the year convert to the accrual basis by recording obligations and receivables. The important thing is that the records kept are appropriate to the nature of the organization and its needs. Chapter 3 discusses cash and accrual accounting.

(b)   Fund Accounting

Although in commercial enterprises separate accounting for departments or branches is often done, fund accounting is a term that is not used by most businesspersons and can cause real difficulty. In fund accounting, amounts are segregated into categories according to the restrictions placed by donors and designations placed by the organization's governing board on their use. All completely unrestricted amounts are in one fund, all endowment funds in another, all building funds in a third, and so forth. Typically in reporting, an organization using fund accounting presents separate financial statements for each "fund." Fund accounting is widely used by not-for-profit organizations because it provides the ability to ensure compliance with legal restrictions and to report on the organization's stewardship of amounts entrusted to it by donors. While this concept of separate funds in itself is not particularly difficult, it does cause problems in presenting financial statements that are straightforward enough to be understood by most readers, that is, to pass the "non-accountant test." Chapter 4 is devoted to a discussion of fund accounting.

(c) Transfers and Appropriations

In not-for-profit organizations, transfers are frequently made between "funds." Unless carefully disclosed, such transfers tend to confuse the reader of the financial statements. Some organizations make "appropriations" for specific future projects (i.e., set aside a part of the fund balance for a designated purpose). Often these appropriations are shown, incorrectly, as an expense in arriving at the excess of income over expenses. This also tends to confuse. Transfers and appropriations are not accounting terms used by commercial enterprises. Each is discussed in Chapter 5.

(d) Treatment of Fixed Assets

In commercial enterprises, fixed assets are almost always recorded as assets on the balance sheet, and are depreciated over their expected useful lives. In not-for-profit accounting, fixed assets may or may not be recorded.

The handling of fixed assets, and depreciation, probably causes more difficulty and confusion than any other type of transaction because everyone seems to have a different idea about how fixed assets should be handled, and there is no single generally accepted principle or practice to follow. Some organizations "write off" or expense the asset when purchased; others record fixed assets purchased at cost and depreciate them over their estimated useful life in the same manner as commercial enterprises. Still others "write off" their fixed asset purchases, and then turn around and capitalize them on the Balance Sheet. Some depreciate; some do not. All of this presents the treasurer with the need for some practical suggestions as to when each approach is appropriate. Fixed asset accounting and depreciation are discussed in Chapters 6 and 7, respectively.

(e)   Contributions, Pledges, and Noncash Contributions

In commercial or business enterprises, there is no such thing as a "pledge." If the business is legally owed money, that amount is recorded as an account receivable. A pledge to a not-for-profit organization may or may not be legally enforceable, or even if technically enforceable, the organization may (for public relations reasons) have a policy of not taking legal action to attempt to enforce unpaid pledges. Some not-for-profit organizations record pledges because they know from experience that they will collect them. Others do not because they feel they have no legally enforceable claim. A related problem is where and how to report both restricted and unrestricted contributions in the financial statements. Contributions and pledges are discussed in Chapter 10.

Noncash contributions include donations of securities, equipment, supplies, and services of volunteers. Commercial enterprises seldom are recipients of such "income." When and at what values it is appropriate to record such noncash contributions is discussed in Chapter 10.

2.3   CONCLUSION

The five areas just discussed are the principal differences in accounting found between not-for-profit and commercial organizations. While each of these can cause real problems for the casual reader if the statements are not carefully prepared, there are only these five areas, and often not all of these differences will be present in any given organization. Part of the reason for these differences stems from the different objectives in not-for-profit and commercial organizations. In not-for-profit organizations, accountability for program activities and stewardship is the objective. In commercial organizations, the objective is to match revenue and costs to measure profitability. The treasurer familiar with commercial financial statements should have no difficulty preparing not-for-profit financial statements once the nature of each of these five areas of accounting differences is understood. If the objectives of financial statements are kept in mind, the treasurer should be able to prepare financial statements that meet the "non-accountant test" for clarity and effectiveness in communicating with their readers.

The new accounting and reporting standards discussed in Chapters 10 and 13 will require certain changes in how organizations handle the last four of these five areas.

CHAPTER 3

Cash versus Accrual
Basis Accounting

In Chapter 2 it was noted that although many of the medium and larger not-for-profit organizations are now keeping their records on an accrual basis, most smaller organizations still keep their records on the cash basis of accounting. The purpose of this chapter is to illustrate both bases of accounting and to discuss the advantages and disadvantages of each.

3.1 CASH AND ACCRUAL STATEMENTS ILLUSTRATED

Perhaps the easiest way to fully appreciate the differences between cash and accrual statements is to look at the financial statements of a not-for-profit organization prepared both ways. The Johanna M. Stanneck Foundation is a "private" foundation with assets of about $200,000. The income from these assets plus any current contributions to the foundation are used for medical scholarships to needy students. Exhibit 3–1 shows the two basic financial statements that, in one form or another, are used by nearly every profit and not-for-profit organization, namely, a Balance Sheet as of the end of a given period and a Statement of Income and Expenses for the period. Exhibit 3–1 shows these statements on both the cash basis and the accrual basis, side-by-side for ease of comparison. In actual practice, an organization would report on one or the other basis, and not both bases, as here.

As can be seen most easily from the Balance Sheet, a number of transactions not involving cash are reflected only on the accrual basis statements. These transactions are:

1. Uncollected dividends and accrued interest income at December 31, 19X2, of $3,550 is recorded as an asset on the Balance Sheet. Since there were also uncollected dividends and accrued interest income at December 31, 19X1, the effect on the accrual basis income as compared to the cash basis income is only the increase (or decrease) in the accrual at the end of the year. In this example, since the cash basis income from this source is shown as $8,953 and the accrual basis as $9,650, the increase during the year must have been the difference, or $697, and the amounts not accrued at December 31, 19X1, must have been $2,853.

2. An uncollected pledge at December 31, 19X2, of $2,000 is recorded as an asset on the Balance Sheet; and because there were no uncollected pledges at the end of the previous year, this whole amount shows up as increased income on an accrual basis.

3. Unpaid expenses of $1,354 at the end of the year are recorded as a liability on the accrual basis Balance Sheet, but on the accrual basis expense statements are partially offset by similar items unpaid at the end of the previous year.

4. The federal excise tax not yet paid on 19X2 net investment income is recorded as a liability and as an expense on the accrual basis. The $350 tax shown on the cash basis expenditure statement is the tax actually paid in 19X2 on 19X1 net investment income. (See Chapter 26 for a discussion of taxes as they affect private foundations.)

5. Unpaid scholarships granted during the year are recorded as an obligation. Most of these scholarships will be paid within the following year but one scholarship has been granted that extends into 19X4. As in the case of the other items just discussed, it is necessary to know the amount of this obligation at the prior year end and to take the difference into account in order to relate accrual basis scholarship expenses to cash basis expenditures.

As a result of these noncash transactions, there are significant differences in the amounts between the cash and accrual basis. On the cash basis, expenditures of $17,600 for scholarships are shown, compared to

EXHIBIT 3–1   Cash basis and accrual basis statements side-by-side to highlight the differences in these two bases of accounting.

THE JOHANNA M. STANNECK FOUNDATION
BALANCE SHEET*
December 31, 19X2

	Cash Basis	Accrual Basis
Assets:		
Cash	$ 13,616	$ 13,616
Marketable securities at cost		
(market value $235,100)	186,519	186,519
Dividends and interest receivable	—	3,550
Pledge receivable	—	2,000
Total assets	$200,135	$205,685
Liabilities:		
Accrued expenses payable	—	$ 1,354
Federal excise tax payable	—	394
Scholarships payable—19X3	—	12,150
Scholarships payable—19X4	—	2,000
Total liabilities	—	15,898
Net assets**	$200,135	189,787
Total liabilities and net assets	$200,135	$205,685

* On a cash basis the title should be "Statement of Assets and Liabilities Resulting from Cash Transactions."
** This was previously called "fund balance."

$21,800 on the accrual basis; excess of income of $3,258 compared to $506; and a fund balance (net assets) of $200,135 compared to $189,787. Which set of figures is more appropriate? In theory, the accrual basis figures are. What then are the advantages of the cash basis, and why might someone use the cash basis?

(a)   Advantages of Cash Basis

The principal advantage of cash basis accounting (as previously stated in Chapter 2) is its simplicity, and the ease with which non-accountants can understand and keep records on this basis. The only time a transaction is recorded under this basis of accounting is when cash has been received or expended. A simple checkbook may be all that is needed to keep the financial records of the organization. When financial reports are required,

EXHIBIT 3–1   *Continued.*

THE JOHANNA M. STANNECK FOUNDATION
STATEMENT OF INCOME, EXPENSES, AND SCHOLARSHIP GRANTS*
For the Year Ended December 31, 19X2

	Cash Basis	Accrual Basis
Income:		
Dividends and interest income	$ 8,953	$ 9,650
Gain on sale of investments	12,759	12,759
Contributions	5,500	7,500
Total	27,212	29,909
Administrative expenses:		
Investment advisory service fees	2,000	2,200
Bookkeeping and accounting expenses	2,350	2,500
Federal excise tax	350	394
Other expenses	1,654	2,509
Total	6,354	7,603
Income available for scholarships	20,858	22,306
Less: Scholarship grants	(17,600)	(21,800)
Excess of income over expenses and		
scholarship grants	$ 3,258	$ 506

* On a cash basis the title should be "Statement of Receipts, Expenditures and Scholarships Paid" to emphasize the "cash" aspect of the statement. There would also have to be a note to the financial statement disclosing the amount of scholarships granted but not paid at the end of the year.

the treasurer just summarizes the transactions from the checkbook stubs. This sounds almost too easy, but a checkbook can be an adequate substitute for formal bookkeeping records, provided a complete description is recorded on the checkbook stubs.[1] The chances are that someone with no bookkeeping training could keep the records of the Johanna M. Stanneck Foundation on a cash basis, using only a checkbook, files of paid bills, files on each scholarship, etc. This would probably not be true with an accrual basis set of books.

Many larger organizations, including many with bookkeeping staffs, also use the cash basis of accounting primarily because of its simpler nature. Often the difference between financial results on a cash and on an accrual basis are not materially different, and the accrual basis provides a

[1] Chapter 30 discusses cash basis bookkeeping and illustrates how this checkbook approach can be used.

degree of sophistication not needed. For example, in Exhibit 3–1, what real significance is there between the two sets of figures? Will the users of the financial statements do anything differently if they have accrual basis figures? If not, the extra costs to obtain accrual basis statements may not be worthwhile.

Another reason organizations often keep their records on a cash basis is that they feel uneasy about considering a pledge receivable as income until the cash is in the bank. These organizations frequently pay their bills promptly, and at the end of the period have very little in the way of unpaid obligations. With respect to unrecorded income, they also point out that because they consistently follow this method of accounting from year to year, the net effect on income in any one year is not material. Last year's unrecorded income is collected this year and tends to offset this year's unrecorded income. The advocates of a cash basis say, therefore, that they are being conservative by using this approach.

(b) Advantages of Accrual Basis

What are the advantages of the accrual basis? In many instances, the cash basis just does not present accurately enough the financial picture of the organization. The accrual basis of accounting becomes the more appropriate basis when the organization has substantial unpaid bills or uncollected income at the end of each period and these amounts vary from period to period. If the cash basis were used, the organization would have great difficulty in knowing where it actually stood. These unpaid bills or uncollected income would materially distort the financial statements.

In Exhibit 3–1, there probably is not a great deal of difference between the two bases. But assume for the moment that toward the end of 19X2 the foundation had made a grant of $100,000 to a medical school, to be paid in 19X3. Not recording this large transaction would distort the financial statements of both years.

Not-for-profit organizations are becoming more conscious of the need to prepare and use budgets as a control techniques.[2] It is very difficult for an organization to effectively use a budget without being on an accrual basis. A cash basis organization has difficulty because payment may lag for a long time after incurring the obligation. For this reason organizations that must carefully budget their activities will find accrual basis accounting essential.

[2] Budgets are discussed in detail in Chapter 20.

3.2   COMBINATION CASH ACCOUNTING AND ACCRUAL STATEMENTS

One practical way to avoid the complexities of accrual basis accounting, and still have meaningful financial statements on an annual or semi-annual basis, is to keep the books on a cash basis but make the necessary adjustments on worksheets to record the accruals for statement purposes. These "adjustments" could be put together on worksheets without the need to formally record the adjustments in the bookkeeping records.[3]

It is even possible that monthly or quarterly financial statements could be prepared on the cash basis, with the accrual basis adjustments being made only at the end of the year. In this way, it is possible to have the simplicity of cash basis accounting throughout the year, while at the end of the year converting the records through worksheets to accrual basis accounting.

Exhibit 3–2 gives an example of the type of worksheet that can be used. It shows how the Johnstown Orphanage converted a cash basis statement to an accrual basis statement at the end of the year. Cash basis figures are shown in column 1, adjustments in column 2, and the resulting accrual basis amounts in column 3. The financial statement given to the board would show only column 3. Adjustments were made to the cash statement in column 2 as follows:

- *Investment income*—$20,000 of dividends and interest that were received during the current year applicable to last year were deducted. At the same time at the end of the year there were dividends and interest receivable of $25,000 which were added. Therefore, on an accrual basis, a net adjustment of $5,000 was added.

- *Fees from the city*—This year the city changed its method of paying fees for children sent to the orphanage by the courts. In prior years the city paid $15 a day for each child assigned at the beginning of the month. This year because of a tight budget the city got behind and now pays in the following month. At the end of the year the city owed $25,000, which was added to income.

- *Expenses*—All the unpaid bills at the end of the year were added up and compared to the amount of unpaid bills as of last year

---

[3] A simplified accrual bookkeeping system is discussed in Chapter 31 in which the records are kept on a cash basis except at the end of the period when accrual entries are recorded in the books.

(which were subsequently paid in the current year). Here is a summary of these expenses:

	Add unpaid at end of this year	Less paid in current year applicable to last year	Net add (deduct)
Salaries	$15,000	$20,000	$(5,000)
Food	12,000	10,000	2,000
Fuel	3,000	2,000	1,000
Maintenance	5,000	4,000	1,000
Children's allowances	—	—	—
Other	1,000	1,000	—

As can be seen, it is not difficult to adjust a cash basis statement to the accrual basis in a small organization. The bookkeeper just has to go about it in a systematic manner, being very careful not to forget to remove similar items received, or paid, in the current year that are applicable to the prior year.

EXHIBIT 3–2   An example of a worksheet that converts a cash basis statement to an accrual basis statement.

JOHNSTOWN ORPHANAGE
WORKSHEET SHOWING CONVERSION OF CASH TO ACCRUAL BASIS
For the Year Ended December 31, 19X1

	Cash Basis (Col. 1)	Adjustments: Add (Deduct) (Col. 2)	Accrual Basis (Col. 3)
Income:			
Investment income	$225,000	$ 5,000	$230,000
Fees from city	290,000	25,000	315,000
Total	515,000		545,000
Expenses:			
Salaries and wages	430,000	(5,000)	425,000
Food and provisions	50,000	2,000	52,000
Fuel	15,000	1,000	16,000
Maintenance	40,000	1,000	41,000
Children's allowances	10,000	—	10,000
Other	15,000	—	15,000
Total	560,000		559,000
Excess of expenses over income	$ 45,000		$ 14,000

Actually, in this illustration there is relatively little difference between the cash and accrual basis except for the $25,000 owed by the city due to its change in the timing of payments. Possibly the only adjustment that need be made in this instance is the recording of this $25,000. However, until this worksheet has been prepared there is no way to be sure that the other adjustments aren't significant. It is recommended that a worksheet similar to this one always be prepared to insure that all significant adjustments are made.

3.3 MODIFIED CASH BASIS

Some not-for-profit organizations use a "modified cash basis" system of accounting. On this basis of accounting, certain transactions will be recorded on an accrual basis and other transactions on a cash basis. Usually, on a modified cash basis all unpaid bills will be recorded on an accrual basis but uncollected income on a cash basis. However, there are many different variations.

Sometimes only certain types of unpaid bills are recorded. Payroll taxes that have been withheld from employee salaries but which have not yet been paid to the government are a good example of the type of transaction, not involving cash, which might be recorded. These taxes are just as much an obligation as the salaries.

On a modified cash basis it is not necessary for the organization to have a complex set of books to record all obligations and receivables. In small and medium-sized not-for-profit organizations, it is sufficient to keep the records on the cash basis and then at the end of the month tally up the unpaid bills and the uncollected receivables and either record these formally in the books through journal entries or record them through a worksheet in the manner described above.[4] Under the cash basis, one of the practical ways some smaller organizations use to record all accrued expenses is to hold the disbursement record "open" for the first four or five days of each month. This allows the bookkeeper to pay last month's bills as they arrive about the first of the month and record them in the prior month's records. While the organization actually pays such amounts in the first few days of the new period, it considers the payment as having been made on the last day of the prior period. This means that the organization does not show accounts payable but instead a reduced cash balance. This is frequently a useful practice for reporting internally to the board because it gives reasonable assurance that all expenditures

---

[4] Chapters 31 and 32 discuss the bookkeeping procedures to formally record accrual basis adjustments in the accounts.

incurred are recorded in the proper period. In financial statements prepared for external use, such payments subsequent to the end of the period should be shown as accounts payable instead of a decrease in cash.

(a) When Accrual Basis Reporting Should Be Used

There are many advantages of cash basis accounting and reporting, but the accrual basis is ordinarily necessary for fair presentation of the financial statements. Unless the organization does not have any significant amounts of unpaid bills or uncollected income at the beginning or end of the period, accrual basis reporting is required to present an accurate picture of the results of operations and of the financial position of the organization.

Accrual basis reporting is also required if an organization is trying to measure the cost of a product or service. It is impossible to know what a particular activity cost during the year if unpaid bills have not been included as an expense in the statement. The same is true where services are provided for a fee but some fees have not been billed and collected during the period. If a board or its membership is trying to draw conclusions from the statements as to the cost or profitability of a particular service, accrual basis statements are essential. The same is true when an organization is on a tight budget and budget comparisons are made with actual income and expenses to see how effectively management has kept to the budget. Without including unpaid bills or uncollected income, such a comparison to budget can be very misleading and useless.[5] Generally accepted accounting principles (GAAP) for both commercial and not-for-profit organizations include the use of accrual basis accounting. Organizations that have their books audited by certified public accountants, and who wish the CPA to report that the financial statements are prepared in accordance with generally accepted accounting principles, have to either keep their records on the accrual basis, or make the appropriate adjustments at the end of the year to convert to this basis.[6]

3.4 LEGAL REQUIREMENTS

For some organizations soliciting funds from the public, there are legal requirements with respect to using the accrual basis of accounting. In New York State, for example, not-for-profit organizations which are

[5] Budgets are discussed in Chapter 20.
[6] See Chapter 24 for a discussion of generally accepted accounting principles, independent audits, and auditors' opinions.

required to report to the state must use the accrual basis. However, even in New York the requirement is not that the records be kept on an accrual basis, but only that the organization file reports prepared on an accrual basis. This means the organization could still keep cash basis records throughout the year, provided it adjusts them to accrual basis for report purposes. Chapters 26 to 28 discuss the legal reporting requirements for not-for-profit organizations. If an organization is required to file reports with one or more state agencies, it should examine the instructions accompanying the report very carefully to see what the reporting requirements are.

3.5   CONCLUSION

There are two bases for keeping records—the cash basis and the accrual basis. The vast majority of small not-for-profit organizations use the cash basis of accounting, and this is probably an acceptable and appropriate basis for such organizations. The chief reason for using the cash basis is its simplicity. Where there are no significant differences between the cash and accrual basis, the cash basis should be used. Where there are material differences, however, the records should either be kept on an accrual basis, or cash basis statements should be modified to reflect the major unrecorded amounts.

Fund Accounting and Internal Financial Reporting

Fund accounting is peculiar to not-for-profit organizations.[1] Most readers of commercial financial statements are not familiar with this type of accounting. As a consequence, fund accounting more than any other single

---

[1] Readers are cautioned against trying to apply the principles and terminology used in *governmental* accounting to not-for-profit accounting. While both types of accounting follow fund accounting concepts, their application and terminology are different. It is in large measure because of these differences that this book has been written. Readers interested in governmental accounting will find a number of useful texts available.

    There are also certain parallels to fund accounting in the accounting techniques used by some businesses. For example a bank with several branches, a retail store with several departments, or a corporation with several subsidiaries will account for each of its separate units in much the same way as a not-for-profit organization accounts for its various funds. The main differences are in the terminology used by the different types of organizations, the legal status of the resources of the units, and that financial statements of businesses prepared for external distribution rarely present details of the individual units—rather they show only the combined totals of all the units.

concept of not-for-profit accounting, tends to confuse the reader. The purpose of this chapter is to explain this concept and how it can be not only necessary, but can also prove to be useful.

A *fund* is a certain part of an organization, defined in accounting terms. Some organizations have only one fund; some have many. Funds can exist with different characteristics: some are legally unrestricted, that is, available for any organizational purpose. Some are legally restricted as a result of stipulations placed by donors on the gifts that make up the fund. Usually, all gifts with the same kind of restriction (for example, all gifts for the purpose of doing research on cancer or all gifts restricted for permanent endowment) are grouped together in a separate fund for accounting purposes. In addition, the governing board of an organization may decide to set aside certain available resources into one or more separate funds (for example, for investment). These "board-designated" funds are normally legally unrestricted.

Many people confuse "funds" with "assets" (especially cash), or with what is called by accountants, "fund balance." The three terms are very different:

- A *fund* is any part of an organization for which separate accounting records are kept.
- *Assets* are valuable things owned or controlled by the organization. Types of assets include cash, investments, property, and amounts owed to the organization.
- *Fund balance* is the mathematical number obtained by subtracting total liabilities from total assets; it is a numerical representation of the net worth of the organization, but has no other significance. Fund balances do not exist except on paper; unlike assets, they have no intrinsic value and cannot be spent. Both assets and fund balances (as well as liabilities, revenues, and expenses) are part of the accounting records of a fund.

As discussed further in Chapter 13, in 1993 the accounting profession issued new standards which change the manner in which financial information for not-for-profit organizations is to be presented in their external financial statements. One aspect of these new standards is a reduction in the amount of detail that is required to be shown in financial statements issued to the public. Rather than showing the traditional "funds," organizations must report their resources as segregated into three "classes" (or groups) of "net assets."[2] This is really no more than

[2] "Net assets" is computed by subtracting liabilities from assets. It is what would be left if all the assets were converted into cash, and all the liabilities paid off. This amount is called "fund

a change in terminology; "funds" correspond to "classes," and "fund balances" to "net assets." The concept of fund accounting is still valid and will continue to be appropriate for many organizations for keeping their books and for internal reporting to management and the governing board. In addition, the fund accounting financial records will be the basis for preparation of the financial statements used for reporting to the public.

This distinction between internal *accounting* and external financial *reporting* is important to understand. Accounting standards issued by the accounting profession deal only with external financial reporting, not how the internal books are kept. Organizations are free to use any method of recordkeeping they wish, as long as the final result—the financial statements seen by the public—are in the proper form.

Accounting information has many users; not all of their needs are the same. Thus the information they should look at and the way that information should be presented are not uniform. An example of this is the recordkeeping related to the acquisition of fixed assets, the allocation of the cost of those assets over the periods that benefit from their use (Depreciation is discussed in Chapter 7.) and the need to make proper provision for their care and eventual replacement. The rules governing external reporting require that this acquisition cost be recognized as depreciation expense ratably over the life of the asset. This approach recognizes the using up of the service potential of an asset as a cost of operating the organization. However, in some organizations, management and/or the governing board may feel that including depreciation as an expense in the measure of operations distorts the way they want to look at the financial results of operations of the organization. This is especially true in those cases where the cash basis of accounting (discussed in Chapter 3) is preferred. Further, in a time of severe inflation, simple allocation of historical cost may not facilitate, from their perspective, planning for future replacement—in fact it may hide real problems.

Thus external reports should conform to the rules of generally accepted accounting principles. Internal reports (for management and the governing board) should include information and be formatted in such a way that they are most useful to the decision-making process of those receiving the reports. For example, reports to the board should facilitate the effective execution of its governance function. The organization's

---

balance" in the context of a fund accounting system. FASB Statement of Financial Accounting Standards No 117, *Financial Statements of Not-for-Profit Organizations*, describes three classes of net assets: unrestricted, temporarily restricted, permanently restricted. These are further discussed in Chapters 10 and 13. The term, net assets, is more likely to be understood by non-accountants than the old term, fund balance.

recordkeeping system must allow all these sets of statements to be easily prepared.

Traditional fund accounting has often led to an organization being viewed as a collection of disparate pieces (funds) rather than as a cohesive whole. The new accounting standards approach financial reporting from the point of view that an organization is a single entity, controlled by a single governing board, despite the fact that individual donors may have imposed certain restrictions on how the board may utilize some of the resources at its disposal. Therefore, under these standards, an organization's external financial statements should mirror this point of view and not be fragmented.

Internally, and for the purposes of reporting to certain constituencies (i.e., donors), an organization may, for very good reasons, wish to report only on one or more segments (funds) of the organization, much as a commercial organization might wish to issue an internal management report on an operating division or cost center.

This chapter deals with internal recordkeeping and reporting; Chapters 11 to 13 will deal with external financial reporting to the public.

4.1 FUND ACCOUNTING DEFINED

Fund accounting is a system of accounting in which separate records are kept for:

- Resources donated to an organization which are restricted by donors or other outside parties to certain specified purposes or use,
- Portions of an organization's unrestricted resources which the board has set aside for some specified future use, and
- All other unrestricted amounts.

With appropriate explanations, there is nothing difficult about fund accounting other than mechanics. It reflects an accountability or stewardship concept, used principally by not-for-profit and governmental organizations that are legally responsible for seeing that certain resources are used only for specified purposes or during specified time periods. This need for separate accountability arises whenever a not-for-profit organization receives restricted contributions. For example:

- The Johnstown PTA receives a special contribution of $15,000 which the donor specifies is to be used only in connection with an educational program on drug abuse.

- The Bethesda Methodist Church decides that they need an addition to the Church, and a building fund drive is established to raise $200,000. Contributors are told the money will be used only for this building addition.
- The Boy Scout Council of Arlington receives a $250,000 gift from an ex-Boy Scout to be kept as a permanent endowment fund.
- The Kennebunkport Civic League receives a gift specified by the donor as being for use in the following year only.

In each instance, the donor's stipulation has created a legal restriction on the contribution, and by accepting such a restricted gift, the organization has incurred an obligation to follow the donor's instructions. One of the responsibilities of the treasurer is to be sure that controls are established to ensure that restricted funds are used only for the purpose intended. (In these examples: the Johnstown PTA cannot spend its gift for any purpose other than drug abuse education; the Bethesda Methodist Church must spend all amounts raised by its fund drive only for the addition; the Arlington Boy Scout Council can never spend the gift itself—only the future investment income earned by the gift is available for use; the Kennebunkport Civic League cannot spend the gift this year, nor after the end of next year.) Usually this control is established through the use of fund accounting. Every new treasurer in an organization should review the disbursement procedures to be sure that restricted funds cannot be inadvertently spent in violation of the restriction.

In addition, some organizations, as a matter of convenience, establish by board action additional funds in order to segregate certain amounts that the board intends to use for specified purposes in the future. An example of a board-created fund would be an Unrestricted Investment Fund or a Quasi-Endowment Fund. The important thing to note about these board-designated funds is that they carry no legal restrictions[3] and represent only an internal designation for the convenience of the organization. By contrast, donor-restricted funds do carry legal restrictions, and the approval of the original donor or a court of law would usually be

---

[3] Sometimes an organization will create a board-designated investment fund using resources which a donor has restricted for some operating purpose, but which the board prefers not to spend right away. The resources retain their legal restriction, and take on the additional designation specified by the board that they will be held for investment for some period of time. The investment income generated by the assets is then used for the purpose specified by the donor. The board may at some future time decide to spend the original amount of the gift for the restricted purpose. The term "quasi-endowment—restricted" is used to describe this kind of fund; colleges and universities are the type of not-for-profit organization that most often use it.

required should the board of the organization wish to divert these contributions from their stipulated purpose.

Internal financial statements or management reports may follow this separate accountability, both for donor-imposed restrictions and for designations imposed by its governing board. Often separate statements are prepared for each "fund."

Note that fund accounting does not itself require physical segregation of the assets of each fund. For example, separate bank accounts need not be maintained for the cash attributable to each fund. (Although the treasurer *may* do so if this would be considered a convenience, and sometimes a donor of some of the assets may require such a separate account.) Usually, all the organization's cash may be kept in a single bank account, and the separate accountability maintained through the fund accounting bookkeeping system. This also saves on bank fees and on the time needed to keep the books and reconcile the monthly bank statements.

4.2 CATEGORIES OF FUNDS

An organization that receives many restricted contributions, each having a different kind of restriction, is faced with the practical problem of having to keep track of and report on many separate funds. While it is possible to keep separate records on any number of restricted funds, these funds are usually grouped by the type of donor restriction. For example, in a college building fund drive, one donor may specify that a gift is to be used for a new chemistry building; another may specify a dormitory. Both represent restricted contributions to a category of fund generally referred to as *Building Funds.*

In the past, a wide variety of names has been given to various categories of funds. However, four categories or groupings of funds have historically been most frequently used by not-for-profit organizations for reporting purposes. The description or title indicates the general type of restriction on the funds. The following are the four groupings most commonly encountered. Chapter 13 includes a discussion of how the four traditional fund groupings relate to the three classes of net assets defined in the new accounting standards issued in 1993.

(a) Current Unrestricted Fund

Several titles are given to the fund that includes the general activities of the organization. It may be known as the *Unrestricted Fund, Operating Fund, General Fund, Current Fund, Current General Fund,* or most commonly the *Current Unrestricted Fund.* This fund contains no restricted resources, and the board can use amounts in the fund as it chooses, to carry out the purposes for which the organization exists.

All unrestricted contributions, gifts, and other income should be recorded in this fund. Except for transactions involving one of the other categories of funds, all transactions of the organization are included in this fund. If the organization never receives restricted gifts or contributions, this fund would show all activity.

Board-Designated Funds

Board-designated funds are a subcategory of unrestricted funds. They are established when the board acts to transfer or segregate part of the unrestricted funds into a fund that the board intends to use for a specific purpose. Remember that the board cannot create legal restrictions, for it can always change its mind later. The board designates certain resources for certain purposes, indeed, this is what it does in the budgeting process. Occasionally, the board may wish to formally (although not legally) segregate the resources it wishes to utilize for a specific purpose, especially when that purpose may extend over a long period of time.

(b)   Current Restricted Fund

Various titles are given to the fund that accounts for resources given to an organization to be spent as part of the normal activities, but only for certain specified purposes. It may be known as *Current Restricted Fund, Fund for Specified Purposes, Donor Restricted Fund,* or just plain *Restricted Fund.* For example, the $15,000 given to the Johnstown PTA for public education on drug abuse would be added to such a fund. In some organizations, such amounts are relatively small and they are often used in the year received or in the following year.

Many restricted gifts are for a particular purpose that the organization normally carries out as a part of its current activities. However, a contribution may be for a purpose that is not normally part of the organization's regular activities, or perhaps it will be some time before the money is needed. Contributions restricted by donors for purposes other than current activities (for example, a contribution to a building fund or an endowment fund) are usually accounted for in a separate fund category.

Note that the current restricted fund should not include board-designated funds. Chapter 5 discusses accounting for board-designated amounts, and Chapter 10 further discusses accounting for current restricted contributions.

(c)   Restricted Endowment Fund

This title is given to the fund that contains resources donated to the organization with the stipulation by the donor that only the income earned by these assets can be used while the original gift is kept intact, either forever (permanent endowment) or for a stated time (term endowment). Generally the income itself is not restricted and can be used to carry out the organization's ongoing activities, but some endowment gifts also have restrictions on the uses to be made of the income.

If term endowment gifts are received, they must be kept in the endowment fund for a period of time, after which the original amount can be used as desired by the board, unless some other purpose was specified by the donor. Another possibility is a gift, the income from which is paid to the donor until death; the gift then becomes available for other uses.[4]

Some donors, while not formally placing restrictions, may express a "preference" that the gift be put in the endowment fund. However, if the actual decision is left to the board, such amounts are legally unrestricted and should be added to the current unrestricted fund. (The board may, if it wishes, then transfer such gifts to an unrestricted board-designated fund as noted earlier.) Legally unrestricted gifts should not be added to a restricted endowment fund. All amounts in a restricted endowment fund should bear legal restrictions that the board cannot normally alter without a *cy pres* ruling from a court of law.

(d)   Fixed Asset Fund

Several titles may be given to the fund in which the cost of fixed assets (land, buildings, furniture and fixtures, equipment, etc.) is recorded. This fund may be referred to as the *Land, Building, and Equipment Fund, Fixed Asset Fund,* or *Plant Fund.* Such a fund will usually also include unexpended restricted building fund contributions.[5]

The principal reason for using this fund is that the board wants to separate these assets from the unrestricted fund (see the earlier discussion on fixed asset reporting). The unrestricted fund will then represent more closely the current activity of the organization, that is, the funds available for current program use (see also the discussion of expendable versus nonexpendable below). Fixed assets such as buildings are not

---

[4] These gifts are variously referred to as "deferred," "split interest," "life income," or "annuity" gifts. See Chapters 10 and 15 for a discussion of these funds.

[5] The AICPA Statement of Position applicable to certain not-for-profit organizations provided that unexpended building fund gifts be reflected in a "deferred income" account until such time as the restriction is met through the acquisition of the building or asset. That approach has been changed by the new accounting standard discussed in Chapter 10.

really available in the sense that they cannot be readily converted to cash and expended. Therefore, many boards believe that fixed assets should be placed in a separate fund.

The use of a separate fixed asset fund is largely a board decision, and there is no reason why a separate fund must be established.[6] Because a separate fixed asset fund is more likely to create considerable confusion for the reader of the statements, without offering any real advantage, we do not recommend the use of a separate fixed asset fund in external financial statements even though this is presently the predominant practice. (If a separate fixed asset fund is not maintained, unexpended gifts restricted by donors for the acquisition or improvement of fixed assets would be included in the current restricted fund until spent for the intended purpose, at which time the amounts would be transferred to the unrestricted fund.)

Fixed assets are a necessary part of the resources that are available to the board for achieving the purposes for which the organization was formed; creating a separate fixed asset fund may imply to some that fixed assets are somehow not related to the day-to-day operations of the organization.

Segregating fixed assets into a separate fund also causes considerable bookkeeping problems. This is particularly true if the organization records depreciation on its fixed assets in the current unrestricted fund. As is explained in more detail in Chapter 7, charging depreciation in the current unrestricted fund and then transferring this depreciation to the fixed asset fund is very confusing to most readers.

There is an extended discussion of accounting for fixed assets and depreciation in Chapters 6 and 7.

(e) Other Types of Funds

Other specialized fund groupings may be encountered reflecting either donor restrictions or board decisions regarding the use of unrestricted resources. For example, colleges and universities often have *Loan* or *Scholarship Funds, Custodian* or *Agency Funds, Annuity and Life Income Funds,* and *Retirement of Indebtedness Funds.* Usually the title is descriptive of the nature of these resources or their intended use.

Occasionally a donor will give such a large sum of money, often for endowment purposes, that the board will want to create (or the donor

---

[6] The AICPA Health Care Providers Audit Guide provides that fixed assets should be reported in the "unrestricted" fund and not as a separate fund. The AICPA Audit Guides for Colleges and Universities and Voluntary Health and Welfare Organizations both illustrate the use of a separate fixed asset fund. The 1978 AICPA Statement of Position indicates either approach is acceptable.

asks the board to create) a separate fund bearing the name of the donor (or some other name specified by the donor), rather than merely burying this separate fund in the financial statements with all other similar funds. Examples would be the *Howard Geckler Scholarship Fund* or the *Agnes Christiansen Memorial Fund*. The principal reason for this separate reporting is to be able to track and give the donor public recognition for a substantial gift.

4.3   ALTERNATIVE FUND GROUPINGS

(a)   Expendable and Nonexpendable

In some cases, statement users may find it useful to see funds classified based on their availability for current expenditure to further the organization's objectives:

- Expendable
  Current unrestricted funds
  Current restricted funds
- Nonexpendable
  Fixed asset funds[7]
  Endowment funds

The theory behind this approach is that the board has basically only two kinds of funds—those that are currently expendable for the organization's program, and those that are not. The nonexpendable are more in the nature of "capital-type" funds.

(b)   Managed Fund Groups

Some organizations prefer to group their funds according to the use made of the resources. These organizations typically have three groups:

1. Operating funds (including current unrestricted and current restricted funds).
2. Plant funds (as described earlier).

---

[7] The reader may wonder why fixed assets are considered nonexpendable here, whereas the authors treated them as unrestricted earlier. The logic of this approach deals more with whether they could be expended, that is, directly spent, than with the question of legal restriction. As previously discussed, fixed assets are used in the current activities of the organization and in this sense are "spent." Yet on balance when using the expendable/nonexpendable classification, it is more meaningful to treat fixed assets as nonexpendable.

3. Endowment funds (which, in this format *only*, may include board-designated endowment funds).

If this format is used, all fund balances must be clearly labelled as to the extent they are unrestricted or donor-restricted.

4.4   A TYPICAL SET OF "FUND" FINANCIAL STATEMENTS

Exhibit 4–1 shows the simplified statements of a not-for-profit organization having the traditional four separate funds—a current unrestricted fund, a current restricted fund, a fixed asset fund, and an endowment fund. (This example reflects only part of the new format and terminology discussed in Chapter 13 where fund accounting financial statements that do present the new format are discussed.) This presentation is typical of a small organization using fund accounting. The format makes separate

EXHIBIT 4–1   A typical set of income statements where each fund is reported in a separate statement.

McLEAN COMMUNITY SERVICE CENTER
CURRENT UNRESTRICTED FUND
STATEMENT OF INCOME, EXPENSES, AND CHANGES
IN NET ASSETS
For the Year Ended August 31, 19X1

Income:		
Contributions and gifts	$ 85,000	
Service fees	110,000	
Investment income from Endowment Fund	20,000	
Other income	13,000	
Total income		$228,000
Expenses:		
Program services	140,000	
Administration	43,000	
Fund raising	12,000	
Total expenses		195,000
Excess of income over expenses		33,000
Net assets, beginning of year		7,000
Less—Transfer to Fixed Asset Fund		(25,000)
Net assets, end of year		$ 15,000

EXHIBIT 4–1 *Continued.*

McLEAN COMMUNITY SERVICE CENTER
CURRENT RESTRICTED FUND
STATEMENT OF CONTRIBUTIONS, EXPENSES, AND CHANGES
IN NET ASSETS*
For the Year Ended August 31, 19X1

Contributions		$ 24,000
Expenses:		
Athletic awards	$15,000	
Citizenship program	5,000	
Other	3,000	
Total expenses		23,000
Excess of contributions over expenses		1,000
Net assets, beginning of year		10,000
Net assets, end of year		$ 11,000

McLEAN COMMUNITY SERVICE CENTER
FIXED ASSET FUND
STATEMENT OF CHANGES IN NET ASSETS
For the Year Ended August 31, 19X1

Net assets, beginning of year	$ 50,000
Add–Transfer from General Fund	25,000
Net assets, end of year	$ 75,000

McLEAN COMMUNITY SERVICE CENTER
ENDOWMENT FUND
STATEMENT OF INCOME AND CHANGES IN NET ASSETS*
For the Year Ended August 31, 19X1

Income:	
Contributions and gifts	$ 25,000
Gain on sale of investments	46,000
Total	71,000
Net assets, beginning of year	250,000
Net assets, end of year	$321,000

* The title used in actual practice would probably be "Statement of Changes in Net Assets."
See Chapter 13 for a discussion of this type of statement.

accountability of each fund quite evident. It also shows the main problem associated with fund accounting—the difficulty in getting an overall picture of the organization's affairs without a careful review of all the statements.

The principal advantage of fund accounting is that the activities of each fund are reported separately. Accountability is quite evident since the reader can see exactly what has taken place. This is the stewardship aspect.

The principal disadvantage of fund accounting is that it is difficult to comprehend the total activities of the organization without a careful review of all the statements and perhaps a little bit of pencil pushing. For example, what was the total excess of income over expenses for all funds? To answer this question it is necessary to add three figures. Be careful to pick out the *right* figures ($33,000 + $1,000 + $71,000 = $105,000).

The statement presentation in Exhibit 4–1 is a quite simple form. Some organizations incorrectly record unrestricted investment income in the endowment fund and then transfer this income to the current unrestricted fund below the caption "excess of income over expenses." In this exhibit, $20,000 would have been shown in the endowment fund and would then have been shown in the current unrestricted fund as a transfer. This would have been incorrect. Unrestricted endowment income is by definition unrestricted, and all such income should be reported directly in the current unrestricted fund. If this income had been handled incorrectly as a transfer, the excess of income in the current unrestricted fund would appear to have been an excess of only $13,000, because the transfer-in of the $20,000 would have appeared after the excess-of-income caption. Few readers would realize from this incorrect presentation that the current unrestricted fund actually had an excess of income of $33,000.

One way to simplify fund accounting statements is to show all funds on a single statement in columnar format. In this format, each fund is shown in a separate column side-by-side. These statements have been recast in this columnar format and are shown in Exhibit 13–1.

(a) Interfund Borrowing

As was previously noted, one of the problems with having a number of separate funds is that there is sometimes difficulty in keeping all the transactions completely separate. For example, in the McLean Community Service Center illustration, the current unrestricted fund often runs out of cash over the summer months and the board authorizes a cash loan from the other funds. In theory one can easily keep track of these borrowings, but it does create one more area where the reader who is not careful or knowledgeable can become confused. Exhibit 4–2 shows the Balance

EXHIBIT 4-2 A typical Balance Sheet where each fund is reported separately.

McLEAN COMMUNITY SERVICE CENTER
BALANCE SHEET
August 31, 19X1

Assets		Liabilities and Net Assets	
CURRENT UNRESTRICTED FUND			
Cash	$ 50,000	Accounts payable	$ 17,000
Pledges receivable	13,000	Due to other funds	31,000
			48,000
		Net assets	15,000
	$ 63,000		$ 63,000
CURRENT RESTRICTED FUND			
Cash	$ 11,000	Accounts payable	$ 3,000
Due from Current Unrestricted Fund	3,000	Net assets	11,000
	$ 14,000		$ 14,000
FIXED ASSET FUND			
Due from Current Unrestricted Fund	$ 5,000	Net assets	$ 75,000
Equipment	70,000		
	$ 75,000		$ 75,000
ENDOWMENT FUND			
Cash	$ 3,000	Net assets	$321,000
Due from Current Unrestricted Fund	23,000		
Investments	295,000		
	$321,000		$321,000

Sheet for the four funds used by the McLean Community Service Center. Notice the number of interfund transactions.

Note that the current unrestricted fund has borrowed $31,000, that is, $3,000 from the current restricted fund, $5,000 from the fixed asset fund, and $23,000 from the endowment fund. While this is perfectly clear to the person knowledgeable about fund accounting, or to the careful reader, some readers are neither knowledgeable nor careful.

Two words of caution with respect to interfund borrowings:

- A fund should not borrow from another fund unless it is clear that the borrowing fund will, within a reasonable time, have the financial resources to repay. It is not appropriate financial management to finance a deficit operation on an ongoing basis through interfund borrowing.

- Before resources are borrowed from legally restricted funds, advice should be sought from legal counsel as to whether such borrowings are permissible. It would appear entirely inappropriate for an organization to raise funds for a building addition (as in the Bethesda Methodist Church example above) and then "lend" such amounts to help finance general operations of the organization.

The statements presented above were fairly simple statements. There were only four funds, and the restricted funds were carefully combined to eliminate unnecessary detail. Some organizations, however, attempt to break out the restricted funds into a number of separate funds—one for each major donor. As the number of funds increases, there will be more transfers between funds and the complexity will increase. Fund accounting and reporting can become very difficult, not so much because the concepts are difficult but because of the confusion created by so many funds. It is not enough merely to report the activities of the organization; it is equally important that the statements be effective in communicating what has actually happened. If this is not accomplished, the statements have not served their purpose and the treasurer has failed in a most important responsibility.

4.5   ELIMINATION OF FUNDS FOR REPORTING PURPOSES

More and more not-for-profit organizations are re-evaluating the need to report their financial affairs on a "fund accounting" basis, even for internal purposes. Instead they are presenting a consolidated Statement of Income showing all activity for the year, and a consolidated Balance Sheet carefully disclosing in line captions or in footnotes all pertinent information on the restricted funds. This approach gives appropriate recognition that a not-for-profit organization is a single entity and not a series of separate entities called "funds." The new FASB standard on financial reporting, discussed in Chapter 13, specifically requires the reporting of certain financial information by what it calls "classes," rather than funds.

This does not mean the organization will not keep detailed internal bookkeeping records on a fund accounting basis. It will still have to do so, or it will lose track of whether it is complying with donor-imposed restrictions. Rather, it means that for reporting purposes the organization will carefully combine all the activity for the year in a meaningful manner. This is not always easy to do but, if carefully done, adds greatly to the reader's understanding of the organization's overall financial picture. The examples in Chapter 13, reflecting the new accounting standards, are generally simpler, and thus easier to understand.

4.6 CONCLUSION

Fund accounting is simply a common-sense answer to the problem of recording amounts given to an organization for restricted purposes. There is nothing particularly difficult about the concepts involved, but as the number of funds increases, there is considerable risk that the reader of the financial statements will not fully understand the relationship among the funds and therefore will lose sight of the overall financial affairs of the organization. For this reason great care must be taken in preparing the financial statements where fund accounting is involved.

Interfund Transfers and Appropriations

As pointed out in Chapter 4, the use of fund accounting, while often necessary, creates a certain amount of confusion and adds to the problem of meeting the non-accountant test. In this chapter, two other problem areas will be explored: One relates to the use of "transfers" to allocate resources between funds, and the other relates to the use of appropriations to authorize future expenditure of resources for specific purposes. Both add to the complexity of financial statements. Transfers between funds are frequently unavoidable; appropriations, on the other hand, usually serve very little purpose and should be avoided if at all possible.

5.1   TRANSFERS BETWEEN FUNDS

Not-for-profit organizations following fund accounting procedures utilize a number of different funds, some restricted, such as funds for specific purposes, and some unrestricted, such as board-designated funds. The board has the right to transfer assets between unrestricted funds and in certain circumstances between restricted and unrestricted funds. For example, if the board has established a board-designated investment fund within the unrestricted fund, it may from time to time transfer funds from the undesignated portion of the current unrestricted fund to this fund. Or, alternatively, it may find at some time that it needs some of the funds previously transferred and will, in turn, transfer some of these funds back to the current unrestricted fund. Another example would be the transfer of unrestricted assets to the fixed asset fund (if a separate fixed asset fund is maintained) to pay for fixed assets purchased in whole or part with cash from the unrestricted fund.

The new Statement of Financial Accounting Standards No. 117, discussed in Chapter 13, uses the term "reclassifications" to refer to what we are calling transfers. We will continue to use the term *transfers* in this chapter. That Statement also uses the term "net assets" in place of *fund balance.* The text of this and other chapters will use the term "fund balance" when referring to the accounting concept of the excess of assets over liabilities of a particular fund. Illustrative financial statements, and references in the text to financial statements, will use the term "net assets," since that is what will be shown in financial statements prepared for public distribution in the future.

Transfers can very easily confuse the readers of financial statements if they are not properly shown. Special care must be taken in preparing the statements to insure that transfers will be understood.

(a)   Presentation of Transfers

Several principles should be followed in the presentation of transfers in the financial statements. The first and most important is that a transfer should not be shown in a manner that suggests the transfer is an expense to the transferring fund or income to the receiving fund. The easiest way to avoid this is to show the transfer in a separate Statement of Changes in Net Assets or, if that separate statement is not used, in the Statement of Income, Expenses, and Changes in Net Assets after the caption "Net assets, beginning of year."

Transfers should not be shown as an expense or as income because only transactions that result in expense or income to the organization *as a whole* are shown in the expense or income sections of a financial statement. A transfer is purely an internal action involving neither. For this reason great care must be taken to avoid a presentation that suggests the transfer is either an income or an expense item.

For example, suppose a person gives some money to his or her spouse. Although the giver personally now has less net worth and the recipient personally has more net worth than before, the *family* is no richer or poorer than before the gift was made. No income or expense has been received or spent by the family. In this analogy, the husband and wife are like the two funds, and the family represents the not-for-profit organization as a whole. Only if some money were received from or paid to a party *outside* the family unit (for example, wages received from an employer, or rent paid to a landlord) would income or expense have occurred.

FASB Statement 117 indicates that certain of what it calls reclassifications are to be reported as part of the revenue section of the statement of income, expenses, and changes in net assets. This presentation is a departure from the methods generally used in the past, and will be found confusing by some, at least at first. The logic behind the presentation is that the particular items being reported in this way are not really transfers of *net assets;* rather what is happening is that certain *revenue* items previously recorded in the restricted fund (class) are being reclassified to the unrestricted (fund) class to match them with the related expenses being reported in the unrestricted class.

Transfers in a Combined Statement of Income, Expenses, and Changes in Net Assets

The most effective way to present a transfer between funds with a minimal risk of misunderstanding is in a columnar statement, with the activity of each fund shown in a separate column, side by side.[1] This is a desirable format because the reader can easily see both sides of the transfer: the amount going out of one fund and the same amount going into the other fund.

Exhibit 5–1 shows this columnar presentation for a Statement of Income, Expenses, and Changes in Net Assets. The Board of the Corvallis YMCA decided to transfer $40,000 from its current unrestricted fund to an unrestricted investment fund. Notice how this is handled in a columnar format. The transfer is shown after the caption "Net assets, beginning of year." There is no inference that the transfer had anything to do with either income or expenses of the current unrestricted fund for the year. Rather, the reader will understand that a portion of the fund balance accumulated over prior years was transferred to another board-controlled fund.

---

[1] Chapter 13 discusses the use of columnar format statements and their advantages and disadvantages. You may want to refer to this discussion since no attempt will be made to discuss this format in this chapter although it will be used throughout.

EXHIBIT 5–1 Reporting a transfer in a columnar format Statement of Income, Expenses, and Changes in Net Assets.

CORVALLIS YMCA
STATEMENT OF INCOME, EXPENSES, AND CHANGES
IN NET ASSETS
For the Year Ended December 31, 19X2

| | Unrestricted | | Funds for | |
	Current Fund	Investment Fund	Specified Purposes	Combined All Funds
		(in thousands)		
Income:				
Membership	$ 255			$255
Community fund	50			50
Program activities	372			372
Contributions and other income	45		$17	62
Investment income	13			13
Gain on sale of investments	15		___	15
Total income	750		17	767
Expenses:				
Program	326			326
General administration	265			265
Property repairs and maintenance	50			50
Depreciation	35			35
Other	14		7	21
Total expenses	690		7	697
Excess of income over expenses	60		10	70
Net assets, beginning of year	415	$200	10	625
Transfer between funds	(40)	40		
Net assets, end of year	$ 435	$240	$20	$695

Transfers in Statement of Changes in Net Assets

Some organizations do not present a combined Statement of Income, Expenses, and Changes in Net Assets. They have either two separate statements—a Statement of Income and Expenses and a Statement of Changes in Net Assets—or only a Statement of Income and Expenses. If two separate statements are presented, the transfer should be shown in the Statement of Changes in Net Assets. It should not be shown in the Statement of Income and Expenses since a transfer represents an adjustment of the net assets rather than an item of income or expense. Exhibit 5–2 shows the Corvallis YMCA transfer of funds using both statements.

Transfers in Statement of Income and Expenses

A third possibility is that the organization will not show the changes in net assets either in the income statement or as a separate statement. This might occur where the only change between the beginning and ending fund balance is the excess of income for the year. In that instance, it is necessary to report the transfer in the Statement of Income and Expenses. Exhibit 5–3 shows the transfer after the caption "Excess of income over expenses."

This approach is not recommended and is acceptable only if a Statement of Changes in Net Assets is not presented either separately or as part of the income statement and if the income statement is presented in columnar form. In practice, this approach is seldom encountered since most organizations will include a "change in net assets section" at the bottom of the income statement as shown in Exhibit 5–1.

(b) Transfer of Income or Deficit

The boards of some organizations create a separate board-designated investment fund and then use "transfers" as a device to reduce or increase the current unrestricted net asset balance to a predetermined level. The casual reader is likely to be misled where this transfer is reported directly on the Statement of Income and Expenses (rather than on a Statement of Changes in Net Assets). This is often what the board has in mind.

Exhibits 5–4 and 5–5 show two examples of this type of transfer, and at the same time provide illustrations of why fund accounting is so hard for most readers to understand when separate statements are presented for each fund. In each of the examples, the reader may look at only the last figure in the statement: the $500 excess of income over expenses and transfers. These are the wrong figures to focus on. What should be observed is a $15,000 excess of income in Exhibit 5–4 and an $8,000 deficit in Exhibit 5–5.

Transfers are made at the discretion of the board and, if this type of transfer is made, the board can "window dress" the statements to suit its objectives. In Exhibit 5–4 it appears that the board may be somewhat embarrassed by the surplus and has "disposed" of it by transferring it to other funds. Perhaps the motivation is fund raising. Many believe that it

EXHIBIT 5–2 Reporting a transfer when a separate Statement of Changes in Net Assets is presented.

CORVALLIS YMCA
STATEMENT OF INCOME AND EXPENSES
For the Year Ended December 31, 19X2

| | Unrestricted | | Funds for | |
	Current Fund	Investment Fund	Specified Purposes	Combined All Funds
	(in thousands)			
Income:				
Membership	$ 255			$255
Community fund	50			50
Program activities	372			372
Contributions and other				
income	45		$17	62
Investment income	13			13
Gain on sale of				
investments	15		—	15
Total income	750		17	767
Expenses:				
Program	326			326
General administration	265			265
Property repairs and				
maintenance	50			50
Depreciation	35			35
Other	14		7	21
Total expenses	690		7	697
Excess of income over				
expenses	$ 60		$10	$ 70

STATEMENT OF CHANGES IN NET ASSETS
For the Year Ended December 31, 19X2

| | Unrestricted | | Funds for | |
	Current Fund	Investment Fund	Specified Purposes	Combined All Funds
	(in thousands)			
Net assets, beginning				
of the year	$ 415	$200	$10	$625
Excess of income over				
expenses	60		10	70
Transfer between funds	(40)	40	—	—
Net assets, end of the				
year	$ 435	$240	$20	$695

EXHIBIT 5–3   A transfer reported in a Statement of Income and Expenses. This presentation would not be acceptable if a separate Statement of Changes in Net Assets is also presented.

CORVALLIS YMCA
STATEMENT OF INCOME, EXPENSES, AND TRANSFERS
For the Year Ended December 31, 19X2

| | Unrestricted | | Funds for | |
	Current Fund	Investment Fund	Specified Purposes	Combined All Funds
		(in thousands)		
Income:				
Membership	$ 255			$255
Community fund	50			50
Program activities	372			372
Contributions and other				
income	45		$17	62
Investment income	13			13
Gain on sale of				
investments	15		__	15
Total income	750		17	767
Expenses:				
Program	326			326
General adminstration	265			265
Property repairs and				
maintenance	50			50
Depreciation	35			35
Other	14		7	21
Total expenses	690		7	697
Excess of income over				
expenses	60		10	70
Transfer between funds	(40)	$40		
Change in net assets	$ 20	$40	$10	$ 70

is hard to convince contributors that money is needed if the organization shows a big surplus. While the careful reader will recognize the surplus, the casual reader, or the reader who does not understand that transfers are made at the discretion of the board, may think the net income for the year was only $500. In Exhibit 5–5 it could appear that the board allowed expenses to get out of hand and has tried to cover up the deficit. Again, careful reading will show that the transfer is merely a bookkeeping device.

EXHIBIT 5–4   An example of a transfer that reduces the current unrestricted fund income. The reader may confuse this transfer with an expense, and may wrongly conclude the excess of income is $500.

THE JOHNSTOWN MUSEUM

STATEMENT OF CURRENT UNRESTRICTED FUND INCOME,
EXPENSES AND TRANSFERS

For the Year Ended December 31, 19X1

Income		$ 157,000
Less—Expenses		(142,000)
Excess of income over expenses		15,000
Less—Transfers to:		
Building fund	$ 4,500	
Board-designated investment fund	10,000	14,500
Excess of income over expenses and transfers		$ 500

The real problem with these two transfers is not that they were made, but that they were reported in a manner that suggests the transfers were items of income or expenses. This confusion would not exist if the transfer had been made in a separate Statement of Changes in Net Assets, or in a separate "changes in net assets section" of the income statement.

At the same time, where separate board-designated funds are used, transfers should not be made to keep the current unrestricted fund balance at zero or at some artificially low amount. Transfers to board-designated funds should be made only when it is obvious that there are

EXHIBIT 5–5   A transfer that covers a current unrestricted fund deficit for the year. The reader may confuse this transfer with income, and may wrongly conclude the excess of income is $500.

THE SMITHVILLE MUSEUM

STATEMENT OF CURRENT UNRESTRICTED FUND INCOME,
EXPENSES AND TRANSFERS

For the Year Ended December 31, 19X1

Income	$ 102,000
Less—Expenses	(110,000)
Excess of expenses over income	(8,000)
Add—Transfer from board-designated investment fund	8,500
Excess of income and transfers over expenses	$ 500

surplus funds in the current unrestricted fund that are not likely to be needed in the foreseeable future. Likewise, transfers should not be made to the general fund from board-designated funds just to cover a particular year's deficit as long as there is a surplus remaining from prior years. Transfers should be made to the current unrestricted fund only when the balance in that fund has become so small that cash is needed from other funds for operations.

(c) Other Transfers

Occasionally there are other transfers between funds. In some instances, expenditures for "current" activities are made from the current unrestricted fund but are later determined to be covered by a restricted gift. This is often handled for bookkeeping purposes as a transfer. However, it would be more straightforward to record the expense directly as paid for by the current restricted fund, rather than recording it in the unrestricted fund and then recording a transfer. The fact that the bookkeeping took place in one fund does not mean the organization cannot record the expense directly in the fund to which it related and that ultimately paid for it. (Note that this paragraph refers only to the internal *recording* of expenses and transfers. SFAS No. 117 requires all expenses to be *reported* in the unrestricted class of net assets. This requirement need not affect an organization's bookkeeping process however.)

Another type of transfer involves depreciation expense which is shown in the unrestricted fund but is then transferred to the plant fund. Chapter 7 shows illustrations of this type of transfer.

5.2 APPROPRIATIONS

An *appropriation* is an authorization to expend resources in the future for a specific purpose. An appropriation is not an expenditure nor does it represent an obligation that has already been incurred. It is only an internal authorization indicating how the board intends to spend part of the organization's resources. Once amounts have been "appropriated," they are usually set up in a separate account, but as part of the fund balance or net assets of the organization. They are not shown as a liability. All that happens when the board makes an appropriation is that part of the net assets is set aside for a particular purpose. Since appropriations are made by the board, rather than by an outside party, it can subsequently reverse its action and restore these amounts to the general use of the organization.

In many ways, an appropriation is very similar to a "transfer between funds" and often the two terms are used interchangeably. If monies are going from one fund to another fund, a "transfer" is involved. Occasionally the treasurer will use the word "appropriation" instead of the word "transfer." This may confuse the readers, who usually don't understand what an appropriation is. If a transfer is being made between funds, the word "transfer" is correct and should be used.

If amounts are being set aside within a single fund, an appropriation or "designation" of the fund balance is involved. In this circumstance, it is better to use the word "designated" since it is more descriptive of what the board has done.

(a) Reporting Appropriations

Exhibit 5–6 shows a simplified presentation of an appropriation where a separate Statement of Changes in Net Assets is not used. Exhibit 5–7 shows a two-year presentation where a separate Statement of Changes in

EXHIBIT 5–6 Handling an "appropriation" in the financial statements, when a separate Statement of Changes in Net Assets is not used. The authors discourage the use of the term "appropriation."

THE BETHLEHEM SERVICES ORGANIZATION
STATEMENT OF INCOME, EXPENSES, AND UNAPPROPRIATED
NET ASSETS
Year Ended December 31, 19X1
(in thousands)

Income	$ 100
Less–Expenses	80
Excess of income over expenses	20
Unappropriated net assets, beginning of year	80
Less–Appropriated for Project A	(15)
Unappropriated net assets, end of year	$ 85

BALANCE SHEET
December 31, 19X1

Cash		$ 100
Other assets		100
Total assets		$ 200
Accounts payable		$ 100
Net assets		
Appropriated–Project A	$15	
Unappropriated	85	100
		$ 200

EXHIBIT 5–7 **An example of the recommended manner in which to report an appropriation, and the subsequent year's reversal when the actual expenditure is made.**

THE BETHLEHEM SERVICES ORGANIZATION
STATEMENT OF INCOME AND EXPENSES
(in thousands)

	Year Ended December 31,	
	19X1	19X2
Income	$ 100	$ 100
Expenses:		
Other than Project A	80	80
Project A	—	13
Total expenses	80	93
Excess of income over expenses	$ 20	$ 7

STATEMENT OF CHANGES IN NET ASSETS

	Year Ended December 31,	
	19X1	19X2
Appropriated:		
Balance, beginning of year	—	$ 15
Add—Appropriation for Project A	$ 15	—
Less—Appropriation no longer needed	—	(15)
Balance, end of year	15	—
Unappropriated:		
Balance, beginning of year	80	85
Excess of income over expenses for the year	20	7
Less—Appropriated for Project A	(15)	—
Add—Appropriation no longer needed	—	15
Balance, end of year	85	107
Net assets	$ 100	$ 107

BALANCE SHEET

	December 31,	
	19X1	19X2
Assets	$ 200	$ 207
Liabilities	$ 100	$ 100
Net assets:		
Appropriated*: for Project A	15	
Unappropriated	85	107
Total liabilities and net assets	$ 200	$ 207

*Sometimes the word "allocated" or the word "designated" will be used instead of "appropriated."

Net Assets is used; the presentation is prepared in the second year, when the actual expenditure is made.

Appropriation accounting is both confusing and subject to abuse. It is confusing because very few readers understand exactly what an appropriation is. Most readers do not realize that an appropriation is not an expenditure but only a nonbinding, internal "authorization" for a future expenditure. (Some people may also be confused because in governmental accounting, an "appropriation" is often a legally binding act of a legislative body which requires the expenditure of resources in a certain way.) Appropriation accounting is also confusing because the presentation in the financial statements is often not made in a straightforward manner. When the term "appropriation" appears on a financial statement the casual reader is probably uncertain of its meaning.

Appropriation accounting is subject to abuse because it is frequently used to give the appearance of an expenditure of resources out of the income for that year. This can occur when, incorrectly, the appropriation is treated as though it were an expenditure, as shown in Exhibit 5–8. This treatment presents a net income figure which appears lower than it actually is. While it is understandable that a board interested in raising contributions finds it difficult to go "hat-in-hand" if the income statement shows a large excess of income for the preceding year, the presentation is not permitted by authoritative accounting pronouncements because it does not accurately present the truth about what happened during the year.

This is not to suggest that the board may not have a specific and very real project in mind when it makes an appropriation. Many organizations

EXHIBIT 5–8   An example of an improper presentation of an appropriation. Even though the appropriation is clearly disclosed, most readers will assume the excess income for the year is $5,000.

THE BETHLEHEM SERVICES ORGANIZATION
STATEMENT OF INCOME AND EXPENSES
Year Ended December 31, 19X1
(in thousands)

Income		$100
Expenses:		
Total expenses	$80	
Appropriation for Project A	15	
Total expenses		95
Excess of income over expenses and appropriation		$ 5

have sizable projects that only take place every few years. Often the board wants to provide for the needed resources over a period of time. The key point is that financial statements should represent transactions that have taken place in the past and not transactions that may take place in the future.

(b) Appropriation Accounting Is Not Recommended

Appropriation accounting creates more confusion than clarification. It fails the non-accountant test. When an organization wants to set aside resources to provide for some future need, no bookkeeping entry is really required. The board may wish to put the desired amount in a separate savings account or earmark part of the organization's investment securities. Neither action would result in a bookkeeping entry or a presentation problem.

(c) Essential Rules Where "Appropriation" Accounting Is Used

Notwithstanding the reservations about the use of the term appropriations, some organizations will continue to use this term. For these organizations, the following rules must be followed to provide a straightforward and meaningful presentation of what transpires and to conform to "generally accepted accounting principles:"[2]

1. *Appropriations should be made only for specific projects or undertakings.* There should be no appropriations for general, undetermined contingencies or for any indefinite future losses. The unexpended balance of a budget should not be carried over to future period(s) in the guise of an appropriation.

2. *All new appropriations and all remaining appropriations from prior years should be specifically authorized (or re-authorized) by the board each year.* This function should not be delegated. All prior-year appropriations should be carefully reviewed to be certain they are still necessary. If all or part of a prior-year appropriation is no longer applicable, it should be reversed.

3. *The appropriation must not be included as part of expenses.* An example of an improper presentation is shown in Exhibit 5–8.

---

[2] All three AICPA Audit Guides and the Statement of Position indicate that appropriations may not be charged to expense, and are only a form of segregation of fund balance. (See Chapters 14 through 17.) The rules listed here comply with the requirements of these pronouncements.

4. *The appropriation should preferably be reported in a separate Statement of Changes in Net Assets, as illustrated in Exhibit 5–7.* If a separate Statement of Changes in Net Assets is not used, the appropriation should be reported in the separate "change in net assets section" of the income statement. Under no circumstances should the appropriation be reported before the caption "Excess of income over expenses."

5. *When an expense is incurred in a subsequent period out of the resources previously appropriated, such expense must be included in the Statement of Income and Expenses for that year, as illustrated in Exhibit 5–7.* It is not proper to charge such expense directly against the appropriation since to do so has the effect of concealing the expense. The reader has a right to know what expenses have been incurred.

6. *When an expenditure has been made, and charged to expense as provided in rule 5 above, the appropriation must be reversed in the same manner as it was set up.* Exhibit 5–7 shows this reversal.

7. *The appropriation on the Balance Sheet must appear in the net assets section, not in the liability section (see Exhibit 5–7).*

(d) Footnote Disclosure

There is one final alternative for the organization wanting to use the term appropriation but not wanting to confuse the reader. That is to make no reference to appropriations on any of the statements and handle the disclosure only in footnotes. If this approach is followed, the footnotes to the Balance Sheet would disclose the amount appropriated. For example such a footnote might read:

> Of the total net assets of $100, $15 has been appropriated by the board for future use in Project A.

Even clearer wording would result if the word "designated" were substituted for the word "appropriated." This fully discloses the appropriation but eliminates all of the confusion on the statements. This approach is easiest to understand and therefore is recommended.

5.3 CONCLUSION

One of the major reasons why appropriation accounting or the use of the term "appropriation" should be avoided is that it is both confusing and complicated. Appropriation accounting serves little legitimate purpose and usually confuses readers, including the board members themselves.

If a board is truly concerned about setting aside a "reserve" or appropriation for some future year, it need only decide that it will not spend that amount currently. Furthermore, there is no reason why the monies represented by the appropriation can't be invested or put in a separate savings account. This is not to minimize the practical problem of actually setting this money aside and not spending it. This discipline is always difficult. But appropriation accounting is not the answer.

Fixed Assets—Some Accounting Problems

Fixed assets and their depreciation may present accounting and reporting problems for some not-for-profit organizations. Some organizations record and report fixed assets, some do not. Some record and report depreciation, some do not. Until recently, this was an area of not-for-profit accounting where practice was sharply divided. This chapter summarizes current accounting thinking and presents alternatives for recording fixed assets. Chapter 7 discusses the related problem of depreciation.

6.1 NATURE OF THE PROBLEM

Fixed assets can present a problem because many not-for-profit organizations handle their affairs on a cash basis. When these organizations need to purchase a new building or equipment they turn to their constituents to raise cash for these purchases in a building or equipment fund drive. Having raised the money and purchased the building, they feel there is relatively little significance in having the fixed asset on the organization's Balance Sheet except as a historical record of what it cost. This is in contrast to a commercial enterprise that is dependent on recovering the cost of the fixed asset through the sale of goods or services to outsiders. In a commercial business, it is entirely appropriate to record the asset on the Balance Sheet and to depreciate (i.e., to systematically allocate) the cost of the asset over its estimated useful life. Depreciation is an expense that is charged against income for the period. If income from the sale of goods or services is not large enough to recover all the expenses, including depreciation charges, the commercial enterprise is considered to have suffered a loss. If such losses occur over an extended period of time, the enterprise will go bankrupt.

One of the principal reasons why recording fixed assets is so controversial in the not-for-profit community is that the nature of these organizations is such that there often is perceived to be no compelling need to record the asset and then to depreciate it over a period of time. The element of matching income and costs has historically been of little interest to many not-for-profit organizations. This is changing.

Another factor is that some not-for-profit organizations have as their principal asset buildings acquired many years ago. Because of inflation and growth in real estate values, these buildings and land are frequently worth several times their cost. To many it seems incongruous to depreciate a building on the basis of original cost when the building is known to be presently worth more than this amount.

Further, if fixed assets were originally purchased out of a special building or equipment fund drive, some find it difficult to justify recording them on the books and then depreciating them since this depreciation represents a charge against current income. Effectively, it appears that the cost of the building has been reported (and incurred) twice, once when the funds were originally raised and once when the assets are written off through the depreciation charge. Some believe it is unethical to raise funds for fixed assets in a building fund drive and subsequently to seek to recover the costs of such assets from the users of the facility or from future donors. The building or asset can be recorded and not depreciated but this goes against the grain of accounting for fixed assets as used by commercial enterprises. The result of all this is that many approaches are followed and there is much confusion.

6.2   ALTERNATIVES FOR HANDLING FIXED ASSETS

There are two basic alternative approaches for recording fixed assets, and a third, not recommended, hybrid approach.[1] These are:

1. Immediate write-off approach, where assets are written off as purchased, in the Statement of Income and Expenses.
2. Capitalization approach, where the full cost of the asset is capitalized and recorded on the Balance Sheet. This is now the "generally accepted" accounting principle.
3. Write-off, then capitalize, approach, where the asset is written off in the Statement of Income and Expenses but then capitalized on the Balance Sheet. This hybrid approach is not recommended because it is confusing to most readers.

Each of these three approaches is discussed in detail in the following sections. Each can theoretically be used by both accrual basis and cash basis organizations.

(a)   Immediate Write-Off Method

The "immediate write-off" approach is the simplest and is frequently used. The organization treats all fixed asset purchases as any other category of expense, and does not capitalize the purchases as assets. The purchase is included as another expense in the Statement of Income and Expenses for the period in which the asset is purchased.

An example is the Rathskeller Youth Center,[2] which raised $25,000 for building alterations in 19X1. In 19X2, the Center purchased furniture and fixtures for $5,000. In this illustration, the Center is on an accrual basis of accounting, but the principles would be the same if it were on a cash basis.

The Rathskeller Youth Center's Statement of Income and Expenses and Balance Sheet for these two years are shown in Exhibit 6–1.

---

[1] Part III of this book discusses the various published Audit Guides for not-for-profit organizations as well as the AICPA Statement of Position. These documents prescribe the fixed asset and depreciation procedures that are acceptable for certain categories of organizations. Readers should refer to this discussion if the financial statements prepared by their organizations are to be described as being prepared in accordance with generally accepted accounting principles. See Chapter 24 for a discussion of the significance of generally accepted accounting principles.

[2] The Rathskeller Youth Center is located in a small town and provides a place where teenagers can congregate. The center occupies a small building donated for this purpose. Operating expenses are covered principally from donations from the general public, although each teenager pays a small membership fee to belong.

EXHIBIT 6–1   An example of the statements of an organization that follows the immediate write-off method of handling fixed assets.

RATHSKELLER YOUTH CENTER
STATEMENT OF INCOME AND EXPENSES

	Year Ended December 31,	
	19X1	19X2
Income:		
Membership fees	$ 4,000	$ 5,000
Contributions:		
General	37,900	39,600
Building Fund	25,000	—
Total income	66,900	44,600
Expenses:		
Salaries	11,000	10,000
Building maintenance	5,000	5,200
Coffee and food	12,800	12,600
Music and entertainment	2,000	2,400
Other	8,000	5,900
Building alterations	25,000	—
Furniture and equipment	—	5,000
Total expenses	63,800	41,100
Excess of income over expenses	3,100	3,500
Net assets:		
Beginning of year	2,000	5,100
End of year	$ 5,100	$ 8,600

BALANCE SHEET

	December 31,	
	19X1	19X2
Assets:		
Cash	$ 2,000	$ 4,000
Pledges receivable	6,500	6,700
Total assets	$ 8,500	$10,700
Liabilities:		
Accrued salaries	$ 3,000	$ 2,000
Accounts payable	400	100
Total liabilities	3,400	2,100
Net assets	5,100	8,600
Total liabilities and net assets	$ 8,500	$10,700

Advantages

The principal advantage is simplicity. In the first year, a building fund drive was conducted to raise income for the building alterations, and this statement shows clearly the income and expenditures for this purpose. The amount shown as excess of income over expenses represents the actual amount that remained after all bills were paid and pledges collected. While this is not the cash balance of the Center, it has much the same significance. With this presentation, there is no confusion as to the amount available for the board to spend.

This approach recognizes that while the Center has a building that is essential to its continued operation, the building has no value in terms of meeting its day-to-day cash requirements.

Disadvantages

The principal disadvantage is that the historical cost of the Center's building is not reflected on the Balance Sheet and therefore the reported net assets amount does not truly represent the "net worth" of the organization. In addition, the Balance Sheet does not account for the asset by reflecting its existence; thus the organization seems much smaller in size than it actually is. Most members take pride in seeing fixed assets reflected in the financial statements. The absence of a building in the statements can be upsetting to many people, particularly those who have made large contributions toward its construction.

Another disadvantage, although not applicable in this case, is that by writing off the asset all at one time, no allocation of cost is made against future years' revenue-producing projects. This is discussed in Chapter 7. A related problem is that by writing off fixed assets as purchased, there can be considerable fluctuation in such expenditures between years. In this instance, observe that the furniture and equipment purchases of $5,000 in 19X2 were not matched by similar purchases in 19X1.

A further disadvantage is that this method is not "generally accepted" and an organization could not describe its financial statements as being prepared in accordance with generally accepted accounting principles. A CPA would therefore be required to qualify the opinion on these statements and to indicate that the statements were not prepared in accordance with generally accepted accounting principles. See Chapter 24 for a discussion of the significance of qualified opinions.

(b) Capitalization Method

The second approach is for the organization to capitalize all of its fixed asset purchases. However, even when fixed assets are capitalized, it still is appropriate to write off small purchases to avoid the paperwork of keeping track of them. Many organizations "expense" amounts under $100; others have higher limits of $500 or $1,000 depending on their size.

Exhibit 6–2 shows the Statement of Income and Expenses and Balance Sheet under this capitalization approach. Organizations that want an unqualified opinion from their CPA will have to follow this method. Under this capitalization approach, depreciation could be taken, or, alternatively, the fixed assets could be written down from time to time as their value decreases. This subject is covered in Chapter 7.

Advantages

The principal advantage is that the fixed assets purchased are reflected on the Balance Sheet. This makes it possible for the reader to see the amount of assets for which the board is responsible. In this instance it will be noted that prior to 19X1 the Center had acquired land and a building for $90,000 and furniture and fixtures for $20,000. The fund balance reflects the cost of these significant assets.

A major advantage is that by reflecting fixed assets on the Balance Sheet, the organization can then follow depreciation accounting techniques. As discussed in Chapter 7, this results in a more accurate reflection of the cost of services rendered.

Many businesspersons feel more comfortable when financial transactions are recorded on this capitalization method since commercial businesses also capitalize (and depreciate) their fixed assets.

Disadvantages

Some readers may find this income statement more difficult to understand. The biggest risk is that they will confuse the large excess of income over expenses with the amount of "cash" available to the board for use. The readers may be left with the incorrect impression that in 19X1 the Center has excess income of $28,100, and therefore does not need any more contributions. This is a risk.

Another related concern is that the reader will look at the net assets on the Balance Sheet and will likewise confuse the $140,100 net assets with an amount that is available for current spending.

(b) Write-Off, Then Capitalize Method

An organization can combine these two approaches and write off purchases of fixed assets on its Statement of Income and Expenses and then

EXHIBIT 6–2   An example of the statements of an organization that follows the capitalization method of handling fixed assets.

RATHSKELLER YOUTH CENTER
STATEMENT OF INCOME AND EXPENSES

	Year Ended December 31,	
	19X1	19X2
Income:		
Membership fees	$ 4,000	$ 5,000
Contributions:		
General	37,900	39,600
Building Fund	25,000	—
Total income	66,900	44,600
Expenses:		
Salaries	11,000	10,000
Building maintenance	5,000	5,200
Coffee and food	12,800	12,600
Music and entertainment	2,000	2,400
Other	8,000	5,900
Total expenses	38,800	36,100
Excess of income over expenses	28,100	8,500
Net assets:		
Beginning of year	112,000	140,100
End of year	$140,100	$148,600

BALANCE SHEET

	December 31,	
	19X1	19X2
Assets:		
Cash	$ 2,000	$ 4,000
Pledges receivable	6,500	6,700
Land and original building	90,000	90,000
Building alterations	25,000	25,000
Furniture and equipment	20,000	25,000
Total assets	$143,500	$150,700
Liabilities:		
Accrued salaries	$ 3,000	$ 2,000
Accounts payable	400	100
Total liabilities	3,400	2,100
Net assets	140,100	148,600
Total liabilities and net assets	$143,500	$150,700

turn around and capitalize or record the assets on its Balance Sheet. It is a hybrid approach and is not recommended because of its complexity.[3]

The theory is that a not-for-profit organization should charge off all purchases as incurred but still show the asset on the Balance Sheet. This allows the organization to show the expenditure for the fixed assets, which reduces the amount of the excess of income over expenses. One of the disadvantages of the capitalization method just discussed is thus eliminated. In this case, the building alterations have been paid for from contributions that are reflected in the Statement of Income and Expenses and the organization does not look to recover the building cost through charges to income over a period of years through depreciation.

The second part of this approach is to "reinstate" or add back these written-off assets on the Balance Sheet. This adding back can be seen in the net assets section of Exhibit 6–3, where $25,000 is added to the net assets in 19X1 to reinstate the assets written off on the Statement of Income and Expenses. In this way, the Balance Sheet reflects the cost of the assets and more fairly shows the net worth of the organization. From time to time, these assets are removed from the Balance Sheet as the assets decline in value by directly reducing the carrying value on the Balance Sheet.[4] The most confusing part of this approach is the adding back or capitalizing of the fixed assets in the net assets section of the Balance Sheet.

Advantages

Most of the advantages of both the immediate write-off and the capitalization methods are present in this hybrid approach. The reader sees the expenditure for the fixed assets in the Statement of Income and Expenses, and the excess of income over expenses has been reduced by this purchase, offset by any contributions that may have been received for such asset purchases in the current year. Accordingly, the reader is not misled into thinking there is a large excess of income that can be expended. At the same time, by capitalizing the asset in the Balance Sheet, the accountability for the asset is not lost.

---

[3] This method of handling fixed assets was originally recommended in certain accounting literature, and was widely followed prior to the 1970s. However, all current literature states that not-for-profit organizations are required to capitalize fixed assets and follow depreciation accounting. Although this method is no longer generally accepted, it has not completely disappeared, and for this reason a discussion of it is included in this chapter.

[4] This direct write-down is illustrated on page 58.

EXHIBIT 6–3 **An example of the statements of an organization that follows the write-off, then capitalize, method of handling fixed assets.**

RATHSKELLER YOUTH CENTER
STATEMENT OF INCOME AND EXPENSES

	Year Ended December 31,	
	19X1	19X2
Income:		
Membership fees	$ 4,000	$ 5,000
Contributions:		
General	37,900	39,600
Building Fund	25,000	—
Total income	66,900	44,600
Expenses:		
Salaries	11,000	10,000
Building maintenance	5,000	5,200
Coffee and food	12,800	12,600
Music and entertainment	2,000	2,400
Other	8,000	5,900
Building alterations	25,000	—
Furniture and equipment	—	5,000
Total expenses	63,800	41,100
Excess of income over expenses	$ 3,100	$ 3,500

BALANCE SHEET

	December 31,	
	19X1	19X2
Assets:		
Cash	$ 2,000	$ 4,000
Pledges receivable	6,500	6,700
Land and building	90,000	90,000
Building alterations	25,000	25,000
Furniture and equipment	20,000	25,000
Total assets	$143,500	$150,700
Liabilities:		
Accrued salaries	$ 3,000	$ 2,000
Accounts payable	400	100
Total liabilities	3,400	2,100
Net assets:		
Beginning of year	112,000	140,100
Excess of income over expenses	3,100	3,500
Building and equipment capitalized	25,000	5,000
End of year	140,100	148,600
Total liabilities and net assets	$143,500	$150,700

Disadvantages

The capitalizing of the asset directly in the fund balance is very confusing, and there is a high degree of risk that the reader won't understand it. It appears to mix apples and oranges in that it is saying purchases of fixed assets should be handled on more or less a cash basis in the Statement of Income and Expenses but on an accrual basis in the Balance Sheet. This is inconsistent and seems illogical.

Another related disadvantage is that under this method there is no way to provide depreciation charges in the Statement of Income and Expenses since the asset has already been written off. As more fully discussed in Chapter 7, it is frequently appropriate to provide depreciation charges in order to try to match income and costs. While depreciation may or may not be appropriate in the case of the Rathskeller Youth Center, it is appropriate for many not-for-profit organizations. Accordingly, this method should not be used by organizations where depreciation is appropriate. Another related disadvantage is that if asset purchases fluctuate from year to year, they can have a significant effect on the excess of income over expenses. This would not be so if the assets were capitalized and depreciated. Only the depreciation charge would then appear in the Statement of Income and Expenses.

Finally, it should again be noted that this method does not follow generally accepted accounting principles, and organizations following this approach will find that their CPAs will be required to qualify their opinion.

6.3   FIXED ASSETS WHERE TITLE MAY REVERT TO GRANTORS

Some organizations purchase or receive fixed assets under research or similar grants in which legal title to the assets remains with the grantor. At the completion of the grant period, the right to these fixed assets technically reverts to the grantor.

Should these assets be recorded on the grantee's balance sheet? Typically the grant period closely approximates the useful life of these assets, and the grantor in fact seldom asks for their return. The right to reclaim these assets usually is in the grant award mainly to protect the grantor in the event the grant is prematurely terminated. Under these circumstances, a fixed asset, whether purchased or donated, should be recorded as an asset and depreciated as with any other asset. If the aggregate amount of these assets that might have to be returned were material, disclosure of the relevant facts would be appropriate.

6.4 SEPARATE BUILDING FUND

No distinction has been made in the illustrations in this chapter between restricted and unrestricted contributions for the building fund. These contributions have been treated as though they were unrestricted, for ease in illustrating the various ways in which fixed assets can be handled. If, however, these contributions were restricted for building acquisition, they would normally be reported in a separate restricted fund, or in a building or fixed asset fund as discussed in Chapter 4.

(a) Immediate Write-Off

If a separate building or fixed asset fund were used, the principles outlined in this chapter would still apply. In the immediate write-off approach, restricted building fund contributions would be added to a separate building fund when received. As expenditures were made, they would be shown as expenses of that fund. The amount remaining in the fund at any time would be the unexpended restricted gifts. Since under this approach assets are not capitalized, the Balance Sheet would normally only have unexpended cash and the corresponding net assets in the building fund. Effectively, the building fund would follow the procedures discussed in Chapter 4 for current restricted funds (see Exhibit 4–1).

In some instances, the organization might purchase fixed assets with unrestricted resources, as is the case with the $5,000 of furniture and equipment purchased in 19X2. Since unrestricted amounts are involved, the $5,000 would be shown as an expense of the unrestricted fund.

(b) Capitalization

If the capitalization approach were followed, the fixed assets on the Balance Sheet would be reflected in a separate fixed asset fund in a manner similar to that shown in Exhibit 6–4.

Observe in this approach that restricted contributions are reflected directly in the fixed asset fund at the time they are received. Observe also that the fixed assets purchased with these restricted resources are reflected directly in this fund.

But reflecting fixed assets in a separate fund creates a problem. What should be done with fixed assets purchased with unrestricted resources, in this case the $5,000 of furniture and equipment in 19X2? Should the fixed assets be left in the current unrestricted fund (since they were purchased with unrestricted resources) or transferred into the fixed asset fund? The answer is to transfer the assets to the fixed asset

EXHIBIT 6–4   An example of statements of an organization that records contributions and fixed assets in a separate Fixed Asset Fund.

RATHSKELLER YOUTH CENTER
STATEMENT OF INCOME AND EXPENSES
For the Years Ended December 31, 19X1 and 19X2

	December 31, 19X1		December 31, 19X2	
	Current Unrestricted	Fixed Assets	Current Unrestricted	Fixed Assets
Income:				
Membership fees	$ 4,000		$ 5,000	
Contributions	37,900	$ 25,000	39,600	
Total income	41,900	25,000	44,600	
Expenses:				
Salaries	11,000		10,000	
Building maintenance	5,000		5,200	
Coffee and food	12,800		12,600	
Music and entertainment	2,000		2,400	
Other	8,000		5,900	
Total expenses	38,800		36,100	
Excess of income over				
expenses	3,100	25,000	8,500	
Net assets:				
Beginning of year	2,000	110,000	5,100	$135,000
Interfund transfer	—	—	(5,000)	5,000
End of year	$ 5,100	$135,000	$ 8,600	$140,000

fund since it may be confusing to have fixed assets spread among several funds. This transfer is shown in the net assets section of the Statement of Income. This results in a fixed asset fund which contains a combination of restricted and unrestricted amounts—unexpended restricted contributions, and fixed assets purchased using both restricted and unrestricted contributions. While this makes it more difficult to characterize the fund as either restricted or unrestricted, the presentation is less confusing. However, observe that the fixed asset fund should not contain any unexpended unrestricted amounts. The transfer from the current unrestricted fund should take place only at the time fixed assets are purchased with unrestricted resources.

The authors do not recommend the use of a separate fixed asset fund in external financial statements, for the reasons discussed in Chapter 4, but prefer that fixed assets be included in the unrestricted fund. If the

EXHIBIT 6–4 *Continued.*

	BALANCE SHEET			
	December 31, 19X1		December 31, 19X2	
	Current Unrestricted	Fixed Assets	Current Unrestricted	Fixed Assets
Assets:				
Cash	$ 2,000		$ 4,000	
Pledges receivable	6,500		6,700	
Land and original building		$ 90,000		$ 90,000
Building alterations		25,000		25,000
Furniture and equipment		20,000		25,000
Total assets	$ 8,500	$135,000	$ 10,700	$140,000
Liabilities:				
Accrued salaries	$ 3,000		$ 2,000	
Accounts payable	400		100	
Total liabilities	3,400		2,100	
Net assets:	5,100	$135,000	8,600	$140,000
Total liabilities and net assets	$ 8,500	$135,000	$ 10,700	$140,000

organization follows this recommendation, it will still record restricted contributions in a separate restricted building fund. However, at the time fixed assets are purchased with these restricted resources, a transfer would be made from the restricted building fund to the unrestricted fund for the cost of the assets purchased. This transfer would also be reported in the manner shown in Exhibit 6–4 but the transfer would be in the opposite direction. The column headings would then change to "unrestricted fund" and "building fund."

(c) Write-Off, Then Capitalize

If the hybrid write-off, then capitalize, approach to handling fixed assets were followed, a combination of the above procedures would also apply. Restricted contributions received would be reported in a separate fixed asset fund, and the disbursement for the assets would be reported as an expense. The Balance Sheet would then show—in a separate fixed asset fund—the capitalization of the assets as illustrated in Exhibit 6–3. Assets purchased with unrestricted resources would be transferred to the fixed asset fund as shown on Exhibit 6–4.

6.5 CONCLUSION AND RECOMMENDATIONS

As discussed in the first chapter, the most important principle to be considered in keeping records and preparing financial statements is that they be successful in communicating to their readers what has happened during the year. If the statements are too complicated, they fail in this respect and their usefulness is limited. The organization should adopt methods of accounting and reporting appropriate to its activities and to the needs of the users of its statements.

The first approach (i.e., immediate write-off) would appear appropriate for small or possibly medium-sized organizations with relatively unsophisticated readers or for organizations on the cash basis. This is particularly so if the primary concern is raising enough cash each year to cover expenses, whether the organization is on the cash or accrual basis. The bookkeeping complexities of the capitalization method just do not seem warranted, particularly because the financial statements prepared on an accrual basis may leave the reader with the wrong impression of the results of operations.

On the other hand, if the organization is larger, or is already on the accrual basis, the second approach (i.e., capitalization) is probably appropriate. If the organization merely writes off, or expenses, all fixed assets as purchased, the reader could lose track of what assets the organization has and part of the stewardship potentially is lost. Also, a larger organization is less likely to keep its fixed assets for an indefinite period of time. It is more likely to outgrow its building, sell it, and buy a new one. It may also have other types of fixed assets which will be replaced from time to time, such as office equipment and vehicles.

Organizations should capitalize their assets if they have a reason to match revenues and costs or if they want to determine cost of services being rendered. A direct write-off approach distorts the results of operations for these organizations. Instead, assets should be capitalized and the costs allocated through depreciation charges. The capitalization method is the only one that can be considered as a "generally accepted accounting principle" and for this reason is the method which must be followed by organizations wanting an unqualified opinion from their CPAs.

The third approach (i.e., write-off, then capitalize) is not recommended. This approach departs too much from generally accepted accounting principles. Very few readers will understand it. Furthermore, this method effectively precludes an organization from depreciating its assets through its income statement, which means that organizations for which it is important to know the total costs of a service each year cannot use this method.

Finally, where an organization follows the recommended capitalization approach, the authors do not recommend reporting the fixed assets in a separate fixed asset fund in external financial statements. As more fully discussed in Chapter 4, carrying fixed assets in a separate fund causes confusion for most readers, particularly where depreciation accounting techniques are followed.

C H A P T E R   7

Fixed Assets—Depreciation

Depreciation, a subject related to fixed assets, can be difficult for not-for-profit organizations to handle. If the organization follows the immediate write-off method of handling fixed assets (discussed in Chapter 6), there are no assets on the Balance Sheet to depreciate. But many organizations do record fixed assets and are faced with the basic question of whether to depreciate these assets. This has been a controversial question until recently; depreciation accounting is now becoming more generally accepted and is required for most not-for-profit organizations if they want their statements to be in conformity with generally accepted accounting principles. This requirement was formalized in FASB Statement No. 93, "Recognition of Depreciation by Not-for-Profit Organizations."

7.1 ARGUMENTS AGAINST TAKING DEPRECIATION

A number of reasons are advanced for not taking depreciation. Probably the most relevant is that depreciation is a concept associated with commercial enterprises, which determine profit through the matching of income and cost. Many not-for-profit organizations are not as concerned with determining "profit" nor with a direct matching of income and cost. For them, depreciation is viewed as serving little purpose.

Another reason often suggested is that not-for-profit organizations frequently raise the resources they need for major fixed asset additions through special fund drives. When it comes time for the replacement of these assets, additional amounts will be raised through similar drives. Therefore, there is no perceived need to recover the costs of such assets from income in the form of a depreciation charge.

Another consideration is that, with inflation, the market value of fixed assets often increases as fast or faster than the decline in asset value associated with deterioration through passage of time. Depreciation is often thought of, incorrectly,[1] as a method of trying to measure loss in value. Many ask, why depreciate an asset that is worth twice what it cost 25 years ago?

Another practical argument is that depreciation can be confusing to show in the financial statements, particularly when fund accounting is followed. If depreciation is viewed as serving no real purpose, why confuse the reader with bookkeeping entries that don't involve cash?

7.2 WHY DEPRECIATION SHOULD BE RECORDED

Depreciation accounting is now required for most not-for-profit organizations that want to describe their financial statements as being in conformity with "generally accepted accounting principles."[2] But aside from these requirements, the authors believe that depreciation accounting is desirable for most not-for-profit organizations for a number of reasons.

Not-for-profit organizations provide services, or, less often, furnish goods, that are measured in terms of costs. Depreciation is a cost. By not including this cost in the financial statements of each year in which the services are rendered or the goods furnished, the reader is misled into thinking the actual costs were less than they really were. The board of an organization is charged with the responsibility of efficiently using all of the resources available to it to carry out the programs of the organization. By excluding a significant amount from the identified costs of the

[1] Depreciation is defined by the Committee on Terminology of the American Institute of Certified Public Accountants as follows: "Depreciation accounting is a system of accounting which aims to distribute the cost or other basic value of tangible capital assets, less salvage (if any), over the estimated useful life of the unit (which may be a group of assets) in a systematic and rational manner. It is a process of allocation, not of valuation. Depreciation for the year is the portion of the total charge under such a system that is allocated to the year. Although the allocation may properly take into account occurrences during the year, it is not intended to be a measurement of the effect of all such occurrences." Copyright (c) 1961 by the American Institute of Certified Public Accountants, Inc.

[2] There is an exception in Statement No. 93 for certain works of art, if criteria specified in the Statement (par. 6) are met.

programs, the board gives the reader the impression that the program has been carried out more efficiently than is actually the case.

Most not-for-profit organizations, even those that raise funds for major fixed asset additions through special fund-raising drives, must replace certain assets out of the recurring income of the organization. If no depreciation is taken and these assets are written off as purchased, two things happen. First, the organization deludes itself into thinking its income is sufficient to cover its costs whereas, in reality, it may not be. Second, the excess of income over expenses of the organization will fluctuate widely from year to year relative to the timing of asset replacement and the replacement cost of the asset.

This will precipitate disproportionately high expenses in some years, which will depress the excess of income over expenses; in other years, the amount written off will be unrealistically low, inflating net income, and will not reflect the true cost to the organization of providing programs or services that year.

Some not-for-profit organizations sell products or provide to outsiders services that are also available from commercial enterprises. Depreciation is especially appropriate for those assets involved with this revenue-producing function. Once the organization engages in the sale of goods or services, it has an interest in matching income and costs in a manner similar to commercial enterprises. If no depreciation is taken, there is an appearance of profit that may not be realistic.

A not-for-profit organization that receives payment for products or services from government agencies, health insurance companies such as Blue Cross, or other organizations where a "reimbursement formula" is involved or potentially involved, should always charge depreciation. The reasons for taking depreciation are much the same as those noted in the preceding paragraph. If no depreciation is taken on the books, it is always difficult to justify using a depreciation factor in a rate-setting or reimbursement situation. On the other hand, if depreciation has consistently been recorded on the books over a period of time, it will be more difficult for the governmental or other agency to argue against using a depreciation factor in setting the rate or reimbursement base.

Even though an organization does not now sell a service to a governmental agency, perhaps it will in the future. It is conspicuous to start taking depreciation only when a product or service is first charged to an agency. Many organizations have found, much to their surprise, that at some point they have undertaken a project involving government reimbursement. A good example is a professional engineering society that undertakes to do research under a government grant on a cost-reimbursement basis.

Furthermore, a not-for-profit organization may be subject to federal income taxes on "unrelated business income." Depreciation is a cost that should be recorded to reduce the profits subject to tax. Depreciation should be charged even if there is no profit in a year because there may be profits in the future. It is always difficult to change accounting principles at a later date and start taking depreciation if the activity starts becoming profitable. Chapter 26 discusses the problems of unrelated business income.

Depreciation is appropriate for most organizations that follow the practice of recording fixed assets on their Balance Sheet.[3] Since depreciation is a concept that is used by commercial organizations, it should cause relatively little confusion in financial statements.

7.3   PRESENTATION IN THE FINANCIAL STATEMENTS

The presentation of depreciation in the financial statements is straightforward and similar to that used by commercial enterprises. Exhibit 7–1 shows depreciation in the financial statements of the Corvallis YMCA.[4] The Corvallis YMCA has both its own building and substantial amounts of equipment. While it receives some support from the public, most of its income is received from program fees. Accordingly, the organization follows the practice of capitalizing all fixed assets and depreciating them. The building is depreciated over a fifty-year life, and all equipment over a five-year life. Depreciation has been included in the Statement of Income and Expenses, calculated as follows:

	19X1	19X2
Building (50 years):		
Cost: $450,000 (2%/year)	$ 9,000	$ 9,000
Equipment (5 years):		
Cost: $120,000 (20%/year)	24,000	
Cost: $130,000 (20%/year)		26,000
Total	$33,000	$35,000

The captions and presentation are familiar and should cause no problem in a single-fund organization. Considerable difficulty arises, however, if the organization has a separate plant fund and wishes to provide the depreciation charge in the current unrestricted fund. The problem is a mechanical one of transferring the accumulated depreciation

---

[3] Depreciation is not applicable, however, to those organizations following the hybrid write-off, then capitalize method discussed in Chapter 6 because the asset has already been written off at the time it was purchased.

[4] The Corvallis YMCA financial statements were presented in greater detail in Exhibit 4–1.

EXHIBIT 7–1 An example of the financial statements of an organization that records depreciation.

CORVALLIS YMCA
STATEMENT OF INCOME AND EXPENSES
(Condensed)

	Year Ended December 31,	
	19X1	19X2
Income (in total)	$ 721,000	$ 767,000
Expenses:		
Other than depreciation	676,000	662,000
Depreciation	33,000	35,000
Total expenses	709,000	697,000
Excess of income over expenses	$ 12,000	$ 70,000

BALANCE SHEET
(Condensed)

	December 31,	
	19X1	19X2
Current assets (in total)	$ 68,000	$ 78,000
Investments in marketable securities at cost (market value $135,000 in 19X1 and $183,000 in 19X2)	132,000	176,000 .
Fixed assets:		
Land	50,000	50,000
Building	450,000	450,000
Equipment	120,000	130,000
Total	620,000	630,000
Less–Accumulated depreciation	(106,000)	(141,000)
Net fixed assets	514,000	489,000
Total assets	$ 714,000	$ 743,000
Liabilities (in total)	$ 89,000	$ 48,000
Net assets (in total)	625,000	695,000
	$ 714,000	$ 743,000

created by the depreciation charge from the current unrestricted fund to the plant fund, since the accumulated depreciation has to be in the plant fund where the assets are recorded.

Here is an example of how this transfer can be made where there is a separate plant fund:

STATEMENT OF INCOME, EXPENSES, AND TRANSFERS

	Current Unrestricted Fund	Plant Fund	Total All Funds
Income	$ 100,000	$ 8,000	$ 108,000
Expenses:			
Other than depreciation	(90,000)		(90,000)
Depreciation	(5,000)		(5,000)
Excess of income over expenses	5,000	8,000	13,000
Net assets, beginning of			
year	50,000	100,000	150,000
Transfer of depreciation to			
plant fund	5,000	(5,000)	—
Net assets, end of year	$ 60,000	$ 103,000	$ 163,000

Things would be simpler if the depreciation charge were included directly in the plant fund and not shown as a transfer. The principal reason why this is usually not done is that the organization wants to show depreciation in the current unrestricted fund to match income and costs. Here is how the statement would look if the depreciation were included directly in the plant fund:

STATEMENT OF INCOME AND EXPENSES

	Current Unrestricted Fund	Plant Fund	Total All Funds
Income	$ 100,000	$ 8,000	$ 108,000
Expenses:			
Other than depreciation	(90,000)		(90,000)
Depreciation		(5,000)	(5,000)
Excess of income over expenses	10,000	3,000	13,000
Net assets, beginning of year	50,000	100,000	150,000
Net assets, end of year	$ 60,000	$ 103,000	$ 163,000

This simplifies the presentation. Furthermore, in a columnar approach the reader's attention is probably going to focus primarily on the "total all funds" column, and the figures are exactly the same for both presentations in this column.

The real confusion occurs when, instead of preparing the statements in a columnar approach, the organization prepares separate statements for each of the funds, as was illustrated in Exhibit 4–1. It is difficult for the readers of the statements to fully understand transfers between funds. This is particularly true with depreciation because the concept of transferring depreciation back and forth is a difficult one to comprehend.

Because of these problems of presentation, it is recommended that whenever depreciation expense is shown in the current unrestricted fund, all fixed assets should be included in this same fund. There would be no separate plant fund and thus there would be no need to transfer depreciation between funds. The financial statement presentation becomes greatly simplified. This approach is recommended by the Health Care Audit Guide and is illustrated in Exhibits 16–1 and 16–2.

7.4 DIRECT WRITE-DOWN OF FIXED ASSETS CAPITALIZED

Some organizations capitalize fixed asset purchases but do not write off such assets through regular depreciation charges in the Statement of Income and Expenses. Instead they continue to carry these assets in the Balance Sheet at their original cost. Where this approach is followed, it may still be necessary to periodically write down the carrying value of these assets so that the Balance Sheet is not overstated.

There are two approaches for handling this write-down in value. The first is to directly reduce both the asset carrying value and the net assets by the amount of the write-down. Under this approach the write-down does not appear at all in the Statement of Income and Expenses. The write-down would appear in a Statement of Changes in Net Assets.[5] This is the approach followed in the 1973 AICPA Audit Guide for Colleges and Universities discussed in Chapter 15.

The other approach is to show the write-down in the Statement of Income and Expenses, appropriately labeled. Here is how this latter approach would appear:

STATEMENT OF INCOME AND EXPENSES

Income		$108,000
Expenses:		
Operating expenses	$90,000	
Write-down of worn-out office equipment and automobile	3,500	93,500
Excess of income over expenses		$ 14,500

---

[5] If a Statement of Changes in Net Assets is not used, the write-down could appear directly on the Balance Sheet, in the net assets section (see Exhibit 7–2).

If the direct write-down method is used, this second approach is the one preferred by the authors because the reader is clearly shown all expenses in one statement. If the write-down were made directly to the net assets, the reader is not as likely to know the total expenses of the organization. At the same time, if this second approach is followed, the organization should rethink its policy of not providing depreciation. The advantage of periodic depreciation charges is that they are regular, and no one year is charged with a disproportionately high amount of expense.

If the organization follows the write-off, then capitalize method, discussed and not recommended in Chapter 6, fixed assets are written off in the Statement of Income and Expenses when purchased and then capitalized on the Balance Sheet. In this case, it is not appropriate to make a charge for depreciation on the income statement since the asset was completely written off when purchased. But the Balance Sheet amount should be reduced from time to time to reflect any decrease in value of the fixed assets. The reduction of the fixed asset amount must be recorded directly on the Balance Sheet. Exhibit 7–2 shows the Balance Sheet of the Rathskeller Youth Center where a direct reduction in asset values is made. The figures are the same as in Exhibit 6–3. Since the Statement of Income and Expenses is not affected by this direct write-down, the statement shown in Exhibit 6–3 is still applicable.

7.5 FUNDING DEPRECIATION

Some organizations, in addition to depreciating their fixed assets, also set aside cash (or other income-producing assets) to be used for subsequent replacement of their fixed assets. This is referred to as "funding" the depreciation, and it involves simply the physical segregation of the assets, often in a separate account. The only bookkeeping entry would be to record the movement of the assets from one account to the other. The Balance Sheet would probably show this segregation, as follows:

BALANCE SHEET
(In Part)

Assets:	
Cash	$15,000
Savings account (for replacement of equipment)	10,000
Receivables	10,000
Equipment (net of accumulated depreciation of $10,000)	40,000
Total assets	$75,000

EXHIBIT 7–2   An example of a Balance Sheet for an organization that periodically writes off fixed assets in the Balance Sheet as a direct reduction of net assets.

	RATHSKELLER YOUTH CENTER	
	BALANCE SHEET	
	December 31,	
	19X1	19X2
Assets:		
Cash	$ 2,000	$ 4,000
Pledges receivable	6,500	6,700
Land and building	90,000	90,000
Building alterations	25,000	25,000
Furniture and equipment	10,000	13,000
Total assets	$ 133,500	$ 138,700
Liabilities:		
Accrued salaries	$ 3,000	$ 2,000
Accounts payable	400	100
Total liabilities	3,400	2,100
Net assets:		
Beginning of year	112,000	130,100
Excess of income over expenses	3,100	3,500
Building and equipment capitalized ...	25,000	5,000
Write-off of worn-out equipment	(10,000)	(2,000)
End of year	130,100	136,600
Total liabilities and net assets	$ 133,500	$ 138,700

At the time the equipment is replaced, the amount of cash in the savings account reserved for this equipment would be used toward the cost of its replacement.[6] The cash has been segregated as a matter of convenience. The only advantage of this "funding" is that cash has been physically set aside, and will be less likely to be used for other things. This technique is primarily a form of self-discipline.

(a)   Separate Plant Fund

Sometimes depreciation will be charged in the plant fund and a transfer of cash made from the current unrestricted fund to the plant fund to fund the depreciation. When this is done, the effect is to transfer part of

---

[6] It should be noted that because of inflation or technological advances the setting aside of funds equal to depreciation on a historical cost basis will probably not cover the cost of replacement.

the net worth of the current unrestricted fund to the plant fund. This can be very confusing, particularly if separate statements are presented for the current unrestricted fund and the plant fund. If, on the other hand, the statements are shown in columnar form, the reader can clearly see what has happened. The following condensed income statement shows depreciation in the plant fund and the transfer of an equal amount of the net assets (in the form of cash) from the current unrestricted fund to the plant fund:

STATEMENT OF INCOME, EXPENSES, AND CHANGES
IN NET ASSETS

	Current Unrestricted Fund	Plant Fund	Total All Funds
Income	$ 100,000	$ 8,000	$ 108,000
Expenses:			
Other than depreciation	(90,000)		(90,000)
Depreciation		(5,000)	(5,000)
Excess of income over expenses	10,000	3,000	13,000
Net assets, beginning of year	50,000	100,000	150,000
Transfer to plant fund	(5,000)	5,000	—
Net assets, end of year	$ 55,000	$ 108,000	$ 163,000

Another possibility is that the organization will record depreciation in the current unrestricted fund and then transfer this depreciation to the plant fund as illustrated on page 75, and also "fund" the depreciation as illustrated above. If this were done, the combination would look like this:

STATEMENT OF INCOME, EXPENSES, AND CHANGES
IN NET ASSETS

	Current Unrestricted Fund	Plant Fund	Total All Funds
Income	$ 100,000	$ 8,000	$ 108,000
Expenses:			
Other than depreciation	(90,000)		(90,000)
Depreciation	(5,000)		(5,000)
Excess of income over expenses	5,000	8,000	13,000
Net assets, beginning of year	50,000	100,000	150,000
Transfer of depreciation expense to plant fund	5,000	(5,000)	—
Transfer of assets to plant fund	(5,000)	5,000	—
Net assets, end of year	$ 55,000	$ 108,000	$ 163,000

The effect of these transfers is a wash as far as their effect on the net assets of each of these two funds. However, the board need not necessarily transfer an amount exactly equal to the depreciation. If it is desired to provide for future purchase of a replacement unit at an anticipated higher cost, a larger amount would be transferred. There is no reason why both transfers can't be netted for statement presentation. If, as in this instance, they net out to zero, no transfer need be shown at all. The entries would still be made on the books but to show both transfers in the statement would be confusing.

The use of "funding" techniques for depreciation is acceptable under present usage but the authors feel the complexities, particularly when a separate plant fund is involved, outweigh the advantages. Therefore this approach is not recommended.

7.6   TRANSFERS OF REPLACEMENT FUNDS TO THE PLANT FUND

Some organizations do not provide depreciation at all in the income statement. Instead, they transfer an amount (usually cash) from the current unrestricted fund to the plant fund as a "replacement fund" to build up cash for future acquisitions. As in the preceding example, this transfer is not an expense but represents a transfer of part of the net assets of the current unrestricted fund to the separate plant fund. Here is an example:

STATEMENT OF INCOME, EXPENSES, AND CHANGES
IN NET ASSETS

	Current Unrestricted Fund	Plant Fund	Total All Funds
Income	$ 100,000	$ 8,000	$ 108,000
Less expenses (excludes depreciation)	(90,000)		(90,000)
Excess of income over expenses	10,000	8,000	18,000
Net assets, beginning of year	50,000	100,000	150,000
Transfer to plant fund replacement fund	(5,000)	5,000	—
Net assets, end of year	$ 55,000	$113,000	$ 168,000

The amount transferred to the plant fund builds up over the years and represents resources from which future purchases or replacement of present buildings and equipment can be made. The amount of this transfer can vary from year to year. The board may choose to establish a policy to transfer amounts exactly equal to a charge for depreciation even though no depreciation has been charged against income. The effect on the net assets of the current unrestricted fund in such circumstances is exactly the same as though depreciation had been taken. The difference is that the reported excess of income over expenses excludes depreciation.

The use of a replacement fund without depreciation is not recommended. If the board deems it prudent to set aside resources for future replacement, this suggests it should be depreciating its assets. While replacement cost may be greater than the original cost being depreciated, depreciation should still be taken and charged against income each year. To the extent that the board wants to set aside additional amounts it may do so, but these amounts should not be confused with depreciation.

Further, by making a transfer of unrestricted net assets to the plant fund, the board has mixed restricted and unrestricted amounts. This violates the principles in several of the Audit Guides and the Statement of Position discussed in Part III. If the board wants to use a "replacement fund" concept, it should do so as part of the unrestricted fund (i.e., a segregation of part of the unrestricted net assets).

7.7 CONCLUSION

Once the question of capitalizing or writing off fixed assets when purchased has been resolved, the question of whether to depreciate the assets recorded on the Balance Sheet is also largely resolved. If the asset has been written off, no depreciation is appropriate. If fixed assets have been recorded and the organization wants to follow "generally accepted accounting principles," depreciation accounting is required for most not-for-profit organizations. Depreciation accounting is clearly applicable where an organization is trying to measure the cost of services rendered or where the organization must look to replacing its assets periodically from current income.

Investment Income, Gains and Losses, and Endowment Funds

Recently, increasing attention has been given to investments and the rate of return on endowment funds, particularly in view of inflation and rising costs. Traditionally, organizations with endowments tended to invest largely in fixed-income bonds or preferred stocks. When common stocks were acquired only the bluest of blue chips were considered.

Beginning in the late 1960s, more and more not-for-profit organizations reduced their dependence on fixed-income investments (e.g., bonds) and began investing sizable portions of their portfolios in common stock. Common stock possesses higher risk than bonds but was purchased because of its potential for future growth. Although this primarily resulted in substantially less current income from interest and dividends, these organizations felt it would be more than offset over a period of years by capital gains resulting from both inflation and real growth. This is often referred to as the "total return" approach to investing. However, this new emphasis created accounting and reporting problems. In this chapter, we discuss the accounting principles that are generally followed by not-for-profit organizations in recording their investments held by endowment and other restricted and unrestricted funds. The accounting implications of the emphasis on total investment return are also reviewed.

8.1 ACCOUNTING PRINCIPLES

In discussing the accounting principles followed for investment return, it is important to distinguish between the two types of return that arise from investments. The first is interest and dividends, which are usually referred to as investment income. The second is the capital gain (or loss) resulting from changes in the market value of investments. "Realized" gains and losses occur when individual securities are sold at a price which differs from their original cost. "Unrealized" gains and losses arise from changes in value of securities still held in the organization's portfolio. Traditionally, gains or losses have not been thought of as "income" but rather as part of principal. In the discussion that follows, the accounting principles applicable to each of these two types of return will be discussed.

(a) Investment Income on Unrestricted Funds

All dividends and interest income on unrestricted funds, including board-designated endowment (quasi-endowment) funds, should be recorded in a current unrestricted fund Statement of Income and Expenses or in the income section of a combined Statement of Income, Expenses, and Changes in Net Assets. It is not appropriate to record such income directly in a separate Statement of Changes in Net Assets; such income must be shown in a Statement of Income and Expenses so the reader will be fully aware of its receipt.

(b)   Unrestricted Investment Income on Restricted Endowment Funds

Unrestricted investment income on restricted endowment funds should also be reported directly in the current unrestricted fund, in the same manner as other unrestricted investment income. It is not appropriate to first report such unrestricted investment income in the endowment fund and then to transfer it to the current unrestricted fund. The reason for this is that only income that is donor-restricted may be recorded in a restricted fund. If the terms of the donor's endowment gift are that the income is automatically unrestricted income, then this income is never restricted and should not be recorded in the endowment fund. This rule applies even where a columnar statement presentation is used in which all funds are shown side by side.

Some argue that with a columnar statement format it is acceptable to report the income first in the restricted endowment column and then to transfer it to the current unrestricted column, perhaps showing the transfer in the income section rather than below the caption "Excess of income over expenses." Their argument is that in this way it is easier for the reader to see the total endowment income in relation to the size of the endowment fund, and thus to form a judgment on management's investment skill. While this argument has merit, the chance of the reader's being confused when a transfer is shown is too great to justify such a presentation. The amount of investment income arising from endowment funds can still be shown as a separate line item in the income statement, to distinguish it from other sources of unrestricted investment income (see Exhibit 4–1).

(c)   Restricted Investment Income

The use of income from certain restricted endowment funds, and usually from all other restricted funds, may be restricted for a specified purpose. This income should be recorded directly in the appropriate restricted fund. For example, the donor may have specified that the investment income from an endowment fund gift is to be used for a specific project. In this situation, the investment income arising from this gift should be recorded directly in the fund for specified purposes and not recorded first in the endowment fund and then transferred.

Some donors will specify that the investment income is to be added to the endowment principal for a period of years, after which time the income, and perhaps the accumulated income and principal, will become unrestricted. In this situation, the investment income would, of course, be retained in the endowment fund, but this is the only circumstance in which such recording is appropriate.

(d) Gains or Losses on Unrestricted Funds

Gains or losses on board-designated and other unrestricted investment funds are not restricted except as the board might designate. For this reason, gains or losses on such unrestricted funds should always be recorded directly in the current unrestricted fund. Except for the college Audit Guide, all of the current AICPA pronouncements concur with this treatment.

There is a difference in practice as to where unrestricted gains should be shown on the statement of income. Some organizations take the position—with which the authors concur—that, in a not-for-profit organization for which income taxes are not normally a concern, there is little real difference among dividends, interest, and capital gains. All represent income to the organization, and traditionally are more or less interchangeable; that is, if high-grade blue chips are held, capital gains will be minimal, but if more speculative low-dividend-paying stocks are held there is the promise of higher gains. When this approach is taken, unrestricted capital gains are usually reported in the same section of the financial statements as dividends and interest income. The other approach is to separate capital gains from dividends and interest income by showing the capital gains in a separate section of the financial statements, but above the "Excess of income over expenses" caption. Either is acceptable.

(e) Gains or Losses on Endowment Funds

The new FASB reporting standard in Statement No. 117 will require many organizations to change their method of reporting gains and losses on endowment funds from the method previously used and described in this section of this book. Briefly, the new method will involve determining which portion of the gains is legally restricted, either by explicit donor restrictions or by applicable laws to which the organization is subject. All gains not so restricted will be reported directly in the unrestricted class of net assets, rather than in the endowment fund as at present. Further discussion of this concept is in Chapter 13.

Under the traditional principles of trust law, gains or losses on endowment investments have not been considered income but as adjustments of the principal of the fund. Thus, gains or losses on an endowment fund are usually added back to the principal of that fund and all of the restrictions associated with the principal are considered applicable to these gains. Presumably the theory for this treatment is that, with inflation, capital gains largely reflect a price-level adjustment of the original principal.[1] In addition, many lawyers have felt that, historically, this treatment was required by law.

As a result, capital gains or losses on endowment funds have usually not been reported as unrestricted gains or losses in the current unrestricted fund. Instead, they have usually been reported in the endowment fund, either in a Statement of Income and Expenses, or in a separate Statement of Changes in Net Assets. The authors' preference is to reflect such gains in a combined Statement of Income, Expenses, and Changes in Net Assets, with the gains shown as part of income in either the permanent endowment fund or the current unrestricted fund, according to the legal facts as to the nature of such gains or losses. An example of this type of presentation is shown in Exhibit 13–1. An alternative approach is shown in Exhibit 17–2 in which such gains are reported as "nonexpendable additions." This latter approach is the one recommended by the AICPA Statement of Position.

It is argued by many that capital gains are not income and therefore must be shown in the changes in net assets section of the statements. This approach, while acceptable under previous guidelines for certain types of organizations, is not recommended. In many ways, gains on investments are income in the same sense that interest and dividends are income, except where by law or donor restriction they are required to be added to principal. As such the reader has a right to clearly see the amount of such gains. When gains are included directly in the changes in net assets section of the statement, the effect is often to bury them. The reader has a right to know the total excess of income over expenses, including such gains. There should be no need to look at two or more parts of the statement.

Some organizations do not keep track of the gains or losses by individual "name" funds within the endowment fund, but place all such gains (or losses) in a separate fund within the endowment fund with the title "Gains or Losses on Investments." This fund is accumulated over a period of years in the endowment fund and is effectively kept in perpetuity. While this may be an easy mechanical approach at the time the gains or losses arise, the authors believe it more appropriate to distribute such gains and losses to each name fund on an equitable basis at the time they

[1] It should be noted that in the case of bonds and other fixed-income securities inflation is usually ignored. If inflation were considered, a portion of the fixed income would have to be retained as an addition to principal if the original purchasing value of the principal were to be maintained. This approach, while logical, is not followed, and would not be considered an acceptable approach for financial reporting purposes.

occur. It is virtually impossible to go back and appropriately allocate such amounts at a future date.

As is discussed later in this chapter, the new FASB standards reach a different conclusion as to whether gains on endowment funds are legally restricted.

(f) Unrealized Gains and Losses

So far our discussion on gains or losses has been focused on realized gains or losses. Gains and losses are realized in an accounting sense only when the investments involved have actually been sold. What about unrealized gains and losses—increases or decreases in market value over original cost of investments currently held?

Prior to 1973, investments could only be carried at cost. Under this method, gains are not recognized until such time as the investment is sold and the gain "realized." In 1973/4, two Audit Guides[2] were issued that indicated these organizations could carry their investments either at cost or at market. In 1978, the AICPA Statement of Position held that not-for-profit organizations not covered by an Audit Guide could carry both their marketable and other types of investments at either market or the lower of cost or market (or amortized cost for certain marketable debt securities). Prior to 1978, hospitals had to carry investments at cost. Subsequent to that date, they can carry equity investments at market only if market value is lower than aggregate cost; otherwise they are still required to carry investments at cost. (See page 292.) When investments are carried at market, gains (and losses) are recognized on a continuing basis.

(g) Investments Carried at Cost

Where an organization carries its investments at cost and not at market, gains can be recorded only when they are realized. The theory behind this is that until such time as an investment is actually sold there can be no assurance that the market value of the investment won't decline to or even below the original cost. Therefore no gain is recorded until such time as the investment is sold and the gain is realized by conversion to cash.[3]

---

[2] Voluntary Health and Welfare Organizations, and Colleges and Universities. (See Chapters 14 and 15.)

[3] There is an exception to this general rule. Where an organization "sells" securities between the organization's own funds, that is, between, say, an unrestricted board designated investment fund and an endowment fund, the transfer is treated as though it were a sale with a third party, and the gain or loss recognized. The rationale is that otherwise the transaction would not be equitable to the funds involved.

On the other hand, if the market value of an investment is less than cost, consideration must be given to writing down the carrying value to the market value. Needless to say, there is a great deal of reluctance to write down investments as market prices decline below cost.[4]

The question is frequently asked whether marketable securities must be written down if it is believed that the decline is merely "temporary." This is difficult to answer. Certainly, market values fluctuate both up and down. It is not the intent of this principle to require a write-down every time market values go below the cost of an investment. The general principle is that if an investment's carrying value is permanently "impaired," either a provision for loss should be set up or the investment written down.

To answer the question of what constitutes "permanent" impairment, it is necessary to look at the nature of the individual securities. If they are being held temporarily or if, based on past buying and selling experience, the probability is that many of the individual stocks or bonds will be sold within the next year or two, then a provision for decline in market value should be set up. On the other hand, this is optional if the decline in value appears truly temporary or if the investments are bonds which, based on past experience, can reasonably be expected to be held until maturity. For example, in the case of stocks, if the loss is caused by a general downward movement in the stock market, as distinct from a downward movement in the price of the particular stock held, there may be little reason to write down the security. A key factor is whether it can be reasonably expected that the organization will sustain a cash loss upon disposal of the security.[5]

Where it appears necessary to write down part of the carrying value of the investments, the provision for decline should appear in the Statement of Income, Expenses, and Changes in Net Assets in the same place in the statement as realized gains or losses are presented in the following table. A caption should be used such as "Provision for decline in market value of investments." The provision set up in this manner should be disclosed in the Balance Sheet and netted against the carrying value of the investments.

---

[4] The Statement of Position discussed in Chapter 17 requires a write-down of marketable securities from cost to market where the aggregate market value of marketable securities by fund group is less than cost. See page 304 for a discussion of the treatment of the write-down.

[5] The Financial Accounting Standards Board (FASB) in its Statement of Financial Accounting Standards No. 115 (which replaced an earlier statement, No. 12), *Accounting for Certain Investments in Debt and Equity Securities*, requires most organizations to carry debt and equity securities at fair value, except for certain debt securities which will be carried at amortized cost. However, paragraph four specifically states that Statement No. 115 does *not* apply to not-for-profit organizations. FASB presently plans to issue guidance at some future date which will apply to not-for-profit organizations.

In subsequent periods, actual losses when realized would be charged to this provision. If it is apparent that some or all of the remaining portion of the provision is no longer required, it should be reversed in exactly the same manner as set up, that is, in the Statement of Income, Expenses, and Changes in Net Assets, with a caption such as "Add reserve for decline in market value no longer needed."

One final observation: There is a tendency to resist setting up a provision when market prices go down since this publicly acknowledges a loss. This is particularly so when one believes the decline is temporary. The alternative is to bury one's head in the sand and pretend there is no loss. This disguises the market value of securities held and may precipitate an even more unfortunate result—inaction with respect to investment decisions. If a loss has already been recognized, there will be no reason not to sell a security at the appropriate time.

(h) Presentation of Gains or Losses in the Financial Statements

The presentation of gains or losses in the Statement of Income, Expenses, and Changes in Net Assets can vary depending on whether such gains or losses are considered unrestricted or restricted, and whether the organization makes a distinction between capital type transactions and other types of transactions.

Unrestricted Realized Gains or Losses

Unrestricted realized gains or losses can be shown in the income section of the statement or toward the bottom of the statement to separate investment income, including gains, from operating income, as shown below:

STATEMENT OF INCOME, EXPENSES, AND CHANGES
IN NET ASSETS (In part)

Operating income (in total)	$ 125,000	
Expenses (in total)	(150,000)	
Excess of expenses over operating income		$(25,000)
Add–Nonoperating income:		
Contributions	20,000	
Interest and dividends	10,000	
Capital gains	25,000	
Total nonoperating income		55,000
Excess of income over expenses		$ 30,000

Sometimes investment income, excluding gains or losses, is shown in the operating income section, with gains or losses shown in the nonoperating income section. This splitting of investment income and gains is acceptable but not recommended by the authors. As discussed next, organizations are increasingly concerned with the total return on invested funds, which includes gains.

Restricted Realized Gains or Losses

Restricted realized gains or losses can be presented in the financial statements in the same manner as unrestricted realized gains, discussed above, except in the appropriate restricted fund column.

Alternatively, some organizations are treating restricted gains and losses separately as "capital additions" or "nonexpendable income," and reporting such amounts as shown below.

Note that in this approach the nonexpendable additions represent only amounts that cannot be spent for current activities—in this case, the endowment gift and the restricted portion of the gain. However, the unrestricted gain of $10,000 is expendable and therefore is reflected outside of the nonexpendable additions section. This approach was introduced by the 1978 AICPA Statement of Position and is discussed more fully in Chapter 17.

	Current Unrestricted	Endowment
Income:		
Unrestricted gains	$ 10,000	
Dividends and interest	5,000	
Other	95,000	
Total	110,000	
Expenses (in total)	(105,000)	
Excess of income over expenses before capital additions	5,000	
Nonexpendable additions:		
Endowment gift	—	$10,000
Gains on investments	—	25,000
Excess of income and capital additions over expenses	$ 5,000	$35,000

Presentation Where Investments Are Carried at Market

Where investments are carried at market, the increase or decrease in market value would be recorded as illustrated on page 91.

STATEMENT OF INCOME, EXPENSES, AND CHANGES
IN NET ASSETS

Income:

Contributions	$ 55,000	
Program activities	115,000	
Interest and dividends	50,000	
Net increase (decrease) in carrying value of investments	(20,000)	
Total income		$ 200,000
Expenses (in total)		(165,000)
Excess of income over expenses		35,000
Net assets, beginning of year		100,000
Net assets, end of year		$ 135,000

BALANCE SHEET
(In Part)

Cash	$ 60,000
Investments at market (cost $275,000)	350,000
Other assets	60,000
Total assets	$470,000

In presenting unrealized gains or losses in the Statement of Income, Expenses, and Changes in Net Assets, there appears little purpose in reporting realized gains or losses separately from unrealized gains or losses. In fact, to report the two separately can result in an awkward presentation.

For example, assume an organization sells for $130 an investment that was purchased in a prior year at a cost of $100, but which had a market value at the beginning of this year of $150. From an economic standpoint, the organization had a loss during this year of $20 (carrying value of $150 vs. sales price of $130). Yet, from the standpoint of reporting realized gains, there is a gain of $30 (cost of $100 vs. sales price of $130). If the realized gain were separately reported, the presentation would be:

Realized gain	$ 30
Less gain previously recognized	(50)
Net loss	$(20)

This presentation is likely to confuse most readers. Since there appears to be no real significance to reporting these two portions separately, the following presentation would appear more appropriate:

Net increase (decrease) in carrying value of investments .... $(20)

8.2 FIXED RATE OF RETURN CONCEPT

As was noted, one of the historical principles followed by many not-for-profit organizations having endowment funds has been that realized gains were added to the principal of the endowment fund, and not reported as "income." Only dividends and interest have been considered income. This created a dilemma. If an organization's $1 million endowment fund is invested in 5 percent bonds, income would be $50,000 a year. If, instead, it were invested in common stocks, that pay 2 percent in dividends but can be expected to double in value every ten years, annual income would be $20,000. If the doubling assumption is correct, over the ten-year period, the organization will realize far more from the common stocks than from the bonds:

	Common Stocks		Bonds
Interest/dividends over 10 years	$ 200,000		$500,000
Increase in value over 10 years	1,000,000	or	—
	$1,200,000		$500,000
Average per year	$ 120,000		$ 50,000

Under these historical accounting practices if the organization wanted maximum current income, the "bonds" in this illustration were the correct choice of investment. But from an economic standpoint, it was the wrong choice. Should the accounting treatment influence an economic or investment decision?

(a) Interfund Transfer of Realized Gains

A number of large institutions have adopted an accounting approach to this problem that involved a transfer to the unrestricted fund of a portion of the previously realized (and unrealized, if investments were carried at market value) gains from the endowment and board-designated investment fund. The amount thus transferred could then be used for current operations. Typically the board determines the amount of the transfer by first deciding what rate of return it could achieve if it emphasized interest and dividends rather than capital growth. This rate of return is often called the "spending rate." This spending rate is then compared to the actual dividends and interest income. The deficiency is the amount transferred.

For example, using the illustration above, if the board felt confident that over a period of time its common stock investments would realize a 5 percent return (the same amount as the bond portfolio described above),

EXHIBIT 8–1 An example of how the transfer from the endowment fund to the unrestricted fund should be presented under the total return approach.

	Unrestricted Fund	Endowment Fund
Income:		
Program income	$ 100,000	
Dividend income	20,000	
Realized gains		$ 50,000
Total income	120,000	50,000
Expenses	(140,000)	
Excess (deficit) of income over expenses	(20,000)	50,000
Net assets, beginning of year	50,000	1,000,000
Transfer of a portion of realized gains from endowment fund	30,000	(30,000)
Net assets, end of year	$ 60,000	$ 1,020,000

after considering inflation, the amount of dividends plus "transfer" should equal 5 percent of the $1 million, or $50,000. Exhibit 8–1 shows how this transfer was presented in both the unrestricted fund and the endowment fund.

Transfer Could Not Be Reported in the Income Section

In Exhibit 8–1 the transfer from the endowment fund is presented in the changes in net assets section, below the caption "Excess of income over expenses." Some organizations have incorrectly presented the transfer in the income section. This incorrect presentation is shown in Exhibit 8–2; it was not (and still is not) acceptable under generally accepted accounting principles.[6]

Many readers have difficulty understanding why accountants would not permit this transfer to be shown as income since the amount transferred is used for current purposes just as though it were dividends and interest. What troubled many accountants was that inclusion of the transfer in the income section (Exhibit 8–2) would allow the board to arbitrarily determine what its excess of unrestricted income over expenses would be. If the board were to consistently transfer all of the legally available realized gains rather than only an arbitrarily determined portion, most accountants would not be troubled by reflecting such amounts as income.

[6] See Chapters 19 and 24 for a discussion of generally accepted accounting principles.

EXHIBIT 8–2 An example of an unacceptable presentation in which the transfer from the endowment fund is reported in the income section of the unrestricted fund.

	Unrestricted Fund	Endowment Fund
Income:		
Program income	$ 100,000	
Dividend income	20,000	
Realized gains		$ 50,000
Transfer of portion of realized gains from		
endowment fund	30,000	(30,000)
Total income	150,000	20,000
Expenses	(140,000)	
Excess of income over expenses	10,000	20,000
Net assets, beginning of year	50,000	1,000,000
Net assets, end of year	$ 60,000	$ 1,020,000

It is when the board decides to transfer only a portion that it appears to the accountant that the potential for income manipulation exists. This is not to suggest that the method the board uses in determining its "spending rate" is not rational, but it is still arbitrary. For this reason, when the board decided to transfer such gains, the presentation of this transfer had to be shown outside of the income section, in the net assets section, as shown in Exhibit 8–1.

It should be emphasized, however, that accountants are not trying to tell the board how to *manage* the organization's investments, or how much of the organization's resources should be utilized for current operations. Those are operating decisions of the board, outside the accountant's purview or interest. However, it is within the accountant's sphere to indicate how the board's action—in this case, the transfer of resources—should be presented in the financial statements so as not to mislead the reader. Looking at Exhibit 8–1 no one can misinterpret the results of the year's activities: an unrestricted deficit of $20,000. However, it would be an unusual reader who would not conclude (erroneously) from Exhibit 8–2 that the there was an unrestricted excess of $10,000.

(b) Fixed Return from an Independent Investment Fund

Because of the popularity of the total return approach, several independent investment funds have been established that provide the not-for-profit organization with a flat "spending rate" amount each year. These are set up in much the same way as mutual funds. Probably the best known of these independent investment funds is The Common Fund in which a number of colleges have invested. If the institution elects, The Common Fund will return annually 5 percent of the market value of the institution's share of the Fund rather than actual dividends, interest, and realized gains.

Accounting for Fixed Annual Payment

The accounting for this 5 percent return must be handled in exactly the same manner as it would be if the organization were making its own investments in its own separate endowment fund. It is not acceptable to record the full 5 percent payment as dividend income. Therefore, it is necessary for the organization to know the amount of its share of the actual dividends and realized gains of the outside investment fund. Its share of the actual dividends is recorded as unrestricted income and its share of the actual total realized gains is recorded as gains, restricted or unrestricted as appropriate, without regard to the 5 percent cash payment received from the investment fund. The carrying value of the organization's share of this investment fund is thus increased or decreased to the investment fund's cost basis just as though there were no separate investment fund.

The excess of the 5 percent cash payment over the dividends and interest earned represents a return of a portion of the organization's investment in this outside fund. If the organization wishes to utilize this excess for general purposes, it should account for this excess in the same way as if it actually owned the underlying securities, as in Exhibit 8–1. In short, the accounting for the dividends and interest and realized gains is completely independent of the 5 percent cash payment. It is dependent on the underlying actual results of the investment fund.

Here is an example. Assume that the organization described above makes a $1 million cash investment in an outside investment fund, which constitutes 10 percent of the total independent investment fund's assets. Here is the activity for the first year:

	Outside Investment Fund	Our Organization's Share (10%)
Balance beginning	$ 10,000,000	$ 1,000,000
Dividend income	200,000	20,000
Realized gains	500,000	50,000
Less 5% payments	(500,000)	(50,000)
Balance ending	$ 10,200,000	$ 1,020,000
Unrealized appreciation	$ 500,000	$ 50,000

The appropriate reporting for our organization, assuming it carries its investments at cost, would be the same as contained in Exhibit 8–1.

Accounting Where Investments Are Carried at Market

If the organization followed the practice of recording its investments at market, then $50,000 would be recorded in the endowment fund as realized gains. The $30,000 transfer would again be handled as in Exhibit 8–1.

(c)   Inflation Index to Protect Principal

It should be noted that the discussion so far has not touched on the budgeting considerations that an organization's board may consider in establishing the amounts to be transferred from the endowment fund to the unrestricted fund. The most common approach is the "spending rate" approach described above, in which the board decides on the amount to be spent in total and then, after deducting actual dividends and interest, transfers the balance. It is referred to as the spending rate because often it is arrived at, in part at least, by determining what income could be achieved if emphasis were placed on current income rather than on growth.

Inflation Protection Approach

The authors believe this spending rate approach is backward. The more appropriate approach is for the board to first establish the rate at which the endowment fund must be increased to protect it from inflation. Transfers to the unrestricted fund should then be made only to the extent that gains exceed the amount which has to be added to principal to protect it from inflation.

There is a significant difference between the spending rate approach and this inflation protection approach. The spending rate approach may or may not protect the principal against inflation, depending on the assumptions used in arriving at the spending rate. Yet the first concern of the board should be to protect the principal against inflation. Only if there are gains in excess of this requirement should transfers be made to the unrestricted fund.

Exhibit 8–3 shows how an inflation index could be used to determine the amount to be transferred. Assuming inflation of 5 percent a year, again our original principal of $1 million, 2 percent dividends, and realized gains of $50,000, $40,000, and $120,000 in each of three years, the amount that would be transferred in each of three years would be calculated as shown in Exhibit 8–3. In this illustration, a constant inflation rate

EXHIBIT 8–3   An example showing how the amount of the transfer would be calculated under the total return approach using an inflation protection approach.

	19X1	19X2	19X3
Principal at beginning of year, adjusted for inflation	$ 1,000,000	$ 1,050,000	$ 1,102,500
Add inflation factor of, say, 5%	50,000	52,500	55,125
Principal end of year as adjusted for inflation	$ 1,050,000	$ 1,102,500	$ 1,157,625
Dividends	$ 20,000	$ 20,000	$ 20,000
Realized gains	50,000	40,000	120,000
Total	70,000	60,000	140,000
Less amount retained as an adjustment for inflation ...	(50,000)	(52,500)	(55,125)
Balance, for current operations	$ 20,000	$ 7,500	$ 84,875

of 5 percent has been assumed. In actual practice, the rate would vary and the board would, of course, peg its rate to the appropriate government index.

The advantage of this approach is that all income—dividends and gains is transferred except that portion that must be retained as an inflation adjustment to protect the value of the endowment fund. This means that the full impact of the board's investment decisions will be felt, whether conservative or speculative.

Income does fluctuate because of the magnitude and timing of realized capital gains. Notice that in Exhibit 8–3 only $7,500 of income is available in 19X2. Possibly one refinement is to provide that the amount of the transfer should be averaged over a three-year period. This would have the effect of dampening large changes due to the timing of the realized gains.

Market Value Approach

An increasing number of not-for-profit organizations carry their endowment fund investments at market value, and the inflation index approach outlined above can be followed by these organizations. Carrying investments at market eliminates the fluctuation due to the timing of realized gains. At the same time, it should be noted that a general stock market

EXHIBIT 8–4   An example showing how the amount of the transfer would be calculated using an inflation protection approach and recognizing unrealized gains in the calculation.

	19X1	19X2	19X3
Dividends	$ 20,000	$ 20,000	$ 20,000
Realized gains	50,000	40,000	120,000
Unrealized gains–increase			
(decrease)	50,000	80,000	(20,000)
Total	120,000	140,000	120,000
Less amount retained as an			
adjustment for inflation			
(see Figure 8–3)	(50,000)	(52,500)	(55,125)
Balance, for current operations	$ 70,000	$ 87,500	$ 64,875

decline at the end of any one year could also result in a loss rather than income. Again, a three-year moving average might be appropriate.

For those not-for-profit organizations that carry their investments at cost, the board could still adopt the market value approach solely for the purpose of determining the amount of realized gains to be transferred. Exhibit 8–4 shows how this would be handled.

Presentation in the Financial Statement

Under the accounting rules that existed prior to the issuance of SFAS No. 117, the board could follow either of the approaches discussed above for determining the amount of realized gains or losses to transfer, but the transfer could not be reported as income. This means that the amounts reported as income in the unrestricted fund calculated as shown in Exhibit 8–3 or 8–4 would be the amounts of actual dividends and the balance would have to be reported as a transfer. In some years it is possible that such dividends would exceed the amount available. When this happens a transfer would be made back to the endowment fund. Exhibit 8–5 shows this presentation for the organization which calculates the amount of the transfer on the basis of realized gains only (as calculated in Exhibit 8–3).[7]

---

[7] Some organizations might object to transferring some of their dividend income to the endowment fund. One modification might be to not make such transfers back to the endowment fund but instead to reduce future years' transfers to the unrestricted fund by the amount of such deficiencies. If this modification were followed, the 19X3 transfer in Exhibit 8–5 would be $52,375 ($64,875 less $12,500).

EXHIBIT 8–5 An illustration showing the presentation in the unrestricted fund of transfers that have been calculated using an inflation protection approach.

	Unrestricted Fund		
	19X1	19X2	19X3
Income:			
Program income	$ 100,000	$ 100,000	$ 100,000
Dividend income	20,000	20,000	20,000
Total	120,000	120,000	120,000
Expenses	(140,000)	(140,000)	(140,000)
Excess of expenses over income	(20,000)	(20,000)	(20,000)
Transfer of portion of realized gains from endowment funds			64,875
Transfer of portion of unrestricted fund to endowment fund to protect principal from inflation		(12,500)	
Change in net assets	$ (20,000)	$ (32,500)	$ 44,875

(d) Transferring Realized Gains

Implicit in the above discussion is the assumption that at least part of the realized gains on funds donated to an organization for endowment purposes are, in fact, legally available for unrestricted use by the organization. Is this a valid assumption?

Changing Attitude on Income Transfer

There has been a tendency to assume that the law requires endowment funds and the realized gains on the sales of endowment fund investments to be inseparable and sacrosanct. There now appears to be authoritative support for the view that the realized gains on endowment funds may also be considered unrestricted under appropriate circumstances. In 1969, in a widely publicized report to the Ford Foundation entitled "The Law and the Lore of Endowment Funds," W. L. Cary and C. B. Bright concluded:

> If the managers of endowment funds wish to seek long-term appreci-
> ation in their investments, the need of their institutions for current yield
> should not dissuade them. We find no authoritative support in the law for
> the widely held view that the realized gains of endowment funds can
> never be spent. Prudence would call for the retention of sufficient gains to

maintain purchasing power in the face of inflation and to guard against potential losses, but subject to the standards which prudence dictates, the expenditure of gains should lie within the discretion of the institution's directors.

Subsequent to Cary and Bright's report, a number of states have adopted legislation which specifically permits most not-for-profit organizations to include capital gains in spendable income to the extent the board deems "prudent." In fact, the model uniform law (the Uniform Management of Institutional Funds Act[8]) provides that not only realized gains may be considered spendable income but also unrealized gains.

Endowment Fund Distinction for Colleges and Universities

There is another important factor to consider. Many colleges and universities[9] for investment management purposes (and, prior to the issuance of SFAS No. 117, also for financial statement purposes) combine two types of endowment funds—board-designated investment funds and true donor-restricted endowments into a single fund. There is a great deal of difference between the two. In the first, the limitation is internally and voluntarily created, whereas in the other the restriction is donor-imposed and cannot be changed by the organization.

There would appear to be no question that the board may transfer to the unrestricted fund not only the realized gains but also the principal of board-designated investments. After all, the board's designation was voluntary and it could therefore reverse its designation and transfer such funds to the unrestricted fund. Board-designated investment funds usually constitute a substantial portion of the endowment funds of most large educational institutions.

---

[8] As of 1994, this act has been passed in some form in 39 states and the District of Columbia. Because the text of the act differs between states, organizations should have their attorneys consult the exact text as it applies to them before acting in accordance with it. In states that have not passed the uniform act, there is likely to be other state law governing gains on restricted endowments.
[9] Most other types of not-for-profit organizations have been prohibited since the 1970s (by the various AICPA audit guides and SOP) from combining board-designated investments and endowment funds for reporting purposes.

CHAPTER 9

Affiliated Organizations

Not-for-profit organizations are often associated with other organizations, either not-for-profit or for-profit. The association may result from many different types of relationships.

In the not-for-profit world, true "ownership" of one entity by another rarely exists (although sometimes a not-for-profit will own an operating business which it either established or had donated to it). Affiliated organizations are more often related by agreements of various sorts, but the level of control embodied in such agreements is usually far short of ownership. For example, the "Friends of the Warsaw Museum" may exist primarily to support the Warsaw Museum, but it is likely a legally independent organization with only informal ties to its "parent." The Museum may ask, but the Friends may choose its own time and method to respond. Further the Museum may have no way to legally compel the Friends to do its bidding if the Friends resists.

The issue for donors is, if I give to the Friends, am I not really just supporting the Museum? Or if I am assessing the financial condition of the Museum, is it not reasonable to include the resources of the Friends in the calculation? Even though the Friends is legally separate, and even though the Friends does not have to turn its assets over to the Museum, isn't it reasonable to assume that if the Museum got into bad financial trouble, the Friends would help?

9.1 TYPES OF RELATIONSHIPS OFTEN FOUND

(a) The Fund-Raising Affiliate of a "Parent" Organization

These are often named something like "The Friends of the [Museum]," "The [Symphony] Guild," "The {x} Foundation," and so on. They are found most often with cultural organizations such as museums, performing arts, and the like, and with health care and educational institutions. College alumni associations often perform this function for the college. Public universities usually use such an affiliate to raise funds which are kept out of the budgetary numbers submitted to the state legislature (which, if the affiliate were combined, might cause a reduction in the governmental appropriation to the college). Hospitals often do the same, with their purpose being to keep the assets out of the base used to calculate Medicare/Medicaid reimbursement rates. Some colleges also have affiliates set up to raise money for a particular college activity—often the athletic department (in which case they are often referred to as booster clubs); this allows the funded activity more financial flexibility than if it were limited to what it would be allocated under the organization's regular budgetary process.

The traditional federated fund-raising organization such as United Way or a Community Arts Fund also performs this kind of function. However the question of consolidation rarely arises with such groups because they are usually completely independent of the groups for which they raise money. (The question of when a fund-raiser is merely acting as an agent for another organization is germane to all of these kinds of organizations (controlled and noncontrolled), but that is a different issue.)

(b) The Asset-Holding Affiliate

Organizations that are in the fortunate position of having more assets than are immediately needed for activities, or that have large endowment funds, avoid having to answer embarrassing questions from prospective and previous donors about the organization's real need for gifts by placing the assets into a separate legal entity. Two other reasons sometimes cited for such an arrangement are that management of the investment portfolio is more efficient, and that the assets are (at least believed to be) protected against possible lawsuits resulting from program activities of the parent organization (especially in areas such as health care, child care, etc.).

A variation on this scenario occurs when a donor establishes a separate legal entity (a trust, foundation, or a fund within a community or private foundation) and stipulates that the income from the fund is to go to a specified organization, usually in perpetuity. The supported organization may or may not have any authority over the investment management of the fund or over the amounts and timing of income distributions to it, or access to any of the principal of the fund.

Another similar situation involves the more common deferred giving arrangements, such as gift annuities, pooled income funds, or remainder trusts, which always terminate at some specified or determinable time (often upon the death of the donor or other life income beneficiary). The assets that fund such arrangements are sometimes under the control of the charity, sometimes of a third party trustee.

(c) The Program Activity Affiliate

Some organizations set up legally separate affiliates to carry out certain program functions within the general area of the organization's activities. A university might have a research foundation specifically to work in a particular area of research. Funding of such organizations sometimes comes wholly from the main organization; sometimes funding is partly or entirely from sources specific to the affiliate. Other examples include a university publishing company or study center (the latter are often geographically separated for the main campus such as Harvard's Villa I Tatti, an art study center in Florence, Italy); a hospital testing laboratory; a cemetery affiliated with a church; a broadcasting station affiliated with a university or with a religious organization; an overseas mission, university, hospital, convent, orphanage, monastery, or charitable organization affiliated with a religious denomination. Most university medical schools that include teaching hospitals have the hospital set up as a separate organization.

A variation on this theme is the affiliate that conducts "program" activities which are peripheral to those of the parent entity. Examples include those commonly referred to as "auxiliary activities" of a university (such as food service, recreational activities, parking facilities), or activities that support the operations of a hospital (such as a laundry, or an office building in which physicians affiliated with the hospital have their private offices). Other examples include pension funds, captive insurance companies, gift shops, welfare benefit plans, investment or management companies. (Harvard University manages its endowment this way.)

Another variation is the "organization" that is legally part of the parent entity but is operated almost as if it were separate. Examples include guilds, circles, and similar church groups, committees set up to carry on certain activities such as annual fairs, dinner-dances, or other fundraising events. These often have separate bank accounts and "governing" boards which act very much like those of legally separate organizations. Accountability for the finances of such groups is often weak.

There are also organizations that are legally separate from the "parent" but are connected by informal relationships stemming from a mandatory organizational affiliation of their members. Examples include on-and off-campus student organizations at a college, such as: fraternities, sororities, cultural organizations (drama club, glee club, etc.), student edited publications, community service organizations, honor societies, academic and athletic clubs, the alumni association. Such affiliated entities are often supported financially by the "parent" in ways such as having their administrative expenses paid by the parent. A variation on this theme is the corporate foundation, a not-for-profit controlled and funded by a for-profit. Most parent companies also pay all or most of their foundation's administrative expenses, in addition to making contributions to it.

(d) Affiliates of a Common Parent

These include the major national charities and service organizations, many of them medically or youth oriented (Cancer, Heart, Lung, United Way, Scouts, etc.). This is also found with some professional and trade associations such as the various medical, dental, legal, accounting, labor, and similar associations, and with national fraternal and civic organizations (Greek letter fraternities and sororities, Rotary, Lions, Kiwanis, etc.). Other examples include the various campuses of a state university system (New York and California are two of the largest). In some cases the state and local "affiliates" have little or no legal relationship with the national organization (AICPA is one example); in other cases the national closely controls the affiliates (Arthritis Foundation is an example); one also sees every gradation in between.

Most religious denominations are also in this category as to the national organization and individual churches/parishes/synagogues/etc. In many denominations there are also intermediate level entities such as archdioceses (Roman Catholic), dioceses (Catholic and Episcopal), synods (Lutheran) or conferences (Methodist). The degree of control of the local entities by the national varies considerably. An additional complicating factor with religious organizations is the existence in some denominations of two different sets of governing rules: theological rules (sometimes referred to as canon law), and secular administrative rules based on civil law.

9.2 DEFINITION OF THE REPORTING ENTITY

There are two issues here but they involve the same concepts. The issues are:

- Gifts to one organization (say, a fund-raising affiliate) which are later passed through to another organization (the organization for which the affiliate raises money).
- When the financial data of affiliated entities should be combined with that of a central or parent organization for purposes of presenting the central organization's financial statements.

Of course if the data are combined, the question of pass-through gifts need not be addressed since the end result is the same regardless of which entity records gifts initially.

(a) Pass-Through Gifts

The question is, should gifts be recorded by the affiliate as its own revenue, followed by gift or grant expense when they money is passed on to the parent organization, or should the gifts be recorded as an amount held on behalf of the parent? Such gifts are often called pass-through gifts since they pass through one entity to another entity.

Although SFAS No. 116 states (in par. 4 and 52–54) that gifts to an organization which is only acting as an agent or intermediary for another organization should not be reported as gifts by the agent, it gives little guidance for distinguishing agents from non-agents in practice. Presumably the criteria would depend on the degree of control over the use of the gift, and active involvement in soliciting, processing, and distributing the gift by the first organization. If it has little control and little active involvement, it is likely an agent and should record the gift as an amount held for the other organization. Appendix 9–A at the end of this chapter is a checklist to help organizations make this distinction in practice.

(b) Combined Financial Statements

The concept underlying the combining of financial data of affiliates is to present to the financial statement reader information that portrays the complete financial picture of a group of entities that effectively function as one entity.

A key determinant of whether consolidation of affiliates is appropriate is the degree of control exercised by one entity over another. Since the normal method of measuring such control (ownership of voting stock) does not usually apply in the not-for-profit environment, other factors must be used. Appendix 9–B at the end of this chapter is a list of factors which the authors consider relevant for this purpose.

In the business setting the determination of when a group of entities is really just a single entity is normally made by assessing the extent to which the "parent" entity has a controlling financial interest in the other entities in the group. In other words, can the parent use for its own benefit the financial resources of the others without obtaining permission from any party outside the parent? When one company owns another company, such permission would be automatic; if the management of the affiliate resisted, the parent would exercise its authority to replace management.

Previously existing accounting literature included only limited guidance for assessing the need for a not-for-profit organization to combine financial data of affiliates. The basic rules for businesses are in Accounting Research Bulletin No. 51, *Consolidated Financial Statements,* Accounting Principles Board Opinion No. 18, *The Equity Method of Accounting for Investments in Common Stock,* and Statement of Financial Accounting Standards No. 94, *Consolidation of All Majority-Owned Subsidiaries.* While, strictly speaking, these rules are generally viewed as not applying to not-for-profits, the concepts embodied therein and the related background discussions are helpful to someone considering the issue. Rules specifically addressed to not-for-profits are in the AICPA audit guides/SOP (par. 7.07–7.11 of *Audits of Voluntary Health and Welfare Organizations;* par. 11.09 of *Audits of Colleges and Universities;* par. 42–48 of SOP 78-10). These rules focus largely on the question of whether one not-for-profit controls another. Considerable judgment is called for, however, in each case to decide whether sufficient control exists to require consolidation.

In September 1994, the AICPA issued a new statement of position (No. 94-3) about when a not-for-profit organization should combine the financial statements of affiliated organizations with its financial statements. This SOP supersedes the rules in the audit guides/SOP 78-10. Briefly, the requirements of the SOP are:

- When a not-for-profit owns a majority of the voting equity interest in a for-profit entity, the not-for-profit must consolidate the for-profit into its financial statements, regardless of whether the activities of the for-profit are at all related to those of the not-for-profit.

- If the not-for-profit owns less than a majority interest in a for-profit but still has significant influence over the for-profit, it must report the for-profit under the equity method of accounting, except that the not-for-profit may report its investment in the for-profit at market value if that is its policy for reporting investments. If the not-for-profit does not have significant influence over the for-profit, it should value its investment in accordance with the applicable audit guide.
- When a not-for-profit organization has a relationship with another not-for-profit in which the "parent" both exercises control (through majority ownership or voting interest) over and has an economic interest in the affiliate, it must consolidate the affiliate, unless control is likely to be temporary. Consolidation is optional if the control is through other than majority ownership/voting interest.
- If the not-for-profit has either control *or* an economic interest but not both, disclosure of the relationship and significant financial information is required.

By "economic interest" is meant generally four kinds of relationship: an affiliate which raises gifts for the parent, an affiliate which holds assets for the parent, an affiliate which performs significant functions for the parent, or an affiliate which is committed to provide resources to or guarantees the debt of the parent.

FASB also has this subject on its agenda for future standard-setting.

APPENDIX 9–A   CHECKLIST

Factors to Be Considered in Deciding Whether a "Pass-Through" Gift Is Truly Revenue and Expense to Charity (C)

Following is a list of factors which may be helpful to:

- Not-for-profit organizations in deciding whether assets received by them are contributions within the meaning of SFAS No. 116, or are transfers in which the entity is acting as an agent, trustee, or intermediary;
- Auditors, in assessing the appropriateness of the client's decision.

No one factor is usually determinative by itself; all relevant factors should be considered together.

D = Original Noncharitable Donor (Individual or Business)

C = Initial Charitable Recipient/Donor (Sometimes there is more than one charity in the chain.)

R = Ultimate Charitable or Individual Recipient

Factors Whose Presence Indicate Recording by C as Revenue and Expense May Not Be Appropriate	Factors Whose Presence Indicate Recording by C as Revenue and Expense May Be Appropriate
General factors—relevant to all gifts:	
1. D has restricted the gift by specifying that it must be passed on to R.*	D has not restricted the gift in this manner.
2. C is controlled by D or by R.	D or R do not control C.
3. Two or more of D, C, and R are under common control, have overlapping boards or management, share facilities or professional advisors.*	Factor not present.
4. Even without the intermediation of C, D would still easily be able to make the gift to R.	Without such intermediation, D would not easily be able to make a gift to R (D is unaware of existence of R or of R's needs, geographic separation, etc.).*
5. The stated program activities of C and R are similar.	The program activities are not particularly similar.

Factors Whose Presence Indicate Recording by C as Revenue and Expense May Not Be Appropriate	Factors Whose Presence Indicate Recording by C as Revenue and Expense May Be Appropriate
6. C has solicited the gift from D under the specific pretense of passing it on to R.*	C has solicited the gift ostensibly for C's own activities.
7. C does not ever obtain legal title to the assets composing the gift.*	C does at some time obtain legal title to the assets.
8. D and/or other entities under common control are major sources of support for C.	Factor not present.
9. R and/or other entities under common control are major destinations for C's charitable resources.	Factor not present.
9a. Both factors 8 and 9 are present.*	One but not both present.
10. The "chain" from D to R consists of several C's.	The chain consists of only one or very few C's.
11. Gifts passed from D to C are frequently in exactly the same dollar amount (or very close) as gifts subsequently passed from C to R.*	Factor not present.
12. Times elapsed between receipt and disbursement of particular amounts by C are short (less than a month).	Times elapsed are relatively long or variable.
13. C makes pledges to R, payment of which is contingent on receipt of gifts from D.	Factor not present.
14. C was created only shortly prior to receiving the gift, and/or C appears to have been created specifically for the sole purpose of passing gifts from D on to R.*	Factor not present.

Factors especially relevant to gifts-in-kind:

15. C never takes physical possession of the gift at an owned or rented facility.	C does have physical possession of the items at some time, at a facility normally owned or rented by it.
16. The nature of the items is not consistent with the program service activities of C as stated in	The nature is consistent with C's stated program activities.

Factors Whose Presence Indicate Recording by C as Revenue and Expense May Not Be Appropriate	Factors Whose Presence Indicate Recording by C as Revenue and Expense May Be Appropriate
its Form 1023, 990, organizing documents, fund-raising appeals, annual report.*	
17. The gift was not solicited by C.	C specifically solicited the particular items from D.
18. The quantity of items is large in relation to the foreseeable needs of C or its donees.	Factor not present.
19. Factor not present.	Members of the board or staff of C have specific technical or professional expertise about the items, and actively participate in deliberations about where to obtain the items and how best to use them.*
20. D appears to be the only source from which C considers acquiring the item. Same for C/R.	C has several potential or actual sources for the item. Same for R.
21. C receives numerous types of items dissimilar in their purpose or use.	Factor not present.
22. C receives items from D and passes them on to R in essentially the same form.	C "adds value" to the items by sorting, repackaging, cleaning, repairing or testing them.*
23. C *and* either or both of D and R have little in the way of program services other than distribution of gifts in kind to other charities.	Either C or *both* D and R have significant program services other than distribution of gifts in kind.
24. The value assigned to the items by D or C appears to be inflated.	Factor not present.
25. There is a consistent pattern of transfers of items along the same "chain" (D to C to R, etc.).	Factor not present.
26. Factor not present.	C incurs significant expenses (freight, insurance, storage, etc.) in handling the items.

* = Factors considered to be generally more significant.

APPENDIX 9–B   CHECKLIST

Factors Related to Control Which May Indicate That an Affiliated Organization (A) Should Be Combined with the Reporting Organization (R), if Other Criteria for Combination Are Met (per AICPA SOP 94-3)

SOP 94-3 defines control as "direct or indirect ability to determine the direction of management and policies through ownership, contract, or otherwise."

Following is a list of factors which may be helpful to:

- not-for-profit organizations, in deciding whether to combine financial statements of affiliated organizations;
- auditors, in assessing the appropriateness of the client's decision.

Many of these factors are not absolutely determinative by themselves, but must be considered in conjunction with other factors.

Factors Whose Presence Indicate Control	Factors Whose Presence Indicate Lack of Control
Organization relationship:	
1. A is clearly described as controlled by, for the benefit of, or an affiliate of R in some of the following: —articles/charter/by-laws —operating/affiliation agreement —fund-raising material/membership brochure —annual report —grant proposals —application for tax-exempt status.	A is described as independent of R, or no formal relationship is indicated.
Governance:	
1. A's board has considerable overlap in membership with R; common officers.	Little or no overlap.
2. A's board members and/or officers are appointed by R, or are subject to approval of R's board, officers, or members.	A's board is self perpetuating with no input from R.

Factors Whose Presence Indicate Control	Factors Whose Presence Indicate Lack of Control
3. Major decision of A's board, officers or staff are subject to review, approval, or ratification by R.	A's decisions are made autonomously; or even if in theory subject to such control, R has in fact never or rarely exercised control and does not intend to do so.

Financial:

1. A's budget is subject to review or approval by R.	Budget not subject to R's approval.
2. Some or all of A's disbursements are subject to approval or countersignature by R.	Checks may be issued without R's approval.
3. A's excess of revenue over expenses or net assets or portions thereof are subject to being transferred to R at R's request, or are automatically transferred.	Although some of A's financial resources may be transferred to R, this is done only at the discretion of A's board.
4. A's activities are largely financed by grants, loans or transfers from R, or from other sources determined by R's board.	A's activities are financed from sources determined by A's board.
5. A's by-laws indicate that its resources are intended to be used for activities similar to those of R.	A's by-laws limit uses of resources to purposes which do not include R's activities.
6. A's fund-raising appeals give donors the impression that gifts will be used to further R's programs.	Appeals give the impression that funds will be used by A.

Operating:

1. A shares with R many of the following operating functions: —personnel/payroll —purchasing —professional services —fund-raising —accounting, treasury —office space	Few operating functions are shared; or reimbursement of costs is on a strictly arms-length basis with formal contracts.
2. Decisions about A's program or other activities are made by R or are subject to R's review or approval.	A's decisions are made autonomously.
3. A's activities are almost exclusively for the benefit of R's members.	Activities benefit persons unaffiliated with R.

Factors Whose Presence Indicate Control	Factors Whose Presence Indicate Lack of Control

Other:

1. A is exempt under IRC Section 501(c)(3) and R is exempt under some other subsection of 501(c), and A's purpose for existence appears to be to solicit tax-deductible contributions to further R's interest.

   A's purposes appear to include significant activities apart from those of R.

2. A qualifies as a publicly-supported organization under IRC Section 509(a)(3) by virtue of being a supporting organization to R.

   Factor not present.

C H A P T E R 10

Contributions, Pledges, and Noncash Contributions

So far we have not discussed the problems of recording and reporting the principal resource most not-for-profit organizations depend on—contributions. An organization can receive contributions with a wide range of restrictions attached. First these contributions must be *recorded* in the right fund; then they must be *reported* in such a way that the financial statement reader is fully aware of their receipt and any restrictions on them. In addition there has been, and continues to be, considerable controversy surrounding the timing of the recording of different types of gifts as income.

Some contributions are made in the form of pledges that will be paid off over a period of time or at some future date; the main accounting questions are whether such pledges should be recorded as assets prior to their collection, and when they should be recognized as income. Also, an organization can receive a variety of noncash contributions ranging from marketable securities, buildings, and equipment to contributed services of volunteers and the use of fixed assets. All of these types of contributions present accounting and reporting problems for the organization.

Support for a not-for-profit organization can be received in many different forms. Each of the types of contributions will be discussed in a separate section of this chapter.

In 1993, the controversy about proper accounting for contributions was settled by the issuance of FASB Statement of Financial Accounting Standards No. 116, *Accounting for Contributions Received and Contributions Made.* The details of the requirements of this statement are discussed throughout this chapter. In brief, it says that all contributions, whether unrestricted or restricted, and in whatever form: cash, gifts-in-kind, securities, pledges, or other forms, are revenue in full immediately upon receipt of the gift or an unconditional pledge. (Restricted contributions are not deferred until the restriction is met, as is now the practice by many organizations.) The revenue is reported in the class of net assets (discussed in Chapter 13) appropriate to any donor-imposed restriction on the gift (unrestricted, if there is no donor-imposed restriction). It also contains guidance on accounting for donated services of volunteers, and an exception to the normal rule when dealing with museum collection objects.

10.1   EXPENDABLE CURRENT SUPPORT

(a)   Unrestricted Contributions

This section of the chapter will discuss simple unrestricted cash gifts. Unrestricted gifts in other forms, such as pledges, gifts of securities, and gifts of equipment and supplies, are discussed in later sections. The general principles discussed here apply to all unrestricted gifts, in whatever form received.

Historical Practices

It was noted in Chapter 4 that all unrestricted contributions should be recorded in the current unrestricted fund. This principle is fairly well accepted and followed by most not-for-profit organizations. What has not been uniformly followed is a single method of reporting such unrestricted contributions. Some organizations followed the practice of adding unrestricted contributions directly to the fund balance either in a separate Statement of Changes in Fund Balances, or in the fund balance section where a combined Statement of Income, Expenses, and Changes in Fund Balances was used. Others reported some or all of their contributions directly in an unrestricted investment fund, and worse still, some reported unrestricted contributions directly in the endowment fund as though such amounts were restricted. The result of all these practices has been to make it difficult for the readers of the financial statements to recognize the amount and nature of contributions received. Sometimes this was done deliberately in an attempt to convince the readers that the organization badly needed more contributions.

Accounting for Unrestricted Contributions

All unrestricted contributions should be reported in the unrestricted class of net assets in a Statement of Income and Expenses or, if a combined Statement of Income, Expenses, and Changes in Net Assets is used, such unrestricted contributions should be shown before arriving at the "Excess of income over expenses" caption. It is *not acceptable* to report unrestricted contributions in a separate Statement of Changes in Net Assets or to report such gifts in a restricted class of net assets.

Bargain Purchases

Organizations are sometimes permitted to purchase goods or services at a reduced price that is granted by the seller in recognition of the organization's charitable or educational status. In such cases, the seller has effectively made a gift to the buyer. This gift should be recorded as such if the amount is significant. For example, if a charity buys a widget for $50 that normally sells for $80, the purchase should be recorded at $80, with the $30 difference being reported as a contribution.

It is important to record only true gifts in this way. If a lower price is really a normal discount available to any buyer who requests it, then there is no contribution. Such discounts include quantity discounts, normal trade discounts, promotional discounts, special offers, or lower rates (say, for professional services) to reflect the seller's desire to utilize underused staff, or sale prices to move slow-moving items off the shelves.

Presentation in the Income Statement

The presentation of unrestricted contributions within the Statement of Income and Expenses can be handled in one of several ways. For smaller organizations and for organizations where fees for services rendered are not a significant factor, contributions are usually reported in the top section of the statement along with all other sources of income, as follows:

Income:	
Contributions	$ 50,000
Other income	10,000
Total	60,000
Expenses (in total)	(55,000)
Excess of income over expenses	$ 5,000

For some other organizations, it may be more appropriate to separate contributions from service fee income in order to arrive at an excess or deficit before contributions are added. The following is a simplified example of this type of presentation:

Service fees	$ 150,000
Less expenses	(175,000)
Excess of expenses over service fees before contributions	(25,000)
Contributions	40,000
Excess of income over expenses	$ 15,000

Note that in both examples contributions are shown above the excess of income over expenses for the period so the reader can see the net results of all unrestricted activities.

Multicolumn presentation.   Some organizations prefer to present unrestricted (board-designated, see Chapter 5) investment amounts separately in a columnar presentation. Some organizations have a policy of treating the entire amount of certain kinds of gifts, for example all bequests (or all gifts above a certain amount) this way. Other organizations periodically determine an amount to be maintained in such a designated account and reclassify enough assets to reach the desired amount. An alternative method of computation is to determine how much to leave behind in the operating column, and reclassify all operating amounts above the target amount. This is done to emphasize that these assets are considered by the directors to be unavailable (at least in the immediate future) for operating expenses. An example of this type of presentation would be:

| | Unrestricted | | |
	Operating	Investment	Total
Support and revenue:			
Other unrestricted income	$ 200,000		$ 200,000
Bequests	125,000		125,000
Total	325,000		325,000
Expenses (in total)	(195,000)		(195,000)
Excess of support and revenue			
over expenses	130,000		130,000
Transfer bequests to investment			
fund	(125,000)	$125,000	
Net assets:			
Beginning of year	60,000	300,000	360,000
End of year	$ 65,000	$ 425,000	$ 490,000

Several points should be noted. First, observe that all three columns are clearly labeled "unrestricted" so the reader will not mistake the investment column for restricted endowment. Second, note that a "total" column is included. The purpose is to clearly show the reader the total of all unrestricted amounts available to the organization. Third, note that all unrestricted income is reported in the "operating" column. This is because, prior to a board decision to designate amounts for other purposes, all unrestricted income is legally available for operations. The board designation of bequests to be held for investment is reflected as an reclassification to the designated investment column.

(b)   Current Restricted Contributions

Current restricted contributions are contributions that can be used to meet the current expenses of the organization, although restricted to use for some specific purpose, or during or after some specified time. An example of the former would be a gift "for cancer research" (a "purpose restriction"), and of the latter, a gift "for your 19X6 activities" (a "time restriction"). In practice, the distinction between restricted gifts and unrestricted gifts is not always clear. In many cases, the language used by the donor leaves doubt as to whether there really is a restriction on the gift. Appendix 10–A contains a checklist to help readers make this distinction in practice.

Current restricted contributions cause reporting problems, in part because the accounting profession took a long time to resolve the appropriate accounting and reporting treatment for these types of gifts. The resolution arrived at is controversial because many believe it is not the most desirable method of accounting for such gifts.

The principal accounting problem relates to the question of what constitutes "income" or "support" to the organization. Is a gift that can only be used for a specific project or after a specified time "income" to the organization at the time the gift is received, or does this restricted gift represent an amount which should be looked on as being held in a form of escrow until it is expended for the restricted purpose (cancer research in the above example), or the specified time has arrived (19X6 in the above example)? If it is looked on as something other than income, what is it—deferred income or part of a restricted net asset balance?

If a current restricted gift is considered income or support in the period received—whether expended or not—the accounting is fairly straightforward. It would be essentially the same as for unrestricted gifts, described earlier, except that the gift is reported in the temporarily restricted class rather than in the unrestricted class of net assets. But if the other view is taken, the accounting can become quite complex.

Historical Practices

Inherent in the discussion of this issue is the question of whether a not-for-profit organization is a single entity, or a series of separate entities called "funds." If the latter view is taken, the organization's primary reporting focus is on the individual funds and more particularly on the unrestricted fund, with the restricted fund reporting being more to show stewardship of these unexpended resources.

Since the question of how to account for current restricted contributions has now been settled by the issuance of SFAS No. 116, an extensive discussion of the various methods previously used is not required here. Interested readers can find a full discussion in Chapter 9 of the fourth edition of this book.

Let's look at an example: The Johnstown Eye Foundation received a contribution of $50,000 to be used for salary costs of the staff of a mobile eye clinic that visits elementary schools to test children's vision in the greater Johnstown area. In the first year, only $40,000 of the $50,000 was expended for this purpose. In addition to the mobile clinic contribution, the Johnstown Eye Foundation had other unrestricted contributions and income of $320,000 and expenses of $315,000. The area of reporting difference relates to how and where to report the $50,000 contribution, and how that relates to the $40,000 of expenses. There are three alternative approaches, all of which have been in common use by different types of organizations:

1. Report the current restricted gift of $50,000 as income in total in the year received, and then reflect the unexpended amount of $10,000 as temporarily restricted net assets at the end of the year (Exhibit 10–1). This is the method historically used by voluntary health and welfare organizations, and which is called for by SFAS No. 116.

2. Report the current restricted gift of $50,000 initially as a direct addition to temporarily restricted net assets and then recognize as income the $40,000 actually expended during the period. This method has been used extensively by colleges, universities, and hospitals. It is not in accordance with SFAS No. 116.

3. Report the current restricted gift of $50,000 initially as a deferred contribution in the Balance Sheet, and then recognize as income the $40,000 actually expended during the period. This method was required by Statement of Position No. 78-10, covering all other types of not-for-profit organizations. It is also not in accordance with SFAS No. 116. However, many persons believe that it is the most appropriate method to use, because it best matches the reporting of restricted revenue with the expenses paid for out of that revenue.

Accounting for Current Restricted Contributions: Report as Income in Full in the Year Received

The approach required by SFAS No. 116 is to report a current restricted gift as income or support in full in the year received, in the temporarily restricted class of net assets. In this approach, gifts are recognized as

EXHIBIT 10–1   An example of a set of financial statements in which current restricted income is reported as income in total in the year received, in the temporarily restricted class.

THE JOHNSTOWN EYE FOUNDATION
STATEMENT OF INCOME, EXPENSES, AND CHANGES
IN NET ASSETS
For the Year Ended June 30, 19X1

	Unrestricted	Temporarily Restricted	Total
Income:			
Restricted contributions		$50,000	$ 50,000
Other income	$320,000		320,000
Net assets released from			
restrictions	40,000	(40,000)	—
	360,000	10,000	370,000
Less—Expenses	(355,000)		(355,000)
Excess of income over expenses . .	5,000	10,000	15,000
Net assets, beginning of year . . .	100,000	25,000	125,000
Net assets, end of year	$105,000	$35,000	$140,000

BALANCE SHEET
June 30, 19X1

	Unrestricted	Temporarily Restricted	Total
Cash	$ 40,000	$38,000	$ 78,000
Other assets	85,000	—	85,000
Total	$125,000	$38,000	$163,000
Accounts payable	$ 20,000	$ 3,000	$ 23,000
Net assets	105,000	35,000	140,000
Total	$125,000	$38,000	$163,000

income as received and expenditures are recognized as incurred. The unexpended income is reflected as part of temporarily restricted net assets. Exhibit 10–1 shows the Statement of Income, Expenses, and Changes in Net Assets and the Balance Sheet for the Johnstown Eye Foundation, following this approach.

The reader can clearly see that the Johnstown Eye Foundation received gifts of $50,000 and expended $40,000 and that the organization had unspent current restricted gifts of $25,000 from previous years.

The implication of this presentation is that the $50,000 is income at the time received, and that while there may be restrictions on the use of the amount, the board truly considers the $50,000 as resources of the Johnstown Eye Foundation, reportable as such.

Observe, however, that in this approach a current restricted gift received on the last day of the reporting period will also be reflected as income, and this would increase the excess of support over expenses reported for the entire period. Many boards are reluctant to report such an excess in the belief this may discourage contributions or suggest that the board has not used all of its available resources. Those who are concerned about reporting an excess of income over expenses are therefore particularly concerned with the implications of this approach: a large unexpected current restricted gift may be received at the last minute, resulting in a large excess of income over expenses.

Others, in rejecting this argument, point out that the organization is merely reporting what has happened and to report the gift otherwise is to obscure its receipt. They point out that in reality all gifts, whether restricted or unrestricted, are really at least somewhat restricted and only the degree of restriction varies; even "unrestricted" gifts must be spent realizing the stated goals of the organization, and therefore such gifts are effectively restricted to this purpose even though a particular use has not been specified by the contributor.

There are valid arguments on both sides. The approach shown in Exhibit 10–1 is the one recommended in the AICPA Audit Guide for Voluntary Health and Welfare Organizations and therefore has been very widely followed. It will now become the method used by all not-for-profit organizations if they want their independent auditor to be able to say that their financial statements are prepared in conformity with generally accepted accounting principles.[1]

Grants for Specific Projects

Many organizations receive grants from third parties to accomplish specific projects or activities. These grants differ from other current restricted gifts principally in the degree of accountability the recipient organization has in reporting back to the granting organization on the use of such monies. In some instances, the organization receives a grant to conduct a specific research project, the results of which are turned over to the grantor. The arrangement is similar to a private contractor's

---

[1] Generally accepted accounting principles (GAAP) are discussed in Chapter 19, and auditors' reports in Chapter 24.

performance on a commercial for-profit basis. In that case, the "grant" is essentially a purchase of services. It would be accounted for in accordance with normal commercial accounting principles, which call for the revenue to be recognized as the work under the contract is performed.[2] In other instances, the organization receives a grant for a specific project, and while the grantee must specifically account for the expenditure of the grant in detail and may have to return any unexpended amounts, the grant is to further the programs of the grantee rather than for the benefit of the grantor. This kind of grant is really a gift, not a purchase.

The line between ordinary current restricted gifts and true "grants" for specific projects is not important for accounting purposes because the method of reporting revenue is now the same for both. What can get fuzzy is the distinction between grants and purchase of services contracts. Most donors of current restricted gifts are explicit as to how their gifts are to be used, and often the organization will initiate a report back to the donors on the use of their gifts. However, restricted gifts and grants usually do not have the degree of specificity that is attached to purchase contracts. Appendix 10–B contains a checklist to help readers distinguish between gifts and purchase contracts in practice.

Prepayment versus cost-reimbursement.   Grants and contracts can be structured in either of two forms: in one the payor remits the amount up front and the payee then spends that money. In the other, the payee must spend its own money from other sources and is reimbursed by the payor.

In the case of a purchase contract, amounts remitted to the organization in advance of their expenditure should be treated as deferred income until such time as expenditures are made which can be charged against the contract. At that time, income should be recognized to the extent earned. Where expenditures have been made but the grantor has not yet made payment, a receivable should be set up to reflect the grantor's obligation.

In the case of a true grant (gift), advance payments must be recognized as revenue immediately upon receipt, as is the case with all contributions under SFAS No. 116. Reimbursement grants are recognized as revenue as reimbursements become due, that is, as money is spent which the grantor will reimburse. This is the same method as is used under cost-reimbursement purchase contracts.

Some organizations record the entire amount of the grant as a receivable at the time awarded, offset by deferred grant income on the liability side of the Balance Sheet. This is no longer appropriate under SFAS

---

[2] Purchase of service contracts are explicitly excluded from coverage of SFAS No. 116 by par. 3.

No. 116. If the entire grant amount qualifies as an unconditional pledge (see below), then that amount must be recorded as revenue, not deferred revenue.

(c) Investment Securities

Frequently an organization will receive contributions that are in the form of investment securities: stocks and bonds. These contributions should be recorded in the same manner as cash gifts. The only problem usually encountered is difficulty in determining a reasonable basis for valuation in the case of closely-held stock with no objective market value.

The value recorded should be the fair market value at the date received. Marketable stocks and bonds present no serious valuation problem. They should be recorded at their market value on the date of receipt or, if sold shortly thereafter, at the amount of proceeds actually received. However, the "shortly thereafter" refers to a sale within a few days or perhaps a week after receipt. Where the organization deliberately holds the securities for a period of time before sale, the securities should be recorded at their fair market value on the date of receipt. This will result in a gain or loss being recorded when the securities are subsequently sold (unless the market price remains unchanged).

For securities without a published market value, the services of an appraiser may be required to determine the fair value of the gift.

10.2 GIFTS-IN-KIND

(a) Fixed Assets (Land, Buildings, and Equipment), and Supplies

Contributions of fixed assets can be accounted for in one of two ways. SFAS No. 116 permits such gifts to be reported as either unrestricted or temporarily restricted income at the time received. If the gift is initially reported as temporarily restricted, the restriction is deemed to expire ratably over the useful life of the asset: that is, in proportion to depreciation for depreciable assets. The expiration is reported as a reclassification from the temporarily restricted to the unrestricted class of net assets. This method of reporting is illustrated in Exhibit 13–2. Nondepreciable assets such as land would remain in the temporarily restricted class indefinitely—until disposed of. (Recognizing the gift as income in proportion to depreciation recognized on the asset is not in conformity with generally accepted accounting principles.)

Supplies and equipment should be recorded at the amount which the organization would normally have to pay for similar items. A value for used office equipment and the like can usually be obtained from a dealer in such items. The valuation of donated real estate is more difficult, and it is usually necessary to get an outside appraisal to determine the value.

(b) Museum Collections

SFAS No. 116 makes an exception for recording a value for donated (and purchased) museum collection objects, if certain criteria are met and certain disclosures are made. Owners of such objects do not have to record them, although they may if they wish. This subject is discussed further in Chapter 18.

(c) Contributed Services of Volunteers

Many organizations depend almost entirely on volunteers to carry out their programs, and sometimes supporting functions. Should such organizations place a value on these contributed services and record them as "contributions" in their financial statements?

Criteria for Recording

The answer is yes, under certain circumstances. These circumstances exist only when *either* of the following conditions is satisfied:

1. The services create or enhance nonfinancial assets; or
2. The services:
   a. Require specialized skills,
   b. Are provided by persons possessing those skills, and
   c. Would typically have to be purchased if not provided by donation.

If neither criterion is met, SFAS No. 116 precludes recording a value for the services, although disclosure in a footnote is encouraged. These criteria differ considerably from criteria in the earlier audit guides/statement of position.

Creating or enhancing fixed assets.   The first criterion is fairly straightforward. It covers volunteers constructing or making major improvements to buildings or equipment. It would also cover things like building sets or making costumes for a theater or opera company, and writing computer programs, since the resulting assets could be capitalized on the balance sheet. The criterion says "nonfinancial" assets so as *not* to cover volunteer fundraisers who, it could be argued, are "creating" assets by soliciting gifts.

Specialized skills.   The second criterion has three parts, all of which must be met for recording to be appropriate. The first part deals with the nature of the services themselves. The intent is deliberately to limit the types of services that must be recorded, thus reducing the burden of tracking and valuing large numbers of volunteers doing purely routine work, the aggregate financial value of which would usually be fairly small. SFAS No. 116 gives very little guidance about how to identify, in practice, those skills which would be considered "specialized," as opposed to nonspecialized. There is a list of skills that are considered specialized, but it merely recites a list of obvious professions such as doctors, lawyers, teachers, carpenters. What is lacking is an operational definition of specialized that can be applied to all types of services. Appendix 10–C contains a checklist to help readers make this distinction in practice.

The second part of the criterion will usually cause no problems in practice, as persons practicing the types of skills contemplated should normally possess the skills (if not, why are they performing the services?)

Would otherwise purchase.   The third part of the criterion will be the most difficult of all to consider, as it calls for a pure judgment by management. Would the organization or would it not purchase the services? This is similar to one in SOP No. 78-10, which reads as follows:

> The services performed are significant and form an integral part of the efforts of the organization as it is presently constituted; the services would be performed by salaried personnel if donated services were not available . . . ; and the organization would continue the activity.

Probably the most important requirement is that the services being performed are an essential part of the organization's program. The key test is whether the organization would hire someone to perform these services if volunteers were not available.

This is a difficult criterion to meet. Many organizations have volunteers involved in peripheral areas which, while important to the organization, are not of such significance that paid staff would be hired in the absence of volunteers. But this is the acid test: If the volunteers suddenly quit, would the organization hire replacements? Appendix 10–D contains a checklist to help readers assess this criterion.

Basis on Which to Value Services

An additional criterion that is not explicitly stated in SFAS No. 116 in connection with donated services is that there must be an objective basis on which to value these services. It is usually not difficult to determine a reasonable value for volunteer services where the volunteers are performing professional or clerical services. By definition, the services to be recorded are only those for which the organization would in fact hire paid staff if volunteers were not available. This suggests that the organization should be able to establish a reasonable estimate of what costs would be involved if employees had to be hired.

In establishing such rates, it is not necessary to establish individual rates for each volunteer. Instead, the volunteers can be grouped into general categories and a rate established for each category.

Some organizations are successful in getting local businesses to donate one of their executives on a full-or part-time basis for an extended period of time. In many instances, the amount paid by the local business to the loaned executive is far greater than the organization would have to pay for hired staff performing the same function. The rate to be used in establishing a value should be the lower rate. This also helps to get around the awkwardness of trying to discern actual compensation.

An organization may wish not to record a value unless the services are significant in amount. There is a cost to keep the records necessary to meet the reporting requirements and unless the resulting amounts are significant it is wasteful for the organization to record them.

Accounting Treatment

The dollar value assigned to contributed services should be reflected as income in the section of the financial statements where other unrestricted contributions are shown. In most instances, it is appropriate to disclose the amount of such services as a separate line.

On the expense side, the value of contributed services should be allocated to program and supporting service categories based on the nature of the work performed. The amounts allocated to each category are not normally disclosed separately. If volunteers were used for constructing fixed assets, the amounts would be capitalized rather than being charged to an expense category. Unless some of the amounts are capitalized, the recording of contributed services will not affect the excess of income over expenses, since the income and expense exactly offset each other. Exhibit 10–2 shows a simplified example of reporting for contributed services.

The footnotes to the financial statements should disclose the nature of contributed services and the valuation techniques followed.

(d) Use of Facilities

Occasionally a not-for-profit organization will be given use of a building or other facilities either at no cost or at a substantially reduced cost. A value should be reflected for such a facility in the financial statements, both as income and as expense. The value to be used should be the fair market value of facilities which the organization would otherwise rent if

EXHIBIT 10–2   An example of a Statement of Income, Expenses, and Changes in Net Assets in which a value is reported for contributed services of volunteers.

THE KANAB COMMUNITY SERVICE ORGANIZATION
STATEMENT OF INCOME, EXPENSES, AND CHANGES
IN NET ASSETS
For the Year Ended June 30, 19X1

Income:		
Service fees	$200,000	
Contributions	50,000	
Value of contributed services	75,000	
Total income		$325,000
Expenses:		
Program services:		
Assistance to the elderly	100,000	
Assistance to the poor	100,000	
Assistance to youth	50,000	
Total program		250,000
Supporting services:		
Administration	40,000	
Fund raising	10,000	
Total supporting		50,000
Total expenses		300,000
Excess of income over expenses		25,000
Net assets, beginning of year		100,000
Net assets, end of year		$125,000

the contributed facilities were not available. This means that if very expensive facilities are donated the valuation to be used should be the lower value of the facilities which the organization would otherwise have rented. Implicit in this rule is the ability to determine an objective basis for valuing the facilities. If an organization is given the use of facilities that are unique in design and have no alternative purpose, it may be impossible to determine what they would have to pay to rent comparable facilities. This often occurs with museums that occupy elaborate government-owned buildings.

Where a donor indicates that the organization can unconditionally use such rent-free facilities for more than a one-year period, the organization should reflect the arrangement as a pledge, and record the present value of the contribution in the same way as other pledges.

10.3   SUPPORT NOT CURRENTLY EXPENDABLE

(a)   Endowment Gifts

Donor-restricted endowment fund contributions should be reported as revenue upon receipt in a restricted class of net assets: temporary in the case of a term endowment gift, otherwise permanent. There are different approaches for reporting endowment gifts in a Statement of Income and Expenses. Usually a multicolumn presentation is followed to separate unrestricted from restricted income as shown here:

	Unrestricted	Permanently Restricted	Total
Support and Revenue:			
Contributions	$ 125,000	$50,000	$ 175,000
Other	200,000	—	200,000
Total	325,000	50,000	375,000
Less—Expenses (in total)	(310,000)	—	(310,000)
Excess of support and revenue			
over expenses	$ 15,000	$50,000	$ 65,000

Another approach which was described in the AICPA Statement of Position 78-10 (discussed in Chapter 17) is the use of a "nonexpendable additions" section in the statement. In this approach such gifts are reflected in a section titled "Nonexpendable additions" or "Capital additions." (See Exhibit 17–2 and the related discussion.) The new FASB standard for financial reporting (SFAS No. 117) does not discuss this approach, but it does not prohibit it either. Thus an organization that wishes to follow it may do so, as long as the gift is clearly identified as restricted.

Gifts of term endowment are later reclassified to the unrestricted class when the term of the endowment expires. (If upon expiration of the endowment restriction, the gift is still restricted—likely for some operating purpose—it would not be reclassified until money was spent for that purpose. If upon expiration of the term endowment restriction, the gift becomes permanently restricted, it should be recorded in that class initially.)

(b)   Pledges (Promises to Give)

A pledge[3] is a promise to contribute a specified amount to an organization. Typically, fund-raising organizations solicit pledges because a donor either does not want to or is not able to make a contribution in cash in the amount desired by the organization at the time solicited. In giving, as with consumer purchases, the "installment plan" is a way of life. Organizations find donors are more generous when the payments being contributed are smaller and spread out over a period of time.

A pledge may or may not be legally enforceable. The point is largely moot because few organizations would think of trying to legally enforce a pledge. The unfavorable publicity that would result would only hurt future fund raising. The only relevant criteria are: Will the pledge be collected and are pledges material in amount?

If these criteria are satisfied, then there are two accounting questions: Should a pledge be recorded as an asset at the time the pledge is received? If the answer is "yes," the next question is: When should the pledge be recognized as income?

Recording as an Asset

For many organizations, a significant portion of their income is received by pledge. The timing of the collection of pledges is only partially under the control of the organization. Yet over the years most organizations find they can predict with reasonable accuracy the collectible portion of pledges, even when a sizable percentage will not be collected. Accounting literature requires that unconditional pledges the organization expects to collect be recorded as assets and an allowance established for the portion that is estimated to be uncollectible.

Historically, there was considerable difference of opinion on this subject, with the AICPA Audit Guides and the Statement of Position

---

[3] SFAS No. 116 uses the term "promise to give" to refer to what is more commonly called a pledge.

taking different positions. The college audit guide said recording of pledges was optional, and most colleges did not record them until collected. The other three guides required recording pledges, although their criteria and method of recording differed slightly. Now, SFAS No. 116 requires *all* organizations to record unconditional pledges.

Conditions versus Restrictions

The requirement in SFAS No. 116 is to record *unconditional* pledges as assets. Unconditional means, without conditions. What is meant by conditions? FASB defines a condition as "a future and uncertain event" that must occur for a pledge to become binding on the pledgor. There are two elements to this definition: future and uncertain. Future means it hasn't happened yet; this is fairly clear. Uncertain is, however, more subject to interpretation. How uncertain? This will be a matter of judgment in many cases.

If a donor pledges to give to a charity "if the sun rises tomorrow," that is not an uncertain event; the sun will rise tomorrow, at a known time. If a donor pledges to give $10,000 to the Red Cross, "if there's an earthquake in California," that is very uncertain (a geologist will say the eventual probability of an earthquake happening is 100 percent, but the timing is completely uncertain). This latter pledge would be conditional upon an earthquake occurring. Once an earthquake occurs, then the donor's pledge is unconditional (the condition has been removed), and the pledge would be recorded by the Red Cross.

Another example of a condition is a matching pledge (also known as a challenge grant). A donor pledges to give an amount to a charity if the charity raises a matching amount from other sources. (The "match" need not be one for one; it can be in any ratio the donor specifies.) In this case, the charity is not entitled to receive the donor's gift until it has met the required match. Once it does, it will notify the donor that the pledge is now due.

A third type of donor stipulation sounds like a condition, but it may or may not actually be one. A donor pledges to contribute to a symphony orchestra "if they will perform my favorite piece of music [specified by name]. (A cynical person would call this a bribe.) Yes, this is an uncertain future event, since the piece of music has not yet been performed, but how uncertain is it? If the orchestra might very well have played the piece anyway, then the "condition" is really trivial, and the event would not be considered uncertain. However, if the piece were one that the orchestra would be very unlikely to perform without the incentive represented by the pledge in question, then the event would be considered uncertain, and the pledge conditional. In this case, the condition is fulfilled when the orchestra formally places the music on its schedule and so informs the donor.

Note that the concept of a condition is quite different from that of a restriction. Conditions deal with events which must occur before a charity is entitled to receive a gift. Restrictions limit how the charity can use the gift after receipt. Unconditional pledges can be either unrestricted or restricted; so can conditional pledges. Donor stipulations attached to a gift or pledge must be read carefully to discern which type of situation is being dealt with. For example, "I pledge $20,000 *if* you play my favorite music" is conditional but unrestricted (the donor has not said the gift must be used to pay for the performance). Whereas "I pledge $20,000 *for* [the cost of] playing my favorite piece of music" is restricted, but unconditional. In the latter case, the donor has said the pledge will be paid, but can only be used for that performance. The difference in wording is small, but the accounting implications are great. The conditional pledge is not recorded at all until the condition is met; the unconditional restricted pledge is recorded as revenue (in the temporarily restricted class) upon receipt of notification of the pledge. Appendix 10–E contains a checklist to help readers determine whether an unconditional pledge actually exists. Appendix 10–F contains a checklist to help distinguish conditions from restrictions.

Discounted to Present Value

Prior to SFAS No. 116, pledges were recorded at the full amount which would ultimately be collected. None of the accounting literature for not-for-profit organizations talked about discounting pledges to reflect the time value of money. There had been for many years an accounting standard applicable to business transactions which does require such discounting,[4] but not-for-profit organizations universally chose to treat this as not applicable to them, and accountants did not object.

SFAS No. 116 does require recipients (and donors) of pledges payable beyond the current accounting period to discount the pledges to their present value, using an appropriate rate of interest. Thus, the ability to receive $1,000 two years later is really only equivalent to receiving about $900 (assuming about a 5% rate of interest) now, because the $900 could be invested and earn $100 of interest over the two years. The higher the interest rate used, the lower will be the present value of the pledge, since the lower amount would earn more interest at the higher rate and still be worth the full $1,000 two years hence.

---

[4] Accounting Principles Board Opinion No. 21, *Interest on Receivables and Payables*, issued in 1971. This statement is silent about its possible application to charitable pledges.

The appropriate rate of interest to use in discounting pledges will be a matter of some judgment. In many cases, it will be the average rate the organization is currently earning on its investments or its idle cash. If the organization is being forced to borrow money to keep going, then the borrowing rate should be used. Additional guidance is in SFAS No. 116 and APB No. 21.

As the time passes between the initial recording of a discounted pledge and its eventual collection, the present value increases since the time left before payment is shorter. Therefore, the discount element must be gradually "accreted" up to par (collection) value. This accretion should be recorded each year until the due date for the pledge arrives. The accretion is recorded as contribution income. (This treatment differs from that specified in APB No. 21 for business debts for which the accretion is recorded as interest income.)

Pledges for Extended Periods

There is one limitation to the general rule that pledges be recorded as assets. Occasionally, donors will indicate that they will make an open-ended pledge of support for an extended period of time. For example, if a donor promises to pay $5,000 a year for 20 years, would it be appropriate to record as an asset the full 20 years' pledge? In most cases, no; this would distort the financial statements. Most organizations follow the practice of not recording pledges for future years' support beyond a fairly short period. They feel that long-term open-ended pledges are inherently conditional upon the donor's continued willingness to continue making payments, and thus are harder to collect. These arguments have validity, and organizations should consider very carefully the likelihood of collection before recording pledges for support in future periods beyond five years.

Allowance for Uncollectible Pledges

Not all pledges will be collected. People lose interest in an organization; their personal financial circumstances may change; they may move out of town. This is as true for charities as for businesses, but businesses will usually sue to collect unpaid debts; charities usually won't. Thus another important question is how large the allowance for uncollectible pledges should be. Most organizations have past experience to help answer this question. If over the years, 10 percent of pledges are not collected, then unless the economic climate changes, 10 percent is probably the right figure to use. Care must be taken, however, because while an organization's past experience may have been good, times do change—as many organizations have discovered to their sorrow.

Another factor to consider is the purpose for which the pledge will be used. Some people will hesitate to default on a pledge for a worthwhile current year's project but may be less conscientious about a pledge for a building fund or a long-term project.

Another point to keep in mind in setting up an allowance is that a pledgor who defaults on an installment once is likely to do so again. If the default brings no notice from the organization, the pledgor assumes the contribution is not really needed, and it will be easier to skip the next payment. So once a donor becomes delinquent on even a single installment, a 100 percent allowance for that total pledge, not just for the delinquent portion, should be considered. In addition, the organization should review the amount of allowance needed for other nondelinquent pledges; once there are signs of any delinquency, the overall collection assumptions may be in doubt. If so, the organization should be conservative and set up additional allowances.

Recognition as Income

The second, related question is: When should a pledge be recognized as income? This used to be a complicated question, requiring many pages of discussion in earlier editions of this book. Now, the answer is easy: immediately upon receipt of an unconditional pledge. This is the same rule that applies to all kinds of gifts under SFAS No. 116. Conditional pledges are not recorded until the condition is met, at which time they are effectively unconditional pledges. Footnote disclosure of unrecorded conditional pledges should be made.

Under the earlier audit guides/statement of position, pledges without purpose restrictions were recorded in the unrestricted class of net assets. Only if the pledge has a purpose restriction would it be recorded in a restricted class. Even pledges with explicit time restrictions were still recorded in the unrestricted class, to reflect the flexibility of use that would exist when the pledge was collected. Under SFAS No. 116, all pledges are considered implicitly time-restricted, by virtue of their being unavailable for use until collected. Additionally, time-restricted gifts, including all pledges, are now reported in the temporarily restricted class of net assets. They are then reclassified to the unrestricted class when the specified time arrives.

This means that even a pledge not payable for 10 years, or a pledge payable in many installments is recorded as revenue in full (less the discount to present value) in the temporarily restricted class in the year the pledge is first received. This is a major change from earlier practice, which generally deferred the pledge until the anticipated period of collection.

Sometimes a charity may not want to have to record a large pledge as immediate revenue; it may feel that its balance sheet is already healthy and recording more income would turn off other donors. If a pledge is unconditional, there is no choice: The pledge must be recorded. One way to mitigate this problem is to ask the donor to make the pledge conditional; then it is not recorded until some later time when the condition is met. Of course, there is a risk that the donor may not be as likely ever to pay a conditional pledge as one that is understood to be absolutely binding, so nonprofit organizations should consider carefully before requesting that a pledge be made conditional.

SFAS No. 116 requires that donors follow the same rules for recognition of the expense of making a gift as recipients do for the income: that is, immediately upon payment or of making an unconditional pledge. Sometimes a charity will find a donor reluctant to make a large unconditional pledge, but willing to make a conditional pledge. Fund raisers should be aware of the effect of the new accounting principles in SFAS No. 116 on donors' giving habits, as well as on recipients' balance sheets.

(c)   Bequests

A bequest is a special kind of pledge. It is the ultimate conditional pledge: a very uncertain future event must occur for it to become payable. Accordingly, bequests should never be recorded before the donor dies—not because death is uncertain, but because a person can always change a will, and the charity may get nothing. (There is a special case: the pledge payable upon death. This is not really a bequest, it is just an ordinary pledge, and should be recorded as such if it is unconditional.)

After a person dies, the beneficiary organization is informed that it is named in the will, but this notification may occur long before the estate is probated and distribution made. Should such a bequest be recorded at the time the organization first learns of the bequest or at the time of receipt? The question is one of sufficiency of assets in the estate to fulfill the bequest. Since there is often uncertainty about what other amounts may have to be paid to settle debts, taxes, other bequests, claims of disinherited relatives, and so on, a conservative, and recommended, approach is not to record anything until the probate court has accounted for the estate and the amount available for distribution can be accurately estimated. At that time, the amount should be recorded in the same manner as other gifts.

Thus, if an organization is informed that it will receive a bequest of a specific amount, say $10,000, it should record this $10,000 as an asset. If instead the organization is informed that it will receive 10 percent of the estate, the total of which is not known, nothing would be recorded yet although footnote disclosure would likely be necessary if the amount could be sizeable. Still a third possibility exists if the organization is told that while the final amount of the 10 percent bequest is not known, it will be at least some stated amount. In that instance, the minimum amount would be recorded with footnote disclosure of the contingent interest.

(d) Split-Interest Gifts

The term "split-interest" gifts is used to refer to irrevocable trusts and similar arrangements (also referred to as deferred gifts) where the interest in the gift is split between the donor (or another person specified by the donor) and the charity. These arrangements can be divided into two fundamentally different types of arrangements: lead interests and remainder interests. Lead interests are those in which the benefit to the charity "leads" or precedes the benefit to the donor (or other person designated by the donor). To put this into the terminology commonly used by trust lawyers, the charity is the "life tenant," and someone else is the "remainderman." The reverse situation is that of the "remainder" interest, where the donor (or the donor's designee) is the life tenant and the charity is the remainderman, that is the entity to which the assets become available upon termination (often called the maturity) of the trust or other arrangement. There may or may not be further restrictions on the charity's use of the assets and/or the income therefrom after this maturity.

Under both types of arrangement the donor makes an initial lump-sum payment into a fund. The amount is invested, and the income during the term of the arrangement is paid to the life tenant. In some cases, the arrangement is established as a trust under the trust laws of the applicable state. In other cases, no separate trust is involved, rather the assets are held by the charity as part of its general assets. In some cases involving trusts, the charity is the trustee; in other cases, a third party is the trustee. Typical third-party trustees include banks and trust companies or other charities such as community foundations. Some arrangements are perpetual, that is, the charity never gains access to the corpus of the gift; others have a defined term of existence that will end either upon the occurrence of a specified event such as the death of the donor (or other specified person) or after the passage of a specified amount of time.

To summarize to this point, the various defining criteria applicable to these arrangements are:

- The charity's interest may be a lead interest or a remainder interest.
- The arrangement may be in the form of a trust or it may not.
- The assets may be held by the charity or held by a third party.
- The arrangement may be perpetual or it may have a defined term.

- Upon termination of the interest of the life tenant, the corpus may be unrestricted or restricted.

Lead Interests

There are two kinds of such arrangements as normally conceived.[5] These are:

1. Charitable lead trust
2. Perpetual trust held by a third party

In both of these cases, the charity receives periodic payments representing distributions of income, but never gains unrestricted use of the assets which produce the income. In the first case, the payment stream is for a limited time; in case two, the payment stream is perpetual.

A *charitable lead trust* is always for a defined term, and usually held by the charity. At the termination of the trust, the corpus (principal of the gift) reverts to the donor or to another person specified by the donor (may be the donor's estate.) Income during the term of the trust is paid to the charity; the income may be unrestricted or restricted. In effect, this arrangement amounts to an unconditional pledge, for a specified period, of the income from a specified amount of assets. The current value of the pledge is the discounted present value of the estimated stream of income over the term of the trust. Although the charity manages the assets during the term of the trust, it has no remainder interest in the assets.

A *perpetual trust held by a third party* is the same as the lead trust, except that the charity does not manage the assets, and the term of the trust is perpetual. Again the charity receives the income earned by the assets, but never gains the use of the corpus. In effect there is no remainderman. This arrangement is also a pledge of income, but in this case the current value of the pledge is the discounted present value of a perpetual stream of income from the assets. Assuming a perfect market for investment securities, that amount will equal the current quoted market value of the assets of the trust or, if there is no quoted market value, then the "fair value," which is normally determined based on discounted future cash flows from the assets.

Some may argue that since the charity does not and never will have day-to-day control over the corpus of this type of trust, it should only record assets and income as the periodic distributions are received from

---

[5] It is also possible to consider both a simple pledge and a permanent endowment fund as forms of lead interests. In both cases, the charity receives periodic payments, but never gains unrestricted use of the assets which generate the income to make the payments. A pledge is for a limited time; an endowment fund pays forever.

the trustee. In fact, that is the way the income from this type of gift has historically been recorded. In the authors' view, this is overcome by the requirement in SFAS No. 116 that long-term unconditional pledges be recorded in full (discounted) when the pledge is initially received by the pledgee. Since SFAS No. 116 requires that the charity immediately record the full (discounted) amount of a traditional pledge, when all the charity has is a promise of future gifts, with the pledgor retaining control over the means to generate the gifts, then the charity surely must record immediately the entire amount (discounted) of a "pledge" where the assets that will generate the periodic payments are held in trust by a third party, and receipt of the payments by the charity is virtually assured.

A variation of this type of arrangement is a trust held by a third party in which the third party has discretion as to when and/or to whom to pay the periodic income. Since in this case the charity is not assured in advance of receiving any determinable amount, no amounts should be recorded by the charity until distributions are received from the trustee; these amounts are then recorded as contributions.

Remainder Interests

There are four types of these arrangements. These are:

1. Charitable remainder annuity trust
2. Charitable remainder unitrust
3. Charitable gift annuity
4. Pooled income fund (also referred to as a life income fund)

These arrangements are always for a limited term, usually the life of the donor and/or another person or persons specified by the donor—often the donor's spouse. The donor or the donor's designee is the life tenant; the charity is the remainderman. Again, in the case of a trust, the charity may or may not be the trustee; in the case of a charitable gift annuity, the charity usually is the holder of the assets. Upon termination of the arrangement, the corpus usually becomes available to the charity; the donor may or may not have placed further temporary or permanent restrictions on the corpus and/or the future income earned by the corpus.

In many states, the acceptance of these types of gifts is regulated by the state government—often the department of insurance—since, from the perspective of the donor, these arrangements are partly insurance contracts, essentially similar to a commercial annuity.

A *charitable remainder annuity trust* (CRAT) and *charitable remainder unitrust* (CRUT) differ only in the stipulated method of calculating the payments to the life tenant. An annuity trust pays a stated dollar amount that remains fixed over the life of the trust; a unitrust pays a stated percentage of the then current value of the trust assets. Thus, the dollar amount of the payments will vary with changes in market value of the corpus. Accounting for the two types is the same except for the method of calculation of the amount of the present value of the life interest payable to the life tenant(s). In both cases, if current investment income is insufficient to cover the stipulated payments, corpus may have to be invaded to do so; however, the liability to the life tenant is limited to the assets of the trust.

A *charitable gift annuity* (CGA) differs from a CRAT only in that there is no trust; the assets are usually held among the general assets of the charity (some charities choose to set aside a pool of assets in a separate fund to cover annuity liabilities), and the annuity liability is a general liability of the charity—limited only by the charity's total assets.

A *pooled income fund* (PIF, also sometimes called a life income fund) is actually a creation of the Internal Revenue Code Section 642(c)(5), which, together with Sec. 170, allows an income tax deduction to donors to such funds. (The amount of the deduction depends on the age(s) of the life tenant(s), and the value of the life interest and is less than that allowed for a simple charitable deduction directly to a charity, to reflect the value which the life tenant will be receiving in return for the gift.) The fund is usually managed by the charity. Many donors contribute to such a fund, which pools the gifts and invests the assets. During the period of each life tenant's interest in the fund, the life tenant is paid the actual income earned by that person's share of the corpus. (To this extent, these funds function essentially as mutual funds.) Upon termination of a life interest, the share of the corpus attributable to that life tenant becomes available to the charity.

Accounting for Split-Interest Gifts

The essence of these arrangements is that they are pledges. In some cases, the pledge is of a stream of payments to the charity during the life of the arrangement (lead interests). In other cases, the pledge is of the value of the remainder interest. Calculation of the value of a lead interest is usually straightforward, as the term and the payments are well-defined. Calculation of remainder interests is more complicated, since life expectancies are usually involved and the services of an actuary will likely be needed.

SFAS No. 116 gives very little guidance specific to split-interests. The AICPA not-for-profit organizations committee will be including more definitive guidance in the new audit guide to be issued in 1995.

APPENDIX 10–A   CHECKLIST

Factors to Be Considered in Deciding Whether a Particular Gift (for Operating Purposes) Should Be Classified as Purpose-Restricted or Not

The following list of factors is to be considered by:

- Not-for-profit organizations, in deciding how to classify operating gifts;
- Auditors, in assessing the appropriateness of the client's decision.

In some cases, no one of these factors will be determinative by itself; all applicable factors should be considered together. These factors are intended to facilitate consideration of the appropriate classification of operating gifts which may be purpose-restricted. This list is not intended to deal with how to account for gifts, nor with questions regarding time-restricted gifts or non-operating gifts, although some factors may be helpful in those areas.

Factors Whose Presence in the Grant Document, Donor's Transmittal Letter, or Other Gift Instrument, or in the Appeal by the Recipient Would Indicate the Gift Is Purpose-Restricted	Factors Whose Presence Would Indicate the Gift May Not Be Purpose-Restricted
1. The purpose of the gift is very specifically set forth.[1] (This factor, if judged to be present, would normally be considered determinative.)	The purpose is described in general or vague terms.
2. The donor expects a detailed report of how the gift was used.	No special reporting to the donor is expected.
3. Refund to the donor of any unspent amount is specifically called for.	No mention is made of the disposition of any unspent amount.
4. The recipient would likely not have conducted the activity at all, or to the same extent, in the absence of the gift.	The recipient would likely have conducted the activity anyway.
5. The donor specifies that the gift can only be used to expand existing activity.	Factor not present.

Factors Whose Presence in the Grant Document, Donor's Transmittal Letter, or Other Gift Instrument, or in the Appeal by the Recipient Would Indicate the Gift Is Purpose-Restricted	Factors Whose Presence Would Indicate the Gift May Not Be Purpose-Restricted
6. The terms of the gift are set forth in a formal written document.	The terms are set forth only orally or informally.
7. The activities funded by the gift are similar to activities funded by previous gifts from the same donor, where the previous gifts were clearly restricted.	Factor not present.
8. The expressed intention of the recipient in soliciting the gift was to solicit restricted gifts.	The solicitation was silent as to the use of the gift or described the use in general terms.
9. In describing the purpose of the gift, the solicitation or the gift instrument includes words such as: restricted must; will only expect certain promise; agree	These documents include words such as: general; operating should any; if intend; hope several plan
10. Based on the overall tone of the language describing the gift, it can reasonably be inferred that the donor's expectation is that the gift is restricted. (See other factors.)	The overall tone does not lead to such an inference.
11. For management control and reporting purposes, the recipient is divided into operating units to conduct different programs;[2] the gift is explicitly directed to one of those units.	Factor not present.
12. The terms of the gift include nonprogrammatic "compliance"—type requirements (often found with government grants).[3]	Factor not present.

[1] The purpose may be described in various ways. Examples include:
- Geographic location (e.g., a city, neighborhood, etc.)
- Population to be served or otherwise benefit (e.g., the visually handicapped, children)

- Anticipated outcome of the activity (e.g., reduction in teen-age pregnancy, performance of a certain opera)
- Precise use of the particular gift (e.g., to pay the salary of a suicide counselor, to repair a blood-mobile)

[2] Examples include:

- An organization serving handicapped children runs a daycare center and a summer camp.
- A university has a law school and a medical school.
- A symphony orchestra has a separate department which operates a youth orchestra.

[3] Examples include compliance with regulations governing:

- Purchasing and hiring
- Affirmative action and civil rights
- Lobbying and political activity
- Drug-free workplace
- Cash management
- Allowable costs and overhead rates
- Subgrants
- Fixed assets
- Audits and financial reports

APPENDIX 10–B   CHECKLIST

Factors to Be Considered in Distinguishing Contracts for the Purchase of Goods or Services from Restricted Grants

The following is a list of factors that may be helpful to:

- Not-for-profit organizations, in deciding how to account for the receipt of payments which might be considered as being either for the purchase of goods or services from the organization, or as restricted-purpose gifts or grants to the organization (as contemplated in par. 3 of SFAS No. 116);
- Auditors, in assessing the reasonableness of the client's decision

Additional discussion of this distinction can be found in the instructions to IRS Form 990, lines 1a–c; and in IRS Regulation 1.509(a)-3(g). No one of these factors is normally determinative by itself; all relevant factors should be considered together.

Factors Whose Presence Would Indicate the Payment Is for the Purchase of Goods or Services	Factors Which Would Indicate the Payment Is a Gift
Factors related to the agreement between the payor and the payee:	
1. The expressed intent is for the payee to provide goods/services to the payor, or to other specifically identified recipients, as determined by the payor.	The expressed intent is to make a gift to the payee to advance the programs of the payee.
2. There is a specified time and/or place for delivery of goods/services to the payor, or other recipient.	Time and/or place of delivery of any goods/services is largely at the discretion of the payee.
3. There are provisions for economic penalties, beyond the amount of the payment, against the payee for failure to meet the terms of the agreement.	Any penalties are expressed in terms of required delivery of goods/services, or are limited to return of unspent amounts.
4. The amount of the payment per unit is computed in a way which explicitly provides for a "profit" margin for the payee.	The payment is stated as a flat amount, or a fixed amount per unit based only on the cost (including overhead) of providing the goods/service.

Factors Whose Presence Would Indicate the Payment Is for the Purchase of Goods or Services	Factors Which Would Indicate the Payment Is a Gift
5. The total amount of the payment is based only on the quantity of items delivered.	The payment is based on a line item budget request, including an allowance for actual administrative costs.
6. The tenor of the agreement is that the payor receives approximately equivalent value in return for the payment.	The payor does not receive approximately equivalent value.

Factors related to the goods/services (items) covered by the payment:

7. The items are closely related to commercial activity regularly engaged in by the payor.	The items are related to the payee's program services.
8. There is substantial benefit to the payor itself from the items.	The items are normally used to provide goods/services considered of social benefit to society as a whole, or to some defined segment thereof (e.g., children, persons having a disease, students), which might not otherwise have ready access to the items.
9. If the payor is a governmental unit, the items are things the government itself has explicitly undertaken to provide to its citizens; the government has arranged for another organization to be the actual service provider.	The government is in the role of subsidizing provision of services to the public by a non-governmental organization.
10. The benefits resulting from the items are to be made available only to the payor, or to persons or entities designated by the payor.	The items, or the results of the activities funded by the payment, are to be made available to the general public, or to any person who requests and is qualified to receive them. Determination of specific recipients is made by the payee.
11. The items are to be delivered to the payor, or to other persons or entities closely connected with the payor.	Delivery is to be made to persons or entities not closely connected with the payor.
12. Revenue from sale of the items is considered unrelated business income (IRC Sec. 512) to the payee.	Revenue is "related" income to the payee.

Factors Whose Presence Would Indicate the Payment Is for the Purchase of Goods or Services	Factors Which Would Indicate the Payment Is a Gift
13. In the case of sponsored research, the payor determines the plan of research and the desired outcome, and retains proprietary rights to the results.	The research plan is determined by the payee; desired outcomes are expressed only in general terms (e.g., to find a cure for a disease), and the rights to the results remain with the payee or are considered in the public domain.
14. The payment supports applied research.	The payment supports basic research.

APPENDIX 10–C   CHECKLIST

Factors to Be Considered in Assessing Whether Contributed Services Are Considered to Require Specialized Skills (per Par. 9 of SFAS No. 116, *"Accounting for Contributions Received . . ."*)

The following is a list of factors which may be helpful to:

- Recipients of contributed services of volunteers, in assessing whether the skills utilized by the volunteers in the performance of their services are considered to be "specialized" within the meaning of Paragraph 9 of SFAS No. 116;
- Auditors, in assessing the appropriateness of the client's judgment.

This list of factors is not intended to be used in determining how to value or account for such services. In some cases, no single factor is necessarily determinative by itself; all relevant factors should be considered together.

Factors whose presence is often indicative that skills are "specialized":

1. Persons who regularly hold themselves out to the public as qualified practitioners of such skills are required by law or by professional ethical standards to possess a license or other professional certification, or specified academic credentials. Alternatively, if possession of such license/certification/credentials is optional, the person performing the services does possess such formal certification.
2. Practitioners of such skills are required, by law or professional ethics, to have obtained a specified amount of technical pre-job or on-the-job training, to obtain specified amounts of continuing professional education, a specified amount of practical work experience, or to complete a defined period of apprenticeship in the particular type of work.
3. Proper practice of the skills requires the individual to possess specific artistic or creative talent and/or a body of technical knowledge not generally possessed by members of the public at large.
4. Practice of the skills requires the use of technical tools or equipment. The ability to properly use such tools or equipment requires

training or experience not generally possessed by members of the public at large.

5. There is a union or professional association whose membership consists specifically of practitioners of the skills, as opposed to such groups whose members consist of persons who work in a broad industry, a type of company, or a department of a company. Admission to membership in such organization requires demonstrating one or more of the factors 1, 2, or 3, above. (Whether or not the person whose skills are being considered actually belongs to such organization is not a factor in assessing whether the skills are considered to be specialized; it may be relevant in assessing whether the person possesses the skills.)

6. Practitioners of such skills are generally regarded by the public as being members of a particular "profession."

7. There is a formal disciplinary procedure administered by a government or by a professional association, to which practitioners of such skills are subject, as a condition of offering their skills to the public for pay.

8. Practice of the skills by persons who do so in their regular work is ordinarily done in an environment in which there is regular formal review or approval of work done by supervisory personnel or by professional peers.

APPENDIX 10–D CHECKLIST

Factors to Be Considered in Determining Whether or Not an Organization Would Typically Need to Purchase Services if Not Provided by Donation

The following is a list of factors which may be helpful to:

- Not-for-profit organizations, in deciding whether or not contributed services meet the third part of the criterion in par. 9b of SFAS No. 116;
- Auditors, in assessing the reasonableness of the client's decision.

No one of these factors is normally determinative by itself; all relevant factors and the strength of their presence should be considered together.

Factors Whose Presence Would Indicate the Services Would Typically Need to Be Purchased	Factors Whose Presence Would Indicate the Services Would Typically Not Need to Be Purchased
1. The activities in which the volunteers are involved are an integral part of the reporting organization's ongoing program services (as stated in its IRS Form 1023/4, fundraising material, and annual report), or of management or fundraising activities that are essential to the functioning of the organization's programs.	The activities are not part of the reporting organization's program, or of important management or fundraising activities, or are relatively incidental to those activities; the services primarily benefit the program activities of another organization.
2. Volunteer work makes up a significant portion of the total effort expended in the program activity in which the volunteers are used.	Volunteer work is a relatively small part of the total effort of the program.
3. The program activity in which the volunteers function is a significant part of the overall program activities of the organization.	The program activity is relatively insignificant in relation to the organization's overall program activities.
4. The reporting organization has an objective basis for assigning a value to the services.	No objective basis is readily available.

Factors Whose Presence Would Indicate the Services Would Typically Need to Be Purchased	Factors Whose Presence Would Indicate the Services Would Typically Not Need to Be Purchased
5. The organization has formal agreements with third parties to provide the program services which are conducted by the volunteers.	Factor not present.
6. The reporting organization assigns volunteers to specific duties.	Assignment of specific duties to volunteers is done by persons or entities other than the reporting organization, or the volunteers largely determine for themselves what is to be done within broad guidelines.
7. The volunteers are subject to ongoing supervision and review of their work by the reporting organization.	The activities of the volunteers are conducted at geographic locations distant from the organization, or factor otherwise not present.
8. The organization actively recruits volunteers for specific tasks.	Volunteers are accepted but not actively recruited, or, if recruited, specific tasks are not mentioned in the recruiting materials.
9. If the work of the volunteers consists of creating or enhancing nonfinancial assets, the assets will be owned and/or used primarily by or under the control of the reporting organization after the volunteer work is completed. If the assets are subsequently given away by the organization to charitable beneficiaries, the organization decides who is to receive the assets.	The assets will immediately be owned or used primarily by other persons or organizations.
10. If there *were* to be a net increase in net assets resulting from the recording of a value for the services (even though in practice, there usually is not), the increase would better meet the criteria for presentation as revenue, rather than a gain, as set forth in SFAC No. 6, par. 78–79, 82–88, and 111–113.	The net increase would better meet the criteria of a gain, rather than revenue.

Factors Whose Presence Would Indicate the Services Would Typically Need to Be Purchased	Factors Whose Presence Would Indicate the Services Would Typically Not Need to Be Purchased
11. Management represents to the auditor that it would hire paid staff to perform the services if volunteers were not available.	Management represents that it would not hire paid staff; or it is obvious from the financial condition of the organization that it is unlikely that financial resources would be available to pay for the services.

Auditors are reminded that management representations, alone, do not normally constitute sufficient competent evidential matter to support audit assertions; however they may be considered in conjunction with other evidence.

Factors particularly relevant in situations where the volunteer services are provided directly to charitable or other beneficiaries of the reporting organization's program services (e.g., Legal Aid society), rather than to the organization itself:

12. The reporting organization assumes responsibility for the volunteers with regard to workers compensation and liability insurance, errors or omissions in the work, satisfactory completion of the work.	The organization has explicitly disclaimed such responsibility.
13. The reporting organization maintains ongoing involvement with the activities of the volunteers.	The organization functions mainly as a clearinghouse for putting volunteers in touch with persons or other organizations needing help, but has little ongoing involvement.

APPENDIX 10–E CHECKLIST

Factors to Be Considered in Assessing Whether a Donor Has Made a Bona Fide Pledge to a Donee

The following is a list of factors which may be helpful to:

- Donees, in assessing whether a pledge (unconditional promise to give—as contemplated in par. 5–7, 22, 23 of SFAS No. 116) has, in fact, been made;
- Auditors, in assessing the appropriateness of the client's judgment.

This list of factors is not intended to be used in deciding on proper accounting (for either the pledge asset or the related revenue/net assets), or to assess collectibility, although some of the factors may be relevant to those decisions as well. In many cases, no single factor is necessarily determinative by itself; all relevant factors should be considered together.

Factors Whose Presence May Indicate a Bona Fide Pledge Was Made	Factors Whose Presence May Indicate a Bona Fide Pledge Was Not Made
1. Factors related to the solicitation process:	
a. There is evidence that the recipient explicitly solicited formal pledges.	The "pledge" was unsolicited, or the solicitation did not refer to pledges.
b. Public announcement[1] of the pledge has been made (by donor or donee)	No public announcement has been made.
c. Partial payment on the pledge has been made, (or full payment after balance sheet date).	No payments have yet been made, or payments have been irregular, late, or less than scheduled amounts.
2. Factors related to the "pledge" itself:	
a. There is written evidence created by the donor which clearly supports the existence of an unconditional promise to give. (This factor, if present, would normally be considered determinative.)	There is no written evidence[2], the only written evidence was prepared by the donee, or written evidence is unclear.

Factors Whose Presence May Indicate a Bona Fide Pledge Was Made	Factors Whose Presence May Indicate a Bona Fide Pledge Was Not Made
b. The evidence includes words such as: promise agree will binding, legal	There is written evidence, but it includes words such as: intend, plan hope may, if expected
c. The pledge appears to be legally enforceable. (Consult an attorney if necessary.) (Note also factor 4a.)	Legal enforceability is questionable, or explicitly denied.
d. There is a clearly defined payment schedule, stated in terms of either calendar dates or the occurrence of specified events whose occurrence is reasonably probable.	A payment schedule is not clearly defined, or events are relatively unlikely to occur.
e. The calendar dates or events comprising the payment schedule will (are expected to) occur within a relatively short time[3] after the balance sheet date (or in the case of events, have already occurred.)	The time (period) of payment contemplated by the donor is relatively far in the future.
f. The amount of the pledge is clearly specified or readily computable.	The amount is not clear or readily computable.
g. The donor has clearly specified a particular purpose for the gift, e.g., endowment, fixed assets, loan fund, retire long-term debt, specific program service. The purpose is consistent with ongoing donee activities.	The purpose is vaguely or not specified, or inconsistent with donee activities.

3. *Factors relating to the donor:*

a. There is no reason to question the donor's ability or intent to fulfill the pledge.	Collectibility of the gift is questionable.
b. The donor has a history of making and fulfilling pledges to the donee of similar or larger amounts.	Factor not present

Factors Whose Presence May Indicate a Bona Fide Pledge Was Made	Factors Whose Presence May Indicate a Bona Fide Pledge Was Not Made

4.   Factors relating to the donee:

    a. The donee has indicated that it would take legal action to enforce collection if necessary, or has a history of doing so.

       It is unlikely (based on donee's past practices) or uncertain whether the donee would enforce the "pledge."

    b. The donee has already taken specific action in reliance on the pledge or publicly[1] announced that it intends to do so.[4]

       No specific action has been taken or is contemplated.

---

[1] The announcement would not necessarily have to be made to the general public; announcement in media circulated among the constituency of either the donor or donee would suffice. Examples include newsletters, fundraising reports, annual reports, a campus newspaper, and so on. In the case of announcements by the donee, there should be a reasonable presumption that the donor is aware of the announcement and has not indicated any disagreement with it.

[2] Oral pledges can be considered bona fide under some circumstances. In the case of oral pledges, much greater weight will have to be given to other factors if the existence of a bona fide pledge is to be asserted. Also, the auditor will have to carefully consider what audit evidence can be relied on.

[3] What constitutes a relatively short time has to be determined in each case. The longer the time contemplated, the more weight will have to be given to other factors (especially 2b, c, 3a and 4a) in assessing the existence of a pledge. In most circumstances, periods longer than 3 to 5 years would likely be judged relatively long.

[4] Types of specific action contemplated include:

- Commencing acquisition, construction or lease of capital assets or signing binding contracts to do so;

- Making public announcement of the commencement or expansion of operating programs used by the public (e.g., the opening of a new clinic, starting a new concert series, a special museum exhibit);

- Indicating to another funder that the pledge will be used to match part of a challenge grant from that funder;

- Soliciting other pledges or loans for the same purpose by explicitly indicating that "x has already pledged;"

- Committing proceeds of the pledge in other ways such as awarding scholarships, making pledges to other charities, hiring new staff, etc., (where such uses are consistent with either the donee's stated purposes in soliciting the pledge or the donor's indicated use of the pledge);

- Forbearing from soliciting other available major gifts (e.g., not submitting an application for a foundation grant) because, with the pledge in question, funding for the purpose is considered complete;

- Using pledge as collateral for a loan.

APPENDIX 10–F   CHECKLIST

Factors to Be Considered in Deciding Whether a Gift or Pledge Subject to Donor Stipulations Is Conditidnal or Restricted (as discussed in SFAS No. 116, par. 7, 22–23, 57–71, 75–81)

Donors place many different kinds of stipulations on pledges and other gifts. Some stipulations create legal *restrictions* which limit the way in which the donee may use the gift. Other stipulations create *conditions* which must be fulfilled before a donee is entitled to receive (or keep) a gift.

In SFAS No. 116, FASB defines a condition as an uncertain future event which must occur before a promise based on that event becomes binding on the promisor. In some cases, it is not immediately clear whether a particular stipulation creates a condition or a restriction. (Some gifts are both conditional and restricted.) Accounting for the two forms of gift is quite different, so it is important that the nature of a stipulation be properly identified so that the gift is properly categorized.

Following is a list of factors to be considered by:

- Recipients (and donors) of gifts, in deciding whether a pledge or other gift which includes donor stipulations is conditional or restricted;
- Auditors, in assessing the appropriateness of the client's decision.

In many cases, no one of these factors will be determinative by itself; all applicable factors should be considered together.

Factors Whose Presence in the Communication from the Donor or the Donee-Prepared Pledge Card Would Indicate the Gift May Be Conditional	Factors Whose Presence in the Grant Document, Donor's Transmittal Letter, or Other Gift Instrument, or in the Appeal by the Recipient Would Indicate the Gift May Be Restricted
Factors related to the terms of the gift/pledge:	
1. The document uses words such as:	The document uses words such as:
If;*	Must;
Subject to;*	For;
When;	Purpose;
Revocable.*	Irrevocable.

Factors Whose Presence in the Communication from the Donor or the Donee-Prepared Pledge Card Would Indicate the Gift May Be Conditional	Factors Whose Presence in the Grant Document, Donor's Transmittal Letter, or Other Gift Instrument, or in the Appeal by the Recipient Would Indicate the Gift May Be Restricted
2. Neither the ultimate amount nor the timing of payment of the gift are clearly determinable in advance of payment.	At least one of the amount and/or timing are clearly specified.
3. The pledge is stated to extend for a very long period of time (over, say, 10 years) or is open-ended. (Often found with pledges to support a needy child overseas, or a missionary in the field.)	The time is short and/or specific as to its end.
4. The donor stipulations in the document refer to *outcomes* expected as a result of the activity (with the implication that if the outcomes are not achieved, the donor will expect the gift to be refunded, or will cancel future installments of a multi-period pledge.[1a]* (Such gifts are likely also restricted.)	The donor stipulations focus on the *activities* to be conducted. Although hoped-for outcomes may be implicit or explicit, there is not an implication that achievement of particular outcomes is a requirement.[1b]*
5. There is an explicit requirement that amounts not expensed by a specified date must be returned to the donor.	There is no such refund provision, or any refund is required only if money is left after completion of the specified activities.
6. The gift is in the form of a pledge.	The gift is a transfer of cash or other non-cash assets.
7. Payment of amounts pledged will be made only on a cost-reimbursement basis.(D)	Payment of the gift will be made up front, or according to a payment schedule, without the necessity for the donee to have yet incurred specific expenses.
8. The gift has an explicit matching requirement (D), or additional funding beyond that already available will be required to complete the activity.	Factor not present.

Factors Whose Presence in the Communication from the Donor or the Donee-Prepared Pledge Card Would Indicate the Gift May Be Conditional	Factors Whose Presence in the Grant Document, Donor's Transmittal Letter, or Other Gift Instrument, or in the Appeal by the Recipient Would Indicate the Gift May Be Restricted

Factors relating to the circumstances surrounding the gift:

9. The action or event described in the donor's stipulations is largely outside the control of the management or governing board of the donee.[2a]*	The action or event is largely within the donee's control.[2b]*
10. The activity contemplated by the gift is one which the donee has not yet decided to do, and it is not yet certain whether the activity will actually be conducted.*	The donee is already conducting the activity, or it is fairly certain that the activity will be conducted.*
11. There is a lower probability that the donor stipulations will eventually be met.	There is a higher probability.
12. The activities to be conducted with the gift money are similar to activities normally conducted on a for-profit basis by the donee or by other organizations.	The activities are not similar
13. As to any tangible or intangible outcomes which are to be produced as a result of the activities, these products will be under the control of the donor. (In such cases, the payment may not be a gift at all; rather it may be a payment for goods or services.)	Any outcomes will be under the control of the donee.

D-Presence of this factor would normally be considered determinative. Absence of the factor is not necessarily determinative.
*-Factors which would generally be considered more important.
[1a] Examples of outcomes contemplated by this factor include:
- Successful creation of a new vaccine;
- Production of a new television program;
- Commissioning a new musical composition;
- Establishing a named professorship;
- Reduction in the teenage pregnancy rate in a community;
- Construction of a new building;
- Mounting a new museum exhibit.

[1b] Examples of activities contemplated by this factor include (but see Factor 10**):
- Conduct of scientific or medical research;
- Broadcasting a specified television program;

- Performing a particular piece of music;
- Paying the salary of a named professor;
- Counseling teenagers judged at risk of becoming pregnant;
- Operating a certain facility;
- Providing disaster relief.

[2a] Examples of events contemplated by this factor include:
- Actions of uncontrolled third parties, e.g.:
  - other donors making contributions to enable the donee to meet a matching requirement of this gift;
  - a government granting approval to conduct an activity (e.g., awarding a building or land use permit, or a permit to operate a medical facility);
  - an owner of other property required for the activity making the property available to the organization (by sale or lease);
- Natural and manmade disasters;
- Future action of this donor (such as agreeing to renew a multi-period pledge in subsequent periods);
- The future willingness and ability of a donor of personal services to continue to provide those services (see SFAS No. 116, par. 70, third sentence).

(Events outside of the donee's control, but which are virtually assured of happening anyway at a known time and place (e.g., astronomical or normal meteorological events), and the mere passage of time, are not conditions.)

[2b] Examples of events contemplated by this factor include (but see Factor 10**):
- Eventual use of the gift for the specified purpose (e.g., those listed in Note 1b above), or retention of the gift as restricted endowment;
- Naming a building for a specified person;
- Filing with the donor routine performance reports on the activities being conducted.

**-There is a presumption here that the right column of Factor 10 applies.

PART TWO

Financial Statement Presentation

Cash Basis
Financial Statements

Most small and some medium-sized not-for-profit organizations keep their records on a cash basis of accounting.[1] As we discussed in some detail in Chapter 3, for many organizations, the cash basis is the best one. Probably the most important reason for this is the simplicity of record keeping. Another reason is that cash basis financial statements are the easiest type of statements to prepare and understand.

---

[1] Note, however, that "generally accepted accounting principles" require accrual basis statements. Organizations that want an opinion from their CPA that states that their financial statements are prepared in accordance with "generally accepted accounting principles" must prepare their statements on an accrual basis.

11.1 SIMPLE CASH BASIS STATEMENT

Exhibit 11–1 shows the financial statement of a typical small church that keeps cash basis records. It also follows the principle of writing off all fixed assets as purchased so there are no fixed assets to be reflected in a Balance Sheet.

(a) Characteristics.

This statement shows not only cash receipts and disbursements but also the cash balance of the church. Since there are no receivables or payables in cash basis accounting, the only asset reflected is cash. This being so, this presentation shows the readers everything they would want to know about the cash transactions for the 12 months.

The words "Receipts" and "Disbursements" have been used, rather than the words "Income" and "Expenses." Traditionally "Receipts" and

EXHIBIT 11–1 An example of a simple cash basis statement that combines both the activity for the year and the ending cash balance.

ALL SAINTS CHURCH
STATEMENT OF CASH RECEIPTS, DISBURSEMENTS, AND CASH BALANCE
For the Year Ended December 31, 19X2

	Actual	Budget
Receipts:		
Plate collections	$ 4,851	$ 5,000
Envelopes and pledges	30,516	32,200
Special gifts	5,038	4,000
Nursery school fees	5,800	6,000
Total	46,205	47,200
Disbursements:		
Clergy	14,325	15,000
Music	8,610	8,400
Education	6,850	7,000
Church office	5,890	6,200
Building maintenance	4,205	4,300
Missions	2,000	2,000
Other	3,318	1,600
Total	45,198	44,500
Excess of cash receipts over disbursements	1,007	$ 2,700
Cash balance, January 1, 19X2	4,300	
Cash balance, December 31, 19X2	$ 5,307	

"Disbursements" are used in cash basis statements since both words signify an event that has taken place (i.e., cash has been received or disbursed). The words "Income" and "Expense" usually refer to accrual basis statements. Also, note that the words "Net Income" have not been used since they usually refer to profit-oriented (i.e., business) entities.

(b)   Budget Comparison

One of the first principles to be remembered in preparing financial statements—whether cash basis or accrual basis—is that the reader should be given a point of reference to help in judging the results. This can be a comparison with last year's statement or it can be a comparison with the budget for the current year. The important thing is that the reader's attention is directed to deviations from either past experience or anticipated results. In Exhibit 11–1 a comparison with the budget gives the reader a point of reference. A careful examination will show where receipts and disbursements have deviated from what was expected. In this illustration, "Envelopes and pledges" has not met expectations. Most expenditures (except "other" disbursements) have been close to the budget.

11.2   SIMPLE STATEMENT WITH LAST YEAR'S FIGURES AND BUDGET

While the statement in Exhibit 11–1 has a comparison with the budget, some organizations also add last year's figures. An even more elaborate statement would contain a column showing the amount of deviation of actual receipts and disbursements from the budget. Exhibit 11–2 shows the same statement but with these additional columns to help the reader quickly pinpoint problem areas.

Quickly look down the column labeled "Actual Better (Worse) Than Budget." See how rapidly the three significant items that have deviated from the budget can be spotted. This is the advantage of the deviation column.

(a)   Comparison with Last Year's Actual Figures

The 19X1 comparison column gives additional information to help the reader interpret the current year's statement. For example, note that in 19X2 every category of receipts is up from 19X1, as is every category of disbursements. The thoughtful reader has to ask whether the board wasn't overly optimistic in budgeting receipts of almost $7,000 more than the prior year. Perhaps on that basis, the less than budget envelope and pledge receipts for 19X2 do not look as bad. At the same time, the reader will observe that the board went ahead and spent more than was

EXHIBIT 11–2 An example of a simple cash basis statement that shows last year's actual figures and this year's budget to give the reader a basis for drawing a conclusion.

ALL SAINTS CHURCH
STATEMENT OF CASH RECEIPTS, DISBURSEMENTS, AND CASH BALANCE
(SHOWING A COMPARISON WITH LAST YEAR AND BUDGET)
For the Year Ended December 31, 19X2

	Actual 19X1	Actual 19X2	19X2 Budget	Actual Better (Worse) Than Budget
Receipts:				
Plate collections	$ 4,631	$ 4,851	$ 5,000	($ 149)
Envelopes and pledges	28,722	30,516	32,200	(1,684)
Special gifts	1,650	5,038	4,000	1,038
Nursery school fees	5,650	5,800	6,000	(200)
Total	40,653	46,205	47,200	(995)
Disbursements:				
Clergy	13,400	14,325	15,000	675
Music	7,900	8,610	8,400	(210)
Education	5,651	6,850	7,000	150
Church office	4,317	5,890	6,200	310
Building maintenance	3,105	4,205	4,300	95
Missions	1,500	2,000	2,000	—
Other	3,168	3,318	1,600	(1,718)
Total	39,041	45,198	44,500	(698)
Excess of cash receipts over disbursements	1,612	1,007	$ 2,700	($1,693)
Cash balance, January 1	2,688	4,300		
Cash balance, December 31	$ 4,300	$ 5,307		

budgeted. This comparison with both last year's actual and this year's budget helps the reader to obtain insight into the financial situation.

At the same time, including last year's actual figures may be more distracting than helpful for some readers. In preparing financial statements, careful consideration must be given to the needs and limitations of the reader. Careful thought must be given to the degree of sophistication that is appropriate. Accordingly, statements for the board might contain this full four-column presentation while the statements for the church membership could contain only the two-column presentation in Exhibit 11–1. Or, perhaps the appropriate information for the membership may be the two "Actual" columns.

11.3 COMBINED CASH BASIS INCOME STATEMENT AND BALANCE SHEET

In Chapter 2 it was noted that cash basis accounting reflects only transactions involving cash. This means that a cash basis Balance Sheet does not show accounts receivable or accounts payable since no cash has been involved. However, there are assets and liabilities that do result from cash transactions and these assets and liabilities should be reflected on the Balance Sheet. Three types of transactions are frequently reflected in a cash basis Balance Sheet: those involving securities or investments, fixed assets, and loans payable.

Securities or investments can arise either from an outright purchase for cash, or as a result of a donation. If they result from a donation, they should be treated as "cash" income and be recorded as an asset. Fair market value at the date of receipt should be used for valuation purposes.

The purchase of fixed assets for cash may or may not be reflected on the Balance Sheet depending on the principles being followed for fixed asset accounting. Chapter 6 discussed alternatives for accounting for fixed assets.

Occasionally, a cash basis organization will borrow money from a bank or from an individual. A good example is a church that has a drop in contributions over the summer months and needs a short-term loan to tide it over until fall pledge collections pick up. These loans are "cash" transactions and should be reflected on the Balance Sheet.

Exhibit 11–3 shows an example of a statement showing assets resulting from cash transactions. The Friends of Evelyn College is a small not-for-profit organization whose function is to raise funds among alumnae for the ultimate benefit of their alma mater.

(a) Characteristics

Note the third line of the title—Net Assets Resulting from Cash Transactions. Normally the use of the words "Balance Sheet" is avoided since these words imply the accrual basis.

This format provides a description of the assets held at the end of year right on the Statement of Income Collected and Expenses Disbursed. This makes it possible for the reader to obtain a total picture of the organization by looking at only one statement. This simplicity is a real advantage.

This organization has used the words "Income Collected" and "Expenses Disbursed" whereas in Exhibits 11–1 and 11–2 the words "Receipts" and "Disbursements" were used. It was previously noted that the words "Income" and "Expense" generally refer to accrual basis accounting and should be avoided in cash basis statements. Here, however,

EXHIBIT 11–3   An example of a simple cash basis financial statement which combines in a single statement both income and expenses for the year and the assets and liabilities at the end of the year.

THE FRiENDS OF EVELYN COLLEGE, INC.
STATEMENT OF INCOME COLLECTED, EXPENSES DISBURSED,
AND NET ASSETS RESULTING FROM CASH TRANSACTIONS
For the Year Ended December 31, 19X2

Income collected:		
Contributions received	$146,797	
Interest income	2,150	
Total		$ 148,947
Expenses disbursed:		
Grants to Evelyn College	125,000	
Audit fee	573	
Other expenses	832	
Total		126,405
Excess of income collected over		
expenses disbursed		22,542
Net assets, January 1, 19X2		20,604
Net assets, December 31, 19X2		$ 43,146
Net assets consisted of:		
Cash	$ 943	
U.S. treasury bills, at cost which		
approximates market	47,211	
Marketable securities at contributed		
value (market value $6,958)	4,992	
		$ 53,146
Less: Loan payable to bank		(10,000)
		$ 43,146

the use of the words "Collected" and "Disbursed" clearly indicate that cash transactions are involved and therefore there is no reason not to use these titles.

The term "Net income" is more familiar to most than the phrase used in this illustration, "Excess of income collected over expenses disbursed" or the phrase used in Exhibits 11–1 and 11–2, "Excess of cash receipts over disbursements." As was previously noted, the words "Income" and "Expense" usually refer to accrual basis transactions. Still, many like to use the words "Net income" in cash basis statements because they feel the reader understands this term better than one of the other expressions. If the organization wants to use the words "Net income," it should then add the words "on a cash basis" so there can be no confusion.

Note that the market value is shown parenthetically on both the U.S. treasury bills and the marketable securities. As is discussed in Chapter 8, marketable securities are often carried at cost. However, it is important to show the market value on the statements so that the reader can see how much unrealized appreciation (or depreciation) there is.

11.4 SEPARATE STATEMENT OF RECEIPTS AND DISBURSEMENTS AND STATEMENT OF NET ASSETS

It is not always possible to combine a Statement of Net Assets with the Statement of Receipts and Disbursements. This is particularly true where the Statement of Receipts and Disbursements is long and complicated or where the assets and liabilities are voluminous. Exhibit 11–4 shows the first two years' operation of a private swim club that purchased land and built a pool, borrowing part of the monies needed. Two statements are used although the cash balance is also shown on the Statement of Cash Receipts and Disbursements.

(a) Cash Basis Emphasized

All cash transactions have been included in this Statement of Cash Receipts, Disbursements, and Cash Balance, but all transactions not involving income or expenses as such have been segregated to aid the reader. If these transactions had not been segregated, it would have been more difficult to see what the on-going pattern of income and expenses would be.

Notice that in this presentation, the statement comes down to the cash balance at the end of the year. The purpose of this is to emphasize the most important asset. The statement could have stopped at the "Excess of cash receipts over disbursements" caption, but by showing the cash balance the importance of cash is emphasized. This is important for organizations with constant cash problems.

(b) Mortgage Repayments

The mortgage principal repayment is shown as an "Other cash" transaction. This allows the reader to see the cash position at the end of the year. On an accrual basis, neither the loan proceeds nor the mortgage principal repayment would be shown on this statement.

EXHIBIT 11–4   Cash basis statements where cash balance is shown in the Statement of Cash Receipts and Disbursements, and a separate Statement of Net Assets is also presented.

CROMWELL HILLS SWIM CLUB

STATEMENT OF CASH RECEIPTS, DISBURSEMENTS, AND CASH BALANCE
RESULTING FROM CASH TRANSACTIONS
For the Years Ended December 31, 19X1 and 19X2

	19X1	19X2
Income collected:		
Membership dues	$ 25,000	$ 25,000
Interest income	125	300
Total	25,125	25,300
Expenses disbursed:		
Salary of manager	2,000	2,200
Salaries of life guards	12,000	13,000
Payroll taxes	1,071	1,130
Pool supplies	2,000	2,200
Mortgage interest	1,200	2,300
Lawn furniture	800	—
Other miscellaneous	1,129	270
Total	20,200	21,100
Excess of income collected over expenses disbursed	4,925	4,200
Other cash transactions-receipts (disbursements):		
Mortgage principal repayments	(3,800)	(5,700)
Members' capital contributions	50,000	—
Bank loan received	40,000	—
Land acquisition	(25,000)	—
Pool construction cost	(62,500)	—
Net other cash transactions	(1,300)	(5,700)
Excess of cash receipts over (under) disbursements for the year	3,625	(1,500)
Cash balance, beginning of the year		3,625
Cash balance, end of the year	$ 3,625	$ 2,125

EXHIBIT 11–4 *Continued.*

CROMWELL HILLS SWIM CLUB
STATEMENT OF NET ASSETS RESULTING FROM CASH TRANSACTIONS
December 31, 19X1 and 19X2

Net Assets	19X1	19X2
Cash	$ 3,625	$ 2,125
Fixed assets, at cost:		
Land	25,000	25,000
Pool	62,500	62,500
Total assets	91,125	89,625
Less–Bank Loan	(36,200)	(30,500)
Net assets	$ 54,925	$ 59,125
Represented by		
Capital contributions	$ 50,000	$ 50,000
Excess of income collected over expenses disbursed:		
Beginning of the year	—	4,925
For the year	4,925	4,200
	4,925	9,125
End of the year	$ 54,925	$ 59,125

(c) Certain Assets Not Capitalized

Notice that the lawn furniture has not been considered a fixed asset. This is because lawn furniture will be replaced every year or two and therefore there is little point in setting it up as a fixed asset. Cash basis organizations normally do not depreciate assets and, if these assets were recorded, they probably would have to be depreciated very rapidly since they have such a short life.

11.5 STATEMENT OF INCOME WITH CERTAIN CASH TRANSACTIONS OMITTED

There is still another way to show the Cromwell Hills Swim Club statements. In this presentation, certain cash transactions that affect the Balance Sheet are not shown in the Statement of Income. In 19X1 these are the loan of $40,000, repayment of $3,800, and the purchases of land and pool of $87,500. Exhibit 11–5 shows how statements presented on this basis would look.

EXHIBIT 11–5 An example of cash basis statements where certain cash transactions are not reflected in the Statement of Income Collected, Expenses Disbursed, and Capital Contributed.

CROMWELL HILLS SWIM CLUB
STATEMENT OF INCOME COLLECTED, EXPENSES DISBURSED,
AND CAPITAL CONTRIBUTED
For the Years Ended December 31, 19X1 and 19X2

	19X1	19X2
Income collected:		
Membership dues	$ 25,000	$ 25,000
Interest income	125	300
Total	25,125	25,300
Expenses disbursed:		
Salary of manager	2,000	2,200
Salaries of life guards	12,000	13,000
Payroll taxes	1,071	1,130
Pool supplies	2,000	2,200
Mortgage interest	1,200	2,300
Lawn furniture	800	—
Other miscellaneous	1,129	270
Total	20,200	21,100
Excess of income collected over expenses disbursed	4,925	4,200
Capital contributed	50,000	—
Excess of income collected and capital contributed over expenses disbursed	$ 54,925	$ 4,200

STATEMENT OF NET ASSETS RESULTING FROM CASH TRANSACTIONS
December 31, 19X1 and 19X2

	19X1	19X2
Cash	$ 3,625	$ 2,125
Fixed assets, at cost:		
Land	25,000	25,000
Pool	62,500	62,500
Total assets	91,125	89,625
Less–Bank loan	(36,200)	(30,500)
Net assets	$ 54,925	$ 59,125

(a) Characteristics

As noted, the Statement of Income Collected, Expenses Disbursed, and Capital Contributed does not contain all cash transactions. Those transactions affecting only the Statement of Assets are not reflected. As a result, the last line on the Statement of Income is no longer the cash balance, but "Excess of income collected and capital contributed over expenses disbursed." This means that the emphasis on the cash balance is gone, and this creates a risk that the reader may misinterpret the meaning of this "Excess" line. Most will readily recognize that the $54,925 in 19X1 is not the cash balance at the end of the year, but some may think the club had a "cash" surplus in 19X2 of $4,200. Many will fail to realize that there was a mortgage principal repayment of $5,700 and that the actual cash balance decreased $1,500 during the year.

In this presentation, the Statement of Assets could have been added at the bottom of the Statement of Income in a manner similar to that of Exhibit 11–3. Exhibit 11–6 shows how this would look in condensed form.

EXHIBIT 11–6 An example of a cash basis statement in which the Statement of Income is combined with a Statement of Net Assets.

CROMWELL HILLS SWIM CLUB
CONDENSED STATEMENT OF INCOME COLLECTED, EXPENSES DISBURSED, CAPITAL CONTRIBUTED, AND NET ASSETS
For the Years Ended December 31, 19X1 and 19X2

	19X1	19X2
Income collected	$ 25,125	$ 25,300
Expenses disbursed	(20,200)	(21,100)
Excess of income collected over expenses disbursed	4,925	4,200
Capital contributed	50,000	—
Excess of income collected and capital contributed over expenses disbursed	54,925	4,200
Net assets, beginning of the year	—	54,925
Net assets, end of the year	$ 54,925	$ 59,125
Net assets comprised:		
Cash	$ 3,625	$ 2,125
Land (at cost)	25,000	25,000
Pool (at cost)	62,500	62,500
Total assets	91,125	89,625
Less—Bank loan	(36,200)	(30,500)
Net assets	$ 54,925	$ 59,125

This is a better approach because the reader does not have to make the transition from one statement to another, or to understand the title at the top of the second statement.

11.6   MODIFIED CASH BASIS STATEMENTS

In Chapter 2 it was noted that cash basis organizations often reflect certain noncash transactions in their financial statements. This may be a large receivable from a brokerage house for securities that have been sold at the end of the year, or it may be a large bill owed to someone that would materially distort the statements if omitted. In each case, these transactions are reflected in the statements to avoid material distortions.

There is absolutely nothing wrong with an organization's including such noncash transactions in the statements. The important thing is that the statements be meaningful. Care should be taken, however, to label noncash transactions in the statement so the reader knows they have been included.

11.7   CONCLUSION

More not-for-profit organizations use cash basis than accrual basis accounting. Except where fixed assets and loans are involved, cash basis statements are very simple to prepare and understand. Even with the complication of fixed assets and loans, it is possible to present meaningful statements that most readers will understand. In developing the appropriate financial statement presentation, the treasurer should consider carefully what emphasis is desired. If the cash position of the organization is the crucial item, then the statement should come down to the cash balance at the end of the period. If cash is not a problem, the last line could be either the caption "Excess of income over expenses on the cash basis" or "Net assets at the end of the year." This is largely a matter of judgment and knowing the sophistication of the readers of the statements.

CHAPTER 12

Accrual Basis
Financial Statements

In the previous chapter, several cash basis statements were illustrated. One of the reasons cash basis accounting is followed is the simplicity of record keeping. Unfortunately for many organizations, cash basis accounting is just not appropriate. They have too many unpaid bills at the end of the year or too much uncollected revenue. The only meaningful basis of accounting for these organizations is the accrual basis.[1]

Accrual basis accounting is more complicated, but this does not mean that the financial statements prepared on an accrual basis need be

---

[1] Generally accepted accounting principles require accrual basis statements. Organizations that want an opinion which states that their financial statements are prepared in accordance with generally accepted accounting principles from their CPA must prepare their statements on an accrual basis.

complicated or hard to understand. The key, however, is careful planning—the laying out of the financial-statement format so that the statements tell the organization's story as simply and effectively as possible. Easy-to-understand financial statements do not just happen; they must be carefully prepared with the reader in mind.

In this chapter, three sets of accrual basis financial statements are discussed. Each has been prepared with the reader in mind. Many of the accounting principles discussed in previous chapters are also illustrated in these statements.

12.1 SIMPLE ACCRUAL BASIS STATEMENTS

Camp Squa Pan is a typical medium-sized boys' camp sponsored by a local YMCA but operated as a separate entity. It was started in the late 1940s with a contribution of $50,000 from the local YMCA, and over the years has broken even financially. Exhibits 12–1 and 12–2 show the financial statements on an accrual basis.

(a) Income

The principal transaction reflected in these statements, which would have been handled differently on a cash basis, is the receipt in the current year of camp deposits for the following year. In 19X1, the camp notices were sent out in October and many deposits had been received by December 31. In 19X2, however, the notices didn't go out until almost Christmas and very few deposits had been received. If Camp Squa Pan had been on a cash basis, the income for 19X2 would have been substantially less, since the $18,275 of deposits received in 19X1 for 19X2 camp fees would have been 19X1 income. Offsetting this would have been the $1,610 of deposits received in 19X2 for 19X3 camp fees. Here is what 19X2 income would have looked like on a cash basis:

19X2 accrual basis income	$214,400
Less 19X2 deposits received in 19X1	(18,275)
Plus 19X3 deposits received in 19X2	1,610
19X2 cash basis income	$197,735

As can be seen, there is a $16,665 difference between the cash and accrual bases. This difference is significant when measured against the excess of expenses over income in 19X2 of $1,502. On a cash basis, this excess would have been $18,167 and the cash basis statements would have been misleading.

EXHIBIT 12–1 An example of a simple accrual basis Statement of Income, Expenses, and Changes in Net Assets.

CAMP SQUA PAN, INC.
STATEMENT OF INCOME, EXPENSES, AND CHANGES
IN NET ASSETS
For the Years Ended December 31, 19X1 and 19X2

	19X1	19X2
Income:		
Campers' fees	$203,760	$ 214,400
Interest	212	412
Total income	203,972	214,812
Expenses:		
Salaries	89,606	93,401
Food	36,978	40,615
Repair and maintenance	25,741	29,415
Horse care and feed	3,983	4,010
Insurance	6,656	6,656
Advertising and promotion	2,563	2,201
Depreciation	12,570	13,601
Other miscellaneous	21,141	26,415
Total expenses	199,238	216,314
Excess of income over (under) expenses	4,734	(1,502)
Net assets, beginning of year	55,516	60,250
Net assets, end of year	$ 60,250	$ 58,748

(b) Depreciation

Depreciation is recorded by Camp Squa Pan. As is more fully discussed in Chapter 7, not-for-profit organizations that capitalize their fixed assets should also depreciate them. In this case, the camp director felt the building and equipment would deteriorate with time and he knew there was little likelihood that the YMCA would make another major contribution for new buildings or equipment. Accordingly, he concluded that it was appropriate to depreciate the fixed assets and to include depreciation as an expense so that he would be forced to set camp fees high enough to recover these depreciation costs.[2]

[2] There are a number of accounting policies that each organization must determine. The handling of fixed assets and depreciation is a good example. Since there are a number of alternatives, each organization should disclose the accounting policies it has adopted in its notes to the financial statements so that all readers will be fully aware of them.

EXHIBIT 12–2   An example of a simple accrual basis Balance Sheet.

CAMP SQUA PAN, INC.
BALANCE SHEET
December 31, 19X1 and 19X2

ASSETS	19X1	19X2
Current assets:		
Cash	$ 13,107	$ 9,997
U.S. treasury bills at cost which approximates market	10,812	—
Accounts receivable	1,632	853
Prepaid insurance	2,702	1,804
Total current assets	28,253	12,654
Fixed assets, at cost:		
Land	13,161	13,161
Buildings	76,773	76,773
Furniture and fixtures	22,198	23,615
Automobiles	13,456	14,175
Canoes and other equipment	12,025	12,675
	137,613	140,399
Less: Accumulated depreciation	(71,242)	(76,629)
Net fixed assets	66,371	63,770
Total assets	$ 94,624	$ 76,424
LIABILITIES AND NET ASSETS		
Current liabilities:		
Accounts payable and accrued expenses	$ 4,279	$ 3,416
Camp deposits	18,275	1,610
Total current liabilities	22,554	5,026
Deferred compensation payable	11,820	12,650
Net assets:		
Original YMCA contribution	50,000	50,000
Accumulated excess of income over expenses	10,250	8,748
Total net assets	60,250	58,748
Total liabilities and net assets	$ 94,624	$ 76,424

(c) Net Assets

The camp uses the term "net assets" on its Balance Sheet. This term is similar in meaning to "stockholders' equity," "net worth," "capital," or "fund balance." Since not-for-profit organizations do not normally have stockholders as such, the term "stockholders' equity" is not appropriate.

However, the terms "net worth," "fund balance," or even "capital" are all terms that are used to represent the aggregate net value of the organization. In this case, Camp Squa Pan has kept the composition of the net assets segregated on the Balance Sheet between the original YMCA contribution and the accumulated excess of income over expenses of the camp. Many organizations keep amounts separated in this way on their financial statements, although this is a matter of preference more than anything else. From a practical standpoint, the historical source of the resources is of little significance for a not-for-profit organization except where there are restrictions that relate to these amounts. In the example here, there is no reason why a single line could not have been shown with the title "net assets" and the amount $58,748.

A minor point to note is that the camp has set up a deferred compensation liability for its caretaker who lives at the camp year round. This will be paid to him sometime in the future, probably when he retires. The point to note is that if the organization has a commitment for this type of expense, it should be recorded currently on an accrual basis.

12.2   ACCRUAL BASIS STATEMENTS—FUND-RAISING ORGANIZATION

The United Fund Drive of Richmond Hill is a typical community fund-raising organization. It solicits contributions on behalf of about 20 agencies serving the Richmond Hill area. Its annual drive takes place in late September. A substantial portion of the contributions is raised through pledges to be paid from payroll deductions over the period October through May. After the annual drive is completed and the board knows how much has been received or pledged, it makes allocations to the various agencies that will receive funds. As the cash is received, it is turned over to these agencies. The records are kept on an accrual basis and pledges are recorded. The fiscal year ends on July 31. Exhibits 12–3 and 12–4 show the comparative financial statements for the six-month periods ended January 31, 19X1 and 19X2.

(a)   Pledges

The Statement of Income, Allocations, and Net Assets clearly shows both the total pledges and the amount that is estimated to be uncollectible. Many organizations are reluctant to record pledges until received. Yet experience shows that a fairly consistent pattern of collection will usually exist for most organizations. There is no reason why pledges, less the anticipated uncollectible portion, should not be recorded. In this case, if pledges were not recorded, the financial statements would have little meaning.

EXHIBIT 12–3   An example of an accrual basis Statement of Income and Allocations for a typical united fund drive.

UNITED FUND DRIVE OF RICHMOND HILL, INC.
STATEMENT OF INCOME, ALLOCATIONS AND NET ASSETS

	Six Months Ended January 31,	
	19X1	19X2
Income available for allocation:		
Pledges	$ 597,342	$ 726,661
Interest income	90	765
Less–Provision for uncollectible		
pledges	(31,161)	(39,192)
	566,271	688,234
Less–Administrative expenses	(25,344)	(27,612)
Income available for allocation	540,927	660,622
Allocations to agencies:		
American Red Cross	42,759	50,000
Richmond Hill Area Urban League	17,640	28,025
Big Brothers	—	13,971
Boy Scouts of America	70,220	72,385
Camp Fire	40,531	40,905
Black Affairs Council	13,816	15,000
Child Guidance Clinic	6,010	—
Day Care Center	—	15,000
Family and Children's Service	107,026	116,760
Girl Scouts	40,422	56,000
Goodwill Industries	30,650	32,700
Legal Aid Society	11,719	10,700
Salvation Army	36,757	40,967
Summer Youth Program	—	10,000
Visiting Nurse Association	4,010	6,689
Hebrew Community Center	25,783	28,038
Y.M. and Y.W.C.A.	42,392	43,075
Richmond Hill Hospital	68,127	65,069
	557,862	645,284
Excess of income over (under) allocations	(16,935)	15,338
Net assets, August 1	24,237	9,502
Net assets, January 31	$ 7,302	$ 24,840

EXHIBIT 12–4   An example of an accrual basis Balance Sheet for a typical united fund drive.

UNITED FUND DRIVE OF RICHMOND HILL, INC.
BALANCE SHEET

	January 31,	
ASSETS	19X1	19X2
Cash	$ 38,727	$ 59,805
Pledges receivable, less allowance for uncollectible pledges of $31,161 in 19X1 and $39,192 in 19X2	168,516	229,517
Total assets	$ 207,243	$ 289,322
LIABILITIES AND NET ASSETS		
Allocated to agencies	$ 557,862	$ 645,284
Less: Payments to date	(361,536)	(389,517)
Net unpaid	196,326	255,767
Payroll taxes and accounts payable	3,615	8,715
Total liabilities	199,941	264,482
Net assets	7,302	24,840
Total liabilities and net assets	$ 207,243	$ 289,322

(b)   Fiscal Period

The organization's fiscal year-end should not fall in the middle of the period when both collections and payment of the allocations are in process. This is what would happen if December 31 were the year-end. In this case, the year-end is July 31 since all pledges are normally paid by May 31. At July 31, the organization will have collected and paid to agencies all of the previous year's fund drive pledges. (For newly formed organizations, the year-end date must be elected on a timely basis for federal tax reporting purposes. Page 477 discusses this requirement.)

(c)   Income Statement Format

There is considerable detail on the Statement of Income, Allocations, and Net Assets, but it all concerns the principal function of the drive, allocations to agencies. While there are some administrative expenses, no details have been shown because to do so would distract from the main purpose of the statement. The board, and anyone else who might ask, should receive a supporting schedule accounting for these expenses.

Notice the caption "Income available for allocations." It is important in statements of fund-raising organizations that the amount which is actually available for the purposes for which the organization exists be clearly shown. An alternative presentation would be:[3]

	19X2
Income	$688,234
Expenses:	
Allocations to agencies (in detail) ...	645,284
Administrative expenses (in detail) ..	27,612
Total	672,896
Excess of income over expenses	$ 15,338

There is certainly nothing wrong with this format except that it is too easy to get lost in the details of the administrative expenses and miss the central point, that $645,284 was distributed to agencies out of an available amount of $660,622 ($688,234 less $27,612). The administrative expenses are a real cost of raising the income for this kind of organization, and should be shown as a deduction from the gross income raised.

(d)   Functional Reporting

The Voluntary Health and Welfare Organization Audit Guide discussed in Chapter 14, as well as SFAS No. 117 provide for reporting of expenses on a functional basis, with a distinction between program and supporting functions and a further division of the supporting function into administrative and fund raising. Exhibit 12–3 does not specifically use the words "program" and "supporting"; however, since the program function of a community fund-raising drive is to collect and allocate funds, its entire fund-raising effort is in reality the program. The only fund-raising costs which would be "supporting" would be efforts made to raise funds for the organization itself, as, for example, a building fund drive.

(e)   Balance Sheet Format

Notice that, to make it easier for the reader, on the Balance Sheet the gross amount allocated to agencies has been shown and then payments-to-date

---

[3] The Third Edition of *Standards of Accounting and Financial Reporting for Voluntary Health and Welfare Organizations* illustrates a presentation similar to this one. See Chapter 14, page 250.

have been deducted to arrive at the net amount still payable. It would certainly be correct to show only one figure, the remaining $255,767, but then it would be more difficult for readers to understand exactly what that figure represented. They might mistakenly conclude this was the total amount allocated.

Notice that the estimated uncollectible amount of pledges is shown on the Balance Sheet. This gives the readers some idea as to the percentage that is expected to be collected.

12.3   ACCRUAL BASIS STATEMENTS—INTERNATIONAL ORGANIZATION

There are many large not-for-profit organizations, some of which have international operations. This does not mean, however, that the financial statements are necessarily complex or involved. The financial statements of Children Overseas Inc. are a good example. Children Overseas Inc. is a large organization serving poor and destitute children in 11 countries. Its resources are raised principally by encouraging contributions toward the support of particular children. Exhibits 12–5, 12–6, and 12–7 show the financial statements of this organization.

One of the first things that may strike the reader is that the figures are shown only in thousands of dollars. There is no point in carrying figures out to the last dollar. Round off to the significant figure. The extra digits only make the reader work harder and incorrectly suggest that there is significance in the detail. Where there is concern that the absence of the extra digits reduces the impact of the numbers, an alternative is to use zeros to replace amounts rounded (i.e., $8,206 becomes $8,206,000). In this way readability is retained along with the visual impact of the amounts.

(a)   Income Statement Format

The Consolidated Statement of Income, Expenses, and Changes in Net Assets (Exhibit 12–5) shows some detailed sources of income, but only total expenses. A separate supporting statement (Exhibit 12–6) shows the details of the expenses by country, for the interested reader. It would have been possible to include much of this "by country" detail on the Statement of Income, but this could very well have confused the reader by having too much detail. The supporting schedule has been carefully prepared to help the reader see how it ties into the income statement ($8,206, $2,353, $583, and $11,142). This makes it easy for the reader to become quickly oriented when looking at this supporting schedule. If

EXHIBIT 12–5   An example of a comparative Statement of Income, Expenses, and Changes in Net Assets for a large international not-for-profit organization.

CHILDREN OVERSEAS INC.
CONSOLIDATED STATEMENT OF INCOME, EXPENSES, AND CHANGES
IN NET ASSETS
(in thousands)

	For the Year Ended June 30	
	19X1	19X2
Income:		
Pledges for children	$ 9,210	$ 9,073
Gifts for special purposes	1,372	1,514
Contributions, endowment gifts, and bequests	450	661
Government grants	155	82
Investment and miscellaneous income	44	74
Provision for unrealized loss on investments	(44)	—
Reduction in provision for unrealized loss on investments no longer needed	—	92
Total income	11,187	11,496
Expenses (Figure 12–6):		
Aid and services to children	8,649	8,206
Supporting operations	2,081	2,353
Promotion and advertising	454	583
Total expenses	11,184	11,142
Excess of income over expenses	3	354
Net assets (deficit), beginning of year	(514)	(511)
Net assets (deficit), end of year	$ (511)	$ (157)

EXHIBIT 12–6 An example of a supplementary statement showing details of expenses. This statement would provide details not shown on the Statement of Income and Expenses.

CHILDREN OVERSEAS INC.
ANALYSIS OF EXPENSES BY COUNTRY
(in thousands)
Year Ended June 30, 19X2

Country	Aid and Services to Children	Supporting Operations	Promotion and Advertising	Total	19X1 Total
United States	—	$1,287	$425	$ 1,712	$ 1,767
Canada	—	192	70	262	122
Australia	—	74	88	162	7
Bolivia	$ 165	59	—	224	107
Brazil	419	59	—	478	392
Colombia	1,116	85	—	1,201	1,223
Ecuador	841	65	—	906	907
Greece	957	100	—	1,057	1,214
Hong Kong	851	80	—	931	1,226
Indonesia	67	38	—	105	43
Korea	1,308	98	—	1,406	1,438
Peru	588	85	—	673	592
Philippines	1,165	61	—	1,226	1,257
Vietnam	729	70	—	799	889
19X2 Total	$8,206	$2,353	$583	$11,142	
19X1 Total	$8,649	$2,081	$454		$11,184

183

EXHIBIT 12–7   An example of a Balance Sheet for a large international not-for-profit organization.

CHILDREN OVERSEAS INC.
CONSOLIDATED BALANCE SHEET
(in thousands)

	June 30	
ASSETS	19X1	19X2
Cash	$ 563	$ 704
Investments, at cost less provision for unrealized loss of $137,000 in 19X1 and $45,000 in 19X2 which approximates market	1,066	1,331
Accounts receivable:		
Estimated unpaid pledges and gifts due from foster parents	155	135
Foreign government grants	24	18
U.S. government grants	3	3
Other receivables	—	22
Prepaid expenses	73	35
Land, building, and equipment, net of allowance for depreciation of $85 in 19X1 and $105 in 19X2	60	65
Total assets	$ 1,944	$ 2,313
LIABILITIES AND NET ASSETS		
Liabilities:		
Advance payments for children	$ 1,963	$ 1,992
Accounts payable and accrued payroll taxes	84	48
Estimated statutory severance pay liability	92	101
Unremitted gifts for special purposes	316	329
Total liabilities	2,455	2,470
Net assets (deficit)	(511)	(157)
Total liabilities and net assets	$ 1,944	$ 2,313

the organization had wanted to give even more detail in this supporting schedule, it could have used a wide sheet of paper and listed the details by type of expenses down the side and by country across the page. It would have taken a wide sheet, but here (in part) is the way it would have looked:

	Total	Bolivia	Brazil	Colombia
Aid and services to children:		(in thousands)		
Monthly cash grants	$4,317	$ 68	$200	$ 542
Purchased goods	636	8	49	107
Gifts for special purposes	1,461	15	40	143
Health services	650	29	38	158
Special services and projects	305	17	25	50
Social workers	472	14	37	65
Shipping and warehousing	145	6	6	18
Translation costs	220	8	24	33
Total	$8,206	$165	$419	$1,116

The key thing to remember is that if details are going to be given they should have totals that tie in to the main schedule so the reader knows exactly what the details represent. For example, in this partial schedule, the $8,206 ties in to the Statement of Income.

(b)   Provision for Unrealized Losses

In Chapter 8 it was noted that not-for-profit organizations should consider setting up a provision for a decline in value in investments where the market is less than cost. These statements present an example of how to set up such a provision and how to reverse it when it is no longer needed. In 19X2 the market value went back up and part of the reserve was no longer needed. Note that it has been reversed in exactly the same manner as it was set up.[4]

As was discussed in Chapter 8, many consider investment income and gains on investments to be similar in nature and both reportable in the same section of the statement. In Exhibit 12–5, investment income and the provision for unrealized loss are reported in the same section.

---

[4] In this example it could be argued that the provision should not have been set up since part of it was not ultimately needed. However, in this instance because of a fund deficit the board felt it prudent to provide a provision since there appeared to be a possibility that part of the investments would have to be sold.

12.4   CONCLUSION

The illustrations in this chapter show many of the features of accrual basis financial statements for not-for-profit organizations. There are many
possible format variations, but readability is the key consideration that
must be considered when preparing financial statements. What does the
organization want to tell its reader? Once it is determined what information to include, it should be possible to design a statement format that
will communicate this information to both sophisticated and unsophisticated readers.

Multiclass Financial Statements

One of the characteristics of not-for-profit organizations is that they have a stewardship responsibility for the resources they receive both to their members and to the public. This stewardship frequently results in a type of accounting referred to as "fund accounting." The principles of fund accounting were discussed in Chapter 4. That chapter explained that while fund *accounting* will still be used by many organizations for recordkeeping and internal reporting, for external financial *reporting*, funds will usually not be used. Instead, this reporting will utilize the three-class structure defined in the new FASB Statement of Financial Accounting Standards No. 117, *Financial Statements of Not-for-Profit Organizations.* Since the reporting units defined in that statement are called classes, financial statements prepared in accordance with it should logically be called "class" financial statements. No such term has yet come into general use, however, since the standard is so new.

Fund accounting offers many advantages if the resulting class financial statements are carefully prepared. This presentation can clearly show the reader what financial activity has taken place within each of the individual classes. Unfortunately, all too often instead of clarifying the financial situation, fund accounting confuses the reader because the statements are not put together with the reader in mind. They may be technically accurate statements but they fail in their principal objective, communication.

On pages 34, 35, and 37, the financial statements of McLean Community Service Center, showing information about each of its funds, were presented. Refer back to these statements, and observe that there are four separate income statements, one for each fund. Note there is a transfer between funds, and that to determine the overall excess of income of the Center the reader really has to have a pencil or a calculator to add up several numbers. There may be some hesitation in even knowing which numbers to combine.

This presentation is typical of organizations that use fund accounting, and no technical fault can be found with these statements. However, the reader may have some difficulty in ascertaining the overall financial picture of the Center. The important question is, therefore, not whether the statements are technically accurate, but whether the reader will understand them. If the reader gives up after only a quick review, then the statements have failed to accomplish their objective. This is the problem with financial statements that present several subunits of an organization—they can be so complex that the reader gets lost or doesn't understand the terminology of the statements. The objective of this chapter is to show how to present class accounting statements that will have the maximum chance of being understood by the average reader. First, the provisions of the new FASB standard dealing with financial statement format will be discussed.

13.1   STATEMENT OF FINANCIAL ACCOUNTING STANDARDS NO. 117—*FINANCIAL STATEMENTS OF NOT-FOR-PROFIT ORGANIZATIONS*

The Financial Accounting Standards Board (FASB) is the body within the accounting profession that determines what are to be considered as "generally accepted accounting principles."[1] In 1993, it issued Statement of Financial Accounting Standards (SFAS) No. 117, *Financial Statements of Not-for-Profit Organizations.*

This statement (frequently referred to as the "display" standard) requires organizations to present, at a minimum, aggregated financial data: total assets, total liabilities, total net assets (excess of assets over liabilities—similar to fund balances), and total change in net assets. Some not-for-profits already do, but many have not done this in the past. Organizations are free to present separate data for the classes of net assets (or funds), but, except that donor-restricted revenue, net assets by class, and change in net assets by class must be shown, no other detail by class or fund is explicitly required.

Three classes of net assets are defined in SFAS No. 117: Unrestricted, temporarily restricted, permanently restricted. The three terms mean exactly what they say: permanent restrictions are those which will never expire or be fulfilled by the organization; temporary restrictions will eventually either expire with the passage of time or will be fulfilled through action by the organization. Net assets of the two restricted classes are created *only* by donor-imposed restrictions on their use. All other net assets, including board-designated or appropriated amounts, are legally unrestricted, and must be reported as part of the unrestricted class, although they may be separately identified within that class as designated for some purpose, if the organization wishes. An example of a balance sheet showing such a designated unrestricted investment fund is shown in Exhibit 13–3.

The permanently restricted net asset class will usually consist mainly of amounts restricted by donors as permanent endowment. Some organizations may also have certain capital assets on which donors have placed perpetual restrictions.[2] Temporarily restricted net assets will often contain a number of different types of donor-restricted amounts: unspent gifts restricted for specified operating purposes, pledges payable in future periods, unspent gifts restricted for use in a specified future time period, unspent amounts restricted for the acquisition of fixed assets,

---

[1] FASB and generally accepted accounting principles (GAAP) are discussed further in Chapter 19.
[2] For example, a donor might give a painting to a museum, with a restriction that the museum can never dispose of it. Another example would be land given to a conservation organization that must be kept as a nature preserve forever.

certain fixed assets, unmatured annuity and life income funds, and term endowments.[3]

Sample financial statements, illustrating formats that contain the disclosures required by SFAS No. 117, are shown in Appendix C to the Statement.

(a) Rearrangement of Funds into Classes

To present their financial statements in accordance with SFAS No. 117, organizations must assess each component of each fund on an individual basis to determine into which class (or classes) that fund balance (net assets) should be classified. This assessment, as to the temporarily and permanently restricted classes, is based only on the presence or absence of donor-imposed restrictions. All funds without donor-imposed restrictions must be classified as unrestricted, regardless of the existence of any board designations or appropriations.

Exhibit 13–1 is a chart showing typical classes into which various types of fund balances will normally be classified.

(b) Expenses Are Always Unrestricted

One requirement of SFAS No. 117 that will be a significant change for many organizations is the reporting of all expenses in the unrestricted class, regardless of the source of the financing of the expenses. Since expendable restricted revenue will be reported in the temporarily restricted class, when these amounts are spent, a reclassification (transfer) will be made to match the restricted revenue with the unrestricted expenses. (An example of this reclassification is shown in Exhibit 13–4.) This practice is presently followed by hospitals, but not by other types of organizations.

(c) Capital Gains Are Normally Unrestricted

A second new requirement is that all capital gains or losses on investments (and other assets or liabilities) will be reported in the unrestricted class. This includes gains on endowment investments, even if the endowment is donor-restricted. There are two exceptions to this general rule: gains must be reported in a restricted class if, (1) there are explicit donor restrictions on the gains (in addition to those on the underlying assets), or (2) applicable state law is judged by the organization's governing board to require the retention of some or all of the capital gains/losses in a restricted class. Adoption of this practice will often

---

[3] A discussion of the different types of temporary restrictions is in Chapter 10 (contributions).

EXHIBIT 13–1 Rearrangement of funds into classes of Net Assets.

Funds	Unrestricted	Temporarily Restricted	Permanently Restricted
Endowment	Quasi-endowment	Term endowment	Permanent endowment
Specific purpose, or current restricted	Board-designated	Donor-restricted	N/A
Loan	Board-designated	Donor-restricted	Revolving[1]
Split-interest (annuity, life income, etc.)	Voluntary excess reserves	Unmatured	Permanent[2]
Fixed asset	Expended[3]; Board-designated	Donor-restricted unexpended; Expended donated[3]	[4]
General/Operating	Unrestricted	Donor-time restricted	N/A
Custodian	All (on balance sheet only)[5]	N/A	N/A

[1] A permanently restricted loan fund would be one where only the income can be loaned, or, if the principal can be loaned, repayments of principal by borrowers are restricted to be used for future loans. A loan fund in which principal repayments are available for any use would be temporarily restricted until the loans are repaid, at which time such amounts become unrestricted.

[2] For example, an annuity fund which, upon maturity, becomes permanent endowment.

[3] Expended donor-restricted plant funds will be either unrestricted or temporarily restricted, depending on the organization's choice of accounting principle under par. 16 of SFAS No. 116 (discussed in Chapter 10).

[4] Fixed assets could be permanently restricted if a donor has explicitly restricted the proceeds from any future disposition of the assets to reinvestment in fixed assets. Museum collection items which were received subject to a donor's stipulation that they be preserved and not sold might also be considered permanently restricted.

[5] Note that since no transactions related to custodian funds are reported in the income statement of the holder of the assets, and since there is never a net asset amount (assets are always exactly offset by liabilities), reporting of such funds as separate items only becomes an issue when a balance sheet is disaggregated into classes. The logic for reporting the assets and liabilities of custodian funds in the unrestricted class is that such assets are not the result of *donor*-restricted *gifts*, which is normally a requirement for recording items in one of the restricted classes.

have the effect of increasing the reported unrestricted net asset balance (and decreasing the other net asset balances) compared with the present reporting method.

(d) Functional Expense Reporting

All organizations must report expenses by functional categories (program, management, fund-raising). Voluntary health and welfare organizations must also report expenses by natural categories (salaries, rent, travel, etc.) in a matrix format;[4] other organizations are encouraged to do so. Reporting in functional categories will be new for some organizations, mainly those which do not raise significant amounts of contributions from the general public, such as trade associations, country clubs, and many local churches.

(e) Statement of Cash Flows

A new financial statement for many organizations will be a statement of cash flows, showing where the organization received and spent its cash. Cash flows will be reported in three categories: operating cash flows, financing cash flows (including receipt of nonexpendable contributions), and investing cash flows. This statement has been required for businesses for several years by SFAS No. 95, *Statement of Cash Flows*, which should be consulted for further information.

SFAS No. 95 permits either of two basic methods for preparing the statement of cash flows: the "direct" and the "indirect" methods. Briefly, the indirect method starts with the excess of revenues over expenses and reconciles this number to operating cash flows. The direct method reports operating cash receipts and cash disbursements, directly adding these to arrive at operating cash flows. The authors recommend using the direct method which is much more easily understood by readers of financial statements.

Much of the information used to prepare a statement of cash flows is derived from data in the other two primary financial statements, some of it from the preceding year's statements. Thus, when planning to prepare this statement for the first time it will be helpful to start a year in advance so that the necessary prior year data will be available when needed.

---

[4] This matrix is illustrated in Exhibit 14–4.

13.2 "CLASS" FINANCIAL STATEMENTS EXPLAINED

(a) Balance Sheet

The Balance Sheet should show the total amounts of assets, liabilities, and net assets, as well as the aggregate net assets for each of the three classes: unrestricted, temporarily restricted, permanently restricted. However, the requirement is for disclosure of these amounts in the net assets section of the Balance Sheet, and not for disclosure of the specific assets and liabilities associated with each class. Accordingly, a Balance Sheet in which all assets and liabilities are commingled is acceptable (and recommended for all but very large, complex organizations) provided the net assets section clearly discloses the amounts of net assets that are unrestricted and amounts that are temporarily and permanently restricted. Exhibit 13–2 shows an example of such a Balance Sheet.

(b) Classes of Net Assets Subdivided

The requirement to disclose the aggregate of the net assets of each of the three classes does not preclude subdividing any or all of the net assets amounts into two or more subcategories. However, where this is done, these subcategories must be aggregated to show the total net assets of

EXHIBIT 13–2 An example of a Balance Sheet showing the three classes of Net Assets.

	August 31	
THE McLEAN COMMUNITY SERVICE CENTER BALANCE SHEET		
	19X1	19X0
Cash	$ 64,000	$ 37,000
Pledges receivable	13,000	10,000
Investments	295,000	230,000
Equipment	70,000	65,000
Total assets	442,000	342,000
Less—Accounts payable	(20,000)	(25,000)
Net assets:		
Unrestricted	130,000	57,000
Temporarily restricted	11,000	10,000
Permanently restricted	281,000	250,000
Total	$422,000	$317,000

EXHIBIT 13–3   An example of a Balance Sheet showing subdivisions of unrestricted Net Assets.

BALANCE SHEET	
August 31, 19X1 (condensed)	
Total assets	$442,000
Accounts payable	$ 20,000
Net assets:	
Unrestricted:	
Designated for investment	25,000
Net equity in fixed assets	70,000
Available for operations	35,000
Total unrestricted	130,000
Temporarily restricted	11,000
Permanently restricted	281,000
Total net assets	422,000
Total liabilities and net assets	$442,000

that class. Exhibit 13–3 shows an example of such subdividing of the unrestricted class.

Some not-for-profit organizations choose to segregate their fixed assets in a separate fixed asset category. The resources that are used to purchase such fixed assets can be both restricted and unrestricted. Although SOP 78-10 indicates that where the organization chooses to report fixed assets as a separate category, it need not subdivide the fixed asset balance into its restricted and unrestricted components, SFAS No. 117 does require that all net assets amounts be categorized into one of the three classes.

(c)   Showing Liquidity

SFAS No. 117 requires not-for-profit organizations to present on their balance sheets information about the "liquidity" of their financial position. In other words, are they likely to have enough cash in the near future to pay their bills as these come due? The most common way to give this information is to present assets and liabilities in a sequence representing, in the case of assets, their nearness to conversion to cash, and, in the case of liabilities, the approximate order in which they will have to be paid. In this format, shown in Exhibit 13–2, the most liquid items (closest to cash/have to be paid soonest) are at the top of the balance sheet, and the least liquid (longest time to convert to cash/last to be paid) at the bottom.

Another way to show this is to classify assets and liabilities as short-term and long-term. This will result in a so-called "classified" Balance Sheet in which current assets and current liabilities are clearly shown. Also in some cases, liquidity will be evident from the nature of the classes of net assets which imply the current or long-term nature of the related assets and liabilities: for example, investments reported as part of permanent endowment are not very liquid.

(d) Interclass Borrowings

A significant interclass borrowing which is intended to be repaid must be disclosed even where the reporting is on a combined or consolidated basis. This can be done either on the face of the Balance Sheet or in the footnotes thereto. However, "borrowing" where there is no intention to repay, or where the borrowing class is unlikely to have the financial ability to repay is in effect a reclassification and should be reported as such.

(e) Statement of Activities

"Statement of Activities" is the name given in SFAS No. 117 to a statement that shows all of the organization's financial activity from the beginning to the end of the year. The title of the statement could be any one of a number of different names, including "Statement of Revenue, Expenses, and Changes in Net Assets," "Statement of Changes in Net Assets," "Statement of Revenue, Expenses, Capital Additions, and Changes in Net Assets," or "Statement of Income and Expenses." The title is not particularly important as long as the statement clearly shows all relevant activity.

At the same time, the Statement of Activities could be broken into two sections, and each treated as a separate statement, that is, a section showing revenue, expenses, and nonexpendable additions, and a section showing changes in net assets. However, there seems little purpose in creating a separate Statement of Changes in Net Assets since the only types of transactions normally shown in the "changes in net assets" section of the Statement of Activities are the addition of the excess for the year and any reclassifications between classes not shown earlier.[5] The authors would expect that most organizations will prepare a single all-inclusive Statement of Activities.

---

[5] SOP 78-10 required unrealized losses on noncurrent investments which are carried at the lower of cost or market would also be reflected as a change in a "change in fund balance" section of the statement. Under SFAS No. 117 this amount will be presented above the "Change in Net Assets," but below an "Excess of revenues over expenses" line, if one is presented.

(f) Other Types of Groupings

Groupings other than the more traditional ones may be entirely appropriate. For example, "Unrestricted/restricted" or "Expendable/nonexpendable" could be used. The requirement is for appropriate disclosure, not the specifics of the classifications to be utilized.

(g) Total of All Classes

One of the controversial issues in not-for-profit accounting is the use of a "Total of all classes" column in the financial statements where a multicolumn presentation is shown. As noted earlier, many believe that the use of such totals is misleading since a total column may imply that interchanges and substitutions between assets are always possible, despite restrictions on certain net assets, or even occasionally on certain individual assets.

SFAS No. 117, consistent with the Statement of Position, while not requiring a total *column*, indicates that it is preferable to include one. It does require presentation of the total change in net assets for all classes together. This is another significant step toward recognizing that not-for-profit organizations are single entities and not a series of separate entities called funds. At the same time, the document notes that care must be taken to assure that all appropriate disclosures are made either in the net assets section or in the footnotes to the financial statements, to make certain the captions are not misleading.

(h) Excess of Revenue over Expenses

SFAS No. 117 does not require this caption as such, nor does it forbid one to be shown. The Statement does require a caption called "Change in Net Assets" which is the final change after all items of revenue, expense, gains/losses, and reclassifications have been shown. The question is whether an organization wishes to present any subtotals *above* the final change number. One possibility is to categorize revenues and expenses into so-called "operating" and "nonoperating" groups, and present a subtotal after the operating revenues and expenses. SFAS No. 117 discusses this approach, but neither requires nor forbids it. The authors believe this approach will be found desirable by those organizations having many items of income or expense that are only peripherally related to their main purposes.

Whether or not an operating/nonoperating subtotal is shown, if there are reclassifications other than those resulting from the release of temporary restrictions on net assets (which are usually shown in the revenue section—as illustrated in Exhibit 13–4), the authors recommend

EXHIBIT 13–4 An example of a columnar Statement of Income, Expenses, and Changes in Net Assets.

THE McLEAN COMMUNITY SERVICE CENTER
STATEMENT OF INCOME, EXPENSES, AND CHANGES IN NET ASSETS
For the Year Ended August 31, 19X1

	Unrestricted	Temporarily Restricted	Permanently Restricted	Total
Income:				
Contributions and gifts	$ 85,000	$24,000	$ 25,000	$134,000
Service fees	110,000			110,000
Investment income from endowment	20,000			20,000
Gains on sale of investments	40,000		6,000	46,000
Other	13,000			13,000
	268,000	24,000	31,000	323,000
Net assets released from restrictions	23,000	(23,000)		—
Total income	291,000	1,000	31,000	323,000
Expenses:				
Program services	163,000			163,000
Administration	43,000			43,000
Fund raising	12,000			12,000
Total expenses	218,000			218,000
Excess of income over expenses	73,000	1,000	31,000	105,000
Net assets, beginning of year	57,000	10,000	250,000	317,000
Net assets, end of year	$130,000	$11,000	$281,000	$422,000

that organizations show a subtotal before such reclassifications. This will clearly distinguish between those items in the statement which are revenues and expenses, thus changing the overall net worth of the organization, and those which are only shifts of resources from one class to another and have no effect on the overall net worth. This is also shown in Exhibit 13–4.

(i)   Reclassifications (Formerly Transfers between Funds)

Reclassifications between classes of net assets are shown in two places in the statement. One type of reclassification results from the release of temporary restrictions through the passage of time or fulfillment of the restricted purpose. These are normally shown in the revenue section of the statement, although it is not required that this be done; they could be shown elsewhere.

The second type is all other reclassifications. Under the new, simplified format called for in SFAS No. 117, there will be very few of these, compared to past practice. The reason for this is that by showing fewer categories in the statement, there are fewer transactions that affect more than one category. The most common types of "other" reclassification will result from, (1) the use of unrestricted resources to meet matching requirements of challenge grants where the donor of the challenge grant has restricted the gift, and (2) reclassifications of unrestricted amounts between subcategories of the unrestricted class, such as to or from an unrestricted investment fund. These reclassifications are shown after the "Excess of Revenue over Expenses" caption in the Statement of Activity. It is not acceptable to reflect a reclassification above this line, except for those reclassifications resulting from the release of restrictions on temporarily restricted net assets shown in the revenue section of the statement.

(j)   Statement of Cash Flows

As discussed in Chapter 14, this statement is required by SFAS No. 117. Further discussion is at pages 248–249.

13.3   COLUMNAR FORMAT PRESENTATION

One of the things that can be done to simplify financial statements resulting from the use of fund accounting is to present the activities of all units of the organization in a columnar format, using as few columns as possible, while still achieving the required disclosures. In this type of presentation, the activity of each class of net assets is shown in a separate column, side by side. In this manner, it is possible to see all the classes at one time. Exhibits 13–4 and 13–5 show the McLean Community Service Center's statements in this columnar format.

(a) Characteristics and Advantages

Once the reader has become oriented to this format, it is possible to see at a glance the total activity of the Center. It is significant that the Center received net income of $105,000 for the year, and not $33,000, which is the first impression that the reader gets when looking at only the separate current unrestricted fund statement in Chapter 4. In this presentation the total income of the other funds can also be seen, and by being given a total the reader doesn't have to work to get the overall results of operations. While the $31,000 of permanently restricted class (endowment) income may not be available for general purposes, it represents a real asset that will generate unrestricted income in the future. The reader should be fully aware of this amount.

Some accountants argue against showing a total column. They point out that this implies that all of the organization's resources can be used for any purpose, whereas in reality there are restrictions. In this example, one-third of the excess of income of $105,000 is permanently restricted

EXHIBIT 13–5 An example of a columnar Balance Sheet.

McLEAN COMMUNITY SERVICE CENTER
BALANCE SHEET
August 31, 19X1

	Unrestricted	Temporarily Restricted	Permanently Restricted	Total
Cash	$ 55,000	$ 9,000		$ 64,000
Pledges receivable ...	2,000		$ 11,000	13,000
Investments	25,000		270,000	295,000
Equipment	70,000			70,000
Due from (to)				
other classes	(2,000)	2,000		—
Total assets	150,000	11,000	281,000	442,000
Less—Accounts				
payable	(20,000)			(20,000)
Net assets	$130,000	$11,000	$281,000	$422,000

gifts and gains that cannot be used currently.[6] They feel that to add the two together is mixing apples and oranges. This is true to a point, but as long as the column headings across the page are descriptive as to the type of restrictions involved, no one can be seriously misled by this columnar approach.[7] Furthermore, the reader who doesn't understand the significance of the separate statement presentation is more likely to be misled and may come away thinking the excess of income was only $33,000.

(b)   Reclassification and Net Assets Section

Notice the ease in handling the reclassification from the temporarily restricted class to the unrestricted class. While any reclassification can cause confusion, the confusion is minimized when both sides of the transaction are shown in a single statement as they have been here.

When more than one class is shown in a columnar format, one or two of the classes may have very little activity and a number of the captions will not be applicable to them. This is particularly so in this instance with the temporarily restricted class. Yet the blank spaces should not detract from the statement, and the very absence of figures in this column is informative because it tells the reader that, in fact, there has been little activity.

Expenses are grouped according to functional category. In this instance, all of the expenses in the program expense category are shown together, and no detail is given. This may not be satisfactory, in which case a supporting schedule could be prepared showing the details of the $163,000. But even if a supporting schedule is prepared the figures should still be shown "in total" in the columnar statement. Otherwise the reader will not be able to see the total picture. There is a risk of confusion in having the same figures in two statements but this can be minimized by putting a caption on the separate supporting statement along the lines "Included in total on Statement of Income, Expenses, and Changes in Net Assets."

(c)   Statement Omitting Changes in Net Assets

It will be noted that in Exhibit 13–4 the statement is labeled Statement of Income, Expenses, and Changes in Net Assets. Some organizations prefer

[6] With respect to gains on endowment fund investments, SFAS No. 117 states that these should be shown in the unrestricted class unless restricted by the donor or by law. The amount shown in the permanently restricted class is that portion of the gains which is considered restricted. (See Chapter 8.)

[7] If there is any question about the reader's understanding the restrictions, a detailed description should be included in the notes to the financial statements, appropriately cross-referenced to the column heading.

to omit reference to "Changes in net assets" and present only a Statement of Income and Expenses, and a Balance Sheet. When this is done, the change in net assets for the year is shown in a separate Statement of Changes in Net Assets.

13.4 A COMPLICATED SET OF CLASS FINANCIAL STATEMENTS

The McLean Community Service Center statements are relatively straightforward and not particularly complicated. In many organizations, this simplicity is not possible. The thing that often complicates the statements is wanting to show a number of "name" funds. These are frequently permanently restricted endowment, but may also include amounts restricted for specified purposes, and possibly unrestricted investments. One characteristic of "name" funds is that the donor's name is associated with the fund. As was discussed in Chapter 4, the use of "name" funds, if carried to an extreme, can cause confusion because it adds detail. The real risk is that the reader will not see the forest for the trees.

There are two principal financial statements that most readers want to see. Most important is a Statement of Income and Expenses and, of lesser importance, the Balance Sheet. If all transactions have been skillfully summarized on these two statements, it is then possible to provide a third schedule that shows the appropriate detail of the information on the two primary statements. The key to successful presentation in this third schedule is showing totals that tie back into the Statement of Income and Expenses.

The J. W. M. Diabetes Research Institute financial statements are a good example of how substantial detail can be provided on "name" funds without detracting from the reader's overall understanding of the results of operations. While these statements relate to a medical service and research institute, the form would essentially be the same for almost any type of organization. Exhibits 13–6, 13–7, and 13–8 show these statements.

(a) Overall Impression of Complexity

The reader's first impression of these statements may be that they "look" complicated and will be hard to understand. This is particularly so with respect to Exhibit 13–8 which shows changes in the individual "name" funds. Before studying this statement, however, take a few minutes to study the first two statements (Exhibits 13–6 and 13–7) to get an overall impression of what has happened during the year. Look first at the

EXHIBIT 13–6 An example of a columnar Balance Sheet.

J. W. M. DIABETES RESEARCH INSTITUTE
BALANCE SHEET
June 30, 19X2

ASSETS	Unrestricted General Fund	Unrestricted Investment Fund	Temporarily Restricted	Permanently Restricted	Total
Current assets:					
Cash	$ 174,860	$ 2,315	$ 20,515	$ 15,615	$ 213,305
Marketable securities, at cost (market value $3,250,000)		256,610	255,310	2,231,080	2,743,000
Contract receivables	7,500				7,500
Other receivables	2,345				2,345
Inventories of books and supplies	14,200				14,200
Total current assets	198,905	258,925	275,825	2,246,695	2,980,350

Fixed assets at cost:					
Land	100,000				100,000
Buildings	1,749,250				1,749,250
Vehicles	25,500				25,500
Total	1,874,750				1,874,750
Less: Accumulated Depreciation	(1,056,200)				(1,056,200)
Net fixed assets	818,550				818,550
Total assets	$1,017,455	$258,925	$275,825	$2,246,695	$3,798,900

LIABILITIES AND NET ASSETS

Accounts payable	$ 47,845				$ 47,845
Withholding taxes	6,300				6,300
Grants paid in advance	42,085				42,085
Payable (receivable)	35,000	$ (42,119)	$ (4,970)	$ 12,089	—
Total liabilities	131,230	(42,119)	(4,970)	12,089	96,230
Net assets:					
Restricted			280,795	2,234,606	2,515,401
Unrestricted	886,225	301,044			1,187,269
Total	886,225	301,044	280,795	2,234,606	3,702,670
Total liabilities and net assets	$1,017,455	$258,925	$275,825	$2,246,695	$3,798,900

EXHIBIT 13–7 An example of a columnar Statement of Income, Expenses, and Changes in Net Assets in which activity for all classes is reported.

J. W. M. DIABETES RESEARCH INSTITUTE
STATEMENT OF INCOME, EXPENSES, AND CHANGES IN NET ASSETS
For the Year Ended June 30, 19X2

	Unrestricted		Temporarily Restricted	Permanently Restricted	Total
	General Fund	Investment Fund			
Income:					
Grants and contracts	$ 424,701				$ 424,701
Contributions and legacies	341,216		$ 27,515	$ 122,504	491,235
Investment income	92,793		16,556	1,640	110,989
Gain on sales of investments	263,660		3,486	29,344	296,480
Net Assets released from restrictions	54,356		(54,356)		
Total	1,176,726		(6,799)	153,478	1,323,405
Expenses:					
Client services	482,813				482,813
Research	275,844				275,844
Administration	112,044				112,044
Total	870,701				870,701
Excess of income over expenses for the year	306,025		(6,799)	153,478	452,704
Reclassifications	(35,000)	$ 42,119		(7,119)	—
Change in net assets	271,025	42,119	(6,799)	146,359	452,704
Net assets, beginning of the year	615,200	258,925	287,594	2,088,247	3,249,966
Net assets, end of the year	$ 886,225	$301,044	$280,795	$2,234,606	$3,702,670

"Total" column on the Statement of Income and Expenses and the description of the items of income and expense. The reader should focus on the total picture before looking at some of the detail by individual funds. The same thing should be done with the Balance Sheet. Look first at the total, and only then at the detail by funds.

The statement of activity by individual "name" funds (Exhibit 13–8) is more difficult. The stewardship concept has been introduced in considerable detail on this statement. Apart from the many individual "name" funds, this statement also shows these funds segregated by the type of restriction associated with each fund. Some funds contain restrictions only with respect to the original principal; others restrict both the income and the principal. While this statement is complicated, there is a great deal of information on the statement that the reader should be able to understand if some time is taken to study it. On the other hand, if the reader isn't interested in this detail, the overall Statement of Income and Expenses still clearly summarizes all income and expenses. This is a key point—everything is summarized in total, and readers are required to look at detail only to the extent they wish to do so.

One final observation about the overall impression these statements make. If these same statements had been presented in a separate statement format, including separate statements for each "name" fund, the resulting set of statements would most certainly have discouraged and probably confused all but the most determined readers. There would be just too much detail; few readers would be able to get any meaningful understanding of the overall financial picture of this organization. So while the supplementary summary on individual "name" funds may seem complex, the alternative would be far less comprehensible.

(b)   Statement of Income, Expenses, and Changes in Net Assets

On the Statement of Income, Expenses, and Changes in Net Assets, the number of columns is only what is needed to show the three classes of net assets, with the unrestricted class being subdivided into an investment fund and the operating fund. While there are varying types of restrictions associated with the various restricted amounts, no attempt is made to indicate these on the face of the statement because this represents a detail that can best be left to a supporting statement. It is important that the reader not get lost in detail on the summary statement.

(c)   Reclassifications

There are two reclassifications in the bottom part of this statement. The first is a reclassification from the permanently restricted class of an

EXHIBIT 13–8   An example of a supplementary statement illustrating how changes in individual name funds can be presented for a fairly complex fund accounting structure.

J. W. M. DIABETES
STATEMENT OF CHANGES IN INDIVIDUAL UNRESTRICTED
(TEMPORARILY RESTRICTED)
For the Year Ended
(All income and expenses have been shown in total on the

		Investment Income		Capital Gains
	Contributions and Legacies	Reported Directly in General Fund	Other	Reported Directly in General Fund
*Unrestricted Investment Fund:				
Elmer C. Bratt Fund		$11,651		$ 33,660
*Funds for specified purposes:				
Charity Fund	$ 3,000		$ 6,683	$ 15,821
Library Fund	18,615		603	1,756
Staff pensions	4,150		3,742	10,811
Malmar Repair Fund	700		5,078	312
100th Anniversary Fund	1,050		450	1,300
Total funds for specified purposes	$ 27,515		$16,556	$ 33,486
Endowment funds:				
Principal and income restricted:				
The Malmar Fund				$ (3,015)
Clyde Henderson Fund ...			$ 1,150	8,165
Evelyn I. Marnoch Fund ...			490	(2,156)
			1,640	2,994
*Principal only restricted:				
The Roy B. Cowin Memorial Fund		$73,859		184,035
The Lillian V. Fromhagen Fund		2,392		6,911
Donna Comstock Fund ...	$ 16,153	1,670		3,661
Josephine Zagajewski Fund	100,000	2,250		
The Peter Baker Fund	6,351	688		1,580
	122,504	80,859		225,521
*Restrictions released by donor in 19X1:				
The Alfred P. Koch Fund ..		283		819
Total endowment funds ...	$122,504	$81,142	$ 1,640	$233,660

* Funds have been "pooled" for investment purposes. See Chapter 24 for a discussion of pooled investments.

EXHIBIT 13–8 *Continued.*

RESEARCH INSTITUTE
INVESTMENT FUND, FUNDS* FOR SPECIFIED PURPOSES
AND ENDOWMENT FUNDS
June 30, 19X2
Statement of Income, Expenses and Changes in Net Assets)

(Losses)

Left in Fund	Disbursed for Specified Purpose	Other Interfund Transfers Add (Deduct)	Net Change in Fund	Net Assets Beginning of Year	Net Assets End of Year
		$42,119	$ 42,119	$ 258,925	$ 301,044
$ 3,486	$ (9,200)		$ 3,969	$ 164,337	168,306
	(18,156)		1,062	15,267	16,329
	(21,500)		(13,608)	93,978	80,370
	(5,500)		278	2,712	2,990
			1,500	11,300	12,800
$ 3,486	$(54,356)		$ (6,799)	$ 287,594	$ 280,795
				$ 107,685	$ 107,685
			$ 1,150	33,766	34,916
			490	8,715	9,205
			1,640	150,166	151,806
$29,334			29,334	1,825,335	1,854,669
				60,076	60,076
			16,153	31,821	47,974
			100,000		100,000
			6,351	13,730	20,081
29,334			151,838	1,930,962	2,082,800
		$ (7,119)	(7,119)	7,119	—
$29,334		$ (7,119)	$146,359	$2,088,247	$2,234,606

endowment on which the restrictions were released by the donor. This reclassification of $7,119 went directly to the unrestricted class since this amount became unrestricted. The second reclassification is from the unrestricted general fund to the unrestricted investment fund, in the amount of $42,119. In the unrestricted general fund column, only the net amount of $35,000 is shown.

It should be noted that there are no contributions or gains shown directly in the unrestricted investment fund. All unrestricted contributions or gains are shown in the unrestricted general fund. The board can then transfer any portion of such income to the unrestricted investment fund but it should not show such income directly in that fund. Unrestricted income must be reported initially in the unrestricted general fund.

(d)   Unrestricted Investment Income

It will be noted that unrestricted investment income of $92,793 ($81,142 from endowment and $11,651 from unrestricted investment funds) has been shown directly in the unrestricted general fund. It would not have been appropriate for the board to have left this amount in the endowment and unrestricted investment funds since this income contains no restrictions as to its use. To assist the reader in seeing how much income each separate fund earned, this unrestricted income is also shown in the Statement of Changes in Individual Funds in the column "Reported directly in general fund." Inclusion of this column in the statement is optional.

(e)   Gains and Losses

Endowment gains aggregating $296,480 have been shown partly in each of the three classes, as discussed in Chapter 8. Unrestricted investment fund gains should be reported entirely in the unrestricted general fund. These gains, as with investment income, represent unrestricted income and should be reported as such. There is no reason why the board can't reclassify all or part of these gains back to the unrestricted investment fund, but this should be handled as a reclassification.

(f)   Comparison with Last Year's Figures

An additional column may be added to the Balance Sheet and the Statement of Income and Expenses to show last year's actual figures so the reader has a point of reference. This comparison is usually to the total column, although sometimes a comparison is made only to the unrestricted general fund. If the comparison column is to the total column, then this additional column should be next to the current year's total column to make it easier for the reader. If the comparison is only to the unrestricted general fund, it should be set up with heads as shown below. Instead of a comparison to last year's figures, the comparison could have been to this year's budget.

Unrestricted					
General Fund		Investment	Temporarily	Permanently	
Last Year	This Year	Fund	Restricted	Restricted	Total

(g) Balance Sheet

Fixed assets have not been set up as a separate category. Instead, they have been included as a part of the unrestricted class. This greatly simplifies the problem of depreciation since depreciation can then be handled in exactly the same manner as it would be handled by a commercial enterprise. The presentation problems in handling depreciation if a separate fixed asset category is used are discussed more fully in Chapter 7.

One of the principal reasons why many prefer to see fixed assets in a separate category is that the unrestricted general fund balance then represents the current assets of the organization. In our illustration the net assets of $886,225 is mostly represented by fixed assets. If the fixed assets had been shown separately, the unrestricted general fund balance would have been only $67,675. But this lower figure has limited significance because there are other unrestricted current assets that are available for general purposes if the board chooses to use them. These other unrestricted current assets are the $301,044 of unrestricted investment funds.

Some will argue that the fixed asset amounts should not be included in the "unrestricted" figure since the organization could not exist without its buildings. This may be so, but there is no reason why the institute has to use its present buildings. They could be sold and new ones built on less expensive land or in a better location. Or property could be rented. These are all decisions that the board is free to make and, being free to make them, the assets are unrestricted.

An alternative presentation that avoids the problem of mixing currently available net assets with the fixed assets is to show the fixed assets on a separate line as in Exhibit 13–3. The authors recommend this approach whenever fixed assets are a significant part of total assets, and especially if the financial condition of the organization is not very liquid. If an organization has a large total unrestricted net assets balance, but most of it is represented by fixed assets, there might not be enough cash available to pay current bills as they come due.

Sometimes an organization will even have a fixed assets balance in excess of its total unrestricted net assets. In this case, there is effectively a deficit in available resources, and serious financial trouble may not be far away.

In the McLean Community Service Center statements, the Balance Sheet (Exhibit 13–2) was set up to show total assets less liabilities equaling net assets:

Total assets	$442,000
Less—Liabilities	(20,000)
Net Assets	$422,000

In the J. W. M. Diabetes Research Institute statements (Exhibit 13–6), the more conventional Balance Sheet approach was followed showing total assets equaling the sum of the liabilities and net assets:

Total assets	$3,798,900
Liabilities	$ 96,230
Net assets	3,702,670
Total liabilities and net assets	$3,798,900

Either approach is acceptable. The first is more appropriate for organizations with relatively few categories of liabilities, and therefore for smaller organizations.

(h)   Statement of Changes in Individual Funds

Notice the line at the top of Exhibit 13–8, "All income and expenses have been shown in the total on the Statement of Income, Expenses, and Changes in Net Assets." This or a similar statement helps readers to recognize that they don't have to add the income and expenses shown on this statement to the amounts shown on the Statement of Income, Expenses, and Changes in Net Assets (Exhibit 13–7) in order to get total income and expenses. While technically there is no requirement that this type of caption be shown, it helps in understanding the nature of this statement. Most of the totals shown on this statement can be tied in directly to the Statement of Income, Expenses, and Changes in Net Assets.

(i)   Restricted Income from Endowments

Income on permanent or term endowment that is restricted to a specified purpose should be recorded directly in the fund for that purpose. Note that in the Malmar endowment fund no investment income has been shown. Actually $4,970 of income was received but it was reported directly in the fund for specified purposes in a separate fund maintained for this income (Malmar Repair Fund). This $4,970 plus $108 of income earned on this restricted fund balance is the $5,078 reported as investment income.

There are two other endowment funds with restrictions on the income. In both instances, the income has been left in the endowment fund. Presumably the donor specified that the income was to be accumulated for a period of time before it could be spent. There is no disclosure of the terms of the fund on the statement, but if they were significant a footnote could be added to tell the reader. However, unless the terms of the restriction are significant, footnote details should be avoided.

There is no reason why unrestricted investments couldn't also have "names" associated with them. Here all of the unrestricted investments are shown as the Elmer C. Bratt Fund. The board could also have had other "name" funds, all part of the total unrestricted investment fund.

While it is not obvious from this statement, most of the investments are "pooled" together and individual funds have a percentage or share interest in the total investment portfolio. Since all of the individual funds are "pooled" together, each gets its proportionate share of income and gains or losses on the sale of investments. Chapter 25 discusses the mechanics of "pooling" investments.

(j)   Other Supporting Statements

There are other statements that could be included with the three statements we have just discussed. For example, many readers might want to see a great deal more of the details of the expense categories than are shown in total on the Statement of Income and Expenses, and perhaps also a comparison with the budget or last year's actual figures. Exhibit 13–9 shows an example of this type of supporting schedule. Again, as with all supporting or supplementary statements, the format must be so designed that the reader clearly sees how the figures tie into the main statement.

The reader interested in detail gets a great deal of information from looking at this type of analysis. There is comparison both with budget for the year and with last year's actual expenses, by type of expense and function. It must be remembered that the more detail provided, the greater the risk that the reader will get lost in the detail. Financial statements are not necessarily improved by providing details or additional supporting schedules. In fact, often they detract from the overall effectiveness.

EXHIBIT 13–9 An example of an analysis of expenses by both function and types of expense, along with a comparison to both budget and last year's actual.

J. W. M. DIABETES RESEARCH INSTITUTE
ANALYSIS OF EXPENSES AND COMPARISON WITH BUDGET AND LAST YEAR'S ACTUAL
For the Year Ended June 30, 19X2

	Actual Last Year	Budget This Year	Actual This Year	Client Services	Research	Administration
Salaries and payroll taxes	$581,615	$615,000	$618,686	$425,851	$133,588	$ 59,247
Retirement benefits	23,151	33,000	33,833	21,463	8,720	3,650
Major medical	3,656	4,500	4,578	3,155	1,013	410
Clinic supplies	34,616	42,000	41,374	29,488	11,886	
Office supplies	3,518	6,900	8,356		5,500	2,856
Laboratory supplies	47,717	40,000	33,596		33,596	
Insurance	5,751	6,000	5,951			5,951
Telephone	3,748	5,000	6,116		3,800	2,316
Depreciation	39,516	43,000	43,525	2,856	30,309	10,360
Contracted repairs and maintenance	14,819	9,600	15,054			15,054
Utilities and fuel	19,151	20,000	19,268		11,316	7,952
Other	36,118	35,000	40,364		36,116	4,248
Total	$807,376	$860,000	$870,701	$482,813	$275,844	$112,044
Budget		$860,000		$480,000	$280,000	$100,000
Actual last year	$807,376			$451,254	$251,348	$104,774

13.5 SUMMARY OR CONDENSED STATEMENTS

Frequently for fund-raising purposes or for the general information of the membership, the board will want to distribute summary or condensed financial statements. Often the board will prefer not to show a large excess of income since this might discourage fund raising. In the case of the J. W. M. Diabetes Research Institute, the board might want to show only the unrestricted general fund activities, which as will be recalled, had an excess of income of $306,025. Yet actually the institute had a total "all funds" excess of $452,704.

The board may prefer issuing statements for only the unrestricted general fund. This is not recommended. At some point, the credibility of the board and its statements may come into question if some of the readers feel information is being withheld. Also, if the board wished to have an auditor's opinion accompany the financial statements of the unrestricted general fund, the auditor would have to call attention in the report to the fact that other funds of the organization were not included.

EXHIBIT 13–10 An example of a condensed Statement of Income and Expenses for all funds, suitable for inclusion in an annual report or fund-raising literature.

J. W. M. DIABETES RESEARCH INSTITUTE
CONDENSED STATEMENT OF INCOME AND EXPENSES
For the Year Ended June 30, 19X2
(in thousands)

Income:		
Grants and contracts	$425	
Contributions and legacies	491	
Investment income	111	
Gain on sale of investments	296	
Total income		$1,323
Expenses:		
Client services	483	
Research	275	
Administration	112	
Total expenses		870
Excess of income over expenses		$ 453
Excess restricted by donor	147	
Unrestricted	306	
Total		$ 453

This requirement is to alert readers that they are not seeing the whole picture.

There is an acceptable approach open to the board. This is to present a condensed statement showing income and expenses for the entire organization but clearly indicating the amount of the excess of income that was donor-restricted. Exhibit 13–10 shows this presentation.

It would be entirely inappropriate, however, to eliminate the unrestricted investment fund activities from the condensed statement. Unrestricted investment funds have all of the characteristics of unrestricted general funds since the board can act at any time to convert unrestricted investment funds back into unrestricted general funds. These funds must be considered part of general unrestricted funds any time when condensed financial statements are presented.

13.6   CONCLUSION

This chapter discussed in detail the significant changes in financial reporting by not-for-profit organizations brought about by SFAS No. 117, including how funds relate to classes of net assets.

The chapter then presented a number of illustrations to help the reader more readily understand the complexities of presenting financial statements that include details for multiple classes and/or funds. The use of the columnar approach has been discussed because it offers many advantages over presenting separate statements for each category, the approach followed by many organizations. It is extremely important that these statements be all-inclusive so that the reader can get a broad overall picture of the activities of the organization before getting down into the detail. Several illustrations were given showing how typical detail can be presented with a minimum risk of confusing the reader. Finally, condensed or summary financial statements were discussed and the importance of disclosing all income, either in the body of the statement or in footnotes was emphasized. Failure to do so creates a credibility gap that can only hurt the organization.

PART THREE

Accounting and Reporting Guidelines

C H A P T E R   14

Voluntary Health and Welfare Organizations

The term, "Voluntary Health and Welfare Organization" first entered the accounting world with the publication in 1964 of the first edition of the so-called "Black Book," *Standards of Accounting and Financial Reporting for Voluntary Health and Welfare Organizations,* by the National Health Council and the National Social Welfare Assembly. The term has been retained through two successor editions of that book, and was used by the American Institute of Certified Public Accountants (AICPA) in the title of its "audit guide," *Audits of Voluntary Health and Welfare Organizations,* first published in 1967.

In 1974, the AICPA issued a revised audit guide, prepared by its Committee on Voluntary Health and Welfare Organizations. This Audit Guide was prepared to assist the independent auditor in examinations of voluntary health and welfare organizations. Included in the revised Audit Guide is a discussion of accounting and reporting principles that were considered appropriate for this type of organization. Since 1974, the audit guide has been slightly revised to reflect certain technical changes in the wording of auditors' reports.

In 1993, the Financial Accounting Standards Board (FASB) issued two new accounting pronouncements, SFAS No. 116, *Accounting for Contributions Received and Contributions Made,* and No. 117, *Financial Statements of Not-for-Profit Organizations,* which supersede many provisions of the AICPA audit guide.[1] Also, as this book is being written, the AICPA Not-for-Profit Organizations Committee is preparing a new audit and accounting guide that will replace the existing guides for voluntary health and welfare organizations, colleges, and universities (discussed in Chapter 15), and other not-for-profit organizations (discussed in Chapters 17 and 18).

This chapter summarizes the accounting and reporting principles discussed in the new FASB standards, and, to the extent that they have not been superseded by the new FASB standards, the provisions of the AICPA voluntary health and welfare audit guide. For the most part, the FASB standards prescribe the same accounting treatment for a given transaction by all types of not-for-profit organizations. One exception to that rule is a requirement that voluntary health and welfare organizations continue to present a statement of functional expenses. Other types of organizations are not required to present this statement, although they may if they wish. More detailed discussions of certain accounting and reporting standards in the new FASB documents will also be found in other chapters of this book. For example, a full discussion of accounting for contributions is in Chapter 10.

"Voluntary health and welfare organizations" are those not-for-profit organizations that "derive their revenue primarily from voluntary contributions from the general public to be used for general or specific purposes connected with health, welfare, or community services."[2] Note that there are two separate parts to this definition: first, the organization must derive its revenue from voluntary contributions from the general public, and second, the organization must be involved with health, welfare, or community services.

---

[1] Chapter 19 discusses in more detail the formal rule-making procedures of the accounting profession, and in particular the relationship of the FASB and the AICPA.

[2] Page v. *Audits of Voluntary Health and Welfare Organizations.* Copyright (c) 1974 by the American Institute of Certified Public Accountants, Inc. Hereafter in this chapter the word "Guide" refers to this publication.

Many organizations fit the second part of this definition, but receive a substantial portion of their revenues from sources other than public contributions. For example, an opera company would not be a voluntary health and welfare organization because its primary source of income is box office receipts, although it exists for the common good. A YMCA would be excluded because normally it receives most of its revenues from dues and program fees. On the other hand, a museum would be excluded, even if it were to receive most of its revenue from contributions, since its activities are educational, not in the areas of health and welfare.

14.1 FUND ACCOUNTING

(a) Classification of Funds

This topic was discussed in detail in Chapter 4. There it was noted that, after the issuance of SFAS No. 117, this concept relates only to internal bookkeeping and reporting, not to external financial reporting. External reporting and the relationship of funds to classes of net assets are discussed in Chapter 13. The Guide lists the funds commonly used, and the types of transactions normally associated with each fund. The fund groupings listed by the Guide and the type of transactions recorded in each are discussed below. When this and subsequent chapters refer to funds, the reference is to how a transaction is *recorded*. When discussing how information is *reported* in financial statements issued to the public, references will be to the three classes of net assets in SFAS No. 117.

Current Unrestricted Fund

This fund "accounts for all resources over which the governing Board has discretionary control to use in carrying on the operations of the organization . . . except for unrestricted amounts invested in land, buildings, and equipment that may be accounted for in a separate fund."[3] These are all of the completely unrestricted resources of the organization, including board-designated endowment funds or other resources allocated by the board for some specific purpose.

Prior to the issuance of this Guide, many voluntary health and welfare organizations set up separate board-designated funds which were reported on separately from the other unrestricted activities of the organization. This Guide, and SFAS No.117, specifically provide that all such unrestricted income, and net assets must be reported in a single category

[3] Page 2, *ibid.*

so that the reader can quickly see the total amount the organization's board has at its disposal. At the time, this was a major and significant change. It means that for these organizations, board-designated amounts must be included in the unrestricted class for financial statement purposes. The prior practice followed by many organizations of "designating" certain gifts as endowments (and then reporting these gifts directly in a restricted endowment category) is not permissible.

This does not prevent the board from "designating" certain portions of the current unrestricted net assets *balance* for specific purposes, but such designations must be reported only in the net assets section of the Balance Sheet. (See the discussion in Chapter 5 and below on "Appropriations.")

Current Restricted Fund

These are the amounts that have been given to the organization for a specific "operating" or "current" purpose. Excluded from this classification would be amounts given for endowment purposes or for acquisition of fixed assets.

Current restricted funds would include only amounts given to the organization by outside persons or organizations. They would not include amounts which the board had "designated" for some future purposes.

Land, Building, and Equipment Fund

If this fund is maintained, it is used to record the organization's net investment in its fixed assets. Also included in this fund are donor-restricted contributions that have been given for the purpose of purchasing fixed assets.

While the Guide provides for this separate land, building, and equipment fund, it does not prohibit the organization from combining this fund (excluding unexpended donor-restricted building fund gifts) with the current unrestricted fund. Many organizations in the past have preferred to use a separate fixed asset fund, principally so that the current unrestricted fund would exclude long-term assets such as fixed assets or other funds. This meant that the current unrestricted fund was then a form of "current working capital" fund. Under this Guide, however, the presentation outside of the unrestricted fund of separate board-designated endowment or other funds is no longer permitted. As a result, many organizations have concluded that there is no practical reason for segregating fixed assets in a separate fund and have combined their fixed asset fund and their current unrestricted fund. When this is done the title of the current unrestricted fund would become "unrestricted fund."

EXHIBIT 14–1 A Balance Sheet prepared in columnar format.

NATIONAL ASSOCIATION OF ENVIRONMENTALISTS
BALANCE SHEET
December 31, 19X2 and 19X1

| | December 31, 19X2 | | | | | December 31, 19X1 |
| | Current Funds | | Endowment Funds | Fixed Asset Funds | Total All Funds | Total All Funds |
	Unrestricted	Restricted				
ASSETS						
Current assets:						
Cash	$ 58,392	$17,151	$ 8,416	$ 2,150	$ 86,109	$ 11,013
Savings accounts	40,000				40,000	
Accounts receivable	3,117				3,117	918
Investments, at market	86,195		226,119		312,314	269,289
Pledges receivable	4,509	1,000			5,509	769
Total current assets	192,213	18,151	234,535	2,150	447,049	281,989

normally the property of the organization, their activity is not reflected in the Statement of Support, Revenues, and Expenses, and Changes in Net Assets. Their assets and offsetting liabilities are reported in the Balance Sheet.

14.2   ACCOUNTING PRINCIPLES

Summarized in the following paragraphs are the accounting principles (or practices) that are prescribed by the Audit Guide and by SFAS No. 116 and No. 117 for voluntary health and welfare organizations.

(a)   Accrual Basis

The Guide concludes that the accrual basis of accounting is normally necessary for financial statements prepared in accordance with generally accepted accounting principles. While cash basis statements are not prohibited, the auditor cannot issue an opinion on cash basis financial statements which states that the statements are prepared in accordance with generally accepted accounting principles, unless these financial statements do not differ materially from the statements prepared on the accrual basis. The same caution is made with respect to modified accrual basis statements (discussed in Chapter 3).

14.3   ACCOUNTING FOR CONTRIBUTIONS

(a)   Unrestricted Gifts

All unrestricted gifts are recorded as revenue or "support" of the current unrestricted fund. As noted above, some organizations may choose to internally "restrict" certain donations but such self-imposed "restrictions" (which are really just designations) in no way change the characteristics of the gift and such gifts must be recorded in the current unrestricted fund and reported in the unrestricted class of net assets.

(b)   Restricted Gifts

Most organizations receive up to three types of restricted gifts: gifts for a "current" purpose (recorded in the current restricted fund); gifts for building fund purposes (recorded in the land, building, and equipment fund); and gifts for endowment (recorded in the endowment fund).

Current Restricted Gifts

The Guide and SFAS No. 116 state that all current restricted gifts and other income should be recorded as revenue in the year in which a gift or an unconditional pledge is received (or pledged). If a donor makes a contribution for a current restricted purpose of $50,000 but the organization expends only $40,000 during the current year, the full $50,000 would still be reported as income in the temporarily restricted class. This is contrary to the practice provided in the Audit Guides for colleges and health care providers and in the AICPA Statement of Position for certain nonprofit organizations (SOP 78-10), as discussed in Chapters 15, 16, and 17; however those practices have been superseded by SFAS No. 116, as discussed in Chapter 10.

Building Fund Gifts

These gifts would be recorded in the fixed asset fund. As was noted above, however, the Guide does not prohibit combining the fixed asset fund and the current unrestricted fund. If this combining is done, receipt of restricted building fund gifts would then be recorded in the current restricted fund.[5]

Endowment Fund Gifts

As noted above, these gifts would be recorded in a separate endowment fund; only legally restricted gifts should be recorded here. Gifts of term endowment, or the various types of split-interest gifts, would be reported in the financial statements in the temporarily restricted class of net assets. Gifts of permanent endowment would be reported in the permanently restricted class.

(c) Donated Services

In the past, many organizations have not recorded donated services. This subject is discussed further in Chapter 10. SFAS No. 116 sets forth fairly specific criteria which, if met, require the recording of donated services, or, if not met, preclude their recording. Even if the criteria are met, donated services would still only be recorded when there is an objective and clearly measurable basis for the amount.

Certain categories of services would not normally be recorded; these include supplementary efforts of volunteers which are in the nature of

---

[5] If a significant amount of restricted building fund gifts were received, the title of the fund would probably have to be changed, or possibly two separate funds used (i.e., current restricted fund and restricted building fund gifts).

incidental services to beneficiaries of the organization, volunteers assisting in fund-raising drives, and members of the organization's governing board when serving in their capacity as board members.

But where the requirements of SFAS No. 116 are met, and where the amounts are material, there is no option. Donated services must be recorded or the CPA will be required to qualify the opinion.

(d) Donated Materials

Donated materials are normally recorded as a contribution at their fair market value, appropriately disclosed. The principal exception would be where the amounts are not significant or where there is no readily measurable basis for valuing such materials. In addition, donated materials that merely pass through the hands of the organization to a beneficiary are normally not recorded since the organization is merely acting as an agent for the donor.

(e) Donated Securities

Donated securities are treated in the same way as donated cash; that is, if the donated securities are to be used for a donor-specified purpose or endowment then the gift would be recorded as revenue in the appropriate fund at the fair market value at the date of receipt. If the gift is not restricted by the donor, the gift would be recorded directly in the current unrestricted fund in the same manner as any other cash gift.

(f) Donated Equipment and Fixed Assets

Donated fixed assets would be recorded at their fair market value as revenue of the fixed asset fund, provided a separate fixed asset fund were used. If, on the other hand, the donated asset will be sold shortly after receipt and the cash received therefrom will be unrestricted, these fixed asset gifts would be recorded in the current unrestricted fund at the time of initial receipt.

(g) Timing of Reporting of Gifts

Current unrestricted and restricted gifts are reported as income in full in the year for which the gift is intended. If the donor is silent as to intent, the presumption is that the gift is intended for the year in which made. Before the adoption of SFAS No. 116, for gifts with a donor-imposed *time* (as opposed to purpose) restriction, recording the gift as revenue would have been deferred to a future period, and the gift would be reported in the Balance Sheet as a "deferred credit" in the unrestricted fund. Since

SFAS No. 116 no longer allows this method of recording, even time-restricted gifts (and pledges) will be recorded as revenue in the period the gift or pledge is received (not the period the pledge is collected) and reported in the financial statements in the temporarily restricted class of net assets.

Even if a calendar-year organization normally solicits contributions late in its fiscal year with the clear understanding in its solicitation literature that the amounts raised will be used for the organization's following year, or if a large unsolicited gift is unexpectedly received toward the end of the year (say, on December 28), the entire amount of these gifts should be recorded as income in the current year. The fact that a contribution is an extraordinarily large one or that it is received toward the end of the year does not justify deferring its recognition as income.

Bequests

A special problem occurs with respect to bequests. Often the organization will be notified that it is a beneficiary under a will but a significant period of time will elapse before the organization receives the cash. The exact amount of the bequest may not be known until shortly before it is received. Accounting for bequests is discussed on pages 135–136.

Pledges

Unconditional pledges (called "promises to give" in SFAS No. 116) are something valuable that will benefit the organization, and thus should be recorded as assets. The same is true with allocations from "United Fund" campaigns that have been made but not received in cash at the end of the period. Under SFAS No. 116, pledges are discounted to their estimated present value to reflect the time value of money. The discount is then accreted (or built up) to par value over the period between the time the pledge is made and the time it is due to be paid. This accretion is reported as additional contribution income. In addition, an appropriate provision for estimated uncollectible pledges should be established based on prior experience.

14.4 ACCOUNTING FOR OTHER INCOME

(a) Investment Income

All unrestricted investment income (dividends and interest) must be recorded directly in the current unrestricted fund in the revenue section. Endowment income that has been restricted to a specified purpose would be recorded directly in the current restricted fund. Investment income from current restricted fund investments or plant fund investments is normally considered "restricted" and would be recorded in the fund generating the income.

(b)   Gains or Losses on Investments

Gains or losses (and appreciation or depreciation where investments are carried at market; see below) on all unrestricted and restricted investment funds would be recorded in the unrestricted class—unless donor stipulations or state law require otherwise (as discussed in Chapter 8)—in the revenue section. This will be a major change for many organizations. Although the total excess of revenue over expenses and the total net assets will not be different as a result of this change, those amounts will be higher in the unrestricted class, and lower in the restricted classes than before. This will have the effect of making an organization *appear* better off financially than it would have under the old rules, thus creating more of a challenge for fund-raisers to convince prospective donors that the organization is truly in need of their gifts.

Prior to SFAS No. 117, gains or losses (and appreciation or depreciation) on restricted endowment funds were usually considered to be restricted and would be recorded directly in the endowment fund. Likewise, gains or losses on current restricted fund investments and plant fund investments would normally have been reported in the respective fund.

As can be seen in Exhibit 14–2, gains or losses on investments are reported in the "revenues" section of the Statement of Support, Revenue and Expenses, and Changes in Net Assets. Prior to the issuance of the Guide, gains or losses on endowment funds were typically added directly to the fund balance of that fund and not reported as income (i.e., revenue).

Where an organization carries its investments at market, the unrealized appreciation or depreciation would also be reported in the "revenue" section of this statement. It would not be appropriate, for example, to report a realized gain in the "revenue" section and then the unrealized appreciation (representing the increase in market value during the year) at the bottom of the statement after the caption "Excess of revenues over expenses." When an organization decides to carry investments at market, its appreciation (or depreciation) is "revenue" and is reported in the same manner as realized gains or losses.

(c)   Total Return Concept

Prior to SFAS No. 117, some organizations followed the so-called "total return" concept in which the board was able to transfer some of the realized

EXHIBIT 14–2 Income statement in the columnar format recommended in the AICPA Audit Guide for Voluntary Health and Welfare Organizations, which meets the requirements of SFAS 117.

NATIONAL ASSOCIATION OF ENVIRONMENTALISTS
STATEMENT OF SUPPORT, REVENUE AND EXPENSES, AND CHANGES IN NET ASSETS
For the Year Ended December 31, 19X2

	Unrestricted	Temporarily Restricted	Permanently Restricted	Total
Support:				
Contributions and gifts	$174,600	$38,400	$ 10,000	$223,000
Bequests	60,000		21,500	81,500
Total support	234,600	38,400	31,500	304,500
Revenues:				
Membership dues	20,550			20,550
Research projects	127,900			127,900
Advertising income	33,500			33,500
Subscriptions to nonmembers	18,901			18,901
Dividends and interest income	14,607			14,607
Appreciation of investments	30,000		3,025	33,025
Total revenues	245,458		3,025	248,483
Total support and revenues	480,058	38,400	34,525	552,983
Net assets released from restriction	26,164	(26,164)		

Expenses:				
Program services:				
"National Environment" magazine	110,500			110,500
Clean-up month campaign	126,617			126,617
Lake Erie project	115,065			115,065
Total program services	352,182			352,182
Supporting services:				
Management and general	33,516			33,516
Fund raising	5,969			5,969
Total supporting services	39,485			39,485
Total expenses	391,667			391,667
Excess (deficit) of revenues over expenses	114,555	12,236	34,525	161,316
Other changes in net assets:				
Transfer of unrestricted resources to meet challenge grant	(10,000)		10,000	—
Change in net assets	104,555	12,236	44,525	161,316
Net assets, beginning of year	124,631	5,915	190,010	320,556
Net assets, end of year	$229,186	$18,151	$234,535	$481,872

or unrealized gains on endowment fund investments to the current unrestricted fund (assuming it had the legal right to do so). This is discussed further in Chapter 8. SFAS No. 117 has made this method obsolete for financial reporting purposes, although it may still be used for internal investment management purposes.

14.5 ACCOUNTING FOR EXPENSES

Because this subject is more related to financial statement presentation, it is discussed in Section 14.8.

14.6 ACCOUNTING FOR ASSETS

(a) Carrying Value of Investments

The Guide provides that an organization can carry its investments either at market or at cost. Previously, marketable securities could be carried only at cost or, in the case of donated securities, at the fair market value at the date of receipt. As of 1994, FASB has issued a new standard (SFAS No. 115) on accounting for marketable securities, but it does not apply to not-for-profit organizations. Currently, FASB is working on a project to establish new accounting standards for marketable securities for not-for-profits.

Carried at Cost

If an organization carries its investments at cost, market value should be disclosed in the financial statements. If the market value of the portfolio as a whole is less than cost and such decline is of a permanent nature, it may be necessary to write down the portfolio or to provide a provision for loss. This same approach can be taken with respect to an individual investment where there is a permanent impairment. But note that this is necessary only where the decline is of a "permanent" nature; short-term fluctuations normally do not require a write down or establishment of a provision for loss.

Carried at Market

If the organization carries its investments at market, it must do so for all of its investments. It may not pick and choose which investments to carry at market.[6] Unrealized appreciation or depreciation would be reported in the same manner as realized gains or losses on investments. See the discussion on gains and losses above.

(b)   Fixed Asset Accounting

Prior to the issuance of the Guide, the practices followed by voluntary health and welfare organizations in handling fixed assets included every conceivable combination of methods. The Guide, however, provides that an organization must capitalize its fixed assets *and* must follow depreciation accounting procedures.[7] This means that this category of organization should follow fixed asset accounting practices similar to those followed by business entities.

Reason for Depreciation

In discussing the question of depreciation accounting, the Guide states:

> The relative effort being expended by one organization compared with other organizations and the allocation of such efforts to the various programs of the organization are indicated in part by cost determinations. Whenever it is relevant to measure and report the cost of rendering current services, depreciation of assets used in providing such services is relevant as an element of such measurement and reporting process. Although depreciation can be distinguished from most other elements of cost in that it requires no current equivalent cash outlay, it is not optional or discretionary. Assets used in providing services are both valuable and exhaustible. Accordingly, there is a cost expiration associated with the use of depreciable assets, whether they are owned or rented, whether acquired by gift or by purchase, and whether they are used by a profit-seeking or by a not-for-profit organization.
>
> Where depreciation is omitted, the cost of performing the organization's services is understated. Depreciation expense, therefore, should be recognized as a cost of rendering current services and should be included as an element of expense in the Statement of Support, Revenue, and Expenses of the fund in which the assets are recorded and in the Statement of Functional Expenses.[8]

There are arguments for not recognizing depreciation and these are discussed at some length in Chapter 7. However, these arguments are

---

[6] This is a different position from that taken in the Statement of Position for not-for-profit organizations not covered by the three Audit Guides. See page 307.
[7] See Chapters 6 and 7 for a comprehensive discussion of fixed assets and depreciation accounting.
[8] Page 12 of the Guide.

moot because the Guide, as well as SFAS No. 93 require that depreciation accounting be followed. If depreciation accounting is not followed, the CPA will be required to qualify the opinion.

Retroactive Recording

This does not mean that every $10 purchase must be capitalized and depreciated. The cut-off point is left to the organization to determine and many may conclude that this cut-off should be fairly high to minimize record keeping. While each organization will have to make its cut-off decision based on its size and extent of fixed asset activity, most organizations will establish a cut-off between $100 (for a small organization) and $5,000 (for a large one).

The Guide also recognized that there would be some initial implementation problems when the Guide became effective in 1974. It provided that the organization should reconstruct the amount of fixed assets and accumulated depreciation as though the organization had followed this accounting principle all along.

The Guide also provided that if an organization were unable to reconstruct its cost basis for its fixed assets (or the fair market value at the date of receipt in the case of donated fixed assets), it could use a "cost" appraisal. A cost appraisal differs from a current value appraisal in that the appraiser attempts to determine what the asset would have cost at the time it was originally acquired, and not at today's prices.

Fixed Assets Where Title May Revert to Grantors

As noted in Chapter 6, some organizations purchase or receive fixed assets under research or similar grants which provide that, at the completion of the grant period, the right of possession of these fixed assets technically reverts to the grantor. If the grantor is not expected to ask for their return, a fixed asset, whether purchased or donated, should be recorded as an asset and depreciated as with any other asset.

14.7   NET ASSETS

(a)   Appropriations

The board is permitted to "appropriate" or designate a portion of the unrestricted net assets for some specific purpose. This appropriation or designation, however, would be reported only in the net assets section of the Balance Sheet. The appropriation or designation may *not* be shown as a deduction on the Statement of Support, Revenue and Expenses, and Changes in Net Assets. This is discussed further in Chapter 5.

Accordingly, it is not appropriate for an organization to charge expenditures directly against "appropriated" balances. The expenditure must be included in the Statement of Support, Revenue and Expenses, and Changes in Net Assets. All an appropriation does is to allow the board to designate *in the net assets section* of the Balance Sheet how it intends to spend the unrestricted net assets in the future.

For example, the unrestricted net assets of the National Association of Environmentalists of $135,516 (Exhibit 14–1) could be split into several amounts, representing the board's present intention of how it plans to use this amount. Perhaps $50,000 of it is intended for Project Seaweed, and the balance is available for undesignated purposes. The net assets section of the Balance Sheet would appear:

Net assets:

Designated by the board for Project Seaweed	$ 50,000
Undesignated, available for current purposes	85,516
	$135,516

As monies are expended for Project Seaweed in subsequent periods, they would be recorded as an expense in the Statement of Support, Revenue and Expenses, and Changes in Net Assets. At the same time, the amount of the net assets designated by the board for Project Seaweed would be reduced and the amount "undesignated" would be increased by the same amount. See Chapter 5 for a comprehensive discussion of appropriation accounting techniques.

14.8   FINANCIAL STATEMENTS

Additional discussion of financial statement presentation is in Chapters 11 to 13, especially Chapter 13. SFAS No. 117 provides for four principal financial statements for voluntary health and welfare organizations, thus superseding the financial statements discussed in the Guide. The first two of those have already been discussed in Chapter 13. Additional examples are shown in this chapter, tailored to the particular types of organizations covered by this chapter and Chapter 17. Also the last two of the four statements are discussed for the first time here. These four statements are:

1. Balance Sheet (Exhibit 14–1, page 222–223)
2. Statement of Support, Revenue and Expenses, and Changes in Net Assets (Exhibit 14–2, page 230–231)
3. Statement of Cash Flows (Exhibit 14–3, page 237)
4. Statement of Functional Expenses (Exhibit 14–4, page 238)

The sample financial statements presented in SFAS No. 117 are for illustrative purposes only, and some variation from the ones presented may be appropriate, as long as the required disclosure elements are shown.

(a) Balance Sheet

Exhibit 14–1 shows a Balance Sheet for the National Association of Environmentalists. Although SFAS No. 117 only requires (and illustrates) a single-column balance sheet showing the totals of assets, liabilities, and net assets (and net assets by class), many organizations will wish to show more detail of assets and liabilities, but not necessarily by class. As discussed in Chapter 13, this is acceptable.

The statement illustrated in the Audit Guide presents the more conventional Balance Sheet format in which each managed fund group is reported as a separate sub-Balance Sheet. Exhibit 4–2 on page 37 is an example of such a Balance Sheet. Exhibit 14–1 has been presented in a columnar format because this presentation is more meaningful to most readers. The Guide does not prohibit a columnar presentation but indicates that care must be taken to ensure that the restricted nature of certain resources is clearly shown.

Funds versus Classes

Note that the columns on the balance sheet reflect the funds used for bookkeeping purposes. This is permissible, as long as the net asset amounts for each of the three classes defined in SFAS No. 117 are shown in the net assets section of the balance sheet.

Comparison Column

In Exhibit 14–1 we have shown the totals for the previous year to provide a comparison for the reader. SFAS No. 117 does not require presentation of a comparison column, but it is recommended. The authors strongly recommend such a comparison. In a columnar presentation it is practical to show this comparison with the previous year for only the "total all

EXHIBIT 14–3   Statement of Cash Flows, derived from data included in Exhibits 14–1 and 2.

NATIONAL ASSOCIATION OF ENVIRONMENTALISTS
STATEMENT OF CASH FLOWS
For the Year Ended December 31, 19X2

Operating cash flows:
  Cash received from:

Sales of goods and services	$198,835
Investment income	14,607
Gifts and grants:	
Unrestricted	230,860
Restricted	37,400
Cash paid to employees and suppliers	(265,854)
Cash paid to charitable beneficiaries	(83,285)
Interest paid	(350)
Net operating cash flows	132,213

Financing cash flows:

Nonexpendable gifts	31,500
Proceeds from borrowing	5,000
Repayment of debt	(5,000)
Net financing cash flows	31,500

Investing cash flows:

Purchase of building and equipment	(38,617)
Purchase of investments	(60,000)
Proceeds from sale of investments	50,000
Net investing cash flows	(48,617)
Net increase in cash	115,096
Cash: Beginning of year	11,013
End of year	$126,109

Reconciliation of Excess of Revenues over Expenses to
Operating Cash Flows:

Excess of Revenues over Expenses	$161,316
Add: Depreciation expense	13,596
Less: Appreciation of investments	(33,025)
Changes in: Receivables	(6,939)
Payables and deferred income	28,765
Nonexpendable contributions	(31,500)
Operating cash flows	$132,213

238

EXHIBIT 14–4 An analysis of the various program expenses showing the natural expense categories making up each of the functional or program categories.

NATIONAL ASSOCIATION OF ENVIRONMENTALISTS
STATEMENT OF FUNCTIONAL EXPENSES
For the Year Ended December 31, 19X2

	Total All Expenses	Program Services				Supporting Services		
		"National Environment" Magazine	Clean-up Month Campaign	Lake Erie Project	Total Program	Management and General	Fund Raising	Total Supporting
Salaries	$170,773	$ 24,000	$ 68,140	$ 60,633	$152,773	$15,000	$3,000	$18,000
Payroll taxes and employee benefits	22,199	3,120	8,857	7,882	19,859	1,950	390	2,340
Total compensation	192,972	27,120	76,997	68,515	172,632	16,950	3,390	20,340
Printing	84,071	63,191	18,954	515	82,660	1,161	250	1,411
Mailing, postage, and shipping	14,225	10,754	1,188	817	12,759	411	1,055	1,466
Rent	19,000	3,000	6,800	5,600	15,400	3,000	600	3,600
Telephone	5,615	895	400	1,953	3,248	2,151	216	2,367
Outside art	14,865	3,165	11,700	—	14,865	—	—	—
Local travel	1,741	—	165	915	1,080	661	—	661
Conferences and conventions	6,328	—	1,895	2,618	4,513	1,815	—	1,815
Depreciation	13,596	2,260	2,309	5,616	10,185	3,161	250	3,411
Legal and audit	2,000	—	—	—	—	2,000	—	2,000
Supplies	31,227	—	1,831	28,516	30,347	761	119	880
Miscellaneous	6,027	115	4,378	—	4,493	1,445	89	1,534
Total	$391,667	$110,500	$126,617	$115,065	$352,182	$33,516	$5,969	$39,485

funds" column, although it is possible also to show a comparison for a second column, as is illustrated on page 209.[9]

Designation of Unrestricted Net Assets

While it is a little more awkward to show when the Balance Sheet is presented in a columnar fashion as in Exhibit 14–1, it is still possible to disclose the composition of the unrestricted net assets of $135,516. This is shown earlier in this chapter, on page 235.

Investments Carried at Market

As previously noted, the National Association of Environmentalists carries its investments at market rather than at cost. The Guide indicates that where this is done the statement should disclose the unrealized appreciation (or depreciation). This particular organization has disclosed this information in footnotes to the financial statements rather than on the face of the statement itself.

(b) Statement of Support, Revenue and Expenses, and Changes in Net Assets

Exhibit 14–2 shows a Statement of Support, Revenue and Expenses, and Changes in Net Assets for the National Association of Environmentalists. This is the format shown in SFAS No. 117, with some modifications (discussed below).

(c) Reporting of Expenses

Functional Classification of Expenses

Traditionally, not-for-profit organizations used to report in terms of amounts spent for salaries, rent, supplies, etc. (called a "natural" expense classification). The Guide took a major step forward when it stated that not-for-profit organizations exist to perform services and programs and therefore should be reporting principally in terms of individual program activities or functions. SFAS No. 117 also reaches the same conclusion. Exhibit 14–2 shows the expenses of the National Association of Environmentalists reported on a functional basis. This type of presentation

---

[9] Many accountants object to including this total comparison column, saying that sufficient information on the nature of the restricted portions is not reported. There is some validity to this argument, but the authors feel this total column is preferable to no comparison.

requires management to tell the reader how much of its funds were expended for each program category and the amounts spent on supporting services, including fund raising.

Further, SFAS No. 117 and the Guide state that this functional reporting is not optional. Although SFAS No. 117 requires that disclosure of expenses by function must be made either in the primary financial statements or in the footnotes, the Guide requires that the Statement of Support, Revenue and Expenses, and Changes in Net Assets must be prepared on this functional or program basis or the CPA will be required to qualify the opinion, stating that the statements were not prepared in accordance with generally accepted accounting principles.

In many instances, the allocation of salaries between functional or program categories should be based on time reports and similar analyses. Other expenses such as rent, utilities, and maintenance will be allocated based on floor space. Each organization will have to develop time and expense accumulation procedures that will provide the necessary basis for allocation. Organizations have to have reasonably sophisticated procedures to be able to allocate expenses between various categories. An excellent reference source is the third edition (1988) of the "Black Book," *Standards of Accounting and Financial Reporting for Voluntary Health and Welfare Organizations,* discussed at 14.10. United Way of America has also published a comprehensive book to guide "human service organizations" in identifying their program classifications. This book is referred to as *UWASIS—United Way of America Services Identification System.*

Program Services

Not-for-profit organizations exist to perform services either for the public or for the members of the organization. They do not exist to provide employment for their employees or to perpetuate themselves. They exist to serve a particular purpose. The Audit Guide re-emphasizes this by requiring the organization to identify major program services and their related costs. Some organizations may have only one specific program category, but most will have several. Each organization should decide for itself into how many categories it wishes to divide its program activities.

Supporting Services

Supporting services are those expenses which do not directly relate to performing the functions for which the organization was established, but which nevertheless are essential to the continued existence of the organization.

The Statement of Support, Revenue and Expenses, and Changes in Net Assets must clearly disclose the amount of supporting services.

These are broken down between fund raising and administrative (management and general) expenses. This distinction between supporting and program services is required, as is the separate reporting of fund raising. Absence of either the functional reporting approach or information on fund raising would result in a qualified opinion by a CPA.

Management and general expenses. This is probably the most difficult of the supporting categories to define because a major portion of the time of top management usually will relate more directly to program activities than to management and general. Yet many think, incorrectly, that top management should be considered entirely "management and general." The Statement of Position (#78-10, discussed in Chapter 17) defines management and general expenses as follows:

> Management and general costs are those that are not identifiable with a single program or fund-raising activity but are indispensable to the conduct of those activities and to an organization's existence, including expenses for the overall direction of the organization's general board activities, business management, general recordkeeping, budgeting, and related purposes. Costs of overall direction usually include the salary and expenses of the chief officer of the organization and his staff. However, if such staff spend a portion of their time directly supervising program services or categories of supporting services, their salaries and expenses should be prorated among those functions. The cost of disseminating information to inform the public of the organization's "stewardship" of contributed funds, the publication of announcements concerning appointments, the annual report, and so forth, should likewise be classified as management and general expenses.

Some suggested methods of computing the allocation of certain types of expenses to the various functions are described in the Statement of Position. Other methods may also be appropriate and could be used.

Fund-raising expenses. Fund-raising expenses are a very sensitive category of expense because a great deal of publicity has been associated with certain organizations that appear to have very high fund-raising costs. The cost of fund raising includes not only the direct costs associated with a particular effort, but a fair allocation of the overhead of the organization, including the time of top management.

Fund-raising expenses are normally recorded as an expense in the Statement of Activity at the time they are incurred. It is not appropriate to defer such amounts. Thus the cost of acquiring or developing a mailing list that has value over more than one year would nevertheless be expensed in its entirety at the time the list was purchased or the costs incurred. The reason for this conservative approach is the difficulty accountants have in satisfying themselves that costs that might logically be deferred will in fact be recovered by future support related thereto. Further, if substantial amounts of deferred fund-raising costs were permitted, the credibility of the financial statements would be in jeopardy, particularly in view of the increased publicity surrounding fund-raising expenses.

If fund-raising is combined with a program function, such as educational literature that also solicits funds, the total cost should be allocated between the program and fund-raising functions on the basis of the use made of the literature, as determined from its content, reason for distribution, and audience, if the criteria of Statement of Position No. 87-2 are met. These criteria are discussed in the next section.

Cost of obtaining grants.   Organizations soliciting grants from governments or foundations have a cost that is somewhat different from fund-raising costs. Where such amounts are identifiable and material in amount, they should be separately identified and reported as a supporting service.

Allocation of Joint Costs of Multipurpose Activities

In 1987, the AICPA issued a Statement of Position (No. 87-2), amending the Voluntary Health and Welfare Audit Guide and SOP 78-10, thus covering the great majority of not-for-profit organizations. It provides that if it can be demonstrated that a bona fide program or management function has been conducted in conjunction with an appeal for funds, joint costs should be allocated between fund raising and the appropriate other function. Otherwise, such joint costs are to be reported as fund-raising expense. Allocation, when made, should be on the basis of content of the activity; the audience to whom the activity is targeted; the action, if any, requested of the audience; and other evidence as to the intent of the activity.

Typically such costs are for a mailing which contains both educational information and an appeal for contributions. The direct cost of printing the educational information is reported as a program service expense, and that of printing the appeal is reported as fund-raising expense. The difficult questions are whether and, if so, how to allocate the joint costs: the envelope and (mainly, as it is usually the largest cost component) the postage to send the piece. The accountant must also consider what costs are properly allocable; for example should part of the salary of the person who organizes the mailing be included as a joint cost? The accounting profession has given considerable attention to the question of whether, but very little to what and how.

Charities, understandably, want to allocate as much as possible to program expense, as they believe this will make a better impression on donors and prospective donors, thus motivating them to greater giving to the charity. Those who regulate charities and who assess the performance of charities are concerned that some charities may be over-allocating to program, to make their reported expenses more appealing than is actually the case.

The requirements of SOP 87-2 are that joint costs are presumed to be fund-raising unless it can be demonstrated that a bona fide program or management function has also been conducted. Demonstrating this requires verifiable indications such as the nature of the content of the activity, the characteristics of the audience targeted by the activity, and the nature of any action requested of the recipients. This is the "whether to allocate" part of the question. If this is answered no, the other two parts are moot.

As to what and how to allocate, the not-for-profit accounting literature has heretofore offered very little guidance. Standard books on cost accounting may be helpful in discussing general principles useful for answering these questions. A proposed new SOP amending No. 87-2 will include some guidance: the "what" question is answered rather broadly by saying that production and distribution costs as well as measurable applicable indirect costs can be allocated. Types of costs mentioned include salaries, postage, utilities, rent and telephone. How to allocate is dealt with by describing three standard methods and noting that they generally result in a reasonable allocation. The user is left to decide which is most appropriate in a given situation. The three methods are physical units, stand alone costs, and relative direct costs. The physical units method is the one most commonly used, but it is subject to much judgment as to just which portions of an activity in fact constitute fund raising versus other purposes and how to measure the units (lines, square inches, etc.) This method is also subject to abuse by a charity that stuffs a mailing, for example, with quantities of ostensibly educational material, which is however of little real value to the recipient.

Since it was issued, many people have found the guidance in SOP 87-2 not as specific as they would like, and believe that some charities are abusing the rules by allocating an inappropriately large portion of joint costs to program services. As this book is written, the AICPA is close to issuing a new statement of position which will update and clarify, although not significantly change the import of, the requirements of SOP 87-2.

Appendix 14–A contains a checklist prepared by one of the authors, which may be helpful to charities and their auditors in applying the rules of SOP 87-2 and, eventually, its replacement. The theme of the list is that being the passive recipient of information is, in and of itself, of no value to someone, no matter how useful the information might potentially be. The potential usefulness of the information is realized only if the recipient is urged to take some beneficial action based on the information. The action need not be taken immediately, as long as the recipient is urged to take it at some later appropriate time, for example, when the symptoms of a disease appear. Nor need the action directly benefit the recipient; it might be something that benefits others: specific groups, humanity, or the environment generally.

All Expenses Reported as Unrestricted

This is a new requirement in SFAS No. 117, and a significant change for almost all not-for-profit organizations (except hospitals, see Chapter 16). In the past, expenses were reported in the same fund as the revenue which was used to pay for the expenses. Thus unrestricted revenue, and expenses paid for out of that revenue, were shown together in the unrestricted fund. Current restricted revenue, and the expenses paid for out of that revenue, were in the current restricted fund. (No expenses could ever be paid out of the permanent endowment fund, due to the nature of the restriction of those amounts.)

With the adoption of SFAS No. 117, all expenses, regardless of the origin of the resources used to finance the expenses, will be shown in the unrestricted class of net assets; no expenses will be in the temporarily restricted class. This is shown in Exhibit 14–2. The method of relating the restricted revenue to the expenses financed out of that revenue is to reclassify an amount of temporarily restricted net assets equal to the expenses to the unrestricted net assets class ($26,164 in Exhibit 14–2).

(d) Columnar Presentation

The statement presentation is in a columnar format and, as can be observed in Exhibit 14–2, includes all three classes on one statement. This format is very similar to the format recommended in earlier chapters of this book. It is also possible to present the information in a single column. In this format, information for the three classes is shown sequentially, including the change in net assets for the class, followed by the total change in net assets for the year. An advantage of such a format is the ease of showing comparative prior year information for each class; a disadvantage is the inability to present a total column.

It should be noted that this statement provides a complete picture of all activity of this organization for the year—not just the activity of a single class or fund. Further, by including a "total" column on the statement, the reader is quickly able to see the overall activity and does not have to add together several amounts to get the complete picture. This represents a major advance in not-for-profit accounting.

The illustrated financial statements in the Guide show figures in the "total" column for both the revenues and expenses categories. The illustrated statements do not, however, show figures in this total column for the caption "Excess of revenues over expenses," or for the captions that follow. SFAS No. 117 requires the statements to show total net assets, and the total change in net assets; thus most organizations will choose to present a complete total column if a columnar format is used. There is no reason not to do so.

Unrestricted Activity in a Single Column

One of the most significant features of this presentation is that all legally unrestricted revenues and all expenses are reported in the single column representing the unrestricted class of net assets. The use of a single column in which all unrestricted activity is reported greatly simplifies the presentation and makes it more likely that a nonaccountant will be able to comprehend the total picture of the organization.

Many organizations, of course, will want to continue to keep board-designated accounts within their bookkeeping system. This is fine. But, for reporting to the public, all unrestricted amounts must be combined and reported as indicated in this illustration.

While not recommended, there would appear to be no prohibition to an organization's including additional columns to the *left* of this total "unrestricted" column to show the various unrestricted board-designated categories of funds which make up the total unrestricted class. However, where an organization does so it must clearly indicate that the total unrestricted column represents the total unrestricted activity for the year and that the detailed columns to the left are only the arbitrarily subdivided amounts making up this total. Probably an organization is better advised to show such detail in a separate supplementary schedule, if at all.

Where an organization chooses to show its unrestricted class broken into two columns and has only one class with restricted resources, it may be acceptable to eliminate the total unrestricted column in the interest of simplicity. An example of the column headings might be:

Unrestricted			
General Fund	Investment Fund	Temporarily Restricted	Total All Classes

The key to whether this would be acceptable is the extent of activity in the various columns. For example, if the temporarily restricted class in the above illustration were relatively minor in amount, then the total column would largely reflect the unrestricted class (i.e., the general fund and the investment fund). This is a judgmental question.

Temporarily Restricted Column

The "temporarily restricted" column represents those amounts which have been given to the organization for a specified purpose other than for permanent endowment. It should be observed that the amounts reported as revenues in this fund represent the total amount the organization received during the year, and not the amount that was actually expended.

Use of Separate Fixed Asset (Plant) Fund

The Guide provides for the use of a separate plant fund, although, as noted earlier, it does not require its use. SFAS No. 117 does not mention a separate fixed asset category; rather it includes amounts related to fixed assets in the three classes of net assets discussed earlier. Even though a fixed asset fund is maintained in the organization's bookkeeping system, for external financial reporting purposes, the organization would include most of the amounts of the fixed asset fund in the unrestricted class. This has the additional advantage of reducing the number of columns and eliminating the need for certain reclassifications.

One of the reasons why a separate plant fund was originally presented was that the industry committee[10] objected strongly at the time to the fixed asset capitalization and depreciation accounting requirements. One argument expressed against depreciation was a concern that certain organizations had to budget their income and expenses exclusive of depreciation. For this reason, the industry committee was reluctant to follow depreciation accounting practices, but agreed to do so at the time provided the depreciation provision was reported directly in a separate fixed asset fund column, and not in the unrestricted fund column.

Another argument many made against combining the plant fund with the unrestricted fund is that fixed assets are often purchased with donor-restricted gifts. There is a legal question of whether the original restrictions remain with the fixed assets once purchased. In the event of sale many believe the cash proceeds would remain restricted, and for this reason feel it inappropriate to combine the two funds.

[10] Joint Liaison Committee of the National Health Council, the National Assembly for Social Policy and Development, Inc., and the United Way of America.

Over time, most of the arguments against capitalization and depreciation of fixed assets have waned, and most people now accept the usefulness of the more simplified presentation used in SFAS No. 117.

(e) Appreciation of Investments

This organization has elected to carry its investments at market. This means that the organization must reflect appreciation (or depreciation) on its Statement of Support, Revenue and Expenses, and Changes in Net Assets. In this instance, the net appreciation of investments was $33,025. Assuming there were no sales or purchases of investments during the year, this amount would have been determined by comparing the market value of the investments at the end of the year with the market value at the beginning of the year. Normally, however, there will be some realized gain or loss during the year. While there is no technical objection to reporting the realized gain or loss separately from the unrealized appreciation (or depreciation), there seems little significance to this distinction. (See page 91 for a discussion of the reasons why.)

Activity of Restricted Funds Recorded as Revenues and Expenses

It is significant to note that the Guide called for recording changes in the restricted funds in an income statement format, including their excess of revenues over expenses. (In the past, many argued that such restricted activity should not be reported in an income statement format but rather as individual "changes" in net assets without any indication of the overall net change for the year.)

This approach is significant because it permits the reader to see the total activity of the organization—both restricted and unrestricted. Thus the Guide appears to be saying that we have a single entity on which we are reporting as distinct from several subentities for which there is no total. SFAS No. 117 also has adopted this philosophy. In this example, the total excess of revenues over expenses was $161,316, whereas the activity of the unrestricted class resulted in an excess of only $114,555. Certainly the reader has a right to know of these other amounts in a manner that will permit seeing a total picture.

Other Changes in Net Assets

This section represents certain reclassifications. Since all unrestricted amounts are reported as a single column there are very few of these. In this illustration, $10,000 was reclassified from the unrestricted class to the permanently restricted class to match a challenge grant received that year.

Operating Statement

A variation on this statement which some may wish to use is to present a subtotal of "operating" revenue in excess of "operating" expenses. This would focus the reader's attention on what the organization considers its core "operations," as distinguished from matters which it considers peripheral or incidental to its operations. SFAS No. 117 permits, but does not require, this presentation. If an organization chooses this presentation, it will decide for itself what it considers to be its operations, versus other activities. Appendix 14–B contains a checklist to help organizations decide what they wish to consider as operating versus nonoperating transactions.

(f) Statement of Cash Flows (Formerly Changes in Financial Position)

A Statement of Cash Flows is a summary of the resources made available to an organization during the year and the uses made of such resources. Until 1978, no similar statement was required for not-for-profit organizations, but commercial organizations have had to prepare a Statement of Changes in Financial Position for many years.[11] In 1978, Statement of Position 78-10 added a requirement for organizations covered by it to prepare a Statement of Changes in Financial Position.

Beginning in 1988, businesses were required to prepare a Statement of Cash Flows in place of a Statement of Changes in Financial Position. However, the accounting standard[12] which mandated this change excluded not-for-profit organizations from its coverage. This effectively left them under the earlier rule requiring only organizations following the Statement of Position to prepare a Statement of Changes in Financial Position. Other not-for-profits could prepare such a statement but were not required to. Now SFAS No. 117 requires presentation of a Statement of Cash Flows by all not-for-profit organizations. Full discussion of preparation of this statement is in SFAS No. 95.

Exhibit 14–3 shows a Statement of Cash Flows. In some ways it is similar to a Statement of Cash Receipts and Disbursements, such as that shown in Exhibit 11–4 (pages 168–169), in that it presents cash received and spent. It differs by grouping transactions into three groups:

[11] Required by Accounting Principles Board Opinion No. 19.
[12] FASB Statement of Financial Accounting Standards No. 95.

Operating, Investing, and Financing cash flows. Also, there is less detail of specific types of operating cash flows, since such detail is already shown for revenue and expenses in Exhibit 14–2.

(g)   Statement of Functional Expenses

Exhibit 14–4 is a statement that analyzes functional or program expenses and shows the natural expense categories which go into each functional category. It is primarily an analysis to give the reader insight as to the major types of expenses involved. In order to arrive at the functional expense totals shown in the Statement of Support, Revenue and Expenses, and Changes in Net Assets, an analysis must be prepared that shows all of the expenses going into each program category. The Statement of Functional Expenses merely summarizes this detail for the reader.

Depreciation

In the illustrative financial statement in the Guide, depreciation expense is shown as the very last item on the statement, and all other expenses are subtotaled before depreciation is added. This presentation was illustrated in the Guide because of the concern of many not-for-profit organizations in showing depreciation as an expense. By subtotaling all expenses before adding depreciation, the Guide emphasizes the somewhat different nature of depreciation expense. The authors disagree and for this reason have included depreciation among the other expense categories in Exhibit 14–4. Either presentation is acceptable.

14.9   RECOMMENDED SIMPLIFIED PRESENTATION

Earlier editions of this book illustrated and recommended simplified formats for the presentations of the balance sheet and statement of income. The authors find it noteworthy that the substance of almost all of their recommendations has now been adopted by the accounting profession in SFAS No. 117, as discussed earlier. Accordingly, the material which was in this section of the fourth edition is no longer needed and has been deleted.

14.10   THE EVOLUTION OF STANDARDS

In 1964, two national organizations in their respective fields of health and social welfare, the National Health Council and the National Assembly for Social Policy and Development, published a book for use by affiliated organizations to assist them in establishing uniform standards of accounting and reporting. This book, *Standards of Accounting and Financial Reporting for Voluntary Health and Welfare Organizations*, was one of the first major attempts to analyze the needs of the readers of financial statements of voluntary health and welfare organizations and to prescribe standards of both accounting and reporting for member organizations.

This book, commonly referred to as the "Black Book," was revised in 1974 and again in 1988. United Way of America participated in these two revisions and has also published an accounting guide, *Accounting & Financial Reporting, A Guide for United Ways and Not-for-Profit Human Service Organizations*. As this book is written, a committee of industry accounting leaders, including one of the authors, is in the process of preparing an update to the Black Book to reflect the new standards of SFAS No. 116 and No. 117.

(a)   A Useful Reference

The Black Book provides considerable assistance to the reader and offers much more detailed instruction than does the Audit Guide. The Audit Guide is intended to be only an outline of principles for the CPA's guidance. The Black Book is intended to be a manual for the accountant within an organization applying these principles. It is a very useful reference book for organizations following the principles in the AICPA Audit Guide.[13]

---

[13] It can be obtained from the National Health Council, 1730 M Street, N.W., Washington D.C. 20036.

APPENDIX 14–A   CHECKLIST

**Factors to Be Considered in Deciding Whether Allocation of
Joint Costs of Multi-Purpose Activities
(Under Paragraphs 15-20 of AICPA SOP 87-2) Is Appropriate**

The following is a list of factors which may be helpful to:

- Charities, in deciding whether to allocate joint costs of multipurpose activities;
- Auditors, in assessing the appropriateness of the client's decision.

No one of these factors is normally determinative by itself; all applicable factors should be considered together (SOP 87-2, par. 21). These factors relate only to the question of whether to allocate at all, not to determining which costs are allocable or how to allocate.

Factors Whose Presence Would Indicate Allocation May Be Appropriate	Factors Whose Presence Would Indicate Allocation May Not Be Appropriate
1. Activity is directed at a broad segment of the population, or at a population specifically in need of the program services of the organization.	Activity is directed primarily at individuals with higher income, or at previous contributors.[1]
2. The group intended to benefit from the "program" activity and the benefits to be derived are well-defined.	The group and/or the benefits are not well-defined.
3. Specific tangible action by the recipient, which will benefit the recipient or other parties, is explicitly urged; the action is unrelated to providing financial or other support to the organization itself.[2]	Action urged is not specific, tangible, or explicitly stated, or consists primarily of supporting the organization itself.[3]
4. The "program" activity urged is consistent with the organization's stated mission.	The "program" activity urged is inconsistent with or only marginally related to the mission.
5. The "program" content of the activity is high.	The fund-raising content is high.

Factors Whose Presence Would Indicate Allocation May Be Appropriate	Factors Whose Presence Would Indicate Allocation May Not Be Appropriate
6. It is likely the activity would be carried on (in some form) even if the fund-raising component were not present.	It is doubtful the activity would be carried on if the fund-raising component were not present.
7. There is tangible evidence to support the existence of a bona fide program component of the activity.[4]	Evidence of program content is only intangible, hearsay, speculative, management assertions, etc.
8. The person actually supervising the activity is not a professional fundraiser, and is compensated by a fee or salary.	The person is a professional fundraiser or is compensated by a bonus or a percent of amounts raised.
9. The person within the organization responsible for overseeing the activity is part of the program staff.	The person is part of the development staff.

[1] However this factor would not necessarily be a bar to allocation if it can be demonstrated that higher-income persons or previous contributors in fact are in a better position to make use of or benefit from the "program" content of the activity. For example, previous contributors to an organization whose program is to change public policy are presumably especially likely to act on an appeal to write to government officials.

[2] Examples of such action (or, in some cases, refraining from an action) include:
- If you are suicidal, *call* our hot line.
- If you notice these symptoms, *go* to your doctor.
- *Write or call* your legislator, other public officials, etc.
- *Eat* more healthy foods (examples given).
- *Stop* smoking.
- *Give* blood. (This is not considered a request to support the blood bank as it is merely acting as an agent for the ultimate recipient. Requests to give to the charity cash or commercially available items (clothing, food, etc.) are considered fund raising even if the items are passed on to others, whereas requests to give such items directly to those in need (e.g., victims of disaster) are not fund raising for the charity. Blood is a special case due to its unique source of supply and special processing requirements.)
- *Volunteer* to help out at your local nursing home. (Fund raising if urged by the nursing home; program if urged by a charity whose purpose is to make life better for the elderly.)
- *Don't drink and drive.*
- *Say no* to drugs.
- *Protest.* (Must describe object of protest and specific method of protest, such as a time and place to demonstrate, a person/organization to communicate with, or other specific action; a general call to protest against something is too vague to qualify as program.)
- *Pray.* (If urged by an organization connected with a religious denomination for which prayer is a central focus of activity.)
- *Boycott* some specific company or product.
- *Complete and return* the enclosed questionnaire, *only* if the questionnaire is an essential part of a bona fide scientific research project, the results of which will be broadly used to further some social good. If the results will merely be compiled and disseminated by the organization itself as a matter of interest, or if the questionnaire is included only as a method of motivating recipients to respond, it does not qualify as a program activity.
- *Contribute* to a charity in no way affiliated with the entity conducting the activity.

[3] Examples of actions which are too vague to qualify as "program" activity include:
- Support your local police. (To qualify as program, there would have to be specific suggestions as to how such support should be manifested.)
- Wear a ribbon (or other item). (To qualify as program, there would have to be specific suggestions as to how wearing a ribbon would, in and of itself, contribute to achieving some social good. Usually this would happen only through other specific actions such as demonstrating, lobbying, boycotting, etc.)
- Protest. (Unless specific time/place/method of protest is specified.)
- Read (the accompanying literature). (Learning about a problem may be helpful, but is of no public or personal benefit unless the learner proceeds to take some action based on the knowledge gained. To qualify as program, the activity would have to urge some specific subsequent action.)
- Save energy. (To qualify as program, there would have to be specific examples of things to do to save energy.) Similarly for "Don't pollute," "Drive safely" and other general slogans.

[4] Examples of such tangible evidence include:
- Written instructions to other persons/organizations regarding the purpose of the activity, audience to be targeted, method of conducting the activity, etc.
- Contracts with unrelated scriptwriters, mailing houses, list brokers, consultants, etc.
- Content of the activity.
- Mission of the organization as stated in its IRS Form 1023/4, fund-raising material, annual report, etc.
- Restrictions imposed by donors (who are not related parties) on gifts intended to fund the activity.

Other tangible evidence which may be helpful, but, because it is solely internal to the organization, is not so persuasive as audit evidence:
- Minutes of board of directors, committees, etc.
- Internal management memoranda.
- Budget, long-range plan, operating policies.
- Job descriptions of organization staff.

APPENDIX 14–B   CHECKLIST

Consideration of Whether Items May Be Reported as Operating or Nonoperating (Within the Context of ¶ 23 of SFAS No. 117)

Paragraph 23 of SFAS No. 117 leaves it to each organization (if it wishes to present a subtotal of "operating" results) to determine what it considers to be operating vs. nonoperating items in a statement of activity; if it is not obvious from the face of the statement what items are included/excluded in the operating subtotal, footnote disclosure of that distinction shall be made. Following are some items which might be considered as nonoperating. This is not intended to express any preferences, nor to limit the types of items that a particular organization might report as nonoperating, but merely to provide a list for consideration of various types of items.

Items which would usually be considered nonoperating as to the current period:

- Extraordinary items
- Cumulative effects of accounting changes
- Corrections of errors of prior periods
- Prior period adjustments, generally
- Results of discontinued operations

Items that many persons might consider nonoperating in some situations:

- Unrealized capital gains on investments carried at market value
- Unrelated business income (as defined in the Internal Revenue Code sec. 512), and related expenses
- Contributions which qualify as "unusual grants," as defined in IRS Regulation 1.509(a)-3(c)(3)
- Items which meet some, but not all, of the criteria in APB 30/ SFAS No. 4 for extraordinary items, or APB 30/SFAS No. 16 for prior period adjustments.

Items that some people might consider non-operating in some situations:

- Bequests, and other "deferred gifts" (annuity, life income funds, etc.) received

- Gains and losses, generally (as defined in SFAC 6, par. 82–89)
- Sales of goods/services which, although they are not considered unrelated under the Internal Revenue Code, are nevertheless peripheral to the organization's major activities
- Some "auxiliary activities" of colleges
- Revenue and expenses related to program activities not explicitly listed on the organization's IRS Form 1023
- Revenue and expenses directly related to transactions which are reported as financing or investing cash flows in the statement of cash flows; e.g., investment income not available for operating purposes, interest expense, write-offs of loans receivable, non-expendable gifts (as contemplated by ¶ 30d of SFAS No. 117), adjustment of annuity liability
- Contributions having the characteristics of an "initial capital" contribution to an organization, even though they do not meet the requirements of an extraordinary item, or an unusual grant (above)

The characterization of an item of expense as operating vs. nonoperating is not driven by its classification as program, management, or fund-raising expense. In general, expenses should follow related revenue: e.g., if contributions are considered operating, then fund-raising expenses normally would be also, and vice versa.

CHAPTER 15

Colleges and Universities

Among the most important and influential types of not-for-profit institutions are colleges and universities. The extent of their influence is suggested by the fact that there are more than 14 million students currently attending more than 3,500 colleges and universities in the United States, most of which depend heavily on support from gifts and contributions from alumni and the general public. These institutions have the same need to report on their activities and to effectively communicate their financial needs as do other not-for-profit organizations. The problems of reporting are complicated for these institutions by their historically strong reliance on fund accounting techniques. This chapter outlines and discusses the accounting principles and reporting practices that have been generally accepted for colleges and universities, and explains how the new FASB standards (116 and 117) will affect them.

15.1   AUTHORITATIVE PRONOUNCEMENTS

The American Council on Education published in 1953 *College and University Business Administration*, of which a substantial portion deals with the principles of accounting and reporting. Republished in 1968, 1974, 1982, and, in part, in 1990,[1] this book was until 1973 generally accepted as the most authoritative source of accounting and reporting principles applicable to colleges and universities. Because of its wide use, it became generally known by the acronym "CUBA." This acronym will be used throughout this chapter and refers to the 1990 edition.

(a)   AICPA Audit Guide

In 1973,[2] the Committee on College and University Accounting and Auditing of the American Institute of Certified Public Accountants issued an Audit Guide for use by CPAs in their examination of the financial statements of these institutions. As with the other not-for-profit industry guides (discussed in Chapters 14, 16, and 17) it contains not only guidance to the CPA on auditing procedures, but also a comprehensive discussion of accounting and reporting principles for such institutions. Accordingly, prior to the issuance of the new FASB standards described

---

[1] *Financial Accounting and Reporting Manual for Higher Education*, National Association of College and University Business Officers, Washington, DC, 1990.

[2] In 1974, the Guide was effectively modified through the issuance of a Statement of Position which modified somewhat the description and classification of revenues, expenditures, and transfers of current funds. See page 342 for a discussion of the purpose and function of a Statement of Position.

earlier, the Audit Guide had become the authoritative source for principles of accounting and reporting for colleges and universities.[3]

To a large extent, this Audit Guide codified principles of accounting and reporting discussed in earlier editions of CUBA. In fact, a number of representatives of the National Association of College and University Business Officers (NACUBO) worked with the AICPA Committee throughout the development of this Audit Guide so that the Guide represented a joint effort of both the accounting profession and college and university business officers.

In 1993, the Financial Accounting Standards Board issued Statements of Financial Accounting Standards No. 116 and No. 117, which supersede portions of the Audit Guide and CUBA. These new standards are discussed earlier in this book in the various chapters that discuss the topics covered by the standards (especially Chapters 10 and 13), and are referred to below within the appropriate topic headings.

15.2 FUND ACCOUNTING

Fund accounting is followed by colleges and universities in a classical manner; no other type of institution is as generally wedded to fund accounting. This results from a historical reliance on outside gifts, many of which were large and involved restrictions, and thus the need to keep track of these restricted resources. Also, because of this continuing reliance on outside financial help, these institutions often felt it prudent to set aside funds from current unrestricted resources to function as endowment funds, thus providing both future endowment income and a cushion against hard times. While all of this encouraged the use of fund accounting, it also resulted in problems of communicating clearly with nonaccountant readers of their financial statements.

As discussed earlier in Chapter 4, fund *accounting* will likely continue to be used by many not-for-profits, especially colleges, for their internal bookkeeping and management processes. However, external financial *reporting* will in the future follow the requirements of SFAS No. 117, which prescribes that revenues and net assets be grouped into only three "classes": unrestricted, temporarily restricted, permanently restricted. A discussion of the relationship between funds and classes is in Chapter 13 at page 191.

---

[3] See Chapter 24 for a discussion of the significance of Audit Guides and their relationship to generally accepted accounting principles.

(a) Funds Typically Used in College Fund Accounting

Historically the number of major fund groupings used by colleges for their accounting was six:

1. Current funds
   a. Unrestricted
   b. Restricted
2. Loan funds
3. Endowment and similar funds
4. Annuity and life income funds
5. Plant funds
   a. Unexpended
   b. Renewal and replacement
   c. Retirement of indebtedness
   d. Investment in plant
6. Agency (or custodian) funds

Within some of these major groupings there can be several subgroupings.

Current Funds

These are the resources that are available for the general operations of the institution. Usually a distinction is made between those current funds that are unrestricted and those that are restricted by an outside party for a current purpose. Generally, each type of activity for the year is presented in a separate column, with the columns side by side in the financial statements.

The balance in the current *restricted* fund represents the unexpended balance of amounts that have been received for a specific current purpose and, in theory, these amounts would have to be returned if the institution were not to use the funds for the restricted purpose. This amount is reported in the temporarily restricted class of net assets.

The balance in the current *unrestricted* fund represents only that amount which the board has chosen to leave in this fund. Under the college audit guide, the board could transfer resources into and out of the current unrestricted fund and there was little significance to the balance in this fund at any given time. Unfortunately, few nonaccountant readers understood this and many mistakenly assumed that a low current unrestricted fund balance was an indication the organization was in weak financial condition, which might or might not have been the case.

After the adoption of SFAS No. 117, the true extent of resources available for general institutional use at the discretion of the governing board can be noted by looking at the amount of *net assets* in the unrestricted net asset class in the balance sheet (Exhibit 15–1). This amount includes not only the balance in the current unrestricted *fund*, but also unrestricted amounts held in other funds, such as the endowment fund (quasi-endowment), and the various plant funds.

Loan Funds

These are amounts which are available for granting loans to students and, sometimes, to faculty. These amounts are not available for other uses. The principal of restricted gifts where only the income can be used for loans is part of the endowment fund (permanently restricted); income as earned and available for loans, and principal that can be used to make loans should be recorded in the loan fund. Refundable advances from governmental agencies are reported as liabilities.

Endowment Funds

This fund grouping includes three types of funds traditionally classified as "endowment and similar" funds:

1. Endowment funds—more appropriately called true endowment—where the donor has stipulated that the principal is to be kept intact in perpetuity and only the income therefrom can be expended either for general purposes or for a restricted purpose. Revenue from gifts to these funds and net assets of these funds are now reported in the permanently restricted class of net assets.
2. Term endowments where the donor has provided that upon the passage of time or the happening of a specific event, the endowment principal can then be utilized either for a specific purpose or for the general operation of the institution. Revenue and net assets of these funds are reported in the temporarily restricted class of net assets. Term endowments are usually not reported separately in the principal financial statements except where they are sizable.
3. Quasi-endowment where the board, as distinct from the donor, has set aside unrestricted amounts to be used as endowment, at

least for some time. Quasi-endowment funds are also known as "Board-Designated Endowment," or "Funds Functioning as Endowment." Because a governing board can at any time vote to expend such amounts, quasi-endowment funds should be clearly shown in the financial statements as part of the unrestricted class of net assets.

Annuity and Life Income Funds

These are amounts where only the principal, and not the current income to be earned thereon, has been given to the institution. The income is retained by the donor for a specified period of time, and the institution agrees to pay either a specified sum, or the actual income earned, to the donor (or another person specified by the donor) for this period. The principal of these gifts does represent an asset owned by the institution, but until the income or annuity restrictions lapse, clearly these amounts do not represent resources which have the same value as other institutional resources. For this reason, these amounts should not be combined with endowments or other funds for reporting purposes, unless they are insignificant.

Plant Funds

Plant funds consist of four subgroupings:

1. *Unexpended funds.* These represent amounts which are to be used for plant additions or modernization. Such resources usually consist of cash and other investments which have been donated or transferred to this fund for plant purposes.
2. *Funds for renewal or replacement.* These represent amounts donated or transferred from current funds for renewal or replacement of existing plant. Such amounts represent a form of funding of depreciation. In reporting, often these funds are combined with unexpended funds.
3. *Funds for retirement of indebtedness.* These are the amounts set aside by the board for debt service (interest and principal), either under a mandatory contractual arrangement with the lender or voluntarily at the board's discretion.
4. *Investment in plant.* This represents the cost of plant including land and equipment, net of accumulated depreciation to date. Actual cost, or market value at date of gifts is used. The principal

EXHIBIT 15–1 An example of a columnar presentation of a Balance Sheet for a small college using fund accounting recommended in the AICPA Audit Guide.

MARY AND ISLA COLLEGE
BALANCE SHEET
June 30, 19X1

ASSETS	Current Funds	Loan Funds	Endowment and Similar Funds	Plant Funds	Total All Funds
Current assets:					
Cash	$1,195,000	$16,000	$ 310,000	$ 80,000	$ 1,601,000
Short-term investments	930,000			550,000	1,480,000
Accounts receivable	18,000	80,000			98,000
Inventories	20,000				20,000
Prepaid expenses	25,000				25,000
Total	2,188,000	96,000	310,000	630,000	3,224,000
Long-term investments			4,215,000		4,215,000
Invested in plant, net of depreciation				23,450,000	23,450,000
Interfund receivable (payable)	(560,000)		510,000	50,000	—
Total assets	$1,628,000	$96,000	$5,035,000	$24,130,000	$30,889,000

LIABILITIES AND NET ASSETS

Current liabilities:					
Accounts payable	$ 573,000			$ 35,000	$ 608,000
Current portion of debt				170,000	170,000
Tuition deposits	110,000				110,000
Total	683,000			205,000	888,000
Long-term debt				580,000	580,000
Refundable advances		$30,000			30,000
Net assets:					
Unrestricted	810,000	16,000	$3,010,000	23,025,000	26,861,000
Temporarily restricted	135,000		510,000	320,000	965,000
Permanently restricted		50,000	1,515,000		1,565,000
Total	945,000	66,000	5,035,000	23,345,000	29,391,000
Total liabilities and net assets	$1,628,000	$96,000	$5,035,000	$24,130,000	$30,889,000

amount of mortgages or other debt related to the plant assets is usually recorded in this fund.

All plant or fixed assets are recorded in the plant fund. The current funds include plant activities to the extent that funds for additions, renewal or replacement, and retirement of indebtedness are transferred from the current fund to the plant fund. Also, the current fund will include plant activities to the extent that equipment purchases initially recorded as a direct charge to current fund expenditures will subsequently be recorded in the plant fund as additions to the net investment in plant.

While the Guide illustrates the use of all four subgroupings, some institutions have combined some or all of these for reporting purposes, showing the balances of each subgrouping only in the Balance Sheet.

Agency or Custodian Funds

These are funds that are in the custody of the institution but are not legally its property. An example would be funds belonging to student organizations on deposit with the institution, to be later disbursed on instructions from the student organization. Agency funds are not further discussed or illustrated in this chapter because they are not funds of the institution. Reference should be made to the Audit Guide and to the Manual referred to above by interested readers.

15.3 THE PRINCIPAL FINANCIAL STATEMENTS

Traditionally, three principal financial statements have been used by colleges and universities, as follows:

1. Balance Sheet (new format illustrated at Exhibit 15–1).
2. Statement of Changes in Fund Balances (similar to the statement of revenue, expenses, and changes in net assets, illustrated at Exhibit 15–2). An example of the traditional format of this statement can be found in the college audit guide and in Chapter 14 (page 240) of the fourth edition of this book.
3. Statement of Current Funds Revenues, Expenditures, and Other Changes (not illustrated in this edition; interested readers can find an illustration on page 248 of the fourth edition of this book).

Since the issuance of SFAS No. 117, most institutions will present three statements:

1. Balance Sheet (Exhibit 15–1).
2. Statement of Revenues, Expenses, and Changes in Net Assets (Exhibit 15–2).
3. Statement of Cash Flows (example in Chapter 14—Exhibit 14–3).

There are frequently other supporting statements that provide detail which should tie in with these three principal statements. While the supporting statements provide information which the board or other specific users of the statements may want, it is important not to confuse the general reader of the financial statements by providing more detail than is appropriate. A reader interested in further information should refer to the Financial Accounting and Reporting Manual.

It is important to recognize the premise from which the Audit Guide prescribed accounting and reporting principles. The Guide states:

> Service, rather than profits, is the objective of an educational institution; thus, the primary obligation of accounting and reporting is one of accounting for resources received and used rather than for determination of net income.[4]

It is essential to recognize that the Guide did not attempt to prescribe accounting and reporting principles that would assist the reader in understanding whether the institution had an excess of revenues over expenditures for the period. Prior to the issuance of SFAS No. 117, this was not the purpose. The purpose was only "accounting for resources received and used." On the other hand, SFAS No. 117 does intend to focus readers' attention on the financial soundness of the institution and whether it is better or worse off financially than it was the year before.

The key, then, to understanding college financial statements is to recognize what types of transactions are included in its financial statements, and to understand the principles of fund accounting. The following paragraphs describe the type of transactions in each of the principal statements required by SFAS No. 117. A description of some of the accounting and reporting principles appears in a later section of this chapter.

(a)   Balance Sheet

Exhibit 15–1 shows the Balance Sheet for Mary and Isla College in a columnar format. (The Balance Sheet, as illustrated in the Guide and prepared by many institutions, is set up in a format where the assets are on

[4] Page 5 of the Guide.

EXHIBIT 15–2 An example of an all-inclusive Statement of Revenues, Expenses, and Changes in Net Assets.

MARY AND ISLA COLLEGE
STATEMENT OF REVENUES, EXPENSES, AND CHANGES
IN NET ASSETS
For the Year Ended June 30, 19X1

	Unrestricted	Temporarily Restricted	Permanently Restricted	Total
Operating revenues:				
Tuition and fees	$ 1,610,000			$ 1,610,000
Governmental appropriations	400,000			400,000
Research grants		$ 190,000		190,000
Auxiliary activities	125,000			125,000
Net assets released from restrictions .	550,000	(550,000)		
Total operating revenues	2,685,000	(360,000)		2,325,000
Operating expenses:				
Educational:				
Engineering	930,000			930,000
Arts	410,000			410,000
Business	625,000			625,000
Research	850,000			850,000

266

Supporting:				
Administrative	495,000			495,000
Fund raising	90,000			90,000
Auxiliary activities	95,000			95,000
Total operating expenses	3,495,000			3,495,000
Excess of operating expenses over revenues	(810,000)	(360,000)		(1,170,000)
Other revenues:				
Gifts and bequests	900,000	240,000	$ 395,000	1,535,000
Investment income	350,000	47,000		397,000
Realized and unrealized appreciation	130,000		20,000	150,000
Total other revenues	1,380,000	287,000	415,000	2,082,000
Excess of revenues over expenses	570,000	(73,000)	415,000	912,000
Net assets, beginning of year	26,291,000	1,038,000	1,150,000	28,479,000
Net assets, end of year	$26,861,000	$ 965,000	$1,565,000	$29,391,000

the left side of the page and the liabilities and fund balances are on the right side, with major fund groupings presented as separate Balance Sheets within the Balance Sheet. Exhibit 4–2 at page 37 is an example of this type of Balance Sheet.) The Guide permits the use of a columnar presentation as an acceptable alternative, although it does caution against cross-footing the columns to a total "unless all necessary disclosures are made, including interfund borrowings."[5] While the columnar format used in Exhibit 15–1 has not been used as widely, the authors prefer it because of the ease in seeing the overall picture of the institution. At the same time, it must be recognized that the columnar format can be misleading if the reader does not recognize the limitations on use of most of the assets.

SFAS No. 117 does not require any particular format for a balance sheet as long as certain disclosures are made: total assets, total liabilities, total net assets, and net assets for each of the three classes. SFAS No. 117 illustrates a balance sheet with only a single column (plus a column showing comparative prior-year information). There is no prohibition against presenting additional columns, if an organization desires. If additional columns are presented, they can be columns which show assets, liabilities, and net assets grouped by class of net assets, by operating unit (such as the college, the hospital, etc.), or by managed fund group (roughly equivalent to the traditional fund structure.) Exhibit 15–1 shows managed fund groups as that is the format that is likely to be adopted by many colleges.

(b)   Statement of Revenues, Expenses, and Changes in Net Assets

The most important of the three financial statements is the Statement of Revenues, Expenses, and Changes in Net Assets. This statement summarizes all of the activity of the institution for the entire period. Exhibit 15–2 shows the Statement of Revenues, Expenses, and Changes in Net Assets for Mary and Isla College.

Notice that this format essentially follows an income statement format (i.e., revenues less expenses equals change in net assets for the year). This is a significant change from the format of the Statement of Changes in Fund Balances previously recommended by CUBA. That form of statement was the more typical Statement of Changes in Fund Balances in which the first line was the balance at the beginning of the year, then the additions were shown, then the deductions, and finally, the fund balance

---

[5] *Audits of Colleges and Universities*, AICPA, 1973, page 57.

at the end of the year. An example of this superseded format can be seen in Exhibit 12–5 of the fourth edition of this book.

The significance of the new format is that it presents a reasonably concise summary of the net change in the financial picture of the institution for the entire year. While most business officers (and many accountants) flinch at the comparison, this "net change" has much the same significance as "net profit" in a business, particularly when all funds are viewed together.

"Total" Column

The illustrative financial statements in the Audit Guide do not show a "total" column, as is illustrated in Exhibit 15–2, and the Guide discourages such a total column. The Guide indicates, however, that the use of a total column is permitted provided care is taken to ensure that the restricted nature of certain of the resources is clearly shown. As has been repeatedly noted, the authors recommend the use of a total column and accordingly have included one in this and subsequent illustrations.[6] SFAS No. 117 does not require a total *column,* but it does require the presentation of the total change in net assets for the year. This disclosure can be made using either a multicolumn format with a total column, or a single-column format; both are illustrated in SFAS No. 117. Whichever format is chosen must, however, present revenues, as well as the change in net assets for the year, separately for each of the three classes of net assets.

Revenues and Expenses

This statement differs from the statement of changes in fund balances previously used by colleges in several significant ways besides the titles of the statement and of the columns composing it. For a discussion of the classes of net assets and how they relate to the traditional funds, see Chapter 13, pages 189–191.

The revenue and expense sections of the statement now include only items which are truly revenue and expense to the organization, that is inflows and outflows of resources which change the total net assets of the organization. The old statement of changes in fund balances included many items which looked like revenues or expenses, were presented in sections captioned "*revenues* and other additions" and "*expenses* and other deductions," but were neither revenues nor expenses. Many of these items were really interfund transfers related to fixed assets and its associated

---

[6] Those readers not familiar with the arguments for and against the inclusion of such a "total" column will find a discussion in Section 13.3.

debt. These items are now presented in the statement of cash flows (page 237).[7]

The restricted gifts and bequests recorded in the current restricted fund represent the total amount which has been received during the year, and not the amount actually expended. In the old "Statement of Current Funds Revenues, Expenditures, and Other Changes" (no longer presented), the amount reported as current restricted revenues was the exact amount actually expended. This inconsistency in presentation caused considerable reader confusion. For a more complete discussion of the principles followed in reporting current restricted amounts, the reader should refer to Chapter 10, pages 119–124.

Net Increase (Decrease) before Transfers

This caption is *not* included in the illustrated Statement of Changes in Fund Balances in the Audit Guide, perhaps in part because the authors of the Guide were reluctant to imply that these amounts represented anything similar to "excess of revenues over expenditures," which certainly they are not. Those who argue against this subtotal point out that some of the transfers are required under mandatory debt arrangements and have many of the characteristics of an expenditure.

The Guide does not prohibit such a subtotal and in fact several members of the Audit Guide Committee felt that the Guide's illustrated statements should include this subtotal. The authors believe this caption is useful and would encourage all colleges and universities to include it. Such a subtotal—called "excess of revenues over expenses"—is shown in Exhibit 14–2.

Change in Net Assets for the Year

The inclusion of this caption is quite important because, appropriately, it tells the reader what the net change was for the year in each class and for the institution as a whole.

In addition to this statement, institutions may wish to present a statement of functional expenses, as illustrated in Chapter 14. Although required for voluntary health and welfare organizations, under SFAS

---

[7] Many persons associated with colleges also argue that the gifts, bequests, capital gains, and other "revenue" recorded in the funds other than the current unrestricted fund are also "other additions." They feel that these amounts are not revenue and are only additions to the fund balance which should not be looked upon as revenue. The authors disagree and feel that such amounts do represent revenue. Note that the same basic format is used in the Audit Guide for voluntary health and welfare organizations (see Exhibit 14–2), and Statement of Position 78-10, and the authors of those documents considered the "revenue" caption appropriate.

No. 117 this statement is optional for colleges and other types of not-for-profits.

Mandatory Transfers

Fund accounting, as practiced by colleges, includes a type of transaction called mandatory transfers. Mandatory transfers are those inter-fund transfers which are required under debt or other agreements with outside parties. The most typical mandatory transfer involves debt service, that is, interest on indebtedness *and* repayment of debt principal. Also, some institutions are required under contractual arrangements to put aside in a renewal and replacement fund certain amounts every year. Mary and Isla College is making a mandatory transfer, but the amount does not appear in the new format of the financial statements because it is entirely within the unrestricted class.

The important point to note here is that while these transfers are "required" the nature of these transactions is not that of an *expenditure* in a conventional accounting sense. Debt repayment, while requiring an *expenditure* of cash, is not considered an *expense* in an accounting sense any more than the proceeds from a bank borrowing is considered income. Thus, these mandatory transfers tend to frustrate the reader who is trying to learn what excess, if any, there was of revenues over expenses in a traditional sense. This could not be determined without some rearrangement of the Exhibits shown in the traditional statement.

Operating versus Nonoperating

If an institution wishes, it may report "operating" revenues and expenses separately from "nonoperating" revenue and expenses. The definition of what is considered operating and non-operating is up to each institution. This subject is discussed further in Chapter 14.

(c) Statement of Cash Flows

This statement is discussed in Chapter 14.

(d) Statement of Current Funds Revenues, Expenditures, and Other Changes

The Statement of Current Funds Revenues, Expenditures, and Other Changes, discussed in CUBA and in the Audit Guide, but not in SFAS No. 117, was a very difficult statement for most readers to understand or to correctly interpret. It was an attempt to show on one statement all of the activity involving "current" funds—that is, the funds available for current use by the college in performing its primary objectives. Since all of the information previously included in this statement is now shown, in more understandable format in the statement of revenues, expenses, and changes in net assets, this statement will likely be discontinued, and is not further discussed here. Interested readers can find a discussion of it on pages 251–256 of the fourth edition of this book.

15.4 ACCOUNTING PRINCIPLES

Summarized below are the accounting principles prescribed by SFAS No. 116 and, where they do not conflict with SFAS No. 116, by the Audit Guide for colleges and universities, a number of which were discussed in earlier chapters.

(a) Accrual Basis

The Guide concludes that the accrual basis of accounting is normally necessary for financial statements prepared in accordance with generally accepted accounting principles. Items such as investment income and an allowance for uncollectible receivables should be recorded on an accrual basis unless unrecorded amounts would not be material. Also, revenues and expenses relating to a summer session should be reported in the fiscal year in which the summer session principally occurs.

(b) Encumbrance Accounting

Implicit in the use of accrual basis accounting is the presumption that the only amounts to be recorded as expenses will be those for which materials or services have been received as of the balance sheet date. Some institutions in the past have followed a governmental accounting approach in which expenses were charged at the time purchase orders or other commitments were issued, without regard to the actual date of receipt. This is another form of "appropriation" accounting which is discussed in detail in Chapter 5.

The Guide states quite clearly that encumbrance accounting is not acceptable and that such amounts should not be reported as expenses, nor as liabilities in the Balance Sheet. If the institution wishes to designate or allocate a portion of unrestricted net assets, it may do so but such designation would appear only in the net assets section of the Balance Sheet.[8]

---

[8] See Section 5.2 for a discussion of fund balance designations.

(c)   Unrestricted Gifts

All unrestricted gifts, donations, and bequests are recorded as revenue in the current unrestricted fund in the year received. While the board is free to designate any portions of such unrestricted gifts or bequests as "board-designated endowment," such gifts must nonetheless be reported initially in the unrestricted class of net assets. After being so reported, these amounts may then be segregated within the unrestricted class as quasi-endowment.

(d)   Current Restricted Gifts

Restricted gifts for current purposes are reported in their entirety in the Statement of Revenue, Expenses, and Changes in Net Assets. Under the traditional method of reporting, while the Statement of Changes in Fund Balances showed this amount, the amount of current restricted gifts reported as revenues in the Statement of Current Funds Revenues, Expenditures, and Other Changes was only the amount which had been actually expended for such restricted purposes during the year. Thus, depending on the statement being looked at, the reader would see either the total amount received during the year or the amount which had actually been expended.

(e)   Other Restricted Gifts

All other categories of legally restricted gifts would be reported directly in the class to which they applied. If a donor made a contribution of permanently restricted endowment, it would be reported directly in that class (assuming that the donor had made clear the intention, presumably in writing).

(f)   Pledges

While the Guide was flexible with respect to handling pledges, SFAS No. 116 is not. Under the Guide, the institution could elect to record such amounts before the cash (or other assets used to fulfill the pledge) was received, but this was not required, and most colleges did not do so. With the adoption of SFAS No. 116, all not-for-profit organizations will be required to record unconditional promises to give (pledges) as assets and revenue at the time notification of the pledge is received by the institution. In addition it must disclose in the footnotes the amount of conditional pledges received but not recorded as of the financial statement date if they are material. Further discussion of accounting for pledges is in Chapter 10.

(g) Investment Income

All investment income (dividends and interest) must be reported as revenues directly in the class of net assets appropriate to any restrictions of the revenue. Prior to the issuance of the Guide the use of an income stabilization reserve was permitted. This is no longer considered acceptable, and all investment income must be reported as revenue in the year in which earned.

Endowment fund investment income is normally considered unrestricted income unless the donor has specified a restricted use for the investment income. Accordingly, unrestricted endowment income should be reported directly in the unrestricted class.

(h) Gains or Losses on Investments

Gains or losses (and appreciation or depreciation where investments are carried at market; see below) have previously been normally considered adjustments of the carrying value of the investment and were reported in the Statement of Revenues, Expenses, and Changes in Net Assets in the fund holding the investment which gave rise to the gain. SFAS No. 117, however, requires that gains and losses be reported in the unrestricted class, unless a restriction is stipulated by the donor of the principal or by state law. This is discussed further in Chapter 8.

Where an organization carries its investments at market, the unrealized appreciation or depreciation would be reported in the same manner as the realized gains or losses.

(i) Carrying Value of Investments

The Guide provides that a college or university can carry its investments at either market or cost. (For donated investments, "cost" is the market value at the date of the gift.) If an institution elects market, however, it must carry all of its investments at market. It cannot carry some at market and some at cost. If investments are carried at cost, the market value must be disclosed. FASB is currently studying the subject of valuation of investments, and will issue guidance for not-for-profit organizations in the near future.

(j) Total Return Concept

Since SFAS No. 117 requires all capital gains which are available for general use to be reported directly in the unrestricted class of net assets, use of the total return concept is now obsolete, at least as far as external financial reporting is concerned. The concept may still be used for internal investment management if an institution wishes. It is discussed further in Chapter 8.

(k)   Fixed Asset Accounting

The Guide follows the CUBA approach to handling fixed assets and requires that all fixed assets (purchased or donated) be capitalized and carried on the Balance Sheet. This means that a college or university should not "expense" material fixed asset purchases in the year in which acquired. This is discussed further in Chapter 6.

(l)   Depreciation Accounting

Effective in 1990, FASB Statement No. 93, *Recognition of Depreciation by Not-for-Profit Organizations,* requires non-governmental[9] not-for-profit organizations, including colleges and universities, to depreciate their fixed assets. This is a major change from the practice historically followed by most colleges and universities. Institutions using the traditional financial statement format illustrated in the fourth edition of this book (Exhibits 14–1 and 14–2 of that edition) presented depreciation as a reduction of fixed assets on the Balance Sheet and a deduction in the Investment-in-Plant column on the Statement of Changes in Fund Balances. After an organization adopts SFAS No. 117, it will include depreciation along with other expenses in the unrestricted class of the Statement of Revenues, Expenses, and Changes in Net Assets. If expenses are shown by functional categories, depreciation will be allocated among the various functions (e.g., education, research, academic support) that benefit from use of depreciable assets.

15.5   SIMPLIFIED FORMAT FOR FINANCIAL STATEMENTS

The principles of accounting and reporting historically followed by most colleges and universities, as recommended by the Guide, were, in the authors' opinion deficient in that the average reader, not knowledgeable in either accounting or college reporting, had considerable difficulty in understanding exactly what had taken place during the year. A large part of the difficulty arose because of the use of separate columns for each

---

[9] Governmental colleges are under the accounting jurisdiction of the Governmental Accounting Standards Board (GASB). Since GASB has not required governmental entities to depreciate fixed assets, governmental colleges may elect either approach. GASB is discussed further in Chapter 19.

fund, normally without a total column, making it difficult for the reader to see an overall picture. This derived from the legal accountability such institutions have to see that funds entrusted to them for specific uses are expended in the manner designated by the donor. This legal accountability, however, does not mean that the institution must report to the public on a detailed separate-statement basis for each fund grouping. There is no reason why financial statements cannot be presented in a format which will permit the reader to see easily the overall picture.

The premise that a set of financial statements for a college should not show results of operations certainly had to be questioned. True, the college is not expected to make a "profit" in the commercial sense, but it is expected over a period of time to take in enough money to be able to sustain its operations. If it doesn't, clearly it is headed for serious trouble. It may very well be that the financial plight that many institutions are presently in can be traced, at least in part, to financial reporting that really did not tell it "as it is."

Further, college financial statements as prescribed in the Guide give very little useful information to the reader or trustee as to the costs of operating the institution. Most institutions, for example, have a number of educational programs—different colleges within the university, different departments. It would appear that the trustees should be told what the costs are for each type of major program of the institution; otherwise, though they are charged with the responsibility for the institution, they have no way of really making an informed judgment.

Price Waterhouse, in a major policy paper in 1975 urged that colleges and universities prepare financial statements following a simplified approach recommended in earlier editions of this book. Further, Price Waterhouse indicated they would give an unqualified audit opinion on financial statements prepared in this format. It is interesting that, while the recommended format for financial statements of not-for-profit organizations contained in the new FASB Statement No. 117 is not identical to that recommended by Price Waterhouse, it is very similar in most major respects, and will thus constitute a significant improvement in the understandability of college financial statements.

Health Care Providers

(i) Contributions
(j) Malpractice Contingencies
(k) Related Organizations
(l) Timing Differences

16.1 INTRODUCTION

One very important segment of the not-for-profit industry is the health care industry. Health care in the United States is provided by entities operating in all sectors of the economy. Some health care providers are investor-owned, some are operated as not-for-profit organizations (either business-oriented or eleemosynary), and some are operated by federal, state, and local governments. The largest number of health care providers are organized as not-for-profit organizations. These are also known as "voluntary" providers; they consist mainly of health care entities that are organized, sponsored, or operated by communities, religious groups, or private universities and medical schools.

Voluntary health care entities are usually exempt from federal and state income taxes if they are operated exclusively for religious, charitable, scientific, or educational purposes and if no part of their net earnings inures to the benefit of any private shareholder or individual. However, they may be subject to taxes on income that is derived from activities not related to their tax-exempt purpose. Voluntary providers are allowed to generate profits in order to meet financial obligations, improve patient care, expand facilities, and participate in research, training, education, and other activities that benefit the provider's community.

Although many voluntary health care entities may receive support from religious and fraternal organizations, individuals, corporations, and other donors or grantors, most are essentially self-sustaining; that is, they finance their capital needs primarily from the proceeds of debt issues and their operating needs largely from revenues derived from health care services provided. As a result, accountability to creditors is more of a driving force in matters pertaining to financial statement presentation and disclosure of not-for-profit health care providers than it is for not-for-profit organizations that rely primarily on contributions. Comparability with financial statements of providers in the governmental and investor-owned sector is also important. Not-for-profit health care providers must keep up with accounting standards of both the business sector and the not-for-profit sector. For this reason, if the financial statements of not-for-profit organizations were arrayed along a continuum based on complexity, the financial statements of most health care providers would be among the most complex.

16.2   AUTHORITATIVE PRONOUNCEMENTS

(a)   AICPA Audit Guide

The AICPA has been and continues to be the primary source of guidance relating to specific accounting principles for health care organizations. Throughout this chapter, the principles outlined will be those contained in the AICPA audit and accounting guide *Audits of Providers of Health Care Services* that was issued by the Institute's Health Care Committee in 1990.

This Guide applies to all entities whose principal operations involve providing health care services to individuals. This includes hospitals, nursing homes, health maintenance organizations (HMOs) and other providers of prepaid care; continuing care retirement communities (CCRCs); home health agencies; ambulatory care organizations such as clinics, medical group practices, individual practice associations, and individual practitioners; freestanding emergency care facilities; surgery centers; integrated delivery systems that include one or more of these types of entities; and organizations whose primary activities are the planning, organization, and oversight of entities providing health care services (such as parent or holding companies of health care providers). The provisions of the Guide are applied somewhat differently with regard to governmental health care providers; however, that matter is beyond the scope of this book.

As noted earlier in this book, in 1993 the FASB issued two new accounting pronouncements, SFAS No. 116 and SFAS No. 117 that affect many of the provisions of the 1990 guide. As a result, the Health Care Committee is preparing a new audit and accounting guide for health care providers that, when issued in final form, will supersede the 1990 guide.[1]

The new guide proposes to resolve a long-standing difficulty stemming from an apparent overlap in the scope of the audit guide for health care entities and the audit guide for voluntary health and welfare organizations. The controversy concerns health care organizations that are funded largely by public support; for example, certain drug abuse centers or Shriner's hospitals for crippled children. Although these "eleemosynary providers" provide health care services, their primary source of income is contributions, rather than fees for services performed or premiums for agreeing to provide prepaid health care services.

---

[1] This guide will be entirely separate from the new guide being prepared by the AICPA's Not-for-Profit Committee to replace the existing guides for voluntary health and welfare organizations, colleges and universities, and other not-for-profit organizations (as discussed in Chapters 14, 15, and 17).

SFAS No. 116 provided guidance that allows this confusing area to be clarified. It defined a voluntary health and welfare organization as one which derives its revenue primarily from voluntary contributions from the general public to be used for general or specific purposes connected with health, welfare, or other community services. Eleemosynary not-for-profit health care providers clearly fall within this definition. As a result, issuance of the proposed new guide may result in such providers being "reclassified" as voluntary health and welfare organizations for purposes of determining which audit guide should be followed for external financial reporting purposes. The not-for-profit providers that remain within the scope of the health care guide would be those that are essentially self-sustaining from fees charged for services (as defined in FASB Concepts Statement No. 4, para. 18). In effect, providers that are operated as "charities" follow more closely the accounting and reporting prescribed for "nonbusiness not-for-profit organizations," while business-oriented not-for-profit providers follow principles comparable to the investor-owned segment. Eleemosynary providers should be aware that this was merely a proposed change at the time this book was being written; therefore, they should not switch until a new guide incorporating that change is issued.

(b)   HFMA Principles and Practices Board

In 1975, the Healthcare Financial Management Association (HFMA) founded a "Principles and Practices Board" (P&PB). This committee consists of distinguished individuals in the field of health-care accounting and finance who set forth advisory recommendations on health care accounting and reporting issues which are not addressed in FASB statements or the Guide. Although the P&PB's statements have no authoritative status, they are valuable to the health care community because they disseminate well-thought-out opinions, along with views on the issues and relevant background information, regarding issues on which information would not otherwise be available. At the time of this writing, seventeen statements have been issued by the P&PB.

16.3   FUND ACCOUNTING

While fund *accounting* may be used by many not-for-profit organizations for recordkeeping and internal reporting, for external *financial reporting,* funds will not be used; rather, this reporting will utilize the three-class structure defined in the new SFAS No. 117. (Fund accounting is discussed in Chapter 4.)

It is a broad generalization to state that health care providers have placed less emphasis on maintenance of separate funds than have other types of not-for-profit organizations. SFAS No. 117 requires not-for-profit entities to classify and report their resources as pertaining to one of three broad categories: unrestricted net assets, temporarily restricted net assets, and permanently restricted net assets. These classifications are related to the existence or absence of any *donor-imposed restrictions* and are discussed in more detail in Chapters 10 and 13, and are basically new names for the same fund groupings that have traditionally been used: *general funds* and *donor-restricted funds*.

(a) Unrestricted Net Assets

Unrestricted net assets (formerly general funds) represent the portion of total net assets that are free from any donor-imposed restrictions. They represent the net assets available for any purpose, at the discretion of the NPO's board. All assets and liabilities without donor-imposed restrictions must be classified as unrestricted. This generally includes the provider's working capital, assets whose use is limited (as discussed below), facility debt, property and equipment, and long-term debt.

The balance sheet caption "assets whose use is limited" includes assets whose use is *contractually limited* under terms of debt indentures, trust agreements such as self-insurance arrangements, and assets required to be set aside to meet statutory reserve requirements (such as those required under state law for many HMOs). Information about significant contractual limits such as debt covenants or self-insurance trusts is generally disclosed in the notes to the financial statements.

Prior to the issuance of SFAS No. 117 many providers set up separate board-designated funds which were reported on separately from the other unrestricted activities of the organization. The proposed new guide would change the reporting for self-imposed (as opposed to externally-imposed) limits, such as board designated assets. Information about self-imposed limits that is considered useful may be presented in notes to the financial statements, if desired; however, it would no longer be appropriate to include such funds in assets whose use is limited.

(b) Donor-Restricted Funds

Assets that are specifically restricted to use for a particular purpose by an external donor or grantor, along with any related obligations, are included in this fund grouping. Although donor-imposed restrictions may require individual gifts or grants to be kept separate for record-keeping purposes, as a general rule they may be grouped for financial reporting purposes. Groupings are determined based on whether the restrictions are temporary or permanent, and on the uses for which the resources are intended. The nature of restrictions on donor-restricted resources, if such amounts are material, should be disclosed in the financial statements.

16.4 FINANCIAL STATEMENTS

Four primary financial statements traditionally have been used by health care entities:

1. Balance Sheet
2. Statement of Revenue and Expenses of General Funds
3. Statement of Changes in Fund Balances
4. Statement of Cash Flows of General Funds

With the issuance of SFAS No. 117 (discussed in Chapter 13), many of the 1990 audit guide's requirements relating to financial statement content and format have been superseded. SFAS No. 117 requires not-for-profit organizations to prepare their general-purpose external financial statements in a "single fund" format; to include cash flows related to donor-restricted contributions in income and expense; to prepare a "statement of activity" as a basic financial statement; and to report expenses on a "functional" basis, among other things. Guidance as to how providers should implement SFAS 117's new requirements will be contained in the proposed new guide under preparation by the AICPA Health Care Committee. Therefore, the following discussion of financial statements will compare existing guidance with that tentatively set forth in the proposed new guide at the time this book was written.

Single-Fund Reporting

The majority of the illustrative statements contained in the 1990 guide are prepared using fund reporting principles. With the issuance of SFAS 117, a not-for-profit organization's basic financial statements must be prepared in a three class format.

Basic Financial Statements

The proposed new audit guide would require health care entities to prepare the following basic financial statements:

1. Balance Sheet
2. Statement of Operations
3. Statement of Net Assets
4. Statement of Cash Flows

The 1990 Guide (and its proposed replacement) provide illustrative financial statements for six types of health care providers: a hospital, nursing home, continuing-care retirement community, home health agency, health maintenance organization, and an ambulatory care facility. The sample financial statements illustrate how to apply the reporting practices contained in the guide; however, they are not intended to represent the only types of disclosure or statement formats that are appropriate. Health care providers should use financial statement formats that are most informative for their individual circumstances, provided the Guide's accounting and reporting guidelines are met.

(a)   Balance Sheet

The primary change for health care providers is the elimination of the fund reporting used by many not-for-profit health care entities in favor of a single-column format. For most providers, the only balance sheet reference to "funds" will be in the net assets (formerly fund balance) section. SFAS states that a balance sheet in which all the assets and liabilities are commingled is acceptable, provided the net assets section clearly discloses amounts of unrestricted and restricted net assets. Net assets should be displayed as unrestricted, temporarily restricted, or permanently restricted amounts as appropriate.

SFAS 117 requires that information about liquidity of assets and liabilities be provided in the balance sheet. Unlike many other types of not-for-profit organizations, most health care entities (with the exception of some CCRCs, as discussed later) traditionally have prepared a "classified" balance sheet—that is, one in which assets and liabilities are categorized as "current" or "noncurrent." The proposed new guide is expected to require all providers other than CCRCs to meet the liquidity requirements by preparing a classified balance sheet.

Much of the fund raising conducted by health care entities (particularly hospitals) is directed toward capital projects; however, those capital projects usually are predominantly financed with debt. If cash contributions restricted for acquisition of long-lived assets such as property, plant, and equipment (PP&E) are included with other cash and cash equivalents in the balance sheet, the entity's ability to repay debt as indicated by compliance with any restrictive debt covenants may be distorted. As a result, the proposed guide states that in a classified balance sheet, assets restricted by donors for acquisition of long-lived assets are differentiated from other cash and contributions receivable, such as by reporting them in a separate category (for example, "assets restricted to investment in PP&E") sequenced near the PP&E section of the balance sheet. Similarly, cash and claims to cash that are designated for expenditure in the acquisition or construction of noncurrent assets or are required to be segregated for the liquidation of long-term debt are reported separately and excluded from cash and cash equivalents.

(b)   Statement of Operations and Net Assets

SFAS No. 117 requires not-for-profit organizations to present a "statement of activity." In essence, it combines the "statement of revenue and expenses" and "statement of changes in fund balances" traditionally presented by health care providers into a single statement that shows all of the organization's activity—both restricted and unrestricted—from the beginning to the end of the year. The substance of this change is that all changes in restricted funds, which in the past showed up as increases and decreases in a restricted fund balance (rather than income or expense) are now reported in an income statement format. (See Chapter 13 for more on the reasons for this change.)

The display model set forth in SFAS No. 117 is geared more toward organizations that are primarily supported by contributions from the general public. As stated earlier, the primary users of the financial statements of business-oriented health care providers are providers of capital to the industry, who are more interested in gauging the entity's ability to repay its debt than they are in seeing what resources flowed through the organization during the year.

Consequently, in the proposed new guide the AICPA would require health care entities to present somewhere in the statement of activities an "operating indicator." This may be achieved by carving out a separate "statement of operations" from the statement showing overall changes in net assets. Although it will not exactly parallel the statement of revenue and expense number of the traditional provider income statement, it will produce financial statements that more closely resemble the traditional income statement presentation used by providers.

What income statement elements should be included in the statement of operations? The proposed new guide would state that operating results should be reported separately from:

- Equity transfers involving other entities that control the reporting entity, are controlled by the reporting entity, or are under common control with the reporting entity

- Receipt of restricted contributions, including temporary or permanent restrictions
- Contributions of long-lived assets
- Other items required by GAAP to be reported separately, such as extraordinary items, the effects of discontinued operations, and the cumulative effect of accounting changes.

An example of the new Statement of Operations/Statement of Net Assets contrasted to the former Statement of Revenues and Expenses is shown in Exhibit 16–1.

Expense Reporting

The new guide also proposes implementing guidance with regard to SFAS No. 117's new expense reporting requirements. The first new requirement is that all expenses must be shown in the unrestricted class of net assets; no expenses may be reported in the temporarily or permanently restricted classes. This will not be a significant change for most health care providers, who traditionally have run most expenses through the income statement of the unrestricted fund.

The second new requirement has to do with functional reporting of expenses. Traditionally, providers have reported expenses classified along revenue/cost center lines (e.g., nursing services, other professional services, general services) or natural lines (e.g., salaries and wages, employee benefits, supplies, purchased services). As discussed in Chapter 13, SFAS No. 117 requires not-for-profit organizations to report expenses by functional categories such as "program," "management," and "fund raising." Not-for-profit health care organizations may continue their traditional presentation on the face of the financial statement, as long as the functional reporting requirements are presented in the notes to the financial statements. The functional reporting requirements may not be as onerous to implement as may first appear. A great deal of flexibility is allowed in the degree to which the functional information is reported. Some providers may choose to present only two categories: "health services" and "general and administrative." Others may desire more detail. Whatever degree of detail is selected, the functional allocations should be based on full cost allocations.

The Statement of Operations has the potential to become an extremely detailed document. Some facilities present a great deal of detail; other present income statements that are highly condensed, providing only summary totals of major classifications of revenue and expense. Details, if desired, may also be presented in the accompanying notes or in supplemental schedules or statements. Each provider must determine the level of detail that it feels is most meaningful for full disclosure.

EXHIBIT 16–1   An example of a Statement of Revenue and Expenses prepared in traditional format (left) and prepared in accordance with proposed new audit guide (right).

JOHNSTOWN HEALTH SYSTEM Statement of Revenue and Expenses of General Funds Year Ended December 31, 19x7 (in thousands)	JOHNSTOWN HEALTH SYSTEM Statement of Operations Year Ended December 31, 19x7 (in thousands)

Net patient service revenue	$4,000	
Other revenue[a]	115	
Total revenue	4,115	
Expenses:		
Nursing services	1,800	
Other professional services	1,300	
General services	1,000	
Fiscal services	200	
Administrative services	380	
Interest	20	
Provision for bad debts	100	
Provision for depreciation	200	
Total operating expenses	5,000	
Loss from operations	(885)	
Nonoperating gains:		
Unrestricted gifts and bequests	470	
Unrestricted income from endowment funds	300	
Income on investments whose use is limited:		
By board for capital improvements	40	
By agreements with third-party payors for funded depreciation	30	
Under indenture agreement	45	
Other investment income	50	
Total nonoperating gains	935	
Revenue and gains in excess of expenses	$ 50	

Unrestricted revenues, gains and other support:	
Net patient service revenue	$4,000
Other, primarily interest income	1,075
Net assets released from restriction	50
	5,125
Expenses and losses:	
Operating expenses	4,780
Depreciation and amortization	200
Interest	20
	5,000
Operating income	125
Contributions of long-lived assets	200
Increase in unrestricted net assets	$ 325

[a] Includes $50,000 from specific-purpose funds and $15,000 investment income on malpractice trust.

286

(c)   Statement of Cash Flows of General Funds

All four statements would incorporate both restricted and unrestricted funds, if applicable. Previously the Statement of Operations (formerly the Statement of Revenue and Expenses) and Statement of Cash Flows involved only unrestricted (general) funds.

Unlike other not-for-profit organizations, health care providers have been required to prepare a Statement of Cash Flows, as do other business organizations, since the issuance of the 1990 audit guide. SFAS No. 117 continues that requirement and also broadens the scope of the flows to be included in the statement. Previously, the statement was prepared using only unrestricted cash inflows and outflows (i.e., the general fund). Now the statement must be extended to include restricted cash inflows and outflows as well.

16.5   ACCOUNTING PRINCIPLES

(a)   Generally Accepted Accounting Principles

Although AICPA Accounting Research Bulletin No. 43 states that authoritative accounting pronouncements are directed primarily to business enterprises organized for profit, the AICPA has concluded that financial statements of health care entities should be prepared in accordance with generally accepted accounting principles. Accordingly, FASB Statements and Interpretations, APB Opinions, and AICPA Accounting Research Bulletins are applicable to financial statements prepared by health care entities.

(b)   The Earnings Cycle

Parties to Health Care Transactions

One unique aspect of health care operations is that revenue transactions primarily involve more parties than the traditional "buyer" and "seller," or "donor" and "donee." As many as four parties may be involved in a revenue-generating transaction within a health care provider. These include: (1) the individual who receives the care; (2) the physician who orders the required services on behalf of the patient; (3) the health care entity that provides the setting or administers the treatment (e.g., hospital, home health company); and (4) the third-party payer that provides payment to the health care provider(s) on behalf of the patient.

Types of Revenue

Health care revenue is classified based on the type of services rendered or contracted to be rendered. Examples include:

- Premium revenue, derived from capitation-type arrangements;
- Patient service revenue, derived from fees charged to patients;
- Resident service revenue, derived from fees charged to residents of a long-term care facility.

Providers that have more than one primary source of revenue (for example, significant amounts of both patient service revenue and premium revenue) should report them separately in the Statement of Operations.

FASB Concepts Statement No. 6

The guide instructs each provider to determine, within certain guidelines, what transactions constitute revenues, expenses, gains, and losses (as defined by the FASB) for their individual facility. Each facility's definitions are tied to its interpretation of which of its activities are "ongoing, major, and central" and which are "peripheral and incidental" to providing health care services. The Guide applies the FASB's guidance to health care providers as follows:

- Activities associated with the provision of health care services constitute the ongoing, major, or central operations of providers of health care services. *Revenues* and *expenses* arise from these activities. Revenues and expenses generally are displayed as gross amounts.
- Transactions that are peripheral or incidental to the provision of health care services, and from other events stemming from the environment that may be largely beyond the control of the entity and its management, result in *gains* and *losses*. These occur casually or incidentally in relation to the provider's ongoing activities. Gains and losses generally are displayed as net amounts.

Under the Guide, each provider must define its central mission and how that will affect its reporting of revenues, expenses, gains, and losses. If material amounts of gains and losses are present, a policy note discussing the entity's definitions of "ongoing, major, and central" and "peripheral and incidental" may be needed in order for the financial statements to be meaningful. Once this policy is established, it should be consistently applied from period to period.

Timing of Revenue Recognition

Revenue is recognized in the financial statements when the provider has fulfilled that which is required to be done under the terms of the contractual agreement that exists among the parties to the transaction. For example, premium (or "capitation") revenue is recognized when coverage is provided to an enrollee in a prepaid health care plan. Patient service revenue is recognized when actual services are provided to a patient and may take many forms: per diem, per case, per occasion of service.

Patient (or Resident) Service Revenue

A significant portion of health care services is paid for by third parties such as Medicare, Medicaid, Blue Cross, commercial insurance companies, and prepaid health care plans such as HMOs. Under many of these payment arrangements, providers receive payment amounts that are less than their full established rates.

For internal record-keeping purposes, providers should record revenue (and the related receivables) from providing services to patients or residents at their established rates, regardless of how much the provider actually expects to collect in payments. The revenue should be recorded on an accrual basis; in other words, it should be recognized as services are rendered. Any differences between the established rates for covered services and the amounts paid by third parties should be accounted for as a contractual adjustment. These adjustments should also be recorded on an accrual basis; to do so, an estimate of this allowance should be made and recorded at the time of billing.

Because providers often receive less in payment than their full established rates, and the amounts received bear little relationship to established charges, reporting gross charges in the financial statements has little meaning for many financial statement users. Consequently, the Guide instructs providers to report only the amount of their net patient service revenue (i.e., gross charges less contractual adjustments and other deductions from revenue) in the Statement of Operations. (This differs from the reporting practices of other not-for-profit organizations.)

Some facilities may choose to provide information concerning gross patient service revenue and deductions from revenue in either the notes to the financial statements or in a supplemental schedule. They believe that doing so allows the reader to see what portion of the provider's full rate structure is being collected. If this type of financial statement disclosure is made, the amount shown as gross patient service revenue may not include charges attributable to services provided to charity patients, and deductions from revenue may not include either the provision for bad debts or the provision for charity care.

Premium Revenue

Providers may also earn income from accepting a fixed, predetermined amount in exchange for *agreeing to provide services* to a specified group of individuals (regardless of the level of services actually provided). This type of revenue constitutes the primary income of prepaid health care plans, such as HMOs and PPOs, and of integrated delivery systems. The Guide reflects such income as "premium revenue."

(c)   Bad Debts

The Guide defines bad debt expense as "the provision for actual or expected uncollectibles resulting from the extension of credit." The provision for bad debts should be determined on an accrual basis and reported as an expense; it is not appropriate to report this amount as a component of net patient service revenue. Bad debts may be reported as a separate line item or included with other expenses in a summary caption.

(d)   Charity Care

According to the Guide, charity care results from an entity's policy to provide health care services free of charge to individuals who meet certain financial criteria. Because no cash flows are expected from these services, they do not qualify for recognition as receivables or revenue in the provider's financial statements. Similarly, receivables for health care services and the related valuation allowance should not include amounts related to charity care. This would hold true on the face of the balance sheet and in any note disclosures or supplemental schedules that accompany the financial statements.

   The Guide does not intend for all mention of charity care to disappear from the financial statements. Charity care represents an important element of the services provided by many facilities. Accordingly, the Guide requires that specific disclosures regarding charity care be made in the notes to the financial statements. A statement of management's policy with regard to providing charity care, and the fact that charity services do not result in the production of revenue, should be included in the entity's "summary of significant accounting policies." The level of charity care provided for each of the years covered by the financial statements must be disclosed in the notes to the financial statements. The level of care provided may be measured in a variety of ways, such as at established rates, costs, patient days, occasions of service, or other statistics. The method used to measure the charity care should also be disclosed.

The Guide recognizes that distinguishing charity care writeoffs from bad debt writeoffs is not easy. As charity care results from an entity's policy to provide health care services free of charge to individuals who meet certain financial criteria, the establishment of a formal management policy clearly defining charity care should result in a reasonable determination, according to the AICPA.

These provisions apply only to financial statement presentation. Both gross charges attributable to charity patients and the corresponding provision for charity care would continue to be recorded for internal recordkeeping purposes.

(e) Settlements with Third-Party Payers

Payments under contracts with third-party payers such as Medicare, Medicaid, and HMOs are often based on estimates. In most cases, these payments are subject to adjustment either during the contract term or afterward, when the actual level of services provided under the contract is known. Oftentimes, final settlements are determined after the close of the fiscal period to which they apply. Such settlements have the potential to materially affect the health care entity's financial position and results of operations. The health care entity must make its best estimate of these adjustments on a current basis, and reflect these amounts in the Statement of Operations. To the extent that the subsequent actual adjustment is more or less than the estimate, such amounts should be reflected in the Statement of Operations for the period in which the final adjustment becomes known; it is not appropriate to reflect such amounts as prior period adjustments.

(f) Agency Funds

Health care entities may act as agents for other parties; as such, they receive and hold assets that are owned by others. In accepting responsibility for these assets, the entity incurs a liability to the owner either to return them in the future or to disburse them as instructed by the owner. Transactions involving agency funds should not have any economic impact on the provider's operations. Consequently, they should not be included in the provider's Statement of Operations.

(g)   Investments

Investments of health care entities are initially recorded at acquisition cost or, if received as a donation or gift, at fair market value at the date of the gift. The investments should subsequently be reported in financial statements as follows:

- *Marketable Equity Securities.* These investments are reported at the lower of aggregate cost or market value in accordance with the requirements of SFAS No. 12, *Accounting for Certain Marketable Equity Securities.*[2] Any writedown from cost to market is a function of both the type of fund that is carrying the securities (i.e., restricted or unrestricted) and the classification of the investment as current or noncurrent. The write-down on unrestricted investments classified as current assets is reflected in the Statement of Operations. The write-down on unrestricted investments classified as noncurrent assets, and the write-down on all restricted investments, are reflected in the Statement of Changes in Net Assets.

- *Debt Securities.* These investments are reported at amortized cost if there is the intent and ability to hold to maturity. If they are not intended to be held to maturity, they should be carried at the lower of cost or market. If the market value of the securities is less than their cost, and the impairment in value is not considered to be temporary, the carrying amount should not exceed market value.

- *Unconsolidated Affiliates.* Investments in unconsolidated affiliates (such as joint ventures) are accounted for in accordance with APB Opinion No. 18.

- *Other Securities.* Other types of investments not addressed above (such as real estate or oil and gas interests) should be reported at the lower of amortized cost or a reduced amount if an impairment in their value is deemed to be other than temporary.

    Not-for-profit health care entities may pool resources of various funds for investment purposes, or invest some resources separately and pool other resources. When investment funds are

---

[2] SFAS 12 was superseded by the issuance of SFAS 115 in 1993; however, not-for-profit organizations are explicitly excluded from the scope of SFAS 115.

pooled, the market value method is used to equitably allocate investment income and gains and losses on pooled investments.

In certain cases, donors and grantors may impose restrictions on investment practices and may require separate accounting for principal and income transactions.

- *Investment Income.* All unrestricted investment income should be reported in the Statement of Operations in the period in which it is earned. Investment income earned which is restricted should be reported in the Statement of Net Assets in the period in which it is earned.

(h) Property and Equipment

If health care providers were ranked along a continuum of capital-intensity, we would see a wide variation among the different types of providers. Some types of providers generally have little investment in capital assets, for example, physicians or home health companies. Others, such as acute-care hospitals, are extremely capital-intensive.

Property and equipment should be recorded at cost, or at fair market value if donated. Where historical cost records are not available, an appraisal at "historical cost" should be made and the amounts recorded in the provider's books.

Depreciation should be recognized by all health care entities, in accordance with both the Guide and with SFAS No. 93. The amount of depreciation expense should be shown separately (or combined with amortization of leased assets) in the Statement of Operations. The Guide states that the American Hospital Association's "Estimated Useful Life" guidelines may be helpful in determining the estimated useful lives of fixed assets of health care providers.

Property that is not used for general operations (such as real estate held for future expansion or investment purposes) should be presented separately from property used in general operations.

(i) Contributions

As stated earlier, the proposed new health care audit guide would "scope out" (e.g., exclude) health care providers that receive material amounts of contributions from the general public and would instead require those organizations to follow the financial reporting requirements applicable to voluntary health and welfare organizations. Providers remaining under the scope of the guide would not be those that receive material amounts of contributions. Such providers that need guidance on accounting for and reporting contributions (including donated services and promises to give in future periods) they do receive should consult Chapters 10 and 14.

SFAS No. 116 promulgated a significant change in the way that not-for-profit providers will recognize "capital" contributions, that is, donations received or pledged toward upgrading or replacing the facility's land, buildings, and equipment. In the past, gifts or grants that are restricted for construction or renovation projects; property or equipment purchases; or for capital debt retirement were added to restricted net assets (formerly fund balance) when the assets are received and reclassified to the unrestricted (general) fund balance when placed in service. Under SFAS No. 116, such contributions must instead be reported as income. The proposed new guide would require health care providers to report such contributions *below the operating indicator* in the Statement of Operations. Furthermore, the proposed guide would require providers to recognize the expiration of donor-restrictions at the time the asset was placed in service. This is a narrowing of the options available to other types of not-for-profit organizations under SFAS No. 117.

(j) Malpractice Contingencies

The Guide states that the ultimate costs of malpractice claims should be accrued when the incidents occur that give rise to the claims, if certain criteria are met. These criteria include a determination that a liability has been incurred and an ability to make a reasonable estimate of the amount of the loss. In particular, the Guide indicates clearly that health care providers that have not transferred to a third party all risk for medical malpractice claims arising out of occurrences prior to the financial statement date will probably be required to make an accrual. The Guide provides guidance in accounting for uninsured asserted and unasserted medical malpractice claims, claims insured by captive insurance companies, claims insured under retrospectively-rated or claims-made insurance policies, and claims paid from self-insurance trust funds.

(k) Related Organizations

Many health care entities are independently owned or operated. However, a growing number of not-for-profit health care entities have restructured in order to protect assets, provide themselves with increased access to capital, and gain new sources of revenue to offset dwindling third-party reimbursement. In anticipation of health care reform, many not-for-profit entities are becoming part of integrated delivery systems, merging both horizontally (that is, with like-kind entities) and vertically (that is, becoming part of a continuum-of-care).

Frequently, not-for-profit health care entities will create separate "foundations" to raise and hold funds for their benefit. The primary motivation of setting up these separate organizations has been to insure that third-party payers could not insist that unrestricted gifts be used to offset hospital costs in determining third-party settlement amounts. Although many health care providers would prefer not to include (or even disclose) the assets of the foundation in their financial statements due to concerns that this would defeat the purpose of setting up the separate foundation, this view ignores the facts of the situation—that is, that the separate foundation exists to benefit the provider and represents a resource available to it. Further, most donors will not even be aware of the separate existence of the foundation and therefore may very well be misled by the hospital's financial statements if they do not disclose information pertaining to the related foundation.[3]

The Guide provides guidance in determining the circumstances in which not-for-profit organizations should be considered to be "related" to a not-for-profit health care entity for financial statement purposes, and sets forth disclosure requirements concerning those organizations in the health care entity's financial statements. This guidance is helpful in determining whether or not the health care entity must combine its financial statements with those of related fund-raising foundations (or make disclosures of those relationships).

However, the guidance described above is of limited use in determining the appropriate financial statement presentation of other complex organization structures now being encountered (such as multiple not-for-profit organizations and taxable entities under not-for-profit parents). To remedy this situation, the FASB is working on a project that is expected to provide a concept of the reporting entity for not-for-profit organizations, but the timetable for its completion is undetermined. Until such guidance is available, not-for-profit health care entities should evaluate the economic substance of transactions among affiliated entities; apply their best judgment in interpreting the applicability of existing GAAP to determine the financial statement presentation that would be most relevant to statement users; and clearly disclose the method of presentation selected along with extensive disclosures of entities not consolidated, combined, or shown as an investment using the equity method.

---

[3] When separate financial statements are required to be issued for the foundation only, the proposed new guide would require that those statements be prepared based on principles contained in the AICPA audit and accounting guide *Audits of Not-for-Profit Organizations*. When the foundation financial statements are consolidated or combined with a health care business enterprise or integrated delivery system, the reporting principles of the controlling entity should apply.

(l) Timing Differences

For Medicare cost-reporting purposes, certain items are accounted for in different periods than they are reported in for financial reporting purposes. The "timing differences" that arise from these items are recognized in the periods in which the differences arise and the periods in which they reverse. Common examples involve deferred compensation arrangements, use of different depreciation methods for financial reporting and cost reporting purposes, malpractice expense, and reporting of gains or losses on debt extinguishments.

Changes in Medicare regulations may cause some of these timing differences to become permanent. In such cases, the Guide states that the effect should be recorded in the period when it's determined they won't be recovered or realized. However, the Guide does not state whether the effect should be included in operations or classified as an extraordinary item in the financial statements.

Timing differences may exist for other types of third-party payers as well. The provisions discussed above would be applicable to those types of timing differences as well as Medicare timing differences.

C H A P T E R 17

Accounting Standards for Other Not-for-Profit Organizations

In 1978, the American Institute of Certified Public Accountants (AICPA) issued a Statement of Position (SOP No. 78-10), "Accounting Principles and Reporting Practices for Certain Nonprofit Organizations," applicable to all not-for-profit organizations that are not covered by one of the three previously issued Industry Audit Guides discussed or referred to in the three preceding chapters. This Statement of Position was addressed to the Financial Accounting Standards Board (FASB). As discussed more fully in Chapter 19, only the FASB presently has authority to issue accounting principles that are binding on organizations wishing to describe their financial statements as being in accordance with "generally accepted accounting principles." However, the AICPA can issue a Statement of Position which, in the absence of FASB standards to the contrary, represents the most authoritative pronouncement of the accounting profession on a given subject. Thus the Statement of Position has much the same authority as the Industry Audit Guides previously discussed.[1]

The Statement of Position did not contain an effective date. It acknowledged that the FASB was at that time developing a conceptual framework policy statement applicable to all nonbusiness entities (see Chapter 19) and was cognizant that differences, if any, between the principles outlined in the Statement of Position and those in the completed conceptual framework policy statement would have to be eliminated. In the interim, however, the Statement of Position represents the most authoritative literature concerning these other types of not-for-profit organizations.[2]

The Statement of Position (SOP) is applicable to all not-for-profit organizations not covered by one of the three Audit Guides other than governmental units and such business-oriented entities as mutual savings banks, insurance companies, and employee benefit plans. Included in

---

[1] This SOP has since been reissued as part of the Audit Guide, *Audits of Certain Nonprofit Organizations.*
[2] See Chapter 19 for a discussion of the rule-making procedures in the accounting profession and the level of authority inherent in a SOP.

the many categories of organizations for which this SOP is applicable are cemetery organizations, civic organizations, fraternal organizations, labor unions, libraries, museums, other cultural institutions, performing arts organizations, political parties, private elementary and secondary schools, private and community foundations, professional associations, public broadcasting stations, religious organizations, research and scientific organizations, social and country clubs, trade associations, and zoological and botanical societies.

Use of the accounting principles and reporting practices discussed in the SOP is required only for organizations that want to describe their financial statements as being prepared in accordance with "generally accepted accounting principles."[3] For many smaller organizations, adoption of some of the recommended accounting principles may be neither practical nor economical.

Unlike the earlier Industry Audit Guides, this SOP deals primarily with underlying accounting principles, leaving financial statement format largely up to each organization to develop as best suits its needs. In fact, over 70 pages of illustrative financial statements are presented in the SOP to document the wide differences in format that are possible. This is not to suggest that complete freedom has been granted in terms of statement format; in some instances, the accounting principles prescribed effectively dictate format.

Most of the accounting principles in the SOP are also discussed in the earlier Industry Audit Guides. In most instances, the principles are in agreement, but in some cases they are not and, as noted in Chapters 13 and 19, some of these differences have been reconciled by the issuance of SFAS No. 116 and No. 117; eventually the remaining differences will be reconciled by the new AICPA audit guide which will replace SOP 78-10.

Where the accounting principles discussed in this chapter have already been covered in earlier chapters, the treatment herein is abbreviated, and readers wanting further information should refer back to the earlier discussions. Also, since with the issuance of SFAS No. 117, there are no longer any differences between the financial statement format recommended for organizations covered by the AICPA voluntary health and welfare guide and those covered by the SOP, the discussion of this topic in Chapter 14 is not repeated here. Readers should refer to Chapters 13 and 14 for a general discussion of financial statement format, and to Chapter 18 for mention of a few areas where SOP organizations may wish to use a format peculiar to their needs.

---

[3] See page 420 for discussion of the concept of generally accepted accounting principles.

17.1   ACCOUNTING PRINCIPLES

(a)   Accrual Basis of Reporting

Probably the most far-reaching of the accounting principles addressed is the requirement that not-for-profit organizations report on the accrual basis of accounting. As noted in Chapter 3, this conflicts with the reporting practices of a large number of small and medium-sized nonprofit organizations, which presently use cash basis accounting for purposes of reporting.

This accrual basis requirement specifically applies to financial reporting and does not necessarily apply to internal *bookkeeping*. Many not-for-profit organizations find it more practical to keep their records on a cash basis throughout the period, and then prepare accrual basis financial statements through worksheet adjustments or formal journal entries.[4]

(b)   Fund Accounting

The Statement of Position indicates that the use of fund accounting (discussed in Chapter 4) for reporting purposes may be helpful, but is not required. Emphasis is on the clarity and usefulness of the information disclosed rather than on the use of fund accounting to disclose the information.

This subtle distinction cannot be overemphasized. As noted throughout this book, it is widely assumed that fund accounting is mandatory for not-for-profit organizations, and that the use of fund accounting for recordkeeping dictates the use of detailed multifund reporting formats. Unfortunately, financial statements prepared on the basis of fund accounting are confusing to most readers. The SOP has redirected emphasis from the form of disclosure to the appropriateness and clarity of the disclosure. While it reaffirms that financial statements utilizing traditional fund-by-fund disclosure may, in many instances, still be the most appropriate way to communicate certain information, it does not mandate the use of a fund accounting format.

SFAS No. 117, discussed in Chapter 13, continues this emphasis on clarity of reporting by focusing on the organization as a whole rather than the individual funds or classes.

---

[4] See Section 3.2.

(c) Unrestricted Gifts, Grants, and Bequests

Unrestricted gifts, grants, and bequests are to be recorded as income at the time received (see the section on "pledges" for a discussion of the timing of recording pledges, unrestricted gifts, and grants).

(d) Current Restricted Gifts

SFAS No. 116, discussed in Chapter 10, has changed the required method of reporting for organizations covered by SOP 78-10. After adoption of SFAS No. 116, all not-for-profit organizations will recognize all gifts, whether restricted or unrestricted, as revenue immediately upon receipt of the gift, or of an unconditional pledge.[5]

The SOP previously provided that current restricted gifts be recorded as deferred income on the Balance Sheet until the organization expended funds which met the restriction imposed by the donor. Only after expenditures had been made that met the terms of the restriction, would such gifts have been reflected as income in the Statement of Activity.

(e) Pledges (Unconditional Promises to Give)

Recorded as an Asset

Under SFAS No. 116, unconditional promises to give (usually called pledges) are to be recorded as an asset and reported at their estimated realizable value, that is, discounted to present value, and net of an appropriate allowance for estimated uncollectible amounts. This is consistent with SOP 78-10, except that the SOP does not discuss discounting to present value. Note that the requirement for recording pledges does not depend on the willingness or intention of the organization to actually take legal action to attempt to enforce an unpaid pledge. Few organizations would, in fact, ever take legal action. Rather, it is the ability to do so which mandates recording the pledge. Pledges to which unfulfilled conditions are attached could not be legally enforced until the conditions have been met, and should not be recorded until that time.

Those organizations wanting to avoid recording pledges can, therefore, include on their pledge card a condition which must be met, or an explicit statement to the effect that the pledgor can unilaterally withdraw the pledge at any time. As long as it is clear that the pledge is conditional

---

[5] See Chapter 10 for a complete discussion of current restricted gifts, including pledges.

upon some unfulfilled occurrence, or that the pledgor retains the right to cancel the pledge, the pledge would be unenforceable and therefore not recorded as an asset.

This treatment also applies to unrestricted grants by foundations and others, which are payable over several years. These subjects are discussed in more detail in Chapter 10.

Pledges Recorded as Income

Under SFAS No. 116, the timing of recording the pledge as income is now the same as for other types of gifts, discussed previously.

(f) Donated Services

The SOP was the first pronouncement that clearly indicated that donated services should be recorded if certain specified criteria were met. SFAS No. 116 establishes new, and somewhat different, criteria for recording of donated services, and prohibits recording services which do not meet its criteria. These criteria are discussed on pages 125–127.

(g) Donated Materials

Donated materials, if significant in amount, should be recorded at their fair value at the date of receipt. The one proviso is that the organization must have a reasonable basis for valuation. Where the organization receives materials that are difficult to value, then no amount should be recorded. Examples of items that would be difficult to value include used clothing, furniture, and similar items. However, if a value can be reasonably determined, donated materials should be recorded. If the materials are sold soon after receipt as in a thrift shop or bookstore, the sale price can be used as their value. Essentially the position taken is similar to the Industry Audit Guide for voluntary health and welfare organizations.

(h) Donated Facilities

Some not-for-profit organizations receive rent-free or reduced-rent offices, warehousing, and similar facilities. The fair value of such facilities should be recorded as a contribution and as an expense in the period utilized.

The value recorded should be based on the use actually being made of the facility. Accordingly, if a donor makes available high-cost office space, but the organization would normally rent low-cost office space, the organization should record as a contribution an amount representing the rent that the organization would pay if the donated facilities were not available. If the donation is in the form of reduced rent, only the excess of what the organization would normally pay over the reduced rent would be recorded.

Donated facilities should be recorded as income in the period the facilities are actually used. Accordingly, if a donor gives the organization a five-year, rent-free lease, under SOP 78-10 the value of the donated rent would be recorded in each of the five years as the facility is used. The new AICPA audit guide will require the organization to record the full five-year rental as income in the year in which the donor gave the five-year lease.

(i)   Investment Income

Unrestricted investment income is reported as income as earned. Unrestricted investment income includes income from endowment or other restricted funds where no restriction has been placed by the donor on the use to be made of the investment income.

For reporting purposes, some organizations may choose to segregate investment income from other types of income, which is acceptable provided it appears above the caption "Excess of revenue over expenses" (see the discussion on statement format below).

The reporting of *restricted investment income* depends on the nature of the donor's restriction. If the investment income is from investment of current restricted investments, or from endowment investments where the donor has specified that the income shall be used for a current restricted purpose, then such income would be recorded as revenue in the appropriate restricted fund, regardless of whether or not the restriction has yet been met. Once the restriction is met, the related temporarily restricted net asset amount is reclassified to unrestricted net assets on the Statement of Activity.

This treatment differs from that specified in SOP 78-10, which called for restricted investment income to be deferred until the restriction was met. The reason for this change is that the original treatment was designed to parallel that for current restricted contributions on the basis that restricted *income* from contributed restricted gifts was conceptually the same as the *gift* itself. With the change in the method of recording restricted gifts, mandated by SFAS No. 116 (discussed above), a similar change is appropriate for restricted investment income.

Where investment income arises from endowment funds containing a donor-imposed requirement that the income be accumulated as part of the endowment fund, such investment income would be reflected as income in the permanently restricted class of the Statement of Activity as discussed on page 211.

(j)   Gains and Losses

Realized gains and losses on investments would generally be treated in a manner similar to the treatment of investment income, discussed above, as far as the timing of revenue recognition.

Unrealized Losses on Investments Carried at the Lower of Cost or Market

Where investments in marketable securities are carried at the lower of cost or market, recognition must be given to unrealized losses when the total market value of all marketable securities in a fund group is less than cost. When this occurs, the write-down of investments classified as current assets would be reflected as charges in the Statement of Activity in the same manner as realized losses. However, if the write-down is of investments classified as noncurrent assets, the charge would be reflected in the "changes in net assets section" of the Statement of Activity as a direct reduction of net assets. This means unrealized losses from the noncurrent investments would be below the "excess" caption for the period. In future periods, if the aggregate market value increases, similar adjustments, reported in this same section of the statement, should be made to increase the carrying value back to original cost, but no higher.

Change in Method of Reporting Gains and Losses

SFAS No. 117, discussed in Chapter 13, now requires that all gains and losses on investments be reported in the unrestricted class of net assets, unless either of two exceptions applies. These exceptions are: if the donor of the assets explicitly stipulated that gains are to be restricted, or if applicable state law (in the state where the organization operates) requires that some portion (or all) of the gains be retained in the restricted fund. These are also discussed in Chapter 8. This will be a change for almost all organizations which have been following the practice of recording gains and losses in the same fund as that which holds the assets which gave rise to the gains or losses.

Investments at Market

As noted below, marketable investments may be reported at either the lower of cost or market (or amortized cost for certain marketable debt securities) or at market. If reported at market, no distinction is made between realized and unrealized gains. Rather, the amount of gain or loss reported each year will be equal to the change in carrying amount during the reporting period. As more fully discussed on page 91, it is not meaningful to separate the period's gains and losses into the realized and unrealized portions. Chapter 8 contains a full discussion of gains and losses of investments carried at market.

Nonmarketable investments such as real estate or mineral rights may continue to be reported at either the lower of cost or market or at market, and gains and losses would be handled in the same manner as discussed above.

Total Return Approach

SFAS No. 117, by requiring most gains to be reported directly in the unrestricted class, has made the total return approach obsolete for external financial reporting purposes, although it may still be used for internal financial management purposes. (See the discussion of this subject in Chapter 8.)

(k)   Membership and Subscription Income

Membership organizations receiving dues in advance of furnishing services to members should allocate the dues as revenue over the period of time in which the members will receive the services. This is a significant requirement. Until recognized as revenue, dues are reported as deferred revenue in the liability section of the balance sheet.

Observe that under this requirement, dues are recognized as income over the period to which they relate, but not necessarily on a pro rata basis. If the organization can show that the services being rendered are not performed ratably over time, another basis of income recognition can be used. For example, if an organization incurs substantial membership renewal costs, the portion of the membership dues applicable to these costs could be recorded currently with only the remainder deferred over the membership year.

Some membership organizations that have not previously deferred unearned dues will find as a result of this requirement that their net assets will drop into a deficit position. This is likely to happen where the organization has little working capital and spends its dues as soon as it receives them.

Some organizations use the term "membership" as a fund-raising device, and no real economic or other direct benefit accrues to the member by virtue of membership. Such "dues" should be treated as contribution income. Alternatively, if the membership dues are really a combination of dues and contribution, the payment should be appropriately allocated between these two categories. Appendix 17–A contains a checklist to help organizations distinguish between dues and contributions in practice.

Subscription income should be prorated over the period to which the subscription applies. Where there are significant costs of obtaining the subscription, or renewal, only the net subscription income need be prorated. [6]

Life Membership and Initiation Fees

Some organizations offer life memberships which represent a prepayment of dues. These life membership dues should also be recognized as income in the periods during which the member will receive services. If the number of life memberships is significant, the amortization would probably be based on the collective life expectancy of the members.

Initiation fees that are not in fact a prepayment for services to be rendered in the future and that are not refundable should be reflected as income in the period in which the fees are payable. If the entire initiation fee is payable at the time a member joins, the entire fee would be recorded at that time. Some organizations provide for the payment of the initiation fee over a several-year period, in which case the fee should be recognized as it becomes due, that is, it should be spread over the several-year period corresponding to the payment schedule. The theory behind this deferral is that very few membership organizations will collect unpaid initiation fees if the member withdraws before the due date of the second or subsequent installments.

Where the initiation fee is a prepayment for services to be rendered in the future, the fee should be amortized over the period in which the services are to be rendered. In some instances, an initiation fee is charged and, in addition, a fee will be assessed in future years to cover all or part of the cost of the services to be rendered. Where the future year's fee can reasonably be expected to cover the cost of such future year's services, then the initiation fee should be reflected as income currently; otherwise all or part of the initiation fee should be amortized as appropriate.

(l) Grants to Others

Some not-for-profit organizations such as foundations make grants to other organizations. Grantor organizations should record both as a

---

[6] However, at a minimum, the deferred amount should at least equal the cost of fulfilling the subscription obligation. If the subscription is sold at a price insufficient to pay all costs, the subscription income which is deferred should be sufficient to cover the future period costs of fulfilling the subscription. The effect in this latter case will be to record a loss on subscriptions in the current period.

liability and as an expense the amount of grants awarded at the time the grantee is "entitled" to the grant. Normally this is either at the time the board of trustees approves a specific grant or at the time the grantee is notified that it has been awarded the grant. This method of accounting for grants made was first set forth in SOP 78-10, and later reaffirmed in SFAS No. 116.

Some grants provide for payment over several years. Where the grantee will routinely receive such payments without the necessity of more than a cursory subsequent review by the grantor, the full amount of the grant, including the amounts payable in future years, should be recorded at the time of the initial award. If, instead, the grantor indicates that the future payments are contingent upon an extensive review and formal decision process by the grantor prior to making payment, subsequent payments would not be recorded as a liability and expense until this subsequent decision process is completed. In these circumstances, each subsequent payment would effectively be treated as a new grant. (See pages 331–334 for a further discussion.)

It should be observed that under SOP 78-10, the accounting treatment by the grantor making a restricted grant was different from that of the grantee receiving the grant. In the case of the grantor, the grant was treated as an expense at the time the award is made, while from the grantee's standpoint the grant was recorded as deferred income until the restrictions were met. This inconsistency was removed by SFAS No. 116 which required the same treatment (i.e., immediate recognition as revenue or expense, as appropriate) by both the donor and donee of a gift or grant.

(m)   Reported Valuation of Investments

Marketable securities may be reported at either the lower of cost or market (or amortized cost for certain marketable debt securities) or at market. Marketable securities include both stocks and bonds. Whichever election is made for stocks, this same basis must be used for all stocks of the organization, and similarly for bonds.

Other types of investments which are not readily marketable, such as oil and gas interests and real property, may also be reported at either the lower of cost or market or at market, but the basis selected does not have to be the same basis as that selected for marketable securities.

(n)   Fixed Assets

Consistent with all three Industry Audit Guides, the SOP provides that fixed assets must be capitalized. However, it recognizes the implementation problem for organizations that have previously been writing off their fixed assets as expenses. It provides that if historical cost records are not reasonably available at the time of initial implementation, other bases may be used such as a cost-based appraisal, replacement costs, property tax assessments, and so forth.

The SOP discusses the desirability of reporting a value for museum and similar collections, but concludes that this is not required because it is often not practical to do so. Museums are nonetheless encouraged to value their collections if circumstances permit. SFAS No. 116 continues this treatment, if certain conditions are met. (This is discussed further in Chapter 18.)

(o)   Depreciation Accounting

The SOP requires the use of depreciation accounting techniques, except for inexhaustible assets such as collections, landmarks, cathedrals, and houses of worship. The exception for houses of worship was removed, effective in 1990, by FASB Statement No. 93. Refer to Chapter 7 for a complete discussion of the arguments for depreciation accounting.

(p)   Life Income and Annuity Funds

The present value of the liability arising from life income and annuity gift contracts should be recorded as a liability at the time the gift is received. The excess of the gift over such liability is then recognized as income, also at the time the gift is received. Normally there would be no excess for life income funds since by definition the donor receives the income generated by the gift. Accounting for these types of gifts is not discussed very much in either SOP 78-10 or in SFAS No. 116. A somewhat more extensive discussion is in the AICPA college audit guide, discussed in Chapter 15. Additional guidance will be included in the new AICPA audit guide, discussed in Chapter 19.

17.2   FINANCIAL STATEMENTS

With the issuance of SFAS No. 117, discussed in Chapter 13, many of the requirements of SOP 78-10 relating to financial statement content and format have been superseded. Accordingly, only a limited discussion of these matters is retained in this chapter. Also, rather than repeat the more extensive discussion and illustrations of financial statements in Chapter 14 (on voluntary health and welfare organizations), readers are referred to that chapter, as the requirements for those organizations are now essentially the same as for SOP 78-10 organizations.

(a) Required Financial Statements

Three financial statements were identified in the SOP as usually required: Balance Sheet, Statement of Activity, Statement of Changes in Financial Position. Under SFAS No. 117, the Statement of Changes in Financial Position has now been superseded by the Statement of Cash Flows.

Both SFAS No. 117 and the SOP make clear that what is required is the disclosure of certain information, and not the specific format of the financial statements. Each organization is encouraged to develop a format suitable to its needs. The key is disclosure, not format.

(b) Balance Sheet

Both SFAS No. 117 and the SOP state that a Balance Sheet in which all assets and liabilities are commingled is acceptable provided the net assets (formerly fund balance) section clearly discloses amounts of unrestricted and restricted net assets. Exhibit 14–1 shows an example of such a Balance Sheet.

Interfund Borrowings

A significant interfund borrowing that is intended to be repaid must be disclosed even where the reporting is on a combined or consolidated basis. This can be done either on the face of the Balance Sheet or in the footnotes thereto. However, "borrowing" where there is no intention to repay or where the borrowing fund is unlikely to have the financial ability to repay is in effect an interfund transfer and should be reported as a reclassification.

(c) Statement of Activity

"Statement of Activity" is the name given in the Statement of Position to a statement that shows all of the organization's financial activity from the beginning to the end of the year. The title of the statement could be any one of a number of different names, including "Statement of Revenue, Expenses, and Changes in Net Assets," "Statement of Changes in Net Assets," "Statement of Revenue, Expenses, Capital Additions, and Changes in Net Assets," or "Statement of Income and Expenses." The title is not particularly important so long as the statement shows all relevant activity.

The Statement of Activity could be broken into two sections, and each treated as a separate statement; that is, a section showing revenue, expenses, and nonexpendable additions, and a section showing changes in net assets. However, there seems little purpose in creating a separate Statement of Changes in Net Assets since the only types of transactions normally shown in the "changes in net assets" section of the Statement of Activity are the addition of the excess for the year and certain reclassifications.[7] Most organizations will prepare a single all-inclusive Statement of Activity.

Required Disclosures

The SOP requires that a number of specific disclosures be made in the Statement of Activity:

1. The amount of unrestricted revenue by major category.
2. The amount of unrestricted support by major source.
3. The amount of current restricted revenue and support by major source.
4. The amount of gifts and other income restricted for nonexpendable purposes.
5. The excess of revenue and support over expenses.
6. The excess of revenue, support, and nonexpendable additions over expenses.

Note that there is no requirement that the aggregate of unrestricted support and unrestricted revenue be shown. Under SFAS No. 117, all of these items will be shown, except that there is no requirement to show "nonexpendable additions" and the excess before that amount, separately.

Exhibit 14–2 is an example of a Statement of Activity that illustrates the required disclosures.

(d)   Nonexpendable Additions

The SOP distinguished between support for current operations and support not intended directly for operations. It provided different reporting treatments for each category. SFAS No. 117 does not discuss this concept. Rather it distinguishes between "revenues and expenses" and "gains and losses," and requires separate reporting of each. The distinction between revenues and gains is not the same as between expendable and nonexpendable additions. SFAS No. 117 would not prohibit reporting

---

[7] Unrealized losses on noncurrent investments which are carried at the lower of cost or market would also be reflected as a change in the "Change in net assets" section. See the discussion above on unrealized losses on investments carried at the lower of cost or market.

nonexpendable additions separately if an organization wishes, as long as the other requirements of SFAS No. 117 were met. Only donor-restricted amounts can be considered nonexpendable, so all such items will be reported in one of the two restricted classes of net assets, never in the unrestricted class.

Nonexpendable additions—also referred to as capital additions—are defined in SOP 78-10 as gifts and other income restricted for purposes other than current activities. The two most common types of nonexpendable additions are gifts for endowment and gifts for purchase of fixed assets. Neither type is available directly for current activities. The SOP provides that these nonexpendable gifts be reported separately from expendable gifts, and shown after the "Excess of revenue and support over expenses" caption.

The Statement of Position requires that nonexpendable additions be segregated from other sources of support because the transactions resemble capital transactions; that is, they are similar to capital stock transactions in a commercial entity. In the past, some have advocated showing nonexpendable additions as direct additions to net assets to distinguish between the two-types of transactions. Others have taken the position that such gifts increase the net worth of the organization and should be reflected as income along with other sources of current support. The approach taken in this SOP was a compromise between these two extremes. The additions are shown before the final excess for the year, but after the excess from current activities.

Two Excess Captions

One unusual provision of the SOP is that the organization show the excess of revenue and support over expenses before and after nonexpendable additions. While at first this may seem awkward, both captions—the Excess from current activities, and the Excess from all activities of the organization—provide useful information for the reader. Since SFAS No. 117 does not include this requirement, it would now be considered mandatory only if the organization chooses to distinguish between expendable and nonexpendable additions in its Statement of Activity.

(e) Reclassifications (Transfers between Funds)

In the SOP, transfers between funds are illustrated after the "Fund balances, beginning of the period" caption in the Statement of Activity. It was not acceptable to reflect a transfer between funds above this line, either before or immediately after the second "excess" caption. Thus it was not acceptable to report a transfer after the caption "Excess of income and nonexpendable additions over expenses," but before the caption "Fund balances, beginning of the period."

Under SFAS No. 117, all reclassifications must be shown above the caption "Change in net assets." Some reclassifications are shown in or near the revenue section. Other items which would formerly have been reported as interfund transfers will no longer be shown at all, since the two funds involved in the transfer will now be included in a single class of net assets for reporting purposes. There will, however, still be a few reclassifications not related to revenue which will be reported after revenue and expenses, such as unrestricted amounts used as the matching portion of a restricted challenge grant. These reclassifications should be presented immediately above the "Change in Net Assets" caption, preceded by a subtotal called "Excess or revenue over expenses" or something similar. This is shown in the sample Statement of Activity in Chapter 13.

(f) Expenses

The general rules for reporting expenses were discussed in Chapter 14. Normally fund-raising costs must be reported as expenses in the period incurred. The SOP discussed one very limited circumstance when fund-raising expenses could be deferred. If a donor had made a gift or pledge which was not reflected as income in the current period but was recorded as deferred income, *and* if the donor had specifically indicated that the contribution could be used for paying the fund-raising costs of obtaining the gift, then identifiable expenses associated with the gift could be deferred. Since SFAS No. 116 no longer allows the deferral of restricted gifts, this provision for dealing with related fund-raising expenses is now obsolete and cannot be followed.

If fund raising is combined with a program function, such as educational literature which also solicits funds, the total cost should be allocated between the program and fund-raising functions on the basis of the use made of the literature, as determined from its content, reason for distribution, and audience, if the criteria of SOP No. 87-2 (discussed in Chapter 14) are met.

Membership Development Costs

Membership organizations that incur significant expense obtaining new members and renewing existing memberships should report these costs as a separate category of support service, with a caption such as "Membership development expenses."

This category is only for bona fide memberships and is not applicable for memberships which are in reality contributions (see the discussion of this topic above at page 305). Members must be receiving services commensurate with their dues. It is possible for membership dues to represent both a fee for services and a contribution. If so, membership development costs should be allocated between the fund-raising and membership development categories.

(g) Statement of Cash Flows (Formerly Changes in Financial Position)

In 1978, the SOP added a requirement for organizations covered by it to prepare a Statement of Changes in Financial Position. SFAS No. 117 changed this into a requirement to present a Statement of Cash Flows (Exhibit 14–3). Full discussion of preparation of this statement is in Chapter 14 and in FASB Statement of Financial Accounting Standards No. 95.

17.3 COMBINED FINANCIAL STATEMENTS

The new SOP No. 94-3 discusses when it is appropriate to prepare combined (or consolidated) financial statements; the question of combined financial statements arises when the reporting organization is affiliated or has a close working relationship with other organizations. There are many types of affiliations between not-for-profit organizations, and the question of whether it is appropriate or necessary to present combined financial statements of legally separate organizations is a difficult one. A full discussion of the current status of this subject is in Chapter 9.

(a) Religious Exemption

A difficult question which the AICPA had to wrestle with is the question of combination of financially interrelated religious organizations. There are many complex and unique relationships among religious organizations, and after trying for almost two years to write words which made no specific reference to religious organizations, but which would clearly exempt them, the AICPA put in SOP 78-10 the following statement (par. 48):

> In view of the unique and complex organizational relationships and degrees of local autonomy common in religious organizations, there may be many circumstances in which application of this section on combination would not result in meaningful financial information. Thus, if a

religious organization concludes that meaningful financial information would not result from the presentation of combined financial statements, the provisions of this section need not be applied.

This exception is not continued in the new accounting standard in SOP 94-3.

(b) Funds Held in Trust by Others

Some organizations are beneficiaries under trusts or other arrangements where the organization itself doesn't have direct control over the assets. The SOP indicates that under these circumstances the assets should not be combined with those of the organization. The key is control. If the organization has no ability to control the investment of the assets, the timing of income distribution, and the like, the combination of assets is not appropriate. This topic also will be the subject of further AICPA and FASB guidance.

APPENDIX 17–A   CHECKLIST

Factors to Be Considered in Deciding Whether a Payment Described as Membership Dues Is Properly Recorded by the Recipient as Dues or as a Contribution

Following is a list of factors which may be helpful to:

- Organizations, in deciding how to record "dues" receipts;
- Auditors, in assessing the appropriateness of the client's decision.

No one of these factors is normally determinative by itself; all applicable factors should be considered together. Additional discussion of this distinction can be found in the instructions to IRS Form 990, line 3; and in IRS Regulation 1.509(a)-3(h).

Note: If the payment genuinely contains elements of both membership dues *and* contributions, it may be appropriate to allocate the payment between the two items, based on the relative proportions of each which are present. For example, a payment of $100 which meets enough criteria to be considered a genuine dues payment, except that the value of the benefits received by the member is only $65, might be recorded as dues of $65, and a $35 contribution.

Factors Whose Presence Would Indicate the Payment Should Be Recorded as Membership Dues	Factors Whose Presence Would Indicate the Payment Should Be Recorded as a Contribution
Status and operation of the organization:	
1. The organization is tax-exempt under IRC Sec. 501(c)(5–8, or 10).[1]	The organization is exempt under IRC Sec. 501(c)(3).[1]
2. The stated purposes of the organization (as set forth in its IRS Form 1023 and/or 990, annual report, etc.) are mainly to serve members' personal, social, or economic ends.	The stated purposes are mainly to serve public welfare purposes.
3. A "member" must meet specific criteria[2] to be permitted to join the organization.	Factor not present.

Factors Whose Presence Would Indicate the Payment Should Be Recorded as Membership Dues	Factors Whose Presence Would Indicate the Payment Should Be Recorded as a Contribution

Characteristics of the solicitation:

4. The solicitation refers specifically to membership dues.

The solicitation refers specifically to contributions, gifts, etc.

5. Factor not present.

The payment is described as an amount in addition to a basic dues payment, but there is no significant increase in the benefits available to the member.

6. The solicitation describes the use of the proceeds as to provide benefits to the member, or to other persons or organizations related to the member.

The solicitation describes the use of the proceeds as being for broad social, public, etc. purposes.

7. The payment is (partly) refundable in case of the member's withdrawal from membership.

The payment is not refundable to the payor.

Benefits to "members":

8. Benefits vary with differing levels of payment.

Factor not present.

9. Benefits, whose values are objectively measurable,[3] have value approximately commensurate with the amount of the payment. (See also the Note above.)

Benefits to the payor (or related parties) are negligible or not objectively measurable.

10. The payment confers benefits for a defined period, after which benefits cease unless another payment is made.

Although the payment may be stated as covering a certain period, benefits do not necessarily cease at the end of the period.

11. Benefits are directly related to matters which are central concerns of members' daily activities; e.g. one's employment or profession, place of residence, organized social and recreational activities, hobbies, religious practices, political views, etc.

Benefits are peripheral or unrelated to the central concerns of daily life.

12. The organization operates a facility, such as a clubhouse, regularly used by members.

Factor not present.

Factors Whose Presence Would Indicate the Payment Should Be Recorded as Membership Dues	Factors Whose Presence Would Indicate the Payment Should Be Recorded as a Contribution
13. Membership in this organization is a prerequisite to receiving benefits from other entities (e.g., a lawyer must join a bar association before being licensed by the government to practice law.)	Factor not present.

[1] Having tax exemption under Sec. 501(c)(4) is not considered as a factor particularly indicative of either treatment.

[2] Types of membership criteria often found include:

- Age;
- Present or former place of ownership of property, of residence, or of employment;
- Professional qualifications (such as having certain levels of formal education, having passed an examination, having certain amounts and/or types of work experience, possessing a professional license);
- Having attended or graduated from a particular educational institution;
- Having demonstrated certain academic, athletic, or other abilities;
- Having been subjected to a formal initiation ritual (as with fraternities, sororities, and similar organizations);
- Professing formal allegiance to certain religious, political, or similar beliefs;
- Having been formally approved by a membership committee or similar body (whether or not criteria similar to these are a factor in the approval process).

[3] Examples of objectively measurable benefits include:

- Receipt of magazines and other forms of communication with a significant amount of genuinely educational content;
- The right to participate in substantive organized gatherings, open only to members, or available to members at a reduced fee, such as educational conferences, social activities, worship services, performances, etc.;
- The right to purchase substantive goods or services from the organization, available only to members, or at a discount from the "non-member" price;
- The right to use certain facilities such as those devoted to social or athletic purposes;
- The right to receive (with or without additional payments) measurable benefits from other entities by virtue of being a member of the organization;
- The right to enter formal competitions for prizes awarded by the organization.

Examples of "benefits" which are not normally considered objectively measurable include:

- The right to vote for officers, or in other elections, or to hold office;
- The right to attend gatherings which are denoted as "membership meetings" but at which no substantive matters are decided by those present;
- Receipt of publications of little or no educational value;
- The privilege of listing one's membership in the organization on one's resume;
- The privilege of wearing or otherwise displaying the organization's insignia;
- Having one's name appear in a roster of the organization's members;
- The possibility of receiving non-competitive prizes or awards made only to members;
- Feelings of satisfaction from supporting a cause, or of enjoyment from associating with certain people or participating in informal social or recreational activities.

C H A P T E R 18

Special Accounting Problems of Specific Organizations

In the preceding chapter we discussed the SOP 78-10 issued by the AICPA in 1978 for not-for-profit organizations not covered by one of the three AICPA Industry Audit Guides discussed in Chapters 14 through 16. This chapter discusses some of the specialized accounting and reporting problems of specific types of organizations covered by this SOP. It identifies the unique accounting problems of these organizations and gives the authors' views on how the SOP applies. It also points out where the new Statements of Financial Accounting Standards (SFAS), Nos. 116 and 117, will particularly affect these types of organizations.

The chapter does not attempt to examine in detail subjects covered earlier in the text. Accordingly, readers should use this chapter primarily as a reference to subjects that are more fully discussed in earlier chapters.

18.1 ASSOCIATIONS AND PROFESSIONAL SOCIETIES

Associations and professional societies are membership organizations that have been formed for other than a religious or social purpose. They include trade associations, engineering and academic societies, business leagues, and the like. Dues or other fees charged to the membership, revenue from trade shows, and subscriptions to publications of the organization are the main sources of revenue for these organizations.

(a) Reporting on a Functional Basis

Associations and professional societies can exist only so long as their membership is convinced that the services being rendered justify the dues and other payments being made. The members must see a benefit for their money. This means an association has a real need to communicate with its members. Functional reporting is one of the most effective ways of communicating since it requires the board to identify the association's programs and then to report the cost of each of these programs.

While the SOP encourages associations to use functional reporting, but does not require it, SFAS No. 117 requires functional reporting. Although SFAS No. 117 permits the detail of expenses by function to be reported in a footnote (with the primary financial statement showing expenses by natural classification), the authors urge all not-for-profit organizations to present the functional expenses in the primary financial statement where they will be more readily noticed by readers. Information by natural classification (salaries, rent, travel, etc.) can be shown in a footnote if desired.

(b)   Reporting of Sections or Groups

Many national and regional professional societies establish separate sections, groups, chapters, or other form of local units which operate within certain geographical regions or within certain disciplines. These units often operate more or less autonomously, although they are legally part of the main organization. The board of directors of the main organization usually has final legal responsibility for both their activities and their financial affairs. The question often is asked: Should the financial affairs of these sections and groups be reported on a combined basis with those of the main organization? Generally such combination would *not* be required. The general subject of combination of affiliated organizations and SOP 94-3 are discussed in Chapter 9.

The most typical situation for associations and professional societies is when the section or group receives part of its funds from the national organization as a dues rebate and part from local assessments and fees for local events. Alternatively, the local organization may collect and process members' entire dues payments, and remit a portion up to the national organization. While technically the board of the national organization may have final legal responsibility with respect to this local section, the financial interrelationship is usually not analogous to that contemplated in SOP 94-3 as warranting consolidated financial statements. Accordingly, combination is not normally required.

Some organizations are structured so that all of the activities of the local organization are financed entirely by the national organization, and on the surface it might appear that the financial interrelationship is such that combination is appropriate. Here is where the element of control becomes critical. If the local section is totally under control of the national organization, with its activities totally dependent on specific direction from the national organization, *and* if the activities being performed are a delegated function of the national organization, then—and only then— would combination be required.

Before combination is required, therefore, the national organization must control and provide support to the local unit, and the local activities must be the responsibility of the national organization. Most local sections have their own boards, with considerable flexibility as to program activities and emphasis, and the authors would expect that in most cases combination would not be required.

Nevertheless, there are some advantages of preparing combined financial statements, at least for internal use. Many associations have substantial activity at the local level and a reader can see the total picture only by looking at combined statements.

The major problem with preparing combined financial statements relates to the cost and difficulties of getting the local units to prepare financial statements on a uniform and timely basis. But the association anxious to present a comprehensive view of its activities should consider combined financial statements. One way to do this is to present the combined statements as an exhibit to the primary statements that show only the parent organization.

(c) Use of Appropriation Accounting

For internal budgetary purposes, associations and professional societies often follow appropriation accounting techniques under which an expense is recorded at the time purchase orders are issued for goods or services to be received in future periods. This is not an acceptable method of accounting for external financial reporting purposes under the SOP.

Some associations and professional societies incorrectly use the term "appropriation" when they really mean "expense." The use of the term "appropriation" is easily misunderstood and should be avoided.

(d) Separate Charitable Organizations

Most associations are organized as noncharitable, tax-exempt organizations, usually under Section 501(c)(6) of the Internal Revenue Code.[1] As such, contributions received are not tax deductible by the donor (although dues may be deductible as a business expense). Often, an association will set up a second, separate "501(c)(3)" organization that is charitable in nature and can receive tax-deductible contributions. This charitable organization must then carefully conduct its affairs so that all of its activities are for purposes which qualify as charitable or educational. Usually, the boards of both organizations are substantially the same, and both organizations may occupy the same quarters (with appropriate inter-organization expense charges).

---

[1] See Chapter 26 for a discussion of federal tax aspects of not-for-profit organizations.

The reporting questions is: Should the financial statements of the two organizations be combined? The answer is almost always "yes" because the distinction between the two organizations is basically a legal and tax distinction, and effectively the combination of the two organizations is what most members think of when the association's name is mentioned. In fact, members will often be unaware that the second organization is a legally separate entity. Members have a right to see the total financial picture of both organizations.

There are two ways to present the financial affairs in such circumstances. The most common is to use columnar statements with a separate column for each organization, with a total or consolidated column. The other approach is to combine the two organizations and present only the combined figures disclosing the existence of the charitable organization in the footnotes. Either is acceptable, although the authors believe the second approach will usually provide adequate disclosure and be more readily understood.

(e)   Lobbying

Under the tax reform act of 1993, associations must comply with strict new rules surrounding their lobbying activities. These are discussed in detail in Chapter 26.

18.2   CHURCHES

In this section, we are discussing individual parishes, churches, or synagogues as distinct from religious organizations discussed later in this chapter. Virtually all revenue is typically received as contributions directly from the membership.

(a)   Cash Basis Accounting

Most churches keep their accounting records on a cash or modified cash basis of accounting, mainly for ease of record keeping. This is usually appropriate, at least for interim internal financial statement purposes. However, if there are any material amounts of unrecorded liabilities or assets at the end of the accounting period, these should be reflected on the financial statements. The key word is "material."

It is not suggested, for example, that uncollected dividends or interest on investments be recorded where such amounts are not in the aggregate significant. Perhaps the easiest way to determine whether accruals are needed is to ask whether the board might make different decisions about the governance or management of the organization if it saw financial statements in which all accruals were reported. If the answer is "yes," then they are material and should be recorded.

Many churches will continue to present cash basis reports, and there is no reason to change as long as the board recognizes the limitation of this type of reporting. If this is done, we recommend disclosing in a footnote the major items of unrecorded assets and liabilities at year end. At the same time, it is important to recognize that if the financial statements of the church are audited, the independent accountant will not be able to say that the financial statements have been prepared in accordance with generally accepted accounting principles if they are prepared on a cash basis (unless, in the accountant's view, unrecorded amounts are immaterial).

(b)   Fixed Assets and Depreciation

Fixed asset and depreciation accounting is a difficult area for churches because of the complexity of the bookkeeping. Most churches do not capitalize fixed assets and even fewer follow depreciation accounting practices. Nevertheless, the SOP makes clear that fixed assets should be recorded as assets, and SFAS No. 93 requires that depreciation accounting be followed. (The SOP originally permitted houses of worship not to be depreciated, but SFAS No. 93 removed that permission, and mandates depreciation of all depreciable assets.)

(c)   Adequacy of the Bookkeeping Staff

Another problem is that churches often have bookkeeping difficulties. Typically, the treasurer of a small church will be the person actually keeping the records. The quality of the record keeping and financial statements is directly related to that individual's competency and availability of time. Also, treasurers come and go and some are more skilled than others. Thus it is important that the system be kept simple or it is likely to fall apart at some time in the future.

18.3   CLUBS

Clubs include many types of organizations ranging from small social clubs that meet informally to much larger clubs that own buildings and property. Country clubs and city "luncheon" clubs are typical of this latter category. Chapter 31 illustrates accrual bookkeeping using a country club as an example.

(a)   Capital Shares and Initiation Fees

Most clubs charge a fee to new members—an initiation fee, or payment for capital shares, or sometimes a combination of the two. Should such amounts be treated as revenue and reported as part of the excess of revenue over expenses for the period? The answer depends on the nature of the payment.

Capital Shares

Clubs are normally the only type of not-for-profit organization which have capital shares representing members' equity in the organization. Normally clubs provide for redemption of capital shares upon termination of membership, or the right of direct transfer of ownership of the shares to others. Thus payment for capital shares is not revenue and should be reported as a direct addition to the net assets of the organization. This addition would be shown after a caption "Excess of revenue over expenses," and before the caption "Change in net assets." Because these payments are not *contributions* to the club, they cannot be shown in one of the restricted classes of net assets. Thus, by default, they must go in the unrestricted class, even though they are rather in the nature of additions to the capital of the club. The authors recommend that the amount of unrestricted net assets attributable to these capital receipts be shown as a separate component of unrestricted net assets on the balance sheet. In the statement of cash flows, these cash flows would be financing cash flows.

Initiation Fees

Initiation fees are nonrefundable charges which are usually considered more like a contribution and should be reported as revenue. Most clubs with significant turnover look upon initiation fees as additional, spendable income which should be reported as such. Initiation fees would be reported in the unrestricted class of net assets, unless, as is the practice with some clubs, initiation fees are explicitly understood by members to be restricted for capital acquisitions and improvements. In that case, the fees are considered temporarily restricted.

Alternatively, some argue that initiation fees are similar to capital stock payments which should be reported as a direct addition to net assets, like contributed capital. They argue that such fees represent the new member's share of equity.[2] The SOP indicates that initiation fees should be reported as revenue in the Statement of Activity. In this way, the reader sees all the "revenue" the club receives. Since initiation fees are not refundable, clearly such fees represent revenue to the club, albeit revenue of a different type than regular annual revenue from dues or sale of goods.

Some clubs provide for installment payment of initiation fees over a several-year period. The SOP indicates that a club should report initiation fees as the installment payments are due. It is not appropriate to record the entire initiation fee at the time the member joins the club since, in most instances, the club would not insist upon payment if the member resigns prior to the due date of the subsequent installments.

(b)   Fixed Asset Accounting

The SOP requires that clubs having buildings and other major fixed assets capitalize these assets and follow depreciation accounting practices. This is appropriate since clubs need to know the cost of particular services being rendered to insure that the pricing structure recovers all costs. Fixed assets wear out and depreciation represents the process of allocating the costs of the assets over their useful lives. To do otherwise is to leave the club management and membership with an inadequate understanding of the costs of providing particular services, with a possible need for a special assessment at the time new fixed assets are purchased. Further, if nonmembers are served by the club, with resulting "unrelated business income," depreciation is an expense which is deductible when arriving at taxable income.

(c)   Unrelated Business Income

Many clubs provide services not only to their membership but to guests of members, and in some instances to the public at large. If unrelated business income becomes sizable, it can jeopardize the club's tax-exempt status, as well as create taxable income (see Chapter 26). Accordingly, it is very important that clubs keep track of revenue from nonmembers and applicable expenses. This usually involves a fairly elaborate reporting and bookkeeping system, and most clubs are well advised to get competent advice from a CPA.

---

[2] This is the approach taken in *Uniform System of Accounts for Clubs,* published by Club Managers Association of America, 1967.

18.4   LIBRARIES

Libraries as contemplated are all not-for-profit, nongovernmental libraries. Libraries run by a government usually follow fund accounting principles common to government entities.

(a)   Recording a Value for Books

Although there is no explicit requirement one way or the other about library books being recorded as an asset on the financial statements, a
strong theoretical argument can be made that they should be recorded
and there is no objection to doing so. One way to simplify the recordkeeping process for library books is, rather than track the actual cost or fair
value of every individual book acquired, to use a standard amount as the
value of each volume. Then the only data needed is the number of volumes, which is always known.

When library books are recorded as an asset, depreciation accounting practices are normally appropriate since most books are dated. While
it is difficult to establish a composite life for all types of books, a three-to
ten-year life is not unreasonable. Depreciation practices should not be followed for a collection or rare books which is likely to maintain its value
over a considerable period of time. Rare books which increase in value
should continue to be recorded at the value on the original date of acquisition and not written up to a higher value.

18.5   MUSEUMS

Museums include all nongovernmental institutions which maintain a collection exhibited to the public, with or without an admission charge.
Some museums which do not collect a mandatory admission charge do
suggest that visitors make specified "contributions."

(a)   Valuing the Collection as an Asset

The most controversial question is whether it is meaningful and practical
to include on the balance sheet of a museum or similar organization (zoo,
arboretum, library, etc.) a value for its permanent collection. SOP 78-10
left such presentation optional. Practice varies; although most museums
do not include such an amount (or use a nominal amount such as one dollar), a significant minority do capitalize their collections or parts of them.

Those who favor such capitalization argue that the collection does
meet the definition of an asset (in FASB Concepts Statement 6), and there-

fore should be presented so as not to omit significant valuable resources from the financial statements.

Those who oppose capitalization, including many in the museum community, make several arguments:

- Any value reported subsequent to initial acquisition has no meaning due to wide fluctuations in the markets for such items and the difficulty of disposing of some types of collection items at all;
- It would be virtually impossible for a museum of any size to perform the appraisal work which would be required to establish an initial value for its collection, if not previously capitalized, (some museum collections number in the tens of millions of individual objects), nor to maintain the ongoing records which would result;
- Even if accurate values could be obtained, to include them on the balance sheet would be at best meaningless (because most collections cannot or would not ever be sold, nor do lenders look to collections as security for loans), or at worst detrimental (because financial statement readers would be diverted by the huge collection value from focusing on the real operating assets of the institution).

The FASB initially proposed to make capitalization mandatory, including retroactive capitalization of existing collections. Because this position met with so much opposition, SFAS No. 116 essentially continues the present optional capitalization standard for collection items which meet certain criteria. For those which do not capitalize, purchased acquisitions would be shown as decreases in net assets, and donated items would *not* be reported as either increases or decreases in net assets. Certain disclosures about the collection would be required.

(b) Fixed Asset Accounting

Except for collections, museums should capitalize and depreciate their fixed assets.

(c) Contributed Facilities

The SOP indicates that museums receiving rent-free (or reduced-rent) facilities should reflect the value of such facilities both as a contribution and as an expense. This will be applicable to museums that occupy city-owned buildings, except that in some cases where the building is itself virtually a work of art, it may not be possible to objectively determine a rental value. SFAS No. 116 has a similar requirement.

(d) Museum Accounting Manual

In 1976, the Association of Science-Technology Centers published *Museum Accounting Guidelines* for the use of museums in preparing financial statements. Individuals from many museum associations participated in this project and it has been widely recognized as the accounting manual which museums should be following. For the most part, this manual is in agreement with the SOP and SFAS No. 116. However, in some areas there are differences. Some of the major differences are outlined below:

1. *Museum Accounting Guidelines* provides that current restricted fund gifts be reported as income when available for expenditure, whereas the SOP provided that such gifts be deferred until the restrictions have been met. (As discussed earlier, SFAS No. 116 has changed this requirement to essentially the same as *Museum Accounting Guidelines.*)

2. *Museum Accounting Guidelines* provides that recording pledges is "preferable" whereas the SOP and SFAS No. 116 indicate that unconditional pledges *must* be recorded.

3. The SOP and SFAS No. 116 provide that contributed facilities be recorded, whereas *Museum Accounting Guidelines* does not require such recording.

4. *Museum Accounting Guidelines* discusses the total return concept of investment management but does not provide a clear prescription regarding its application. The SOP is very specific (however, as discussed in Chapter 8, this concept is no longer applicable to external financial statements, although it may still be used for internal recordkeeping).

5. *Museum Accounting Guidelines* does not require depreciation accounting whereas the SOP and SFAS No. 93 do (as discussed in Chapter 7).

6. The SOP provides that: "The nature and the cost or contributed value of current period accessions and the nature of and proceeds from deaccessions should be disclosed in the financial statements." There is no such requirement in *Museum Accounting Guidelines.* SFAS No. 116 requires disclosure of deaccessions and of purchased, but not donated, accessions.

7. The SOP provides for reporting nonexpendable additions separately from operating income. *Museum Accounting Guidelines* (and SFAS No. 117) do not discuss this subject.

8. *Museum Accounting Guidelines* requires all transfers between funds to be reported after the "Excess or deficit of revenue and support over expenses," whereas the SOP provides that transfers be reported after the "Fund balance, beginning of the year." SFAS No. 117 would require transfers to go above the "Change in Net Assets."

18.6 PERFORMING ARTS ORGANIZATIONS

Performing arts organizations include a wide variety of organizations: theatrical groups, ballet and opera companies, symphonies, and the like. In most instances, they rely on ticket sales as their primary source of revenue but are usually heavily dependent on public support as well. They range in size from all-volunteer companies to such professional groups as the Metropolitan Opera and the Los Angeles Philharmonic.

(a) Recognition of Expenses

A basic reporting problem for many performing arts organizations is the timing of expense recognition for particular productions that have not as yet been performed. Should a theatrical company which has incurred costs for the performance of a new play that will not be opening until the following period report such costs in the current period or should they be deferred until the following period? The general rule is that costs should be deferred so as to match the costs with revenues.

The annual reporting period for most performing arts organizations should conclude shortly after the close of the season, to minimize this kind of issue as well as a good number of bookkeeping problems.

(b) Recognition of Ticket Revenue

A related question is when to recognize ticket revenue—when the tickets are sold or on the date of the performance? Ticket revenue income should be recorded when earned, that is, on the date of the performance. This is particularly important for organizations having advance ticket sales for the following season.

The revenue from sales of "season" tickets and subscriptions should be prorated over the performances covered by the subscription. Sometimes ticket prices for special events such as "opening night" or "gala" performances will be higher than normal and include what is in effect an element of contribution. Since the contribution element must be disclosed separately to patrons (for tax-deduction purposes), the organization should record this portion of the ticket price as a contribution.

(c)   Recording Costumes and Stage Scenery as Fixed Assets

The SOP provides for recording fixed assets. Does this apply to costumes and scenery? In principle, the answer is "yes," but in practice this is rarely done. The SOP does not specifically speak to this question and it would appear such assets should be recorded. However, the implication in recording a fixed asset is that it does have a future value and that there will be revenue which will absorb the costs of such assets. This is probably fine where a performing arts company has a production that is given season after season; in this instance, the costumes and scenery should be recorded as an asset and depreciated over their expected useful life.

But most performing arts companies do not perform the same production on a regular schedule and effectively the costumes and scenery have assured value only for the initial season. If so, they should be expensed currently.

(d)   Financial Statement Presentation

Since contributions are usually an essential part of their income, performing arts organizations should consider a statement format that emphasizes the role these gifts play toward keeping the organization solvent. A recommended format is to show first the loss from operations and then the contribution income. Here in very abbreviated form is an example:

Ticket sales		$500,000
Less—Expenses:		
Production costs	$(600,000)	
Administration and general	(50,000)	(650,000)
Loss from operations		(150,000)
Contribution income	170,000	
Fund-raising costs	(10,000)	160,000
Excess for the year		$ 10,000

A more complete example is at Exhibit 6 in the Statement of Position.

18.7   PRIVATE FOUNDATIONS

The term "private foundation" is used here as defined in the Tax Reform Act of 1969. The tax aspects of private foundations are discussed in detail in Chapter 26. Such organizations generally do not solicit funds from the public but are supported mainly by endowment income. Occasionally, private foundations receive new gifts but, by definition, these come from relatively few individuals.[3]

(a) Timing of Recording Liability for Grants Awarded to Others

While this is not unique to foundations, it is more of an issue to them than to most organizations. Many times foundations will make a grant award payable in installments, often over several years. Typically, subsequent payments are dependent upon satisfactory performance or compliance with the original grant agreement, and as such, the "liability" for future payments is somewhat "conditional." The accounting question relates to the timing of recording these grant liabilities and the related expense by the foundation.

Historically, three possible approaches have been taken by foundations. Some have preferred to treat payments to grantee institutions on a "cash" basis. That is, they recorded future grant obligations as an expense only when they are paid (no liability is ever recorded in this case as the cash payment coincides with the recording as expense).

The second approach was for the foundation to record both as an expense and as a liability the full commitment at the time the grantee institution is informed of the foundation's intention to make specific payments.

A few foundations recorded both as an expense and as a liability amounts which the board of trustees "appropriated" for particular areas of interest (for example, cancer research). This board action usually occurs before grantees have been selected and is a nonbinding action indicating only where the trustees would like to see the foundation spend its money. Where such "appropriations" are recorded, the foundation effectively treats as an expense the amount which the board has concluded it will spend in a given area in the future. This recording is at the time of appropriation, as distinct from recording at the time the grantee is informed or the grant is awarded.

While sound accounting arguments can be cited for both the first and second approaches and a sound business reason advanced for the last approach, the SOP is fairly explicit in saying that the second approach is appropriate for private foundations that wish to describe their financial statements as being prepared in accordance with generally

---

[3] Community foundations, another type of foundation, do receive gifts from the general public.

accepted accounting principles. (SFAS No. 116 contains the same requirement as SOP 78-10.) The SOP provides:

> Organizations that make grants to others should record grants as expenses and liabilities at the time recipients are entitled to them. That normally occurs when the board approves a specific grant or when the grantee is notified.
>
> Some grants stipulate that payments are to be made over a period of several years. Grants payable in future periods subject only to routine performance requirements by the grantee and not requiring subsequent review and approval for continuance of payment should be recorded as expenses and liabilities when the grants are first made . . . . (Par. 101–102 of the SOP)

The real problem is determining when a grant is subject ". . . only to routine performance requirements . . . and not requiring subsequent review and approval. . . ." As noted, most multipayment grant awards contain language that requires certain interim reporting by the grantee and review by the foundation. When do these "routine performance requirements" stop being routine, and instead become a basis for re-evaluation of the foundation's grant commitment every time it receives a report by the grantee?

There is no easy answer to this question, and it is necessary to examine very carefully the wording in the grant notification document. If from the terms of that document it is clear that the foundation has made the decision to make future years' payments conditional only upon the grantee institution doing what it says it will do, and it is reasonably clear that the grantee has the capacity to do so, then the grant is essentially unconditional and the full amount of future payments should be recorded. On the other hand, if the grant document merely indicates the foundation's general intent to consider favorably future requests, subject to a full review at that time, future payments would be conditional, and would not be recorded until the condition is met. This would not constitute the type of grant obligation which should be reported since the commitment is contingent on a future decision by the foundation. Footnote disclosure of significant unrecorded amounts should be made.

Perhaps key to this discussion is the phrase "subject only to routine performance." All foundations reserve the right to revoke unpaid grants if the grantee institution fails to live up to its past performance, to submit routine financial reports of the use of such funds, and the like. Grants made subject to these routine performance requirements would not normally constitute language sufficiently restrictive to avoid the recording of the future grant payments. On the other hand, grants containing language such as the following would not be recorded:

The D. E. Martin Foundation Board of Trustees hereby grants to the Karen J. Sylvestre Home for Battered Women the sum of $100,000 to establish a program for runaway teenage girls in the Detroit area. The staff of the Foundation will review carefully the uses made of this money during the first twelve months, and based upon their evaluation of the effectiveness of the program will consider additional annual requests for $100,000 to fund the second and third years' programs.

It is clear that next year the Foundation will investigate the uses made of the money and will then make a decision as to future support. Yet, on the basis of the Foundation's intent, this organization can plan its program on the assumption that it is likely to get the additional support in the following two years.

On the other hand, wording such as the following would appear to require recording in full:

The D. E. Martin Foundation Board of Trustees hereby grants $300,000 to the Karen J. Sylvestre Home for Battered Women, payable $100,000 by check herewith and additional payments of $100,000 in each of the next two years. The payment of these future amounts is contingent upon receipt by the Foundation of a report by the Home which details the uses made of the monies received in the preceding year, an evaluation of the results of the program, and detailed budgets at the beginning of each program year.

In this instance, it appears fairly clear that the Foundation has committed itself for a three-year period and that it should record the full $300,000 (discounted to present value, as discussed in Chapter 10) both as an expense and as a liability at the time the grant is made. (The recipient would record a corresponding asset and revenue, as also discussed in Chapter 10.)

There are many gray-area grants where the answer will not be as clear as in these illustrations. The intent of SFAS No. 116 and the SOP is for the foundation to record the grant if in all likelihood future payments will be routinely made. However, if the foundation has not made a final judgment on future payments, they should not be recorded. At the end of Chapter 10 are two checklists to help readers determine when, in fact, an unconditional pledge exists.

Rationale

Some question why the obligation should be recorded both as a liability and as an expense in the current year. They point out that foundations derive their revenue primarily from endowment income, and that the future years' payments should be recorded as an expense at the time the income that will be used to pay the grant obligation is generated.

The reason the SOP and SFAS No. 116 take the approach discussed above is that, historically, such amounts are in fact paid and are, therefore, obligations. If a foundation that had committed itself to making future payments were not to record such amounts as an obligation, it would be presenting a rosier financial picture than is in fact the case. For example, one use of the financial statements is for the board to be aware of how much money is available for future grants. Amounts already committed, even if to be paid in future years, are clearly not available for new grants.

(b)   Investments at Market

Foundations typically have large investment portfolios. Under the SOP, investments in marketable securities may be carried at either the lower of cost or market or market value (or amortized cost for certain marketable debt securities). Nonmarketable investments, such as oil and gas interests, real estate, and so on, can continue to be carried at either the lower of cost or market or at market. Reference should be made to Chapter 8 for a discussion of the appropriate accounting and reporting procedures for investments.

(c)   Distinction between Principal and Income

One accounting distinction that private foundations often make is the distinction between principal and income in their net assets. Where such a distinction is made, the original principal and usually all capital gains thereon are accounted for separately from the accumulated, unspent income arising from investment of this principal. This distinction appears to be arbitrary and except where legal restrictions are involved usually serves no purpose to the readers of the financial statements.

This distinction between principal and income seems even less meaningful since the Tax Reform Act of 1969 and its requirement that minimum distributions be made (which will have the effect of dipping into capital gains and principal if dividends and income are not sufficient). The authors recommend that in the absence of legal restrictions these two amounts be combined and reported simply as net assets. If an organization wishes to maintain the distinction, then the only place where the distinction should be made is in the net assets section of the Balance Sheet as illustrated in the following abbreviated example:

Unrestricted Net Assets:
  Original donor contribution $1,000,000
  Accumulated undistributed income   200,000
      Total unrestricted net assets $1,200,000

(d)   Community Foundations

Community foundations differ from private foundations mainly in that their source of contributions is the community at large rather than one person or family. This gives rise to certain tax and legal considerations that do not really affect financial accounting or reporting. Thus, all of the accounting and reporting principles discussed above and in Chapter 14 are applicable to community as well as private foundations.

18.8   RELIGIOUS ORGANIZATIONS OTHER THAN CHURCHES

The term "religious organization," as contemplated here, excludes individual churches that were discussed earlier in this chapter. Organizations that exist to service the particular needs of organized religion on a regional or national basis are included, as are organizations involved in the national administration of churches or their domestic and foreign missionary activities.

(a)   Combined Financial Statements

One of the difficult questions for a religious organization is to determine which entities are so financially interrelated that combined financial statements should be prepared as required by SOP 94-3. (See the discussion in Chapters 9 and 17.)

The key to determining when combination would be appropriate under SOP 94-3 rests heavily on the financial interrelationship. There is no requirement for preparing combined financial statements unless substantially all of the funds collected by the secondary unit will be transferred to the reporting organization or used for its benefit. Thus, for example, a diocese would not be required to combine the financial statements of the individual church units within its jurisdiction for purposes of its reporting. While the individual church units may raise funds in the name of the church, such funds will largely be used for local purposes, and only a portion transmitted to the diocese.

(b)   Allocations from Other Organizations

Religious organizations frequently receive allocations from affiliated local or regional organizations. Usually the allocation is established by the
"parent" organization at the beginning of the fiscal year. An accounting
question often arises as to timing of income recognition. Should it be at
the beginning of the year when the allocation is determined, at the time
it is paid, or pro rata throughout the year?

Unless the amount to be paid by the parent organization qualifies
as an unconditional pledge (as discussed in Chapter 10), recognition
normally should be on a pro rata basis throughout the year since it is
effectively payment for services which are presumably being rendered
throughout the year. Where experience shows that the full allocation or
assessment will not be paid, only the amount that can reasonably be expected to be paid should be recorded on this pro rata basis. Unpaid collections at the end of the year must be reviewed for collectibility.

18.9   RESEARCH AND SCIENTIFIC ORGANIZATIONS

Research and scientific organizations are those not-for-profit organizations existing primarily to do research in particular areas, usually under
contract with government agencies, private foundations, or third parties.

(a)   Timing of Recording Contract Revenue

The major question most research and scientific organizations have relates to the timing of recording contract revenue. Under the SOP, contract
revenue should be recorded as revenue at the time the contract terms
are met. In most instances, this is as expenses are incurred that can be
charged against the contract.

Some research and scientific organizations receive grants unrestricted as to use to assist the organizations in conducting their programs or meeting their general expenses. Usually these organizations
submit budgets to the granting organization indicating the time frame
and the type of activities that will be carried out with these unrestricted
funds. When such grants are tantamount to a purchase of services by the
grantor, recognition of such unrestricted grants should be on a time-
frame basis; that is, pro rata over the period which the grant specifies.
Where the research or scientific organization has submitted a budget to
the grantor indicating an uneven use of these unrestricted funds, the
grant revenue should be recognized in the time period provided in
the submitted budget. If the grant amounts to an unconditional gift to

the grantee, it should be recognized like all gifts; that is, immediately upon receipt of the gift or pledge. At the end of Chapter 10 is a checklist to help readers distinguish between contributions and purchases of services in practice.

The recognition of revenue is independent of the actual receipt of cash under the grant. In some instances, grantors pay the entire grant in advance, and in others, in arrears. When a grant which is a purchase of services is paid in advance, it would be reflected as "deferred grant revenue" on the Balance Sheet. If it is essentially a contribution, it is recorded as revenue immediately upon receipt. When the grant is paid in arrears, a receivable would be set up at the time of revenue recognition.

(b) Recording Future Grant Awards

A related question arises as to the appropriateness of recording both as a receivable and as deferred grant revenue the amounts which the organization has been told it will receive for future activities—either restricted or unrestricted. Should an organization reflect large future years' grants on the Balance Sheet?

This is a difficult question to answer, but the general answer is "no," unless the grant amounts to an unconditional pledge, discussed in Chapter 10, and the organization could enforce payment. If the grant has language in it such that the grantor can change its mind, with or without cause, such future grants are conditional and would not be recorded. On the other hand, where a grantor has made the grant unconditional and it is clear that the only condition is the passage of time, there is justification for recording the grant both as a receivable and revenue. The burden, however, is on showing that the grant is unconditional and could be legally enforced. In many ways, such future grants are similar to "pledges." SFAS No. 116 and the SOP provide that unconditional pledges should be recorded; otherwise, not. The same applies to future grants. Note that this accounting principle is the same as that discussed previously for foundations making grants.

18.10 PRIVATE ELEMENTARY AND SECONDARY SCHOOLS

Private elementary and secondary schools are those institutions that provide education below the college level, and which are supported by tuition and contributions from private sources. Excluded from this category are government supported school systems.

(a) Depreciation Accounting

Traditionally, private elementary and secondary schools tended to follow the accounting principles in the College and University Audit Guide, which discourages reporting depreciation. However, the SOP and SFAS No. 93 clearly indicate that private schools should be using depreciation accounting.

Unfortunately, most private elementary and secondary schools had not been following depreciation accounting techniques in the past. In the authors' opinion, one of the reasons many private schools have run into financial difficulties is that boards of trustees have not been fully aware of the true cost of operating their schools, and accordingly have set their tuition fees too low. Depreciation is a cost, albeit not a cash cost, and should be reported as an expense if financial statements are to accurately reflect the actual costs of a school.

(b) Accounting Manual

The National Association of Independent Schools published the third edition of *Business Management for Independent Schools* in 1987. It is widely recognized as the accounting manual private elementary and secondary schools should follow. For the most part, this manual is in agreement with the SOP and SFAS No. 116; however, in some areas there are differences. Some of the major differences are:

1. The SOP provides that current restricted gifts and plant fund gifts are reported as income when the restrictions are met, whereas *Business Management for Independent Schools* permits them to be reported as income when received. SFAS No. 116 agrees with NAIS on this point.

2. The SOP and SFAS No. 117 provide that board-designated endowment is reported as part of the unrestricted class and not combined with the restricted endowment. *Business Management for Independent Schools* provides that board-designated endowments are reported as part of the endowment fund.

3. As noted above, depreciation accounting is required by the SOP and SFAS No. 93, whereas *Business Management for Independent Schools* states depreciation is not recommended.

4. The SOP and SFAS No. 116 provide for unconditional pledges being recorded, whereas *Business Management for Independent Schools* provides that pledges are not recorded.

5. The SOP and SFAS No. 117 provide that investment income is recorded directly in the fund to which the income applies, whereas *Business Management for Independent Schools* recommends that such income should initially be recorded in the fund having the investments.

6. The SOP requires interfund transfers to be shown in the fund balance section after the caption "Fund balance beginning of the year." *Business Management for Independent Schools* provides that interfund transfers are reported before the final caption, "Net change for the year." SFAS No. 117 has made this difference moot.

7. A Statement of Changes in Financial Position is required by the SOP; this requirement is now superseded since a Statement of Cash Flows is required by SFAS No. 117, but no such statement is recommended by *Business Management for Independent Schools.*

Presumably, the National Association of Independent Schools will, in due course, revise its manual to incorporate the changes brought about by SFAS No. 116 and No. 117 and by the SOP. In the meantime, institutions following the third edition of *Business Management for Independent Schools* should be aware that CPAs making an examination of the school's financial statements will not be able to say that the statements are in accordance with generally accepted accounting principles.

CHAPTER 19

The Financial Accounting Standards Board and Future Trends in Not-for-Profit Accounting

So far the discussion of accounting principles and reporting practices has dealt with existing authoritative literature to which accountants and CPAs refer when determining appropriate treatment of accounting questions.

This chapter deals with probable future developments. The chapter first discusses the impact on not-for-profit accounting of the activities of the Financial Accounting Standards Board (FASB). The later portion deals with some of the trends and developments which the authors see as likely to take place during the next few years. It should be emphasized that much of the discussion in this chapter is conjecture, based on the authors' close involvement with many of the recent developments in this field, and reasonable expectations as to future developments. A great deal of the now-existing literature was first discussed in this chapter of earlier editions.

19.1   FINANCIAL ACCOUNTING STANDARDS BOARD

Beginning in 1977, the Financial Accounting Standards Board has been involved in rule making for not-for-profit organizations. With the issuance in 1993 of Statements of Financial Accounting Standards Nos. 116 and 117, discussed in earlier chapters of this book, the FASB has started to have a significant impact on not-for-profit accounting. To put this development into perspective, it is first necessary to describe the accounting profession's existing rule-making machinery, and detail its enforcement.

(a)   Establishment of Accounting Rules

Until 1973, the senior rule-making body was the Accounting Principles Board (APB) of the American Institute of Certified Public Accountants (AICPA). Accounting principles formally established by the Accounting Principles Board or its successor represent "generally accepted accounting principles," and CPAs reporting on financial statements of their clients cannot indicate that their clients are following generally accepted accounting principles unless they are, in fact, following the principles established by this Board or its successor. CPAs who report on a contrary treatment without appropriate indication in their opinion can be disciplined by both the accounting profession and the state licensing boards, with a possible loss of their CPA certificates.

The Accounting Principles Board never formally established accounting principles for not-for-profit organizations as such. However, the Board did authorize publication of the Industry Audit Guides discussed in Chapters 14 and 16 and the *Hospital Audit Guide* referred to in Chapter 15. These Guides have some authoritative status although they do *not* formally constitute generally accepted accounting principles. This means that accountants would not necessarily be disciplined for violating the principles in these Guides. However, they could be called on to justify a departure from the Guides, since they represent the most authoritative literature on the subjects covered. Embarrassing as this could be, seldom would it result in loss of a CPA certificate. However, all of the major accounting firms and most conscientious CPAs look upon these Guides as authoritative and are reluctant to violate them. (The above description applies only to audit guides and statements of position issued before 1992. Documents issued after 1992 carry a higher level of authority. Since all of the relevant not-for-profit documents were issued before that date, the above discussion is the relevant one here.)

Technically there are two levels of accounting rules: those rules that formally constitute generally accepted accounting principles from which departures cannot occur without CPAs calling attention to them as such in their opinions, and those rules that represent the best thoughts of the accounting profession from which departures can occur without CPAs identifying them in their opinions, although they may later have to justify a failure to do so.

Formation of FASB

In 1973, the Accounting Principles Board turned over its rule-making authority to a new and totally independent organization, the Financial Accounting Standards Board, usually referred to as the FASB. The Accounting Principles Board was disbanded. Since then, only the FASB is empowered to issue standards that formally constitute generally accepted accounting principles. Prior to 1993, the FASB issued only one accounting principle specifically addressed to the not-for-profit sector (SFAS No. 93, referred to below).

AICPA's Statement of Position

At the time the FASB was established in 1973, the AICPA set up an ongoing committee to make recommendations to the FASB on accounting issues. This ongoing AICPA body is the Accounting Standards Executive Committee (AcSEC). Its recommendations are made in the form of "Statements of Position" addressed to the FASB for its consideration. These Statements of Position (SOP) are widely publicized; in no sense are they private communications. In the absence of FASB statements to the contrary, these SOP's represent the best thoughts of the accounting profession on a given subject.

Upon receipt of a proposed SOP, the FASB has two basic options. The FASB can conclude that the subject matter of the Statement is sufficiently important that the FASB will place the subject on its agenda and consider it in the near future. When this is done the SOP has little authority pending the FASB's resolution.

Alternatively, the FASB can indicate that it does not intend to consider the matter covered in the SOP in the near future. When this happens the SOP becomes the "most authoritative" discussion of the accounting principles on that subject, and has much the same authority as the Industry Audit Guides discussed above. As with the Audit Guides, a violation of an SOP by a CPA would not necessarily result in disciplinary action by the accounting profession or by state licensing boards. At the time of issuance of the SOP discussed in Chapter 17, the FASB had not yet placed on its agenda the consideration of formal accounting standards for not-for-profit entities. Accordingly, that SOP continues to be the most authoritative discussion of accounting principles for not-for-profit organizations not covered by one of the Industry Audit Guides, except for those matters covered by one of the Statements of Financial Accounting Standards described below. It will continue to have this authority until the FASB issues further specific accounting standards for not-for-profit organizations, or until the AICPA issues the new audit guide described below.[1]

(b)   FASB Conceptual Framework

In 1977, the FASB indicated that it was exploring the possibility of issuing a financial reporting "conceptual framework policy statement" applicable to not-for-profit organizations. A conceptual framework policy statement is a document that attempts to establish the framework on which individual, specific accounting principles (referred to by the FASB as "standards") can be developed which will facilitate consistency among principles. The conceptual framework policy statement, however, would not represent detailed accounting standards as such; these would be adopted subsequently as a separate procedure. In an earlier document,[2] the FASB summarized the purposes of such a framework as follows:

> To establish the objectives and concepts that the Financial Accounting Standards Board will use in developing standards of financial accounting and reporting.

[1] The FASB has announced a proposed procedure for ultimately transforming existing AICPA Audit Guides and Statements of Position into FASB standards, but no action has yet been taken with respect to any of the not-for-profit Guides or the Statement of Position as such. Rather the FASB has issued three specific standards (Nos. 93, 116, 117) dealing with particular matters covered in the audit guides and statement of position, thus amending those documents as to those matters only. The remaining principles in those documents remain in effect until changed.

[2] Financial Accounting Standards Board, Exposure Draft, *Objectives of Financial Reporting and Elements of Financial Statements of Business Enterprises* (Stamford, CT: FASB, 1977), p. 1.

To provide guidance in resolving problems of financial accounting and reporting that are not addressed in authoritative pronouncements.

To enhance the assessment by users of the content and limitations of information provided by financial accounting and reporting and thereby further their ability to use that information effectively.

The FASB commissioned Dr. Robert Anthony of Harvard to develop a research study that would identify the issues he believed should be considered by the FASB in such a conceptual framework policy statement. His assignment was not to discern specific answers but rather to identify the issues and the alternatives he felt the FASB should consider.

The FASB also decided to include within the scope of this research study all entities not organized on a for-profit basis, that is, all "nonbusiness" entities. Initially it was the intention of the FASB to include governmental units in the scope of the study. Later, at the request of various groups connected with governmental accounting, the FASB agreed to remove governmental units from this study and make them the subject of separate concepts and standard-setting processes, under the control of a separate Government Accounting Standards Board.

Dr. Anthony's study was published in 1978 under the title: *Financial Accounting in Nonbusiness Organizations—An Exploratory Study of Conceptual Issues.* Subsequently, the FASB put the conceptual framework policy statement on its formal agenda. In doing so, the FASB exposed for public comment a formal Discussion Memorandum describing the issues it intended to cover. Late in 1980, the FASB published Statement of Financial Accounting Concepts No. 4, *Objectives of Financial Reporting by Nonbusiness Organizations.*

In 1985, the FASB published another Concepts Statement, Number 6, *Elements of Financial Statements*, containing further material relating to FASB's views on accounting and financial reporting by not-for-profit entities.

It is important to note that, while these conceptual framework policy statements set the framework under which formal financial accounting standards are written, a conceptual framework policy statement itself is *not* a rule book. The development of specific financial accounting standards is a separate, formal process usually taking several years.

(c)   FASB Not-for-Profit Projects

Originally the FASB identified five areas in which it intended to set accounting and reporting standards for not-for-profit entities. As of late 1994, the FASB has issued three accounting standards specifically applicable to not-for-profit organizations:

1. Number 93, *Recognition of Depreciation by Not-for-Profit Organizations*. This was discussed in Chapter 7.
2. Number 116, *Accounting for Contributions Received and Contributions Made*. This was discussed in Chapter 10 (especially) and in Chapters 14–18.
3. Number 117, *Financial Statements of Not-for-Profit Organizations*. This was discussed in Chapter 13 (especially) and in Chapters 14–18.

Two other not-for-profit projects are under way which will have major impacts on the not-for-profit sector:

1. One will specify when financial data of affiliated entities should be combined for financial statement presentation; (topic discussed in Chapter 9)
2. The other will set common standards for accounting for investments, to replace the various standards currently in use as discussed in Chapters 14–17.

The first of these two projects is not very far along and final standards are not expected for at least two years. The second project may be completed by late 1995.

(d) AICPA Projects

Now that these three statements have been issued, large parts of the various AICPA Audit Guides and Statement of Position are obsolete. In anticipation of that, and in recognition of the fact that these documents are many years old and in need of updating, the AICPA not-for-profit organizations committee established a task force to update, revise, and combine the documents. (The Health Care Providers Audit Guide will remain as a separate document, as much of its subject matter is peculiar to these types of organizations.) The new Guide will contain interpretive information about the new accounting and reporting standards, as well as guidance for auditors of financial statements in which the standards are applied.

The next AICPA project deals with joint costs of multipurpose activities, as discussed in Chapter 14. Accountants have tried to create rules that permit fair allocation but preclude improper allocation of these costs. The existing accounting rules are contained in AICPA Statement of Position 87-2, *Accounting for Joint Costs of Informational Materials and Activities of Not-for-Profit Organizations That Include a Fund-Raising Appeal*. As of late

1994, the AICPA is preparing a new SOP that will replace 87-2, but not change its basic requirements. Rather the new SOP will clarify and amplify some of the rules in 87-2 as well as provide examples of recommended practices in this area.

The third project is one to issue guidance on combination of related entities when one is a not-for-profit organization. This subject is discussed in detail in Chapter 9. In September 1994, the AICPA issued a new statement of position (No. 94-3) that expands and clarifies guidance on this subject.

(e) Relationship of the AICPA to the FASB

This raises the obvious question of the relationship of the AICPA Statement of Position discussed in Chapter 17, and the various Industry Audit Guides, to the FASB and its conceptual framework policy statement and present and future accounting and reporting standards.

When formal accounting and reporting standards are issued by the FASB, they supersede any contrary provisions of the Industry Audit Guides and SOP's. However, until superseded, the provisions of the Industry Audit Guides and SOP's continue to represent the most authoritative pronouncements on the subject by the accounting profession. Thus for the immediate future they continue to have great impact.

When the new AICPA Audit Guide is issued it will supersede and then have the same status as the now-existing guides. Because its issuance will follow issuance of the new FASB standards, its accounting positions will be completely consistent with these standards. In accounting areas not dealt with by FASB, the AICPA Guide will be the most authoritative pronouncement.

19.2 TRENDS IN NOT-FOR-PROFIT ACCOUNTING

The balance of this chapter is devoted to discussing some of the reporting and accounting trends that the authors noted in earlier editions of this book and continue to see, with the hope that readers may find these observations useful as they explore ways to strengthen the reporting of organizations with which they are associated.

(a) The Organization as a Reporting Entity

Perhaps the most significant reporting trend is toward reporting on the organization as a whole, and away from reporting on the individual funds of the organization. SFAS No. 117 and SOP 94-3 have accelerated this trend. For too long, organizations have been reporting on a fund-by-fund basis either in multicolumn format or on separate statements;

confusion has resulted for most readers. In the future, more and more emphasis will be placed on reporting on the organization as a single entity. The use of multicolumn, layered, or separate fund-by-fund financial statements will give way to more reporting on a combined basis where the individual funds making up the entity will not be separately shown in each financial statement.

This is not to suggest that monitoring the restrictions and limitations placed on resources by outside parties will not continue to be important. Of course, it will. However, the use of fund accounting for bookkeeping purposes does not dictate the use of fund accounting for reporting purposes; this is the significance of the trend.

Combining Affiliated Organizations

A related trend is that of requiring more combination of financial information of affiliated organizations for public reporting purposes. The theory here is also that readers should see the "big picture" rather than just a part or a collection of parts. In recent years, the FASB has required business entities to combine more of their affiliates into the parent company's financial statements. It is reasonable, and desirable, to expect the same for not-for-profit entities. This topic is discussed further in Chapter 9.

(b) Reporting Certain Assets at Current Value

Recent years have seen a trend toward more reporting of some assets at current fair market value, rather than just at historical cost. All of the AICPA audit guides and the statement of position permit valuing marketable securities at current market value as an option. More and more organizations are following this option. The FASB recently issued Statement of Financial Accounting Standards No. 115, *Accounting for Certain Investments in Debt and Equity Securities*. This standard requires market value accounting for some investments owned by businesses.[3] While SFAS No. 115 does not apply to not-for-profit organizations, it is indicative of the thinking of FASB on the subject. It appears likely that the new standard FASB eventually issues for not-for-profits will require market value accounting for, at least, marketable securities.

(c) Use of a Bottom Line

Another trend is toward reporting a "bottom line," that is, reporting the excess of revenue and support over expenses. This is now required by

---

[3] In addition, businesses in certain other specialized industries: banks, insurance, mutual funds, pension funds, and others have long been required to value some or all of their investments at market rather than cost.

SFAS No. 117. Some not-for-profit organizations have resisted this, believing that there is no significance to the fact or size of such an excess. However, boards and other readers are recognizing with increasing frequency that an important indicator of financial health is the "bottom line." The axiom that over time you can't spend more than you receive applies to all organizations, including not-for-profit organizations.

Further, many readers find they are able to get a better overall understanding of the organization's financial statements if they first see a clearly labeled bottom line. The bottom line pulls together financial details and helps the reader to focus on the overall results of activities. It is similar in effect to the perspective astronauts achieve when looking at the North American continent from space. Once the overview is comprehended it is much easier to focus on the specifics.

(d) Similarity to Profit-Oriented Reporting

Another related trend is that not-for-profit reporting will become more similar in appearance to reporting by profit-oriented entities. This is not to suggest that there aren't transactions unique to not-for-profit organizations; rather, it reflects the fact that readers of financial statements of not-for-profit-oriented entities feel more comfortable—that is, more confident in their interpretive ability with reporting formats that closely parallel those of profit-oriented entities. As a result, except where unique transactions suggest contrary treatment, the trend will be toward profit-oriented reporting.

(e) Emphasis on Functional Reporting

Consistent with SFAS No. 117 and the earlier accounting pronouncements, reporting for not-for-profit organizations will continue to emphasize program or functional reporting. Not-for-profit organizations exist to perform services, not to pay salaries. Thus, there will be greater emphasis on appropriately reporting the cost of services being rendered. Cost accounting techniques will become a standard tool in not-for-profit accounting.

(f) A Single Set of Accounting Principles for All Not-for-Profit Organizations

With the entry of the FASB, and increased awareness on the part of CPAs of the awkwardness of applying different principles to the same transaction for different types of organizations, we are seeing a gradual reconciliation of existing accounting pronouncements and the evolution of a single set of basic underlying accounting principles and reporting practices for all not-for-profit organizations. The three statements listed above are part of this trend.

As with the Statement of Position discussed in Chapter 17, this does not mean that there will be a single reporting format applicable for all nonprofit organizations. This is neither practical nor appropriate, and it can reasonably be expected that there will continue to be many different reporting formats. But there will be greater uniformity in the basic information disclosed in the statements.

(g) Development of "Industry" Accounting Manuals

The development of a single set of accounting principles will not decrease the need for individual manuals for each of the various types of not-for-profit organizations; rather, it will increase the need. Just as the development of accounting principles in the not-for-profit sector was initiated by industry groups, so too it can be expected that the various industry associations of different types of not-for-profit organizations will continue to develop detailed accounting manuals to assist their own membership. Recent examples such as *Museum Accounting Guidelines*, developed for museums, and *Accounting and Financial Reporting Guide for Christian Ministries*, for religious organizations, will be emulated by other industry groups.

(h) Uniform State Reporting

As is more fully discussed in Chapter 28, many states have reporting requirements for charitable organizations soliciting funds within their jurisdiction. Unfortunately, the reporting requirements differ from state to state, as have some of the reporting formats that must be used. This constituted a great expense for a national charity that may have had to file different reports in each of the various states. It was also awkward since the accounting principles applicable in one state often differed from those of another state.

As a result of efforts on the part of the Internal Revenue Service, state regulators, charities, the accounting profession, and others, starting in 1982, almost all the states agreed to accept a copy of IRS Form 990 in satisfaction of the basic financial statement reporting requirements. Most states require additional schedules and some an auditor's opinion; but using a single set of financial statements is a cost saving for national charities.

(i) Federal Reporting Requirements

As discussed in Chapter 27, present federal reporting requirements relate primarily to filing information with the IRS to enable it to determine the tax status of activities of not-for-profit organizations. The present IRS form (990) is largely a statistical report and is not particularly useful from a financial analysis perspective. Contributors and other interested parties get relatively little information from this tax report.

With the increased emphasis on full disclosure and accountability in recent years and an occasional newspaper headline about a charity that has abused its public trust, legislation has been introduced at various times in Congress which would, if adopted, require additional reporting by charitable organizations soliciting funds from the public. The legislation proposed has fallen basically into two alternative categories: regulatory and disclosure. Since each is distinctively different they are discussed separately below.

Regulatory-Type Legislation

The regulatory-type legislation basically provides for filing financial statements and other information with a regulatory body to allow that body to determine the organization's conformity to certain standards established either by the legislation or by the regulatory body. Typically, the regulatory body is given authority to discipline the organization if transgressions occur which are deemed to be not in the public interest. The financial statements filed with the regulatory agency are usually open for public inspection, although often only at the offices of either the charity or the regulatory agency with the result that they are not easily available to many people. There is currently a proposal before Congress to require not-for-profits to send a copy of their IRS reporting form (Form 990) to anyone who requests it.

Disclosure-Type Legislation

This alternative type of legislation basically provides that certain information be disclosed on the face of all fund-raising literature, including a statement that financial statements will be sent directly to the contributor upon request. Typically such legislation does not require the routine filing of a financial statement with a regulatory body, or the passing of judgment on these statements or on the charity by a regulatory body. The presumption is that, with access to financial information, the contributor can make a wiser decision than a regulatory body on which charity to support.

As can be seen, these two approaches are quite different. In the one, the presumption is that a regulatory body can better make the judgment as to the worthiness of an organization. In the other, the presumption is that the contributor can make the better judgment.

The authors believe that the *disclosure* approach would eliminate 95 percent of the credibility problems currently experienced by charitable organizations simply because charities will know that their financial affairs will routinely become public. Few will abuse public trust if they know with certainty they will be found out. In addition, the authors endorse recognition of the individual contributor, equipped with adequate information, as the best arbiter of worthiness among organizations competing for funds.

The authors expect that in the coming years our lawmakers, both federal and state, will pay increased attention to charitable organizations and their reporting practices, and that some legislation will be passed. Unfortunately, it is far from clear which type of legislation will be enacted; in large measure, the climate at the time of passage will be the determining factor. If legislation is passed as a result of newspaper headlines about the abuse of public trust by charities, an emotional outcry will likely produce a regulatory-type bill. Philanthropic organizations would be well advised to anticipate the problem by working toward passage of disclosure-type legislation.

19.3 CONCLUSION

With the introduction of the Financial Accounting Standards Board into the not-for-profit accounting sector, and with increased attention directed at *all* of our public institutions, it appears that financial reporting by not-for-profit organizations is bound to undergo increasing scrutiny. Perhaps foremost among the changes that is emerging is a reassessment of the appropriateness of different accounting treatments for the same transaction by different types of organizations.

This trend toward greater openness and accountability is desirable and will continue to accelerate in the coming years. Financial statements will increasingly report on the organization as a whole rather than on a fund-by-fund basis. Our not-for-profit institutions will increasingly find themselves in the "sunshine" environment of the post-Watergate era, and will increasingly recognize their responsibility to provide the public with meaningful financial information.

PART FOUR

Controlling the
Not-for-Profit Organization

C H A P T E R   20

The Importance of Budgeting

A budget, like motherhood, is something very few would argue against. Yet, the art of preparing *and using* budgets in a meaningful manner is completely foreign to many not-for-profit organizations. It is not that the treasurer or board is unaware of their importance, but more that they are uncertain of their skills in budgeting techniques, and often are reluctant to use a budget as a tool to *control* the financial activities. This chapter discusses the *importance* of budgeting, preparing a useful budget, and equally important, *using* the budget to control.

20.1   THE BUDGET: A PLAN OF ACTION

A budget is a "plan of action." It represents the organization's blueprint for the coming months, or years, expressed in monetary terms. This means the organization must have specific goals before it can prepare a budget. If it doesn't know where it is going, it is going to be very difficult for the organization to do any meaningful planning. All too often the process is reversed and it is in the process of preparing the budget that the goals are determined.

The first function of a budget is to record, in monetary terms, what the realistic goals or objectives of the organization are for the coming year (or years). The budget is the financial plan of action that results from the board's decisions as to the program for the future.

The second function of a budget is to provide a tool to monitor the financial activities throughout the year. Properly used, the budget can provide a benchmark or comparison point that will be an early warning to the board that their financial goals may not be met. For a budget to provide this type of information and control, four elements must be present:

1. The budget must be well-conceived and have been prepared or approved by the board.
2. The budget must be broken down into periods corresponding to the periodic financial statements.
3. Financial statements must be prepared on a timely basis throughout the year and a comparison made to the budget with explanations of significant deviations (or lack of deviation where one might be expected).
4. The board must be prepared to take action where the comparison in Step 3 indicates a problem.

Each of these four elements will be discussed in this chapter.

(a)   Steps for Preparation

A budget should represent the end result of a periodic review by the board or by the membership of the organization's objectives or goals, expressed in monetary terms. Often the budget process is a routine "chore" handled by the treasurer to satisfy the board that the organization has a budget, which the board, in turn, routinely ratifies. Frequently, such budgets are not looked at again until the following year, when the next year's budget is prepared. This type of budgeting serves little purpose. A budget, to be effective, must be a joint effort of many people. It must be a working document that forms the basis for action.

Here are the basic steps that, in one form or another, should be followed by an organization to prepare a well-conceived budget:

1. A list of objectives or goals of the organization for the following year should be prepared. For many organizations, this process will be essentially a re-evaluation of the relative priority of the existing programs. Care should be taken, however, to avoid concluding too hastily that an existing program should continue unchanged. Our society is not static and the organization that does not constantly re-evaluate and update its programs is in danger of being left behind.

2. The cost of each objective or goal listed should be estimated. For continuing programs, the actual expense and budget for the previous year, as well as the current year's budget and estimated actual expenses,[1] will be helpful as a starting point in estimating this cost. For new programs or modifications of existing programs, a substantial amount of work may be necessary to accurately estimate the costs involved. This estimating process should be done in detail since elements of a particular goal or objective may involve many categories of salaries and other expenses. Input from the operating staff of the organization is necessary for this step.

3. The expected income of the organization should be estimated. With many organizations, contributions from members or the general public will be a principal source of income and careful consideration must be given to the expected economic climate in the community. A year when unemployment is high or the stock market is down is a poor year to expect increased contributions. With other organizations, the amount of income will be dependent on how successful they are in selling their program. Possibly some of the programs can be expanded if they are financially viable, or contracted if they are not.

   Organizations are often overly optimistic in estimating income. This can prove to be the organization's downfall if there is no margin for error; realism must be used or the budget will have little meaning. The persons preparing a budget should *never* "plug" a predicted deficit by "assuming" that contributions will

---

[1] Note that the expenses for the current year are described as "estimated actual." This is because the preparation of the budget for the next year should be taking place well before the end of the current year—before the current year's final actual data is known.

somehow be found to cover the shortfall. This is a certain recipe for financial disaster.

4. The total expected income should be compared to the expense of achieving the objectives or goals. At this point in the process, usually the expected expenses will exceed income, and this is where some value judgments will have to take place. What programs are most important? Might expected costs be reduced, and, if so, where? Can some additional income be found? This process of reconciling expected income and expenses is probably the most important step taken during the year because it is here that the program's blueprint for the coming year is fixed.

   It is important that consideration be given to the reliability of the estimated income and expense figures. Is it possible that expenses have been underestimated or that income has been overestimated? If expenses have been underestimated by 15 percent and income has been overestimated by 10 percent, there will be a deficit of 25 percent, and unless the organization has substantial available reserves it will likely be in serious difficulty before the year is out. If the organization has small cash reserves or has little likelihood of getting additional resources quickly, then a realistic safety margin should be built into the budget.

5. The final proposed budget should be submitted to the appropriate body for ratification. This may be the full board or it may be the entire membership. This should not be just a formality but should be carefully presented to the ratifying body so that, once ratified, all persons will be firmly committed to the resulting plan of action.

The steps listed may seem so elementary that there is no need to emphasize them here. But elementary as they are, they are often not followed and the resulting budget is of very little value to the organization.

(b) Levels of Reserves

Step 4 referred to cash reserves. What is the appropriate level of reserves to maintain? Most people understand the need for a cushion against an unexpected, or expected, downturn in the organization's financial situation, or for an unanticipated, or anticipated, opportunity to expand services. But there is little guidance available about how large such reserves should be. Although, it would be nice to have enough in the bank to cover any possible problem or opportunity; this is rarely possible, nor is it necessarily desirable. Every dollar held back in reserve is a dollar that is not being used to provide program services to the organization's constituency. If no amounts were held back, more meals could be served to the homeless, more concerts given by the orchestra, more work done to find a cure for cancer—at least in the short run. But without reserves, the organization might not survive for the long run, and then there will eventually be no meals, concerts, or cancer research. Somewhere between is the happy medium; but where?

Reserve levels are necessarily a matter of judgment. The authors suggest the following factors for consideration in making that judgment for a particular organization:

- How predictable are the organization's revenues? How likely is it that there might be a sudden and significant shortfall that could hurt the organization's ability to continue its programs?

- How predictable are the organization's expenses? How likely is it that there might be a sudden and significant need to spend resources beyond those planned for in the budget? Such a need could result from either an unexpected increase in the cost of doing what has been planned (such as a wage increase won by a labor union, or an increase in the price of some commodity purchased), from the need to respond to a natural or man-made disaster such as a fire, flood, or earthquake, or from an unexpected opportunity to meet a new community need by expanding the organization's program activities into new areas.

- If one (or both) of the preceding two scenarios occurs, how certain is management and the board of their ability to tap new or increased sources of financial resources quickly? Are there existing donors who would readily respond to an emergency appeal for support? Are there other donors, maybe a local foundation, a United Way, or a governmental unit, who would help? Could revenues from sales of goods or services (if such exists) be rapidly expanded? Would creditors be willing to postpone debt payments? Are there other assets that could be sold for cash on short notice? Are there lenders (either individual or commercial) who would make a loan to the organization? Does the organization already have an available line of credit with its bank? (If not, why not?)

- Could planned expenditures be reduced or deferred, at least for a while, without long-term harm to the organization's programs? Many not-for-profits are quite labor-intensive. Payroll expenses are often not easy to cut, and payroll taxes have to be paid to the government.

- How risk averse is the organization's management? How willing is it to "run close to the edge" and count on its ability to deal with problems or opportunities as they arise without having much in the way of ready reserves to draw on?

None of this has yet directly answered the question of reserve size. Unfortunately, there is no answer that works for all organizations all of the time. Each organization has to make its own determination based on its own circumstances. Some people use as a rule of thumb somewhere between three and six months' expenditures as a desirable reserve level. Consider *all aspects* of your particular situation before making this determination.

Once the decision as to desired size is made, the actual reserve can be handled in several different ways. One way is to do nothing beyond monitoring the level of unrestricted net assets for conformity with the established reserve level. Some organizations like to place an amount of cash or other liquid assets equal to the reserve amount in a separate bank or investment account. This may serve as a form of self-discipline by making it less easy to spend the reserve assets. A more formal procedure is to have the board vote to designate an amount of the unrestricted net assets as an operating reserve on the balance sheet, as shown in Exhibit 5–6, although, as noted in that chapter, the authors caution that such a procedure may be confusing to financial statement readers.

A final question that sometimes comes up is whether there is some upper level of reserves which, if exceeded, will attract unwelcome attention from the Internal Revenue Service. The answer is almost always, no. The tax laws tell the IRS to be concerned with how an organization uses its resources to further its tax-exempt purpose, but do not mention any limits on how much the organization may accumulate. Some major universities and foundations have assets in the billions of dollars, without raising any concern. The point is that these organizations are using these assets, in many cases to generate annual income which is used for the organizations' purposes. Only if an organization were not even using the investment income from its assets, or were holding large amounts of non-income-producing and otherwise unused assets, would the IRS ask questions about reserve levels.

Questions about apparently high levels of reserves are far more likely to come from those who support the organization financially: donors, members, students, or others. A donor who is asked to contribute to an organization that appears to already have sufficient resources for its needs might fairly ask why further contributions are still being sought. Members may question dues levels; students may ask why tuition is so high. Organizations must be prepared to respond to such questions in a way which will convince the questioner that there is truly a need for additional resources.

(c)   Responsibility for Budget Preparation

The next concern is, who should follow these steps in preparing the budget? The preparation of a budget involves policy decisions. The treasurer may be the person best qualified to handle the figures, but is usually not the person to make policy decisions. For this reason, a "budget committee" should consist of persons responsible for policy decisions. Usually this means that either the board should itself act as the budget committee, or it should appoint a subcommittee of board members. The treasurer may, probably should, be a member of this committee, but should take care not to dominate the process.

This doesn't mean that the detailed estimated cost studies and revenue estimates for various activities can't be delegated to staff members. In fact, they normally should be. But the final decisions as to what are the goals and their relative priority has to be a board-level function.

Take, for example, a private independent school. At first glance, there might not appear to be many board-level decisions to make. The purpose of a school is to teach, and it might seem that the budget would be a most routine matter. But there are many decisions that have to be made. For example:

1. Should more emphasis be placed on science courses?
2. Should the school purchase more sophisticated equipment to help teach computer science?
3. Should the school hire a foreign language teacher for grades 2–4?
4. Should the school increase salaries in the coming year and try to upgrade the staff?
5. Should the athletic field be resodded this year?
6. Should a professional fund raiser be hired?
7. Should the extracurricular music program be expanded?
8. Must tuition be increased? If so, how much?

These questions and many more face the board. Undoubtedly they may rely on the paid staff to make recommendations, but the board is responsible for policy and the budget represents "policy." This responsibility cannot be delegated.

20.2   MONTHLY AND QUARTERLY BUDGETS

After the organization has prepared an annual budget, the budget must be divided into meaningful segments that can be compared to interim financial statements prepared on a monthly or quarterly basis. Some organizations attempt to do this by dividing the total budget by twelve and showing the resulting amounts as a monthly budget, which is then compared to actual monthly income and expenses. While this is better than not making any budget comparison, it can produce misleading results when the income or expenses do not occur on a uniform basis throughout the year, as is usually the case. Consider the following abbreviated statement of a small church:

	Annual Budget	Three Months Ending March 31	
		Annual Budget ÷ 4	Actual
Contributions ...	$ 120,000	$ 30,000	$ 35,000
Less Expenses ..	(120,000)	(30,000)	(30,000)
Excess	—	—	$ 5,000

The logical conclusion that might be drawn is that the church will have a surplus at the end of 12 months of approximately $20,000: four times the quarterly excess of $5,000. If this conclusion were reached, the temptation would be to slacken off on unpaid pledge collection efforts and to be a little less careful in making purchases. This would be a very serious mistake if, in fact, the normal pattern of pledge collections were such that $40,000 should have been collected in the first quarter instead of the $35,000 actually received. A monthly or quarterly budget can produce misleading conclusions unless considerable care is taken in preparing it.

(a)   Allocating an Annual Budget to Monthly or Quarterly Periods

One of the best and easiest ways to allocate an annual budget into shorter periods is to first analyze the actual income and expense for the prior year, and then allocate this year's budget based on last year's actual expenses.

To illustrate, assume the church's income last year was $100,000 but is expected to be $120,000 this year. A budget for the new year could be prepared as follows:

	Actual Last Year	Percent of Last Year's Total	New Budget
Income:			
First quarter	$ 30,000	30%	$ 36,000
Second quarter ..	25,000	25%	30,000
Third quarter	25,000	25%	30,000
Fourth quarter ...	20,000	20%	24,000
	$100,000	100%	$120,000

In this illustration, we have assumed that the increase in income of $20,000 will be received in the same pattern as the prior year's income was received. If this assumption is not correct, then adjustment must be made for the anticipated income which will depart from past experience. For example, if it is anticipated that a single gift of $10,000 will be received in the first quarter and the other $10,000 will be received in about the same pattern as last year's income, the calculations to arrive at a new budget would be somewhat different, as shown below:

	Actual Last Year	Percent of Last Year's Total	New Budget Other Than Special	Special Gifts	Total Budget
First quarter	$ 30,000	30%	$ 33,000	$10,000	$ 43,000
Second quarter	25,000	25%	27,500	—	27,500
Third quarter	25,000	25%	27,500	—	27,500
Fourth quarter	20,000	20%	22,000	—	22,000
	$100,000	100%	$110,000	$10,000	$120,000

If at the end of the first quarter, income of only $35,000 had been received compared to a budget of $43,000, it would be apparent that steps should be taken to increase contributions or the church will fall short of meeting its budget for the year.

The expense side of the budget should be handled in the same way. Generally, expenses tend to occur at a more uniform rate, although this is not always so. In many ways the expense side of the budget is more important than the income side since it is easier to increase expenditures for things that weren't budgeted than to raise additional contributions. If the budget is regularly compared to actual expenditures for deviations, it can be an effective tool to highlight unbudgeted expenditures.

The more frequently year-to-date actual information is compared with the budget for the same period, the better able management and the board will be to respond to changing circumstances before small problems become big ones. If possible, the budget, and actual data, should be prepared on a monthly basis. If this proves to be too cumbersome, consideration could be given to quarterly or bimonthly budgets and statements. However, if the organization's cash position is tight, monthly statements become almost a necessity.

(b)   Illustrative Expense Budget

The Valley Country Club is a good example of an organization that has to be very careful to budget its income and expenses. While the club has a beautiful clubhouse and a fine golf course, all of its money is tied up in these fixed assets and there is no spare cash to cover a deficit. Accordingly, each fall when the board starts to wrestle with the budget for the following year, it is aware that it cannot afford the luxury of a deficit. Since the budget is so important, the entire board sits as a budget committee to work out the plans for the following year. The club manager, with the help of the treasurer, prepares a worksheet in advance of the budget meeting. This worksheet indicates the actual expenses for the current year to date, the estimate of the final figures for the year, and the current year's budget to show how close the club will come. The board through discussion and debate attempts to work out a budget for the coming year. Exhibit 20–1 shows the worksheet for the expense budget.

In looking at this worksheet, notice first that the expenses are grouped by major function so that the board can focus attention on the activities of the club. The alternative presentation would have been to list expenses by type—salaries, supplies, food—but this doesn't tell the board how much each of the major activities is costing. Knowledge of the cost of each activity is needed to know whether the club is making or losing money on them, so that intelligent decisions can be made about levels of charges to be assessed to members for participation.

There are three columns for the proposed budget—the minimum, the maximum, and the final amount. As the board considers each item, it records both the minimum and the maximum it feels is appropriate. No attempt is made at the beginning to fix a "final" budget amount. Instead, all budget items are considered, listed as to the minimum and maximum cost, and totals arrived at. It is only after all items have been considered, and only after a preliminary review of potential income has been made, that the board is in a position to make judgments.

After the board has completed this worksheet showing final figures for the year, the next step is to break down the budget into monthly pieces. As with many organizations, the Valley Country Club's expenses (and income) are seasonal. In this case, the budget is broken down into monthly segments assuming that the expenses will be incurred in the same pattern as expected for the current year, in the manner discussed earlier.

20.3 TIMELY INTERIM STATEMENTS

The most carefully thought out budget will be of little value if it is not compared throughout the year with the actual results of operations. This means that the interim financial statements must be prepared on a timely basis.

What is timely? This depends on the organization and how much "slippage" or deviation from budget the organization can afford before serious consequences take place. If the cash balance is very low, an organization can't afford the luxury of not knowing where it stands on a very timely basis. Guidelines are dangerous, but if an organization is unable to produce some form of abbreviated monthly or quarterly financial statement within 20 days of the end of the period, the likelihood is that the information is "stale" by the time it is received by those who depend on it for decision making. If 20 days is the length of time it takes then the board should plan to meet shortly after the twentieth of the month so as to be able to act on deviations while there is still time to act.

This is not to suggest that monthly financial statements are always necessary for all not-for-profit organizations. But even if prepared on a bimonthly or quarterly basis, they should still be prepared on a timely basis.

(a) Importance of Budget Comparison

The internal financial statement should also show the budget, and for the same period of time. Interim figures for the three months cannot easily be compared to budget figures for twelve months. The budget must also be for three months. Last year's actual figures for the same period, and the current full-year's budget, may also be shown if that is considered helpful. However, the more information a reader of a financial report has to absorb, the greater the chance that added information could detract from rather than help the reader's understanding of the information presented.

Exhibit 20–2 shows the Valley Country Club Statement of Income and Expenses for both the month of June and for the six months, with budget comparisons to highlight deviations from the budget.

EXHIBIT 20–1   Worksheet used in preparing an expense budget for a country club.

THE VALLEY COUNTRY CLUB
WORKSHEET FOR PREPARING 19X1 EXPENSE BUDGET
(in thousands)

	Actual Current Year			Budget Current Year	Budget for New Year		
	To Date (10 Months)	Estimate Balance of Year	Estimate for Year		Proposed Minimum	Proposed Maximum	Final
Maintenance of greens and grounds:							
Salaries and wages	$ 47	$ 3	$ 50	$ 46	$ 50	$ 65	$ 55
Seeds, fertilizer and supplies ..	14		14	13	14	14	14
Repairs, maintenance and other	12	2	14	10	10	15	15
Maintenance of clubhouse:							
Salaries and wages	20	4	24	23	24	28	26
Supplies, maintenance and repair	10	1	11	12	11	11	11
Golf activities:							
Salaries and wages	10		10	11	12	20	20
Tournament costs	14		14	15	15	15	15
Golf cart maintenance	8		8	5	5	5	5

Swimming pool expenses:					
Salaries and wages	4	4	4	5	10	5
Supplies and maintenance	2	2	1	2	2	2
General and administrative						
salaries	35	41	40	44	51	44
Property taxes	33	40	38	42	42	42
Other expenses	41	48	40	40	50	50
Total, excluding restaurant	250	280	258	274	328	304
Restaurant expenses:						
Food and beverages	96	109	67	110	150	130
Salaries and wages:						
Kitchen	32	38	30	45	60	50
Dining room	20	24	19	26	39	32
Bartender	11	13	10	14	19	16
Supplies, repairs and maintenance	13	17	8	15	25	18
Total restaurant	172	201	134	210	293	246
Total expenses	$422	$481	$392	$484	$621	$550

EXHIBIT 20–2 Statement of income and expenses, showing a comparison with budget.

VALLEY COUNTRY CLUB

STATEMENT OF INCOME AND EXPENSES, AND COMPARISON WITH BUDGET

For the Month of June and the 6 Months Ended June 30, 19X1

	Month			6 Months		
	Actual	Budget	Deviation Favorable (Unfavorable)	Actual	Budget	Deviation Favorable (Unfavorable)
Income:						
Annual dues	$15,650	$17,000	($1,350)	$ 81,900	$ 90,000	($ 8,100)
Initiation fees	2,100	2,000	100	6,600	4,500	2,100
Greens fees	4,750	4,000	750	11,000	8,000	3,000
Swimming	3,300	3,000	300	2,300	2,000	300
Other	6,710	8,000	(1,290)	18,250	14,000	4,250
Total, excluding restaurant	32,510	34,000	(1,490)	120,050	118,500	1,550
Restaurant	37,850	34,000	3,850	168,500	180,000	(11,500)
Total income	70,360	68,000	2,360	288,550	298,500	(9,950)
Expenses:						
Maintenance of greens and grounds	14,650	12,000	(2,650)	37,650	36,000	(1,650)
Maintenance of clubhouse	3,450	3,000	(450)	18,100	19,000	900
Golf activities	13,500	10,000	(3,500)	19,500	16,000	(3,500)
Swimming pool	3,400	3,000	(400)	5,100	4,000	(1,100)
General and administrative	4,200	3,700	(500)	24,150	22,000	(2,150)
Payroll taxes	3,700	3,500	(200)	23,500	21,000	(2,500)
Other expenses	4,150	5,000	850	19,560	20,000	440
Total, excluding restaurant	47,050	40,200	(6,850)	147,560	138,000	(9,560)
Restaurant	29,550	27,000	(2,550)	145,650	153,000	7,350
Total expenses	76,600	67,200	(9,400)	293,210	291,000	(2,210)
Excess of income over (under) expenses	($ 6,240)	$ 800	($7,040)	($ 4,660)	$ 7,500	($12,160)

This financial statement gives the reader a great deal of information about the club's activities for the two periods. It should have the effect of alerting the reader to the fact that unless something happens, there may be a deficit for the year. For instead of having a small excess for June, there was a deficit of $6,240, and instead of having an excess of $7,500 for the six months, there was a deficit of almost $5,000. The board member reading the statement should be concerned about these deviations from the budget. This form of presentation makes it easy to see deviations. Unfavorable deviations can be quickly pinpointed and the reasons for them can be explored to determine the action that must be taken to "make up" (if possible) for their effects and to prevent their recurrence.

Notice that both the current month and the year-to-date figures are shown on this statement. Both are important. The monthly figures give a current picture of what is happening, which cannot be learned from the six-month figures. If only the six-month figures were shown the reader would have to refer to the previous month's statements showing the first five months to see what happened in June. Likewise, to show only the month, with no year-to-date figures, puts a burden on the reader. Some calculating using previous monthly statements would be required to get a total and see where the club stood cumulatively. Year-to-date budget comparisons are often more revealing than monthly comparisons because minor fluctuations in income and expenses tend to offset over a period of months. These fluctuations can appear rather large in any one month.

(b) Restaurant Operation

Restaurant income and expenses have been shown "gross" in the statements. It would be equally proper for the club to show net income for the club before the restaurant operation was considered. Here is how this would look:

Income (excluding restaurant)	$ 120,050
Expenses (excluding restaurant)	147,560
Excess of expenses over income excluding restaurant	(27,510)
Restaurant	
Gross income	168,500
Expenses	(145,650)
Net restaurant income	22,850
Excess of expenses over income	$ (4,660)

Another possibility is to show only the net income of the restaurant in the statements, perhaps in the income section. In condensed form here is how the statements would look:

Income
 Other than restaurant .... $ 120,050
 Restaurant net income 22,850
  Total income 142,900
 Expenses (other than restaurant) .... (147,560)
 Excess of expenses over income .... $ (4,660)

Either presentation, or the one in Exhibit 20–2, is acceptable. The appropriate presentation depends on the importance of highlighting the restaurant activities.

(c) Variable Budget

One technique that is often used in budgeting an operation where costs increase as the volume of activity increases is to relate the budgeted costs to income. For example, the final expense budget (Exhibit 20–1) and the relationship to budgeted income for the restaurant operation is as follows:

	Amount	Percent of Income
Income	$290,000	100%
Food and beverages	$130,000	45%
Salaries and wages		
Kitchen	50,000	17
Dining room	32,000	11
Bartender	16,000	6
Supplies, repairs and maintenance	18,000	6
	$246,000	85%

If all costs increase proportionately as income increases, it is a simple matter to create new budget figures each month based on actual income. Using the six-month figures shown in Exhibit 20–2, our budget comparison for the restaurant activity for the six-month period would look like this:

	Actual	Variable Budget	Deviation from Variable Budget	Deviation from Original Budget Shown in Figure 19–2
Income	$168,500	$180,000[a]	$(11,500)	$(11,500)
Expenses (in total)	145,650	143,225[b]	(2,425)	7,350
Net	$ 22,850	$ 36,775	$(13,925)	$ (4,150)

[a] Original budget for six months.
[b] 85% of actual income for the six months, based on the relationship of budgeted expenses to budgeted income as shown above.

The significant observation here is that while the original budget comparison in Exhibit 20–2 showed an unfavorable deviation from budget of only $4,150, the unfavorable deviation using this variable budget is significantly higher, $13,925. If the variable budget is accurate, the club manager has not been watching costs carefully enough.

The financial statements would show only the variable expense budget. The original expense budget would not be used. This kind of budget is more difficult to work with because each month the treasurer or bookkeeper has to recalculate the expense figures to be used based on actual income. At the same time by doing so, a more meaningful budget comparison can then be made. It would be very difficult otherwise for the board to judge the restaurant's results.

One final observation about this variable budget. Certain costs are not proportional to income. For example, the club cannot have less than one bartender or one chef. Accordingly, in preparing a variable budget sometimes the relationships that are developed will not be simple percentage relationships. For example, perhaps the relationship of bartender salary will be, say, $5,000 plus 5 percent of total income over $75,000. If so, then if restaurant income is $350,000, the budget will be $18,750 ($5,000 + 5 percent of $275,000).

(d) Narrative Report on Deviations from Budget

Much of the detail shown in the budget (Exhibit 20–1) has not been shown on the interim financial statement (Exhibit 20–2). If the board felt it appropriate, supporting schedules could be prepared giving as much detail as desired. Care should be taken, however, not to request details that won't be used since it takes time and costs money to prepare detailed supporting schedules, even when the mechanics of preparation are done by computer.

It may be that a more meaningful supporting schedule would be a narrative summary of the reasons for the deviations from budget for the major income and expense categories. The club manager, in the case of the Valley Country Club, would probably be the one to prepare this summary. It should then be reviewed by the treasurer prior to the full board meeting so that questions that are likely to be asked in that meeting can be anticipated and answers obtained. The amount of detail and description that might be put in this summary would vary from account to account. The report should discuss only reasons for the major deviations. This report should accompany the financial statements so that questions raised by the statement are answered immediately. Exhibit 20–3 is an example of the type of summary that might be prepared to explain the expense deviations from budget (in part).

This type of report can be as informal as you want to make it as long as it conveys why there have been deviations from the original budget.

EXHIBIT 20–3   An example of a narrative report prepared by the manager of a country club explaining why certain major deviations have occurred from budget.

VALLEY COUNTRY CLUB
CLUB MANAGER'S REPORT TO THE BOARD
EXPENSE DEVIATIONS FROM BUDGET, JUNE 19X1

Maintenance of Greens and Grounds ($2,650)
As you will recall, April and May were fairly wet months. This coupled with other unfavorable soil conditions required that we treat about 25% of the course with a fungicide which had not been budgeted ($1,850). We also had some unexpected repairs to the sprinkler system ($1,500). For the six months to date we have exceeded budget by only $1,650 and I am confident that our annual budget will not be exceeded.

Maintenance of Clubhouse ($450)
We had scheduled painting the Clubhouse for May but because of the rains were not able to get it done until this month. Year-to-date expenses are $900 under budget.

Golf Activities ($3,500)
After the budget had been approved the Board decided to have an open tournament with a view toward attracting new membership. With promotion and prizes this came to $2,850. So far the membership committee has received thirteen new applications for membership.

But it should be in writing, both to ensure that the board knows the reasons, and to force the club manager to face squarely the responsibility to meet the projected budget. This report is a form of discipline for the manager.

(e)   Action by the Board

The best-prepared budget serves little purpose if the board is unwilling to take action once it becomes apparent that expenses are exceeding budget or that income has not been as high as anticipated. To be useful, the budget must be a planning device that *everyone* takes seriously. There must be follow-up action.

The type of reporting discussed in this chapter will give the board information on where the plan is not being followed. But the board must be prepared to take action when the deviations indicate the existence of serious problems. Perhaps all that will be necessary is for the board to discuss the budget deviations with the club manager. A club manager who knows that the board fully expects performance within the budget will take appropriate action. If some matters are beyond the control of the manager, he or she may suggest alternatives to the board for its action.

The board must be prepared to take action to modify its plans if it becomes apparent that the budget cannot be met. If the organization has substantial resources to fall back on, it can afford to accept some deviations from the original budget without serious financial consequences. For most organizations, this is not the case. The board must be willing to face unpleasant facts once it becomes apparent from interim financial statements that corrective action must be taken. Many budgets fail, not because there is not enough information available to the board, but because the board fails to take aggressive, corrective action. In these instances, the board is not fulfilling its responsibilities and the budget is a meaningless formality. Chapter 21 discusses this topic further.

20.4   A FIVE-YEAR MASTER PLAN

So far our discussion has centered on budgeting techniques for the current year. Almost as important are the techniques for planning even further into the future than the twelve-month period most budgets show. As will be discussed more fully in the next chapter, organizations must be constantly alert to changing conditions that may alter their goals or objectives and thus their sources of income. Otherwise, they may find themselves in unexpected financial difficulty. One of the more effective ways organizations can avoid the unexpected is to prepare, and periodically update, a five-year master plan. The purpose of this five-year plan is to force the board to look ahead and anticipate not only problems but goals and objectives that it wants to work toward achieving.

The development of a five-year plan requires considerable effort. The treasurer can be the person who initiates and pushes the board toward developing such a plan but cannot single-handedly prepare it. As discussed earlier, to be effective any plan of action involving the organization's program and allocation of resources must be developed by all of the people who will have to live with the resulting plans. To unilaterally prepare a five-year plan risks the strong possibility that the treasurer's conceptions of the important objectives are not consistent with those of the conceptions of the rest of the board or the membership.

(a) Suggested Procedures

There is no "standard" way to go about preparing a five-year plan. Probably the best way to start is to set up a committee of, say, three persons. The persons chosen for this five-year planning committee should be persons who are in policy-making roles within the organization. There is little point in putting a person on this committee who is not both knowledgeable and influential within the organization. Otherwise the resulting document will be of relatively little value to the organization.

Setting Goals

Before meeting as a committee, each member should be instructed to list all of the goals or objectives that are considered important for each of the next five years. The list can be specific or general. The important thing is to get down some thoughts as to what the organization should be doing during each year, particularly as they might be different from what is being done currently. No consideration should be given at this point to dollar costs—only goals or objectives.

Once each member of the committee has independently prepared this conception of the future goals or objectives of the organization, the committee should meet and discuss these projections jointly. There may or may not be initial agreement among the three, and if not, there should be extended discussions to try to establish a plan of objectives that all members can agree on as being reasonable. If, after extended discussions, the committee cannot agree on these broad objectives, they should go back to the board for direction. All of this is *before* any figures have been associated with each specific objective or goal. The organization must decide what its goals or objectives are before it starts worrying about costs.

Estimating Costs

Once the committee has agreed upon objectives for each of the five years, then it is appropriate to start to estimate the costs involved in reaching each of these goals. This can be difficult because there are always many unknowns and uncertainties as to the details of how each goal will be accomplished. Nevertheless, it is important that the best estimate be made by the committee. The treasurer and club manager are key people in this estimating process. Among other things, it is up to the treasurer to try to factor inflation and realism as to costs into these figures.

After the committee has associated dollar costs with each objective for the five years, the next step is to add up the total to see how much income will have to be raised. Notice that until this point, no real consideration has been given to how the goals will be financed. This is important because in long-range planning an organization should set its objectives and then look for the means to reach them. If the objectives are good ones which the membership or public will agree should be accomplished, the financial support should follow. An organization gets into difficulty when it does not periodically re-evaluate its direction and thus finds itself out of step with those who support the organization financially and in other ways. The procedure to follow is first to define the objectives and goals, then to associate dollar amounts with each, and finally to determine how to raise the necessary income.

Plan for Income

This final step of determining how the income will be raised is usually not as difficult as it may sound provided the goals and objectives are ones that the board and the membership believe are sound. It is possible that as a result of this five-year plan new sources of income may be required. Perhaps a foundation will be approached, or perhaps a major capital improvement fund drive will be started. There are many possibilities. The important thing is that the organization has no right to exist except as it serves societal or members' interests. So if the organization keeps up with the times, it should be able to get sufficient support to achieve its objectives; if it does not, this is clear evidence that the objectives or goals are not sufficiently important to justify support. At that point the organization should either change its goals or should seriously consider the desirability of discontinuing its existence.

(b) Illustrative Master Plan

The result of this whole process is a master plan that should guide the board in its planning. It should be reviewed at least every year or two and

EXHIBIT 20–4   An example of a five-year master plan which emphasizes the objectives and goals of the organization.

CENTER FOR THE DEVELOPMENT OF HUMAN RESOURCES
Master Plan—19X2 THROUGH 19X6

	19X2	19X3	19X4	19X5	19X6
Goals or objectives:					
Develop and run management program	$ 17,000	$ 22,000	$ 25,000	$ 27,000	$ 30,000
Reprogram receptive listening program	12,000	—	—	—	—
Continue receptive listening program	35,000	35,000	45,000	45,000	45,000
Work with other "centers" across country	—	12,000	15,000	15,000	15,000
Develop and run child day care training center	8,000	15,000	20,000	20,000	20,000
Explore Project "A"	20,000	10,000	—	—	—
Run other programs	40,000	45,000	50,000	55,000	55,000
Purchase building for center	—	150,000	—	—	—
Total	132,000	289,000	155,000	162,000	165,000
Sources of income:					
Contributions from members	60,000	45,000	60,000	60,000	60,000
Special gifts and legacies	10,000	10,000	—	—	—
Building fund drive	—	100,000	—	—	—
Program fees:					
Management	10,000	15,000	18,000	20,000	22,000
Receptive listening	30,000	35,000	45,000	45,000	45,000
Child care	—	5,000	10,000	10,000	10,000
Other	38,000	40,000	45,000	45,000	45,000
Foundation grants:					
Child care	10,000	—	—	—	—
Building fund	—	50,000	—	—	—
Total	158,000	300,000	178,000	180,000	182,000
Projected surplus	$ 26,000	$ 11,000	$ 23,000	$ 18,000	$ 17,000

should be updated and extended so that it represents, at all times, a five-year plan for the future. Exhibit 20–4 shows an example of a simple master plan for the Center for the Development of Human Resources. The Center for the Development of Human Resources exists to help individuals "grow" through interaction in study groups. The center has a professional staff organizing and running programs, which are held in a rented building.

Note that on this master plan the center has indicated future expenses not in terms of the type of expenses (salaries, rent, supplies, etc.) but in terms of the goals or objectives of the organization. This distinction is important because the center pays its expenses only to further some goal or objective. Thus, in a master plan it is entirely appropriate to associate costs with each goal or objective. This means that a certain amount of allocation of salaries and other costs between goals will be necessary.

Another observation is that the format of this master plan did not start off with the traditional approach of showing income and then deducting expenses. Instead, the goals or objectives were stated first, and only after the organization agreed on what it wanted to do did it start to work on how to raise the necessary income. This point has been emphasized because the organization does not exist to raise money and pay expenses; it exists to accomplish certain objectives, and unless these are spelled out clearly and are constantly kept in mind, the organization may lose sight of the reason for its existence.

No attempt was made in this master plan to balance the amounts of income and expense except in a general way. In each year, there is an indicated surplus. This recognizes that while the board has made its best guess as to how it will raise its income, there are a great many unknowns when working with a five-year budget. As each year passes and this five-year plan is updated (and extended), the sources of income will become more certain, as will costs, and these figures will be refined and adjusted. The important thing, however, is that the board has set down what it plans to do in the future, and how it now expects to be able to finance such plans.

20.5 CONCLUSION

A budget can be an extremely important and effective tool for the board in managing the affairs of the organization. However, to prepare a meaningful budget the organization must know where it is heading and its goals and objectives. Priorities change, and this means that many people should be involved in the budget preparation and approval process to insure the resulting budget is fully supported. Once prepared, the budget must be compared to actual results on a timely basis throughout the year to insure that the board knows where deviations are occurring. Equally important, the board must promptly take corrective action if problems are discovered. The foundations of a sound financial structure are a well-conceived budget, a timely reporting system, and a willingness by the board to take corrective action.

The importance of planning into the future cannot be overemphasized. In this fast-moving age, worthy not-for-profit organizations can quickly get out of step with the times, and when this happens contributions and other income quickly disappear. A five-year master plan is one technique to help ensure this won't happen.

C H A P T E R 21

Avoiding Bankruptcy

"Bankruptcy?" "It can't happen to us!" Of course it can; don't think that your organization is immune. Whether the organization is a commercial or a not-for-profit one, insolvency will be the fate of some organizations that are today vigorous and healthy. An organization's importance and reputation will not protect it. Avoiding bankruptcy takes effort and real skill.

21.1 EARLY RECOGNITION OF PROBLEMS

While the final responsibility for the financial health of the organization is the board's, the treasurer is the person charged with watching both the day-to-day and long-term financial picture. One of the most important functions of the treasurer is to recognize potential problems while there is still time to act. While it might seem like a simple task to recognize that the organization is in, or is headed for, financial trouble, the fact is that many people fail to recognize the symptoms at a time when they might still be able to do something.

379

Recognizing that there is a problem on a timely basis is important because most not-for-profit organizations have so little cash. They cannot afford the luxury of waiting until after the problem has fully manifested itself. If they do, they may run out of cash. If there are substantial reserves in the bank, an organization can afford several years of deficits before it really has to become concerned about the future. But few organizations have this comfortable level of cash reserves. Organizations usually have enough cash for only three or four months' operations if all income were to cease.

A balanced budget, based on conservative revenue estimates, is an effective means to avoid financial calamity. A balanced budget requires that difficult decisions, such as program curtailment or elimination, be made during each budget cycle, rather than deferring them until a future date, at which time a genuine crisis may have developed and the future of the organization itself may be imperiled.

There is no perpetual life for not-for-profit organizations. And this is as it should be. Not-for-profit organizations have a privileged place in our society. Most have been granted certain tax privileges which means that society as a whole has a right to demand that they perform their function in the public interest. If the organization fails to be responsive, no matter how "worthwhile" its program may be when viewed objectively from afar, the organization will have a short life. This is as true of churches and religious organizations as it is of other types. The organization must be responsive, and the contributor is the final judge of whether it is or not. This means the treasurer must be alert to indications that the health of the organization may be declining either as shown in historical financial statements, or as projected into the future.

(a)   Historical Statements as a Guide

Many look upon past financial statements only as a historical bookkeeping record that has little significance for the future. This is a mistake. Often, there is a clear indication in these statements of potential problems for the future. This can often be seen by comparing several years' statements, because relationships may become obvious that were not apparent when looking at only one year's statements.

An example can best illustrate this point. The five-year operating statement of the Center for World Peace is shown in Exhibit 21–1.

This statement offers a great deal of information to the observant treasurer and should help in anticipating problems. The obvious and most serious problem revealed is that there has been a large deficit in 19X5 which, if repeated, would wipe out the organization. But beyond this obvious observation, a number of other important clues can be seen.

EXHIBIT 21–1 An example of a five-year Statement of Income, Expenses, and Cash Balances which can assist the reader in spotting trends.

CENTER FOR WORLD PEACE

SUMMARY OF INCOME, EXPENSES, AND CASH BALANCES RESULTING
FROM CASH TRANSACTIONS

For the Five Years Ended December 31, 19X5

	19X1	19X2	19X3	19X4	19X5
Income:					
Contributions	$ 53,000	$ 65,000	$ 56,000	$ 66,000	$ 49,000
Program fees	46,000	48,000	48,000	50,000	52,000
Other	3,000	3,000	2,000	3,000	2,000
Total income	102,000	116,000	106,000	119,000	103,000
Expenses:					
Salaries	68,000	72,000	76,000	78,000	80,000
Rent	14,000	16,000	18,000	20,000	24,000
Supplies	9,000	10,000	14,000	18,000	22,000
Other	3,000	3,000	4,000	5,000	6,000
Total expenses	94,000	101,000	112,000	121,000	132,000
Excess of income over (under) expenses	8,000	15,000	(6,000)	(2,000)	(29,000)
Cash balance, beginning of the year	34,000	42,000	57,000	51,000	49,000
Cash balance, end of the year	$ 42,000	$ 57,000	$ 51,000	$ 49,000	$ 20,000

Note first the relationship between expenses and program fees over the years. From 19X1 to 19X5 expenses have gone up almost 40 percent, but program fees have gone up only 13 percent. Either the organization is not charging enough for its programs, or the programs are not responsive to the membership and therefore attendance is down. Alternatively, perhaps the center has gotten too sophisticated in its programming, with too many paid staff for the size of fees that can be charged. These are the kinds of questions that have to be asked.

Another question that should concern the treasurer is why contributions have fluctuated so much from year to year. Is there significance in the decline in contributions received, from $66,000 in 19X4 to $49,000 in 19X5? Does this represent a strong "vote" by the membership that they are not interested in the programs of the center or that something is wrong? This question concerned the treasurer and after some digging, these facts were found:

Year	Recurring Contributions	Special or One-Time Gifts	Total
19X1	$43,000	$10,000	$53,000
19X2	45,000	20,000	65,000
19X3	47,000	9,000	56,000
19X4	55,000	11,000	66,000
19X5	49,000	—	49,000

From this analysis it is easy to see what happened. The center had been living off special or one-time gifts and these gifts were not received in 19X5. Most of the special gifts had come from half a dozen people, some now deceased. The earlier five-year summary did not tell the whole story, and the treasurer recast this statement showing these special gifts separately. Exhibit 21–2 shows these revised statements in condensed form.

From Exhibit 21–2, it was easy for the treasurer and the board to see that they had been living off special gifts in every year except 19X5. Hard decisions had to be made as to whether the center should count on receiving such special gifts in the future and, if not, how expenses could be cut or additional income gained.

(b) Analysis of Interim Statements

It is not necessary (or wise) to wait for the completion of a full year's activities before starting to draw conclusions from the trends that should be obvious to the careful analyst. Exhibit 21–3 is a worksheet showing a comparison of actual with budget for three months, and a projection for

EXHIBIT 21–2 A five-year Statement of Income and Expenses in which nonrecurring special gifts are shown separately to highlight continuing income.

CENTER FOR WORLD PEACE

SUMMARY OF INCOME AND EXPENSES

For the Five Years Ended December 31, 19X5

	19X1	19X2	19X3	19X4	19X5
Recurring income:					
Contributions	$ 43,000	$ 45,000	$ 47,000	$ 55,000	$ 49,000
Program fees	46,000	48,000	48,000	50,000	52,000
Other	3,000	3,000	2,000	3,000	2,000
Total	92,000	96,000	97,000	108,000	103,000
Expenses (total)	94,000	101,000	112,000	121,000	132,000
Excess of expenses over recurring income	(2,000)	(5,000)	(15,000)	(13,000)	(29,000)
Special nonrecurring gifts ..	10,000	20,000	9,000	11,000	—
Excess of income over (under) expenses	$ 8,000	$ 15,000	($ 6,000)	($ 2,000)	($ 29,000)

the entire year based on the assumption that the experience for the first three months compared to budget is a good indication of what can be expected for the next nine months.

Based on this worksheet, unless something happens to change the pattern, instead of being ahead of budget the center is headed for a deficit of $23,000. As will be recalled, the center had only $20,000 in cash at the beginning of the year, and cannot afford to have a deficit of $23,000. The board can hardly spend money it does not have, and yet it appears that some time during the fourth quarter this is exactly what is going to happen.

The point should be obvious. If the treasurer does not stay on top of the finances of an organization, serious trouble may be discovered only after it is too late to do anything about it.

The following checklist may be helpful in identifying financial problems before they endanger the organization.

Signs That May Indicate Financial Trouble for Not-for-Profit Organizations

Community Support:

- Decline in utilization of organization's services by the local community (fewer students, patients, visitors, members, or other users).
- Decline in real dollar support through gifts, bequests, and membership dues.
- Decline in hours of time made available by volunteers.

EXHIBIT 21-3 An example of a worksheet projecting income and expenses for the year based on only the first three months' actual experience.

CENTER FOR WORLD PEACE

WORKSHEET SHOWING CALCULATION OF PROJECTED INCOME AND EXPENSES

For the Year 19X6

| | 3 Months to March 31 | | | 9 Months April to December | | 12 Months | |
	Actual	Budget	Percentage Actual to Budget	Budget	Projected Based on Actual[a]	Budget	Projected
Recurring income:							
Contributions	$18,000	$20,000	90%	$ 38,000	$ 34,200	$ 58,000	$ 52,200
Program fees	17,000	18,000	95%	42,000	39,900	60,000	56,900
Other	500	500	100%	1,500	1,500	2,000	2,000
Total	35,500	38,500	92%	81,500	75,600	120,000	111,100
Expenses:							
Salaries	22,000	21,000	105%	63,000	66,100	84,000	88,100
Rent	6,000	6,000	100%	18,000	18,000	24,000	24,000
Supplies	4,500	2,500	180%	7,500	13,500	10,000	18,000
Other	1,000	500	200%	1,500	3,000	2,000	4,000
Total	33,500	30,000	111%	90,000	100,600	120,000	134,100
Excess of income over (under) expenses	$ 2,000	$ 8,500		($ 8,500)	($ 25,000)	—	($ 23,000)

[a] I.e.: percentage actual to budget for three months times budget for nine months (90% × 38,000 = $34,200).

- Increasing incidence of turndown of grant requests.
- Criticism of the organization or its programs by public figures or media.

Financial Independence:

- A growing percentage of expenditures for basic operations financed by restricted grants.
- A growing percentage of own-source unrestricted revenues committed to meet matching requirements, or needed to supplement restricted revenues for special projects.
- Increasing reliance on very few different sources of support.
- A growing debt burden.
- Rapid increases in fixed cash costs (salaries and fringes, rent, debt service, others).
- Continuing decline or deficit in operating income or unrestricted net assets.
- Continuing decline or overdraft in cash and equivalents.

Productivity:

- Cost per unit of service rising rapidly.
- Number of employees per unit of service rising rapidly.
- User fee rates rising rapidly (unless resulting from a deliberate management decision to reduce the amount by which such fees are subsidized from other revenue sources).

Deferred Current Costs:

- Proceeds of long-term debt or sales of long-term investments being used for current purposes.
- Deferring needed maintenance of capital assets.
- Low or declining funding of replacement of capital assets near the end of their useful life.
- Default on debts (bonds, notes, mortgages, interest).
- Failure to pay payroll or other taxes when due.
- Inability to pay salaries or other current expenses when due, or borrowing to cover such amounts shortly before payment.
- Borrowing of cash or other assets from restricted funds or other diversion of restricted resources to inappropriate purposes.

Management Practices:

- A pattern of budget cost overruns, either overall or in specific programs/departments.
- Increasing incidence of revenue shortfalls.
- Earnings on investments declining disproportionately to general trends of investment yields.

- Interest rates charged by lenders increasing disproportionately to general trends of interest rates, unwillingness of lenders to lend to organization, or insistence by lenders on burdensome debt covenants.
- Levels of receivables, inventory, or prepaid expenses increasing faster than related activity would dictate.
- Increasing incidence of funding source challenge or disallowance of expenses.
- Financial and operating data being provided to board members and management is delayed, unclear, or incomplete. Explanations of key items and variances are unavailable or of doubtful validity.
- Failure on the part of board members or management to understand and accept the seriousness of the financial situation.

(c) Treasurer's Duty to Sound the Alarm

With all of these warning signs, the treasurer must call for help—loudly! The treasurer's job is to call the situation to the attention of the board. The real responsibility for solving the problem, however, is the board's. The treasurer may be able to offer recommendations on how to solve the problem. As the person closest to the finances, the treasurer will probably have some sound ideas. But under the laws of most states, it is the full board that is responsible for the continuation of the organization.

There is another very practical reason for calling for help as loudly as possible. Sometimes calling attention to a problem is all that is really necessary to start the wheels in motion to solve it. Perhaps some of the members who have been lax in making contributions or attending programs will start doing so.

21.2 REMEDIAL ACTION

Once the board has been forced to recognize the problem, what are the alternatives or courses of action that can be taken? There are perhaps six or seven, some of which may not be available to all organizations.

(a) Increasing Contributions

The most obvious solution to many organizations' financial problems is to raise additional contributions. However, this is usually much easier said than done. If contributions are received mainly in small amounts from many donors, it is not realistic to expect that the organization will be able to increase contributions by a very large amount. Unless the organization really motivates its donors, contributions tend to remain fairly constant from year to year except for small increases attributable to general cost of living increases, increased personal income, and so on.

This is not as true with donors making large contributions. If the organization can sell its program (called "making its case" in fund-raising parlance), often these larger donors will make additional special contributions. The key is that the organization must convince these large donors that the extra amount it needs to solve this year's crisis will not be needed again next year, and the year after, and so on. This means that in presenting its case, the organization must be able to show how it can and will avoid a similar difficulty next year. Otherwise, to the donor it will appear that a contribution is not really helping to solve the problem but only postponing it.

Credibility is an important aspect of the ability to raise additional funds. The board will have a greater chance of success if over the years it has presented meaningful financial statements to all donors and has not created doubts about the true financial condition. But even with good statements, an organization that is in serious difficulty will probably find that the first place to look is not at contributions. Contributions can be increased, but usually the response rate is too slow and the amounts too modest.

(b) Increasing Fees

Another source of increased income is raising fees charged for services being rendered. Modest increases usually can be "sold" if there has not been a recent increase. Most people recognize the effect of inflation. At the same time, increasing fees may decrease the number of persons using the services.

For example, in the case of the Center for World Peace, if the board were to increase charges by only 10 percent effective April 1, almost $4,000 would be added to income assuming nobody dropped out as a result of the increase. This represents almost 20 percent of the projected deficit for the year. If the programs are worthwhile, the board should be able to convince the membership that the alternative to increasing fees is discontinuing the organization's activities. If the board is unable to "sell" this, then perhaps it should question the need for these programs.

(c) Cutting Expenses

If it appears that there will be a deficit, and this deficit cannot be covered by increasing income, then most likely it will be necessary to reduce expenses. This is always difficult for the board of a not-for-profit organization to accept. A board often finds it difficult to accept the fact that sometimes an organization cannot do all that it wants to do, no matter how worthy.

Whatever the reason, not-for-profit organizations seem to have particular difficulty in recognizing that as with any individual, they must spend within their means. This is one reason why the treasurer can offer only suggestions and should not attempt to dictate solutions. The board has to wrestle with the policy question of which programs are in fact most "indispensable." The treasurer may have suggestions, but if these are forced on the organization without the board's full concurrence, the suggestions either will not "stick" or the treasurer's efforts will be sabotaged. Remember that not-for-profit organizations, unlike commercial ones, are heavily dependent on volunteer help and these volunteers must be in agreement with what is going on or they will stop volunteering their time and effort.

The conclusion is obvious. When the organization is threatened with insolvency, the board must either raise income or cut expenses. Cutting expenses, however unpleasant, is often the only practical solution to an immediate crisis.

(d)   Borrowing

One source of emergency funds that many organizations use is the bank. They will borrow to cover short-term emergency needs, particularly when they have fluctuations in their income. Short-term borrowing is fine if used only to cover fluctuating income, and if the treasurer is sure that there will be income from which to pay these monies back. On the other hand, what should not be done without some serious thought is to mortgage the organization's physical property to raise money to pay for current operations. It is one thing to borrow money for capital additions but it is an entirely different thing to borrow money that will be used for the day-to-day operations of the organization. If this becomes necessary, the treasurer and board should consider very carefully how they can reasonably expect to repay these loans. If repayment is in doubt, the board must seriously consider the future of the organization, and why it is prolonging the organization's life. Keep in mind that the board of a not-for-profit organization has a responsibility to act prudently on all matters. If it mortgages the "cow" to pay for its fodder with the full knowledge that it is going to have to sell the "cow" to pay the bank back, perhaps it should sell the "cow" to start with.

Many times a bank will lend funds to an organization on the basis of the members of the board being well-known and influential in the business community. This means an organization may be able to borrow money even though the banker may have some doubts about the organization's ability to repay. The banker knows, however, that the board members will not let the organization default. The board members should carefully consider the repayment problem. They will not want their personal reputations tarnished by subsequent difficulties with the bank.

(e) Applying for Foundation Grants

Grants from foundations are other potential sources of financial help. There are approximately 35,000 foundations in the United States, and under the Tax Reform Act of 1969, these foundations are required to distribute a minimum of 5 percent of their assets every year. While there are limitations regarding to whom such money can be given, generally any organization that is exempt under Section 501(c)(3)[1] (which excludes social clubs) and is not a "private foundation" can receive grants from foundations. Most people think of foundations as being only the large ones—the Ford Foundation, the Carnegie Foundation. While these giant foundations are giving millions of dollars to worthwhile organizations every year, there are thousands of lesser known foundations that are also granting millions.[2]

Each foundation receives many more requests than it can possibly handle, so it is important that application be made only to those whose stated interests coincide with the organization's. There is no point in wasting time in submitting a request for funds that will not receive serious consideration because it is outside of the foundation's scope of interest.

The formal application itself is very important. There are usually no standard forms as such to fill out. Instead, the application should outline succinctly and with feeling what the objectives of the organization are. It should document why the foundation's gift would be of significant help *and* how it would further the foundation's stated objectives. Keep both of these points in mind—why the grant would be significant, and how it would further the foundation's stated objectives. An application that cannot answer both of these points is defective.

The application should contain evidence that the board is effective and that the foundation won't be wasting its money if it makes a grant.

---

[1] Tax-exempt status is discussed in Chapter 26.

[2] The Foundation Directory, published by The Foundation Center, is a good source of information, especially about larger foundations. They are listed geographically by state. Included in each listing is a brief description of the foundation, the size of its assets, the amount of grants made, and the purposes for which the foundation will consider making a grant. In trying to find foundations to approach, an advantage may be gained where members of the organization's board already know one or more of the trustees of the foundation. There is no question that the chances are improved if the board's message can be informally presented to individual members of the foundation's board of trustees in advance of their considering the formal request. This does not mean that such personal contacts can assure success, but it certainly will improve the chances.

The application should contain complete financial information in a format that clearly indicates that the board has financial control of the organization. In the case of the Center for World Peace, the application would include the five-year summary of income and expenses, the budget for the current year, the projections based on the first quarter's results, and a projection for five years. This five-year projection is important to show that the crisis is truly under control, or will be under control, and that the foundation's grant will not necessarily have to be a continuing one.

The application should specify explicitly how the money will be used. Most foundations will not consider requests for money that will be merely added to the "pot" and used for general purposes. In the 1971 edition of *The Foundation Directory*, this point was emphasized:

> Fund-raisers need to be warned that at least the larger foundations do not usually make grants toward the operating budgets of agencies, whether national or local, or for individual need. Many foundations have accepted the doctrine that their limited funds should be used chiefly as the venture capital of philanthropy, to be spent in enterprises requiring risk and foresight, not likely to be supported by government or private individuals. In their fields of special interest they prefer to aid research, designed to push forward the frontiers of knowledge, or pilot demonstrations, resulting in improved procedures apt to be widely copied.
>
> Support for current programs, if it comes at all from foundations, must usually be sought from the smaller organizations, and especially those located in the area of the agency, well acquainted with its personnel and its needs. Most small foundations, and some larger ones, restrict their grants to the local community or state. Immense variety exists; the interests and limitations of each foundation need to be examined before it is approached.

Care must be taken to plan exactly how these funds will be used. This should not be done hastily. It takes many months to get foundation help and an organization that has not carefully thought out its needs may find that when it receives the grant it really would have preferred to spend the money in some other way. Foundations look with disfavor on organizations that ask that their grants be used for different purposes than originally specified.

Another thing to keep in mind is that many foundations like to make grants on a matching basis. That is, they will make the grant at such time as the organization has raised an equal or greater amount from other sources. This is in line with many foundations' concern that recipients not become dependent on foundation help.

Timing is important. Many foundations will approve grants only once or twice a year. This means that unless the application is received on a timely basis there may be a long delay before there is an answer. Foundation grants are not very likely to get an organization out of an immediate cash bind. But foundations can be very helpful to the organization that truly plans for its future and knows what it wants and how to accomplish its objectives. For these organizations, foundation help should be carefully considered because there are monies available.

(f) Merging with Another Organization

One of the alternatives that the board must consider if bankruptcy looms on the horizon is the possibility that the organization should merge with another organization having similar or at least compatible objectives. This is not a course of action that is always appealing but if the alternative is bankruptcy, then the only real question is how the objectives and programs of the organization can best be salvaged. It is probably better to have a combined program with another organization than to have no program at all. If the board doubts that this is true, then the reason for the continued existence of the organization is in doubt, and perhaps bankruptcy is the appropriate answer.

Where do you look for other candidates for merger? There is no easy answer. Basically you have to know the field that your organization is working in, and then you have to approach all possible candidates. Do not hesitate to do so, for it may turn out that there are other organizations in similar financial straits, which if combined with yours would make the resulting organization stronger than either was before. Keep in mind that unless you personally know the board members of the other organization you are not likely to know of their problems before you approach them. Perhaps they are also looking for a merger candidate.

There are other considerations that must be taken into account. One of the more important is to determine whether any of your donor-restricted funds contain restrictions that would prohibit use by a combined organization. Ideally the board could find a compatible organization with similar enough goals and objectives so that any restricted amounts could be effectively used. If there are problems in this area, ask the original donor for permission to change the restrictions.

Another consideration is whether the merged organization can accomplish the organization's objectives more effectively and at less cost than if it remained a separate entity. The merger may provide more resources that will probably make possible economies of scale. The chances are that there will be some opportunity for cost saving, perhaps through sharing staff, or facilities, or a combination of both. The board, however, should be sure that it looks very carefully before it leaps. It must analyze the other organization's financial statements and five-year plan very carefully. It serves very little purpose to trade one set of problems for another if several years from now the combined organization will again be on the verge of bankruptcy.

21.3   CONFRONTING BANKRUPTCY

Another possibility is that the board will conclude that the organization has accomplished the purposes for which it was set up, or that times have changed and the original objectives are no longer appropriate. If so, perhaps the humane thing to do is to let the organization "die," but in a controlled manner so as not to leave a trail of debts behind it. Although this may not seem like a very practical suggestion at first, it is one that must be considered by every thoughtful board member. If the members and contributors are not supporting the organization, then why not? If it is only a temporary problem of a poor economy, it is perhaps appropriate to try to wait for better times. But the board must be cautious in drawing this conclusion. It must not get so emotionally involved in the mechanics of the organization's programs that it loses sight of the need to respond to today's conditions, which are different from yesterday's. In this "throw away" society that we are in, not-for-profit organizations are not exempt, and those that do not serve society's current needs will find that bankruptcy will always be close by.

As the board gets closer and closer to a decision to curtail operations, the individual members of the board, as well as the treasurer, have to consider carefully the steps that should be taken to ensure that actual bankruptcy as such does not take place. No board wants to incur financial obligations that cannot be met. This includes salary obligations (and especially payroll taxes as those will become a personal obligation of the board members and management). As the time for going out of existence looms nearer, consideration must be given to an orderly dismissal of the staff with appropriate termination benefits to help them over the period of relocation. This is expensive, because once the decision to terminate operations is made, sources of income will dry up promptly. This means that the board members cannot wait until the bank account is empty to face these difficult decisions. If they do, either the board members themselves are going to personally face the prospects of making sizable contributions to cover their moral obligations, or they are going to leave unpaid debts and recriminations. Most board members have personal reputations at stake and this last alternative is not very attractive.

One area that must be carefully watched as cash gets low is the payment of payroll withholding taxes to the various levels of government. Usually the federal government can sue the treasurer personally, and all other persons responsible for nonpayment of such withholding taxes. These amounts are not usable funds of the organization as such, but are held in escrow until paid to the government. To use these funds to pay other bills is a very serious offense that can result not only in recovery from responsible persons, but also in subjection to fine and/or imprisonment.

Another consideration, if it is decided to discontinue operations, is that any funds or other assets that remain must either be given to another exempt organization or to the state. This is true for all tax-exempt organizations except social clubs. When thinking about discontinuing operations, competent legal help is needed to consider all ramifications. Timing is of major importance. The point at which operations will be discontinued must be anticipated and this must be before the bank account is empty. No board member wants the stigma of having been on a board of an organization that actually went bankrupt and could not pay its bills.

21.4 CONCLUSION

This chapter has discussed the ever present threat of bankruptcy many not-for-profit organizations face at one time or another. It was noted that one of the characteristics of such organizations is that they receive support only so long as they serve the needs of the public or their members. Since most organizations find it difficult to build up large cash reserves, they must be responsive.

If they are not, support will drop and unless the organization responds quickly, it could very well find itself on the verge of actual bankruptcy.

The treasurer's role of eliminating the unexpected was discussed, and several techniques reviewed to help the treasurer stay on top of the current financial situation. It was emphasized that when trouble looms, the treasurer's first and most important responsibility is to call "loud and clear" so that the board can take appropriate action. It is the board that must take action.

Most organizations in financial trouble find that is difficult to increase income by any substantial amount in a short period of time. Accordingly, when financial troubles loom, one of the first things the board must do is to cut back on its rate of expenditures. If some of the budgeting techniques in the previous chapters have been followed, the board will have plenty of warning that it must cut expenses and should be able to avoid actual bankruptcy.

It may be that the board will find, however, that the organization is not viable, and that the reason for its continuation no longer exists. When this occurs, it is important that the board take action on a timely basis to either merge it into another more viable organization, or to actually discontinue operations and dissolve the organization in a controlled manner. It is also important to constantly remember that a not-for-profit organization does not have a perpetual life. It can continue to exist only so long as it serves a worthwhile purpose which its members or the public will support.

Small Organizations:
Obtaining the Right Bookkeeper

Obtaining and keeping the right bookkeeper is the key to making life easy and routine for the treasurers of small organizations.[1] Unless the treasurer wants to spend substantial time and effort in keeping the records, a good bookkeeper is essential. There is nothing difficult about bookkeeping as such, but the details can become most wearisome to the busy volunteer treasurer. The time they consume can detract from the treasurer's other responsibilities, particularly that of planning. For most not-for-profit organizations, other than the very smallest, a part-or full-time bookkeeper will be hired.

The problem of finding the right bookkeeper is compounded for not-for-profit organizations because traditionally such organizations pay

---

[1] This chapter deals only with the bookkeeping problems of relatively small organizations. Larger organizations are not discussed because to a very large extent they are run like commercial organizations.

low salaries to all of their staff, including the bookkeeper. The salary level frequently results in the organization's getting someone with only minimum qualifications. This is false economy. A good bookkeeper can help the organization save money and can free the time of the volunteer treasurer.

Often the other staff in the organization are extremely dedicated individuals interested in the particular program of the organization and willing to accept a lower than normal salary. Bookkeepers are often not dedicated to the programs of the organization in the same way. They have been hired to provide bookkeeping services and may have no special interest in the program of the organization.

22.1 LEVEL OF BOOKKEEPING SERVICES NEEDED

The first step in obtaining a bookkeeper is to determine what bookkeeping services are needed. Depending on the size of the organization, there are a number of possibilities. If the organization is very small and fewer than 25 checks are issued a month, the treasurer will probably find that a "checkbook" type set of records will be all that is required or appropriate. If so, the treasurer may very well keep the records and not try to find someone to help. In this case the "bookkeeping problem" is merely one of finding enough time to keep the checkbook up-to-date and to prepare financial statements on a timely basis.

(a) Secretary as Bookkeeper

For many organizations, the number of transactions is too large for the treasurer to handle but not large enough to justify a full-time bookkeeper. If the organization has a paid full-or part-time secretary, often some of the bookkeeping duties are delegated to the secretary. Usually this means keeping the "checkbook" or perhaps a simple cash receipts and cash disbursements ledger.[2] At the end of the month, the treasurer will summarize these cash records and prepare the financial statements. While this means the treasurer will still have a lot of work to do, the work has been reduced significantly by having the secretary keep the basic records. This is a very practical approach for small organizations with very limited staff and not too many transactions.

---

[2] Chapter 30 discusses both a checkbook system of bookkeeping and a simple cash basis bookkeeping system. A secretary could probably keep most of the records in either of these systems with a minimum of instruction.

(b)   Volunteer as Bookkeeper

Another possibility for the small organization is to find a volunteer within the organization who will help keep the records. While this can occasionally be effective, it often turns out to be less than satisfactory. There is less control over the activities of a volunteer bookkeeper and it is difficult for the treasurer to insist that the records be kept on a timely basis. After all, volunteer bookkeepers are just that—volunteers—with all the rights and privileges that go with volunteers. Volunteers have to work around their own schedules and it is difficult to insist that they perform their duties on as strict a basis as with paid employees. Another problem with volunteers is that their tenure tends to be short. Keeping a set of books is work, and while a volunteer bookkeeper's enthusiasm may be great at the beginning, it tends to diminish in time. The result is that there are often delays, clerical errors, and eventually the need to get another bookkeeper. The volunteer bookkeeper is often not a good solution. A treasurer who cannot handle the bookkeeping should use a paid secretary or consider hiring a part-time bookkeeper.

(c)   Part-Time Bookkeepers

In considering a part-time bookkeeper, the first question is how much time is required. Is the job one that can be handled on a one-day-a-month basis, two-days-a-month, two-days-a-week? For most small organizations, the answer will probably be only a day or two a month, or at the most, a day a week. Where do you go to find a good part-time bookkeeper? This can be difficult.

Some of the best potential may be found among parents, with school children, who were full-time bookkeepers at one time. Since a part-time bookkeeping job can easily fit into a flexible schedule, permitting the parent to be home before and after school, this can be a very good arrangement if the bookkeeping needs are not more than 15 to 20 hours a week.

If the organization wants someone at its office for a full day each week or during hours not suitable for a parent with school children, then a retired bookkeeper or accountant may be a good possibility. Sometimes it is difficult to find a suitable retired person—one with practical bookkeeping experience. For example, a retired assistant treasurer of a large business had bookkeeping in school but may never have used the skills. While this person may have a sophisticated knowledge of business, he or she may not be competent as a bookkeeper. In addition, he or she may find the detail boring, and interest will be short-lived. Also, the hourly rate such persons may demand will probably be higher than that commanded by a competent bookkeeper. An ad in a local newspaper or inquiry of other organizations are probably the best places to start to look for a qualified person.

(d)   Full-Time Bookkeepers

For larger or growing organizations, there is a point when a full-time bookkeeper is needed. An advertisement in the newspaper is probably the best approach to finding a suitable employee. The ad should be explicit and should indicate salary, and the type of experience and competence this person will need. It should also indicate the type of organization since some applicants may not be interested in working for a not-for-profit organization.

Alternatively, an employment agency can be used. A good agency can save time and effort. The agency will place the ad in the paper and will do the initial weeding out of the obvious misfits before forwarding the potential candidates to the organization for review. Agencies also know the job market and will probably be in a good position to advise on the "going" salary. They should also be able to help in checking references.

These agencies charge a fee that is usually paid by the hiring organization, and this can be from two to six weeks' pay. The question that the treasurer must ask is, is it worth this amount for the help an agency can give? There is no sure answer to this question. In many instances, agency help is most valuable. On the other hand, some agencies do very little screening and the organization ends up with almost the same work that it would have had without the agency.

Often a friend of the treasurer knows of someone who is looking for a job and while there is no reason not to consider such a person, the treasurer should also interview others.

If the organization has outside auditors, they may be able to help. Get their advice, and before actually hiring a bookkeeper, let them talk with the candidates. While there is no guarantee that the right person will be hired, the auditors are more likely to be able to judge the candidate's technical skills and background than the treasurer is.

One final thought on hiring a bookkeeper (or any other employee, for that matter): don't skimp on the salary offered in the hope of "getting a bargain." Yes, it is easy to think that every dollar spent on staff (some people read that to mean on "overhead") is a dollar that did not go directly to feeding the hungry, curing cancer, and so on. But without a staff back at headquarters competent to do its job, there won't be much feeding or research going on. In all but the tiniest organizations, volunteers can only do so much without paid staff to back them up. When hiring staff, you usually get what you pay for. If you pay low salaries, you will get underqualified staff.

22.2 PERSONALITY CHARACTERISTICS

There are several personality characteristics that good bookkeepers often have that the treasurer should be aware of. A good bookkeeper is usually a very meticulous and well-organized person. This often means that the bookkeeper will become impatient with other members of the staff who are slow in providing the required information or who are sloppy in providing all of the necessary details. To the rest of the staff the book-keeper often appears to be a "nit picker." If the bookkeeper is not diplomatic, this can be annoying to the rest of the staff, but these are desirable qualities that the treasurer should not discourage.

Another desirable characteristic is that the bookkeeper will often be critical of the spending patterns of the organization, particularly if the organization is apparently not being frugal. This tendency to be critical of spending habits can be a very helpful trait that the treasurer should not discourage. The bookkeeper sees all of the spending of the organization and is bound to have an opinion about how wisely expenditures are made. The conclusion may not always be correct because the bookkeeper's vantage point is limited. Yet, from the treasurer's standpoint, the book-keeper acts as a watchdog and will often have some good ideas. The treasurer should not ignore them.

22.3 ALTERNATIVES TO BOOKKEEPERS

There are many ways to delegate the actual bookkeeping process to sources external to the organization. *Responsibility* for bookkeeping, however, cannot be delegated outside the organization. The treasurer or another employee of the organization must continuously monitor and review the work of an outside bookkeeper.

(a) Outside Preparation of Payroll

One thing that can be done to reduce the burden on the bookkeeper is to let a bank or a service bureau handle the payroll. This is particularly effective where employees are paid the same amount each payroll period.

Some banks will handle the complete payroll function and will use their own bank checks. This eliminates the need for the organization to prepare a payroll bank reconciliation. Others will prepare the payroll but use the organization's checks, which after being cashed are returned to the organization. Banks usually have a minimum fee that ranges from $40 to $50 for each payroll. If there are more than about 20 employees, this amount increases. While the charge may seem high, the time saved can be considerable. Remember that in addition to the payroll preparation the bank will also keep cumulative records of salary paid to each employee and will prepare the various payroll tax returns, W-2 forms, and so on. Having payroll tax matters handled by someone else removes a great burden from the organization's staff.

The use of a bank or service bureau works best where the payroll is regular and routine in amount, that is, where there are not a lot of hourly employees, or changes in rates between periods. While a bank can handle such changes, the "input" to the bank is such that the organization would be faced with the need to have someone act as a payroll clerk to assemble the information for the bank, and this takes time. If there are a lot of changes each period, it may be just as easy for the bookkeeper to handle the complete job and not use an outside service bureau or bank.

(b)   Service Bureau Bookkeeping Records

Another possibility is to have a service bureau keep all the bookkeeping records. If there is any volume of activity, a service bureau can often keep the records at less cost than for an organization to hire a bookkeeper. For example, there are some service bureaus that will enter information from original documents such as the check stubs and invoices. They can then prepare a cash receipts book, cash disbursement book, general ledger, financial statements, and so on, all automatically. All the organization has to provide is the basic information. The costs for such services vary widely depending on the volume and type of records and the geographic area in which the organization is located.

A treasurer starting to think about going to a service bureau should get some outside professional advice on whether it is practical. While talking to the service bureau will provide information on costs, the treasurer must keep in mind that the service bureau will be trying to sell its services and will not describe all the problems that may be encountered or the other alternatives that could be considered. A treasurer who wants to study these alternatives should seek the advice of a CPA. If the organization has no CPA, it should hire one for the express purpose of getting advice on this one area.

(c)   Accounting Service

Another alternative is to hire an outside accounting service to perform the actual bookkeeping. Many CPAs and public accountants provide bookkeeping services for their clients. Under this arrangement, the accountant has one of the staff do all of the bookkeeping but takes the responsibility for reviewing the work and seeing that it is properly done. The accountant usually prepares financial statements monthly or quarterly.

There are still some functions the organization itself usually must perform. The organization will normally still have to prepare its own checks, vouchers, payroll, depositing of receipts, and billings. This means that normally it cannot delegate 100 percent of the bookkeeping to an outside accounting service.

The cost of this type of service is its principal disadvantage. The accountant is in business and has overhead and salaries to pay, including salaries for employees when they are not busy. All of these costs are considered in establishing hourly rates. These rates are generally about twice what it costs to hire a competent bookkeeper on a full-time basis; they will range from $25 to $50 an hour. Nevertheless, it may still be cheaper to hire an outside accountant than to have someone on the payroll. The outside accountant is paid only for work performed with no separate fringe benefits and no overhead. If the work totals 10 hours a month, the pay is for 10 hours. Also, these services are performed by experienced staff, and there should not be a problem of competency.

One problem with this type of service is that the accountant cannot be in two places at the same time. The chances are that sometimes when your books are ready, several other clients will also be ready. This can result in some delay, although, with proper advance planning and adherence to deadlines, usually not an excessive amount.

22.4 TIMING IN HIRING A REPLACEMENT

One question that is frequently asked is when should a replacement be hired if the present bookkeeper is leaving. Should there be an overlap in employment so that the retiring bookkeeper can indoctrinate the new one and, if so, how long a period of overlap is appropriate? Or is it better to have no overlap at all?

It is appropriate to have some overlap, but it should be fairly short. A good bookkeeper can pick up another bookkeeper's set of books and procedures fairly quickly. A bookkeeper can usually get oriented to the broad outlines of the procedures within a few days. Most of these details are learned by experience and not from having the former bookkeeper tell about them.

For most organizations, it is probably best to keep the overlap short and recognize that things will not be entirely smooth for a month or two. Unless the organization is willing to have an overlap period of at least a month, it must expect that it will take some time for the new bookkeeper to get firmly established.

22.5   CONCLUSION

The bookkeeping needs of not-for-profit organizations vary widely. At the one extreme is the small organization that has so few transactions that the treasurer is able to handle all the bookkeeping. On the other extreme is the large national organization that has an accounting or bookkeeping staff of many persons that is run exactly like a commercial organization. In between is every conceivable combination of full- and part-time bookkeeping need.

A variety of sources for bookkeepers were discussed. Often in small organizations, a paid secretary will keep some simple records for the treasurer. Until the records get voluminous, this can be quite satisfactory. On the other hand, "volunteer" bookkeepers are seldom satisfactory because of rapid turnover and the problem of control. It was suggested that part-time bookkeeping jobs could be particularly attractive to parents with children in school who might want to earn some extra money. This assumes previous bookkeeping experience. The procedures to follow in looking for both part- and full-time bookkeepers were discussed and the importance of paying the going salary was emphasized. The use of banks or service bureaus was also suggested as one way to reduce the work load for the bookkeeper. Finally, it was suggested that while some overlap in bookkeepers is necessary, this overlap period should be relatively short.

Small Organizations—Providing Internal Control

"EMPLOYEE ADMITS EMBEZZLEMENT OF TEN THOUSAND DOLLARS." "TRUSTED CLERK STEALS $50,000." These headlines are all too common and many tell a similar story—a trusted and respected employee in a position of financial responsibility is overcome by temptation and "borrows" a few dollars until payday to meet some unexpected cash need. When payday comes, some other cash need prevents repayment. Somehow the employee just never catches up, and borrows a few more dollars, and a few more and a few more.

The reader's reaction may be, "Thank goodness, this kind of thing could never happen to my organization. After all, I know everyone and they are all honest, and besides who would think of stealing from a not-for-profit organization?" This is not the point. Very few who end up as embezzlers start out with this intent in mind. Rather, they find themselves in a position of trust and opportunity and when personal crises arise, the temptation is too much. Not-for-profit organizations are *not* exempt, regardless of size. There is always a risk when a person is put in a position where there is an opportunity to be tempted.

The purpose of this chapter is to outline some of the practical procedures that a small organization can establish to help minimize this risk and thus safeguard the organization's physical assets. For purposes of this discussion, the emphasis is on smaller organizations where one or two persons handle all the bookkeeping. This would include many churches, country clubs, local fund-raising groups, YMCAs, and so on. Internal control for larger organizations is not discussed here because controls for such organizations can become very complicated. The principles, however, are essentially the same. Setting up a set of internal controls requires an understanding of the basic principles plus a great deal of common sense. Larger organizations will probably want professional help in setting up a strong set of controls. Readers who are interested in this subject should refer to the Bibliography (pages 651–654).

23.1 REASONS FOR INTERNAL CONTROL

Internal control is a system of procedures and cross checking that in the absence of collusion minimizes the likelihood of misappropriation of assets or misstatement of the accounts, and maximizes the likelihood of detection if this occurs. For the most part, internal control does not prevent embezzlement but should insure that, if committed, it will be promptly discovered, and the identity of the perpetrator known. This likelihood of discovery usually persuades most not to allow temptation to get the better of them. Very few first-time embezzlers are so desperate that they would steal if they expected to be promptly caught.

There are several reasons for having a good system of internal controls. The first is to prevent the loss through theft of some of the organization's assets. A second reason, equally important, is to prevent "honest" employees and volunteers from making a mistake that could ruin their lives. An employer has a moral responsibility to avoid putting undue temptation in front of its personnel. Internal controls are designed to help remove the temptation.

Aside from this moral responsibility of the employer, there is also a responsibility of the board to the membership and to the general public to safeguard the assets of the organization. The board has an obligation to use prudence in protecting the assets. If a large sum were stolen and not recovered, it could jeopardize the programs of the organization. Furthermore even if only a small amount were stolen, it would be embarrassing to management and the members of the board. Another likely side effect would be a reduction in the amount the public would be willing to contribute to the organization. In either case, the membership or the public would certainly want to know why internal control procedures had not been followed by the board.

23.2   FUNDAMENTALS OF INTERNAL CONTROL

The simple definition of the purpose of internal control noted above relates to small organizations and emphasizes the fraud aspects. For larger organizations, this definition would have to be expanded to include a system of checks and balances over all paperwork to insure that there was no intentional or unintentional misstatement of the accounts.[1] For purposes of this discussion, however, the emphasis is on the physical controls over the organization's assets, principally cash.

One of the most effective internal controls is the use of a budget that is compared to actual figures on a monthly basis. (See Chapter 20.) If deviations from the budget are carefully followed up by the treasurer or executive director, the likelihood of a large misappropriation taking place without being detected fairly quickly is reduced considerably. This type of overall review of the financial statements is very important, and every member of the board should ask questions about any item that appears out of line either with the budget or with what would have been expected to be the actual figures. Many times this type of probing for reasons for deviations from the expected has uncovered problems.

23.3   SOME BASIC CONTROLS

There are a number of other basic internal controls that are probably applicable to most not-for-profit organizations; these are discussed next. However, these are only basic controls and should not be considered all-inclusive. Establishing an effective system of internal control requires knowledge of the particular organization and its operations. The controls discussed here should give the reader some indication of the nature of internal control and act as a starting point for establishing an appropriate system.

In this discussion, we will be considering the division of duties for a small organization, The Center for World Peace, whose financial

---

[1] The American Institute of Certified Public Accountants in an official pronouncement, Statement on Auditing Standards No. 1, defined internal control as follows:

"Internal control comprises the plan of organization and all of the coordinate methods and measures adopted within a business to safeguard its assets, check the accuracy and reliability of its accounting data, promote operational efficiency, and encourage adherence to prescribed managerial policies. This definition possibly is broader than the meaning sometimes attributed to the term. It recognizes that a system of internal control extends beyond those matters which relate directly to the functions of the accounting and financial departments." Statement on Auditing Standards No. 55, "Consideration of the Internal Control Structure in a Financial Statement Audit," also discusses this subject.

statements were discussed in Chapter 21. As will be recalled, this organization sponsors seminars and retreats and has a paid staff to run its affairs. The office staff consists of:

An executive director

The executive director's secretary

A program director

A bookkeeper

The officers of the Center are all volunteers and usually are at the Center only at irregular times. The executive director, treasurer, president, and vice president are check signers. With this background, let us now look at several controls in detail and see how each applies to this organization.

(a)   Control over Receipts

The basic objective in establishing internal control over receipts is to obtain control over the amounts received at the time of receipt. Once this control is established, procedures must be followed to ensure that these amounts get deposited in the organization's bank account. Establishing this control is particularly difficult for small organizations because of the small number of persons usually involved.

1. Prenumbered receipts should be issued for all money (cash and checks) at the time first received. A duplicate copy should be accounted for and a comparison eventually made between the aggregate of the receipts issued and the amount deposited in the bank.

The purpose of this control is to create a written record of the cash (and checks) received. The original of the receipt should be given to the person from whom the money was received; the duplicate copy should be kept permanently. Periodically, a comparison should be made of the aggregate receipts issued, with the amount deposited. The receipts can be issued at the organization's office, or if door-to-door collections are made, a prenumbered receipt can be issued as amounts are received by the collector. It is hoped that all contributors will learn to expect a receipt for cash payments.

It is important that both the duplicate copy and the original be prenumbered in order to provide control over the receipts issued. If a receipt is "voided" by mistake both the original and the duplicate should be kept and accounted for. In this way there will be complete accountability over all receipts that have been issued.

In our illustration, the Center receives a fair amount of cash at its seminars and retreats on weekends when the bookkeeper and treasurer are not available. One of the participants is designated as the fee collector for that session and in turn collects the fees and issues the receipts. After all of the fees are collected, they are turned over, with the duplicate copy of the receipts (along with all unused receipt forms) to the program director. A summary report of the cash collected is prepared and signed in duplicate. One copy of this report is mailed directly to the treasurer's home in an envelope provided, and the duplicate is turned over to the program director. The program director counts the money, agreeing the total received with the total of the duplicate receipts, and with the summary report. The program director puts the money in the safe for the weekend and on Monday morning gives the money, the duplicate receipts, and the copy of the summary report to the bookkeeper for depositing. The bookkeeper deposits the money from each program separately, and files the duplicate receipts and summary report for future reference. Once a month the treasurer compares the copy of each summary report with the deposits shown on the bank statement.

One final note here: While the procedure of issuing prenumbered receipts is certainly desirable, and will reduce the *likelihood* of theft, it *will not guarantee* that all cash receipts will actually make it into the organization's bank account. A person intent on misappropriating some of the receipts need only have a private supply of receipt forms printed, of which there will of course be no record in the organization's office to which to compare bank deposits. This last observation is made, not to serve as a primer on how to steal, as, unfortunately, that seems already to be all too well known, but rather to be a warning to organizations not to become complacent about internal controls. It is all too easy to think that because "we are doing everything the book (or our auditor, or the treasurer) says to do, no one can possibly steal from us." That is a dangerous attitude, sure to be regretted some day.

2. Cash collections should be under the control of two people wherever possible, particularly where it is not practicable to issue receipts.

In the illustration in the previous paragraph, control was established over cash collections by having the person collecting at each seminar issue receipts and prepare a summary report. The program director, in turn, also had some control through knowledge of how many persons attended, and comparison of the amount collected with the amount that should be collected. This provided dual control.

There are many instances, however, where cash collections are received when it is not appropriate to give a receipt. Two examples are church "plate" collections during worship services, and coin canisters placed in stores and public places in a community for public support. To the extent that only one person handles this money, there is always a risk. The risk is not only that some of it will be misappropriated, but also that someone may erroneously think it has been. This is why it is recommended that two people be involved.

With respect to church plate collections, as soon as the money has been collected, it should be locked up until it can be counted by two people together. Perhaps the head usher and a vestryman will count it after the last service. Once the counting is completed, both should sign a cash collection report. This report should be given to the treasurer for subsequent comparison with the deposit on the bank statement. The cash should be turned over to the bookkeeper for depositing intact.

This procedure will not guard against an usher's dipping a hand into the plate before it is initially locked up or counted, but the ushers' duties are usually rotated and the cumulative risk is low. But the bookkeeper and treasurer normally have access to such funds on a regular and recurring basis. This is why their function of counting these cash receipts should be controlled by having a second person involved. It is not because they are not trusted; it is to insure that no one can think of accusing one of them.

Canisters containing cash that are placed in public places should be sealed so that the only way to get access to the cash is to break the canister open. Someone could take the entire canister, but if the canister is placed in a conspicuous place, near the cash register, for example, this risk is fairly low. These canisters should be serially numbered so that all canisters can be accounted for. When the canisters are eventually opened, they should be counted by two people using the same procedures as with plate collections.

3. Two persons should open all mail and make a list of all receipts for each day. This list should subsequently be compared to the bank deposit by someone not handling the money. Receipts in the form of checks should be restrictively endorsed promptly upon receipt.

Two persons should open the mail; otherwise there is a risk that the mail opener may misappropriate part of the receipts. This imposes a heavy burden on the small organization with only one or a few employees but it is necessary if good internal control is desired.[2] One alternative is to have mail receipts go to a bank lock box and let the bank do the actual opening of the mail.

The purpose of making a list of all checks received is to ensure that a record is made of the amount that was received. This makes it possible

---

[2] Organizations that have their financial statements audited by CPAs will find that the CPA cannot give an unqualified opinion if internal control is considered inadequate. (See page 421.)

for the treasurer to later check to see whether the bookkeeper has deposited all amounts promptly.

Checks should be promptly endorsed since once endorsed there is less likelihood of misappropriation. The endorsement should be placed on the check by the person first opening the mail.

In theory if the check has been made out in the name of the organization, no one can cash it. But experience has shown that a clever enough person can find a way to cash it or deposit it in a "personal" bank account opened for the purpose. On the other hand, once the check is endorsed with the name of the bank and the organization's account number it is very difficult for the embezzler to convert the check to personal use.

In our illustration at the Center, the secretary to the executive director together with the bookkeeper jointly open all mail and place the rubber stamp endorsement on the check. They then make a list, in duplicate, of all checks received, with one copy of the list going to the bookkeeper with the checks for depositing. They both sign the original of the list, which goes to the executive director. The executive director obtains the copy to see what amounts have been received. At the end of the month, all of these lists are turned over to the treasurer who then compares each day's lists with the respective credits on the bank statement.

4. All receipts should be deposited in the bank, intact and on a timely basis.

The purpose of this control is to insure that there is a complete record of all receipts and disbursements. If an organization receives "cash" receipts, no part of this cash should be used to pay its bills. The receipts should be deposited, and checks issued to pay expenses. In this way, there will be a record of the total receipts and expenses of the organization on the bank statements.

This procedure does not prevent someone from stealing money but it does mean that a check must be used to get access to the money. This leaves a record of the theft and makes it more difficult for a person to cover up.

In our illustration, it should be noted that the bookkeeper deposits each day's mail receipts intact, and also deposits, separately, the receipts from each seminar. On some days, there are two or three deposits. Making the deposits separately enables the treasurer at the end of the month to compare the copy of the summary of seminar receipts and the daily mail receipts to the bank statement. This comparison by the treasurer does not take more than a few minutes each month but it provides excellent internal control over receipts and it also gives assurance that the bookkeeper is depositing all receipts daily.

(b)   Control over Disbursements

The basic objective in establishing internal controls over disbursements is to ensure that a record of all disbursements is made and that only authorized persons are in a position to withdraw funds. The risk of misappropriation can be significantly reduced if procedures are established to minimize the possibility that an expenditure can be made without leaving a trail, or that an unauthorized person can withdraw money.

5. All disbursements should be made by check and supporting documentation kept for each disbursement.

This control is to insure that there will be a permanent record of how much and to whom money was paid. No amounts should be paid by cash, with the exception of minor petty cash items. For the same reason, no checks should be made payable to "cash." Checks should always be payable to a specific person or organization, including checks for petty cash reimbursement. This makes it more difficult to fraudulently disburse funds.

At the Center, the bookkeeper is the one who prepares all checks for payment of bills. Before a check is prepared, however, the vendor's invoice must be approved by the executive director. If the purchases involved goods that have been received at the Center, the person who received the goods must indicate their receipt, right on the vendor's invoice.

The bookkeeper is not a check signer since, if this were the case, this person could fraudulently disburse funds to him or herself and then cover up the fraud in the books. The check signers are the executive director, the treasurer, the president, and the vice president. Normally the executive director signs all checks. Checks of more than $1,000 require two signatures, but these are very infrequent. The executive director carefully examines all supporting invoices, making sure that someone has signed for receipt of the goods before signing the check. After signing the check, each invoice is marked "paid" so that it won't inadvertently be paid twice. The secretary mails all checks to the vendors as an added control over the bookkeeper. By not letting the bookkeeper have access to the signed checks, the bookkeeper is not in a position to profit from preparing a fraudulent check to a nonexistent vendor.

6. If the treasurer or check signer is also the bookkeeper, two signatures should be required on all checks.

The purpose of this control is to insure that no one person is in a position to disburse funds and then cover up an improper disbursement in the records. In part, this recommendation is designed to protect the organization, and in part, to protect the treasurer.

Two signatures on a check provide additional control only so long as the second check signer also examines the invoices or supporting bills behind the disbursement before signing the check. The real risk of having dual signatures is that both check signers will rely on the other and will review the supporting bills in such a perfunctory manner that there is less control than if only one person signed but assumed full responsibility.

Even when the treasurer is not the bookkeeper, two signatures should also be required on checks of very large amounts and for transfers out of a savings or investment account. This gives some added protection that the treasurer won't be able to abscond with the entire assets of the organization.

As was noted before, the bookkeeper at the Center is not a check signer. This reduces the need for a second signature on checks under $1,000. Where the second signature is required for large checks the treasurer is usually the second signer. The treasurer very carefully inspects all bills involving such payments although usually well aware of the purchase in advance because of the size. The Center has a safe deposit box at the bank, and two signatures are also required for access. The same persons who are authorized to sign checks have access to this box.

7. A person other than the bookkeeper should receive bank statements directly from the bank and should promptly reconcile them.

This control is to prevent the bookkeeper from fraudulently issuing a check for personal use and, as bookkeeper, covering up this disbursement in the books. While the bookkeeper may not be a check signer, experience has shown that banks often do not catch forged check signatures. The bookkeeper usually has access to blank checks and could forge the check signer's signature. If the bookkeeper were to receive the bank statements, the fraudulent and forged canceled checks could be removed and then destroyed, with the fraud covered up through the books.

In most smaller organizations, the bank statement and canceled checks should go directly to the treasurer, who should prepare the bank reconciliations.[3] In those situations where the treasurer is also the bookkeeper, the bank statements should go directly to another officer to

---

[3] In large organizations, the control can be even more effective where the division of duties is such that an employee who is not a check signer or bookkeeper can prepare the bank reconciliation. It is possible for check signers to fraudulently make out a check to themselves and then, if they have access to the returned checks, to remove the canceled check. However, if they don't also have a means of covering up the disbursement, sooner or later the shortage will come out. The person reconciling the bank account is not in a position to permanently "cover up" a shortage although it could be hidden for several months. For this reason, it is preferable to have neither a check signer nor the bookkeeper prepare the reconciliation.

reconcile. The treasurer should insist on this procedure as a protection from any suspicions of wrongdoing.[4]

In the Center's case, the bank statement and canceled checks are mailed directly to the treasurer's home each month. After receiving the bank statement, the treasurer usually spends half a day at the Center's offices to prepare the complete bank reconciliation and compare the lists of mail and program receipts received throughout the month to the deposits shown on the bank statement.

(c) Other Areas of Control

8. Someone other than the bookkeeper should authorize all write-offs of accounts receivable or other assets.

This control is to insure that a bookkeeper who has embezzled accounts receivable or some other assets will not also be in a position to cover up the theft by writing off the receivable or asset. If the bookkeeper is unable to write such amounts off, someone will eventually ask why the "receivable" has not been paid and this should trigger correspondence that would result in the fraud's being discovered.

Generally, write-offs of small receivables should be approved by the treasurer (provided the treasurer is not also the bookkeeper), but if they are large in amount they should be submitted to the board for approval. Before any amount is written off, the treasurer should make certain that all appropriate efforts have been made to make collection, including, possibly, legal action. The treasurer must constantly keep in mind the fiduciary responsibility to take all reasonable steps to safeguard the organization's assets.

The Center only very rarely has accounts receivable. It does have, however, many pledges receivable. Although the Center would not think

---

[4] In those situations, where the treasurer or other officer does not have the time to prepare the reconciliation, then, as a minimum procedure, the treasurer should receive the unopened bank statement directly from the bank. Each check returned by the bank should be checked for both the payee and the purpose of the check. If a check is not recognized a question should be raised about it. After this review, which usually doesn't take very much time, the bank statement and checks are turned over to the bookkeeper (or treasurer) to reconcile. The completed bank reconciliation should be returned to the treasurer (or other officer) for review. The review of the completed reconciliation should consist of reviewing the reconciling items, comparing the balance "per bank" to the bank statement, and the balance "per books" to the general ledger.

This alternative procedure should be used only where it is not practical for the treasurer or other officer to actually prepare the bank reconciliation. While this alternative procedure can be effective, it does not offer the protection that comes from having someone independent of the bookkeeper actually perform all of the steps of a bank reconciliation.

of taking legal action to enforce collections,[5] it does record those pledges as though they were receivables. Occasionally the bookkeeper has to call the treasurer's attention to a delinquent pledge. The treasurer, in turn, usually calls the delinquent pledgor in an effort to evaluate the likelihood of future collection. Once a year a written report is submitted to the board advising it of delinquent pledges, and requesting formal approval to write them off. The board discusses each such delinquent pledge before giving its approval.

9. Marketable securities should be kept in a bank safe deposit box or held by a custodian in an account in the name of the organization.

This control is to insure that securities are protected against loss by fire or theft or from bankruptcy of a brokerage house. For most organizations, marketable securities represent long-term rather than short-term investments and certificates should not be kept in a safe in the organization's office or at the broker's office. The organization should provide the maximum protection for these assets. Either a custodian should keep these securities or they should be kept in the bank safe deposit box under dual signature control. Safeguarding investments is discussed more fully in Chapter 25.

In our illustration, the Center does not have very much in the way of investment funds. What endowments the Center has it keeps in a bank common stock fund. This is a form of mutual fund that the bank set up to handle investments on a pooled basis for a number of not-for-profit organizations. All decisions at the Center to put money into or take money out of this bank fund are made by the executive committee of the board, acting on the advice of the investment committee. The bank insists that the executive committee's minutes accompany any request for withdrawals of or additions to the Center's shares in this fund. There are no share certificates as such although the bank sends quarterly statements to the treasurer showing the number of shares the Center has.

10. Fixed asset records should be maintained and an inventory taken periodically.

These procedures insure that the organization has a complete record of its assets. The permanent record should contain a description of the asset, cost, date acquired, location, serial number, and similar information. Such information will provide a record of the assets that the employees are responsible for. This is particularly important in not-for-profit organizations where turnover of employees and officers is often high. It also provides fire insurance records. An example of the type of fixed asset record that should be kept is shown in Chapter 31 (Exhibit 31–3).

---

[5] Pledges are discussed more fully in Chapter 10.

11. Excess cash should be maintained in a separate bank or investment account. Withdrawals from this account should require two signatures.

Where an organization has excess cash that will not be needed for operations in the immediate future, it should be placed in a separate account to provide an added safeguard. Frequently, this separate account will be an interest-bearing savings account. The bank or investment manager should be advised that the signatures of two officers are required for all withdrawals. Normally in such situations withdrawals are infrequent, and when they are made the funds withdrawn are deposited intact in the regular current checking account. In this way, all disbursements are made from the regular checking account.

In this situation, the officers involved in authorizing a withdrawal should not do so without being fully aware of the reasons for the need of these funds. Approval should not be perfunctorily given.

23.4 FIDELITY INSURANCE

One final recommendation. Fidelity insurance should be carried. The purpose of fidelity insurance is to insure that if a loss from embezzlement occurs the organization will recover the loss. This insurance does not cover theft or burglary by an outside person (which is covered by a different kind of insurance policy). It provides protection only against an employee's or volunteer's dishonesty. Having fidelity insurance also acts as a deterrent because the employees know that the insurance company is more likely to press charges against a dishonest employee than would a "soft hearted" and embarrassed employer.

There is only one "catch" to this type of coverage. The organization has to have good enough records to prove that an embezzlement has taken place. This means that this coverage is not a substitute for other internal controls. If the theft occurs but the employer doesn't know it or if there is no proof of the loss, fidelity insurance will not help.

This protection is not expensive since the risk is usually low. The risk varies from one organization to another, and thus the premium will vary. In the case of the Center, a fidelity policy covering losses of up to $100,000 costs a couple of hundred dollars annually. In any case, the cost is relatively so little that prudence dictates that all not-for-profit organizations, except possibly the very smallest, have this coverage.

Sometimes employees feel that a lack of confidence is being expressed in them if the organization has fidelity insurance. The treasurer should assure them that this is not the case, and that fidelity insurance is similar to fire insurance. All prudent organizations carry such coverage.

23.5 CONCLUSION

Internal control as discussed in this chapter for small organizations is a system of procedures that in the absence of collusion minimizes the likelihood of misappropriation of assets or misstatement of the accounts, and if it has occurred maximizes the likelihood of detection. These controls largely depend on a division of duties such that no one person is in a position to both misappropriate assets and to cover up the theft in the records. These controls are very important even in a smaller organization where it is difficult to provide for this division of duties. One of the principal reasons often overlooked for having good internal control is to remove temptation from normally honest employees.

Even the smallest organization should be able to apply the eleven internal controls that have been recommended in this chapter. The board should insist that these and similar controls be established. It has a responsibility to insure that all practical measures be taken to protect the organization's assets. Otherwise the board is subject to severe criticism if an embezzlement were to occur. Fidelity insurance was also recommended.

The controls discussed in this chapter are basic ones and should not be considered all-inclusive. A complete system of internal control encompasses all of the procedures of the organization. If the organization is a large or complex one, or if it has peculiar problems or procedures, the board will want to retain the services of a professional to help set up and monitor the effectiveness of internal control. The next chapter discusses the services that the certified public accountant can provide, including assistance in establishing internal controls.

CHAPTER 24

Independent Audits

Related to the internal controls discussed in Chapter 23 is the question whether the books and records should be audited, and if so, by whom. Like many other decisions the board has to make, this is a value judgment for which there are no absolute answers. Audits cost time and money, and therefore the values to be derived must be considered carefully.

24.1 FUNCTIONS AND LIMITATIONS

An audit is a series of procedures followed by an experienced professional accountant to test, on a selective basis, transactions and internal controls in effect, all with a view to forming an opinion on the fairness of the presentation of the financial statements for the period. An audit is not an examination of every transaction that has been recorded; it is a series of tests designed to give the accountant a basis for judging how effectively the records were kept and the degree of reliance that can be placed on the internal controls. The end result of an audit is the expression of an opinion by the auditor on the financial statements prepared by the organization's management.

Several things should be underscored. Auditors do not examine all transactions. If they were to do so, the cost would usually be prohibitive. They do look at what they believe is a representative sample of the transactions. In looking at these selected transactions, they are as concerned with the internal controls and procedures that were followed as they are with the legitimacy of the transaction itself. If internal controls are good, the extent of the testing can be limited. If controls are weak, the auditors will have to examine many more transactions to be satisfied. In smaller organizations where internal controls are often less effective, auditors must examine proportionately more transactions.

Another point that should be made is that for the most part the auditors can only examine and test transactions that have been recorded. If a contribution has been received but not deposited in the bank or recorded in the books, there is little likelihood that it will be discovered. This is why Chapter 23 emphasized that controls should be established over all receipts at the point of receipt and all disbursements should be made by check. In this way, a record is made and the auditor has a chance of testing the transaction.

The end product of the audit is not a "certificate" that every transaction has been properly recorded, but an expression of an opinion by the auditor on the fairness of the presentation of the financial statements. The auditor does not guarantee accuracy; the bookkeeper may have stolen $100, but unless this $100 is material in relation to the financial statements as a whole, the auditor is not likely to discover it.

(a) Auditor's Opinion Explained

Exhibit 24–1 represents a typical opinion prepared by a certified public accountant which in this case is on the financial statements of the National Environmental Society.

EXHIBIT 24–1   Independent auditor's report.

We have audited the accompanying balance sheets of National Environmental Society as of December 31, 19X2 and 19X1, and the related statements of revenue and expense, and cash flows for the years then ended. These financial statements are the responsibility of the Organization's management. Our responsibility is to express an opinion on these financial statements based on our audits.

We conducted our audits in accordance with generally accepted auditing standards. Those standards require that we plan and perform the audit to obtain reasonable assurance about whether the financial statements are free of material misstatement. An audit includes examining, on a test basis, evidence supporting the amounts and disclosures in the financial statements. An audit also includes assessing the accounting principles used and significant estimates made by management, as well as evaluating the overall financial statement presentation. We believe that our audits provide a reasonable basis for our opinion.

In our opinion, the financial statements referred to above present fairly, in all material respects, the financial position of National Environmental Society at December 31, 19X2 and 19X1, and the results of its operations and its cash flows for the years then ended in conformity with generally accepted accounting principles.

[*Signature*]

[*Date*]

This opinion is very carefully worded, and each phrase has significance. The wording is designed to tell the knowledgeable reader what responsibility the auditor takes and does not take. Since this opinion is the end product of an audit, it is important to know exactly what the opinion means. Let us look at the opinion phrase by phrase to see what is being said.

Identification of Statements

"We have audited the accompanying balance sheets and the related statements of revenue and expense, and cash flows . . ."

The auditor is carefully identifying the statements covered by the opinion—the "accompanying" balance sheets and statements of revenue and expense and cash flows. These statements and only these statements are the ones referred to.

Responsibility for Statements

"These financial statements are the responsibility of the Organization's management. . . ."

The auditor is pointing out to readers that the financial statements are the client's and not the auditor's.

Audit Standards Followed

"We conducted our audits in accordance with generally accepted auditing standards . . ."

Here the auditor is spelling out in technical language how the examination was conducted. There is a whole body of literature that defines generally accepted auditing standards. These include standards of training, proficiency, independence, planning, supervision of staff, evaluation of internal controls, and obtaining evidential matter to support the audit conclusions. They also provide that the auditor must perform certain specific tests where applicable.

Essential Tests

There are two specific tests which cannot be omitted by the auditor: confirmation of amounts receivable from outside parties (including pledges receivable), and observation of a physical count of items held in inventory. Confirmation of receivables involves writing to those owing money (or who have made pledges) to the organization and asking them to confirm that they do, in fact, owe the stated amount to the organization. Observation of a count of inventories involves going out to the storage facility and personally verifying the existence of the items shown as being held. Both of these tests can require substantial amounts of the auditor's time, and often an organization will ask the auditor to eliminate these tests to save time and cost. If omitted, however, and if receivables or inventories are significant in value, the auditor will not be able to say that the examination has been made in accordance with generally accepted auditing standards. An opinion cannot be expressed on the financial statements "taken as a whole."

The remainder of this paragraph elaborates on what is meant by these standards.

"We believe that our audits provide a reasonable basis. . . ."

This phrase says that in addition to all other auditing requirements spelled out in official pronouncements, the auditor has performed whatever additional tests he or she believes should be performed in the particular client circumstances.

Statements Present Fairly

"In our opinion . . . present fairly, in all material respects, the financial position . . . and the results of its operations and its cash flows . . ."

Here the auditor is saying the statements "present fairly"—not that they are correct or that they are accurate, but that they present "fairly." What does "fairly" mean? It means that there is no *material* misstatement of these figures. The statements may not be 100 percent accurate, but they are not materially inaccurate. The question of what is "material" cannot really be answered with any definitiveness since this is largely a subjective question, and in part depends on what figures you are looking at.[1]

Accounting Principles Followed

". . . in conformity with generally accepted accounting principles."

Here the auditor is defining the principles of accounting that have been followed—generally accepted accounting principles. These words have specific meaning and refer to published pronouncements by the Financial Accounting Standards Board and the American Institute of Certified Public Accountants and to general usage by organizations similar to the one being audited. Where there have been pronouncements of accounting

---

[1] The Securities and Exchange Commission, in referring to reporting requirements for SEC filings defines "material" as ". . . the information . . . [about] which an average prudent investor ought reasonably to be informed before purchasing the security registered."

principles by the FASB or the AICPA, the auditor is saying here that these principles have been followed. Where there have been no pronouncements, the auditor is saying that the principles followed are those generally used by similar organizations. Chapters 2 to 10 discuss some of the principles generally accepted as they relate to not-for-profit organizations. If an opinion is issued without these specific words "in accordance with generally accepted accounting principles" the reader should be certain the principles used are clearly explained and understood. This will be the case, for example, if the cash basis of accounting (discussed in Chapters 3 and 11) is used.

(b) Adequacy of Internal Control over Contributions

The auditor must be satisfied that internal control over contributions is such as to ensure that substantially all contributions intended for the organization have been received and properly recorded. Internal control was discussed in the previous chapter, but one control in particular should again be noted. Normally *two* persons should open all mail to minimize the chance of misappropriation. In the absence of adequate internal control, the CPA cannot issue an unqualified opinion.

(c) Qualified Opinions

A "qualified" opinion is an opinion in which the independent auditor takes exception to some specific aspect of the financial statements as presented, or is unable to form an unqualified opinion because of an inability to obtain audit evidence about a matter which might affect the financial statements. The independent auditor will spell out in the opinion exactly what the nature of the qualification is. A qualification with respect to presentation can result because generally accepted accounting principles were not followed. A qualification because of an inability to obtain audit evidence results when client records are missing or incomplete or it is not possible to obtain needed documents from outside parties.

Adverse Opinion

An "adverse" opinion results when, in the opinion of the auditor, the financial statements taken as a whole do *not* present fairly the financial position in conformity with generally accepted accounting principles. The distinction between a "qualified" opinion and an "adverse" opinion is primarily one of the significance of the departures from generally accepted accounting principles.

Disclaimer

A "disclaimer" of opinion results when the auditor is unable to form an opinion on the financial statements. This could be the result of limitations on the scope of the examination such as the inability to predict the outcome of some event (such as a lawsuit against the organization) that would affect the financial statements in a very material way, or because the organization's records were inadequate and it was not possible to form an opinion one way or the other. When an auditor gives a disclaimer of opinion, the reasons for it are spelled out in the auditor's report.

Any qualification detracts from the credibility of the financial statements. Since one of the functions of an auditor's opinion is to add credibility to the financial statements, an opinion other than a "clean" or unqualified opinion will detract and raise questions about the statements. Wherever it is possible for an organization to take corrective action to eliminate the qualification, it should do so.

24.2   BENEFITS OF AN INDEPENDENT AUDIT

Audits are not free. This means that the board has to evaluate the benefits to be derived from an audit and the cost of this professional service. What are the benefits that can be expected from an audit? There are four: (1) credibility of the financial statements; (2) professional assistance in developing meaningful financial statements; (3) professional advice on internal control, administrative efficiency, and other business matters; and (4) assistance in tax reporting and compliance requirements.

(a)   Credibility of the Financial Statements

We have already touched on credibility. This is the principal benefit of having an independent CPA express an opinion on the financial statements. Unfortunately, over the years, there have been many instances where not-for-profit organizations have been mismanaged and the results buried in the financial statements in a manner that made it difficult, if not impossible, for the reader of the statements to discern them.

It has been noted that the purpose of financial statements is to communicate in a straightforward and direct manner what has happened. The presence of an auditor's opinion helps in this communication process because an independent expert, after an examination, tells the reader that the financial statements present fairly what has happened. Not-for-profit organizations are competing with other organizations for the money of their members or of the general public. If an organization can tell its financial story accurately and completely, and it is accepted at face value, the potential contributor is more likely to feel that the organization is well managed.

(b) Meaningful Statements

Another benefit of having professional help is that the auditor is an expert at preparing financial statements in a format that will be most clear to the reader. All too often financial statements are poorly organized and hard to understand. The CPA has had years of experience in helping organizations prepare financial statements in clear and understandable language.

(c) Advice on Internal Control and Other Matters

Another benefit is that the CPA will be in a position to advise the board on how to strengthen internal controls and simplify the bookkeeping procedures. As an expert, the CPA can also assist the board in evaluating the competency of the organization's bookkeeper or accountant and be able to help the organization when it comes time to hire someone for these positions.

The CPA has had experience in dealing with many different types of organizations and is likely to have a number of general business suggestions. Typically, periodic meetings with senior staff or board members will be held to discuss the problems of the organization and business conditions in general. Many boards arrange annual meetings to ask questions and to be sure that the organization has picked the CPA's brain. This meeting also provides the CPA with an opportunity to call any potential problems to the board's attention.

(d) Assistance in Tax Reporting and Compliance Requirements

As is discussed in Chapters 26 to 28, most not-for-profit organizations are required to submit some form of report to one or more agencies of a state government and the IRS. These reports are almost always technical in format and unless the treasurer is an accountant, the assistance of an expert will probably be required. The CPA is an expert and can either offer advice on how to prepare the returns or can actually prepare them.

24.3 SELECTING A CERTIFIED PUBLIC ACCOUNTANT

Like doctors and lawyers, certified public accountants depend more on word of mouth than advertising to spread their reputation. When it comes time to choose a CPA, talk with your banker, attorney, and fellow members of the board. The chances are that collectively they will know many CPAs practicing in your locality and will know of their reputations. Talk also with officers of other not-for-profit organizations. They will probably have had some experience that may be of help. One significant criterion in the selection should be the CPAs familiarity with not-for-profit entities similar to yours.

In any professional relationship, the interest and willingness of the CPA to serve the organization is one of the most important factors to consider in making a selection. It is always difficult to judge which of several CPAs has the greatest interest in helping the organization. In large part, the treasurer will have to make the decision from impressions formed in personal interviews.

One of the more effective ways to gain an impression is to send the CPA financial statements before an interview. Then, at the time of the interview, ask for comments on the statements. The amount of homework done will be obvious in the response.

During this personal interview, let the CPA take a look at the records to get a general impression of the amount of time that will be necessary, and thus the fee. For the most part the treasurer's judgment should not be swayed significantly by the fee range estimated unless it is out of line with other CPA fees. Like a doctor or lawyer, the accountant expects to receive a fair fee for services. The organization is largely dependent on the honesty and professional reputation of the accountant to charge a fair fee. Appendix 24–A is a checklist that may be helpful in selecting a CPA.

(a) Cost of an Audit

What does it cost to have an audit? This is a difficult question to answer because most CPAs charge on an hourly basis. If the organization's records are in good shape and up to date, the time will be less. There is no way to know how much time will be involved without looking at the records and knowing something about the organization.

The hourly rates vary, depending on the individual assigned and his or her experience. Most examinations involve a combination of experienced and inexperienced staff members. In 1994, the hourly rates ranged from $60 to $300, with an overall average effective rate of between $70 and $125 an hour. This average rate is a composite. Most of the time spent on any audit will be by less experienced staff members whose billing rates will be lower than for the CPA in charge.

The only accurate way to find out what it will cost to have an audit is to call a CPA and ask for an estimate. Even then it will be difficult to know all the problems that may be encountered and the CPA will probably hedge on the estimate by indicating that while it is a best estimate the final amount might be more or less. Keep in mind that the CPA is providing a professional service just as does a doctor or a lawyer.

Sometimes an organization will shop around in an effort to find the CPA that will charge it the least. While understandable, this makes about as much sense as choosing a doctor based on the rate charged for an office visit. You get what you pay for. Since the salaries paid by the various firms are pretty much the same at any given level of competence, each CPA firm will charge about the same amount per hour for a staff member's services. The variable is the length of time it will take to perform the examination. Since the treasurer is not likely to be in a position to judge the quality of the work, there is a risk in choosing a professional accountant solely on the basis of an estimated fee. Choosing a CPA should be on the basis of reputation, expertise, and willingness to serve the organization.

(b) Review Services

A possible alternative to an audit, for an organization that does not have to submit audited financial statements to a state, a funding source, or another organization, is to have its financial statements "reviewed" by a CPA. A review requires less time, hence incurs less cost; however, it results in a lesser degree of assurance by the CPA. Instead of saying that the financial statements "present fairly," the CPA does only enough work to be able to say, "I am not aware of any material modifications that should be made in order for the financial statements to be in conformity." This is called "negative assurance" and does not give as much credibility to the financial statements as an audit does. Nevertheless, a review may meet the needs of some smaller organizations.

(c) The "Big Six" Accounting Firms

Many smaller organizations tend to feel that the major accounting firms, including the "big six," won't be interested in serving a smaller not-for-profit organization. This is not the case with most offices of these firms. There should be no hesitation in soliciting their interest, as well as that of smaller firms.

24.4 PUBLIC ACCOUNTANTS

So far we have talked about the advantages of bringing in a "certified public accountant." There are also "public accountants" in many states. What does the difference in title mean?

Certified public accountants are the "professionals." They have been licensed by the state after proving their competency by passing a rigorous two-and-a-half-day examination, meeting certain educational requirements, and, in most states, working for another CPA for a period of time. The CPA is continually accountable to the state. Only a CPA can join the American Institute of Certified Public Accountants.

Public accountants may or may not be licensed by the state. Where they are licensed, there are usually no examinations to pass or educational requirements to meet, and for the most part they can practice without experience. Nevertheless, public accountants are often quite competent and can provide good and effective service to clients, particularly in keeping the records or preparing financial statements. If an organization is going to hire an accountant to help keep the records, the public accountant may well be the right person to hire. But, as a general rule, it must retain a certified public accountant if it wants an audit to be made.

24.5 AUDIT COMMITTEES

(a) Internal Audit Committee

Many smaller organizations do not feel they can afford a CPA (or a public accountant) and yet want some assurance that all disbursements have been made for properly approved purposes. One solution to this is to set up an "internal audit committee" consisting of several members of the board or of the membership. The purpose of this internal audit committee is usually to review all disbursements "after the fact" to make sure that all have been properly approved and documented. The review can take place at any time, but for convenience it is usually done some time after the payment has been made. The committee may meet on a monthly or bimonthly basis and review all transactions since the last meeting. It may also review bank reconciliations, marketable securities bought, sold, and on hand, and any other matter that could be "sensitive."

The advantage of an internal audit committee is that it strengthens internal control significantly with little cost. This is particularly important where internal control is weak because it is not practical to segregate duties as much as might be desired.

The weakness of an internal audit committee is that it can become so routine and perfunctory that the committee does little effective auditing and is merely a rubber stamp. Probably the best way to see that this doesn't happen is to rotate committee membership. For example, the past president, past treasurer, and a member chosen from the board would constitute an effective and knowledgeable internal audit committee.

Since both the president and treasurer have limited tenure, the composition of the committee would automatically change with time.

There is also a risk that the board will get a false sense of security with an internal audit committee. The committee members are usually not trained accountants and might very well miss clues that a CPA would see. Also, this committee is essentially looking at only disbursements and is making no test of receipts. All of this means that an internal audit committee has some limitations although clearly it is better to have such a committee than to have no review function at all.

(b) External Audit Committee

The institution of external audit committees has now become a common practice for not-for-profit organizations. A properly functioning audit committee goes a long way toward demonstrating that the board of trustees has taken prudent steps to perform its administrative and control functions. Thus, with regard to audit committees, the authors recommend that:

- Every not-for-profit organization that raises funds from the general public or that receives grants or membership dues should have an active and functioning external audit committee.
- For most effective operation, audit committees should be composed of three to five directors, with the majority (including the chairman) being trustees who are not employees.
- Audit committees should be responsible for recommending the appointment of the independent accountants and for discussion of their work with them.
- Audit committees should be responsible for the review and evaluation of the reports prepared by the independent accountants that describe any weaknesses in the organization's internal accounting and management controls and that contain recommendations for improvements in such controls. Audit committees should also determine if management has taken appropriate action on these recommendations.
- Audit committees should be delegated the responsibility to review the annual financial statements with the independent accountants.

Another function of the audit committee can be to ensure that management has used proper accounting standards and made all required disclosures in the organization's financial statements. The checklist in

Appendix B may be helpful both to management and the audit committee in this regard.

In view of the current concern about proper accountability by not-for-profit organizations, the audit committee should conduct a periodic inquiry into the board and management's procedures for ensuring that expenditures (especially in sensitive areas such as professional fees, executive compensation, and travel and entertainment) are appropriate in nature and reasonable in amount. A good test of reasonableness for such expenditures is whether an audit committee member would feel comfortable responding to an inquiry from an investigative reporter or a donor about the expenditures. Another suggestion is to regularly review the organization's conflict of interest policy and the procedures in place to ensure compliance with it.

24.6 CONCLUSION

We have discussed the principal advantages of retaining a certified public accountant to make an audit of not-for-profit organizations. In addition to providing "credibility" to the financial statements, the CPA can provide for improving the format of the financial statements to make them more effective in communicating to the reader and can offer suggestions to improve internal controls and administrative efficiency. In addition, in this increasingly complex society of rules and reports, the CPA is an expert and can help an organization comply with the many reporting requirements.

The importance of hiring the right CPA was discussed and some suggested procedures to follow were outlined. As with any professional, it is important to find a CPA who is both knowledgeable about not-for-profit accounting and interested in serving your organization. This is largely a personal judgment and one that each organization has to make based on interviews and the reputation of the accountant. The difference between a "public accountant" and a "certified public accountant" was discussed. While there are many competent public accountants, the CPA is the professional and therefore is the accountant that should be hired if an audit is needed. The use of an internal or external audit committee was suggested as one way in which internal control could be strengthened.

APPENDIX 24–A CHECKLIST

Criteria for Selection of a CPA

Not all of these criteria will be relevant in every selection process, and their relative importance will vary for different organizations. The order of the items in the list is not intended to indicate an absolute degree of importance to an organization, but criteria listed in the early part of the list are those that are often considered more important. An organization should set tentative criteria at the start of the proposal process, but should not hesitate to change the criteria or their relative importance if considered desirable. (Criteria that have been disseminated to proposing CPAs should not be changed without notifying the CPAs.)

1. Characteristics of the personnel to be assigned to the engagement:
   - *Experience and expertise in the area of not-for-profit organization accounting and auditing on the part of the personnel who will be assigned to the engagement.* These are the people who will be directly responsible for serving the organization's needs, and it is their abilities on which the quality of that service primarily depends. The not-for-profit environment is different in many ways from that of for-profit organizations; a lack of experience with that environment can be only partly offset by experience with other types of clients, except in the most routine circumstances.
   - *Personal ability of the designated key engagement personnel to relate well to and work effectively with organization staff.* This is a hallmark of any successful professional relationship.
2. *Ability of the CPA to respond quickly, effectively and competently to the organization's needs.* This is a more general statement of the previous criterion, as well as reflecting other factors such as the ability of the engagement staff to call upon other resources if needed. Such resources might include other personnel within a firm, reference material, and other persons with appropriate knowledge and skills. It also encompasses the overall attitude with which a CPA approaches service to clients.
3. *Experience with similar organizations* (e.g., medium-size symphony orchestras, Red Cross chapters, large trade associations, community colleges). A long list of a CPA's present clients can be considered positive evidence supporting an ability to meet

criterion 2, but, especially in a larger firm, many of these clients may not be served by the same personnel as would serve your organization. Such a list is certainly a plus but should not be the only basis for choosing a CPA. An organization may wish to request the proposing CPAs to furnish names of client references who may be contacted.

4. *Reputation.* This includes the two previous criteria, as well as a lot of more intangible factors such as how the CPA is looked upon by others in and outside the not-for-profit industry, his or her commitment to serving organizations in the industry, involvement by personnel in professional activities. (What an organization sometimes means by this criterion is, will the presence of a particular CPA's or CPA firm's signature on our accounts help our fund-raising efforts? The answer is, usually, not much.)

5. *Fee.* This should not be the deciding criterion (although it too often is), unless two or more CPAs are perceived as nearly equal in all other respects. A CPA who proposes a fee significantly lower than others' fees is sometimes: (1) not being realistic about the effort required to complete an engagement or (2) "low-balling" to get the work, and will either give a lower quality of service and/or try to raise the fee significantly in future years. When evaluating a proposal of this type, the organization should question the CPA about the basis for the quoted fee.

6. *Proposed approach to the engagement.* What does the CPA believe needs to be done, and how will the engagement be undertaken? A well-thought-out presentation on this subject improves the chances that the CPA meets criteria 1 and 2. The presentation need not be long but should show evidence that the work will be well planned and tailored to the particular needs and circumstances of the organization. There should also be an indication of the commitment of adequate time to the engagement by more senior personnel.

7. *Closeness of the CPA's office to the organization's headquarters.* (In the case of a multilocation organization; closeness of one or more offices of a firm to the principal operating locations of the organization.) This is really just part of criterion 2. Distance can be a negative factor, but it does not have to be if the CPA can compensate for this.

8. *Size of the CPA's firm and/or local office.* Except for an extremely large and complex organization (which usually does require the

services of a large firm), there are no rules on this point. Both larger and smaller firms and individual practitioners can render distinguished service to both larger and smaller organizations, if the conditions of criteria 1 and 2 are well met.

9. *Ability of the CPA to provide other services such as consulting work.* Sometimes this may be important to an organization and sometimes not. An organization should think about this in view of its own current and anticipated future circumstances.

10. *Organization structure of the CPA's firm.* How centralized or decentralized is it? How much authority does the engagement partner have to make decisions? Usually any effect of this factor is far outweighed by criteria 1 and 2, unless a large firm is so centralized that local personnel have little authority.

11. *Continuity of staff assigned to the engagement.* Some amount of staff turnover is inevitable in almost any accounting practice, but excessive turnover is not desirable as it partly defeats the goal of building familiarity with a client. At the same time, some organizations consider orderly slow rotation of personnel desirable as a way of maintaining the CPA's independence and bringing fresh ideas to bear on the engagement.

Other criteria that are not judgment criteria, but rather should be prerequisites for any CPA to be considered for selection:

—Ability to meet reasonable deadlines.

—Willingness to furnish recommendations for proposed improvements in internal controls and management procedures identified during the course of other work.

—Ability to assign the requisite number and experience levels of personnel to work on the engagement.

—Ability to render the desired services in a professional manner.

Investments

Some not-for-profit organizations have an investment program to manage, resulting from receipt of endowment and other restricted gifts. Some organizations also have excess cash in their unrestricted general fund that can be invested. Together all of these investments can be very sizable. They are usually invested in publicly traded securities, although occasionally part may be invested in real estate or in mortgages.

One of the practical problems faced by the not-for-profit organization is how to handle its investment program where there are a number of separate funds, each with amounts available for investment. The question that arises is whether investments should be made on a separate fund-by-fund basis or whether all investments should be pooled. This chapter discusses the concept of pooling of investments and shows how to keep the appropriate records. Some sources of investment advice are given, along with the considerations a treasurer must take into account in providing physical safeguards over the securities themselves.

25.1 POOLING VERSUS INDIVIDUAL INVESTMENTS

Typically, most organizations have a number of different individual funds, each having cash that can be invested. These individual funds may include board-designated endowment funds, as well as donor-restricted endowment funds. Within these fund groupings, there may be a number of individual "name" funds. All of this means that a not-for-profit organization can have a number of separate accounting entities that have assets invested in marketable securities. This is where some practical problems arise.

The organization can invest the money of each individual fund in specific securities and keep track of the actual income and gain or loss associated with these specific investments. If it does so, there is no question about the amount of income, or the gain or loss associated with each separate fund.

But for many organizations, the cash available for investment in each fund is not large enough to make individual purchases. If purchases were made on an individual fund basis, there probably would be little diversification. Yet the aggregate of the available assets of all individual funds could be sizable enough to provide a well-diversified portfolio if all of the assets were pooled and invested together.

This is what many organizations do. They pool all of their investments and prorate the resulting income and gains or losses, like a mutual fund.

(a) Example of Individual Investments for Each Fund

An example will illustrate the difference in these two approaches. The Bradford Museum has investments aggregating about $200,000. It follows the approach of making specific investments for each fund. What the portfolio looked like at December 31, 19X1, is shown in Exhibit 25–1.

As is typical, some of the individual investments have done better than others but on an overall basis, market value is a third above cost. Since the museum keeps track of its portfolio by individual fund, the gain or loss and the income for each of these funds are based on the actual investments in each fund. The board-designated endowment fund had income of $3,900, and if the organization were to sell all of these investments there would be a capital gain of $55,000. On the other hand, the R. A. Adler Fund has had a decline in value of $25,000.

One of the problems of making investments on an individual fund basis is that there are usually some amounts of cash that are too small to be individually invested. In this case the Bradford Museum has a total of $18,500 of uninvested cash in all of its funds, which is large enough to be put to work.

EXHIBIT 25–1   The Bradford Museum Investments—Individual Investments.

	Cost	Market 12/31/X1	Income Year 19X1
Board-designated endowment fund			
1,000 shares of Stock A	$ 20,000	$ 45,000	$ 800
500 shares of Stock B	20,000	40,000	1,200
1,000 shares of Stock C	40,000	50,000	1,000
Uninvested cash	15,000	15,000	900
	95,000	150,000	3,900
Endowment fund–W. H. Miller			
1,000 shares of Stock D	9,000	31,000	1,500
100 shares of Stock E	5,000	3,000	100
Uninvested cash	1,000	1,000	
	15,000	35,000	1,600
Endowment fund–R. A. Adler			
500 shares of Stock F	37,500	12,500	400
Uninvested cash	2,500	2,500	100
	40,000	15,000	500
Total all funds	$150,000	$200,000	$6,000

(b)   Example of Pooled Investments

A fair amount of paperwork is involved in keeping track of specific investments by individual funds. Pooling all investments eliminates the need to keep track of the individual purchases by specific fund. It also provides a larger investment fund that helps to cushion the effect of any single poor investment decision. In the case of the 500 shares of stock F, which has declined in value, the effect on the R. A. Adler Fund is devastating. It is worth a fraction of its original $40,000. On the other hand, if stock F had been pooled with the other stocks, the effect on the Adler Fund would have been only a pro rata portion. Likewise, the large gain on stock D in the Miller Fund would have been spread over all of the funds. The principal advantage of pooling is that it spreads the risk uniformly over all of the pooled funds. A second advantage is that the total uninvested cash is usually lower. And, as noted above, a third advantage is simplified record keeping.

Let us now examine how these funds would have looked if the museum had managed its investments on a pooled basis. For the sake of simplicity, it is assumed that no investments have been sold since the original principal was established in each fund and that all funds were

EXHIBIT 25-2   The Bradford Museum Investments—Pooled Account.

	Number of Shares	Cost	Market 12/31/X1	Income for 19X1
Board-designated fund	95,000	$ 95,000	$126,666	$3,800
Endowment fund				
W. H. Miller	15,000	15,000	20,000	600
R. A. Adler	40,000	40,000	53,334	1,600
	150,000	$150,000	$200,000	$6,000
Per share		$1.00	$1.33	$.04

established on the same date. Accordingly, each fund has been assigned "shares" on the basis of one share for each dollar transferred to the investment pool. Exhibit 25–2 shows how the individual funds would look at December 31, 19X1.

The number of shares in each fund represents the original amount pooled as, in this example, $1.00 per share. The market value per share is simply the aggregate portfolio market value (including uninvested cash) divided by the number of shares (i.e., $200,000/150,000 shares = $1.33). The market value for each individual fund is the value per share of $1.33 times the number of shares in each fund. Likewise, the overall per-share income of $.04 is first calculated ($6,000/150,000 shares) and then the individual fund income amounts are arrived at by multiplying $.04 times the number of shares.

When a comparison is made of the market value of each fund on a pooled basis to the market value on an individual investment basis, there are significant differences. The Adler Fund is the most conspicuous example because the market on the pooled basis is now $53,334 compared to only $15,000 before. Distribution of the income on a pooled basis is also based on shares, and the Adler Fund is again a beneficiary of this method.

25.2 CALCULATING SHARE VALUES IN POOLED INVESTMENTS

The previous discussion was centered on a relatively simple illustration showing the principles involved in pooling. It was assumed that all of the funds pooled their money on the same date, and accordingly each fund received shares with a "cost" of the same amount per share. In practice this doesn't happen except for the single date when the pool is set up. At subsequent dates, the market value per share will be higher or lower, and additions or withdrawals to and from the pool must be at the then existing per share market value.

Let us look at the transactions that took place in the Bradford Museum portfolio in 19X2:

March 31: The board transferred $40,500 from the unrestricted general fund to the board-designated fund.

August 10: The board found it had transferred more than it should have and needed to redeem some of its shares. It transferred $14,300 from the board-designated fund back to the unrestricted general fund as of the end of the calendar quarter.

December 31: The board received a contribution to be added to the R. A. Adler Fund.

Exhibit 25–3 shows a calculation of the share values at the end of each of the calendar quarters. The market value of the portfolio is determined, based on actual market values on these dates plus all uninvested cash.

Generally, organizations calculate share values only at the end of the calendar quarter. If the board wants to buy or redeem shares during a period between quarters, the value of the shares purchased or redeemed is based on the value at the end of the quarter in which the request to purchase or redeem is made. Thus, if the board decides to redeem some of the shares in the board-designated fund on August 10, the transaction does not take place until the next date on which share values are calculated. In this case, this would be the end of the quarter, September 30. Share values could be calculated as of any date, so if the board wanted to calculate share values on August 10, the transaction could be effected on that date.

(a) Cost Basis Accounting

Different types of not-for-profit organizations have different bases for carrying their investments.[1] For organizations on a cost basis, marketable

---

[1] The Audit Guides for voluntary health and welfare organizations and for colleges and universities, and the Statement of Position applicable to many other not-for-profit organizations permit the carrying of investments on a market value basis. In 1978, hospitals were required to carry marketable equity investments at the lower of aggregate cost or market. See Chapter 8 for a more complete discussion.

EXHIBIT 25-3 A worksheet showing how to calculate share values for a pooled investment fund.

BRADFORD MUSEUM

CALCULATION OF SHARE VALUES FOR PURPOSES OF PURCHASING AND REDEEMING SHARES

By Quarter for 19X2

Date	Shares Outstanding before Purchase or Redemption	Market Value before Purchase or Redemption	Value Per Share	Shares Purchased (Redeemed) This Date		Shares Outstanding after Purchase or Redemption	Market Value after Purchase or Redemption
				Shares[a]	Amount		
12/31/X1	150,000	$200,000	$1.33	—	—	150,000	$200,000
3/31/X2	150,000	202,500	1.35	30,000	$40,500	180,000	243,000
6/30/X2	180,000	252,000	1.40	—	—	180,000	252,000
9/30/X2	180,000	257,400	1.43	(10,000)	(14,300)	170,000	243,100
12/31/X2	170,000	238,000	1.40	10,000	14,000	180,000	252,000

[a] The number of shares purchased or redeemed is determined by dividing the amount invested or withdrawn by the value per share.

securities cannot be "written up" to reflect the market value of the port-folio. However, when a stock is sold, the realized gain or loss should be recorded.

There is no difficulty in determining the amount of gain or loss when individual stocks are purchased for a specific fund. It is quite clear which fund realized the gain or loss. On pooled investments, however, each fund shares in all realized gains or losses on a pro rata basis. This necessitates a calculation of the proper allocation. From a practical stand-point, this allocation is usually not made each time a stock is sold unless such sales are made very infrequently. Instead, these gains or losses are accumulated and allocated at the end of the quarter, or at the end of the year if there has been no change in the number of shares outstanding.

An illustration may be helpful. Assume the following transactions took place during 19X2:

March 10: 500 shares of Stock F were sold for $12,500 with a cost of $37,500, and a loss of $25,000.

August 15: 500 shares of Stock C were sold for $30,000 with a cost of $20,000, and a gain of $10,000.

September 15: 100 shares of Stock E were sold for $4,000 with a cost of $5,000, and a loss of $1,000.

At the end of the first and third quarters the loss of $25,000 and net gain of $9,000 are allocated on the basis of shares as shown in the follow-ing statement:

	March 31		September 30	
	Shares Outstanding[a]	Gain/(Loss) Allocated	Shares Outstanding[a]	Gain/(Loss) Allocated
Board-designated fund	95,000	($15,833)	125,000	$6,250
Endowment fund:				
W. H. Miller	15,000	(2,500)	15,000	750
R. A. Adler	40,000	(6,667)	40,000	2,000
	150,000	($25,000)	180,000	$9,000
Gain (loss)		($25,000)		$9,000
Per share		($.16666)		$.05

[a] The purchase and redemption of shares in Exhibit 25–1 have also been reflected here, but notice that the allocation is based on the number of shares before purchases or redemptions on that date.

Here is the balance in each of the individual funds at December 31, 19X2, taking into consideration both gains and losses and purchases and redemptions shown in Exhibit 25–3:

	Number of Shares	Book Cost	Market Value (i.e. Share Value Times Number of Shares)
Board-designated fund	115,000	$111,617	$161,000
Endowment fund:			
W. H. Miller	15,000	13,250	21,000
R. A. Adler	50,000	49,333	70,000
	180,000	$174,200	$252,000

Each of these amounts was calculated at December 31, 19X2, as follows:

	Shares	Book Cost
Board-designated fund		
December 31, 19X1 balance	95,000	$ 95,000
March 31, allocation of loss	—	(15,833)
March 31, purchase of shares	30,000	40,500
September 30, allocation of gain (net)	—	6,250
September 30, redemption of shares	(10,000)	(14,300)
December 31, 19X2 balance	115,000	$111,617
W. H. Miller		
December 31, 19X1 balance	15,000	$ 15,000
March 31, allocation of loss	—	(2,500)
September 30, allocation of gain (net)	—	750
December 31, 19X2 balance	15,000	$ 13,250
R. A. Adler		
December 31, 19X1 balance	40,000	$ 40,000
March 31, allocation of loss	—	(6,667)
September 30, allocation of gain (net)	—	2,000
December 31, purchase of shares	10,000	14,000
December 31, 19X2 balance	50,000	$ 49,333

It should be emphasized that while the calculation of share values for purposes of purchases and redemptions of shares is based on the market value of the portfolio at date of valuation, this calculation is only for purposes of this purchase or redemption and is not recorded in the books. The books are kept on a cost basis adjusted only for realized gains or losses.[2]

---

[2] If an organization carries its investments at market, then the books would be periodically adjusted to reflect unrealized gains and losses.

25.3 ALLOCATION OF POOLED INCOME

There has been no discussion of the handling of income and interest received on pooled funds, but the mechanics of allocation are exactly the same as with the allocation of gains or losses. Generally, allocation of income is also made on a quarterly basis, although some organizations allocate at other intervals. Investment income is usually not added back to the principal of the fund and reinvested. It is expended for the purposes specified by the donor or added to the unrestricted general fund in the case of board-designated endowment funds. This means that as income is received, it is put into a separate account. At the end of each quarter, it is allocated to each fund on a share basis. An organization could allocate more often than quarterly but this would complicate the bookkeeping.

Once the mechanics of these calculations are established they should not cause difficulty. It is important to formalize these calculations in worksheets that become part of the records of the organization.

25.4 PROFESSIONAL INVESTMENT ADVICE

Let us turn now to a practical nonaccounting question. Where should an organization go to get good investment advice? The answer is clear: to a professional, to someone who knows the investment markets, and is in the business of advising others.

You may feel that this skirts the question. Yet many medium and some large organizations try to outguess the market on their own and they usually don't succeed. They make all of the investment mistakes that many individuals do. They tend to rely on their own intuition and try to outguess the professionals. This doesn't make sense when an individual's own money is involved and it makes even less sense when the money belongs to a not-for-profit organization.

Sometimes the board, recognizing its fiduciary responsibilities, will tend to be too conservative in its investment policy, and will purchase high-grade, low-interest-bearing bonds. This conservatism can be almost as risky as purchasing a highly volatile stock, as many holders of bonds discovered in recent years when high interest rates depressed bond prices. This is why professional advice is needed.

(a) Investment Funds

There are a number of places to go for professional advice. If the total investments are relatively small in size (under $100,000), many organizations find that a no-load mutual fund or a bank common stock fund is the answer.[3] In both cases, the organization is purchasing expertise while it pools its funds with those of many other people. Mutual funds offer a convenient way to obtain investment management when the organization has a minimum amount to invest. There are numerous mutual funds with different investment goals and varying degrees of risk. A good place to start looking for a mutual fund is the Forbes Magazine annual review of mutual funds published each August. This review gives a great deal of comparative information that should help pinpoint several funds to study.

Bank-commingled or common stock investment funds are a form of mutual fund. One of the advantages of using a bank fund is that the reputation of the bank is involved and the bank will pay close attention to the investments made. Banks are often more conservative than mutual funds in their investment decisions, but this may be appropriate when one considers the fiduciary responsibility of not-for-profit organizations.

If the investment fund is large in size (over $100,000), the organization may prefer to select a professional to advise on specific stocks and bonds to purchase for its own portfolio. Most brokers are pleased to offer this service. On the other hand, many not-for-profit organizations are reluctant to entrust investment decisions to the brokers who handle the actual purchasing, because they are "wearing two hats." This can be avoided by going to one of the many available investment advisory services that does not handle the actual purchasing or selling.

(b)   Short-Term Investments

Investment professionals can also offer advice on a type of investment that is frequently not given the attention it warrants by not-for-profit organizations—short-term investments. Short-term investments are investments in interest-bearing instruments of that portion of an organization's cash balances which is currently inactive but will be needed to pay for programs and activities in the near future.

An ordinary savings account is one type of short-term investment of cash balances that are temporarily not deployed. Often, however, it is possible to improve on the interest rate available in savings accounts, without substantially increasing risk, by purchasing "money-market" instruments. These vary in interest rate, risk, minimum denomination available, time to maturity, and marketability prior to redemption; included

[3] If an organization has under $100,000 to invest, the board should carefully consider the nature of the resources being invested before buying common stocks. If the resources available are to be invested for only a short period of time, or if investment income is essential, then the organization should not be investing in common stocks. Instead, a savings account or money-market instrument is probably more appropriate.

are U.S. Treasury Bills, "agencies," certificates of deposit, and repurchase agreements.

Treasury Bills are the most marketable money-market instrument. The smallest denomination currently available is $10,000 and the shortest maturity is 13 weeks.

"Agencies" are federally sponsored debt instruments issued by federal agencies or quasi-governmental organizations. Some are explicitly guaranteed by the full faith and credit of the U.S. government while others are not.

Certificates of deposit (CDs) are available directly from commercial or savings banks, or through securities dealers. Only large CDs (over $100,000) are negotiable, and all bear substantial penalties for redemption prior to maturity.

Repurchase agreements are agreements under which a bank or securities dealer agrees to repurchase at a specific date and at a specific premium securities sold earlier to an investor. Interest rates on repurchase agreements are often attractive, and a wide range of maturities is usually available.

(c)   Selecting an Investment Advisor

A list of investment advisory services can usually be found in the classified telephone directory. Bear in mind that, as with all professionals, the investment advisor's reputation should be carefully checked. The bank's trust department is usually also happy to give advice on investment decisions. The point to emphasize is that investment decisions should be made by professionals in the investment business and not by amateurs (this is as true of investments as it is of medicine!). Remember, too, that even professionals sometimes make errors in judgment.

The professional advisor will charge a fee that is generally calculated on the basis of a percentage of the monies invested. The larger the investment fund, the lower the rate charged. This rate will vary depending on the size of the fund, but frequently is in the range of $1/2$ to 1 percent annually. The rate structure follows pretty closely the structure that investment advisors charge mutual funds.

25.5   SAFEGUARDING INVESTMENT SECURITIES

The physical safeguarding of an organization's investment securities is as important as making the right decision as to which stocks to buy or sell. This is often overlooked. The board of directors or the finance committee of the board has general responsibility for all investment instruments owned by the organization. Periodic verification of the existence of the securities should be made, either by independent accountants or the board itself. Verification usually involves a physical counting of the securities at the location where they are deposited. Three areas warrant special attention. The first is that stock certificates aren't lost or misplaced through carelessness or poor handling. The second is that they are not lost through misappropriation by an employee. The third is that the stockbroker doesn't lose the certificates or, worse yet, go bankrupt. Let's look at the risks in each of these three areas.

(a) Careless Handling

If the organization keeps the certificates in its possession, the certificates should be kept in a bank safe deposit box. They should be registered in the name of the organization. The organization should also maintain an investment register that shows the certificate number as well as cost and other financial information.[4] There should be limited access to the safe deposit box, and it is wise to require the presence of two persons (preferably officers) whenever the box is opened.[5]

Some organizations become careless in handling the certificates because they are registered in their name. They know they can "stop transfer" if the certificates are lost. While this is usually true, most transfer agents will require the registered owner to post a bond before a replacement certificate is issued. The purpose of the bond is to protect the agent from any loss that might result from misuse of the lost certificate. The bond can be purchased from an insurance company, but it is expensive, ranging between 1 percent and 4 percent of the market value of the lost certificate. This is a high price to pay for carelessness.

(b) Embezzlement

An organization must always be concerned that someone having access to stock certificates may be tempted to steal them. While the certificates may be registered in the organization's name, there is an underworld market for stolen certificates. Furthermore, if the loss is not discovered promptly and the transfer agent advised to "stop transfer," the organization's rights may be jeopardized.

---

[4] An example of an investment register is shown on page 585.
[5] It is also wise for the board to establish an investment committee charged with the responsibility for authorizing all investment transactions. If an outside advisor is retained, this committee should still review the outside advisor's recommendations before they are accepted. It is not wise to delegate authority to an outside advisor to act except in accordance with an investment policy approved by the investment committee and reviewed by the board.

The best control is to have the broker deliver the stock certificate directly to a custodian for safekeeping. When the stock is sold, the custodian is then instructed to deliver the certificate to the broker. In this way, the organization never handles the certificate. The use of a custodian provides excellent internal control. There is, of course, a charge for this custodian service.

(c) Leaving Certificates with Brokers

Some organizations leave their certificates in the custody of their broker. This has certain risks. One is that the broker will temporarily lose track of the certificates if the back office falls behind in its paperwork or incorrectly records the certificates. If this happens, there might be some delay before the broker straightens out the records. This is a risk that cannot be completely avoided since the broker must buy or sell the stock. But it increases if the organization also has the broker hold the certificate in safekeeping. As long as the broker doesn't go bankrupt, the worst that is likely to happen is that there will be delay in getting the certificates when the organization wants them. This risk can be minimized by making inquiries as to the broker's reputation for handling back office problems.

The other risk is the broker's going bankrupt while holding the stock. Provided the broker has not fraudulently hypothecated the stock, bankruptcy should not result in a loss to an organization. However, there could be considerable delay before the stock is released by a court. On the other hand, if the broker has, without the consent of the organization, pledged the stock for personal borrowings, there is a possibility of actual loss. While the organization might be able to take both civil and criminal action against the broker, this would be of little consolation in bankruptcy. The first $500,000 of such losses, however, would be recovered from the federally chartered Securities Investor Protection Corporation.

While these risks might be relatively small, a not-for-profit organization has a fiduciary responsibility to act with more than ordinary care and judgment. Accordingly, it would be prudent for an organization to have the broker deliver the stock certificates in the organization's name, either to an independent custodian or to the organization.

25.6 CONCLUSION

The board of a not-for-profit organization has an obligation to act prudently in all of its actions. When it comes to handling investments, very few boards are competent to make informed professional decisions. Accordingly, professional advice should be obtained to ensure that the organization's investments are wisely made. For very small organizations, this can be accomplished by choosing a mutual fund or bank common stock fund. For larger organizations, a professional advisor should be retained. Investment counsel should also be sought for short-term investments.

The board should not overlook its responsibility for security of its stock certificates. The most effective arrangement is to have the broker deliver all certificates to a custodian. In this way, neither the employees of the organization nor the broker have access to the certificates.

Tax and Compliance Reporting Requirements

CHAPTER 26

Principal Federal Tax and Compliance Requirements

This chapter discusses two aspects of not-for-profit organizations' relations with the federal government: (1) Qualification for tax-exempt status under the Internal Revenue Code; and (2) reporting requirements applicable to organizations that receive support in the form of federal grants, contracts, loans, loan guarantees, and similar awards.

Congress has imposed an income tax on all individuals and organizations with few exceptions. Those organizations that are exempt from such tax are known as exempt organizations. Generally not-for-profit organizations are exempt organizations if they meet certain specific criteria as to the purpose for which they were formed and if their source of income is related to that purpose. But even an exempt organization can be subject to tax on certain portions of its income and, if the organization is a private foundation, it is subject to a number of very specific rules as well as certain excise taxes. This chapter discusses the types of organizations that are exempt and the general tax provisions of the rules governing such organizations.

This discussion is intended only to give the reader a general understanding of the tax rules and is not intended to be a complete discussion of the law and the tax regulations. Each organization should consult with its own tax accountant or attorney about its status and any specific problems it may have.

26.1 ORGANIZATIONS EXEMPT FROM TAX

The Internal Revenue Code (I.R.C.) provides exemption from tax for certain organizations that meet very specific requirements. The most widely applicable of these exemptions are:

1. Corporations, and any community chest, fund or foundation, organized and operated exclusively for religious, charitable,

scientific, testing for public safety, literary, or educational purposes, or to foster national or international amateur sports competition . . . or for the prevention of cruelty to children or animals, no part of the net earnings of which inures to the benefit of any private shareholder or individual, no substantial part of the activities of which is carrying on propaganda, or otherwise attempting to influence legislation[1] (except as otherwise provided in subsection (h)), and which does not participate in, or intervene in (including the publishing or distributing of statements), any political campaign on behalf of any candidate for public office. (§ 501(c)(3))[2]

2. Clubs organized for pleasure, recreation, and other nonprofitable purposes, substantially all of the activities of which are for such purposes and no part of the net earnings of which inures to the benefit of any private shareholder. (§ 501(c)(7))

3. Business leagues, chambers of commerce, . . . not organized for profit and no part of the net earnings of which inures to the benefit of any private shareholder or individual. (§ 501(c)(6))

4. Corporations organized for the exclusive purpose of holding title to property, collecting income therefrom, and turning over the entire amount thereof, less expenses, to an organization which itself is exempt . . . (§ 501(c)(2))

There are other categories of exempt organizations found in the I.R.C. under sections 501, 521, 526, 527, and 528, but the exemptions listed above cover the majority of not-for-profit organizations. This chapter focuses on the exemption requirements for charities and discusses three other examples of exempt organizations: social clubs, trade associations, and title-holding companies. Other categories of exempt organizations are not discussed here.

26.2 CHARITABLE ORGANIZATIONS

Most exempt organizations are categorized as charitable organizations or § 501(c)(3) organizations. There are four main purposes that organizations exempt under § 501(c)(3) may have: religious, charitable, scientific,

---

[1] The Tax Reform Act of 1976 allows a § 501(c)(3) organization to elect the § 501(h) safe harbor for the amount of lobbying activities in lieu of the subjective "no substantial part" test.
[2] References are to specific sections of the Internal Revenue Code of 1986 from which the quotations were taken. Exempt organizations often refer to the type of exemption they hold by the code section under which they are exempt.

or educational. This covers organizations such as churches, hospitals, schools, community funds, museums, medical research organizations, and YMCAs.

All § 501(c)(3) organizations must be "organized and operated exclusively for" one of these purposes. In order to meet the "organizational test," an organization's charter must limit its purpose to one or more of the exempt purposes allowed and must not expressly empower the organization to engage, other than as an insubstantial part of its activities, in activities that are not in furtherance of the organization's exempt purpose(s). An organization's charter must also contain certain language and restrictions to conform to the requirements for a § 501(c)(3) organization. Organizations that contemplate application for recognition of exempt status under § 501(c)(3) should consult with qualified legal and tax counsel to ensure that the organizing documents meet the requirements of the organizational test.

An organization that meets the organizational test must actually operate within the boundaries established by its charter in order to meet the "operational" test. The operational test requires that organizations engage primarily in activities that further one or more exempt purposes. Also, in order to pass the operational test, organizations must serve a public, rather than private, interest; must not attempt to influence legislation as more than an insubstantial portion of activities, and must not benefit a private shareholder or individual.

The Tax Reform Act of 1969 created two general categories of § 501(c)(3) organizations. Each category is subject to different rules. The two categories are private foundations and public charities, also referred to as publicly supported organizations. All § 501(c)(3) organizations are assumed to be private foundations unless they meet a statutory public support test or are considered not to be private foundations under a specific statutory definition.

- Publicly supported organizations receive broad public support. An individual donor may normally deduct contributions to such organizations in amounts up to 50 percent of the donor's adjusted gross income.

- Private foundations are organizations that do not receive broad public support but instead receive most of their support from a limited number of donors or from investment income. Private foundations are subject to many restrictions on their activities and are subject to certain excise taxes. Normally an individual donor may deduct contributions to private foundations in amounts only up to 30 percent of the donor's adjusted gross income.

A publicly supported organization is defined for this discussion[3] as a "§ 501(c)(3) organization that is not a private foundation."[4] There are three principal categories of organizations that are not private foundations. These three categories are as follows:

1. Organizations formed exclusively for religious, charitable, scientific, literary, or educational purposes, or to foster national or international amateur sports which normally receive a substantial portion of their support from direct or indirect contributions from the general public or from a governmental unit. Also excluded from private foundation status are churches, educational institutions with a faculty and student body, hospitals, and medical research organizations related to a hospital (§ 509(a)(1)).

2. Organizations that meet both of the following mechanical tests, based on actual support during the previous four years (§ 509(a)(2)):

   a. The organization receives not more than one third of its support from gross investment income, and

   b. The organization receives more than one third of its support from a combination of:

      (1) Contributions, gifts, grants, and membership fees, except when such income is received from disqualified persons,[5] and

      (2) Gross receipts from admissions, sale of merchandise, performance of services, or furnishing facilities, all of which must be derived from an activity related to the organization's exempt purpose. Excluded from gross receipts are any amounts from any one person, governmental unit, or company in excess of $5,000 or 1 percent of total support

---

[3] Organizations exempt under another section of the law, such as social clubs, business leagues, etc., are not private foundations.

[4] Some organizations that are not private foundations do not receive broad public support. However, the organizations are subject to the same rules that organizations receiving broad public support are subject to; accordingly, in order to assist the reader in distinguishing between private foundations and other than private foundations, the title "publicly supported" organizations will be used throughout this discussion to refer to all "§ 501(c)(3)" organizations which are not private foundations.

[5] A disqualified person is a substantial contributor, or a foundation manager, or a person (or a person's relatives) having a sizable interest in a corporation, partnership, estate, or trust which is itself a substantial contributor. A substantial contributor is a person who has contributed in either the current or a prior year aggregate amounts exceeding $5,000, if that amount at the time of the contribution was 2 percent or more of total contributions received since formation of the foundation. A foundation manager is any officer, director, or trustee of the foundation.

(whichever is greater) and amounts received from disqualified persons.

3. Organizations organized and operated exclusively for the benefit of, to perform the functions of or to carry out the purpose of a publicly supported charity, or to perform a charitable purpose in support of a § 501(c)(4), § 501(c)(5), and/or a § 501(c)(6) organization (§ 509(a)(3)). These organizations are called "supporting organizations." They are not required, themselves, to meet either public support test as long as the organization which is supported meets one of the support tests discussed above. When the supported organization is a § 501(c)(4), § 501(c)(5), or § 501(c)(6) organization, the supported organization must meet the support test under § 509(a)(2), a test to which the supported organization would not normally be subject.

The law and regulations provide mathematical tests for public support. The tests are very technical and are different depending on whether the organization must meet the test under 1 or 2 above. A detailed discussion of the two different public support tests is beyond the scope of this book.

Simply stated, the test under § 509(a)(1) requires that one-third of an organization's support come from the general public. The test under § 509(a)(2) requires that one-third of an organization's support come from the general public and not more than one-third of an organization's support come from gross investment income. Support is calculated over an aggregated four-year period and the calculations are performed on the cash basis.

Excluded from the calculation under each test are unusual grants. Unusual grants are defined in the regulations under § 509. A grant must meet the following requirements before it may be excluded from the public support calculation as an unusual grant:

- The grant was a substantial contribution from a disinterested party.
- The grant was attracted by reason of the publicly supported nature of the organization.
- The grant was unusual or unexpected in respect to the amount.
- The grant would, by reason of its size, adversely affect the organization's public support test.

This provision enables organizations to receive infrequent large amounts from generous donors without losing public support status.

Organizations exempt under § 501(c)(3) must file Schedule A of Form 990. Schedule A includes a schedule for organizations to complete regarding the support they received for the four years prior to the current taxable year. The Internal Revenue Service performs additional mathematical calculations on the information provided in the schedule to confirm that the organization has met the public support test to which it is subject. A completed Form 990 and Schedule A are included in the next chapter.

This discussion shows generally how these rules are applied. There are a number of exceptions to these rules and each organization should consult with legal or tax counsel to determine exactly how these rules affect it. Also, keep in mind that this mechanical test is applied only to organizations with at least four years' experience. Younger organizations having at least one year's experience can obtain a "temporary" exemption until they have four years' experience, at which time the above tests are applied.

26.3 PRIVATE FOUNDATIONS

Private foundations are charitable organizations that are subject to specific rules and taxes which do not apply to publicly supported organizations. The most important provisions that apply to private foundations are:

1. Payment of an excise tax on investment income.
2. Distribution of at least a minimum amount of income (as defined).
3. Disposition of excess business holdings.
4. Avoidance of certain prohibited transactions.
5. Filing a complex annual information return.

(a) Excise Tax on Investment Income

The Tax Reform Act of 1969 established an excise tax on net investment income:[6] Net investment income includes dividends, interest, rents, royalties, and net capital gains.[7] For purposes of calculating gain on

---

[6] This excise tax was originally established at the rate of 4 percent but was reduced to 2 percent in 1977. When a private foundation makes qualifying distributions which equal or exceed the sum of (1) the fair market value of the foundation's assets multiplied by the foundation's average payout ratio for the 5 prior years; and (2) 1 percent of the foundation's net investment income, the foundation qualifies for a 1 percent excise tax rate for that year.

[7] Capital losses can be offset only against capital gains and not against investment income.

investments acquired prior to December 31, 1969, the tax basis of the property is the higher of the fair market value at December 31, 1969, or the cost. In calculating net investment income, reasonable expenses directly related to the production of investment income can be deducted.

Also, income that is subject to unrelated business income tax is not included in the calculation of net investment income. This would include items of income such as interest or dividends from debt financed stocks and bonds and capital gains from the sale of debt financed assets. An example of the excise tax applied to a private foundation that had stocks and bonds which were acquired both before and after December 31, 1969, follows:

		Taxable Income
Dividends and interest		$ 10,000
Sale of stock A for $45,000 purchased in 1967, at a cost of $20,000, but having a market value at December 31, 1969 of $30,000		
Proceeds	$ 45,000	
December 31, 1969 value	(30,000)	
Gain		15,000
Sale of stock B for $20,000 purchased in 1968 at a cost of $15,000, but having a market value at December 31, 1969 of $25,000		
Proceeds	$ 20,000	
December 31, 1969 value	(25,000)	
Difference, not recognized for tax purposes. No loss is recognized if using the December 31, 1969 market value creates a loss	$ (5,000)	
Sale of stock C for $15,000 purchased in 1970 at a cost of $20,000		
Proceeds of sale	$ 15,000	
Cost	(20,000)	
Loss		(5,000)[a]
Net		20,000
Less investment advisory fees and other expenses		(2,000)
Net investment income		$ 18,000
Tax at 2%		$ 360

[a] The amount of capital loss deductible from taxable income is limited to the amount of capital gain included therein.

It is important to keep accurate accounting records of the cost basis for all investments as well as an accurate segregation of any expenses applicable to investment income. With respect to investments acquired prior to December 31, 1969, it is also important to keep a record of the fair market value as of December 31, 1969.

Foundations are required to pay estimated excise taxes on a quarterly basis.

(b) Tax Consequences of Gifts of Securities

On investments received by gift subsequent to December 31, 1969, the contributor's tax basis is the basis that the foundation must use when calculating taxable gain. For investments received prior to December 31, 1969, the basis is the higher of fair market value at December 31, 1969, or contributor's tax basis. In most instances, the fair market value is higher. Thus, a private foundation must obtain from the donor, at the time a gift of securities is received, a statement of tax basis. This is very important and great care should be taken to obtain this information promptly upon receipt of the gift. At a later date the donor may be difficult to locate or may have lost the necessary tax records. Since donated securities are recorded for accounting purposes at fair market value at date of receipt, the foundation must keep supplementary memo records of the donor's tax basis.

Here is an illustration of how two gifts of the same marketable security can have different tax consequences to the private foundation. Both gifts made in 1980 involve 100 shares of stock A.

Gift 1—Very Low Basis:

Mr. Jones acquired his 100 shares of stock A in 1933 when the company was founded. His cost was only 10 cents a share, and therefore his basis for these 100 shares was only $10. Market value on the date of gift was $90 a share, or a total of $9,000. The tax basis to Mr. Jones of $10 carries over to the private foundation. If the foundation later sells the stock for $10,000 it will pay a 2 percent tax on $9,990 ($10,000 sales proceeds less $10 tax basis), or a tax of $199.80.

Gift 2—Very High Basis:

Mr. Smith acquired his 100 shares of stock A in 1970 at a cost of $110 a share or a total of $11,000. The market value on the date of his gift was also $90 a share, or a total of $9,000. If the private foundation later sells this stock for $10,000 it will have neither a taxable gain or loss. In this instance the donor's basis of $110 a share carries over to the foundation for purposes of calculating taxable gain, but for purposes of calculating *loss*, the fair market value at date of gift ($90 a share) becomes the tax basis. Since the sales price

($100) is more than the fair market value at the date of gift ($90), but less than the donor's cost ($110), there is no gain or loss recognized.

As can be seen from this example, in one instance the private foundation had to pay a tax of $199.80 and in the other instance had no tax. Rather than sell appreciated stock and pay excise tax on the gain, a foundation might consider distributing the stock to a publicly supported organization and letting the distributee organization sell it. The distributee organization would not incur tax on the gain since capital gains are exempt from unrelated business taxable income and publicly supported organizations are not subject to the excise tax on net investment income. To the extent a private foundation has capital losses, they can be offset against capital gains in the same year. If there are no capital gains to offset such losses, the losses cannot be offset against investment income. Capital losses cannot be carried over to another year.

(c) Distribution of Income

A private foundation is required to make qualifying distributions of at least the distributable amount by the end of the year following the current taxable year. Qualifying distributions are those amounts paid to accomplish the exempt purposes of the foundation. If the foundation fails to distribute the required amount, it may be subject to taxes that ultimately have the effect of taxing 100 percent of any amount not distributed.

Starting in 1982, the "distributable amount" is defined as the minimum investment return, less the excise tax and, where applicable, less the unrelated business income tax.

The minimum investment return is 5 percent of the fair market value of all the foundation's assets that are not used in directly carrying out the organization's exempt purpose. Cash equal to 1.5 percent of the total foundation's assets is deemed to be used in carrying out the exempt purpose and is deducted for this calculation. This means that if a foundation has marketable securities and cash with a market value of $1,000,000 it must make minimum qualifying distributions of 5 percent of $985,000 ($1,000,000 less 1.5 percent of $1,000,000) or $49,250 regardless of its actual income. If, for example, actual investment income were only $30,000, the foundation would still have to make qualifying distributions of $49,250.

Note that contributions and gifts received are included in the calculation of the distributable amount only to the extent that they increase the fair market value of the foundation's assets.

This means that the private foundation will not have to make qualifying distributions out of principal provided its investment income plus contributions and gifts equal the distributable amount. In the preceding example, if contributions to the foundation were, say, $50,000, the distributable amount would still be $49,250. These requirements will have little effect on private foundations that receive continuing contribution support.

Here is an illustration showing how these calculations work. Using the condensed financial statements of the A. C. Williams Foundation, the distributable amount is calculated as follows:

A. C. WILLIAMS FOUNDATION
SUMMARY OF RECEIPTS AND EXPENDITURES

Receipts:			
Contributions	$140,000		
Investment income	50,000	$ 190,000	
Expenditures:			
For exempt purposes	70,000		
Excise tax	1,000	71,000	
Net		$ 119,000	

ASSETS

Cash	$ 30,000
Marketable securities	970,000
Net assets	$1,000,000

CALCULATION OF DISTRIBUTABLE AMOUNT:

Investment income	$ 50,000
	$ 50,000
Minimum investment return:	
Average fair market value of securities and cash[8]	$ 1,000,000
Less 1½% of above amount for cash deemed to be used in carrying out the exempt purpose	(15,000)
Net, subject to stipulated minimum investment return	985,000
Stipulated rate of return	5%
	$ 49,250
Distributable amount:	
Minimum investment return	$ 49,250
Less—Excise tax	(1,000)
	$ 48,250

[8] The regulations under § 4942 provide guidance with regard to the methods to be used in calculating the fair market value of a foundation's assets. It would be extremely unusual if the fair market value of a foundation's assets calculated for the distributable amount equalled the fair market value of a foundation's assets as of the balance sheet date.

Thus the distributable amount is $48,250. Qualifying distributions were $70,000, which exceeds the distributable amount by $21,750, and the requirement has thus been met. This excess can be carried over for five years to meet the requirements of a year in which there is a deficiency. Where there is such a carryover, the order of application of the amounts distributed would be: current year, carryover from earliest year, carryover from next earliest year, and so forth.

(d)   Excess Business Holdings

A private foundation is not allowed to own a stock interest in a corporation if the stock it owns together with the stock owned by disqualified persons[9] would exceed 20 percent of the voting stock. The provision also applies to holdings in partnerships, joint ventures and beneficial interests in trusts.

> **Example:** Mr. Scotty owns, together with his family, 15 percent of the voting stock in the A. M. Scotty Company, and he is a substantial contributor to the "Scotty Foundation" and thus is a disqualified person. The maximum amount of stock that the Scotty Foundation can own is 5 percent (20 percent maximum less 15 percent). There are several minor exceptions to this general rule, and there is a transitional period for foundations to dispose of their pre-1969 excess holdings. The transition rule for disposition of excess pre-1969 holdings allowed a 10-, 15-, or 20-year period for initial reduction in excess business holdings depending on the percentage of ownership by the foundation and disqualified persons at May 26, 1969. Private foundations are given an additional 15 years to further reduce excess business holdings to allowable limits.
>
> Failure to comply with these rules will result in taxes which can be as high as 200 percent of the value of the excess stock held.

(e)   Prohibited Transactions

There are several categories of transactions in which private foundations may not engage. They cannot engage in "self-dealing," make investments that jeopardize their exempt function, or make expenditures for certain prohibited purposes (so-called "taxable expenditures"). There is an excise tax on both the foundation and on the foundation manager who engages in these prohibited transactions. For example, the tax on taxable expenditures is initially 10 percent and 2.5 percent on the foundation and foundation manager respectively, but is increased to 100 percent and 50 percent respectively if corrective action is not taken within a specified period of time.

---

[9] A "disqualified person" is defined in footnote 5.

Self-Dealing

The law prohibits private foundations from engaging in certain transactions with disqualified persons, or foundation managers. These prohibited self-dealing transactions include the sale, leasing, or lending of property or money, the furnishing of goods or services on a basis more favorable than that granted to the general public, or the payment of unreasonable compensation. Disqualified persons may continue to support the foundation by lending money without charge and providing goods and services for charitable use without charge. The prohibition against self-dealing prevents disqualified persons from receiving a benefit from their relationship with a foundation but does not generally prevent the foundation from receiving a benefit from the disqualified person.

All transactions involving a disqualified person should be examined very closely to make absolutely certain they do not involve self-dealing.

Investments That Jeopardize Exempt Function

The law provides that the foundation may not make investments that jeopardize the exempt function of the foundation. The foundation is expected to use a "prudent trustee's approach" in making investments. Examples of investments that probably would not be prudent would be investments that have a high level of risk.

Prohibited Expenditures

The law provides that a foundation may not make expenditures to carry on propaganda to influence legislation or the outcome of a public election. It also prohibits making a grant to an individual for travel or study without prior Internal Revenue Service approval of the grant program. The law also provides no grant shall be made to another *private* foundation or to any noncharitable organization unless the granting foundation exercises expenditure control over the grant to see that it is used solely for the purposes granted. Finally, the law prohibits a private foundation from making any grant for any purpose other than a charitable purpose.

(f) Annual Information Return

The annual information return (Form 990-PF) filed with the Internal Revenue Service is considerably longer and more complex than the Form 990 filed by most other not-for-profit organizations. Chapter 27 discusses this annual return and illustrates a completed form.

A private foundation must also publish a notice in a newspaper broadly circulated in the county where its principal office is located. The notice states that a copy of the annual return is available for inspection by anyone desiring to see it at the organization's office within six months of the date of publication of the notice.

26.4 PRIVATE OPERATING FOUNDATIONS

Private operating foundations are private foundations that actively conduct charitable program activities that are the exempt function for which the organization was founded. This is in contrast to private foundations that act only as conduits for funds and have no operating programs as such. Private operating foundations have most of the characteristics of publicly supported organizations but do not meet the public support tests outlined for such organizations that were discussed earlier in this chapter.

(a) Qualifying Tests

In addition to expending substantially all (85 percent) of its income directly for the active conduct of its exempt function, a private foundation, to be a private "operating" foundation, must meet one or more of the following tests:

1. It devotes 65 percent or more of the fair market value of its assets to direct use in its exempt function.
2. Two thirds of its minimum investment return is devoted to its exempt function and used chiefly by the foundation to accomplish that function.
3. It derives 85 percent or more of its support, other than investment income, from the general public and from five or more exempt organizations, no one of which provides more than 25 percent. In addition not more than 50 percent of its total support is from investment income.

(b) Advantages

There are several advantages to being a private operating foundation. The minimum distribution rules imposed on private foundations do not apply to private operating foundations and donors are allowed to deduct a contribution to a private operating foundation up to 50 percent of the donors' adjusted gross income versus the 30 percent of donors' adjusted gross income limitation on contributions to private foundations.

26.5   OTHER CONCERNS FOR CHARITIES

(a)   Contributions Disclosures

Contributions other than cash are subject to special reporting by both donors and recipient charities. Contributors must attach Form 8283 to their tax returns to support noncash charitable contributions of $500 or more to the same donee. The form requires an appraisal by a competent, independent appraiser and, in some cases, the recipient organization is required to sign the form also. If the recipient organization is required to sign the form, and disposes of the property within two years of the date of the gift, then the organization must file Form 8282 with the Internal Revenue Service within 125 days of the disposition. The organization must also supply the donor with a copy of Form 8282. By requiring this reporting, the Internal Revenue Service is better able to monitor sizable charitable deductions on individual returns.

(b)   Contribution Acknowledgments

For single charitable contributions made after December 31, 1993, of property and/or cash of $250 or more, donors will need an acknowledgment from the charity to substantiate a charitable tax deduction. A cancelled check is not sufficient in this case. Charities should be prepared to acknowledge gifts to assist their individual and corporate donors with substantiation of these deductions.

(c)   Solicitation Disclosures

When an organization gives a donor something in return for a contribution, for example, a dinner or a raffle ticket, the amount given may not constitute a charitable contribution. A portion, or all, of the payment may be payment for receipt of a benefit, and not a gift to the organization. Revenue Ruling 67-246 and Revenue Procedure 90-12 provide guidance to organizations that provide a benefit to donors in conjunction with solicitation of funds.

For contributions received after December 31, 1993, organizations must inform their donors, in clearly stated language, how much, if any, of the payment is deductible as a charitable contribution if the total received is greater than $75. An example of this is an organization that sponsors a fund-raising dinner. A comparable dinner in a restaurant would cost a donor $50. In order to attend the dinner, donors pay $200. In this case, the organization must inform donors that $150 of their $200 payment is deductible as a charitable contribution. Charities should print this information on the donors' tickets or receipts thereby providing donors with documentation for the charitable deductions they claim on their tax returns.

There are exceptions for low-cost items that are distributed as part of a fund-raising effort. Charitable organizations should consult the Revenue Ruling and Revenue Procedure and ensure that their solicitation materials comply. The Internal Revenue Service is empowered to impose penalties in cases of failure to comply with the notification requirements.

(d)   Excise Tax Considerations

There are several excise taxes imposed on organizations under certain circumstances. The following provides a short summary of each tax:

- Excess Expenditures to Influence Legislation—§ 4911 imposes a 25 percent excise tax on the excess lobbying expenditures (including grass roots lobbying expenditures) of an organization which has elected to be covered under section § 501(h). The election under § 501(h) provides qualifying organizations with a safe harbor for their lobbying and grass roots expenditures. In any year in which the organization's lobbying expenses exceed the safe harbor amounts, the organization must pay the excise tax under § 4911.

- Tax on Disqualifying Lobbying Expenditures of Certain Organizations—If an organization loses its status under § 501(c)(3) because of making more than an insubstantial amount of lobbying expenditures, § 4912 imposes excise taxes on an organization, and its management. The tax on the organization is 5 percent of the lobbying expenditures in the taxable year in which § 501(c)(3) status is revoked. A separate 5 percent excise tax is imposed on the management of the organization, if the management agreed to the expenditures while knowing the organization might lose its exemption. This excise tax does not apply to private foundations or organizations which elect the safe harbor of section § 501(h). (Note that organizations which lose their § 501(c)(3) status when more than an insubstantial portion of their activities is lobbying may not become exempt under § 501(c)(4).)

- Political Expenditures of § 501(c)(3) Organizations—§ 501(c)(3) organizations are forbidden from participating or intervening in any political campaign on behalf of or in opposition to any candidate for public office. § 4955 imposes a two-level excise tax on the organization and its management that participate in prohibited activities. The first level of tax is imposed on the organization at the rate of 10 percent of the amount of the expenditures; and on the management at the rate of 2.5 percent of the expenditures if the management agreed willfully to the expenditures. If the organization does not correct the political expenditure by obtaining a refund of the amounts spent, a second level tax of 100 percent and 50 percent of the expenditure is imposed on the organization and management, respectively. (Note that if a private foundation makes political expenditures and pays the tax imposed by this section, then the expenditures will not also be taxed under § 4945 as taxable expenditures.)

(e) Summary of Individual Tax Deductions

Charitable organizations depend to a very large extent on individual contributions for support. To the extent that a contributor receives a tax deduction for a contribution, there is more inclination to be generous in the contribution. Accordingly the tax deductibility of a contribution is of real importance. Exhibit 26–1 summarizes the general rules applicable to common types of contributions.

As the Exhibit indicates, the amount of deduction allowed in any year is limited to a percentage of the donor's adjusted gross income. Contributions limited in this manner may be carried forward for five years until fully used. The adjusted gross income limitation depends on the type of donee organization; the type of property donated; and whether the organization will use the property in pursuit of its exempt purpose (related) or will use the property in a way unrelated to its exempt purpose (such as selling the property).

Gifts of appreciated property may have additional tax implications to the donor. Because the charitable contribution rules are somewhat complex, donors should consult with their tax advisors before making a large contribution to any organization. Exhibit 26–1 is intended to be a general guide only.

26.6 NONCHARITABLE EXEMPT ORGANIZATIONS

(a) Social and Recreation Clubs

Another type of organization that is granted exemption from tax is the club "organized for pleasure, recreation, and other nonprofitable

EXHIBIT 26–1 Deductibility of charitable contributions by donors.

CHARITABLE CONTRIBUTION TABLE

Type of Property	Factors			
	Type of Organization	Use by Organization	Amount of Deduction	AGI Limitation
Cash	Public	Any	Actual Amount	50%
	Private	Any	Actual Amount	30%
Long-Term Capital Gain (LTCG):				
Intangible or real property	Public	Any	FMV[a]	30%
	Private	Any	FMV less LTCG[b]	20%
Tangible personal property	Public	Related	FMV[a]	30%
		Unrelated	FMV less LTCG	50%
	Private	Related	FMV less LTCG	20%
		Unrelated	FMV less LTCG	20%
Ordinary income (OI) property	Public	Any	FMV less OI	50%
	Private	Any	FMV less OI	30%
Loss (ordinary or capital loss property)	Public	Any	FMV	50%
	Private	Any	FMV	30%

Key: AGI—Adjusted Gross Income
FMV—Fair Market Value
Public—50% type charities including private operating foundations
Private—30% type charities including private nonoperating foundations
[a] Taxpayer may elect to decrease the amount of deduction to fair market value less long term gain potential and to increse the AGI limitation to 50%
[b] In the case of a contribution of "qualified appreciated stock" to a private nonoperating foundation, the full FMV is deductible.

purposes, substantially all of the activities of which are for such purposes and no part of the net earnings of which inures to the benefit of any private shareholder." Social and recreation clubs are exempt as long as substantially all their activities are for members. Income derived from nonmember activities, such as investment income and nonmember use of the club, can have significant implications for the social club.

Exempt Status

Significant use of the club by nonmembers can result in loss of the club's tax exemption. The congressional committee reports of the Tax Reform Act of 1976 indicate that a social club will retain its exempt status if no more than 35 percent of its gross receipts are from investments and nonmember use of facilities. Within this 35 percent, no more than 15 percent can be derived from nonmember use of facilities.

Gross receipts include receipts from normal and usual activities of the club, including charges, admissions, membership fees, dues, assessments, investment income, and normal recurring gains on investments, but exclude initiation fees and capital contributions.

Gross receipts from nonmembers are amounts derived from nonmember sources such as investment income and amounts paid by members involving nonbona fide guests. Amounts paid by a member's employer can, depending on the situation, be considered as paid by a member or as paid by a nonmember.

The problem of determining whether someone using the club is a bona fide guest of a member has proven troublesome. Most clubs adopt rules which limit use of the facilities to members and their guests. The Internal Revenue Service has taken the position that, in many situations, the member's participation in, or connection with, a function is so limited that the member is merely using the membership to make the club facilities available to an outside group. In many instances, the member is viewed merely as acting as a sponsor.

If a member's charges are reimbursed by an employer, the income will be member income if the event is for a personal or social purpose of the member, or due to a direct business objective of the employer. If there is no direct relationship between the business objective or purpose of the activities, the reimbursement will be considered nonmember income. The distinction is where the member has a direct interest in the company function as contrasted with a situation where the member is merely serving as a sponsor to permit the company to use the facilities.

There are also guidelines to help determine whether group functions hosted by members at which guests are present constitute member or nonmember receipts. In groups of eight or fewer individuals, it is assumed that all nonmembers are guests. In larger groups, it is assumed that all nonmembers are bona fide guests provided 75 percent of the group are members. In all other situations the club must substantiate that the nonmember was a bona fide guest. In the absence of adequate substantiation it will be assumed such receipts are nonmember receipts, even though paid for by the members.

Substantiation Requirements

In order to rely upon the above assumptions regarding group functions, clubs must maintain certain records. Where the "8 or fewer" rule or the "75 percent member rule" is used, it is necessary to document only the total number in the party, the number of members in the party, and the source of the payments. For all other group occasions involving club use by nonmembers, even where a member pays for the use, the club must maintain records containing the following information if it wishes to substantiate that such receipts are not "nonmember" receipts:

1. Date
2. Total number in the party
3. Number of nonmembers in the party
4. Total charges
5. Charges attributable to nonmembers
6. Charges paid by nonmembers

In addition, the club must obtain a statement signed by the member indicating whether the member will be reimbursed for such nonmember use and, if so, the amount of the reimbursement. Where the member will be reimbursed, or where the member's employer makes direct payment to the club for the charges, the club must also obtain a statement signed by the member indicating (a) name of the employer, (b) amount of the payment attributable to the nonmember use, (c) nonmember's name and business or other relationship to the member (or if readily identifiable, the class of individuals, e.g., sales managers), and (d) business, personal, or other purpose of the member served by the nonmember use.

Recordkeeping requirements for other activities such as providing guest rooms, parking facilities, steam rooms, and so on, have not been specifically set forth. Clubs must be careful to ensure that their recordkeeping procedures provide information regarding member and nonmember use of these facilities. All social clubs must be extremely careful not to receive, even inadvertently, nonmember income in excess of allowable limits.

Unrelated Business Income

In addition to jeopardizing its exempt status, receipts from nonmembers have other tax implications for a social club since such receipts constitute unrelated business income. Social clubs are subject to tax at regular corporate tax rates on their unrelated business income. This is calculated on a somewhat different basis than for other types of exempt organizations. The total income of the club from all sources except for exempt function income (dues, fees, etc., paid by the members) is subject to tax. This means that income from nonmembers, as well as investment and other types of income, is subject to tax. Deductions are allowed for expenses directly connected with such income, including a reasonable allocation of overhead. As with other exempt organizations, there is a specific deduction of $1,000 allowed.

It is possible for a social club to have an overall loss but still have a substantial amount of unrelated business income. Here is an example of a country club where this is the case:

	Exempt	Unrelated	Total
Interest on taxable bonds	—	$ 10,000	$ 10,000
Membership fees	$ 100,000	—	100,000
Golf and other fees	40,000	20,000	60,000
Restaurant and bar	200,000	50,000	250,000
Total income	340,000	80,000	420,000
Direct expenses	(320,000)	(30,000)	(350,000)
Overhead	(60,000)	(20,000)	(80,000)
Net income (loss)	$ (40,000)	$ 30,000	$ (10,000)

This club will have taxes to pay on $30,000 of income, which at the 1993 corporate tax rates is $4,350.[10]

One of the real burdens for social clubs is to keep their bookkeeping records in such a manner that it is possible to not only determine direct expenses associated with nonmember income, but also to provide a reasonable basis of expense allocation between member and nonmember activities. Even the largest of corporations has difficulty in making allocation of overhead between functions, so the problems of allocation for social clubs should not be passed over lightly.

Many social clubs charge nonmembers enough to cover the direct costs of the services provided but consistently incur overall losses on nonmember income when they allocate overhead and indirect expenses to nonmember income. This loss enables a club to offset investment income and other unrelated business income when calculating the tax it

---

[10] $30,000 less $1,000 special exclusion, taxed at 15 percent on the first $50,000 of taxable income.

must pay. The Internal Revenue Service has taken the position that an activity that consistently generates losses does not have the requisite profit motive needed for a trade or business. Under this position, the Service contends that the activity is not an unrelated trade or business and the losses from the activity may not be used to offset other types of unrelated income. In *Portland Golf Club v. Commissioner*, 90-1 USTC ¶ 50,332 the Supreme Court agreed with the Service's position. Social clubs should reevaluate their cost allocations and the amounts they charge nonmembers and should consider whether the activity is pursued with a motive for profit.

(b) Trade Associations

Another example of an exempt noncharitable organization is a trade association exempt under § 501(c)(6). Trade associations are membership organizations which function for the common business purpose of their members. The activities of a trade association must be directed toward the improvement of business conditions as opposed to performing particular services for individual persons or members.

Contributions or dues paid to a trade association are not deductible as charitable contributions. Most members, however, are entitled to deduct dues and other fees paid as a business deduction.

Lobbying Expenses

Expenses paid after December 31, 1993, for lobbying activities, that is, activities engaged with the intent to influence legislation, are not deductible for tax purposes. The nondeductibility of lobbying expenses is extended to the portion of business dues paid to trade associations allocable to the trade association's lobbying activities. Trade associations must either notify members as to the portion of member dues that are not deductible, or pay a "proxy tax" equal to the highest corporate income tax rate on amounts expended for lobbying purposes. The provisions governing member notification and payment of the "proxy" tax are complex, and trade associations should consult with their professional advisors on this issue.

Unrelated Business Income

Trade associations are taxed on net unrelated business income the same way that charitable organizations are taxed. Interest, dividends, rents, and royalties are exempt as long as the property which generates the income is not debt financed. Membership dues and meeting and convention receipts are also not income from an unrelated trade or business.

(c)   Title Holding Companies

§ 501(c)(2) provides an exemption for corporations that hold title to property, collect the income therefrom, and remit the net income to another exempt organization annually. These organizations most frequently hold title to real property but may also hold investment portfolios. The organizations are allowed exempt status because of their relationship to the parent exempt organization. Possible abuse situations are avoided by requiring the § 501(c)(2) to remit net income from the property to the exempt parent and forbidding a § 501(c)(2) to participate in any activity except holding title.

Unrelated Business Income

Because § 501(c)(2) organizations are forbidden from any activity other than holding property, the only source of unrelated business income they might have is income from debt financed property under § 514. Unrelated business income is discussed in more detail in the next section.

26.7   UNRELATED BUSINESS INCOME

Virtually every exempt organization, including churches and clubs, is subject to normal corporate taxes on its unrelated business income.

(a)   Definition

There is always difficulty in knowing exactly what is unrelated business income. Here is the way the law reads:

> The term "unrelated trade or business" means . . . any trade or business the conduct of which is not substantially related . . . to the exercise or performance by such organization of its charitable, educational, or other purpose or function constituting the basis for its exemption . . . (§ 513(a) of the Internal Revenue Code).
> . . . the term "unrelated business income" means the gross income derived by any organization from any unrelated trade or business . . . regularly carried on by it, less the deductions . . . which are directly connected . . . (§ 512(a)(1) of the Internal Revenue Code).

There are three key phrases in these definitions. The first is "unrelated," the second is "trade or business," and the third is "regularly carried on." All three criteria must be present for an activity to be categorized as an unrelated trade or business activity. It is not difficult to determine whether the business in question is "regularly carried on," but it is difficult to know what is truly unrelated, and it is sometimes difficult to ascertain what is a trade or business. The burden is on the exempt organization to justify exclusion of any income from this tax.

Exclusions

There are a few exemptions from this tax. They include, among others, income from research activities in a hospital, college, or university, income from a business in which substantially all the people working for the business do so without compensation, and income from the sale of merchandise donated to the organization. There are special rules for social clubs, which were discussed previously, and other special types of exempt organizations not discussed here.

Also excluded from unrelated business income is passive investment income such as dividends, interest, royalties, rents from real property, and gains on sale of property. However, rents that are based on a percentage of the net income of the property are considered unrelated. Also, income (passive investment income and rent) from assets acquired by incurring debt (debt financed property) and rent from personal property may be considered unrelated business income in whole or in part. Private foundations must still pay the excise tax on these items of passive income.

Advertising Income

One example of a wide-spread activity that is generally considered an unrelated business activity is advertising. Many exempt organizations publish magazines that contain advertising. While this advertising helps to pay the cost of the publication, advertising is nevertheless considered to be unrelated business income. The advertising is not directly part of the organization's exempt function, and therefore is taxable. The fact that the activity helps pay for exempt functions is not enough. To be tax-free, it must be itself part of the exempt function. This is the distinction that must be made. The IRS has adopted tough rules with respect to the taxability of advertising income. The rules are complex and professional advice should be sought concerning their application.

Trade Shows

The Tax Reform Act of 1976 provided an exclusion from unrelated business income for certain organizations, such as business leagues, that hold conventions or trade shows as a regular part of their exempt activities. In order for the exclusion to apply the convention or trade show must stimulate interest in, and demand for, an industry's product in general. The show must promote that purpose through the character of the exhibits and the extent of the industry products displayed.

Caveats

The organization is allowed to deduct the costs normally associated with the unrelated business. This places a burden on the organization to keep its records in a manner that will support its business deductions. Overhead can be applied to most unrelated activities, but the organization must be able to justify both the method of allocation and the reasonableness of the resulting amount. Also keep in mind that if after all expenses and allocation of overhead, the organization ends up with a loss, it will have to be able to convincingly explain why it engages in an activity that loses money. Logically no one goes into business to lose money and if there is a loss the allocation of expenses to the taxable activity is immediately suspect.

(b)   Tax Rates on Unrelated Business Income

Unrelated business income is taxed at the same rates as net income for corporations. All exempt organizations having gross income from unrelated business activities of $1,000 or more are required to file Form 990-T within $4^1/_2$ months of the end of the fiscal year (May 15 for calendar year organizations). Extensions can be obtained if applied for before the due date of the return. Organizations are required to pay estimated taxes on a quarterly basis.

(c)   Need for Competent Tax Advice

From the above discussion, it should be obvious that taxes on unrelated business income may be substantial and can apply to most organizations. It must be emphasized that every organization contemplating an income-producing activity should consult with a competent tax advisor to determine the potential tax implications of that activity.

26.8   REGISTRATION AND REPORTING

(a)   Initial Registration

All charitable (§ 501(c)(3)) organizations, except churches and certain charitable organizations having annual gross receipts of less than $5,000, must comply with Internal Revenue Service notification requirements before they may be considered exempt from income tax. Charitable organizations comply with these notification requirements by submitting Form 1023 to the Internal Revenue Service District Director within 15 months of the start of their operations. If the application is approved, the Internal Revenue Service will send the organization a determination letter which recognizes the organization's exempt status and publicly supported (or private foundation) status under one of the law's provisions.

Organizations must file the application within 15 months of the start of business in order to have exempt status apply to the organization's entire period of existence. Organizations which apply after the 15-month period expires will have exempt status recognized only from the date of the application.

Organizations which anticipate they will meet one of the public support tests are given an advance determination letter. This letter allows the organization up to 60 months to meet the public support test without being classified as a private foundation. If, at the end of the 60 months, or advance determination period, the organization fails to meet the support test, it will be characterized as a private foundation retroactive to the date operations began.

Exempt organizations other than § 501(c)(3) charities, may apply for recognition of exempt status by submitting Form 1024. Some noncharitable organizations are required to apply for recognition of exempt status, e.g., Voluntary Employee Benefit Associations (§ 501(c)(9)).

(b)   Annual Information Returns

Almost all exempt organizations are required to file annual information returns. The principal exceptions to this reporting requirement are churches and their integrated auxiliaries, and certain organizations normally having gross receipts of $25,000 or less. Most organizations must file Form 990, Return of Organization Exempt from Tax. Organizations with gross receipts of less than $100,000 for the taxable year *and* total assets at year end of less than $250,000 may file Form 990-EZ. All private foundations must file Form 990-PF without exceptions.

These information returns must be filed by the fifteenth day of the fifth month after the end of the fiscal year (May 15 for calendar year organizations). There is a penalty for failure to file the return on time. Extensions of time for filing can usually be obtained if there is good reason why the return cannot be filed on a timely basis, but application for extension must be made before the filing deadline. These returns do not require certification by an outside auditor.

In addition, all exempt organizations having gross unrelated business income of $1,000 or more must file a separate tax return and pay taxes at regular corporate rates on all taxable income over $1,000. Chapter 27 discusses the annual reporting forms used by exempt organizations.

(c)   Return Inspection

All organizations exempt from tax under § 501(a) or (d) must make their Forms 990 (or 990-PF) available for public inspection. Except for the list of contributors attached to the return, the entire return and all statements filed therewith must be made available for inspection upon request. The Internal Revenue Service makes the annual return, except for lists of contributors, available to the general public. The Internal Revenue Service also makes an organization's Application for Recognition of Exempt Status (Form 1023 or 1024) available for public inspection. The regulations under § 6104 provide procedures for requesting these forms from the Internal Revenue Service.

26.9   REPORTS BY RECIPIENTS OF FEDERAL SUPPORT

Not-for-profit organizations that receive support from the Federal government usually must comply with various audit and reporting requirements. These apply whether the support is received directly from a Federal agency or indirectly through a state or local governmental unit or another not-for-profit organization. Many different kinds of Federal support can trigger these requirements; these kinds of support include grants, contracts, loans, loan guarantees, in-kind gifts (such as agricultural commodities), interest subsidies, and other forms of support.

It is beyond the scope of this book to present a detailed description of all of the audit and reporting requirements applicable to Federal support, as they are numerous and complex. Organizations which receive or are considering applying for such support should take into consideration the time and costs associated with federally required audits, for they can be significant to those organizations. Readers should consult with a CPA or other knowledgeable person about these requirements. Failure to fulfill the requirements can result in severe financial penalties to the organization, including loss of future funding or even being compelled to repay amounts already received.

Chapter 29 contains further information about these requirements.

C H A P T E R 27

Principal Federal Tax Forms Filed

While not-for-profit organizations may be exempt from most federal taxes, they must file annual information returns with the Internal Revenue Service. With few exceptions, all exempt organizations other than private foundations are required to file Form 990 annually. Private foundations are required to file Form 990-PF. Most not-for-profit organizations having "unrelated business" income must also file Form 990-T. Organizations that anticipate incurring a tax liability must pay estimated taxes in quarterly installments. This chapter discusses the three principal returns and comments on some of the less obvious points that the preparer must be aware of while completing these forms.

27.1 FORM 990: RETURN OF ORGANIZATION EXEMPT FROM INCOME TAX

(a) Who Must File

All not-for-profit organizations exempt from income tax must file Form 990 except the following:

476

1. Churches, and certain other religious organizations.
2. Organizations that are part of a federal, state, or local governmental unit.
3. Most employee benefit plans (they file other forms).
4. Organizations other than private foundations with average annual gross receipts normally $25,000 or less.
5. Private foundations (they file Form 990-PF).

Gross receipts means the total income recognized during the year, including contributions, investment income, proceeds from the sale of investments, and sale of goods, before the deduction of any expenses or costs, including the cost of investments or goods sold.

This means that most not-for-profit organizations including social clubs, educational institutions, and membership organizations must file this return. The return is due not later than the fifteenth day of the fifth month after the end of the fiscal year (May 15 for calendar year organizations), and there is a penalty for failure to file unless it can be shown that there was a reasonable cause for not doing so. Continued failure to file can also result in personal penalties imposed on responsible persons associated with the organization.

(b) Contents of Form 990

The return consists of two parts:

- Form 990—Completed by all filing organizations, except that smaller organizations may omit certain sections.
- Schedule A—Completed by all § 501(c)(3) publicly supported organizations.

Exhibit 27–1 shows an example of a completed Form 990 for a small public charity. The circled numbers on this form refer to the comments below.

1. The first fiscal year must end within 12 months of date of inception. The organization can choose any month as the end of its fiscal year, but once the election is made it cannot easily be changed in future years without notification to the Internal Revenue Service and in some instances, only with IRS approval. Thus it is important during the first year to select the year end carefully, keeping in mind the "natural" year end for the organization. The election is made automatically when the first return is filed, which must be on a "timely" basis. This means the

EXHIBIT 27–1

Form **990**	**Return of Organization Exempt From Income Tax**	OMB No. 1545-0047
	Under **section 501(c)** of the Internal Revenue Code (except black lung benefit trust or private foundation) or section 4947(a)(1) nonexempt charitable trust	19**93**
Department of the Treasury Internal Revenue Service	**Note:** The organization may have to use a copy of this return to satisfy state reporting requirements.	This Form Is Open to Public Inspection

A For the 1993 calendar year, OR tax year period beginning ①, 1993, and ending, 19

B Check if:	Please use IRS label or print or type. See Specific Instructions.	**C** Name of organization **Nelle Plains Community Service Society**	**D** Employer identification number 13 : 6213564 ②
☐ Initial return		Number and street (or P.O. box if mail is not delivered to street address) Room/suite **1400 Diamond Avenue**	**E** State registration number ③
☐ Final return ☐ Amended return ☐ Change of address		City, town, or post office, state, and ZIP code **Nelle Plains, NY 10977**	**F** Check ▶ ☐ If exemption application is pending

④ **G** Type of organization ▶ ☒ Exempt under section 501(c)(**3**) ◀ (insert number) OR ▶ ☐ section 4947(a)(1) nonexempt charitable trust

Note: Section 501(c)(3) exempt organizations and 4947(a)(1) nonexempt charitable trusts MUST attach a completed Schedule A (Form 990).

H(a) Is this a group return filed for affiliates? . . . . ☐ Yes ☒ No   **I** If either box in H is checked "Yes," enter four-digit group exemption number (GEN) ▶ **N/A**

(b) If "Yes," enter the number of affiliates for which this return is filed: . . ▶ **N/A**   **J** Accounting method: ☐ Cash ☒ Accrual

(c) Is this a separate return filed by an organization covered by a group ruling? ☐ Yes ☒ No   ☐ Other (specify) ▶

K   Check here ▶ ☐ if the organization's gross receipts are normally not more than $25,000. The organization need not file a return with the IRS; but if it received a Form 990 Package in the mail, it should file a return without financial data. **Some states require a complete return.** ⑤

Note: Form 990-EZ may be used by organizations with gross receipts less than $100,000 and total assets less than $250,000 at end of year.

Part I Statement of Revenue, Expenses, and Changes in Net Assets or Fund Balances

	1	Contributions, gifts, grants, and similar amounts received:			
	a	Direct public support	1a	56,649	
	b	Indirect public support . . . . . . ⑥ .	1b		
	c	Government contributions (grants)	1c		
	d	Total (add lines 1a through 1c) (attach schedule—see instructions) (cash $ **56,649** noncash $)	1d		56,649 ⑦
	2	Program service revenue including government fees and contracts (from Part VII, line 93) .	2		0 ⑧
	3	Membership dues and assessments (see instructions)	3		10,500
	4	Interest on savings and temporary cash investments	4		3,875
	5	Dividends and interest from securities	5		11,316
	6a	Gross rents	6a		
	b	Less: rental expenses	6b		
	c	Net rental income or (loss) (subtract line 6b from line 6a)	6c		0
Revenue	**7**	Other investment income (describe ▶)	7		
	8a	Gross amount from sale of assets other than inventory . . . . . . ⑨ .	(A) Securities 7,000	8a	(B) Other
	b	Less: cost or other basis and sales expenses	2,000	8b	
	c	Gain or (loss) (attach schedule). . . . ⑩ .	5,000	8c	0
	d	Net gain or (loss) (combine line 8c, columns (A) and (B))	8d		5,000
	9	Special events and activities (attach schedule—see instructions):			
	a	Gross revenue (not including $ **300** of ⑪) contributions reported on line 1a) . . .	9a	1,300	
	b	Less: direct expenses other than fundraising expenses	9b	700	
	c	Net income or (loss) from special events (subtract line 9b from line 9a)	9c		600
	10a	Gross sales of inventory, less returns and allowances . . . ⑧	10a		
	b	Less: cost of goods sold . . . . ⑫	10b		
	c	Gross profit or (loss) from sales of inventory (attach schedule) (subtract line 10b from line 10a) .	10c		0
	11	Other revenue (from Part VII, line 103)	11		0
	12	Total revenue (add lines 1d, 2, 3, 4, 5, 6c, 7, 8d, 9c, 10c, and 11)	12		87,940
Expenses	**13**	Program services (from line 44, column (B)—see instructions) . . . . . . ⑬ .	13		66,640
	14	Management and general (from line 44, column (C)—see instructions)	14		6,200
	15	Fundraising (from line 44, column (D)—see instructions) . . . . . . ⑭ .	15		1,700
	16	Payments to affiliates (attach schedule—see instructions) . . . . . . ⑮ . .	16		
	17	Total expenses (add lines 16 and 44, column (A)).	17		74,540
Net Assets	**18**	Excess or (deficit) for the year (subtract line 17 from line 12)	18		13,400
	19	Net assets or fund balances at beginning of year (from line 74, column (A))	19		229,000
	20	Other changes in net assets or fund balances (attach explanation) . . . . . ⑯	20		
	21	Net assets or fund balances at end of year (combine lines 18, 19, and 20) . . . ⑰	21		242,400

For Paperwork Reduction Act Notice, see page 1 of the separate instructions.   84-1128480   Form **990** (1993)

NPCSS.N93

EXHIBIT 27–1 *Continued.*

EIN 13-6213564

Form 990 (1993)   Page **2**

Part II Statement of Functional Expenses — All organizations must complete column (A). Columns (B), (C), and (D) are required for section 501(c)(3) and (4) organizations and section 4947(a)(1) nonexempt charitable trusts but optional for others. (See instructions.)

	Do not include amounts reported on line 6b, 8b, 9b, 10b, or 16 of Part I. ⑱		(A) Total	(B) Program services	(C) Management and general	(D) Fundraising
22	Grants and allocations (attach schedule) ⑲ (cash $ 7,000 noncash $)	22	7,000	7,000		
23	Specific assistance to individuals (attach schedule)	23				
24	Benefits paid to or for members (attach schedule)	24				
25	Compensation of officers, directors, etc. ⑳	25	15,130	10,000	4,930	200
26	Other salaries and wages	26	27,000	26,000		1,000
27	Pension plan contributions	27				
28	Other employee benefits	28	1,655	1,400	210	45
29	Payroll taxes	29	2,940	2,495	375	70
30	Professional fundraising fees	30				
31	Accounting fees	31	200		200	
32	Legal fees	32				
33	Supplies	33	2,580	2,470	110	
34	Telephone	34	555	485	50	20
35	Postage and shipping	35	785	460	25	300
36	Occupancy	36				
37	Equipment rental and maintenance	37	305	305		
38	Printing and publications	38	2,495	2,200	230	65
39	Travel	39	210	210		
40	Conferences, conventions, and meetings	40				
41	Interest	41				
42	Depreciation, depletion, etc. (attach schedule) ㉑	42				
43	Other expenses (itemize): a Insurance	43a	840	800	40	
b	Gas, oil,repairs for bookmobile	43b	8,855	8,855		
c	City band - 3 concerts	43c	3,600	3,600		
d	Miscellaneous	43d	390	360	30	
e		43e				
44	Total functional expenses (add lines 22 through 43) **Organizations** completing columns (B)–(D), carry these totals to lines 13–15.	44	74,540	66,640	6,200	1,700

Reporting of Joint Costs.—Did you report in column (B) (Program services) any joint costs from a combined educational campaign and fundraising solicitation? ▶ ☐ Yes ☒ No   ㉒

If "Yes," enter (I) the aggregate amount of these joint costs $ N/A ; (ii) the amount allocated to Program services $ N/A ; (iii) the amount allocated to Management and general $ N/A ; and (iv) the amount allocated to Fundraising $ N/A .

Part III Statement of Program Service Accomplishments (See instructions.) ㉓

Describe what was achieved in carrying out the organization's exempt purposes. Fully describe the services provided; the number of persons benefited; or other relevant information for each program title. Section 501(c)(3) and (4) organizations and section 4947(a)(1) nonexempt charitable trusts must also enter the amount of grants and allocations to others. | **Expenses** (Required for 501(c)(3) and (4) organizations and 4947(a)(1) trusts; optional for others.)

a Awards for outstanding community service. Each year, awards are given to as many as three citizens of Nelle Plains who are judged to have contributed substantially to the community.
(Grants and allocations $ 4,000) | 4,175

b Operation of Bookmobile. Bookmobile contains about 1,000 books. In 1993 7,200 books were borrowed.
(Grants and allocations $) | 18,590

c Cultural activities. Historical exhibit in the Town Hall. Three outdoor band concerts in River Park. Grant towards rehabilitation of an old firehouse as a museum.
(Grants and allocations $ 3,000) | 43,875

d
(Grants and allocations $)

e Other program services (attach schedule)   (Grants and allocations $)

f Total (add lines **a** through **e**) (should equal line 44, column (B), Program services). ▶ | 66,640

NPCSS.N93

EXHIBIT 27–1 *Continued.*

EIN 13-6213564

Form 990 (1993)   Page **3**

Part IV   Balance Sheets

Note: Where required, attached schedules and amounts within the description column should be for end-of-year amounts only.

			(A) Beginning of year		**(B)** End of year
	Assets				
45	Cash—non-interest-bearing		3,500	**45**	2,250
46	Savings and temporary cash investments		30,000	**46**	28,000
47a	Accounts receivable ㉔	**47a** 1,000			
b	Less: allowance for doubtful accounts	**47b** 0	1,250	**47c**	1,000
48a	Pledges receivable	**48a** 1,000			
b	Less: allowance for doubtful accounts	**48b** 0	0	**48c**	1,000
49	Grants receivable			**49**	
50	Receivables due from officers, directors, trustees, and key employees (attach schedule)			**50**	
51a	Other notes and loans receivable (attach schedule)	**51a**			
b	Less: allowance for doubtful accounts	**51b**	0	**51c**	0
52	Inventories for sale or use			**52**	
53	Prepaid expenses and deferred charges			**53**	
54	Investments—securities (attach schedule)		196,750	**54**	212,900
55a	Investments—land, buildings, and equipment: basis	**55a**			
b	Less: accumulated depreciation (attach schedule)	**55b**	0	**55c**	0
56	Investments—other (attach schedule)			**56**	
57a	Land, buildings, and equipment: basis	**57a**			
b	Less: accumulated depreciation (attach schedule)	**57b**	0	**57c**	0
58	Other assets (describe ▶ _____)			**58**	
59	**Total assets** (add lines 45 through 58) (must equal line 75)		231,500	**59**	245,150
	Liabilities				
60	Accounts payable and accrued expenses		2,500	**60**	1,250
61	Grants payable			**61**	1,500
62	Support and revenue designated for future periods (attach schedule) ㉕			**62**	
63	Loans from officers, directors, trustees, and key employees (attach schedule)			**63**	
64a	Tax-exempt bond liabilities (attach schedule)			**64a**	
b	Mortgages and other notes payable (attach schedule)			**64b**	
65	Other liabilities (describe ▶ _____)			**65**	
66	**Total liabilities** (add lines 60 through 65)		2,500	**66**	2,750
	Fund Balances or Net Assets				
	Organizations that use fund accounting, check here ▶ ☒ and complete lines 67 through 70 and lines 74 and 75 (see instructions). ㉖				
67a	Current unrestricted fund		121,000	**67a**	119,400
b	Current restricted fund			**67b**	
68	Land, buildings, and equipment fund			**68**	
69	Endowment fund		108,000	**69**	123,000
70	Other funds (describe ▶ _____)			**70**	
	Organizations that do not use fund accounting, check here ▶ ☐ and complete lines 71 through 75 (see instructions).				
71	Capital stock or trust principal			**71**	
72	Paid-in or capital surplus			**72**	
73	Retained earnings or accumulated income			**73**	
74	**Total fund balances or net assets** (add lines 67a through 70 OR lines 71 through 73: column (A) must equal line 19 and column (B) must equal line 21)		229,000	**74**	242,400
75	**Total liabilities and fund balances/net assets** (add lines 66 and 74)		231,500	**75**	245,150

Form 990 is available for public inspection and, for some people, serves as the primary or sole source of information about a particular organization. How the public perceives an organization in such cases may be determined by the information presented on its return. Therefore, please make sure the return is complete and accurate and fully describes the organization's programs and accomplishments.

EXHIBIT 27–1 *Continued.*

EIN 13-6213564

Form 990 (1993)   Page **4**

Part V   List of Officers, Directors, Trustees, and Key Employees (List each one even if not compensated (see instructions).)

(A) Name and address	(B) Title and average hours per week devoted to position	(C) Compensation (if not paid, enter –0–)	(D) Contributions to employee benefit plans & deferred compensation	(E) Expense account and other allowances
W. Jonathan Stephens Nelle Plains, NY	Executive Dir. 40 hours/week	15,130	550	㉗ 0
Sean Fessenden, Jr. Waverly, NY	Trustee 2 hours/week	0	0	0
Phyllis Kolowski Nelle Plains, NY	Trustee 2 hours/week	0	0	0

Did any officer, director, trustee, or key employee receive aggregate compensation of more than $100,000 from your organization and all related organizations, of which more than $10,000 was provided by the related organizations? ▶ ☐ Yes ☒ No
If "Yes," attach schedule—see instructions.

Part VI   Other Information

			Yes	No
76	Did the organization engage in any activity not previously reported to the IRS? If "Yes," attach a detailed description of each activity	76		X
77	Were any changes made in the organizing or governing documents, but not reported to the IRS?	77		X
	If "Yes," attach a conformed copy of the changes. ⑧			
78a	Did the organization have unrelated business gross income of $1,000 or more during the year covered by this return?	78a		X
b	If "Yes," has it filed a tax return on **Form 990-T**, Exempt Organization Business Income Tax Return, for this year?	78b		N/A
79	Was there a liquidation, dissolution, termination, or substantial contraction during the year? If "Yes," attach a statement; see instructions.	79		X
80a	Is the organization related (other than by association with a statewide or nationwide organization) through common membership, governing bodies, trustees, officers, etc., to any other exempt or nonexempt organization? (See instructions.)	80a		X
b	If "Yes," enter the name of the organization ▶ _____ and check whether it is ☐ exempt **OR** ☐ nonexempt.			
81a	Enter the amount of political expenditures, direct or indirect, as described in the instructions .	81a	㉘ 0	
b	Did the organization file **Form 1120–POL**, U.S. Income Tax Return for Certain Political Organizations, for this year?	81b		X
82a	Did the organization receive donated services or the use of materials, equipment, or facilities at no charge or at substantially less than fair rental value?	82a	X	
b	If "Yes," you may indicate the value of these items here. Do not include this amount as ㉙ revenue in Part I or as an expense in Part III. (See instructions for reporting in Part III.) .	82b	8,600	
83	Did the organization comply with the public inspection requirements for returns and exemption applications?	83	X	
84a	Did the organization solicit any contributions or gifts that were not tax deductible?	84a		X
b	If "Yes," did the organization include with every solicitation an express statement that such contributions or gifts were not tax deductible? (See General Instruction M.)	84b		N/A
85	Section 501(c)(4), (5), or (6) organizations.—a Were substantially all dues nondeductible by members? . ㉚	85a		N/A
b	Did the organization make only in-house lobbying expenditures of $2,000 or less?	85b		N/A
	If "Yes" to either **85a** or **85b**, do not complete **85c** through **85h** below.			
c	Dues, assessments, and similar amounts from members for January 1994 and later. . . .	85c	N/A	
d	Section 162(e) lobbying and political expenditures after December 1993	85d	N/A	
e	Aggregate nondeductible amount of section 6033(e)(1)(A) dues notices	85e	N/A	
f	Taxable amount of lobbying and political expenditures (line 85d less 85e; see instructions.)) .	85f	N/A	
g	Does the organization elect to pay the section 6033(e) tax on the amount in 85f?	85g		N/A
h	Does the organization elect to add the amount in 85f to its reasonable estimate of dues allocable to nondeductible lobbying and political expenditures for the following tax year?	85h		N/A
86	Section 501(c)(7) organizations.—Enter: ㉛			
a	Initiation fees and capital contributions included on line 12	86a	N/A	
b	Gross receipts, included on line **12**, for public use of club facilities (See instructions.)	86b	N/A	
87a	Section 501(c)(12) organizations.—Enter: Gross income from members or shareholders	87a	N/A	
b	Gross income from other sources. (Do not net amounts due or paid to other sources against amounts due or received from them.).	87b	N/A	
88	At any time during the year, did the organization own a 50% or greater interest in a taxable corporation or partnership? If "Yes," complete Part IX	88		X
89	Public interest law firms.—Attach information described in the instructions.			
90	List the states with which a copy of this return is filed ▶ New York _____			
91	The books are in care of ▶ W. Jonathan Stephens _____ Telephone no. ▶ (914) 521-6790			
	Located at ▶ 1400 Diamond Avenue, Nelle Plains, NY _____ ZIP code ▶ 10977			
92	Section 4947(a)(1) nonexempt charitable trusts filing Form 990 in lieu of **Form 1041**, U.S. Fiduciary Income Tax Return, should check here ▶ ☐ and enter the amount of tax-exempt interest received or accrued during the tax year . . ▶ 92 N/A			

NPCSS.N93

EXHIBIT 27–1 *Continued.*

EIN 13-6213564

Form 990 (1993)   ㉜   Page **5**

| Part VII | Analysis of Income-Producing Activities |

Enter gross amounts unless otherwise indicated.		Unrelated business income		Excluded by section 512, 513, or 514		(E) Related or exempt function income (See instructions.)
		(A) Business code	(B) Amount	(C) Exclusion code	(D) Amount	
93	Program service revenue:					
a	_____					
b	_____					
c	_____					
d	_____					
e	_____					
f	_____					
g	Fees and contracts from government agencies . .					
94	Membership dues and assessments					10,500
95	Interest on savings and temporary cash investments .			14	3,875	
96	Dividends and interest from securities			14	11,316	
97	Net rental income or (loss) from real estate:					
a	debt-financed property					
b	not debt-financed property					
98	Net rental income or (loss) from personal property . .					
99	Other investment income					
100	Gain or (loss) from sales of assets other than inventory			18	5,000	
101	Net income or (loss) from special events			01	600	
102	Gross profit or (loss) from sales of inventory . . .					
103	Other revenue: a _____					
b	_____					
c	_____					
d	_____					
e	_____					
104	Subtotal (add columns (B), (D), and (E))		0		20,791	10,500
105	TOTAL (add line 104, columns (B), (D), and (E)) . . . . ▶					31,291

Note: (Line 105 plus line 1d, Part I, should equal the amount on line 12, Part I.)

| Part VIII | Relationship of Activities to the Accomplishment of Exempt Purposes |

Line No. ▼	Explain how each activity for which income is reported in column (E) of Part VII contributed importantly to the accomplishment of the organization's exempt purposes (other than by providing funds for such purposes). (See instructions.)
94	Members receive quarterly newsletter and membership card for dues.
	Enables members to stay informed about the organization's
	activities and exempt purpose.

| Part IX | Information Regarding Taxable Subsidiaries (Complete this Part if the "Yes" box on line 88 is checked.) |

Name, address, and employer identification number of corporation or partnership	Percentage of ownership interest	Nature of business activities	Total income	End-of-year assets
N/A ㉝	%			
	%			
	%			
	%			

Please Sign Here	Under penalties of perjury, I declare that I have examined this return, including accompanying schedules and statements, and to the best of my knowledge and belief, it is true, correct, and complete. Declaration of preparer (other than officer) is based on all information of which preparer has any knowledge.		
	▶ _____ Signature of officer	Date	▶ _____ Title

Paid Preparer's Use Only	Preparer's signature ▶	Date	Check if self-employed ▶ ☐	Preparer's social security no.
	Firm's name (or yours if self-employed) and address ▶		E.I. No. ▶	
			ZIP code ▶	

return must be filed within four and a half months after the chosen year end. The first return can cover a period as short as one month (or even a fraction of a month) or as long as twelve months. It cannot cover a period longer than twelve months, even though the first part of the period may have been a period of no activity. As a practical matter, many organizations elect a year end following the conclusion of their first fund-raising effort.

2. The "employer identification number" is a number assigned by the Internal Revenue Service upon request by any organization. This number will be used on all payroll tax returns and on all communications with the IRS. It serves the same identification function that the social security number serves for an individual. The preparer of a return should always be careful to use the correct number. An employer identification number should be requested by an organization on Form SS-4 as soon as it is formed even if it has no employees. It takes the IRS a period of time to assign the number; if the organization must file a return before the number is received, it should put "applied for" in this space.

3. The "state registration number" is assigned by state charity registration or taxing authorities and will differ from state to state. Therefore, organizations which plan to use copies of Form 990 to meet state reporting requirements should complete all parts of the form except this item and make as many copies of the form as will be needed. Then the appropriate state registration numbers can be inserted on the copies to be filed with each state. No number is needed on the IRS copy.

4. This refers to the section of the Internal Revenue Code under which the organization was granted exemption. This reference will be in the "exemption letter." Request for exemption should be made as soon as the organization is incorporated and is made on Form 1023 (for organizations which believe they are exempt under § 501(c)(3)) or Form 1024 (for other organizations). If an organization has applied for but not yet received exempt status, the preparer should check the box in Item F.

5. "Gross receipts" means total receipts, including total proceeds from the sales of securities, investments, and other assets before deducting cost of goods sold or the cost of the securities or other assets. It is computed as the sum of lines l(d), 2, 3, 4, 5, 6(a), 7, 8(a) (both columns), 9(a), 10(a), and 11 of part I. Gross receipts for the filing requirement test is not the same as total income.

Total income normally would not include the gross proceeds from the sale of assets, but only the net profit or loss on such sale. The concept of gross receipts used in this return is a tax and not an accounting concept. If gross receipts are normally[1] under $25,000, the rest of the return need not be completed.

6. "Indirect public support" includes amounts received from United Way or similar federated fund-raising organizations, and from organizations affiliated with the reporting organization where the original source of the money is public contributions.

7. A schedule must be attached to the return listing all gifts aggregating $5,000 or more from any one person during the year. This schedule must show the name, address, date received, and value of all gifts received from each such person. For publicly supported organizations, this information is required only if the amount of such gifts from each person is 2 percent or more of the total contributions received during the year (in addition to being over $5,000). There are some specific rules involved, and if the organization had contributions from any one person of $5,000 or more the instructions should be carefully read and followed. In our illustration a schedule is included in Exhibit 27–3, which shows that Mr. Schultz donated $10,000 during the year.

8. Amounts reported as "Program service revenue" (line 2) and "Gross sales" (line 10) should be reviewed to determine if the organization has received income from an unrelated trade or business. If the organization had "unrelated business income" during the year it may have to file Form 990-T and should answer Question 78(a) "yes."

9. "The cost or other basis and sales expenses" of assets sold includes the original cost of securities or other assets. Although the original cost of donated securities is generally the donor's basis, for purposes of this form, the fair market value at the date of gift may be used.

10. A detailed schedule is required showing the type of asset sold, cost, to whom sold, and so on. The instructions must be carefully followed to be sure that all the required information is shown. An example is presented in Exhibit 27–3.

11. Amounts reported on this line will be those resulting from fund-raising events such as dinners, dances, concerts, and sales of merchandise (e.g., cookies, candy), where the attendee or buyer pays more than a fair market price for the item received.

---

[1] "Normally" is defined in the instructions to Form 990.

For example, an organization may sponsor a benefit concert and sell tickets for $50. A normal price for such a concert ticket might be $10. The organization pays the performing group an amount which equals $8 per ticket, and incurs publicity, printing, and other "overhead" costs equal to $3 per ticket. Assuming, for purposes of illustration, that one ticket is sold, these amounts would be reported as follows:

$40   the $50 selling price of the ticket, less $10, (a normal price for such a ticket) will be included with other contributions on line 1 (a), and also shown on the line in the caption for line 9(a).

$10   (the normal price for a concert ticket) on line 9(a).

$ 8   (the direct cost to the organization of providing the benefit received by the ticket buyer) on line 9(b).

$ 2   ($10 on line 9(a) less $8 on line 9(b)) on line 9(c).

$ 3   (indirect costs of the event) are included in fund-raising costs in Column D of Part II.

The $40 reported on line l(a) is included with other contributions, and will not normally be separately identifiable on that line. It is important for organizations which sponsor such fund-raising events to keep records which will allow completion of Form 990 in the above manner. Organizations which participate in fund-raising events in which the donor receives a benefit should inform those who buy tickets or merchandise what portion of the selling price is allowable as a tax deduction on the buyer's personal income tax return. In the above example, this amount is also $40, the "extra" amount paid over the fair value of the ticket. Since a person who wants merely to attend a concert can do so for $10, the presumption is that the extra $40 is intended as a contribution to the sponsoring charitable organization. See IRS Publication 1391 for more information.

12. "Cost of goods sold" refers to the cost of merchandise or goods that were sold, but not selling expenses. Selling expenses are shown in Part II. In the case of a country club, cost of goods sold would include the direct cost of food and drink sold and direct labor. A profit motive for the activity is important. See the discussion in the previous chapter.

13. Expenses incurred for the organization's exempt purpose other than for soliciting contributions should be shown on this line, including applicable overhead expenses. It is important to

remember that the Internal Revenue Service will look at this line to determine whether the organization is spending sufficient amounts of its income for its exempt purpose to justify continuation of the organization's exempt status.

14. All expenses associated with the soliciting of contributions should be shown on this line. A typical example would be the salary of a fund raiser.

15. This line is used by organizations which are affiliated with other charitable organizations to report amounts remitted to or paid on behalf of the affiliated organization. For example, a local branch of a national charity may be required to pass through to the national office a certain percentage of all contributions, or the national office may allocate certain amounts to its local chapters. This line is not intended to be used for reporting allocations by a federated fund-raising organization such as United Way to its member agencies. These allocations should go on line 22.

16. Line 20 will be used to report two main types of transactions:

    a. Unrealized changes in the market value of investments reported at market value (only realized gains may be reported on line 8)

    b. "Capital additions" as defined in Statement of Position No. 78-10

17. The amounts shown as fund balances or net worth at end of year should correspond to line 74 on the Balance Sheet in Part IV.

18. Part II of Form 990 shows allocation of expenses among "Program services," "Management and general," and "Fund raising." This part is very important because the method and amounts of allocation among these three categories become fixed once the return has been filed, and it is very difficult to go back and subsequently change it. The risk is that the Internal Revenue Service could challenge the conclusion that certain gross receipts are related to the exempt purpose. If they were successful in this challenge, the organization would want to be certain that it had already allocated a fair proportion of expenses to this gross income in order to minimize (or even eliminate) the resulting tax. It would be very awkward to go back and claim that a fair allocation of expenses had not been made at the time of initially filing this return. Note that this section of Form 990 is required for all § 501(c)(3) and § 501(c)(4) organizations and § 4947(a)(1) trusts, but is optional for all other exempt organizations.

19. A detailed schedule is required showing, among other things, to whom grants were paid, the relationship to the reporting organization, and the purpose and amount of the grant. The instructions should be carefully followed to be sure that all of the required information is shown. An example is shown in the schedule in Exhibit 27–3.

20. Details of the information requested here are shown in Part V on page 4 of Form 990.

21. A schedule must be attached showing details of depreciation. Form 4562 can be used (this is a schedule giving the details requested) or the required information may be presented on a supplementary schedule.

22. Joint costs from a combined educational and solicitation campaign must be detailed here, including the total costs of the campaign and the amounts separately allocated to the educational, fund-raising, and management and general portions of the campaign.

23. Part III requires a brief description of the activities carried out by the organization which form the basis for the organization's exempt status. Extensive details need not be given, but the descriptions should be informative enough that a person who knows nothing about the organization will obtain a basic understanding of the organization's programs. Many organizations choose to treat this section as a report card of their accomplishments.

24. Where required, information reported in blanks that are part of item captions should be end-of-year information only.

25. In the past, two kinds of amounts were reported on this line:

    a. Gifts and grants specified by the donor or grantor for use in future accounting periods—reported as deferred revenue until the intended period of use.

    b. Gifts and grants specified by the donor or grantor for a current, but restricted, purpose—reported as deferred revenue until the organization carries out the intended purpose. This method of accounting was used by organizations which followed the AICPA Statement of Position, Accounting Principles and Reporting Practices for Certain Nonprofit Organizations. However, FASB Statement of Financial Standards (SFAS) 116 now requires that these items be reported as restricted revenue. Organizations making a change in accounting method for Form 990 should consult their tax advisor.

26. "Net Assets" has the same meaning as "fund balance." The terms are used throughout this book to represent excess of assets over liabilities of the organization. This section allows an organization to report its net assets in whatever way its records are kept. Most not-for-profit organizations use fund accounting and will complete lines 67 to 70. Social clubs will probably have capital stock, and perhaps capital surplus. Foundations often keep their fund balance segregated between principal and unexpended income.

27. Not all expense allowances are reported here, rather only those for which the recipient did not account to the organization, or which exceeded the expense incurred by the recipient. Such amounts are taxable income to the recipient. Generally, all compensation paid to or on behalf of the employee must be included in one of the columns provided. Wages, base salary, and bonuses are included in Column C. All contributions to employee benefit plans including non-qualified plans (§ 457) should be included in Column D. All other compensation payments should be included in Column E.

28. Membership organizations should enter the total amount of direct and indirect expenses for political purposes.

29. The value of donated services may not be reported as revenue or expense in Parts I and II, but may, if the organization wishes, be reported on line 82.

30. In this series of questions, the IRS obtains information about the organization's compliance with the disallowance of lobbying expenses provisions. § 501(c)(4), § 501(c)(5) [except for labor unions] and § 501(c)(6) organizations must either notify their members about the portion of member dues that are not deductible, or must pay a proxy tax on their lobbying expenditures. There are limited exceptions to this provision. Organizations that lobby should consult with tax or legal advisors with regard to these complex requirements.

31. Clubs may be challenged on their exempt status if receipts from the general public, and investment income, exceed 35 percent of gross receipts. However, within this 35 percent limitation is a 15 percent limitation on receipts from the general public.

32. Page 5, parts VII and VIII require a complete and detailed analysis of an organization's revenue from all sources except contributions, gifts, and grants. Organizations should be extremely careful when completing this portion of the Form, since the

information inserted will constitute the organization's tax position with regard to its income. Revenue entered on lines 93 to 103 must tie to revenue on lines 2 to 11 of page 1 of the Form. All revenue must be separated into three categories:

(1) Unrelated business income dollar amounts are entered in column (B) on the appropriate lines. The business code which most closely corresponds to the type of revenue received is entered in column (A). Business codes are listed on the last page of the instructions to Form 990-T. Gross revenue in column (B) should agree to the gross revenue on the organization's Form 990-T except for unrelated business income from rental of property, which is shown net of expenses in this part of Form 990.

(2) Income which is exempt from unrelated business income because of a specific statutory exclusion is entered in column (D) on the appropriate lines. The exclusion code which corresponds to the statutory exclusion is entered in column (C). These exclusion codes may be found on the last page of the instructions for Form 990.

(3) Income which is related to the exempt purpose of the organization is entered in column (E) on the appropriate lines. The exempt purpose for all income entered in column (E) must be explained in Part VIII of Form 990.

This portion of the form establishes the organization's tax position with regard to its income. It also forms the basis for the organization's disclosure of its unrelated and related activities. Adequate disclosure is required on a return in order to avoid penalties for understatement of tax. The requirements for adequate disclosure are complex. Organizations are well advised to supplement the information on Part VII of the 990 with a schedule explaining their tax positions if those positions are not supported by substantial authority.

33. Part IX of the 990 requests information regarding taxable subsidiaries. This part of the form enables the Internal Revenue Service to monitor reporting of taxable income pursuant to § 512(b)(13). This code section states that interest, annuities, royalties, and rents (items of income usually exempt from unrelated business income tax) will constitute unrelated business income if received from an 80% controlled subsidiary. This portion of the form will also allow the Internal Revenue Service to evaluate the extent to which organizations have taxable subsidiaries,

in the event that Congress wishes to require exempt organizations to aggregate their activities.

Schedule A is prepared by all § 501(c)(3) organizations that must file Form 990. This will include most charitable exempt organizations except private foundations. Schedule A, which consists of five pages, is broken down into seven parts. Parts I to IV and VII must be completed, while Part V applies only to schools and Part VI is used to compute the "lobbying limitation" (see Chapter 26).

Exhibit 27–2 shows five pages of Schedule A that have been completed for The Nelle Plains Community Service Society. The information requested in Parts I and II is straightforward and does not require comment. The circled numbers are explained in the following list:

34. Part III attempts to determine whether the organization is engaging in any number of activities which, in certain circumstances, are improper. An affirmative response may indicate possible exposure to loss of exemption.

35. See Exhibit 27–3 for an example of the type of statement that is required.

36. This section is the place where an organization states specifically why it is not a private foundation. The previous chapter discusses the various categories of publicly supported organizations, i.e., nonprivate foundation organizations.

37. This category of publicly supported organization is the most common. See the previous chapter for a discussion of the support test which these organizations must meet. Where an organization can qualify under this category, it should do so.

38. This category of publicly supported organization must meet the second mechanical test of public support discussed in the previous chapter.

39. Lines 26(a) and 26(b) are designed to determine the amount of gifts, grants, and membership fees that must be given special treatment in computing the public support test.

40. Line 27(a) requires the year-by-year detail of gifts, grants, gross receipts, and membership fees from disqualified persons. Such amounts are given special treatment in computing second support test discussed in the previous chapter. See footnote 5 in Chapter 26 for the definition of a disqualified person.

41. Line 27(b) requires the year-by-year detail of gross receipts from admissions, sales of services, and so on, from any one person or

EXHIBIT 27-2

SCHEDULE A (Form 990)	**Organization Exempt Under Section 501(c)(3)** (Except Private Foundation), and Section 501(e), 501(f), 501(k), or Section 4947(a)(1) Nonexempt Charitable Trust **Supplementary Information**	OMB No. 1545-0047 19**93**
Department of the Treasury Internal Revenue Service	▶ **Must be completed by the above organizations and attached to their Form 990 (or 990-EZ).**	

Name of the organization	Employer identification number
Nelle Plains Community Service Society	13 ⋮ 6213564

Part I **Compensation of the Five Highest Paid Employees Other Than Officers, Directors, and Trustees**
(See instructions.) (List each one. If there are none, enter "None.")

(a) Name and address of each employee paid more than $30,000	(b) Title and average hours per week devoted to position	(c) Compensation	(d) Contributions to employee benefit plans & deferred compensation	(e) Expense account and other allowances
NONE				

Total number of other employees paid over $30,000 . . . . ▶

Part II **Compensation of the Five Highest Paid Persons for Professional Services**
(See instructions.) (List each one. If there are none, enter "None.")

(a) Name and address of each person paid more than $30,000	(b) Type of service	(c) Compensation
NONE		

Total number of others receiving over $30,000 for professional services . . . . ▶

Part III **Statements About Activities**   ㉞

		Yes	No
1	During the year, has the organization attempted to influence national, state, or local legislation, including any attempt to influence public opinion on a legislative matter or referendum? **1**		X
	If "Yes," enter the total expenses paid or incurred in connection with the lobbying activities. $ _____		
	Organizations that made an election under section 501(h) by filing Form 5768 must complete Part VI–A. Other organizations checking "Yes," must complete Part VI–B AND attach a statement giving a detailed description of the lobbying activities.		
2	During the year, has the organization, either directly or indirectly, engaged in any of the following acts with any of its trustees, directors, officers, creators, key employees, or members of their families, or with any taxable organization with which any such person is affiliated as an officer, director, trustee, majority owner, or principal beneficiary:		
a	Sale, exchange, or leasing of property? **2a**		X
b	Lending of money or other extension of credit? **2b**		X
c	Furnishing of goods, services, or facilities? **2c**		X
d	Payment of compensation (or payment or reimbursement of expenses if more than $1,000)? Part V, Form 990 . . . **2d**	X	
e	Transfer of any part of its income or assets? **2e**		X
	If the answer to any question is "Yes," attach a detailed statement explaining the transactions.		
3	Does the organization make grants for scholarships, fellowships, student loans, etc.? **3**		X
4	Attach a statement explaining how the organization determines that individuals or organizations receiving grants or loans from it in furtherance of its charitable programs qualify to receive payments. (See instructions.) ㉟		

For Paperwork Reduction Act Notice, see page 1 of the Instructions to Form 990 (or Form 990–EZ).   84-1128480   **Schedule A (Form 990) 1993**

NPCSS.O93

EXHIBIT 27–2 *Continued.*

EIN 13-6213564

Schedule A (Form 990) 1993

Page **2**

| **Part IV** | **Reason for Non–Private Foundation Status** (See instructions for definitions.) |

The organization is not a private foundation because it is (please check only **ONE** applicable box):

5 ☐ A church, convention of churches, or association of churches. Section 170(b)(1)(A)(i).   ㊱

6 ☐ A school. Section 170(b)(1)(A)(ii). (Also complete Part V, page 3.)

7 ☐ A hospital or a cooperative hospital service organization. Section 170(b)(1)(A)(iii).

8 ☐ A Federal, state, or local government or governmental unit. Section 170(b)(1)(A)(v).

9 ☐ A medical research organization operated in conjunction with a hospital. Section 170(b)(1)(A)(iii). **Enter the hospital's name, city, and state ▶** -

10 ☐ An organization operated for the benefit of a college or university owned or operated by a governmental unit. Section 170(b)(1)(A)(iv). (Also complete the **Support Schedule** below.)

11a ☒ An organization that normally receives a substantial part of its support from a governmental unit or from the general public. Section 170(b)(1)(A)(vi). (Also complete the **Support Schedule** below.)   ㊲

11b ☐ A community trust. Section 170(b)(1)(A)(vi). (Also complete the **Support Schedule** below.)

12 ☐ An organization that normally receives: **(a)** no more than 1/3 of its support from gross investment income and unrelated business taxable income (less section 511 tax) from businesses acquired by the organization after June 30, 1975, and **(b)** more than 1/3 of its support from contributions, membership fees, and gross receipts from activities related to its charitable, etc., functions—subject to certain exceptions. See section 509(a)(2). (Also complete the **Support Schedule** below.)   ㊳

13 ☐ An organization that is not controlled by any disqualified persons (other than foundation managers) and supports organizations described in: **(1)** lines 5 through 12 above; or **(2)** section 501(c)(4), (5), or (6), if they meet the test of section 509(a)(2). (See section 509(a)(3).)

Provide the following information about the supported organizations. (See instructions for Part IV, line 13.)

(a) Name(s) of supported organization(s)	**(b)** Line number from above

14 ☐ An organization organized and operated to test for public safety. Section 509(a)(4). (See instructions.)

Support Schedule (Complete only if you checked a box on lines 10, 11, or 12 above.) **Use cash method of accounting.**
Note: You may use the worksheet in the instructions for converting from the accrual to the cash method of accounting.

Calendar year (or fiscal year beginning in) ▶	**(a)** 1992	**(b)** 1991	**(c)** 1990	**(d)** 1989	**(e)** Total
15 Gifts, grants, and contributions received. (Do not include unusual grants. See line 28.)	48,000	42,000	35,000	28,000	153,000
16 Membership fees received	8,700	8,000	6,500	5,000	28,200
17 Gross receipts from admissions, merchandise sold or services performed, or furnishing of facilities in any activity that is not a business unrelated to the organization's charitable, etc., purpose	1,100	900	750	500	3,250
18 Gross income from interest, dividends, amounts received from payments on securities loans (section 512(a)(5)), rents, royalties, and unrelated business taxable income (less section 511 taxes) from businesses acquired by the organization after June 30, 1975.	11,500	9,500	7,950	5,500	34,450
19 Net income from unrelated business activities not included in line 18 .	0	0	0	0	0
20 Tax revenues levied for the organization's benefit and either paid to it or expended on its behalf	0	0	0	0	0
21 The value of services or facilities furnished to the organization by a governmental unit without charge. Do not include the value of services or facilities generally furnished to the public without charge	8,500	7,500	3,500	3,500	23,000
22 Other income. Attach a schedule. Do not include gain or (loss) from sale of capital assets	0	0	0	0	0
23 Total of lines 15 through 22 .	77,800	67,900	53,700	42,500	241,900
24 Line 23 minus line 17 .	76,700	67,000	52,950	42,000	238,650
25 Enter 1% of line 23 .	778	679	537	425	

26 Organizations described in lines 10 or 11:
a Enter 2% of amount in column (e), line 24 . . . . ㊴ | 4,773
b Attach a list (which is not open to public inspection) showing the name of and amount contributed by each person (other than a governmental unit or publicly supported organization) whose total gifts for 1989 through 1992 exceeded the amount shown in line 26a. Enter the sum of all these excess amounts here . . . . ▶ | 35,227

(**Support Schedule** continued on page 3)

NPCSS.O93

EXHIBIT 27–2 *Continued.*

EIN 13-6213564

Schedule A (Form 990) 1993   Page **3**

Part IV Support Schedule (continued) (Complete only if you checked a box on lines 10, 11, or 12.)

27   Organizations described on line 12: ㊵

   a   Attach a list, for amounts shown on lines 15, 16, and 17, to show the name of, and total amounts received in each year from, each "disqualified person." Enter the sum of such amounts for each year:

     (1992) _____0_____ (1991) _____0_____ (1990) _____0_____ (1989) _____0_____

   b   Attach a list to show, for 1989 through 1992, the name of, and amount included in line 17 for, each person (other than a "disqualified person") from whom the organization received, during that year, an amount that was more than the larger of **(1)** the amount on line 25 for the year or **(2)** $5,000. Include organizations described in lines 5 through 11, as well as individuals. After computing the difference between the amount received and the larger amount described in **(1)** or **(2)**, enter the sum of all these differences (the excess amounts) for each year: ㊶

     (1992) _____0_____ (1991) _____0_____ (1990) _____0_____ (1989) _____0_____

28   For an organization described in line 10, 11, or 12, that received any unusual grants during 1989 through 1992, attach a list (which is not open to public inspection) for each year showing the name of the contributor, the date and amount of the grant, and a brief description of the nature of the grant. Do not include these grants in line 15. (See instructions.)

Part V   **Private School Questionnaire**
        (To be completed ONLY by schools that checked the box on line 6 in Part IV)   ㊷

		Yes	No
29	Does the organization have a racially nondiscriminatory policy toward students by statement in its charter, bylaws, other governing instrument, or in a resolution of its governing body? **29**		
30	Does the organization include a statement of its racially nondiscriminatory policy toward students in all its brochures, catalogues, and other written communications with the public dealing with student admissions, programs, and scholarships? **30**		
31	Has the organization publicized its racially nondiscriminatory policy through newspaper or broadcast media during the period of solicitation for students, or during the registration period if it has no solicitation program, in a way that makes the policy known to all parts of the general community it serves? **31**		

     If "Yes," please describe; if "No," please explain. (If you need more space, attach a separate statement.)

32	Does the organization maintain the following:		
a	Records indicating the racial composition of the student body, faculty, and administrative staff? **32a**		
b	Records documenting that scholarships and other financial assistance are awarded on a racially nondiscriminatory basis? **32b**		
c	Copies of all catalogues, brochures, announcements, and other written communications to the public dealing with student admissions, programs, and scholarships? **32c**		
d	Copies of all material used by the organization or on its behalf to solicit contributions? **32d**		

     If you answered "No" to any of the above, please explain. (If you need more space, attach a separate statement.)

33	Does the organization discriminate by race in any way with respect to:		
a	Students' rights or privileges? **33a**		
b	Admissions policies? **33b**		
c	Employment of faculty or administrative staff? **33c**		
d	Scholarships or other financial assistance? (See instructions.) **33d**		
e	Educational policies? **33e**		
f	Use of facilities? **33f**		
g	Athletic programs? **33g**		
h	Other extracurricular activities? **33h**		

     If you answered "Yes" to any of the above, please explain. (If you need more space, attach a separate statement.)

34a	Does the organization receive any financial aid or assistance from a governmental agency? **34a**		
b	Has the organization's right to such aid ever been revoked or suspended? **34b**		

     If you answered "Yes" to either 34a or b, please explain using an attached statement.

35	Does the organization certify that it has complied with the applicable requirements of sections 4.01 through 4.05 of Rev. Proc. 75–50, 1975–2 C.B. 587, covering racial nondiscrimination? If "No," attach an explanation. (See instructions for Part V.) **35**		

NPCSS.O93

EXHIBIT 27–2 *Continued.*

EIN 13-6213564

Schedule A (Form 990) 1993 Page 4

Part VI-A **Lobbying Expenditures by Electing Public Charities** (See instructions.)
(To be completed **ONLY** by an eligible organization that filed Form 5768) ㊸

Check here ▶ a ☐ If the organization belongs to an affiliated group (see instructions).
Check here ▶ b ☐ If you checked a and "limited control" provisions apply (see instructions).

Limits on Lobbying Expenses (The term "expenditures" means amounts paid or incurred)		(a) Affiliated group totals	(b) To be completed for ALL electing organizations
36 Total lobbying expenditures to influence public opinion (grassroots lobbying)	36		
37 Total lobbying expenditures to influence a legislative body (direct lobbying)	37		
38 Total lobbying expenditures (add lines 36 and 37)	38		
39 Other exempt purpose expenditures (see Part VI-A instructions)	39		
40 Total exempt purpose expenditures (add lines 38 and 39) (see instructions)	40		
41 Lobbying nontaxable amount. Enter the amount from the following table—			
If the amount on line 40 is— / **The lobbying nontaxable amount is—**			
Not over $500,000 ... 20% of the amount on line 40			
Over $500,000 but not over $1,000,000 ... $100,000 plus 15% of the excess over $500,000			
Over $1,000,000 but not over $1,500,000 ... $175,000 plus 10% of the excess over $1,000,000	41		
Over $1,500,000 but not over $17,000,000 ... $225,000 plus 5% of the excess over $1,500,000			
Over $17,000,000 ... $1,000,000			
42 Grassroots nontaxable amount (enter 25% of line 41)	42		
43 Subtract line 42 from line 36. Enter -0- if line 42 is more than line 36	43		
44 Subtract line 41 from line 38. Enter -0- if line 41 is more than line 38	44		

Caution: File Form 4720 if there is an amount on either line 43 or line 44.

4-Year Averaging Period Under Section 501(h)

(Some organizations that made a section 501(h) election do not have to complete all of the five columns below. See the instructions for lines 45 through 50.)

	Lobbying Expenditures During 4-Year Averaging Period				
Calendar year (or fiscal year beginning in) ▶	(a) 1993	(b) 1992	(c) 1991	(d) 1990	(e) Total
45 Lobbying nontaxable amount (see instructions)					
46 Lobbying ceiling amount (150% of line 45(e))					
47 Total lobbying expenditures (see instructions)					
48 Grassroots nontaxable amount (see instructions)					
49 Grassroots ceiling amount (150% of line 48(e))					
50 Grassroots lobbying expenditures (see instructions)					

Part VI-B **Lobbying Activity by Nonelecting Public Charities**
(For reporting by organizations that did not complete Part VI-A)

During the year, did the organization attempt to influence national, state or local legislation, including any attempt to influence public opinion on a legislative matter or referendum, through the use of:	Yes	No	Amount
a Volunteers		X	
b Paid staff or management (include compensation in expenses reported on lines c through h)		X	
c Media advertisements		X	
d Mailings to members, legislators, or the public		X	
e Publications, or published or broadcast statements		X	
f Grants to other organizations for lobbying purposes		X	
g Direct contact with legislators, their staffs, government officials, or a legislative body		X	
h Rallies, demonstrations, seminars, conventions, speeches, lectures, or any other means		X	
i Total lobbying expenditures (add lines c through h)			

If "Yes" to any of the above, also attach a statement giving a detailed description of the lobbying activities.

NPCSS.O93

EXHIBIT 27–2   *Continued.*

EIN 13-6213564

Part VII   **Information Regarding Transfers To and Transactions and Relationships With Noncharitable Exempt Organizations**   (44)

51   Did the reporting organization directly or indirectly engage in any of the following with any other organization described in section 501(c) of the Code (other than section 501(c)(3) organizations) or in section 527, relating to political organizations?

		Yes	No
a Transfers from the reporting organization to a noncharitable exempt organization of:			
(i) Cash	**51a(i)**		X
(ii) Other assets	**a(ii)**		X
b Other transactions:			
(i) Sales of assets to a noncharitable exempt organization	**b(i)**		X
(ii) Purchases of assets from a noncharitable exempt organization	**b(ii)**		X
(iii) Rental of facilities or equipment	**b(iii)**		X
(iv) Reimbursement arrangements	**b(iv)**		X
(v) Loans or loan guarantees	**b(v)**		X
(vi) Performance of services or membership or fundraising solicitations	**b(vi)**		X
c Sharing of facilities, equipment, mailing lists, other assets, or paid employees	**c**		X

d   If the answer to any of the above is "Yes," complete the following schedule. Column (b) should always show the fair market value of the goods, other assets, or services given by the reporting organization. If the organization received less than fair market value in any transaction or sharing arrangement, show in column (d) the value of the goods, other assets, or services received.

(a) Line no.	(b) Amount involved	(c) Name of noncharitable exempt organization	(d) Description of transfers, transactions, and sharing arrangements

52a   Is the organization directly or indirectly affiliated with, or related to, one or more tax-exempt organizations described in section 501(c) of the Code (other than section 501(c)(3)) or in section 527?   ☐ **Yes**   ☒ **No**

  b   If "Yes," complete the following schedule.

(a) Name of organization	(b) Type of organization	(c) Description of relationship

NPCSS.O93

EXHIBIT 27–3

13-6213564
THE NELLE PLAINS COMMUNITY SERVICE SOCIETY
1400 DIAMOND AVENUE
NEW YORK, NEW YORK

1993 FORM 990—SUPPLEMENTARY SCHEDULES

Contributions in excess of $5,000
Part I, Line (d) and Schedule A, Part IV, Line 26(b)

B. Leonard Schultz Jr.
2 Butler Road
Scarswood, NY
$10,000 cash received September 11, 1993

Total gifts received from Mr. Schultz during 1989–1992
in excess of 2% of support: $35,227

Part I, Line 8

Gross amount from the sale of assets: Sale of common stock to unknown
parties through Merrill Lynch:

1,000 shares of US
Lockwood Common   Purchased 3/01/70   Sold 10/15/93

Selling Price	$7,000	
Cost	2,000	
Gain	$5,000	

Part I, Line 9

Special Fundraising events: Annual Awards Dinner

Gross receipts	$1,600
Contributions	300
Gross revenue	1,300
Direct expenses	700
Net income	$ 600

EXHIBIT 27–3   *Continued.*

13-6213564
THE NELLE PLAINS COMMUNITY SERVICE SOCIETY
1400 DIAMOND AVENUE
NEW YORK, NEW YORK

1993 FORM 990—SUPPLEMENTARY SCHEDULES

Part II, Line 22

Grants and Allocations paid (none of the recipients is a related person)

Awards for outstanding community service to:

Mrs. Mary Jo Phillips, 18 Birch St., Nelle Plains, NY	$2,500
Mr. Jack Anderson, 50 Chimney Ave, Nelle Plains, NY	1,000
Mr. L. A. Soben, Deerwood Rd, Nelle Plains, NY	500
Grant for rehabilitation of old firehouse to Nelle Plains volunteer Fire Department, Main St., Nelle Plains, NY	3,000
	$7,000

Part IV, Line 54, Investments

Securities at market value:

Corporate stocks:
Non-publicly traded:

JJ Faraway Co., common	$ 700
The Lesch Corp., common	1,800
Total Publicly traded	210,400
	$212,900

Schedule A, Part III, Line 3

Determination of qualifying recipients:

> An independent board headed by the Honorable George Burns, Mayor of Nelle Plains, makes the selection of the individuals who will receive annual awards. These individuals are selected for public recognition based upon their outstanding contributions to Nelle Plains. The basis for the Nelle Plains Community Service Society's tax exemption is to further, encourage, and recognize outstanding achievements of its citizens.

company in excess of $5,000 or 1 percent of the total support, whichever is greater. These amounts are given special treatment in computing second support test discussed in the previous chapter.

42. Part V is completed only by schools.

43. Part VI-A is completed only by organizations that have made an election under § 501(h) to be covered under the safe harbor lobbying activity provisions for publicly supported charities. Part VI-B must be completed by publicly supported charities that have not made the § 501(h) election.

44. Part VII explores the relationship between the reporting charitable organization and noncharitable exempt organizations and political organizations. Transactions with noncharitable exempt organizations must be aggregated through the tax year. If certain transactions with any noncharitable exempt organization exceed $500, then the transactions must be disclosed in this section of Schedule A.

27.2   FORM 990-PF: RETURN OF PRIVATE FOUNDATION

All private foundations must file Form 990-PF by the fifteenth day of the fifth month after the end of the fiscal year (May 15th for calendar year private foundations) and there is a penalty for failure to file, unless it can be shown that there was a reasonable cause for not doing so.

This return consists of 12 pages and to the uninitiated appears to be a difficult form to complete. Most private foundations would be well advised to have a competent professional prepare this form for them. The comments indicated below—while undoubtedly helpful—cannot substitute for the direct assistance of a tax lawyer or accountant knowledgeable in the foundation's particular circumstances.

Exhibit 27–4 shows this form. Again, the numbers on the form refer to the comments below:

1. The fair market value of assets at the end of the year can differ from the net worth as shown in the Balance Sheet on page 2 of Form 990-PF (Exhibit 27–4) because many foundations carry their investments at cost rather than at fair market value. However, in the illustration, investments are carried at market since this treatment is also permitted.

2. Part I (Analysis of Revenue and Expenses) looks more complicated than it actually is. In this section the foundation reports its revenue and expenses as recorded in its books in column (a).

EXHIBIT 27-4

Form **990-PF**	**Return of Private Foundation**	OMB No. 1545-0052
Department of the Treasury Internal Revenue Service	or Section 4947(a)(1) Nonexempt Charitable Trust Treated as a Private Foundation	19**93**

Note: The organization may be able to use a copy of this return to satisfy state reporting requirements.

For calendar year 1993, or tax year beginning _____ , 1993, and ending _____ , 19 ___

Use the IRS label. Otherwise, please print or type. See Specific Instructions.	Name of organization **The Christiansen Foundation**	**A** Employer identification number 13 : 5326271
	Number and street (or P.O. box number if mail is not delivered to street address) Room/suite **60 Broad Street**	**B** State registration number (see instruction F)
	City or town, state, and ZIP code **New York, NY 10017**	**C** If exemption application is pending, check here ▶ ☐

H Check type of organization: ☒ Section 501(c)(3) exempt private foundation
☐ Section 4947(a)(1) nonexempt charitable trust   ☐ Other taxable private foundation

I Fair market value of all assets at end of year (from Part II, col. (c), line 16)   **2,900,461** ①

J Accounting method: ☐ Cash   ☒ Accrual
☐ Other (specify) _____
(Part I, column (d) must be on cash basis.)

D 1. Foreign organizations, check here . ▶ ☐
2. Organizations meeting the 85% test, check here and attach computation ▶ ☐
E If private foundation status was terminated under section 507(b)(1)(A), check here ▶ ☐
F If the foundation is in a 60-month termination under section 507(b)(1)(B), check here . ▶ ☐
G If address changed, check here . . ▶ ☐

Part I   Analysis of Revenue and Expenses (The total of amounts in columns (b),(c), and (d) may not necessarily equal the amounts in column (a) (see instructions).) ②

		(a) Revenue and expenses per books ③	(b) Net investment income ⑥	(c) Adjusted net income ⑧	(d) Disbursements for charitable purposes (cash basis only) ⑨
Revenue	1 Contributions, gifts, grants, etc., received (attach schedule)				
	2 Contributions from split-interest trusts				
	3 Interest on savings and temporary cash investments	8,330	8,330		
	4 Dividends and interest from securities	226,483	226,483		
	5a Gross rents	0	0		
	b (Net rental income or (loss) ____0____)				
	6 Net gain or (loss) from sale of assets not on line 10 ④	20,000			
	7 Capital gain net income (from Part IV, line 2) . . ⑦		2,274		
	8 Net short-term capital gain			0	
	9 Income modifications				
	10a Gross sales less returns and allowances ____0____				
	b Less: Cost of goods sold . . . ____0____				
	c Gross profit or (loss) (attach schedule)	0			
	11 Other income (attach schedule)	0			
	12 **Total** (add lines 1 through 11)	254,813	237,087	0	
Operating and Administrative Expenses	13 Compensation of officers, directors, trustees, etc.	20,395	4,046		16,349
	14 Other employee salaries and wages	13,211	0		13,211
	15 Pension plans, employee benefits	966	0		966
	16a Legal fees (attach schedule)	0	0		0
	b Accounting fees (attach schedule)	0	0		0
	c Other professional fees (attach schedule)	19,138	6,363		12,775
	17 Interest	0	0		0
	18 Taxes (attach schedule) (see instructions)	4,519	0		0
	19 Depreciation (attach schedule) and depletion	0	0		
	20 Occupancy	10,507	722		9,785
	21 Travel, conferences, and meetings				
	22 Printing and publications				
	23 Other expenses (attach schedule)	11,340	0		11,340
	24 **Total** operating and administrative expenses (add lines 13 through 23)	80,076	11,131	0	64,426
	25 Contributions, gifts, grants paid	790,059			790,059
	26 **Total** expenses and disbursements (add lines 24 and 25)	870,135	11,131	0	854,485 ⑩
	27a Excess of revenue over expenses and disbursements (line 12 minus line 26) . . . . . ⑤	(615,322)			
	b Net investment income (if negative, enter "-0-")		225,956		
	c Adjusted net income (if negative, enter "-0-") . .			0	

For Paperwork Reduction Act Notice, see page 1 of the instructions.   84-1128480   Form **990-PF** (1993)

CHRISFDN.X93

EXHIBIT 27–4 *Continued.*

EIN 13-5326271

Form 990-PF (1993)   Page **2**

Part II	Balance Sheets	Attached schedules and amounts in the description column should be for end-of-year amounts only. (See instructions.)	Beginning of year	End of year	
			(a) Book Value	(b) Book Value	(c) Fair Market Value

Assets	1	Cash—non–interest–bearing . . . . (11) .	4,021	5,087	5,087
	2	Savings and temporary cash investments	39,400	227,000	227,000
	3	Accounts receivable ▶ _____			
		Less: allowance for doubtful accounts ▶ _____	47,438	0	
	4	Pledges receivable ▶ _____			
		Less: allowance for doubtful accounts ▶ _____	0	0	
	5	Grants receivable			
	6	Receivables due from officers, directors, trustees, and other disqualified persons (attach schedule) (see instructions)			
	7	Other notes and loans receivable (attach schedule) ▶ _____			
		Less: allowance for doubtful accounts ▶ _____	0	0	
	8	Inventories for sale or use			
	9	Prepaid expenses and deferred charges			
	10a	Investments—U.S. and state government obligations (attach schedule)	3,554,409	2,668,374	2,668,374
	b	Investments—corporate stock (attach schedule)			
	c	Investments—corporate bonds (attach schedule)			
	11	Investments—land, buildings, and equipment: basis ▶ _____			
		Less: accumulated depreciation (attach schedule)▶ _____	0	0	
	12	Investments—mortgage loans			
	13	Investments—other (attach schedule)			
	14	Land, buildings, and equipment: basis ▶ _____			
		Less: accumulated depreciation (attach schedule)▶ _____	0	0	
	15	Other assets (describe ▶ _____)			
	16	Total assets (to be completed by all filers—see instructions) . . .	3,645,268	2,900,461	2,900,461
Liabilities	17	Accounts payable and accrued expenses	33,691	7,175	
	18	Grants payable			
	19	Support and revenue designated for future periods (attach schedule)			
	20	Loans from officers, directors, trustees, and other disqualified persons			
	21	Mortgages and other notes payable (attach schedule)			
	22	Other liabilities (describe ▶ Taxes Payable _____)	10,926	4,519	
	23	Total liabilities (add lines 17 through 22) . . . . ▶	44,617	11,694	
Net Assets or Fund Balances		Organizations that use fund accounting, check here ▶ ☒ and complete lines 24 through 27 and lines 31 and 32.			
	24a	Current unrestricted fund	1,520,029	808,145	
	b	Current restricted fund			
	25	Land, buildings, and equipment fund			
	26	Endowment fund	2,080,622	2,080,622	
	27	Other funds (describe ▶ _____)			
		Organizations not using fund accounting, check here ▶ ☐ and complete lines 28 through 32.			
	28	Capital stock or trust principal			
	29	Paid–in capital or capital surplus			
	30	Retained earnings or accumulated income			
	31	Total net assets or fund balances (see instructions)	3,600,651	2,888,767	
	32	Total liabilities and net assets/fund balances (see instructions)	3,645,268	2,900,461	

Part III	Analysis of Changes in Net Assets or Fund Balances

1	Total net assets or fund balances at beginning of year—Part II, column (a), line 31	1	3,600,651
	(must agree with end–of–year figure reported on prior year's return)		
2	Enter amount from Part I, line 27a . . . . (12) .	2	(615,322)
3	Other increases not included in line 2 (itemize) ▶ _____	3	
4	Add lines 1, 2, and 3	4	2,985,329
5	Decreases not included in line 2 (itemize) ▶ Change in market value of securities _____	5	96,562
6	Total net assets or fund balances at end of year (line 4 minus line 5)—Part II, column (b), line 31	6	2,888,767

CHRISFDN.X93

EXHIBIT 27–4 *Continued.*

EIN 13-5326271

Form 990–PF (1993)   Page **3**

Part IV   Capital Gains and Losses for Tax on Investment Income

(a) List and describe the kind(s) of property sold, e.g., real estate, 2-story brick warehouse; or common stock, 200 shs. MLC Co.	(b) How acquired P—Purchase D—Donation	(c) Date acquired (mo., day, yr.)	(d) Date sold (mo., day, yr.)
1 100 shares AT&T	P	11/01/58	12/11/93
1200 shares Xerox ⑬	D	7/11/67	12/01/93
7500 shares ITT	D	6/01/53	6/01/93
2000 shares GM	P	8/03/71	5/27/93

(e) Gross sales price minus expense of sale	(f) Depreciation allowed (or allowable)	(g) Cost or other basis ⑭	(h) Gain or (loss) (e) plus (f) minus (g)
46,000		22,000	24,000
144,000		176,000	(32,000)
350,000		300,000	50,000
135,000		117,000	18,000

Complete only for assets showing gain in column (h) and owned by the foundation on 12/31/69

(i) F.M.V. as of 12/31/69	(j) Adjusted basis as of 12/31/69	(k) Excess of col. (i) over col (j), if any	(l) Losses (from col. (h)) Gains (excess of col. (h) gain over col. (k), but not less than '-0-')
29,726	22,000	7,726	16,274
			⑮ (32,000)
365,000	300,000	65,000	0
			18,000

2   Capital gain net income or (net capital loss).   { If gain, also enter in Part I, line 7; If (loss), enter "-0-" in Part I, line 7 }   **2**   ⑯   2,274

3   Net short-term capital gain or (loss) as defined in sections 1222(5) and (6):
If gain, also enter in Part I, line 8, column (c) (see instructions). If (loss), enter "-0-" in Part I, line 8 . . . .   **3**   0

Part V   Qualification Under Section 4940(e) for Reduced Tax on Net Investment Income

(For optional use by domestic private foundations subject to the section 4940(a) tax on net investment income.)

If section 4940(d)(2) applies, leave this part blank.   ⑰

Was the organization liable for the section 4942 tax on the distributable amount of any year in the base period? . . ☐ Yes ☐ No
If "Yes," the organization does not qualify under section 4940(e). Do not complete this part.

1   Enter the appropriate amount in each column for each year; see instructions before making any entries.

(a) Base period years Calendar year (or tax year beginning in)	(b) Adjusted qualifying distributions	(c) Net value of noncharitable-use assets	(d) Distribution ratio (col. (b) divided by col. (c))
1992			
1991			
1990			
1989			
1988			

2   Total of line 1, column (d) **2**

3   Average distribution ratio for the 5-year base period—divide the total on line 2 by 5, or by the number of years the foundation has been in existence if less than 5 years **3**

4   Enter the net value of noncharitable–use assets for 1993 from Part X, line 5 . . . .   **4**

5   Multiply line 4 by line 3 . . . .   **5**

6   Enter 1% of net investment income (1% of Part I, line 27b) **6**

7   Add lines 5 and 6 . . . .   **7**

8   Enter qualifying distributions from Part XII, line 4 . . . .   **8**

If line 8 is equal to or greater than line 7, check the box in Part VI, line 1b, and complete that part using a 1% tax rate. See the Part VI instructions.

CHRISFDN.X93

EXHIBIT 27–4 *Continued.*

EIN 13-5326271

Form 990-PF (1993)   Page 4

Part VI — Excise Tax on Investment Income (Section 4940(a), 4940(b), 4940(e), or 4948—see instructions)

1a	Exempt operating foundations described in section 4940(d)(2), check here ☐ and enter "N/A" on line 1.		
	Date of ruling letter: _____ **(attach copy of ruling letter if necessary—see instructions)**		
b	Domestic organizations that meet the section 4940(e) requirements in Part V, check here ☐ and enter 1% of Part I, line 27b . . . . ⑱ . .	1	4,519
c	All other domestic organizations enter 2% of line 27b. Exempt foreign organizations enter 4% of line 27b		
2	Tax under section 511 (domestic section 4947(a)(1) trusts and taxable foundations only. Others enter "-0-")	2	0
3	Add lines 1 and 2	3	4,519
4	Tax under subtitle A (domestic section 4947(a)(1) trusts and taxable foundations only. Others enter "-0-")	4	0
5	**Tax on investment income** (line 3 minus line 4 (but not less than "-0-"))	5	4,519
6	Credits/Payments:		
a	1993 estimated tax payments and 1992 overpayment credited to 1993	6a ⑲	5,000		
b	Exempt foreign organizations—tax withheld at source	6b			
c	Tax paid with application for extension of time to file (Form 2758) . . .	6c			
d	Backup withholding erroneously withheld	6d			
7	Total credits and payments (add lines 6a through d)	7	5,000
8	Enter any **PENALTY** for underpayment of estimated tax. Check here ☐ if Form 2220 is attached . .	8	0
9	**TAX DUE.** If the total of lines 5 and 8 is more than line 7, enter **AMOUNT OWED** . . . . . . ▶	9	0
10	**OVERPAYMENT.** If line 7 is more than the total of lines 5 and 8, enter the **AMOUNT OVERPAID** . . ▶	10	481
11	Enter the amount of line 10 to be: Credited to 1994 estimated tax ▶	481	Refunded ▶	11	0

Part VII — Statements Regarding Activities ⑳

File Form 4720 if the answer is "No" to question 10b, 11b, or 14b or "Yes" to question 10c, 12b, 13a, 13b, or 14a(2), unless an exception applies.

			Yes	No
1a	During the tax year, did the organization attempt to influence any national, state, or local legislation or did it participate or intervene in any political campaign?	1a		X
b	Did it spend more than $100 during the year (either directly or indirectly) for political purposes (see instructions for definition)?	1b		X
	If the answer is "Yes" to 1a or 1b, attach a detailed description of the activities and copies of any materials published or distributed by the organization in connection with the activities.			
c	Did the organization file **Form 1120-POL**, U.S. Income Tax Return for Certain Political Organizations, for this year?	1c		X
2	Has the organization engaged in any activities that have not previously been reported to the IRS?	2		X
	If "Yes," attach a detailed description of the activities.			
3	Has the organization made any changes, not previously reported to the IRS, in its governing instrument, articles of incorporation, or bylaws, or other similar instruments? If "Yes," attach a conformed copy of the changes	3		X
4a	Did the organization have unrelated business gross income of $1,000 or more during the year?	4a		X
b	If "Yes," has it filed a tax return on **Form 990-T**, Exempt Organization Business Income Tax Return, for this year?	4b	N/A	
5	Was there a liquidation, termination, dissolution, or substantial contraction during the year? . . . . ㉑ . .	5		X
	If "Yes," attach the statement required by General Instruction T.			
6	Are the requirements of section 508(e) (relating to sections 4941 through 4945) satisfied either:			
	• By language written into the governing instrument, or ㉒			
	• By state legislation that effectively amends the governing instrument so that no mandatory directions that conflict with the state law remain in the governing instrument?	6	X	
7	Did the organization have at least $5,000 in assets at any time during the year?	7	X	
	If "Yes," complete Part II, column (c), and Part XV.			
8a	Enter the states to which the foundation reports or with which it is registered (see instructions) ▶ New York ㉓			
b	If the answer is "Yes" to line 7, has the organization furnished a copy of Form 990-PF to the Attorney General (or his or her designate) of each state as required by General Instruction G? If "No," attach explanation . . .	8b	X	
9	Is the organization claiming status as a private operating foundation within the meaning of section 4942(j)(3) or 4942(j)(5) for calendar year 1993 or taxable year beginning in 1993 (see instructions for Part XIV)? If "Yes," complete Part XIV ㉔	9		X
10	Self-Dealing (section 4941):			
a	During the year did the organization (either directly or indirectly):			
	(1) Engage in the sale or exchange, or leasing of property with a disqualified person? . . ㉕	10a(1)		X
	(2) Borrow money from, lend money to, or otherwise extend credit to (or accept it from) a disqualified person?	10a(2)		X
	(3) Furnish goods, services, or facilities to (or accept them from) a disqualified person?	10a(3)		X
	(4) Pay compensation to or pay or reimburse the expenses of a disqualified person? . . . ㉖	10a(4)	X	
	(5) Transfer any income or assets to a disqualified person (or make any of either available for the benefit or use of a disqualified person)?	10a(5)		X
	(6) Agree to pay money or property to a government official? (**Exception:** Check "No" if the organization agreed to make a grant to or to employ the official for a period after he or she terminates government service, if he or she is terminating within 90 days.)	10a(6)		X

CHRISFDN.X93

EXHIBIT 27–4   *Continued.*

EIN 13-5326271

Form 990-PF (1993)   Page **5**

Part VII   Statements Regarding Activities (continued)

		Yes	No
10b If the answer is "Yes" to any of questions 10a(1) through (6), were the acts engaged in excepted acts as described in Regulations sections 53.4941(d)–3 and 4, or Notice 93–41, 1993–27 I.R.B. 13?	**10b**	X	
c Did the organization engage in a prior year in any of the acts described in 10a, other than excepted acts, that were acts of self-dealing not corrected by the first day of the tax year beginning in 1993?	**10c**		X
11 Taxes on failure to distribute income (section 4942) (does not apply for years the organization was a private operating foundation as defined in section 4942(j)(3) or 4942(j)(5)):			
a At the end of tax year 1993, did the organization have any undistributed income (lines 6d and 6e, Part XIII) for tax year(s) beginning before 1993? If "Yes," list the years ▶ _____ ' _____ ' _____ ' _____	**11a**		X
b If 11a is "Yes," is the organization applying the provisions of section 4942(a)(2) (relating to incorrect valuation of assets) to the undistributed income for ALL such years? (If "Yes," attach statement—see instructions.)	**11b**	N/A	
c If the provisions of section 4942(a)(2) are being applied to ANY of the years listed in 11a, list the years here. ▶ _____ ' _____ ' _____ ' _____			
12 Taxes on excess business holdings (section 4943):			
a Did the organization hold more than a 2% direct or indirect interest in any business enterprise at any time during the year?	**12a**		X
b If "Yes," did it have excess business holdings in 1993 as a result of (1) any purchase by the organization or disqualified persons after May 26, 1969; (2) the lapse of the 5-year period (or longer period approved by the Commissioner under section 4943(c)(7)) to dispose of holdings acquired by gift or bequest; or (3) the lapse of the 10-, 15-, or 20-year first phase holding period? (Use Schedule C, Form 4720, to determine if the organization had excess business holdings in 1993.)	**12b**	N/A	
13 Taxes on investments that jeopardize charitable purposes (section 4944): ㉗			
a Did the organization invest during the year any amount in a manner that would jeopardize its charitable purposes?	**13a**		X
b Did the organization make any investment in a prior year (but after December 31, 1969) that could jeopardize its charitable purpose that had not been removed from jeopardy on the first day of the tax year beginning in 1993?	**13b**		X
14 Taxes on taxable expenditures (section 4945) and political expenditures (section 4955):			
a During the year did the organization pay or incur any amount to:			
(1) Carry on propaganda, or otherwise attempt to influence legislation (section 4945(e))?	**14a(1)**		X
(2) Influence the outcome of any specific public election (see section 4955); or to carry on, directly or indirectly, any voter registration drive?	**14a(2)**		X
(3) Provide a grant to an individual for travel, study, or other similar purposes?	**14a(3)**		X
(4) Provide a grant to an organization, other than a charitable, etc., organization described in section 509(a)(1), (2), or (3), or section 4940(d)(2)? ㉘	**14a(4)**		X
(5) Provide for any purpose other than religious, charitable, scientific, literary, or educational purposes, or for the prevention of cruelty to children or animals?	**14a(5)**		X
b If the answer is "Yes" to any of questions 14a(1) through (5), were all such transactions excepted transactions as described in Regulations section 53.4945 or Notice 93–41, 1993–27 I.R.B. 13?	**14b**	N/A	
c If the answer is "Yes" to question 14a(4), does the organization claim exemption from the tax because it maintained expenditure responsibility for the grant? If "Yes," attach the statement required by Regulations section 53.4945–5(d).	**14c**	N/A	
15 Did any persons become substantial contributors during the tax year? ㉙ If "Yes," attach a schedule listing their names and addresses.	**15**		X
16 During this tax year, did the organization maintain any part of its accounting/tax records on a computerized system?	**16**	X	
17a Did anyone request to see either the organization's annual return or its exemption application (or both)? ㉚	**17a**	X	
b If "Yes," did the organization comply pursuant to the instructions? (See General Instruction Q.)	**17b**	X	

18 The books are in care of ▶ **The Foundation** _____ Telephone no. ▶ **(212) 785-6423**
Located at ▶ **Address above** _____ ZIP code ▶ _____
19 Section 4947(a)(1) nonexempt charitable trusts filing Form 990-PF in lieu of **Form 1041**, U.S. Fiduciary Income Tax Return.—Check here ▶ ☐
and enter the amount of tax-exempt interest received or accrued during the year. ▶ | **19** |

Part VIII   Information About Officers, Directors, Trustees, Foundation Managers, Highly Paid Employees, and Contractors

1 List all officers, directors, trustees, foundation managers, and their compensation (see instructions):

(a) Name and address	(b) Title, and average hours per week devoted to position	(c) Contributions to employee benefit plans and deferred compensation	(d) Expense account, other allowances	(e) Compensation (If not paid, enter -0-)
Jane Cornell 60 Broad Street, New York, NY 10017	President 40 hours/wk	0	0	18,395
W.H. Larkin III 60 Broad Street, New York, NY 10017	Trustee 2 hours/week	0	0	1,000
Robert Perone 60 Broad Street, New York, NY 10017	Trustee 2 hours/week	0	0	1,000

CHRISFDN.X93

EXHIBIT 27–4   *Continued.*

EIN 13-5326271

Form 990–PF (1993)   Page **6**

Part VIII	**Information About Officers, Directors, Trustees, etc. (continued)**

2   Compensation of five highest paid employees (other than those included on line 1—see instructions). If none, enter "NONE."

(a) Name and address of each employee paid more than $30,000	(b) Title and average hours per week devoted to position	(c) Contributions to employee benefit plans and deferred compensation	(d) Expense account, other allowances	(e) Compensation
NONE				

Total number of other employees paid over $30,000 . . . . ▶   **0**

3   Five highest paid persons for professional services—(see instructions). If none, enter "NONE."

(a) Name and address of each person paid more than $30,000	(b) Type of service	(c) Compensation
NONE		

Total number of others receiving over $30,000 for professional services . . . . ▶   **0**

Part IX-A	**Summary of Direct Charitable Activities**

List the foundation's four largest direct charitable activities during the tax year. Include relevant statistical information such as the number of organizations and other beneficiaries served, conferences convened, research papers produced, etc.	Expenses
1 Not Applicable	
2	
3	
4	

Part IX-B	**Summary of Program–Related Investments (see instructions)**

Describe any program-related investments made by the foundation during the tax year.	Amount
1 Not applicable	
2	
3	

CHRISFDN.X93

EXHIBIT 27–4   *Continued.*

EIN 13-5326271

Form 990-PF (1993)   Page **7**

Part X   Minimum Investment Return (All domestic organizations must complete this part. Foreign foundations, see instructions.)

1	Fair market value of assets not used (or held for use) directly in carrying out charitable, etc., purposes:	(31)	
a	Average monthly fair market value of securities	1a	2,757,412
b	Average of monthly cash balances.	1b	79,830
c	Fair market value of all other assets (see instructions)	1c	23,720
d	Total (add lines 1a, b, and c)	1d	2,860,962
e	Reduction claimed for blockage or other factors (attach detailed explanation) ▶ **1e** 0		
2	Acquisition indebtedness applicable to line 1 assets	2	0
3	Line 1d minus line 2	3	2,860,962
4	Cash deemed held for charitable activities—Enter 1 1/2% of line 3 (for greater amount, see instructions)	4	42,914
5	Net value of noncharitable-use assets—Line 3 minus line 4. (Enter in Part V, line 4.)	5	2,818,048
6	Minimum investment return. (Enter 5% of line 5.)	6	140,902

Part XI   Distributable Amount (see instructions)

(Section 4942(j)(3) and (j)(5) private operating foundations and certain foreign organizations check here ▶ ☐ and do not complete this part.)

1	Minimum investment return from Part X, line 6		1	140,902
2a	Tax on investment income for 1993 from Part VI, line 5 . . . (31)	2a 4,519		
b	Income tax under subtitle A, for 1993	2b 0		
c	Line 2a plus line 2b		2c	4,519
3	Distributable amount before adjustments (line 1 minus line 2c)		3	136,383
4a	Recoveries of amounts treated as qualifying distributions	4a 0		
b	Income distributions from section 4947(a)(2) trusts	4b 0		
c	Line 4a plus line 4b		4c	0
5	Line 3 plus line 4c		5	136,383
6	Deduction from distributable amount (see instructions)		6	0
7	Distributable amount as adjusted (line 5 minus line 6). (Also enter in Part XIII, line 1.)		7	136,383

Part XII   Qualifying Distributions (see instructions)   (32)

1	Amounts paid (including administrative expenses) to accomplish charitable, etc., purposes:		
a	Expenses, contributions, gifts, etc.—total from Part I, column (d), line 26	1a	854,485
b	Program-related investments—total of lines 1–3 of Part IX-B	1b	0
2	Amounts paid to acquire assets used (or held for use) directly in carrying out charitable, etc., purposes	2	
3	Amounts set aside for specific charitable projects that satisfy the:		
a	Suitability test (prior IRS approval required)	3a	
b	Cash distribution test (attach the required schedule) . . . . (33)	3b	
4	Qualifying distributions (add lines 1a through 3b). (Enter in Part V, line 8, and Part XIII, line 4.) . . .	4	854,485
5	Organizations that qualify under section 4940(e) for the reduced rate of tax on net investment income—enter 1% of Part I, line 27b (see instructions) . . . . (17) .	5	
6	Adjusted qualifying distributions (line 4 minus line 5)	6	854,485

Note: The amount on line 6 will be used in Part V, column (b), in subsequent years when calculating whether the foundation qualifies for the section 4940(e) reduction of tax in those years.

CHRISFDN.X93

EXHIBIT 27–4   *Continued.*

EIN 13-5326271

Form 990–PF (1993)   Page **8**

Part XIII   Undistributed Income (see instructions)   ㉞

		(a) Corpus	(b) Years prior to 1992	(c) 1992	(d) 1993
1	Distributable amount for 1993 from Part XI, line 7				136,383 ㉟
2	Undistributed income, if any, as of the end of 1992:				
a	Enter amount for 1992 only				
b	Total for prior years: 19 ____ ,19 ____ ,19 ____				
3	Excess distributions carryover, if any, to 1993:				
a	From 1988	109,357			
b	From 1989	208,751			
c	From 1990 . ㊱	(51,964)			
d	From 1991	79,147			
e	From 1992	101,101			
f	**Total** of lines 3a through e	446,392			
4	Qualifying distributions for 1993 from Part XII, line 4: $ ____854,485____ ㊲				
a	Applied to 1992, but not more than line 2a .			0	
b	Applied to undistributed income of prior years (Election required—see instructions) . .		0		
c	Treated as distributions out of corpus (Election required—see instructions)	0			
d	Applied to 1993 distributable amount . . .				136,383
e	Remaining amount distributed out of corpus	718,102			
5	Excess distributions carryover applied to 1993. (If an amount appears in column (d), the same amount must be shown in column (a).)	0			0
6	Enter the net total of each column as indicated below: ㊳				
a	Corpus. Add lines 3f, 4c, and 4e. Subtract line 5.	1,164,494			
b	Prior years' undistributed income (line 2b minus line 4b)		0		
c	Enter the amount of prior years' undistributed income for which a notice of deficiency has been issued, or on which the section 4942(a) tax has been previously assessed		0		
d	Subtract line 6c from line 6b. Taxable amount—see instructions		0		
e	Undistributed income for 1992 (line 2a minus line 4a). Taxable amount—see instructions . .			0	
f	Undistributed income for 1993 (line 1 minus lines 4d and 5). This amount must be distributed in 1994				0
7	Amounts treated as distributions out of corpus to satisfy requirements imposed by section 170(b)(1)(E) or 4942(g)(3) (see instructions) . .	0			
8	Excess distributions carryover from 1988 not applied on line 5 or line 7 (see instructions) . .	109,357			
9	Excess distributions carryover to 1994 (line 6a minus lines 7 and 8)	1,055,137			
10	Analysis of line 9:				
a	Excess from 1989	208,751			
b	Excess from 1990	(51,964)			
c	Excess from 1991	79,147			
d	Excess from 1992	101,101			
e	Excess from 1993	718,102			

CHRISFDN.X93

EXHIBIT 27–4 *Continued.*

EIN 13-5326271

Form 990–PF (1993)   Page **9**

Part XIV Private Operating Foundations (see instructions and Part VII, question 9)

1a If the foundation has received a ruling or determination letter that it is a private operating foundation, and the ruling is effective for 1993, enter the date of the ruling . . . . . ▶   ㊴

b Check box to indicate whether the organization is a private operating foundation described in section ☐ 4942(j)(3) or ☐ 4942(j)(5).

	Tax year	Prior 3 years			
	(a) 1993	(b) 1992	(c) 1991	(d) 1990	(e) Total
2a Enter the lesser of the adjusted net income from Part I or the minimum investment return from Part X (for 1991 through 1993; previously Part IX)					
b 85% of line 2a					
c Qualifying distributions from Part XII, line 4 (for 1991 through 1993; previously Part XIII, line 6)					
d Amounts included in line 2c not used directly for active conduct of exempt activities . .					
e Qualifying distributions made directly for active conduct of exempt activities (line 2c minus line 2d)					
3 Complete 3a, b, or c for the alternative test relied upon:					
a "Assets" alternative test—enter:					
(1) Value of all assets					
(2) Value of assets qualifying under section 4942(j)(3)(B)(i) . .					
b "Endowment" alternative test—Enter 2/3 of minimum investment return shown in Part X, line 6, (for 1991 through 1993; previously Part IX, line 6)					
c "Support" alternative test—enter:					
(1) Total support other than gross investment income (interest, dividends, rents, payments on securities loans (section 512(a)(5)), or royalties) . . .					
(2) Support from general public and 5 or more exempt organizations as provided in section 4942(j)(3)(B)(iii)					
(3) Largest amount of support from an exempt organization .					
(4) Gross investment income . .					

Part XV Supplementary Information (Complete this part only if the organization had $5,000 or more in assets at any time during the year—see instructions.)

1 **Information Regarding Foundation Managers:**

a List any managers of the foundation who have contributed more than 2% of the total contributions received by the foundation before the close of any tax year (but only if they have contributed more than $5,000). (See section 507(d)(2).)

NONE

b List any managers of the foundation who own 10% or more of the stock of a corporation (or an equally large portion of the ownership of a partnership or other entity) of which the foundation has a 10% or greater interest.

NONE

2 **Information Regarding Contribution, Grant, Gift, Loan, Scholarship, etc., Programs:**

Check here ▶ ☐ if the organization only makes contributions to preselected charitable organizations and does not accept unsolicited requests for funds. If the organization makes gifts, grants, etc., (see instructions) to individuals or organizations under other conditions, complete items 2a, b, c, and d.

a The name, address, and telephone number of the person to whom applications should be addressed:
Jane Cornell - 60 Broad Street, New York, NY 10017   212-678-6423

b The form in which applications should be submitted and information and materials they should include:

Letter describing activities/audited financial statements/Form 990

c Any submission deadlines:

NONE

d Any restrictions or limitations on awards, such as by geographical areas, charitable fields, kinds of institutions, or other factors:

NONE

CHRISFDN.X93

EXHIBIT 27–4 *Continued.*

EIN 13-5326271

Form 990–PF (1993)				Page 10
Part XV Supplementary Information (continued)				
3 Grants and Contributions Paid During the Year or Approved for Future Payment				

Recipient	If recipient is an individual, show any relationship to any foundation manager or substantial contributor	Foundation status of recipient	Purpose of grant or contribution	Amount
Name and address (home or business)				
a Paid during the year				
See attached schedule ㊵				
Total . . . . ▶ **3a**				0
b Approved for future payment See attached schedule				
Total . . . . ▶ **3b**				0

CHRISFDN.X93

EXHIBIT 27-4 *Continued.*

EIN 13-5326271

Form 990-PF (1993)

Page **11**

Part XVI-A Analysis of Income-Producing Activities ④

Enter gross amounts unless otherwise indicated.

	Unrelated business income		Excluded by section 512, 513, or 514		(e) Related or exempt function income (See instructions.)
	(a) Business code	(b) Amount	(c) Exclusion code	(d) Amount	
1 Program service revenue:					
a _____					
b _____					
c _____					
d _____					
e _____					
f _____					
g Fees and contracts from government agencies .					
2 Membership dues and assessments					
3 Interest on savings and temporary cash investments			14	8,330	
4 Dividends and interest from securities			14	226,483	
5 Net rental income or (loss) from real estate:					
a Debt-financed property.					
b Not debt-financed property					
6 Net rental income or (loss) from personal property . .					
7 Other investment income					
8 Gain or (loss) from sales of assets other than inventory			18	20,000	
9 Net income from special events					
10 Gross profit or (loss) from sales of inventory . . .					
11 Other revenue: a _____					
b _____					
c _____					
d _____					
e _____					
12 Subtotal (add columns (b), (d), and (e))		0		254,813	0
13 TOTAL (add line 12, columns (b), (d), and (e)) . . . . ▶ 13					254,813

(See worksheet for line 13 instructions to verify calculations.)

Part XVI-B Relationship of Activities to the Accomplishment of Exempt Purposes

Line No. ▼	Explain below how each activity for which income is reported in column (e) of Part XVI-A contributed importantly to the accomplishment of the organization's exempt purposes (other than by providing funds for such purposes). (See instructions.)
	N/A

CHRISFDN.X93

EXHIBIT 27–4 *Continued.*

EIN 13-5326271

Form 990–PF (1993)   Page 12

Part XVII **Information Regarding Transfers To and Transactions and Relationships With Noncharitable Exempt Organizations**

		Yes	No
1 Did the organization directly or indirectly engage in any of the following with any other organization described in section 501(c) of the Code (other than section 501(c)(3) organizations) or in section 527, relating to political organizations?			
a Transfers from the reporting organization to a noncharitable exempt organization of:			
(1) Cash.	1a(1)		X
(2) Other assets	a(2)		X
b Other Transactions: ㊷			
(1) Sales of assets to a noncharitable exempt organization	b(1)		X
(2) Purchases of assets from a noncharitable exempt organization	b(2)		X
(3) Rental of facilities or equipment	b(3)		X
(4) Reimbursement arrangements	b(4)		X
(5) Loans or loan guarantees	b(5)		X
(6) Performance of services or membership or fundraising solicitations	b(6)		X
c Sharing of facilities, equipment, mailing lists, other assets, or paid employees	c		X

d If the answer to any of the above is "Yes," complete the following schedule. Column **(b)** should always show the fair market value of the goods, other assets, or services given by the reporting organization. If the organization received less than fair market value in any transaction or sharing arrangement, show in column **(d)** the value of the goods, other assets, or services received.

(a) Line no.	(b) Amount involved	(c) Name of noncharitable exempt organization	(d) Description of transfers, transactions, and sharing arrangements

2a Is the organization directly or indirectly affiliated with, or related to, one or more tax-exempt organizations described in section 501(c) of the Code (other than section 501(c)(3)) or in section 527? . . . . ☐ Yes ☒ No
b If "Yes," complete the following schedule.

(a) Name of organization	(b) Type of organization	(c) Description of relationship

Part XVIII **Public Inspection** ㊸

1 Enter the date the notice of availability of the annual return appeared in a newspaper ▶ _ _ _ _ _ _ _ _ _ _ _ _ _ 5/09/94
2 Enter the name of the newspaper ▶ **New York Times**
3 Check here ▶ ☒ to indicate that you have attached a copy of the newspaper notice as required by the instructions. (If the notice is not attached, the return will be considered incomplete.)

Under penalties of perjury, I declare that I have examined this return, including accompanying schedules and statements, and to the best of my knowledge and belief, it is true, correct, and complete. Declaration of preparer (other than taxpayer or fiduciary) is based on all information of which preparer has any knowledge.

Please Sign Here

▶ Signature of officer or trustee   Date   ▶ Title

Paid Preparer's Use Only

Preparer's signature ▶		Date	Check if self-employed ▶ ☐	Preparer's social security no.
Firm's name (or yours if self-employed) and address ▶			E.I. No. ▶	
			ZIP code ▶	

CHRISFDN.X93

Then income and expenses are allocated to the appropriate remaining columns to arrive at certain key amounts that the foundation must use to determine the amount of its excise tax and distributable income.

3. Column (a) (Revenue and expenses per books) is exactly what it says it is, and the foundation should record its revenue and expenses in this column. Record all the figures in column (a) before attempting to complete the other three columns. The foundation can keep its records on either the cash or the accrual basis of accounting and the amounts shown in column (a) will be the amounts on whichever basis is used. However, the amounts included in column (d) must be the amounts actually disbursed during the year (i.e., the cash basis).

4. The net gain or loss from sale of assets will be the book amount of the capital gains or losses from the sale of investments. As noted in the previous chapter, book gain or loss may or may not be the same as taxable gain or loss. The taxable gain will be reported only in column (b) on line 7 (see comment 7 below).

5. Line 27(a) will be the excess of revenue over expenses (or vice versa) as shown on the organization's books.

6. Column (b) looks complicated but it really is not. The amounts shown in the top section are merely those amounts which are subject to the excise tax on investment income. The amounts in the bottom half of this schedule are the allocated expenses which can be deducted in arriving at the amount of net investment income subject to the excise tax. It is for this reason that there are a number of shaded areas in this column in the income section. (No figures should be put in these shaded areas.) For example, contributions, gifts, and grants are not subject to excise tax and therefore the corresponding lines in column (b) have been shaded. The allocation of expenses should be made on the basis of the nature of the expense. The last line in this column ($225,956) is the amount of net investment income subject to the excise tax. The tax is calculated in Part VI.

7. Taxable gain on sale of investments is calculated on page 3 of the form and the calculation on that page must be completed before a figure can be entered on line 7 in column (b).

8. Column (c) provides for the computation of "adjusted net income." Net investment income and adjusted net income are not the same and should not be confused. Private non-operating foundations that do not derive income from the direct conduct of

charitable activities (such as the private foundation in our example) are not required to complete this column. All other private foundations must complete column (c). Private operating foundations use the adjusted net income number further at Part XIV of the return.

9. Column (d) is used to report the amount of expenditures made for an exempt purpose, including a reasonable allocation of administrative and overhead expenses.

10. The amounts reported in column (d) are those that were actually disbursed during the current year (i.e., on a cash basis). Therefore, if a foundation keeps its books on an accrual basis, it must adjust the deductions in column (d) to the cash basis.

11. See comments 24 to 26 on Form 990, which are also relevant to Form 990-PF.

12. Part III reconciles the fund balance at the beginning of the year to the fund balance at the end of the year. In many instances the amount reported on the first page as the excess of revenue over expenses will be the only reconciling item. If the foundation carries its securities at market value, the unrealized change in market value during the year will be shown on either line 3 or line 5.

13. One of the major bookkeeping problems created by the Tax Reform Act of 1969 is that the foundation must determine the donor's basis on all gifts acquired after December 31, 1969, and all prior gifts when the fair market value at December 31, 1969, was less than the donor's tax basis. Gains from the sale of donated property are based on the donor's original tax basis. As was illustrated in the previous chapter, if the donor's tax basis is very low, the foundation could have substantial gain and this gain would be subject to the excise tax. The amounts in Part IV, column (g) refer to donor's tax basis for donated securities.

14. The cost basis shown in column (g) is the cost at which the foundation is carrying this security.

15. Private foundations are not subject to tax on the gain accrued on securities through December 31, 1969. For computing gain on the sale of securities, the foundation uses the higher of its adjusted basis (column (j)) or the fair market value on December 31, 1969 (column (i)).

16. The net capital gain is taxable, but, if there is a net loss, the loss is not deductible from investment income to determine the amount of income subject to excise tax.

17. Part V is where a private foundation calculates whether it qualifies for the 1 percent reduced excise tax on net investment

income. The calculation is based on the average payout ratio of the foundation's 5 prior years. The foundation has the option of paying the 1 percent reduced tax, if it qualifies, or paying tax at the regular 2 percent rate. If the foundation chooses to pay the reduced tax, the amount of the reduction in tax from 2 percent to 1 percent is subtracted from the foundation's qualifying distributions in Part XII.

18. In this section, the foundation calculates the excise tax on net investment income.

19. Private foundations must make estimated tax payments for the amount of excise taxes they will owe (Tax Reform Act of 1986).

20. Part VII must be answered very carefully because it investigates whether any of the many rules affecting private foundations have been violated. If the answer to any of the questions results in filing Form 4720, the foundation should consult with its tax advisor since the foundation and its manager may be subject to escalating taxes.

21. A substantial contraction is defined as disposition of more than 25 percent of the fair market value of the foundation's assets (as distinguished from book value).

22. The 1969 Tax Reform Act required foundations to put certain restrictive language in their governing instruments, or, alternatively, state legislatures could effectively amend these governing instruments for all foundations within the state through legislation. Many states did so, thus eliminating the need for individual foundations to amend their governing instruments. Question 6 is designed to make sure that either state legislation was enacted or the foundation itself amended its governing instruments as appropriate.

23. All private foundations must submit a copy of Form 990-PF to the attorney general in each state in which it is registered or otherwise doing business.

24. There are certain advantages to being an "operating" foundation. See Chapter 26.

25. Questions 10 through 14 are designed to determine whether the foundation is engaged in any "prohibited" transactions. See Chapter 26 for a discussion of prohibited transactions, and footnote 5 in Chapter 26 for a definition of disqualified persons.

26. In most instances the foundation will have paid compensation to the foundation manager and perhaps others who fit the definition of a "disqualified person." In that case, the answer to question 10(a)(4) will be "yes" but this transaction is not a prohibited

transaction as long as the compensation paid is not unreasonable. A "yes" answer to question 10(b) confirms that this is the case.

27. A foundation is expected to follow a "prudent man" approach to investments. However, this does not preclude a foundation from making "program-related" investments. Typically these investments involve a high element of risk and probably would not meet the "prudent man" test. The distinguishing feature of a program-related investment is that it is made to accomplish the exempt function of the organization and not for the purpose of generating income. In reality, these investments are in the nature of a grant.

28. Question 14(a)(4) is asking whether the foundation has made a grant to an organization other than a publicly supported organization. Where grants are made to other than publicly supported organizations the foundation is required to exercise "expenditure responsibility" to ensure that the grant is actually spent for the charitable purpose for which it was granted. Expert tax advice should be obtained to ensure that the procedures followed by the foundation to exercise this expenditure responsibility are adequate to meet the requirements.

29. The only substantial contributors who need be listed in the schedule required by question 15 are those who became substantial contributors in the current taxable year.

30. Private foundations must make their 990-PF available to all who request to see it, if the requests are received within 180 days of the placement in the newspaper of the notice of public availability. See comment 43 below.

31. Parts X and XI calculate the minimum investment return and the distributable amount. See the prior chapter for a complete discussion of these two calculations.

32. Part XII is fairly straightforward. Line 1(b) refers to program related investments, which are discussed in comment 27 above.

33. Very few foundations will have qualifying distributions which conform to the requirements for "Amounts set aside for specific charitable projects." A foundation which wishes to set aside funds for future use and have those funds qualify as a current qualifying distribution must obtain the agreement of the Commissioner of the Internal Revenue Service prior to setting the amounts aside.

34. Part XIII is a complex schedule which requires patience on the part of the preparer. The purpose of the schedule is to determine whether the foundation has made the proper required

distributions. Foundations which have distributed sufficient amounts will find that lines 6 (b), (c), (d), and (e) will be zero. Failure to distribute can result in excise taxes.

35. The first step in filling out this part is to record the distributable amount on line 1. This amount comes directly from Part XI. If the amount was not paid within the current year, then the foundation has the next fiscal year to distribute this amount without paying excise taxes for failure to distribute.

36. The next step is to record the excess or deficit distributions for the prior years (lines 3a through 3e). These amounts are carried over from the prior year's return.

37. Of the $854,485 distributed during 1993 (line 4), $136,383 will be allocated on line 4(d) to meet the current year's distribution requirement. The excess distribution for 1993 of $718,102 is shown on line 4(e).

38. Line 6(a) is used to accumulate the excess distributions for 1993 and 1988–1992. Lines 8 to 10 are used to determine the excess distribution carryover to 1994. Since there is a five-year limitation on carryovers, the 1988 carryover of $109,357 is deducted on line 8, leaving $1,055,137 for carryover to 1994.

39. Most of page 9 is completed only by private operating foundations. The Christiansen Foundation is not a private operating foundation. The previous chapter discusses the general requirements for classification as a private operating foundation and the advantages of that status.

40. The schedule required should provide all the information requested on page 10.

41. See comment on page 5, Form 990.

42. See comment on Schedule A, page 5, Form 990.

43. The notice referred to here is the newspaper notice of public availability of Form 990-PF.

27.3   FORM 990-T: EXEMPT ORGANIZATION BUSINESS INCOME TAX RETURN

Form 990-T must be filed if an exempt organization has unrelated business income and the gross (not net) income was $1,000 or more. Unrelated trade or business income was discussed in Chapter 26, and it was noted that all exempt organizations are subject to this tax. Form 990-T is due the 15th day of the fifth month after the end of the fiscal year (May 15 for calendar-year organizations).

The complete Form 990-T is four pages long, and is complicated. Because of the complicated nature of Form 990-T, only the first and second pages of the return are discussed. Exhibit 27–5 shows the completed first and second pages of a return for an organization having less than $10,000 of gross income and a very small tax. The circled numbers refer to the comments below.

1. Notice the nature of the unrelated income—the operation of a small thrift shop. While the net income from this activity will be used for exempt purposes, the activity of operating a thrift shop does not directly contribute toward the exempt purposes of the church. The thrift shop is operated by paid employees, not volunteers.

2. In addition to the direct expenses, indirect expenses and overhead (such as heat, light, building costs) can also be deducted to determine taxable income.

3. There is a specific deduction of $1,000 for all exempt organizations.

4. An organization with gross income of $1,000 or more is still required to file Form 990-T even if taxable income after deductions is zero.

5. Organizations pay tax at the regular corporate rates.

6. This section of the form is not applicable to exempt organizations of the type we have been discussing in this book. This is for trusts that are treated as though they were "individuals."

7. Organizations are required to pay estimated unrelated business taxes quarterly. Organizations are subject to penalties for underpayment of these taxes if they are not paid on a timely basis.

27.4   CONCLUSION

All exempt organizations must be aware of the requirements of federal tax laws. All exempt organizations except churches and organizations with gross receipts of $25,000 or less must file tax returns with the Internal Revenue Service, and even churches and very small organizations may have to file returns under certain circumstances. For many, this is a traumatic experience because the principal forms that are used—Form 990, Form 990-PF, and Form 990-T—are written in technical language that requires expert knowledge. With few exceptions, exempt organizations are well advised to obtain competent tax advice not only at the time these returns are prepared, but also throughout the year as potential tax issues arise.

EXHIBIT 27–5

Form **990-T**	**Exempt Organization Business Income Tax Return** (and proxy tax under section 6033(e))	OMB No. 1545-0687

Department of the Treasury
Internal Revenue Service

For calendar year 1993 or other tax year beginning _____, 1993, and ending _____, 19____
▶ **See separate instructions.**

1993

A ☐ Check box if address changed	Name of organization	D **Employer identification number** (Employees' trust, see instructions for Block D)
B Exempt under section ☒ 501( )(**3**) or ☐ 408(e)	**Please Print or Type**	**The First Inter-Faith Church**	**13 ¦ 1211947**

Number, street, and room or suite no. (If a P.O. box, see page 4 of instructions.)

632 Main Street

City or town, state, and ZIP code

Spring Valley, NY 10799

C Book value of all assets at end of year

E **Unrelated business activity codes** (See instructions for Block E)

5930

F Group exemption number (see instructions for Block F) ▶

G Check type of organization . . . . ▶ ☒ Corporation ☐ Trust ☐ Section 401(a) trust ☐ Section 408(a) trust

H Describe the organization's primary unrelated business activity. (see instructions for Block H)
  Thrift Shop ①

I During the tax year, was the corporation a subsidiary in an affiliated group or a parent–subsidiary controlled group? . . ▶ ☐ Yes ☒ No
  If "Yes," enter the name and identifying number of the parent corporation. (see instructions for Block I) ▶

Part I	**Unrelated Trade or Business Income**		(A) Income	(B) Expenses	(C) Net
1a	Gross receipts or sales _____ 9,670				
b	Less returns and allowances _____ c Balance ▶	1c	9,670		
2	Cost of goods sold (Schedule A, line 7)	2			
3	Gross profit (subtract line 2 from line 1c)	3	9,670		
4a	Capital gain net income (attach Schedule D)	4a			
b	Net gain (loss) (Form 4797, Part II, line 20)(attach Form 4797)	4b			
c	Capital loss deduction for trusts	4c			
5	Income (loss) from partnerships (attach statement) . . .	5			
6	Rent income (Schedule C)	6			
7	Unrelated debt–financed income (Schedule E)	7			
8	Interest, annuities, royalties, and rents from controlled organizations (Schedule F)	8			
9	Investment income of a section 501(c)(7), (9), (17), or (20) organization (Schedule G)	9			
10	Exploited exempt activity income (Schedule I)	10			
11	Advertising income (Schedule J)	11			
12	Other income (see instructions for line 12—attach schedule) .	12			
13	TOTAL (add lines 3 through 12)	13	9,670	0	9,670

Part II	**Deductions Not Taken Elsewhere** (See instructions for limitations on deductions.) (Except for contributions, deductions must be directly connected with the unrelated business income.)		
14	Compensation of officers, directors, and trustees (Schedule K)	14	
15	Salaries and wages	15	
16	Repairs and maintenance	16	
17	Bad debts	17	
18	Interest (attach schedule)	18	
19	Taxes and licenses	19	
20	Charitable contributions (see instructions for limitation rules)	20	
21	Depreciation (attach Form 4562)	21		
22	Less depreciation claimed on Schedule A and elsewhere on return . . .	22a		22b	
23	Depletion	23	
24	Contributions to deferred compensation plans	24	
25	Employee benefit programs	25	
26	Excess exempt expenses (Schedule I)	26	
27	Excess readership costs (Schedule J)	27	
28	Other deductions (attach schedule) . . . . ②	28	4,135
29	TOTAL DEDUCTIONS (add lines 14 through 28)	29	4,135
30	Unrelated business taxable income before net operating loss deduction (subtract line 29 from line 13).	30	5,535
31	Net operating loss deduction	31	
32	Unrelated business taxable income before specific deduction (subtract line 31 from line 30) . . .	32	5,535
33	Specific deduction . . . . ③ .	33	1,000
34	Unrelated business taxable income (subtract line 33 from line 32). If line 33 is greater than line 32, enter the smaller of zero or line 32 . . . . ④ .	34	4,535

For Paperwork Reduction Act Notice, see page 1 of separate instructions.   84–1128480   Form **990–T** (1993)

1ST_IFC.P93

EXHIBIT 27–5 *Continued.*

EIN 13-1211947

Form 990–T (1993)   Page **2**

Part III **Tax Computation**		
35	Amount from line 34 (unrelated business taxable income)	**35**	4,535

36 Organizations Taxable as Corporations (see instructions for tax computation)
Controlled group members (sections 1561 and 1563)—Check here ☐ and:

a Enter your share of the $50,000, $25,000, and $9,925,000 taxable income brackets (in that order):

(1) |$ _____ | (2) |$ _____ | (3) |$ _____ |

b Enter organization's share of: (1) additional 5% tax (not more than $11,750) . . |$ _____ |

(2) additional 3% tax (not more than $100,000). . . . . |$ _____ |

c Income tax on the amount on line 35 and any other tax. . . . ⑤ . . . . . | **36c** | 680 |

37 Trusts Taxable at Trust Rates (see instructions for tax computation) Income tax on the amount
on line 35 from: ☐ Tax rate schedule or ☐ Schedule D (Form 1041) and any other
tax ▶ | **37** | ⑥ |

Part IV **Tax and Payments**			
38a	Foreign tax credit (corporations attach Form 1118; trusts attach Form 1116) .	**38a**	
b	Other credits. (see instructions).	**38b**	
c	General business credit—Check if from:		
	☐ Form 3800 or ☐ Form (specify) ▶ _____	**38c**	
d	Credit for prior year minimum tax (attach Form 8801 or 8827)	**38d**	
39	Total (add lines 38a through 38d).	**39**	0
40	Subtract line 39 from line 36c or line 37.	**40**	680
41	Recapture taxes. Check if from: ☐ Form 4255 ☐ Form 8611	**41**	
42a	Alternative minimum tax _____ b Environmental tax _____	**42c**	
43	Total tax (add lines 40, 41, 42c)	**43**	680
44	Payments: a 1992 overpayment credited to 1993	**44a**	
b	1993 estimated tax payments . . . . ⑦ .	**44b**	700
c	Tax deposited with Form 7004 or Form 2758	**44c**	
d	Foreign organizations—Tax paid or withheld at source (see instructions) . .	**44d**	
e	Other credits and payments (see instructions)	**44e**	
45	Total credits and payments (add lines 44a through 44e)	**45**	700
46	Estimated tax penalty (see the instructions on page 2). Check ▶ ☐ if Form 2220 is attached	**46**	
47	Tax due—If line 45 is less than the total of lines 43 and 46, enter amount owed . . . . . . ▶	**47**	
48	Overpayment—If line 45 is larger than the total of lines 43 and 46, enter amount overpaid . . . . ▶	**48**	20
49	Enter the amount of line 48 you want: Credited to 1994 estimated tax ▶ _____ Refunded ▶	**49**	20

Part V **Statements Regarding Certain Activities and Other Information** (See instructions on page 9.)		Yes	No
1	At any time during the 1993 calendar year, did the organization have an interest in or a signature or other authority over a financial account in a foreign country (such as a bank account, securities account, or other financial account)?		X
	If "Yes," the organization may have to file Form TD F 90–22.1. If "Yes," enter the name of the foreign country here ▶ N/A		
2	Was the organization the grantor of, or transferor to, a foreign trust that existed during the current tax year, whether or not the organization had any beneficial interest in it?		X
	If "Yes," the organization may have to file Forms 3520, 3520–A, or 926.		
3	Enter the amount of tax-exempt interest received or accrued during the tax year ▶ $ 0		

SCHEDULE A—COST OF GOODS SOLD (See instructions on page 9.)
Method of inventory valuation (specify) ▶ N/A

1	Inventory at beginning of year . .	**1**	N/A	6	Inventory at end of year	**6**		
2	Purchases	**2**		7	Cost of goods sold. Subtract line 6			
3	Cost of labor	**3**			from line 5. (Enter here and on			
4a	Additional section 263A costs				line 2, Part I.)	**7**	0	
	(attach schedule)	**4a**		8	Do the rules of section 263A (with respect to		Yes	No
b	Other costs (attach schedule) . .	**4b**			property produced or acquired for resale) apply			
5	TOTAL—Add lines 1 through 4b .	**5**	0		to the organization?			

The books are in care of ▶ The Organization   Telephone number ▶ (914) 521-6700

Please Sign Here	Under penalties of perjury, I declare that I have examined this return, including accompanying schedules and statements, and to the best of my knowledge and belief, it is true, correct, and complete. Declaration of preparer (other than taxpayer) is based on all information of which preparer has any knowledge.		
	▶ _____ Signature of officer or fiduciary	Date _____	▶ _____ Title

Paid Preparer's Use Only	Preparer's signature ▶	Date	Check if self-employed ▶ ☐	Preparer's social security number
	Firm's name (or yours, if self-employed) and address ▶		E.I. No. ▶	
			ZIP code ▶	

1ST_IFC.P93

C H A P T E R 28

State Compliance Requirements

28.1 Registration for Organizations Soliciting Funds
28.2 Registration for Organizations Having Assets within the State
28.3 Individual State Requirements

In addition to federal filing requirements, most states also require not-for-profit organizations to register with and submit financial reports to one or more agencies of the state government. Some counties and cities have similar requirements. These requirements usually fall into one or more of three areas:

1. Registration requirements for organizations soliciting funds within the state.

2. Registration of not-for-profit organizations (including trusts) holding property in the state.

3. Registration of organizations doing business in the state.

These requirements are basically concerned with legal matters and may vary significantly from state to state. If an organization has operations in, or intends to do business in, a state, it should consult with its tax advisors to get competent advice. The comments that follow in this chapter are intended only as an overview of the compliance reporting requirements as related to the first two areas listed. This overview will give the reader an indication of the financial reporting and, in some cases, the auditing requirements of various states. Because the laws governing not-for-profit organizations' compliance requirements are complex and rapidly changing, the following comments should not in any sense be considered as a substitute for consultations with competent legal and accounting advisors.

28.1 REGISTRATION FOR ORGANIZATIONS SOLICITING FUNDS

A number of states have laws requiring not-for-profit organizations to register with a regulatory agency (or obtain operating licenses or permits) prior to soliciting any funds within the state. Most states make no distinction between resident and nonresident organizations and, in most instances, an organization soliciting funds by mail or through advertisements would have to register, even though it has no office or employees in that state.

This registration often requires yearly renewals, as well as a requirement that an annual financial report be filed. Since 1982, most states accept a copy of IRS Form 990 as the basic financial statement. Form 990 EZ has not gained wide acceptance among the states. The financial statements included in this report must sometimes include an opinion of an independent public accountant and, in some instances, the state will even specify the accounting principles to be followed. Where an organization must provide this type of information, particularly where the organization is not a resident in that state, considerable planning is required. These annual reports are usually due between three and six months after the end of the organization's fiscal year.

Most states exempt certain classifications of not-for-profit organizations from their registration and reporting requirements. These exemptions are usually limited to one or more of the following organizations:

Category 1. Religious organizations.

Category 2. Educational institutions, meeting certain standards.

Category 3. Not-for-profit hospitals.

Category 4. Organizations that solicit funds solely from within their existing membership.

Category 5. Organizations that solicit funds for the relief of any individual specified by name at the time of solicitation, and all or substantially all of the contributions are turned over to the beneficiary for his or her use.

Category 6. Organizations that do not actually raise or receive more than a specified amount, or do not receive contributions from more than a specified number of persons, and where no paid fund raisers are involved, and, in some states, where the organization has no paid staff.

These exemption categories are referred to by number in this chapter's section on individual state requirements. Organizations in Categories 2 and 3 usually are required to file a copy of the fiscal report filed with other state agencies such as the department of education or health.

There are other types of exemptions as well, and their applicability depends upon a number of factors, including dollar limitations on contributions and/or total income, use of professional fund raisers, etc. Most states require that organizations register if they use professional fund raisers, no matter how small the contributions received. For example, in New York not-for-profit organizations receiving annual contributions of less than $10,000 are not required to register at all (providing no professional fund raisers are used), although an annual affidavit must be filed. When more than $10,000 in contributions has been received, but before total income exceeds $150,000, a simplified form of reporting is required. When more than $150,000 has been received, a much more detailed, audited report is necessary.

28.2 REGISTRATION FOR ORGANIZATIONS HAVING ASSETS WITHIN THE STATE

In addition to the registration of organizations soliciting funds, some states also have laws requiring all not-for-profit organizations or charitable trusts to register with a state agency if they have assets or are residents within the state, even if they do not solicit funds. Each organization must be careful to comply with these requirements. Sometimes a different agency of the state is involved, and the reporting requirements may be different from the requirements under the solicitation law.

As with the requirements for organizations soliciting funds, an organization may be required both to register initially and to file an annual report. The principal interest of the state is the proper administration and disposition of assets held by the organization.

Moreover, the Internal Revenue Code and regulations provide that every private foundation is required to submit a copy of its Form 990-PF to the attorney general of each state in which it conducts activities. The intent of this requirement is to encourage state officials to oversee the activities of this type of exempt organization.

28.3 INDIVIDUAL STATE REQUIREMENTS

Summarized in this section are some of the basic solicitation requirements of each state with respect to registration and report filing of charitable and not-for-profit organizations and trusts. (Exemption reference numbers are keyed to the listing given above.) This summary should not be considered all-inclusive or authoritative; its purpose is simply to provide a brief outline of requirements as of the date of publication. Even as this book was in progress, a number of states had statutes pending which, if adopted, will change existing laws.

Alabama

Alabama enacted the "Alabama Nonprofit Corporation Act" in 1984. There are, however, no known requirements for solicitation registration.

Alaska

No statutory registration requirements for soliciting.

Arizona

All organizations which solicit must register with the Secretary of State no later than 3 days after any solicitations except for the following:

1. Categories 1, 2, 3.
2. Various other specific types of entities.

Annual reports are required to maintain initial registration.

Arkansas

All organizations are required to register with the Attorney General prior to soliciting funds, except for the following:

1. Categories 1, 2, 3, 4.
2. Category 6, with limitation of $10,000.

An annual report must be filed to maintain registration.

California

All organizations which solicit are required to register with the Attorney General.

An annual report must also be filed. In addition, most cities or counties in California have statutes regulating charitable solicitations.

Colorado

No statutory requirements for soliciting.

Connecticut

All organizations are required to register annually with the Department of Consumer Protection prior to soliciting funds except for the following:

1. Categories 1, 2, 3.
2. Category 6, with limitation of $25,000.

The annual report must be audited by an independent public accountant if gross revenue is $100,000 or more or if a professional fund raiser is used.

Delaware

No known requirements for solicitation registration.

District of Columbia

All organizations soliciting contributions are required to register annually with the Department of Consumer and Regulatory Affairs except for the following:

1. Categories 1, 4.
2. Category 6, with limitation of $1,500.
3. American Red Cross.

An annual report must be filed at the time of registration and within 30 days after the end of each annual licensing period.

Florida

All organizations soliciting contributions must register with the Department of State prior to soliciting funds and annually thereafter, except:

1. Categories 1, 2, 4, 5.
2. Category 6, with limitation of $25,000.

Georgia

All organizations are required to register with the Secretary of State prior to soliciting funds, except for the following:

1. Categories 1, 2, 4, 5.
2. Category 6, with limitation of $25,000.
3. Various other specified types of entities.

The annual report must be audited by an independent certified public accountant if contributions are in excess of $500,000.

Hawaii

All organizations are required to register annually with the Director of the Department of Regulatory Agencies prior to soliciting funds, except for the following:

1. Categories 1, 2, 3, 4, 5.
2. Category 6, with limitation of $4,000 or 10 contributors.
3. Various other specified types of entities.

Idaho

No known registration requirements for solicitation purposes, although the Attorney General is empowered to supervise and examine charitable organizations.

Illinois

All organizations are required to register with the Attorney General prior to soliciting funds, except for the following:

1. Categories 1, 2, 4, 5.
2. Category 6, with limitation of $10,000.
3. Various other specified types of entities.

The annual report must be audited by an independent certified public accountant if contributions are in excess of $100,000, or if paid fund raisers are used.

Indiana

No known charitable solicitation requirements.

Iowa

All organizations are required to register annually with the Attorney General prior to soliciting funds.

Kansas

All organizations are required to register with the Secretary of State prior to soliciting funds, except for the following:

1. Categories 1, 2, 3, 4, 5.
2. Category 6, with limitation of $10,000.
3. Various other specified types of entities.

An annual report must be filed by organizations receiving contributions in excess of $10,000 or which use paid fund raisers, and the report must be audited by an independent certified public accountant if contributions exceed $100,000.

Kentucky

No known charitable solicitation requirements.

Louisiana

No known charitable solicitation requirements, but the Attorney General is empowered to request certain financial information to enforce the laws against deceptive practices.

Maine

All organizations are required to register with the Secretary of State prior to soliciting funds, except for the following:

1. Categories, 1, 2, 3, 4, 5.
2. Category 6, with limitation of $10,000 or 10 contributors.

An annual report must also be filed.

Maryland

All organizations are required to register annually with the Secretary of State prior to soliciting funds.

The annual report must be audited by an independent certified public accountant if gross income is $200,000 or more.

Massachusetts

All organizations are required to register annually with the Division of Public Charities prior to soliciting funds, except for the following:

1. Category 1.
2. Category 6, with limitation of $5,000 or 10 contributors.

An annual report must be filed (by all public charities except Category 1) and it must be audited if gross receipts are $100,000 or more.

Michigan

All organizations are required to register with the Attorney General prior to soliciting funds, except for the following:

1. Categories 1, 2, 3, 4, 5.
2. Category 6, with limitation of $8,000.
3. Various other specified types of entities.

The annual report must be audited by an independent certified public accountant if public support is in excess of $100,000.

Minnesota

All organizations are required to register annually with the attorney general prior to soliciting except for the following:

1. Categories 1, 2, 5.
2. Category 4 (provided no professional fund raiser is engaged).
3. Category 6, with limitation of $25,000.

The annual report must be audited by a certified public accountant if gross contributions exceed $100,000.

Mississippi

All organizations are required to register with the Secretary of State prior to soliciting except:

1. Categories 1, 2, 4, 5.
2. Category 6 with limitation of $4,000.
3. Various other specific types of entities.

Missouri

No known requirements for solicitation registration.

Montana

No known solicitation requirements.

Nebraska

All organizations are required to register annually with the Secretary of State prior to soliciting funds, except for those organizations soliciting solely within their home county or for "churches and like charitable organizations" in the immediately adjoining counties where part of their membership resides.

An annual financial report must be filed by all voluntary health and welfare organizations within six months after the end of the fiscal year.

Nevada

No known solicitation requirements.

New Hampshire

No known solicitation requirements.

New Jersey

All organizations are required to register annually with the Attorney General prior to soliciting funds, except for the following:

1. Categories 1, 2, 4, 5.
2. Category 6, with limitation of $10,000.
3. Various other specified types of entities.

The annual report must be audited by an independent public accountant if contributions are in excess of $50,000.

New Mexico

All organizations are required to register with the Attorney General before soliciting except:

1. Categories 1, 2.
2. Category 6, with $2,500 limitation.

New York

All organizations are required to register with the Department of State prior to soliciting except:

1. Categories 1, 2, 5.
2. Category 4, limited to certain enumerated types of organizations.
3. Category 6, with limitation of $25,000.
4. Various other specified types of entities.

An annual report must be filed with the Department of State, with a copy to the Attorney General. If total income received is in excess of $150,000, or if paid fund raisers are used, a comprehensive report audited by an independent accountant must be filed.

North Carolina

All organizations are required to register with the Department of Human Resources prior to soliciting funds, except for the following:

1. Categories 1, 2, 3.
2. Category 6, with limitation of $10,000.
3. Various other specific types of organizations.

The annual report must be audited by an independent public accountant if total support and revenue exceed $250,000.

North Dakota

All organizations are required to register with the Secretary of State prior to soliciting funds, except for Category 1.

Ohio

All organizations are required to register with the Attorney General prior to soliciting funds, except for the following:

1. Categories 1, 2, 4.

Oklahoma

All organizations are required to register annually with the State Auditor and Inspector prior to soliciting funds, except for:

1. Categories 1, 2, 4, and 5.
2. Category 6 with limitation of $10,000.

Oregon

No known solicitation registration requirements.

Pennsylvania

All organizations are required to register annually with the Department of State prior to soliciting funds, except for the following:

1. Categories 1, 2, 3.
2. Various other specified types of entities.

The annual report must be audited by an independent public accountant if gross contributions are over $100,000. If contributions are between $25,000 and $100,000, the financial statements must be reviewed or audited.

Rhode Island

All organizations are required to register annually with the Department of Business Regulation prior to soliciting funds, except for the following:

1. Categories 1, 2, 3, 4, 5.
2. Category 6, with limitation of $3,000 or 10 contributors.
3. Various other specified types of entities.

South Carolina

All organizations are required to register with the Secretary of State prior to soliciting funds, except for the following:

1. Categories 1, 2, 3, 4, 5.
2. Category 6, with limitation of $2,000 or 10 contributors.

South Dakota

No requirements for not-for-profit organizations to register or report for solicitation purposes.

Tennessee

All organizations are required to register with the Secretary of State prior to soliciting funds, except for the following:

1. Categories 1, 2.
2. Category 6, with limitation of $5,000.

The annual report must be audited by an independent public accountant or accompanied by Form 990.

Texas

There is no requirement that organizations register for solicitation purposes.

Utah

All organizations are required to register with the Department of Commerce before soliciting funds except for:

1. Categories 1, 2, 4, 5.

Vermont

No known requirements to register for solicitation purposes.

Virginia

All organizations are required to register annually with the Department of Agriculture and Consumer Services prior to soliciting funds, except for the following:

1. Categories 1, 2, 3, 4, 5.
2. Category 6, with limitation of $5,000.
3. Various other specified types of entities.

The annual report must be audited by an independent public accountant.

Washington

All organizations are required to register with the Secretary of State except:

1. Category 1.
2. Category 6, with limitation of $5,000.

West Virginia

All organizations are required to register annually with the Secretary of State prior to soliciting funds, except for the following:

1. Categories 1, 2, 3, 4, 5.
2. Category 6, with limitation of $10,000 or 10 contributors.
3. Various other specified types of entities.

The annual report must be audited by an independent public accountant if contributions are in excess of $50,000.

Wisconsin

All charitable organizations are required to register with the Department of Regulation and Licensing prior to soliciting funds, except for the following:

1. Categories 1, 2, 4, 5.
2. Category 6, with limitation of $5,000.
3. Various other specified types of entities.

The annual report must be audited by an independent certified public accountant if solicited contributions are in excess of $100,000 or if a paid individual performed fund raising.

Wyoming

No known requirements for solicitation registration.

CHAPTER 29

Audits of
Federally-Funded Programs

29.1 BASIC REQUIREMENTS

In 1990, the Office of Management and Budget (OMB) issued Circular A-133, *Audits of Institutions of Higher Education and Other Nonprofit Institutions* (the Circular). The Circular establishes the requirements for organization-wide audits of financial statements and of compliance with laws and regulations, to be performed normally annually,[1] for organizations

---

[1] Annual audits are required if the organization's financial statements are audited annually (see PCIE Statement #6—Question 71), if the financial statements are audited every other year, then biennial audits of federal awards are permitted.

EXHIBIT 29–1   Audit thresholds.

Federal Awards Recorded as Revenue	Single Program	More Than One Program
	Organization-wide or program audit at the organization's option	A-133 audit
$100,000*		
	Organization-wide or program audit(s) at the organization's option	
$25,000**		
	No audit requirement, but records must be available	

* - Threshold probably changing to $250,000 (see 29.4)
** - Threshold probably changing to $100,000 (see 29.4)

receiving $25,000 or more in federal funds in a given year.[2] Audits can be performed on federal programs standing alone or on the organization as a whole ("single audit"), depending upon the amount of federal funds recorded as revenue[3] in a given year and upon the number of federal programs run by the organization (see Exhibit 29–1).

(a) Historical Context

In response to criticism from the General Accounting Office in the 1970s, which cited a laxity of control over not-for-profits' use of taxpayers' money, OMB issued attachments to Circulars A-110 (for not-for-profit organizations) and A-102 (for state and local governments) that tried to establish uniform audit requirements for organizations receiving federal funds. Unfortunately, these attachments did not mandate specific procedures or reporting to be followed and were enforced with differing levels of zeal by different federal agencies. Meanwhile, as the result of a small number of highly publicized problems in the not-for-profit sector, the public and Congress began to bring further pressure

[2] At this writing, this and other thresholds are under review and may change.
[3] Although the Circular itself uses the language "federal funds received", PCIE Statement #6, Question #7, clarified that this amount should be determined using the revenue recognition method normally used by the organization. So, for organizations reporting on the cash basis in their external financial reports, this amount would be the amounts of federal funds actually received. For organizations reporting externally on the accrual basis, it would be the amount recorded as revenue, regardless of the amount actually received.

for accountability by not-for-profit organizations, particularly those receiving and using federal funds.

In addition, it became quite clear that the audit process mandated by Circulars A-102 and A-110 was inefficient and insufficiently implemented by federal agencies. Consequently, Congress passed the Single Audit Act (the Act) in 1984. The Act's principal aims were to eliminate the excessive duplication of effort built into the then current audit process and to make more uniform the reports required by different federal agencies. OMB was charged with implementing the requirements of the Act and it responded with Circular A-128 (A-128), *Audits of State and Local Governments*. The Act and A-128 pertained only to audits of state and local governments. However, OMB made a commitment to Congress to extend the concept to nongovernmental entities receiving federal funds. The result was A-133.

(b)   The Single Audit Concept

Prior to the Act and A-133, audits of federally-funded programs were carried out on a grant-by-grant basis. To an organization receiving multiple awards covering different programs, this often meant that auditors representing each of the funding agencies would shuttle in and out of the organization's doors, each monitoring its own program in its own way. The consequent repetitiveness and confusion over standards and methods required basic changes in how these audits were performed. The Act and both circulars approach the accountability problem from the premise that the organization receiving funding is a single entity, is governed by a single Board, and has a unified management structure. As such, much of the organization's internal control structure and many of the applicable laws and regulations are common to its various programs and, therefore, can be audited in a single, more efficient effort.

(c)   Objectives

Even though A-133 anticipates that this audit will be coordinated with the audit of an organization's financial statements (and possibly performed by the same auditor), the objectives of the two audits are not the same.

Financial Statement Audits

An audit of an organization's financial statements, performed in accordance with generally accepted auditing standards (GAAS), requires that the auditor gather audit evidence sufficient to express an opinion as to whether the financial statements present fairly the financial position and results of operations when taken as a whole. Such an audit usually results in a single report issued by the auditor. This report confines itself to the amounts and disclosures expressed in the financial statements and whether or not they are fairly stated. It is concerned with the numbers reported—not with how they were created. Although separate reports on an organization's internal or administrative controls are often issued along with this report, these additional reports are not a required part of a GAAS audit.

A-133 Audits

An A-133 audit, on the other hand, is much more concerned with how the numbers were created than with the numbers themselves. Although the auditor is required to issue a report on the financial statements and the schedule of federal awards, the auditor must also report on the internal control structure and on the organization's compliance with a wide variety of laws and regulations that we will discuss in more detail later in this chapter. This focus on process rather than results will be unfamiliar to many not-for-profit organizations.

(d) Rationale

There is no question that many view these expanded audit requirements as an unfair and unreasonable burden. They cost money and they absorb a great deal of time. Sometimes, the additional cost can be charged to the grant or contract being audited as either a direct or indirect cost. There are many who feel that even if the cost is partially or wholly defrayed, the audit distracts management's attention from administering programs that are the organization's reason for being.

As a practical matter, the administrative costs of these audits can be viewed as a cost of doing business with the federal government—the government awards the funds and an audit is part of their price. However, the not-for-profit sector should not forget what these requirements reflect. These audits are an outgrowth of the 1980s call for increased accountability in the not-for-profit sector. This call was prompted in part by the public's increasing desire for control over its charitable dollar and by the public's reaction to management problems they perceived within a very small number of high-profile organizations.

In some ways, we in the not-for-profit sector have brought this public relations problem upon ourselves. We have worn a halo of respectability granted by our charitable intent for so long that some of us have lost sight of the need to continually convince the donating public that we are worthy of the trust that they have put in us through their donations, both directly and through tax dollars.

We have welcomed many of the changes in the sector in the last twenty years. Many of them have resulted in not-for-profit organizations that are more efficiently and more professionally managed than at any time in the past. We need to recognize that as part of that increasing professionalism, we should be welcoming the need for accountability and should look forward to the opportunity to demonstrate our credibility.

29.2   REQUIREMENTS AND DEFINITIONS

A-133 audits must be performed on any organization that receives $25,000 or more in federal awards in a given year. Federal awards (or federal financial assistance) can take any of a number of forms:

Grants

Cooperative agreements

Loan guarantees

Interest subsidies

Direct appropriations

Contracts

Loans

Property or commodities

Insurance

Other non-cash assistance

Federal financial assistance does not include direct federal assistance to individuals such as through Aid to Families with Dependent Children (AFDC), crop subsidies, Medicaid, or Medicare, nor does it include procurement contracts awarded to not-for-profit organizations as vendors of goods or services to the federal government.

(a)   Pass-Throughs and Subrecipients

Federal awards do not always come directly from a federal agency. Assistance will often be given in bulk to a single organization along with the responsibility for managing the distribution and monitoring of the funds through a network of subrecipients. In such a case, it is the responsibility of the primary recipient to notify each subrecipient that it has received federal funds and what its responsibilities are as a subrecipient of federal financial assistance. These responsibilities are exactly what they would have been had the subrecipient received the assistance directly from the federal agency plus whatever additional requirements the primary recipient decides to impose. The same thresholds and audit requirements apply.

A primary recipient assumes responsibility to monitor the compliance of its subrecipients with the administrataive and audit requirements of A-133 and with the other requirements imposed by the grant, contract, or other agreement covering the assistance. In order to accomplish this, the primary recipient must have an internal control structure in place to accomplish this monitoring function. This *must* include collecting and reviewing the applicable A-133 reports completed on subrecipients by their independent auditors. The monitoring function may also have to include further procedures performed by the primary recipient depending upon the complexity of the subrecipient structure. If you are faced with such a situation, open discussion with the program officers and inspector general at your funding agency and the primary recipient can help you plan, in advance, how to satisfy the monitoring requirements of such a grant or contract.[4]

(b)   Major and Nonmajor Programs

Under A-133, all "major programs" must be tested for compliance. A major program is defined as either an individual award or group of awards with the same Catalog of Federal Domestic Assistance[5] (CFDA) number for which total annual expenditures of federal funds are the larger of three percent of total federal funds expended or $100,000. Expenditures should include only those of federal funds. The organization's own *matching* funds should be excluded. The CFDA number is important because an organization may receive funding, either pass-through or direct, from different sources supporting the same program. Grants with the same CFDA number should be grouped together for the purposes of A-133 audits. All awards made under either student financial aid (SFA) or research and development (R&D) programs should also be combined and must each be identified collectively in the Schedule of Federal Awards as these two categories are, by definition, considered separate major programs.

For the purposes of calculating the 3 percent threshold for determining a major program, loans, loan guarantees, and insurance programs are ignored. Non-cash awards, including commodity and property awards, should be recorded at fair value. (As this book is written, the government is close to proposing a change in the definition of major program.)

---

[4] Additional guidance can be found in ¶ 3.30–3.41 of SOP 92-9.
[5] The *Catalog of Federal Domestic Assistance* is published by the General Accounting Office of the U.S. government. It lists all domestic assistance programs and assigns a unique number to each. The identifying number has the format XX.XXX.

(c)   The Schedule of Federal Awards

A-133 requires that the Schedule of Federal Awards (see Exhibit 29–2 for an example) cover the same period as the financial statements that it accompanies. The basis of accounting should be consistent with that used in the organization's federal grant reports which means that the schedule may not be consistent with the organization's financial statements. In this case the Schedule should be reconciled to the financial statements. The basis of accounting should be disclosed in a footnote to the schedule. The schedule must show (at a minimum) the following:

- Each major program separately (except for student financial aid and research and development which are each collectively considered one major program), noting the program or grant title, that the program is major, CFDA number, and federal agency.
- Other major awards not having a CFDA number (such as grants from the U.S. Agency for International Development).
- Total federal expenditures for each federal award program (see note above).
- Total federal expenditures for all nonmajor programs (if any) together.
- Total federal award expenditures.
- Federal noncash assistance should be included at its fair market value at the date received.
- Amounts of federal loans, loans subject to federal guarantees, and insurance programs should be disclosed, but not included in total federal expenditures.
- Federal funds passed through a nonfederal organization should be so identified, including the name of the awarding organization, the awarding organization's identifying number, and the CFDA number.

Some additional information, though not required under A-133, may be useful, such as:

- Federal program revenue.
- Program or grant periods and/or total granted amounts.
- Opening and closing advanced (asset) or deferred (liability) balances.
- Nonfederal expenditures used for matching, although this should be clearly separated from the federal funds expended. Note that

EXHIBIT 29–2 Sample Schedule of Federal Awards.

SAMPLE NOT-FOR-PROFIT ORGANIZATION
Schedule for Federal Awards
For the Year Ended June 30, 19XX

Federal Grantor/Pass-Through Grantor/Program Title	Federal CFDA Number	Agency or Pass-Through Number	Federal Expenditures	
U.S. Department of Health and Human Services				
Headstart	93.600	05CH5560/07	$156,327	Note A
	93.600	05CH5560/08	150,000	
			306,327 *	
Pass-through from State Dept. of Human Services—Community Services Block Grant	93.792	K1578	356,456 *	Note B
Weatherization	93.818	K4599		
			662,783	
U.S. Agency for International Development Biden-Pell Grant Program	None	OTR-0230-G-SS-9192-00	246,123 *	Note C
Department of Education Pass-through from City Department of Education	84.151	KLHN45689	78,000	
			$986,906	

* Denotes a major program.

Note A: Although not required, this breakout by grant will facilitate review and make the report more meaningful to users.
Note B: A program can be open without monies having been received or expended during the period under audit. Such programs should be included in the schedule.
Note C: CFDA numbers will not necessarily be available for all programs.

539

the organization's accounting records must be able to segregate the use of federal and nonfederal funds.

- Federal funds passed through to subrecipients.
- Individual SFA or R&D grants as components of the total.
- For organizations with loan programs, the opening and closing outstanding balances along with the new and matured loan activity during the year.
- Matching contributions raised.

29.3   RESPONSIBILITIES OF THE RECEIVING ORGANIZATION

By accepting any donations from individuals or organizations that have attached restrictions to the donation, an organization incurs a legal and moral obligation to adhere to the restrictions imposed by the donor. The clear alternative is not to accept the donation. A federal agency is no different in this respect. The receipt of federal funds in any of the forms noted earlier, implicitly acknowledges acceptance of grant imposed responsibilities. Ignoring or inadequately adhering to these requirements may cause the agency to refuse further funding or even require the return of the federal funds granted.

The responsibilities assumed by the organization fall into two categories, both of which will be reported on by the A-133 auditor, compliance with laws and regulations, and the maintenance of an internal control structure sufficient to ensure that such compliance takes place and the funds granted to the organization are adequately safeguarded.

(a)   Compliance with Laws and Regulations

An exhaustive analysis of the requirements imposed on an organization receiving federal funds is beyond the scope of this book. We will give general background on the kinds of requirements that an organization may find itself subject to and offer some direction for how to go about determining conclusively what the organization must do in meeting the requirements imposed on it.

The A-133 auditor will, in most cases, issue three or four reports on compliance, two or three of which pertain specifically to compliance with the requirements imposed by the receipt of federal funding. The first of these is a report on compliance with the so-called "general requirements." The auditor performs certain specific procedures (in this case those laid out in the *Compliance Supplement for Audits of Institutions of*

Higher Learning and Other Nonprofit Institutions published by OMB) and, in the report, states what he or she has found. The second is an opinion on the organization's compliance with the "specific requirements" of each of its major programs. The third that might be issued is a report on the organization's compliance with nonmajor program transactions. This report is only issued if such transactions have been tested by the auditor.

General Requirements

General requirements are those imposed on the organization simply by virtue of the fact that it has received federal funds. They are not associated with a particular program. These include:

- *Prohibitions against Political Activity.* The use of federal funds to support political activity of any kind is prohibited by the Hatch Act and the Intergovernmental Personnel Act of 1970. (Note also that lobbying activities by tax exempt organizations is very strictly limited and can result in the loss of exempt status.)

- *Davis-Bacon Act Compliance.* This act requires that mechanics and laborers working for contractors on federally-funded construction projects be paid regionally-prevailing wages.

- *Civil Rights Compliance.* No person shall be excluded from participation in nor be subject to discrimination in any program funded, in whole or in part, by federal funds because of race, color, national origin, sex, age, or physical impairment.

- *Drug-Free Workplace Act Compliance.* Organizations receiving federal awards must certify that they provide a drug-free workplace.

- *Allowable Costs/Cost Principles.* These principles (described in various OMB circulars) prescribe the direct and indirect costs allowable as costs of federally-funded programs.

- *Cash Management Requirements.* OMB Circular A-110[6] prescribes certain methods for and limitations on receiving federal cash. For instance, there are very strict limitations on the period of time federal funds can be held by an organization prior to disbursement and on how interest earned on those held funds may be treated and used.

- *Federal Financial Reporting.* OMB Circular A-110 prescribes certain periodic standard financial reports for each federal program.

---

[6] OMB Circular A-110 has recently been revised. The new revision is effective for fiscal or program years beginning after January 1, 1994. Be sure to review your own grant or contract documentation to confirm the revised circular's applicability.

- *Administrative Requirements.* Standard OMB circulars prescribe certain administrative requirements that must be followed.

Specific Requirements

Just as general requirements apply to recipients of federal awards regardless of the programs being funded, specific requirements are imposed on the recipient as a consequence of a specific grant or contract. In general, these specific requirements fall into the following categories:

- Expenditures reported were for allowable services.
- Those receiving benefits were eligible to receive them.
- Certain prescriptions on the use of nonfederal funds or resources such as matching requirements, levels of effort, or earmarking limitations, were met.
- Special reporting requirements included in the grant or contract document were met.
- Any special tests and provisions included in the grant or contract document were met.
- Standard and special reports and claims for advances or reimbursement are supported by the organization's books and records.
- Amounts claimed or used for matching were determined in accordance with the applicable OMB circular(s), the Federal Acquisition Regulations, or other grant or contract documentation.

These specific requirements can vary widely from program to program. There are a number of sources that can be tapped to determine what requirements a program is subject to.

- *The Grant or Contract Document.* The first place to look for these requirements is the grant document itself. Because all of these requirements are imposed by contract (as opposed to being a matter of law), they should all be incorporated into the grant or contract either directly or by reference. So read the document first.
- *Standard Attachments to the Grant.* Many grants or contracts will be quite brief, but will refer to standard attachments that are incorporated by reference into every grant issued by a given agency.
- *Compliance Supplement.* The *Compliance Supplement for Audits of Institutions of Higher Learning and Other Nonprofit Institutions,* noted above in the discussion of general requirements, also includes many of the specific requirements that pertain to many of the

largest federally-funded programs. It is organized by federal agency by program.

- *Other OMB Circulars and Publications.* As noted in the section on general requirements, OMB has issued a number of circulars that may be incorporated completely or partially by reference in a grant or contract. Some of the more important circulars are:

  —A-110—*Uniform Requirements for Grants and Agreements with Institutions of Higher Education, Hospitals, and Other Nonprofit Institutions.* This circular was revised in 1994 and includes many of the administrative requirements pertaining to federally-funded programs.

  —A-21—*Cost Principles for Educational Institutions.*

  —A-122—*Cost Principles for Nonprofit Organizations.* These circulars establish the principles to be used in determining the costs of grants and contracts, including the basic principles of allowable and unallowable costs and the mechanics involved in establishing indirect cost rates.

  —The *President's Council on Integrity and Efficiency Position Statement #6—Questions and Answers on OMB Circular A-133* was written and published in response to many of the early questions raised about the implementation of A-133.

(b)   Internal Controls

A-133 requires that the auditor issue two reports, one on the organization's overall internal control structure and a second on the internal control structure surrounding the organization's use of federal funds. Chapter 23 discusses internal accounting controls, their importance, and some of the procedures that an organization can implement in order to protect the organization's assets and help to ensure that the organization's resources are utilized only as authorized by the Board, but also notes that internal controls often extend beyond those matters relating directly to the functions of the accounting and financial departments.

Internal controls, as envisioned by A-133, extend also to ensuring that the requirements imposed by the receipt of federal funds, both general and specific, are complied with. This will include many matters not normally encompassed in accounting or finance. For example, the organization must have a structure in place to ensure that the drug-free workplace and civil-rights requirements are met, and that nonfinancial grant-specific requirements, such as specific use of personnel or qualitative grant progress reports are submitted.

29.4   WHAT TO EXPECT FROM THE AUDIT

(a)   How Is It Different from a Financial Statement Audit?

We noted earlier some of the differences between a financial statement and an A-133 audit. The focus of the two is very different—the former concentrates on financial statement balances and disclosures, while the latter concentrates on internal accounting controls and on compliance with laws and regulations.

By reading the reports issued, one will note that the audit is performed in accordance with Government Auditing Standards (GAS) issued by the General Accounting Office of the United States. These auditing standards incorporate all of GAAS and extend certain of the auditor's reporting and quality control requirements. 1994 revisions to GAS emphasized the importance of compliance with laws and regulations.

In addition, the testing performed by the auditor will be somewhat different in scope and in objective. Items tested will normally extend beyond those usually covered by a financial statement audit to include the nonfinancial specific requirements of all major grants or contracts. In addition, the concept of materiality changes from the financial statement to the A-133 audit. Because tests of compliance focus on whether or not a requirement was followed, not on attempting to support a given account balance, they usually result in either a "did" or "didn't" comply report, regardless of the amounts, if any, that are involved.

(b)   What Will Be Included in the Report?

The report package can consist of as many as nine reports, including the audit opinion usually expressed by the organization's auditor on the organization's financial statements and footnotes, plus additional sections, as follows:

- Report on the Financial Statements (1)
- Report on the Schedule of Federal Awards (3)
- Report on the Entity's Internal Control Structure based upon an Audit Performed in accordance with Government Auditing Standards (2)
- Report on the Entity's Compliance with Laws and Regulations based upon an Audit Performed in accordance with Government Auditing Standards (2)
- Report on the Internal Control Structure over Federal Awards (3)
- Report on Compliance with General Requirements (3)

- Report on Compliance with the Specific Requirements of Major Programs (3)
- Report on Compliance with the Specific Requirements of Non-major Programs (3)
- Report on Illegal Acts (if any are noted) (2)
- Current Findings, Questioned Costs and Recommendations (3)
- Status of Prior Findings and Recommendations (3)
- Management's Comments and Corrective Action Plan (3), (4)

where (1) Required by Generally Accepted Auditing Standards (GAAS); (2) Required by Government Auditing Standards (GAS); (3) Required by OMB Circular A-133; (4) May be submitted by management separately.

This package of reports must be submitted by the organization to the organization's cognizant or oversight agency (a federal agency designated by OMB—usually an organization's primary federal funder) within one month after being received from the auditor, but in no case more than 13 months after the close of the year being reported on.

(c)   What Do I Do if the Auditor Finds Something?

The final package component, Management's Comments and Corrective Action Plan, is usually submitted to the cognizant or oversight agency after the report package and must include a plan of corrective action taken or planned to address the findings and recommendations noted by the auditor.

A-133 requires that all findings of noncompliance and internal control recommendations be reported in some form. Those that are, in the auditor's judgment, material instances of noncompliance,[7] material weaknesses or reportable conditions,[8] must be included by the auditor in the report package. Those findings and recommendations that in the auditor's judgment are not material can be reported in a separate written

---

[7] Whether an instance of noncompliance is material or not must be evaluated by the auditor not only based on quantitative criteria in relation to the program, but also given qualitative considerations.

[8] A reportable condition is a matter coming to the auditor's attention that, in his or her judgment, should be communicated to the audit committee because it represents a significant deficiency in the design or operation of the internal control structure, which could adversely affect the organization's ability to record, process, summarize and report financial data consistent with the assertions of management in the financial statements.

A material weakness is a reportable condition in which the design or operation of one or more of the internal control structure elements does not reduce to a relatively low level the risk that errors or irregularities in amounts that would be material in relation to the financial statements being audited may occur and not be detected within a timely period by employees in the normal course of performing their assigned functions.

communication to management, which must also be forwarded to the cognizant or oversight agency.

29.5   STEPS BEING TAKEN TO IMPROVE THE PROCESS

Although a distinct improvement over its predecessor, implementation problems have been cited with A-133 since its inception. In 1992, OMB issued *President's Council on Integrity and Efficiency Position Statement #6— Questions and Answers on OMB Circular A-133* which clarified some of the early implementation misunderstandings. Then in 1993, OMB issued *Improving the Single Audit Process,* which made several significant recommendations, including increasing the audit and major program thresholds and implementing a risk-based approach to such audits. These recommendations have not been implemented as of this publishing, but may be in the near future.

29.6   CONCLUSION

Whether we welcome it or not, audits of federally-funded programs are now part of the funding landscape. If an organization receives funds from a federal agency, as with any provider or restricted funding, it must adhere to the requirements imposed. An organization can best minimize the trouble and the possibility of adverse consequences by fully understanding the requirements and working with its funding agency and with its auditor to find the most efficient and expeditious way to meet the requirements.

Setting Up and Keeping the Books

Cash Basis Bookkeeping

Bookkeeping is the process of recording in a systematic manner transactions that have taken place. It is that simple. There is nothing mysterious or complicated about bookkeeping. It is simply maintaining records in a manner that will facilitate summarizing them at the end of a period in the form of financial statements. For small cash basis organizations there is little need to know a great deal about accounting theory. Common sense will dictate the records that must be kept. The purpose of this chapter is to discuss bookkeeping in its simplest form—where everything is recorded on a cash basis.[1]

---

[1] Cash basis accounting and financial statements were discussed in Chapters 3 and 11.

30.1   THREE STEPS IN A BOOKKEEPING SYSTEM

There are basically only three steps involved in any bookkeeping system, whether a simple cash system or a more involved accrual basis system. These are:

1. Recording each transaction in a systematic manner when it occurs. In a simple cash basis system only cash transactions are recorded. This recording could be on the checkbook stub or, for organizations with many transactions, it might be an entry in either the "cash disbursement record" or the "cash receipts record." In accrual basis bookkeeping, transactions not involving cash are also recorded.

2. Summarizing transactions so that all "like" transactions are grouped together. This summarizing can be informally done on a simple columnar worksheet, or it can be more formally handled in a system in which transactions are posted to a formal book called the "general ledger." In either case, the objective is to bring "like" transactions together.

3. Preparing financial statements from the "summary" prepared in step 2. These financial statements can be a simple listing of all the major categories in the summary or they can involve some rearrangement of the figures into a more meaningful presentation. In either case, the financial statements are the end product of the bookkeeping system.

Bookkeeping is truly a matter of common sense. With some thought, a simple bookkeeping system can be devised that will meet the needs of a small, cash-basis organization. The best way to illustrate this is by showing how two organizations keep their records. The first is the Cromwell Hills Swim Club, and the second is All Saints Church. The financial statements of both organizations were illustrated in Chapter 11. The Cromwell Hills Swim Club uses the checkbook system of bookkeeping. All Saints Church uses a somewhat more formal system utilizing a cash receipts book, a cash disbursements book, and a general ledger.

30.2   CHECKBOOK SYSTEM

Most people are familiar with the first step in checkbook record keeping since almost everyone keeps a personal checkbook. The process of recording each check and each deposit on the checkbook stub is the first step in a checkbook system of bookkeeping—the step of initially recording the transaction. The checkbook becomes the "book of original entry." It is important to write down enough description on the stub to properly identify what the receipt or disbursement was for. In the case of disbursements, there is usually reference to a vendor's invoice or some supporting documents. It is also important to keep track of receipts by noting whose checks are included in each deposit, perhaps using the back of the check stub if there isn't room on the front. Or, alternatively, this information can be put on the copy of the deposit slip which can then be kept with the bank statement or in a separate file.

Since the checkbook becomes the source of all bookkeeping entries, it is important that all receipts be deposited intact and all disbursements be made by check. This will ensure that a record is established of all transactions. Exhibit 30–1 shows an example of a checkbook stub.

EXHIBIT 30–1   An example of a checkbook stub.

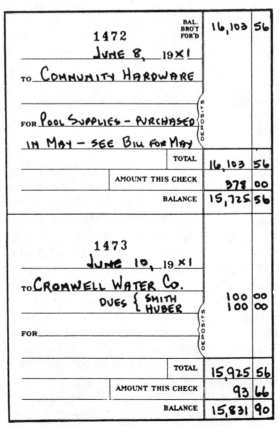

(a) Worksheet Summary

The second step of summarizing all the transactions for the period is almost as easy. Most organizations use a worksheet which has many columns, one for each major category of income or expense. Exhibit 30–2 shows a worksheet for the Cromwell Hills Swim Club.

On this worksheet each month's transactions have been summarized from the checkbook stubs and entered in total. However, each individual transaction could have been entered on this worksheet. If this were done, the worksheet would have been many pages long, depending on the number of transactions. However, if an organization has many similar transactions in a period, the bookkeeper can probably run an adding machine tape of all like items and enter only the total each month from the checkbook stubs, which would be faster than copying each transaction onto the worksheet. Either approach, or even a combination, is appropriate and is a matter of preference.

Notice the reconciliation of the cash account at the bottom of this worksheet. This is the bookkeeper's proof that a mistake hasn't been made in summarizing the transactions on this worksheet. While this is shown for the entire year, in practice the worksheet would be totaled either every month or every time financial statements were prepared. At that point, the bookkeeper would want to prove the cash position in this manner. This reconciliation should not be confused with the bank reconciliation which should be prepared monthly to prove out the checkbook balance.

(b) Payroll Register

The payroll presents a problem because the club must also keep track of the payroll taxes it has to withhold, and it must pay these amounts plus the employer's share to the government, through the local bank. Exhibit 30–3 shows a typical payroll register. A payroll register in a form similar to this one can be obtained from many large stationery stores.

Since the club is following cash basis accounting, no attempt is made to record the liability for the unpaid payroll taxes between the date they were "withheld" and the date they were actually paid.

In our example, employees are paid their summer wages in two equal installments on July 25 and September 5. Notice on the worksheet in Exhibit 30–2 that the net payroll of $5,294.30 is shown as the payroll expense in July. The payroll tax deductions of $1,705.70 are not shown since they weren't paid until August. In August when these withheld taxes are paid, the club will also have to pay employer FICA taxes of $535.70. This is also recorded when paid in August.

EXHIBIT 30–2 Worksheet summarizing checkbook stubs by month.

Cromwell Swim Club
Worksheet Summarizing Checkbook Stubs By Month
For the Year Ended December 31, 19x1

Month	Dues	Deposits — Capital Contributions	Deposits — Loan from Bank	Deposits — Interest	Salaries	Payroll Taxes	Mortgage Interest	Expenditures — Mortgage Principal	Pool Supplies	Other — Description	Other — Amount
January											
February		10,000 00									
March		40,000 00									
April	10,000 00										
May	12,000 00								200 00	Land	25,000 00
										Pool Const.	3,25,000 00
June	3,000 00		40,000 00							Misc.	10,000 00
July				75 00	5,294 30					"	3,0,000
August					1,705 70	5,35,70	200 00			"	27,430
September					5,294 30		200 00			"	3,8,000
October				50 00	1,705 70	5,35,70	200 00			"	7,430
November							200 00			Lawn Furn.	8,000 00
December							200 00	38,0,000			
Total	25,000 00	50,000 00	40,000 00	125 00	14,000 00	1,07,140	1,200 00	38,0,000	200 00		89,428 60
		Total Deposits 115,125 00		Total Deposits 115,125 00	14,000 00	1,07,140	Total Expenditures 111,500 00		111,500 00		

Reconciliation of Cash

Balance at Beginning of Year	–0–
Total Deposits	115,125 00
Less: Expenditures	(111,500 00)
Balance at End of Year	3,625 00

EXHIBIT 30-3 Payroll register.

Cromwell Hills Swim Club
PAYROLL MONTH ENDING JULY, 19X1

NAME OF EMPLOYEE	WAGES			EMPLOYEE DEDUCTIONS				NET AMOUNT PAYABLE
	REGULAR	OVERTIME	TOTAL WAGES	F.I.C.A.	FED. WITH. TAX	OTHER WITH.	TOTAL DEDUCT.	
Jones, W. (Pool Mgr.)	1000.00	—	1000.00	76.50	170.00	—	246.50	753.50
Smith, J. (Lifeguard)	750.00	—	750.00	57.40	125.00	—	182.40	567.60
Brown, J. "	750.00	—	750.00	57.40	125.00	—	182.40	567.60
Samuels, A. "	750.00	—	750.00	57.40	125.00	—	182.40	567.60
McNair, S. "	750.00	—	750.00	57.40	125.00	—	182.40	567.60
Williams, A. "	750.00	—	750.00	57.40	125.00	—	182.40	567.60
Huber, W. "	750.00	—	750.00	57.40	125.00	—	182.40	567.60
Miller, C. "	750.00	—	750.00	57.40	125.00	—	182.40	567.60
McDonald, W. "	750.00	—	750.00	57.40	125.00	—	182.40	567.60
Total	7000.00	—	7000.00	535.70	1170.00	—	1705.70	5294.30

(c) Unpaid Dues

The club will also need to keep track of which members have paid their dues. This can be handled by simply keeping a list of members and indicating the date "paid" after each member's name when payment is received. This common sense approach should be used with any other type of information that the club must keep.

(d) Financial Statements

The third step in the bookkeeping system is preparing financial statements. They can be prepared directly from the worksheet summary of the checkbook stubs (Exhibit 30–2). Look at the Statement of Cash Receipts, Disbursements, and Cash Balance . . . shown on page 168. This statement agrees with the totals on this worksheet. This worksheet becomes, in essence, the general ledger. This in conjunction with the checkbook and payroll register would become the "books" of the club.

(e) Advantages and Disadvantages

The checkbook system of record keeping is very satisfactory for many organizations, but it has limitations on the number of transactions it can handle before it becomes more cumbersome than useful. This system has the disadvantage that it is not a recognized or formal system of bookkeeping and while it may work perfectly well for one treasurer, the next treasurer may find it awkward and too informal. Further, the use of worksheets to summarize the period's transactions has the disadvantage that they are just worksheets, and are likely to get lost or destroyed. When an organization starts to have any volume of financial activity, it should start to consider a more conventional and formal set of records.

30.3 CASH BASIS SYSTEM

The basic difference between the checkbook system and a more formal cash basis system is that in the latter transactions are recorded and summarized in a more formal manner. Otherwise the bookkeeping process is the same.

(a) Basic Records

In the checkbook system we had only the checkbook stubs, worksheets summarizing transactions, and a payroll register. In a more formal cash basis system, we would have the following records:

- Cash Disbursement Book—in which each check disbursed is recorded in almost the same manner as on a checkbook stub.
- Cash Receipts Book—in which each cash receipt is recorded in almost the same manner as on a checkbook stub.
- General Journal—in which certain noncash transactions are recorded. The principal noncash entry is the entry to close the books at the end of the year.
- General Ledger—in which all transactions are summarized.
- Trial Balance—which lists all accounts in the general ledger and proves that the total of the "debits" and "credits" in the general ledger is equal.[2]

Each of these five records is discussed and illustrated below. Before doing so, however, it is necessary to discuss briefly the concept of a "double entry" bookkeeping system and to introduce the terms "debits" and "credits."

(b) Double Entry System

There are five major categories of accounts which a bookkeeping system keeps track of: expense accounts, income accounts, asset accounts, liability accounts, and the net worth, fund balance, or net assets of the organization. For the moment, only the first four will enter into our discussion. The principle of double entry bookkeeping is that every transaction affects two accounts and usually two of these four categories of accounts. For example:

- An organization spends $100 to pay a secretary. The two categories affected are assets and expenses. The asset account is the cash balance (it is decreased) and the expense account is payroll expense (it is increased).
- An organization receives a contribution of $50. The two accounts affected are contribution income (it is increased) and cash account (it is increased).
- An organization spends $10 for stationery supplies. The two accounts affected are stationery supplies expense (it is increased) and cash (it is decreased).

---

[2] Actually the trial balance is not part of the "set of books." Rather it is something prepared from the books. However, since it is important that the trial balance be prepared, it is considered part of the books for this discussion.

- An organization borrows $100 from the bank. The two accounts affected are cash (it is increased) and loans payable (it is increased).

- An organization provides Jones with $100 of service which Jones agrees to pay for at the end of next month. The two accounts affected are the income account—sales of services—(it is increased) and accounts receivable from Jones, an asset account (it is increased).

- Jones pays the organization the $100 owed. The two accounts affected are cash (it is increased) and accounts receivable (it is decreased).

Every transaction affects *two* accounts. This is why the words "double entry" bookkeeping are used. Each bookkeeping entry must affect two accounts.

(c) Debits and Credits

The words "debit" and "credit" are bookkeeping terms that refer to the two sides of a transaction. Asset accounts and expense accounts normally have debit balances. Liability accounts and income accounts normally have credit balances. To increase an asset or expense account one would add a debit amount (i.e., the account would be "debited"); to increase an income or liability account one would add a credit amount (i.e., the account would be "credited"). Here is a summary which shows these debit and credit rules:

Category of account	To increase you would add a	To decrease you would add a	Balance is normally a
Assets (cash, accounts receivable, inventory, prepaid expenses, fixed assets)	debit	credit	debit
Liabilities (accounts payable, accrued liabilities, bank loan payable, long-term debt)	credit	debit	credit
Income (contributions, sales, receipts)	credit	debit	credit
Expenses (salaries, supplies, cost of goods sold, taxes)	debit	credit	debit

All that needs to be remembered is that assets and expenses normally are debits and liabilities and income are normally credits, and that to decrease an account you would reverse the designation. It is also important to remember that there are both debits and credits to every transaction and that in total they must be equal in amount.

Many people are confused by the rule that an asset is a debit. After all, they point out, when you have a "credit" balance in your account with the local department store this is certainly an asset to you. How does this reconcile with the rule that an asset normally has a debit balance? The answer is the perspective from which one looks at a transaction. For every borrower there is a lender. On the borrower's books the amount borrowed shows up as a liability (credit balance). When a customer returns some merchandise and gets credit she is getting credit on the department store's books—they owe her—a liability that is a credit on "their" books. If the customer kept her own set of books they would show that the department store owed her and this is an asset to her, and would be a debit. So when someone talks about having a credit balance with someone what he is really saying is that on the other person's books he has a credit balance.

(d)   Debits on the Left

When there are two columns, by custom the debits are always represented on the left side, and the credits on the right side. The general ledger pages illustrated in Exhibit 30–4 uses a three-column format—a debit column, a credit column, and a "balance" column.

This illustrates both the position of debits and credits, and also how, following the rules above, an asset account would be increased or decreased. Notice that since cash is an asset account it would normally have a "debit" balance. Notice that the beginning balance is a debit. The

EXHIBIT 30–4   General Ledger—3-column format.

increase in cash from receipts is also a debit. The decrease in cash from expenditures is a reduction of a normally debit account and therefore must be a credit. The final column is merely a running balance to aid the bookkeeper.

Some general ledgers do not have this "balance" column and are set up on a somewhat different format. Exhibit 30–5 is the same general ledger account in this other form. This form of general ledger is a little more difficult for the inexperienced person to work with primarily because a running balance is more difficult to obtain. For this reason, it is not recommended. However, either form is equally acceptable.

That is all you must know about the theory of double entry bookkeeping. The rest follows from these relatively straightforward rules. Don't try to figure out logically why assets and expenses are debits, or why liability and income accounts are credits. These are the rules by definition.

With the foregoing explanation about double entry bookkeeping, and debits and credits, let us now turn to the set of books that would be kept by an organization that keeps its records on a simple cash basis. The two principal books that will be substituted for the "checkbook stub" are the Cash Disbursements Book and the Cash Receipts Book. As the names indicate, one is for recording cash disbursements and one for recording cash receipts.

Cash Disbursements Book

The cash disbursements book is a book which provides a place to record all disbursements. Usually this is a wide book with 10 to 15 columns, each column of which represents one of the major categories of expense. As each check is written it is recorded in the cash disbursements book.

EXHIBIT 30–5   General Ledger—2-column format.

Date 19 XL	ITEMS	FOLIO	✔	DEBITS	Date 19 XL	ITEMS	FOLIO	✔	CREDITS
Jan 1	Bal. beginning			100 00	Jan 31	Expenditures			200 00
31	Receipts			300 00	31	To balance			200 00
	total			400 00		total			400 00
31	Balance			200 00					

General Ledger
Cash Account

The amount of the check is "posted"[3] in two places. The first is in the total column which at the end of the month will be "footed"[4] and then posted to the cash account in the general ledger to reduce the cash balance. The second posting will be in the column showing the category of expense which the disbursement represents. At the end of the month each of these expense category columns is footed to get the total disbursements for that particular category. These totals, in turn, are posted to the general ledger. Normally at the start of each month, a new cash disbursements page is started. Exhibit 30–6 shows an example of a cash disbursements book for All Saints Church.

Cash Receipts Book

The cash receipts book is very similar to the cash disbursements book and is used in the same manner. It also has a number of columns to provide for direct posting to the appropriate category of income. Exhibit 30–7 shows an example of a cash receipts book for All Saints Church.

Notice that there is a miscellaneous column for those items of receipts that do not fit into one of the income categories for which there are columns. At the end of the month the bookkeeper can either post all of these amounts in total to a miscellaneous category of income in the general ledger, or alternatively can analyze this column and then post to individual general ledger accounts based on this analysis. It should be observed that there is a similar column in the cash disbursements book for expenses that do not fall under one of the other categories.

General Journal

There are occasions where an entry must be made that does not involve cash. While this is not often necessary for cash basis organizations, there are times when adjustments must be made or when the books are "closed" at the end of the year. A general journal is merely a separate journal (or even a separate section of the cash receipts or cash disbursements book) in which all noncash entries are made. These entries are made in traditional bookkeeping fashion showing the name of the account being "debited" and the name of the account being "credited," the amounts involved and then some explanation of the purpose of the entry. The general ledger account involved is then posted directly from this

---

[3] The word "post" means to record or to transfer an amount from one record to another. In this instance, the check is "posted" or recorded initially in the cash disbursements book. At the end of the month, the column totals are posted or "transferred" in total to the general ledger.

[4] Footed means added together. Appendix A discusses the rules for footing and ruling.

EXHIBIT 30-6   A simple cash disbursements book.

All Saints Church
Cash Disbursements Book
January 19x1
Page 1

Date	Payee	Check No.	Total Disbursements	Clergy	Music	Education	Church Office	Building Maint.	Miscellaneous Amount	Miscellaneous Description
Jan. 3	Community Lumber	125	385.16					385.16		
5	Montana Telephone Co.	126	8.15				8.15			
6	S & S Stationery	127	11.83				11.83			
7	Mrs. Jones	128	100.00		100.00					
7	Ace Piano Repair Co.	129	85.85		85.85					
10	Parish House Publish. Co.	130	50.00		50.00					
11	Bismarck Water Co.	131	23.16						23.16	Water
13	Montana Oil Co.	132	216.15						216.15	fuel
15	Rev. Williams	133	615.89	615.89						
15	Julian Dennison	134	318.50		318.50					
15	D. D. Bell	135	218.75					218.75		
17	Miss Smith	136	419.36				419.36			
17	S & S Stationery Co.	137	387.45			387.45				
20	R & R Roofing	138	74.43			74.43				
		139	250.00					250.00		
	U.S. Post Office		150.00				150.00			
	...ck Nat'l Bank		235.05	8.41	31.50		50.64	31.25		
23	...Leader	142	15.00					15.89		
23		143								
23	Acme									
23	City Lighting									
24	S & S Stationery		12.45.1				12.45			
28	Ace Piano Repair Co.	173	16.30		16.30					
31	Thompson's Hardware	174	13.45		13.45					
31		175	23.00					23.00		
31	Mutual Insurance Co.	176	36.25						36.25	Insurance
			4766.66	950.00	1131.63	511.807	841.83	908.32	411.681	

EXHIBIT 30-7   A simple cash receipts book.

Date	Description	Total Deposited	Plate Collections	Envelopes & Pledges	Special Gifts	Nursery School	Miscellaneous
Jan. 3	Plate Collection	88 25	88 25				
3	Envelope & Pledges	510 66		510 66			
10	Plate Collection	73 80	73 80				
10	Envelope & Pledges	505 66		505 66			
10	Sale of Song Books	15 00					15 00
10	Plate Collection	58 15	58 15				
17	Envelope & Pledges	544 66		544 66			
17	Envelope & Pledges	115 10		115 10			
17	Gift of John D. Smith	200 00			200 00		
17	Nursery School Fees	240 00				240 00	
17	Plate Collections	95 00	95 00				
18	Gift of Mr. & Mrs. Jones	250 00			250 00		
20	Gift of Thomas Brown	250 00			250 00		
20	Gift of the Murray Family	150 00			150 00		
24	Envelope & Pledges	119 20		119 20			
·	Nursery School Fees	00				00	
··	Collections		80 18				
24	Night	13					3 00
24	Sale o.	10 00					
24		36 25				36 25	
	Plate Collections	80 27					
31	Envelope & Pledges	111 00		111 00			
31	Plate Collection	48 30	48 30				
31	Gift of the Choir	50 00			50 00		
		4287 84	585 20	2077 64	1000 00	580 00	45 00

general journal entry. Here is an example of a journal entry that is being made to correct a misposting in the previous month's cash disbursements register which had already been posted to the general ledger when the mistake was discovered:

February 28

Entry #1

Debit Education expense $500.00
Credit Music expense $500.00

> To correct error made in posting to the cash disbursement register in January. Music books purchased for the nursery school were charged to music expense instead of education expense.

Journal entries follow a prescribed format:

1. They are dated and consecutively numbered for identification purposes.

2. The name of the account being debited is entered first and is shown at the left margin. The amount is entered in the left hand column of the two columns. If there is more than one account being debited, all debit entries would be entered before entering the credits. All debit amounts on the page should line up in the same column.

3. The name of the account being credited is indented to the right of the left margin to distinguish it from a debit. The amount is likewise entered in a column to the right of the debit column.

4. A brief narrative explanation is given describing the purpose or reason for the entry.

An example of a general journal entry to close the books at the end of the year is illustrated on page 566. This journal entry has a number of debit and credit amounts within the same entry.

General Ledger

The general ledger is a book or ledger in which all categories of transactions are summarized by specific account. The general ledger will contain a separate page for each of the various asset, liability, income, and expense accounts. Transactions are posted to the general ledger from the cash disbursements and cash receipts books and from the general journal entries at the end of each month. The format of the general ledger account was illustrated on pages 558–559.

The general ledger will also have an account called "net assets," "fund balance" or "net worth" which will represent the cumulative net worth of the organization. The income and the expense accounts are closed out at the end of each year into this "fund balance" account. This is discussed next. New ledger sheets are started at the beginning of each year.

(e) Trial Balance

A "trial balance" should be taken from the general ledger each month after the cash disbursements book, the cash receipts book, and individual entries from the general journal have been posted to the general ledger. A trial balance is simply a listing of every account in the general ledger along with the balance in each account. The trial balance is shown with the debit balance amounts in one column and the credit balance amounts in the other. Again, the debit column is on the left side, and the credit is on the right side. Exhibit 30–8 is an example of a trial balance.

EXHIBIT 30–8   A sample trial balance.

ALL SAINTS CHURCH
TRIAL BALANCE
January 31, 19X1

	Debits	Credits
Cash	$3,859.18	
Fund balance (January 1)		$4,300.00
Plate collections		585.20
Nursery school fees		580.00
Envelopes and pledges		2,077.64
Special gifts		1,000.00
Other income		83.00
Clergy expense	950.00	
Music expense	1,131.63	
Education expense	518.07	
Church office expense	841.83	
Building maintenance	908.32	
Missions	—	
Other expenses	416.81	
Total	$8,625.84	$8,625.84

After the trial balance is prepared, the two columns should be footed. If everything has been posted correctly, the debit and credit columns should be equal. If they are not, it is because an entry has been misposted, or perhaps because there is an arithmetical error in arriving at the balance on an individual ledger account.

The trial balance is the bookkeeper's check to make sure that everything has been properly posted and summarized. Once it "balances"— that is, the debits and the credits in total are in agreement—the bookkeeper can then prepare financial statements directly from the trial balance.

(f)   Closing the Books at the End of the Year

One of the bookkeeping chores that can cause a great deal of confusion is how to close the books at the end of the year. It is not difficult. Exhibit 30–9 shows the December 31, 19X1, trial balance for All Saints Church before the books are closed.

EXHIBIT 30–9 Trial Balance before closing the books.

ALL SAINTS CHURCH
PRECLOSING TRIAL BALANCE
December 31, 19X1

	Debits	Credits
Cash	$ 5,307.00	
Fund balance (January 1)		$ 4,300.00
Plate collections		4,851.00
Envelopes and pledges		30,516.00
Special gifts		5,038.00
Nursery school		5,800.00
Clergy expense	14,325.00	
Music expense	8,610.00	
Education expense	6,850.00	
Church office expense	5,890.00	
Building maintenance	4,205.00	
Missions	2,000.00	
Other expenses	3,318.00	
Total	$50,505.00	$50,505.00

The process of closing the books is simply the transferring of the balances in each of the income and expense accounts to the "fund balance" account. The effect is to transfer the net income into the fund balance. To make the transfer, the debit balance expense accounts must be reduced to zero by "crediting" them in the same amount. This is done for every expense account. The same process is followed with the income accounts, but since they have a credit balance in them, they are "debited." The difference between the aggregate debits and credits will be the amount of excess of income for the year and would be "credited" to the fund balance account.

While separate entries could be made to accomplish this transfer, usually a single journal entry is prepared. Using the trial balance above, the entry would look as shown in Exhibit 30–10.

Each debit and credit above, once posted, would reduce the income and expense account to zero and the accounts would be "closed out." The fund balance account after posting the net income of $1,007.00 would then show a balance of $5,307.00, which is the net worth of the organization at December 31, 19X1, on a cash basis.

EXHIBIT 30–10   Close the books for the year 19X1 by closing out all income and all expense accounts into the Fund Balance Account.

December 31, 19X1

Entry 1

Debit Plate collections .... $ 4,851.00
Debit Envelopes and pledges 30,516.00
Debit Special gifts 5,038.00
Debit Nursery school fees 5,800.00
   Credit Clergy expense $14,325.00
   Credit Music expense 8,610.00
   Credit Education expense 6,850.00
   Credit Church office expense 5,890.00
   Credit Building maintenance 4,205.00
   Credit Missions 2,000.00
   Credit Other expenses 3,318.00
   Credit Fund balance (excess of income over expenses for year) ....
                                                                  1,007.00

(g)   Other Records

As with the checkbook system discussed earlier, a payroll register must be kept in order to keep track of employees' gross salaries, deductions, and withholdings. The same type of payroll register used with a checkbook system of bookkeeping should also be used. In addition, there are forms on which to record such items as employees' salaries and deductions, needed to facilitate preparation of the quarterly payroll tax returns and the annual W-2 statement of wages given to each employee for tax purposes. These forms also can be obtained from stationery suppliers.

   This chapter has not discussed some of the supporting information which the bookkeeper should maintain, giving details of disbursements and receipts. Some organizations follow the practice of making a "voucher" package for each disbursement and assigning it a consecutive number which is cross-referenced on the cash disbursement register. The voucher would contain the vendor's invoice, receiving reports, or other supporting information to show any interested person why the disbursement was made. Other organizations merely file the paid invoices by vendor name, or in check order sequence. A bank reconciliation must, of course, be prepared promptly upon receipt of the monthly bank statement. The internal controls surrounding bank reconciliations were discussed in Chapter 23.

30.4 CONCLUSION

Cash basis bookkeeping is basically a very simple way of keeping records since the only transactions entered into the records are those affecting cash. The principal records in such a system are the records of disbursements and receipts. These records can be informal as in the checkbook system or can be more formal as with the cash receipts and cash disbursements books. What is important is that systematic records be kept and that they be summarized into meaningful classifications. Both the checkbook system and the more formal set of cash basis records presented in this chapter meet these requirements.

Simplified Accrual Basis Bookkeeping

Many not-for-profit organizations keep their records on a cash basis but record accrual entries at the end of each reporting period to convert these records to an accrual basis. These accrual entries are recorded by these organizations because they recognize that their financial statements would be distorted if unpaid bills or uncollected income at the end of the month weren't recorded. At the same time, they want to keep their records as simple as possible. They do this by using what is referred to in this chapter as a simplified accrual basis system. It combines much of the simplicity of cash basis bookkeeping and the advantages of accrual basis reporting.

This chapter discusses such a simplified accrual basis system of bookkeeping. This approach will be appropriate for many small or medium-sized organizations that need accrual bookkeeping with a minimum of sophistication.

31.1 BOOKS AND RECORDS

The following records constitute a "set" of books under the simplified accrual basis system discussed in this chapter:

- Cash Disbursements Book. The same basic format discussed in the previous chapter (Exhibit 30–6) is used. A separate payroll register is used to record payroll expenses and withholding amounts.
- Cash Receipts Book. The format for this book is identical to the one illustrated in Chapter 30 (Exhibit 30–7). The number of columns for the various categories of income can be expanded as appropriate.
- General Journal. The same format illustrated in Chapter 30 is followed. In this accrual system, a number of general journal entries will be made at the end of each month.
- General Ledger. The format illustrated in Chapter 30 is used. However, because of the greater number of general ledger accounts, the account structure is formalized through a "chart of accounts," discussed below.
- Payroll Register. The format of this register differs from that illustrated in the previous chapter in that this register now records directly the cash disbursement of payroll tax and withholding obligations. This will be discussed and illustrated in this chapter.
- Fixed Asset and Depreciation Ledger. This is a summary of all fixed assets and related depreciation. Fixed assets and depreciation cause some bookkeeping problems; these are also discussed below.
- Investments Ledger. This is a summary of all investments.

Most of these records were discussed in the previous chapter on cash basis accounting. The simplified accrual system is not much more complicated than the cash basis system. To a large extent, the simplified accrual system is the worksheet adjustment approach discussed on pages 19–21. However, in the system discussed in this chapter, the adjustments are formally entered in the records.

The handling of cash receipts and disbursements is not discussed in this chapter. The reader should refer to the previous chapter to see the general format of the cash receipts book and the cash disbursements book and the mechanics of their use. In this chapter, only records and procedures not discussed in the previous chapter will be covered.

31.2   CHART OF ACCOUNTS

A chart of accounts is a formal listing of all the different accounts being used by the organization. Usually the chart of accounts has numbers assigned to each account to facilitate account identification and to more readily locate the account in the general ledger. Every account in the general ledger is listed in the chart of accounts—all assets, liabilities, income, and expenses. The chart of accounts is an index to facilitate bookkeeping.

In Chapter 12, the financial statements of Camp Squa Pan were presented to illustrate simple accrual basis financial statements. The chart of accounts for Camp Squa Pan is shown in Exhibit 31–1. This is a simple and straightforward chart of accounts. It uses a two-digit number, and each type of account is grouped together. Thus, all assets are shown in numbers 1–30, liabilities in numbers 31–40, and so forth.

Some numbers are skipped within each grouping; for example, account "1" is cash in bank, but there is no account "2." Instead it skips to account "3. " The reason for this is to allow for future expansion of the chart of accounts as the organization expands. If Camp Squa Pan opens up a second bank account, account "1" might be for the original bank account and account "2" could then be used for the new bank account.

Notice that there are more accounts in the chart than there are accounts listed on the financial statement. This is so detail can be maintained for internal purposes. There is no reason to burden the reader of the financial statements with more details than are needed since they may detract from an overall understanding of the financial picture.

There is no "magic" way to develop a chart of accounts. The important thing is to sit down and think about the financial statement structure, the accounts which will be shown, and the detailed information that might be desired in the books. Then it is a simple matter to group like accounts together and assign numbers to them. The end product of an accounting system is the financial statements, and if the chart of accounts is properly put together it should be possible to prepare the statements directly from the general ledger without numerous reclassifications.

A chart of accounts can obviously be changed from time to time but it is difficult to make major changes in the middle of the year without creating chaos. New accounts can always be added by assigning the new

EXHIBIT 31–1   A simple chart of accounts for an accrual basis organization.

CAMP SQUA PAN, INC.
CHART OF ACCOUNTS

Assets (1–30)
1   Cash in bank
3   Petty cash
4   U.S. Treasury bills
5   Marketable securities
7   Accounts receivable from campers—19X3
8   Accounts receivable from campers—19X4
9   Employee accounts receivable
10 Other accounts receivable
11 Prepaid insurance
12 Other current assets
13 Food inventory
15 Land
16 Buildings
17 Furniture and fixtures
18 Automobiles
19 Canoes
20 Other camp equipment
21 Accumulated depreciation— building
22 Accumulated depreciation— furniture and fixtures
23 Accumulated depreciation— automobiles
24 Accumulated depreciation— canoes
25 Accumulated depreciation— other camp equipment

Liabilities (31–40)
31 Accounts payable
32 Accrued salaries payable
33 Withholding and employer taxes payable

34 Accrued expenses
36 Bank loans payable
38 Camp deposits
39 Deferred compensation payable

Net assets (41–50)
41 Original contribution
42 Retained earnings

Income (51–60)
51 Camp fees
55 Interest income
56 Other income
57 Gain or loss on sale of assets

Expenses (61–99)
61 Salaries—counselors
62 Salaries—food
63 Salaries—camp director
64 Salaries—office
65 Salaries—other
69 Payroll taxes
70 Food
75 Repair and maintenance— buildings
76 Repair and maintenance— automobiles
77 Repair and maintenance— equipment
80 Horse care and feed
90 Insurance
91 Advertising and promotion
92 Depreciation
95 Miscellaneous expenses

account a number not previously assigned. Examples of more complex charts of accounts are shown in Chapters 32 and 33.

31.3   MONTHLY ACCRUAL ENTRIES

The basic approach to this simplified accrual basis system is to keep all records on the cash basis during the month in the manner discussed in the previous chapter but at the end of the month to make adjustments to record accrual items.[1] These adjustments are made through general journal entries following the format discussed in the previous chapter. For most small or medium-sized organizations, there will be 6 to 15 recurring journal entries each month. The recurring journal entries most commonly recorded are:

1. An entry to record unpaid bills.
2. An entry to record unpaid salaries.
3. An entry to record uncollected income from the sale of goods or services.
4. An entry to record uncollected pledge income.
5. An entry to record depreciation expense.
6. An entry to record inventory and prepaid expenses.

Each of these entries and the mechanics involved in determining the amount of the "accrual" are discussed below. For some organizations, only two or three of these entries will be appropriate. If the amounts involved are not material, no adjustment need be made.

(a)   Accrual for Unpaid Bills

An estimate must be made at the end of the month as to the amount of all unpaid bills. This is not difficult to do since most bills from vendors are received around the first of the month. Large expenditures of an unusual nature are usually known well in advance and bills for recurring services such as water, electricity, and so on, can normally be estimated. The bookkeeper should gather all of this information together and summarize the total of these unpaid amounts, and the expense accounts to be charged.

The accrual entry itself is straightforward. The expense accounts for the estimated or actual bills should be debited[2] and "accounts payable"

---

[1] If financial statements are prepared less frequently than monthly, the accrual entries suggested here would be made only at the end of the period covered by the financial statements.

[2] Debits and credits are discussed on pages 557–559.

should be credited for the total. Here is an example using the chart of accounts for Camp Squa Pan.

July 31

Entry No. 1*

Debit No. 70 Food $485.00
76 Repairs—automobile 116.89
80 Horse care and feed 259.00
95 Miscellaneous 184.62
17 Furniture and fixtures 250.00
19 Canoes 485.00
20 Other camp equipment 618.46
Credit No. 31 Accounts payable $2,398.97
To record the liability for unpaid bills at the end of July
and to charge the appropriate expense and asset accounts.

* Journal entries can be numbered consecutively from the beginning of the year, from the beginning of the month, or, as here, by individual date. In this instance, if there were 6 entries dated July 31, they would be numbered from 1 to 6.

The bookkeeper will post each of these amounts directly to the general ledger from this journal entry.

(b) Reversal of Accrual

The related problem is how to handle the actual disbursement when the bills are paid. Since the expense account has already been "charged" as a result of this accrual entry, it cannot be charged a second time when the bill is actually paid. To avoid this double charging, the accrual entry is reversed at the beginning of the following month. In this way, all bills can then be paid and recorded in the usual manner on the "cash" basis. The effect of these accrual entries and the reversal in the following month is to record the accrual only for financial statement purposes.

To reverse the accrual entry shown above, the entry's debits and credits are reversed. Here is how the reversal entry would look:

August 1

Entry No. 1

Debit No. 31 Accounts payable $2,398.97
Credit No. 70 Food $485.00
76 Repairs 116.89
80 Horse care and feed 259.00
95 Miscellaneous 184.62
17 Furniture and fixtures 250.00
19 Canoes 485.00
20 Other camp equipment 618.46
To reverse accrual entry No. 1 set up at July 31.

If at the end of August, several of the bills from July are still unpaid, these bills should be added to the new unpaid bills and recorded as an August 31 accrual. During August when paying bills, no distinction is made between bills that were accrued at the end of July and bills that relate only to August.

Here is the general ledger page for account No. 70, Food expense. It shows both the accrual at the end of each month and the reversal of the accrual at the beginning of the month. Note that actual expenditures for food are posted directly from the cash disbursements book.

Food Expense—Account No. 70

			(Debit)	(Credit)	(Balance)
June	30	Cash disbursements	$ 6,151.00		$ 6,151.00
	30	Accrual of unpaid bills	315.00		6,466.00
	30	To record inventory of food* ..		$4,000.00	2,466.00
July	1	Reversal of accrual		315.00	2,151.00
	1	Reversal of food inventory	4,000.00		6,151.00
	31	Cash disbursements for July ...	13,163.00		19,314.00
	31	Accrual of unpaid bills	485.00		19,799.00
	31	To record inventory of food ...		5,000.00	14,799.00
August	1	Reversal of accrual		485.00	14,314.00
	1	Reversal of food inventory	5,000.00		19,314.00
	31	Cash disbursements for August	10,161.00		29,475.00
	31	Accrual of unpaid bills	1,156.00		30,631.00
	31	To record food inventory		1,000.00	29,631.00

* The entries to record food inventory are discussed below.

In a full accrual system, the organization would use a somewhat different approach which would not require this type of reversal of the accrual entries each month. However, that type of system is more complex. The full accrual system is discussed in Chapter 32.

(c) Accrual for Unpaid Salaries

The easiest way to avoid having to record accruals for unpaid salaries is to pay salaries on the last day of the month. To do this, all employees would have to be paid on a monthly or semi-monthly payroll basis. This should be done, when practical, to avoid the bookkeeping problem of setting up an accrual. This is not always possible, and where it is not, an accrual entry should be set up at the end of the month for the unpaid portion of salaries.

There is usually no problem in determining the amount of the payroll accrual. By the time the bookkeeper is ready to make this accrual, the payroll covering the last week in the month will probably have been paid and the actual expense known. Unless there were unusual payroll expenses during that period, a simple proration based on the number of workdays is all that is needed. For example, Camp Squa Pan pays its employees every other Monday covering the two weeks ending on that date. The last pay date in July was on the 22nd and the first one in August was on the 5th; therefore 9 days of the 14 days paid on August 5th are applicable to July. If the August 5th payroll totaled $14,000, the $9/14$, or $9,000, would be applicable to July and should be recorded in an accrual entry.

The accrual entry that would be made to record this payroll would be:

July 31

Entry No. 2

Debit No. 61 Salaries—counselors	$6,000	
62 Salaries—food help	1,000	
63 Salaries—office	1,000	
64 Salaries—other	1,000	
Credit No. 32 Accrued salaries payable		$9,000
To record accrued salaries payable at July 31, 9/14 of the August 5 payroll is applicable to July.		

As with the accrual entry for unpaid bills, this entry should be reversed in August. The August 5th payroll should be recorded in the same manner as any other payroll.

Withholding taxes and the employer's share of payroll taxes are special problems that can cause difficulty. They are discussed in section 31.4.

(d) Accrual for Uncollected Income

The accrual for uncollected income is made in the same manner as the accruals for unpaid bills and salaries. The bookkeeper must accumulate the appropriate information to determine the estimated amount of uncollected income. In the case of Camp Squa Pan, there are always a few campers who sign up for the first two weeks of the camp season but then stay on for additional weeks. The parents are billed for these additional amounts as soon as they decide to let their children stay for additional periods, but there is often a delay before payment is received. At the end of July, there was a total of 15 campers who had been scheduled to leave on July 15 but had stayed through July 31, and whose fees were still unpaid. Camp fees are $100 a week, so each camper owes $228.57—and a total of $3,428.55 should be recorded as income:

July 31

Entry No. 3

Debit No. 8 Accounts receivable—campers $3,428.55
    Credit No. 51 Camp fees $3,428.55
        To record unpaid camp fees at July 31 arising from
        extended camp periods.

This accrual should also be reversed in August, and all receipts from these campers' parents should be handled in the same manner as all other receipts. A formal accounts receivable subsidiary ledger[3] is not suggested. Instead an informal system should be used keeping a copy of the unpaid bill sent to the parent in a folder until paid. Once paid, the bill should be filed with the paid copies of campers' bills.

(e)   Accrual for Pledges

As discussed in Chapter 10, accrual basis organizations should record all significant pledges. Pledges are not applicable to Camp Squa Pan, but if they were, the entry to record the pledge would be made in exactly the same manner as the other accruals discussed above. The accrual would likewise be reversed in the following month, and all payments received on the pledges would be treated as any other contribution.

(f)   Accrual to Record Depreciation

If depreciation is a significant expense for the organization, it should be recorded on a monthly basis. If it is not, depreciation can be recorded every six months, or even annually.

The easiest way to determine the amount of depreciation that should be recorded is to calculate the annual amount at the beginning of the year and then divide by 12 to get the amount to record each month.[4] This method ignores depreciation on fixed asset purchases during the year. Unless purchases or disposals are sizable, they can be ignored on a monthly basis; at the end of the year an adjustment should be made for such items. The calculation of depreciation itself is discussed in section 31.5.

The accrual entry that should be made monthly would be as follows:

---

[3] An accounts receivable subsidiary ledger is discussed in Chapter 32.
[4] In the case of Camp Squa Pan, depreciation would be recorded over the camp season of two months rather than over twelve months.

July 31

Entry No. 4

Debit No. 92 Depreciation $6,600
    Credit No. 21 Accumulated depreciation–building $1,200
        22 Accumulated depreciation—
            furniture and fixtures 600
        23 Accumulated depreciation—automobiles 3,000
        24 Accumulated depreciation—canoes 1,200
        25 Accumulated depreciation—
            other camp equipment 600
    To record depreciation for the month of July.

This entry, unlike others discussed so far in this chapter, is not reversed in the following month. Instead, depreciation continues to accumulate until such time as it is equal to the cost of the fixed asset, or until the asset is sold. The entries to record the sale of depreciable assets are discussed later in this chapter.

(g)   Accrual for Inventory and Prepaid Expenses

Some organizations purchase inventory for use or resale, part of which may still be on hand at the end of the period. Other organizations prepay certain categories of expenses, such as insurance premiums. The disbursement for these items should be treated as any other category of expense in the cash disbursement book. This means that the full amount is "expensed" at the time it is paid for. At the end of each month, it is necessary to record the amount of any remaining inventory, and the unexpired portion of insurance or similar expense. The entry that should be made would be similar to this:

July 31

Entry No. 5

Debit No. 11 Prepaid insurance $2,800
        13 Food inventory 5,000
    Credit No. 90 Insurance expense $2,800
        70 Food expense 5,000
    To record as an asset prepaid insurance premiums and
    food inventory at July 31.

This entry should be reversed in the following month in the same manner as the other accruals discussed above.

31.4   PAYROLL TAXES

Probably the most difficult "accrual" that has to be made for an organization trying to keep its books on a simple accrual basis is the entry to record payroll taxes. In the previous chapter, it was recommended that payroll taxes be handled strictly on a cash basis. These taxes were recorded when they were paid and not before, and the amount recorded as salary expense on payday was the net amount of payroll after withholding deductions. At the later date, when the withholding and payroll taxes were paid, this additional amount was recorded as salary expense.

This is awkward because most organizations split their payroll into two or more categories of salary expense. If payroll withholding taxes and the employer's share of taxes have to be allocated between salary categories, it is easier to do this at the time the payroll is prepared than at the end of the month in an accrual entry, or in the following month when the taxes are actually paid. In the simplified accrual system recommended in this chapter, a separate payroll disbursement register is used that is designed to record this withholding at the time the payroll is paid.

(a)   Illustrative Treatment

Exhibit 31–2 shows an illustration of the payroll register for Camp Squa Pan. Notice that the amount shown in the salary expense columns for each employee is the full gross amount of salary. The net amount paid after deductions is shown in the net paid column. The withholding taxes are posted in total at the end of the month to the liability account in the general ledger. When such withheld taxes are paid, they are entered as a disbursement in the cash disbursements book with the offset to the withholding tax account. In the cash disbursements book in Chapter 30 (Exhibit 30–6), the offset (or debit) would be recorded in the miscellaneous column (account No. 33—withholding taxes payable). The total payment of withheld taxes for the month will be posted from the cash disbursement book to the general ledger as an offset to the liability account. At any month end, the remaining amount in the liability account should represent the unpaid taxes.

Unlike the payroll register illustrated in Chapter 30 (Exhibit 30–3), the payroll register in Exhibit 31–2 is actually used to record the disbursement of the net pay to each employee. Notice that there is a space for the check number to be indicated. At the end of the month the total amount disbursed will be posted to the general ledger cash account.

EXHIBIT 31-2   A payroll disbursement register.

Camp Squa Pan
Payroll Disbursement Register
19x4

Date	Check No.	Payee	Net Pay	Counselors (61)	Kitchen (62)	Salaries — Camp Director (63)	Office (64)	Other (65)	Withholding Taxes — Income	FICA
July 8	187	John Harris	80 00	100 00					15 00	5 00
8	188	Tom Hannagan	80 00	100 00					15 00	5 00
8	189	Betty Thompson	80 00	100 00					15 00	5 00
8	190	Jim Heary	80 00	100 00					15 00	5 00
8	191	Ken Samuels	100 00					125 00	18 75	6 25
8	192	Tim Bradley	60 00		75 00				11 25	3 75
8	193	Steve McNair	240 00			300 00			45 00	15 00
8	194	Bill Huber	100 00				125 00		18 75	6 25
8	195	Brian Hogan	96 00				120 00		18 00	6 00
8	196	Karl Miller	160 00	100 00				200 00	30 00	10 00
8	197	Dave Johnson	80 00	100 00					15 00	5 00
8	198	Adam Smith	80 00	100 00					15 00	5 00
8	199	Elaine Michaels	80 00	100 00					15 00	5 00
8	200	Susan Bradley	60 00		75 00				11 25	3 75
8	201	Bob McDonald	96 00				120 00		18 00	6 00
8	202	Henry Faber	144 00	180 00						
8	203	Morris	80 00	100 00		8 500				6 25
8	204	Brian	90 00						18 75	4 25
8	205	Al Davidson		180 00					12 75	9 00
8	206	Steve Kline	80 00	100 00	8 000				15 00	5 00
8	207	Ralph Henderson	64 00						32 00	4 00
22	270									
22	271	Ken Samuels	100 00					125 00	18 75	6 25
22	272	Karl Miller	160 00					200 00	30 00	10 00
22	273	Jim Heary	80 00	100 00					15 00	5 00
22	274	Brian Hogan	96 00				120 00		18 00	6 00
			4 11 168 59	37 54500	1 48100	60 0000	36 0200	8 23400	7 22044	2 57197

(b) Employer Taxes

There is one final problem. In addition to withholding taxes, there are some taxes that are employer taxes. An example is the employer share of FICA taxes. These amounts will be paid at the same time as the withholding taxes are paid and probably as part of the same payment. These employer tax amounts should be recorded at the end of each month in an accrual entry similar to the entry recording unpaid bills. The debit, in this illustration, would be to payroll tax expense (account No. 69) and the credit account would be to taxes payable (account No. 33). This entry should *not* be reversed at the beginning of the following period since payment is recorded in the cash disbursements book, the "debit" entry will be directly to the taxes payable account as discussed above.

31.5 FIXED ASSET REGISTER AND DEPRECIATION SCHEDULE

Every organization, including those on a cash basis, should keep a ledger of fixed assets. As was discussed in Chapter 23, the board has a fiduciary responsibility to effectively control the organization's assets. The first step in controlling fixed assets is to know what assets the organization owns. A fixed asset ledger is merely a listing of these assets in a systematic manner. Exhibit 31–3 shows an example of the type of ledger that might be kept by a not-for-profit organization. The first part records details on the asset itself; the second part records the calculation of depreciation.

A separate page of the fixed asset register is usually kept for each major category of asset. This categorization should follow the general ledger account description. For example, Camp Squa Pan has separate ledger accounts for buildings, furniture and fixtures, automobiles, canoes, and other camp equipment. Thus there would be a separate page for each of these categories.

Every time an asset is acquired it should be entered on this ledger. The total dollar amount shown in this ledger should agree with the general ledger account. Thus at December 31, 19X1, the total of the assets listed in the automobile account will equal $13,456, the amount shown on the Balance Sheet on page 176.

In order to do this, entries must be made in the fixed asset ledger to not only record additions but also to record when an asset is sold or junked. Two entries must be made. The first is to record the date of disposal on the line in this ledger on which the original entry was recorded at the time it was acquired. This will indicate that the asset has been

EXHIBIT 31-3   A fixed asset ledger and depreciation schedule.

Camp Squa Pan
Fixed Asset Ledger—Automobiles

Date Acquired	Description	Tag Serial No.	Location	Cost	Depreciable Life	Date Disposed of
(19x1)	Balance Forward			8 756 00		
Jan. 1	Ford Pick-up Truck	1 176 15 17		4 200 00	5	
May 16	Chevrolet Station Wagon	3 165 17 1—AE		3 500 00	5	
July 1	Trade-in Ford Purchased in 19W8	G11 7 661		(3 000 00)		6/15x2
Dec. 31	Balance			13 456 00		
(19x2)	Ford Station Wagon	61 87 G1		4 219 00	5	
June 15	Trade-in Chevrolet Purchased in 19x1	3 165 17 1—AE		(3 500 00)		
Dec. 31	Balance			14 175 00		

Depreciation Schedule—Automobiles (5 Yrs):

Date	Description	Total Cost	Depreciation by Year					
			19x1	19x2	19x3	19x4	19x5	19x6	19x7
(19x1)	Balance Forward	8 756 00	1 751 00	1 751 00	1 27 7 00	6 00 00	2 00 00		
Jan. 1	Pick-up Truck	4 200 00	4 20 00	8 40 00	8 40 00	8 40 00	8 40 00	4 20 00	
May 16	Chevrolet Station Wagon	3 500 00	3 00 00	7 00 00	7 00 00	7 00 00	7 00 00	3 50 00	
July 1	Sale of 19W8 Ford	(3 000 00)	(3 00 00)	(6 00 00)	(3 00 00)				
Dec. 31	Balance	13 456 00	2 22 1 00	2 69 1 00	2 51 1 700	2 14 0 00	1 74 0 00	7 70 00	
(19x2)	Ford Station Wagon	4 219 00		4 21 90	8 43 80	8 43 80	8 43 80	8 43 80	4 21 90
June 15	Sale of 19x1 Chevrolet	(3 500 00)		7 00 00	7 00 00	7 00 00	(3 50 00)	(3 50 00)	
Dec. 31	Balance	14 175 00	2 22 1 00	2 41 2 90	2 66 0 80	2 28 3 80	1 88 3 80	1 26 3 80	4 21 90

disposed of. The second entry is recorded in the current period to remove the original cost of the asset. To do this, the original cost is shown in the amount column, in parentheses to indicate that it should be subtracted rather than added. In this way, the amount column should agree with the general ledger. These two entries can be seen in Exhibit 31–3 where an automobile is sold.

At the time a fixed asset is acquired, the bookkeeping entry to set the asset up in the general ledger will be made automatically through the cash disbursements book. The account charged in the cash disbursements book will be the asset account, using the miscellaneous column.

The entries to record a sale of fixed assets are discussed below.

(a) Depreciation Schedule

The second part of this fixed asset ledger shows depreciation and is used only for accrual basis organizations that capitalize and depreciate fixed assets.[5] This schedule is used to spread depreciation expense over the depreciable life of an asset using a columnar format. As with the fixed asset ledger, a separate page should be used for each general ledger category of assets, and often, as illustrated here, it is shown on the same page as the fixed asset register.

There are several equally correct methods for calculating depreciation in the year of acquisition. If an organization wants to be accurate to the last penny, depreciation should start in the month the asset is acquired. This degree of accuracy is usually not necessary. A more practical approach that many organizations follow is to assume that all assets are purchased half way through the year and therefore charge one half year's depreciation in the year the asset was acquired. Thus, for the automobile with a five-year life, the first year's depreciation in 19X1 would be $350 ($3,500 ÷ 5 years × ¹/₂ year $350). In 19X2, depreciation would be $700.

(b) Depreciation Spread Year by Year

All acquisitions for the year for each category should be summarized and entered on this schedule at the end of the year.[6] All assets with the same depreciable life can be summarized and entered as one amount or each asset can be entered separately. The bookkeeper then calculates the

---

[5] Depreciation is the subject of Chapter 7.

[6] If there have been major acquisitions during the year, such as a building, they can be entered during the year to enable the bookkeeper to start depreciating them, as part of the monthly depreciation entry. If no entry is made until the end of the year, the additional depreciation for the current year is recorded at that time.

amount of depreciation applicable to each future year and enters these amounts in the columns for that year. For example, if an automobile with a five-year life is acquired on July 1, 19X1, for $3,500, $350 depreciation would be shown in the column for 19X1, $700 in each of the columns for 19X2, 19X3, 19X4, and 19X5 and $350 in the column for 19X6. To determine the amount of total depreciation for each year the bookkeeper refers to the total depreciation in each column. In our illustration, depreciation is $2,221.00 for 19X1 and $2,412.90 for 19X2.

An adjustment must also be made to this schedule if the automobile is sold before it has been fully depreciated. Depreciation for future periods must be removed from the appropriate years' columns. This future depreciation is removed by subtracting it from these columns. Exhibit 31–3 shows the removal of depreciation on an automobile sold in 19X1 and one sold in 19X2.

(c) Depreciation on Acquisitions during the Year

At the end of the year, the depreciation column for the current year is totaled. As indicated earlier, the amount of depreciation recorded in the monthly accrual entries will normally not be adjusted throughout the year as assets are purchased or sold. Instead, for the sake of simplicity the same amount is used each month. This means that the amount of depreciation actually charged during the year should be compared to the current year's depreciation column in this schedule. An adjustment should be recorded for any difference.

This is less complicated than it seems. It does require that the bookkeeper systematically keep track of acquisitions and disposals. Since for most organizations purchases of fixed assets are not voluminous, this should not be too difficult.

(d) Entries for Disposal of Assets

Many bookkeepers have difficulty in preparing the bookkeeping entry to record the sale or disposal of a fixed asset. This entry is not difficult if the objective of the entry is kept in mind: namely, to remove the cost of the fixed asset and to remove the accumulated depreciation. Let's take a typical example of an automobile acquired in 19W8 at a cost of $3,000 with a five-year life. It was sold in July 19X1 for $800.

The biggest problem is to calculate the amount of depreciation that has been taken. In 19W8, the year acquired, one-half year's depreciation was taken, a full year's depreciation in 19W9 and 19XO, and half a year's depreciation through June 30, 19X1 (the asset is sold in July so depreciation has been charged only through June). In total, that is three years' depreciation or $1,800 ($3,000 ÷ 5 years = $600 per year × 3 years = $1,800). Here is the entry that records this sale:

July 31

Entry No. 8

Debit No. 10 Accounts receivable .... $ 800
   23 Accumulated depreciation—automobile ...   1,800
   57 Loss on sale   400
 Credit No. 18 Automobiles $3,000
   To record the sale of an auto acquired in 19W8 for $3,000, sold in July for $800, and to remove the accumulated depreciation.

Notice that we have debited accounts receivable for $800, the sales price of the automobile. When the cash is received it will be entered in the cash receipts book and the credit will be to accounts receivable. In this way, the cash receipt is recorded in the cash receipts book. The $400 loss is simply the amount needed to make the entry balance.

A typical variation on the above entry occurs if instead of receiving cash for the old car, this $800 is allowed as a trade-in value on a car costing $3,500. The organization pays $2,700 and its old car and receives a later model. Here is the journal entry that would be made to record this transaction:

July 31

Entry No. 9

Debit No. 18 Automobile .... $ 500
   23 Accumulated depreciation—auto   1,800
   57 Loss on sale   400
 Credit No. 31 Accounts payable $2,700
   To record purchase of an automobile costing $3,500 and trade-in of old automobile with original cost of $3,000.

Notice that the automobile asset account has been increased by $500, the difference in cost between the two automobiles. Instead the entry might have shown a debit of $3,500 to record the purchase, and a credit of $3,000 to remove the old car. Either would be acceptable since the end result is the same. When the organization makes out its check for $2,700 it will be entered in the cash disbursement book in the same manner as any other disbursement except that the account debited will be accounts payable. This will be shown in the miscellaneous column.

With respect to the old automobile, the bookkeeper must not forget to remove the depreciation for future periods from the depreciation

EXHIBIT 31–4 An investment ledger.

The Johanna M. Stannick Foundation

Investment Ledger

Date	Investment Description	No. of Shares/ Par Value	Cert. No.	Location of Cert.	Cost or FMV at Date Rec'd	Date Sold	Sale Proceeds	Gain or (Loss)	How Acquired	Donor's Name & Address	FMV at 12/31/69*	Donor's Tax Basis
2-1x3	IBM	100	11734	Daytona Bank	18,700.00	2-13x4	45,759.00	12,759.00	Gift	J.M. Stannick, Daytona, Fla.		25,000.00
2-1x3	Polaroid	300	34104	"	33,000.00				Gift	J.M. Stannick, Daytona, Fla.		15,000.00
2-1x3	Hercules	1775	10025	"	60,725.00				Gift	J.M. Stannick, Daytona, Fla.		16,000.00
2-1x3	Intl. Nickle	2225	21573	"	81,853.00				Gift	J.M. Stannick, Daytona, Fla.		19,000.00
	Total Dec. 31, 19x3				194,278.00							
2-13x4	Polaroid	300	34104	Daytona Bank	(33,000.00)							
2-23x4	U.S. Steel	935	C8156	"	25,241.00				Purchase			
	Total Dec. 31, 19x4				186,519.00							

*Required only for securities held on that date.

schedule. Notice that depreciation of $300 in 19X1, $600 in 19X2, and $300 in 19X3 has been removed in Exhibit 31–3. If the auto had been sold three months later, in October instead of July, the amount removed from the 19X1 column would have been $150 instead of $300. This amount is calculated right up to the end of the month prior to sale since the monthly accrual entry has recorded depreciation to that time.

31.6   INVESTMENT LEDGER

All organizations must keep a record of the investments they own. Often this record is not formalized and when questions are raised later, the organization has difficulty in providing details. Exhibit 31–4 shows an example of the type of investment ledger that should be kept. The information on this schedule is pretty straightforward, except for information on the tax basis of investments received as gifts. This information is required only with respect to "private foundations" and results from the special tax rules for calculating gains for these organizations.[7] Other organizations can eliminate these columns.

31.7   CONCLUSION

Many organizations will find that the simplified accrual basis system presented here is a practical way to have the advantage of cash basis accounting throughout the period while still recording the necessary adjustments at the end of the period to convert to an accrual basis at that date. The only difficulty with this system is determining the amount of each of these accruals at the end of the period. Nevertheless this is not hard to do if it is done systematically. Most non-bookkeepers can keep books in this fashion if they carefully study and follow the examples shown in this and the previous chapter. Where problems arise that are not discussed, a common sense approach should be used, or help solicited from someone with more experience.

---

[7] See Chapter 26 for a discussion of these requirements.

Full Accrual Basis Bookkeeping

The simplified accrual system discussed in the previous chapter will meet the needs of many smaller, and even some medium-sized organizations. However, there are many other organizations for which this system is too cumbersome because they have a large number of transactions. For these organizations, a "full" accrual system is more appropriate. This chapter discusses such a system and illustrates the principal records that must be kept.

32.1 BOOKS AND RECORDS

The following records constitute a "set" of books for an organization using a full accrual basis bookkeeping system. Listed first are the new or revised books or records discussed in this chapter:

- Sales Register. This records all sales of goods and services at the time they are made (Exhibit 32–3).
- Accounts Payable Register. This book records all purchases and other obligations at the time the bill or invoice is received from the vendor, rather than at the time paid, as in previous systems (Exhibit 32–6).
- Accounts Receivable Subsidiary Ledger. This book records the details of all amounts that others owe to the organization (Exhibit 32–4).
- Cash Receipts Book. This book changes from that discussed in the previous chapter because much of the information previously recorded in this book is now recorded in the sales register (Exhibit 32–5).
- Cash Disbursements Book. This book changes also from that discussed in previous chapters because much of the information previously recorded in this book is now recorded in the accounts payable register (Exhibit 32–7).
- Chart of Accounts. This chart is more complex than previously illustrated (Exhibit 32–1).

Books or records that were discussed elsewhere include:

General ledger (Chapter 30)
General Journal (Chapter 30)
Trial Balance (Chapter 30)
Payroll Register (Chapter 31)
Fixed Asset Register (Chapter 31)
Investment Ledger (Chapter 31)

The new "books" not previously discussed are those in which two types of transactions are now recorded at the time they take place rather than at the time cash is involved—the sales register in which all sales are entered and the accounts payable register in which all bills are entered at the time they are received from the vendors. The basic distinction between a full accrual system and the simplified accrual system discussed in the previous chapter is that transactions are recorded at the time they occur rather than at the end of the month in accrual entries. In all other significant respects, the two systems are similar.

The reader should refer to the previous two chapters for a description of records discussed earlier and for an explanation of how they tie into a total bookkeeping system. These chapters are cumulative and closely interrelated.

(a) Automated Bookkeeping Systems

The discussions in Chapters 31–33 illustrate manual bookkeeping systems—that is, systems not involving electronic or other automated data processing operations. Organizations, especially larger ones, may find it efficient and cost-effective to use partly or fully computerized systems for bookkeeping and the preparation of financial reports.

Computerized bookkeeping can be done on equipment kept in the organization's own office, or data can be sent out to a "service bureau," an organization which uses its equipment to process data for other organizations. There are various existing automated systems available which will meet the needs of most not-for-profit organizations, or an organization with complex or unusual bookkeeping needs can have a custom-made system designed for its use.

Automated bookkeeping systems do not differ at all in concept from the manual systems illustrated, so no separate detailed discussion of them is necessary. Merely, the mechanical aspects of the process are partly or wholly done by automated equipment instead of by human bookkeepers. An important internal control[1] consideration to remember when using automated systems is that the organization must carefully monitor the data processing function, whether performed in-house or at a service bureau, for completeness and accuracy of processing. It is wishful thinking to assume that because a machine is doing the processing, mistakes cannot occur. Such an assumption will inevitably lead to trouble. Chapter 34 discusses the process of automating a manual system.

(b) Background for Illustrative Example

The full accrual system can best be illustrated by using a typical organization as an example, and in this chapter we will study some of the procedures followed by The Valley Country Club. The procedures discussed here are applicable to many other types of not-for-profit organizations and careful readers will be able to see how the books and procedures illustrated here can be adapted to their own organization.

The Valley Country Club's budgeting problems and financial statements were discussed in some detail on pages 364–373 and the reader may want to refer to the financial statements shown on those pages. This club is a typical small-to-medium size club. It has an 18-hole course and an olympic-size swimming pool. The only public building is the clubhouse in which there is a restaurant, a separate bar, and locker rooms. There are several small maintenance buildings.

---

[1] Internal control is discussed in Chapter 23.

Members may bring guests to the club but the member must pay a greens fee of $5 and a swimming-fee of $2 for each guest. The members pay no fees as this is part of the annual dues. Guests are welcome in the restaurant and bar but they must be accompanied by a member and in all cases the member is billed for the fees and charges incurred by a guest. No cash is handled and the member signs a "charge slip" for each charge incurred. No tips are allowed, since 5 percent tax and 15 percent gratuity are added to all charges. The members are billed in the first week of the month for the previous month's charges.

32.2 CHART OF ACCOUNTS

Exhibit 32–1 shows a chart of accounts for The Valley Country Club. This chart of accounts is considerably more complex than the chart shown in Chapter 31. It is complex not only because of the greater number of accounts, but because expenses are kept by type of club activity.

(a) Coding

Look first at the top group of accounts under the major caption, "Expenses." These are the major expense groupings. The subcodes that are immediately below this group are used with each of the major codes. For example, if salaries are to be charged to golf activities the code number would be "410." If salaries are to be charged to the bar then account "710" would be used, and so forth. This type of classification allows the bookkeeper to learn quickly almost all account numbers since only the major group codes and the major subcodes must be learned. There are also a number of specific accounts, mostly involving general and administrative expenses, and these are listed separately.

The income and expense accounts are three-digit codes; the asset and liability accounts are two-digit codes. In this accrual system, the code numbers frequently will be used instead of account names. This is one of the advantages of having a chart of accounts. It cuts down on both the amount of writing and the space involved.

32.3 SALES REGISTER

Exhibit 32–2 shows an example of the charge slip used by The Valley Country Club. Notice that it is prenumbered to ensure that accountability is maintained. Charge slips are prepared for every charge to members.

EXHIBIT 32–1   A chart of accounts for a country club.

THE VALLEY COUNTRY CLUB
CHART OF ACCOUNTS

Assets

10–Cash in bank—main
11–Cash in bank—payroll
12–Cash in bank—savings
20–Members' accounts receivable
21–Employees' accounts receivable
22–Other accounts receivable
23–Allowance for bad debts
32–Inventories—greens and
  grounds
35–Inventories—pool supplies
36–Inventories—restaurant
37–Inventories—bar
40–Prepaid expenses—insurance
41–Prepaid expenses—taxes
42–Prepaid expenses—other
50–Land (original cost)
52–Greens and grounds
  improvements
53–Clubhouse
54–Golf carts
55–Swimming pool
56–Restaurant equipment
57–Bar equipment
58–Automotive equipment
59–Club furniture and fixtures
63–Accumulated depreciation—
  clubhouse
64–Accumulated depreciation—golf
  carts
65–Accumulated depreciation—
  swimming pool
66–Accumulated depreciation—
  restaurant and dining room
67–Accumulated depreciation—bar
68–Accumulated depreciation—
  automotive equipment
69–Accumulated depreciation—
  club furniture

Liabilities

70–Accounts payable
73–Short-term loans payable
74–Accrued expenses
75–FICA and withholding taxes
  payable
76–Sales taxes
77–Real estate taxes
78–Other taxes
79–Wages payable
80–Employees' tip fund
85–Mortgages—long-term
87–Member bonds due 19X8
90–Contributed capital
95–Surplus

Income

110–Initiation fees
111–Dues—full members
112–Dues—social members
120–Golf fees
130–Locker room fees
140–Golf cart rentals
150–Swimming fees
160–Sales—dining room
170–Sales—bar
180–Other
190–Discounts earned
191–Interest income
192–Cash over/short

Expenses

200–Greens and grounds
300–Clubhouse
400–Golf activities
500–Swimming pool
600–Restaurant
700–Bar
900–Administrative

EXHIBIT 32–1 *Continued.*

Subcodes

10–Salaries
20–Supplies
30–Repairs and minor maintenance
40–Other costs
60–Depreciation

Specific Accounts

610–Dining room salaries
611–Kitchen salaries
620–Food
720–Liquor and mixes
911–Club manager's salary
912–Secretarial and clerical
913–Bookkeeping

914–Janitorial
915–Other
940–Interest expense
941–Auditing and legal
942–Postage
943–Telephone
944–Insurance
945–Real estate taxes
946–Income taxes
947–Pension expense
948–Electricity
949–Water
950–Unemployment insurnace
951–Bad debts
952–Employer payroll taxes

At the end of each day, all of the charge slips are forwarded to the bookkeeper in numerical sequence for each activity or location. The bookkeeper should check the sequence carefully. If some of the charge slips were lost before they were recorded, the club would lose income since there would be no way to know whom to charge, or the amount.

After accounting for the sequence of all charge slips, the bookkeeper enters each charge slip in the sales register. Exhibit 32–3 shows an example of a sales register. Each charge slip has been entered individually in the sales register in order to establish a permanent record of all charges.[2] The distribution of the charge, sales tax, and gratuity is shown in the appropriate column.[3] The account numbers shown at the top of the page are the general ledger account numbers.

---

[2] Some clubs do not enter these charge slips individually in the sales register. Instead the bookkeeper, using an adding machine, runs a recap of the charge slips for each day, by account classification. Then only the total of these charges is entered in the sales register. When this procedure is followed, the charge slips will probably be photocopied before being sorted by member number. In this way, a permanent record is created to support the summary entry in the sales register.

[3] While in this illustration the sales tax and gratuity amounts have been posted separately for each charge slip, some time could have been saved by entering only the total amount of the member's charge (including the sales tax and gratuity) and the income account distribution. Since both the sales tax and the gratuity amounts are a fixed percentage (5 percent and 15 percent) of charges, these amounts can be calculated at the end of the month by multiplying the total of all income accounts by these fixed percentages. In Exhibit 32–3 the aggregate of the income accounts (accounts 120–180, or $62,505.27) multiplied by these two percentages would give the amounts shown in the sales tax column ($3,125.26) and gratuity column ($9,375.80). These last two columns could then be eliminated.

EXHIBIT 32–2 An example of a "charge slip" used by a country club.

THE VALLEY COUNTRY CLUB

MEMBER CHARGE SLIP

DESCRIPTION OF CHARGE:

1 Club Sandwich	$ 2.50
1 Ham Sandwich	1.50
1 Steak Sandwich	3.20
3 Coffees	.75

Sub Total	7.95
5% Sales Tax	.40
15% Gratuity	1.19
TOTAL	$ 9.54

Number in Party

Members _1_
Guests _2_

No. 04402

JUL 1 19X1

Name _John Brillon_
Member No. _789_

At the end of the month all columns are totaled and the totals posted to the general ledger. The total sales column figure is posted to the accounts receivable control account in the general ledger. The other columns are posted to the general ledger account indicated at the top of the column. In order to be sure that all accounts are posted, the bookkeeper puts a check mark (✓) beside each column total as it is posted.

32.4 ACCOUNTS RECEIVABLE SUBSIDIARY LEDGER

After being posted to the sales register, all charge slips should be sorted down by member number and accumulated together during the month. Either at the end of the month, or throughout the month as the bookkeeper ᴵᴿᵂᴵᴺ ᴰᴼᴿˢᴱᵞ
ᴺᴼᵀ ᴬᵀ ᴬᴸᴸ

EXHIBIT 32–3 A sales register.

The Valley Country Club
Sales Register

Date (19x1)		Member No.	Charge Slip No.	Total Sales	Golf Fees a/c 120	Locker Room Fees a/c 130	Golf Cart Rentals a/c 140	Swimming Fees a/c 150	Sales—Dining Room a/c 160	Sales—Bar a/c 170	Other a/c 180	Sales Tax a/c 76	Employees' Tip Fund a/c 80
July 1	Jones	369	10861	9 60	5 00	1 00	2 00					40	1 20
1	Smith	700	10862	9 60	5 00	1 00	2 00					40	1 20
1	McDonald	607	10863	2 40			2 00					10	30
1	Slannick	720	8715	2 40				2 00				10	30
1	McNair	605	8716	2 40				2 00				10	30
1	Riley	687	8717	2 40				2 00				10	30
1	Falvey	340	4400	4 60					3 68			23	69
1	Miller	625	4401	21 04						17 53		88	2 63
1	Brillon	89	4402	9 54						7 95		40	1 19
1	Brillon	89	22815	43 39					36 17			1 80	5 42
1	Jackson	372	22816	51 78	10 00					43 15		2 16	6 47
1	Allen	15	22817	56 15	5 00		15 00		3 60	21 80		2 34	7 01
1	Thompson	760	22818	11 52				2 00	2 60			48	1 44
1	Peterson	665	22819	15 84					13 20			66	1 98
1	Davidson	275	15001	7 20					5 50			30	90
1	Kinney	360	15002	30 00		1 00		2 00				1 25	37ᵃ
1			15003	4ᵃᵃ								25	
31	Jamison	390		1 10									
31	Benjoya	81	5112										
31	Williams	905	5113	19 87		1 00				32 10	19 00	1 05	2 49
31	Shames	701	5114	22 80						16 55		83	2 85
31	Jones	385	5115	6 00					5 00			95	75
31	Harris	353	5116	10 20					8 50			25	1 25
31	Johnson	390	5117	55 80						46 51		2 32	6 97
				75000 63³	7500 17	1513 10	1749 71	160 00	16339 01	15001 27	241 01	3125 26	9375 80

EXHIBIT 32–4   An individual accounts receivable ledger card.

DATE	DESCRIPTION	DEBIT	CREDIT	BALANCE
JUNE 30	BALANCE			345.18
JULY 1	# 4402	9.54		
1	22815	43.39		
3	4079	14.53		
3	23019	24.56		
8	11345	14.00		
8	4107	45.44		
14	4314	33.16		
14	PAYMENT		345.18	
22	# 4516	13.15		
22	23990	43.67		
31	BALANCE			241.44

THE VALLEY COUNTRY CLUB

P.O. BOX 144
DAYTONA BEACH, FLORIDA 32017

STATEMENT OF MEMBER'S ACCOUNT

MEMBER NAME
BRILLON, JOHN
MEMBER ADDRESS
2641 ADAMS STREET
DAYTONA BEACH, FLA.
MEMBER NUMBER
89

has time, an accounts receivable ledger card for each member should be posted. Exhibit 32–4 shows an example of the type of accounts receivable ledger which should be maintained. This accounts receivable ledger should be in duplicate, with one copy sent to the member as a monthly bill. This ledger card can be hand posted, or if the volume is sufficient, a small bookkeeping machine or one-write system[4] can be used to post the charge slip to both the sales register and the ledger card simultaneously.

Usually the charge slips are sent to the member with the bill. A few organizations, however, prefer to keep the charge slips as a part of the organization's permanent records and only send the member a copy of the ledger card. They will send a photo copy of the charge slip to the member

---

[4] A one-write system is a system where, through specially designed forms and carbon paper, more than one record is prepared simultaneously.

if there is a question. Obviously there will be fewer questions raised if the charge slip is sent with the bill. Until the Tax Reform Act of 1969, this was largely a matter of preference. But as noted in Section 26.7, the Club must now document certain information for tax purposes. The charge slip is the most logical place to do so, and accordingly, the Club may prefer to keep these slips permanently. One alternative is for the charge slips to be prepared in duplicate or to be photocopied.

There will be, of course, receipts during the month from the member paying a bill from the previous month. As discussed below, all receipts are entered in the cash receipts book and then posted to the accounts receivable ledger cards.[5] The individual accounts to be credited can be either posted directly from the cash receipts book or from a "credit advice" slip prepared at the time the receipt is entered in the cash receipts book. If the credit advice slip approach is followed, the slips are sorted and posted in the same manner as the charge slips. Either approach can be used, but it is important to "control" carefully the postings to be sure they are posted to the right account.

The general ledger accounts receivable account becomes the "control" account for all the individual members' accounts. In the sales register in Exhibit 32–3, the total amount of all charges to the members ($75,006.33) is posted in one amount to the general ledger accounts receivable control account. The same is true with the cash receipts book; $70,001.65 would be posted (Exhibit 32–5). If no mistakes have been made in posting, the aggregate of the individual ledger card balances should be the same as the balance in this control account after all postings since the sources of the postings are the same. Before mailing the members' monthly bills, all individual bills should be added together to be certain that the total of these bills does agree with this general ledger control account. If there is a large volume of activity, this "balancing," as it is called, can be a major job each month. But it must be done, and the individual bills should not be sent out until they are in agreement in total.

32.5   CASH RECEIPTS BOOK

As indicated above, the cash receipts book is the source of postings for the individual members' receivable accounts. This means that the form of cash receipts book discussed in the previous chapters must change in format. Exhibit 32–5 shows an example of the new format.

---

[5] Some clubs will find it impractical to post receipts individually to the cash receipts book because of the large volume. One alternative is to prepare the deposit slip for the bank with the name of the member shown alongside each check listed. A duplicate copy of the deposit slip could be kept permanently, and only the total of the deposit slip entered in the cash receipts book. The copy of the deposit slip would be the posting source for the credits to each member's accounts.

EXHIBIT 32–5   A cash receipts book.

Date (19x1)	Description	Member No.	Total Cash	Members' Acct. Rec. A/C #20	Other Credits a/c #	Amount
July 14	Brillon	89	345.18	345.18		
14	McNair	605	16.21	16.21		
14	Spangle	710	26.41	26.41		
14	Wander	890	18.16	18.16		
14	Rengler	679	86.15	86.15		
14	McNair	605	8.61	8.61		
14	Falvery	340	60.00	60.00		
14	Daytona Trust		1.141		191	11.41
14	Riley	687	214.50	214.50		
14	Jackson	372	150.20	150.20		
14	Allen	15	135.29	135.29		
14	Thompson	760	210.23	210.23		
14	Williamson	905	2100.45	2100.45		
14	McDonald	607	65.00	65.00		
14	Peterson	665	89.15	89.15		
	Hannagan		131.40	131.40		
	...dson		55.95	55.8?		
14		402	15.00			
		701		.45		
		211		17.42		
14	Brillon	89	25.19	25.19		
31	Harris					
31	McNally					
31	Melon	615	1215.16	1215.16		
			70065.16	70001.65		63.51

√ = Posted

AC	AMT.
191	11.41 √
180	52.10 √
	63.51

This is a very simple cash receipt register because The Valley Country Club makes sales only to its members, and only on a charge basis. Therefore there are seldom any receipts from sources other than the members. Since all receipts are posted to the members' accounts, the credit entry is usually to accounts receivable. There is an "other" column in this cash receipts book to provide for the occasional receipt from some other source.

There are two ways to handle the posting to the members' accounts. The first is to post directly from the cash receipts book to an individual member's ledger card. This is probably the most common method where the volume is not too large. One alternative is to prepare an "advice slip"[6] at the time the cash receipts book entry is made and use this advice slip as a posting source.[7] Or, if a bookkeeping machine or one-write system is used, the posting to the member's account can be made simultaneously at the time the posting to the cash receipts book is made.

[6] An illustration of a credit advice slip is not shown. However, the format can be very simple. Some organizations even use the envelope in which payment was received as the advice slip, marking the amount of the payment on the envelope. The bookkeeper can easily work out the preferred method.
[7] See the footnote on page 596 describing the use of a duplicate deposit slip as the posting source.

32.6 ACCOUNTS PAYABLE REGISTER

An accounts payable register is a book in which all bills are formally recorded at the time they are received. In the process of recording these "payables," the expense classification to be charged is also entered, and this book becomes the primary source of charges to the various general ledger expense accounts. Exhibit 32–6 shows an example of the first page of an accounts payable register. The actual register could extend across a double page in order to provide enough columns for all major categories of expense. Using a double page would give about 20 columns.

The date of actual payment is not of significance because the bill will show as an account payable until paid. The "date paid" and "check number" columns are provided in this register to show a record of which accounts have been paid, and which have not been paid. If there is no entry in these two spaces, the bill has not been paid and it is still an account payable. This is a control to keep track of the unpaid accounts payable. Each month after all general ledger postings have been made, an adding machine tape should be taken of these unpaid accounts and the total agreed with the amount in the general ledger. If the total does not agree, an error has been made and the bookkeeper should go back and check to be sure that every cash disbursement involving accounts payable has been posted as being paid in the accounts payable register.

Although it is not necessary to do so, most organizations enter all bills in this register, even those they are going to pay the day they receive them. It is easier to record an expense in this register than in the cash disbursement book since the various expense classifications are in columnar form.

At the end of the month, the accounts payable register is totaled by column. The total of the accounts payable column is posted to the accounts payable liability account. This liability account will be reduced as disbursements are made through the cash disbursement book. The various expense account columns should also be posted, and if there are any amounts in the "other" column, they should be analyzed and posted individually.

32.7 CASH DISBURSEMENTS BOOK

With all bills being entered in the accounts payable register when received, there is no longer a need to have columns for the various expense categories in the cash disbursements register. In fact, the cash disbursements book becomes a much smaller book with only a few columns. Exhibit 32–7 shows an example of this book.

EXHIBIT 32-6 An accounts payable register.

The Valley Country Club
Accounts Payable Register

Date 19x1	Payee	Check No.	Date Paid	Accounts Payable (70) -220-	-220-	-320-	-420-	-520-	-620-	-720-	Other Account	Amount
July 3	Allen's Lawn Needs	160	7/20	515.10	515.10							
3	All Pro's Invitational	162	7/21	1840.75			1840.75					
3	Aquarium Monthly	167	7/24	25.00							#340	25.00
3	McGivern's Sporting Goods	169	7/26	245.30		245.30						
3	Best Food Inc.	170	7/26	1125.13					1125.13			
3	Jones Meat Market	173	7/26	2010.40					2010.40			
5	Ted's Frozen Foods	174	7/26	946.30					946.30			
5	Brown's Seed Supply	175	7/26	412.00	412.00							
5	Business Review	177	7/26	20.00							#340	20.00
5	AC Sporting Goods, Inc.	178	7/26	412.00		412.00						
5	Pickering Pool Supplies	179	7/26	350.00				350.00				
5	Morton Frozen Goods	181	7/27	851.75					851.75			
5	Bill's Produce Market	183	7/27	1141.90					1141.90			
6	Forrest Lawn Service	184	7/27	95.10	95.10							
6	Swimming Pool Goods	185	7/27	115.75				115.75				
6	Ludwig-Lawrence Agency		7/27	86.150							#944	86.150
	... Stationery Store	201	7/2?	51.17							#?20	51.174
6	Cobb ...											
6	Martin & Ro... supplies	226	7/3?	1140.050						1140.050		
6	The Lawn Goods	227	7/31	185.90								
6	... Good											
31	Apex Dry Goods			91.75					917.10		#915	
31	Photo Copy Services			34.45					91.75			34.45
31	Ted's Golf Goods			245.10		245.10						
31	Florida Golf Assoc.			1000.00			1000.00					
				4317.956	1751.90	1333.236	559.000	620.030	2416.144	618.231		354.125

599

EXHIBIT 32-7 A cash disbursements book.

The Valley County Club

Cash Disbursement Book

Date 1961	Payee	Check No.	Disbursement Daytona Bank	Disbursement National Bank	Accounts Payable (Dr)	Discount Earned (Cr)	Payroll Taxes (a/c 75)	Other Account	Other Amount
	Balance Forwarded from Previous Page		7,695.02	1,400.375	1,789.492	45.30	39.875		345.040
July 26	McGiven's Sporting Goods	169	245.30		245.30				
26	Best Food Inc.	170		1,112.513	1,125.13				
26	Volusia Tax Board	171	348.900						348.900
26	Thompson's Hardware	172	85.93		90.45	4.52			
26	Jones Meat Market	173		201.040	201.040				
26	Ted's Frozen Foods	174		94.630	94.630				
26	Brown's Seed Supply	175	412.00		412.00				
26	Johnson's Lumber Co.	176	23.750		25.000	1,250			
26	Business Review	177	20.00		20.00				
26	A.C. Sporting Goods, Inc.	178	412.00		412.00				
26	Pickering Pool Supplies	179	350.00		350.00				
27	Daytona Bank & Trust	180	489.571				489.571		
27	Morton Frozen Goods	181	73.50	85.175	85.175				
27	Williams Printers	182		1,141.190			150		
27	Bill's Produce Market				75.10				
27	~st Lawn Service	185	95.10		115.75				
27	Ludw~ · Pool Goods	186	~15.75		86.150				
27	A.B.C. Static~ Repair Service	187	3~		51.174				
31	Martin & Ross Liquor Supplies	225	1,85.90		140.50		50		
31	Thomas Lawn Goods	226			185.90				
		227	21,23.849	24,087.940	33,85.598	71.95	529.446		83.940

Notice that there are two bank account columns. Many organizations have more than one active bank account and this is how the second bank account is handled. The amount of the check disbursed is entered in the appropriate column depending on the bank on which the check is drawn. The offsetting debit is normally accounts payable since all bills are entered in the accounts payable register. A column for this debit to accounts payable is provided. The total of the accounts payable column is posted to the general ledger at the end of the month which serves to reduce the accounts payable amount recorded as an obligation from the accounts payable register.

There is also a column for discounts earned. If payment is made within the time specified on the vendor's invoice for cash discounts, it should be taken. Thus the amount of the check will be less than the amount of the bill, and, therefore, less than the payable set up in the accounts payable register. The discounts earned column would be the place where this discount would be shown. In this way, the amount entered in the accounts payable column will be the total amount owed. The "discounts earned" column is a credit or income item. For example, note that the July 26 payment to Thompson Hardware was less a 5 percent discount of $4.52, but the credit to accounts payable was the total amount of the bill, $90.45.

A column has been provided to record the payment of FICA and withholding taxes. The obligation to pay these withholding taxes is recorded in the payroll register (Exhibit 31–2), and this column, when posted to the general ledger, serves to reduce the liability.

As with the other books, a column is provided to record transactions not reflected in one of the specific columns. There will be relatively few entries recorded in this column. In our illustration, payment of the sales tax collections in June has been recorded in this column. The actual liability entry setting up the obligation was recorded through the sales register (Exhibit 32–3).

32.8 MONTHLY ACCRUAL ENTRIES

Notwithstanding the use of the various journals and registers discussed above, several entries must still be made on a monthly basis in the general journal. These entries relate principally to adjustment of accounts not involving cash.

(a) Employer Payroll Taxes

The payroll register provides a place to record the amount of withholding and FICA taxes withheld from employees' wages. It does not provide, however, for the recording of the employer's share of such taxes. An accrual entry must be made monthly to record such amounts. The amount of FICA taxes is usually exactly the same amount withheld from employees during the period. At the time the payroll register is totaled at the end of the month, the bookkeeper should note the amount of employee taxes and then make the following entry:

July 31

Entry No. 5

Debit No. 952 Payroll tax expense $2,117.89
    Credit No. 75 FICA and withholding taxes payable $2,117.89
        To record the employer's share of payroll taxes for the
        month of July.

In this illustration, all of this payroll tax expense was charged to a single account. Some organizations prefer to split this expense among all payroll expense accounts. If this is done, it can either be done monthly at the time the above entry is prepared, or it can be done at the end of the year by analyzing total payroll for the year and allocating the total employer taxes charged to account No. 952.

(b) Depreciation

An entry must still be made monthly to record depreciation expense. The procedures outlined in Chapter 31 should be followed.

(c) Inventories

Inventories can be handled in two ways. The first way, which is probably how it would be handled with The Valley Country Club, is to charge all inventory items to expense as the bills are received, and then to adjust, at the end of the month, for any inventory still on hand. This is the method used with the simplified accrual basis system discussed in Chapter 31. The other approach is to record all inventory purchases as assets (i.e., debit to the inventory asset account and credit to accounts payable) and then periodically to reduce the carrying value of this inventory as it is consumed. The entry for this adjustment would be a debit to expense and a credit to the inventory asset account.

(d) Accrued Salary Payable

There is no automatic procedure to record accrued salary payable even with a full accrual system. Accordingly, an accrual entry must still be made for the portion unpaid at the end of the month. The procedures followed in this type of accrual are exactly as discussed in Chapter 31.

(e) Prepaid Expenses

Insurance premiums, taxes, and similar items should be charged to the appropriate prepaid asset account at the time they are recorded in the accounts payable register. Then, at the end of the period, the portion of this prepaid expense which has expired by virtue of passage of time or usage should be written off to expense in a journal entry. The type of entry to be made would be:

July 31

Entry No. 6

Debit No. 944 Insurance expense $100.00
Credit No. 40 Prepaid insurance $100.00
   To record as an expense that portion of the prepaid
   insurance applicable to July.

This type of entry might not be made on a monthly basis if the amounts involved were not large. Often quarterly or even semiannual entries are all that are necessary.

(f) Reserve for Bad Debts

From time to time, a reserve for bad debts will be needed. This type of entry is also handled through the general journal. The entry in the case of The Valley Country Club would be:

July 31

Entry No. 7

Debit No. 951 Bad debts expense $200.00
Credit No. 23 Allowance for bad debts $200.00
   To set up an allowance for bad debts for the portion of
   accounts receivable that are in dispute with estate of
   deceased member.

An alternative approach is to record the bad debt expense only at the time specific accounts receivable are written off. If this approach were followed, then the credit at the time of write-off would be to accounts receivable (account No. 20) rather than to the allowance account.

32.9   CONCLUSION

The two principal books that allow an organization to record certain transactions on an accrual basis are the sales register and the accounts payable register. Both have as their intent, the recording of transactions as they occur rather than when cash is involved. As with the other records discussed in earlier chapters, they are basically commonsense types of records which are designed to record transactions in a systematic manner so as to allow like transactions to be grouped together.

Fund Accounting Bookkeeping

There is only one important difference between fund accounting and the other accounting methods used by not-for-profit organizations. In fund accounting, a number of separate accounting entities are maintained which are referred to as "funds." A fund accounting system presents no special difficulty, except for the problem of keeping the transactions of these funds separated while integrating all of the funds into a total bookkeeping system. An organization using fund accounting can be on the cash basis, a simplified accrual basis, or a full accrual basis. The same types of records discussed in the three previous chapters can be used in fund accounting. This chapter will discuss only the problems related to fund accounting.

For purposes of discussion an accrual basis research institute will be used as an illustration. The J.W.M. Diabetes Research Institute was discussed and financial statements were presented in Chapter 13 (Exhibits 13–6 to 13–11) and the reader may find it helpful to refer back to these statements. This organization uses fund accounting and has five fund "groupings"[1]—unrestricted general fund, unrestricted investment fund, fund for specified purposes, plant fund, and endowment fund. Readers are reminded that for purposes of external reporting, as discussed in Chapter 13, the funds are rearranged into classes of net assets.

33.1   CHART OF ACCOUNTS

The key to a good bookkeeping system is a carefully thought out chart of accounts. This is especially true when fund accounting is used because there are several completely separate accounting entities each of which has its own accounts for assets, liabilities, income, expense, and net assets. Yet these separate entities must be integrated carefully into an overall chart of accounts. Each fund grouping must have an account structure similar to the other groupings, both for ease in keeping the records and for ease in preparing financial statements.

Exhibit 33–1 shows the chart of accounts for the J.W.M. Diabetes Research Institute. This chart is basically a three-digit system with the first digit designating the fund grouping. These fund groupings are shown at the left-hand top column on the chart. All asset, liability, income, and expense codes are two-digit codes and are the second and third digits in the three-digit account code. These two-digit codes are used with the fund grouping code to designate the specific fund grouping they belong to. For example, code 107 is "unrestricted general fund marketable securities" while 507 is "endowment fund marketable securities."

Expense groupings are also used in a similar manner. There are four expense groups (instruction, research, administration, and maintenance). For each of these groups there are six single-digit expense codes and they are the third digit from the left. For example, "0" is salaries. Code 60 is "instruction salaries" while code 90 is "maintenance salaries." In addition to these codes, there are a few other specific codes that are not applicable to these four major expense groups and they are listed separately.

One of the features of this chart of accounts is that it facilitates the preparation of financial statements in columnar format or, if desired, in a consolidated format. All similar items are coded with the same last two digits and this can be a time saver for the bookkeeper.

---

[1] The reader should be careful to distinguish between a fund "grouping" and an individual fund. A fund "grouping" is all of the individual funds having similar characteristics, whereas a "fund" is an individual entity being accounted for as a separate unit. Another expression used in this chapter is "name" fund. A "name" fund is a fund that bears a name, usually of the principal donor. There may be other funds, with identical restrictions but the separate identification by "name" is maintained for any one of a number of reasons. These concepts were discussed in Chapter 4.

EXHIBIT 33–1   A chart of accounts for a research institute that uses fund accounting.

J. W. M. DIABETES RESEARCH INSTITUTE
CHART OF ACCOUNTS

Fund Grouping

100	Unrestricted general fund
200	Unrestricted investment fund
300	Fund for specified purposes
400	Plant fund
500	Endowment fund

Assets

01	Cash in bank
02	Cash in savings bank
03	Petty cash
05	U.S. treasury bills
06	Marketable bonds
07	Marketable securities
08	Investment real estate
09	Other investments
10	Contracts receivable—current year
11	Contracts receivable—prior year
12	Other receivables
13	Inventory—books
14	Inventory—supplies
15	Prepaid expenses
18	Land
19	Buildings
20	Accumulated depreciation— building
21	Equipment
22	Accumulated depreciation— equipment
23	Vehicles
24	Accumulated depreciation— vehicles

Liabilities

30	Accounts payable
31	Short-term loans
32	Payroll taxes
33	Salaries payable
34	Grants paid in advance
35	Other short-term liabilities
36	Long-term debts

Interfund Receivables (Payables)

41	Unrestricted general fund
42	Unrestricted investment fund
43	Fund for specified purposes
44	Plant fund
45	Endowment fund

Net Assets

46	Unrestricted
47	Unrestricted—allocated
48	Restricted

Income

50	Grant and contract income
51	Other fees
55	Contributions and gifts
57	Investment income
58	Interest income
59	Realized gains or losses

EXHIBIT 33–1   *Continued.*

Expense Groups	−4 Books
6− Instruction	−5 Other
7− Research	
8− Administration	Specific Codes
9− Maintenance	86 Insurance
	87 Bad debts
Type Expense	88 Depreciation
−0 Salaries	89 Legal and accounting and investment fees
−1 Retirement benefits	
−2 Major medical	97 Contracted services
−3 Stationery and supplies	98 Utilities and fuel

(a)   Interfund Accounts

In fund accounting, there are frequently interfund receivables and payables. In this chart of accounts, all of these interfund balances are shown in five accounts for each fund grouping. The only distinction between a receivable or a payable with a particular fund is whether it is a debit (receivable) or a credit (payable). For example, if the unrestricted general fund owes the unrestricted investment fund $100, the unrestricted general fund would show a credit of $100 in account 142; the unrestricted investment fund would show a debit balance in account 241. Notice the account numbers 142 and 241. The first digit designates the fund in which the account belongs (1 = unrestricted general fund, 2 = unrestricted investment fund), and the third digit designates the fund which either is owed, or owes, the $100. In the first instance, the 2 designates the unrestricted investment fund. In the other, the 1 designates the unrestricted general fund.

Likewise if the endowment fund owed $50 to the unrestricted general fund and $10 to the fund for specified purposes, the respective fund groupings would look like this in a columnar format:

Unrestricted General Fund		Fund for Specified Purpose		Endowment Fund		Total All Funds
145	$50			541	($50) credit	—
		345	$10	543	(10) credit	—

As can be seen, if all interfund receivables and payables are shown in columnar form in this fashion, the "total all funds" column will net out to zero.

(b) "Name" Funds

No separate listing is shown for the various name funds within the fund for specified purposes or in the endowment fund. As can be seen from Exhibit 13–8, The J.W.M. Diabetes Research Institute has many such funds.

If there are only one or two name funds, probably no separate set of account numbers need be assigned. There are not usually many transactions in each such fund and it will be easier to analyze each name fund separately once or twice a year than to keep a separate set of accounts for each. But if there are many name funds, as is the case here, or if the bookkeeping is done on a bookkeeping machine where account numbers are really needed to facilitate posting, then a further account-number structure should be set up. The easiest way is to assign one more, or even two more, digits to the three-digit code to designate the specific fund involved. These would be the fourth or fifth digits reading from the left. Thus marketable securities in the Malmar endowment fund might be shown as code 507-1: the 507 being the code number for endowment fund marketable securities, and the 1 being the code number assigned to the Malmar Fund. There would be a complete balancing set of accounts maintained for this subcode 1. If more than ten such name funds were used then a second digit would be added (507-11). The same procedure would be followed with the fund for specified purposes. In this way, the organization can have any number of name funds all within the same chart of account structure.

33.2 BOOKS AND RECORDS

The books and records used by fund accounting organizations are basically the same records discussed in Chapters 30 to 32. A completely separate set of books may be maintained for each fund grouping rather than trying to integrate all of the fund groupings into a single set of books. With a separate set of books the unrestricted general fund would have its own cash receipts book, cash disbursement book, accounts payable register, general ledger, general journal, grant income ledger, and so on. Each of the other fund groupings would also have its separate set of books, although not all of the books would be appropriate for each grouping. In the case of The J.W.M. Diabetes Research Institute, separate books are kept for each fund grouping, as shown below.

Even where a fund grouping requires one of these books, the actual format of the book may be much simpler than the format used by the unrestricted general fund. For example, the number of expense categories and volume of transactions applicable to the fund for specified purposes are relatively few, and the cash disbursement book may have only a debit and credit column with each expenditure being posted individually to the general ledger. In fact, if there are only a few cash transactions during the year, the cash receipts book and cash disbursements book may not be used at all. All entries, including cash entries, would then be entered in the general journal and posted directly and individually to the general ledger accounts.

Book	Unrestricted General Fund	Unrestricted Investment Fund	Fund for Specified Purposes	Plant Fund	Endowment Fund
General ledger	x	x	x	x	x
General journal	x	x	x	x	x
Cash disbursement ...	x		x		
Cash receipts	x		x		
Accounts payable register	x				
Tution income ledger	x				
Payroll register	x				
Investment ledger	x	x			x
Fixed asset register ...	x			x	

The plant fund may or may not include assets other than plant or fixed assets. If the board places donor-restricted gifts for plant additions into the fund for specified purposes then only fixed assets would be shown in the plant fund. This type of decision, of course, affects the books that must be kept. In the case of our illustration, only fixed assets are shown in the plant fund.

(a) Books of "Name" Funds

Each individual name fund within each fund grouping will also require separate records but these records will consist only of a set of general ledger pages for the accounts maintained for each name fund. For example, if the fund for specified purposes has two name funds, each with opening net assets represented by cash in a savings account and each having contributions and expenses during the year, then the general ledger accounts would be as follows:

	Name Fund No. 1	Name Fund No. 2
Savings cash	302–1	302–2
Net assets	348–1	348–2
Contributions	355–1	355–2
Interest	358–1	358–2
Expenses	3 ---1	3 ---2

These general ledger accounts would be filed in account number order rather than being segregated by each of the name funds. When a trial balance of the general ledger of the entire fund grouping is needed, the bookkeeper will take a trial balance of the individual general ledger accounts for all of the name funds. For purposes of statement presentation these name accounts would be combined to get the figures for the fund grouping as a whole. Exhibit 33–2 shows an example of a combining worksheet for the endowment fund grouping. Notice how these figures tie into the financial statements in Chapter 13.

(b) Single Set of Books

There is no reason why an organization cannot merge all of the fund groupings into one overall set of books in much the same manner discussed for the name funds above. The chart of accounts is arranged to permit this. If all accounts were combined, the general ledger would be fairly sizable but then it would only be necessary to keep one general journal, one cash disbursement book, one cash receipts book, and so on.

The principal advantage of a single set of books is that there is only one set of records, and this facilitates bookkeeping, particularly if the organization has enough volume to handle its bookkeeping on a bookkeeping machine or some other form of mechanized system. With almost any type of mechanization, it is simpler to have one complex general ledger system than to have many separate general ledgers.

The principal disadvantage is that it is far easier to keep all transactions relating to one fund grouping together in a separate set of records. The bookkeeper is less likely to get confused and will be able to see what is happening more easily when separate books are used for each fund grouping. Accordingly, except when records are handled on some sort of mechanized system or where the organization has an especially competent bookkeeping staff, it is probably better to stick with a separate set of records for each fund grouping.

33.3 INTERFUND TRANSACTIONS

If all transactions involved a single fund, and there were no transactions between funds or fund groupings, the bookkeeping problems of fund accounting would be relatively easy. Unfortunately, these interfund transactions often cause more difficulty than they should partly because a bookkeeper may be uncertain how to record such transactions. There are several fairly common interfund transactions, and each of these is discussed and illustrated in the following paragraphs.

EXHIBIT 33–2 An example of a preclosing worksheet in which individual "name" endowment funds are combined. For financial statement purposes, only the totals would be reported.

J. W. M. DIABETES RESEARCH INSTITUTE

PRECLOSING WORKSHEET COMBINING NAME ENDOWMENT FUNDS

June 30, 19X2

Sub-Code		01/02	06/07	41/45	48	55	57/58	59	61/99
					Accounts				
–1	The Malmar Fund	$ 4,000	$ 108,655	($ 4,970)	($ 110,700)		($4,970)	$ 3,015	$ 4,970
–2	Clyde Henderson Fund		34,916		(25,601)		(1,150)	(8,165)	
–3	Evelyn I. Marnoch Fund		9,205		(10,871)		(490)	2,156	
–4	Roy B. Cowin Memorial Fund	4,496	1,850,173		(1,641,300)			(213,369)	
–5	Lillian V. Fromhagen Fund		60,076		(53,165)			(6,911)	
–6	Donna Comstock Fund		47,974		(28,160)	($ 16,153)		(3,661)	
–7	Josephine Zagajewski Fund		100,000			(100,000)			
–8	The Peter Baker Fund		20,081		(12,150)	(6,351)		(1,580)	
–9	The Alfred P. Koch Fund	7,119		(7,119)	(6,300)			(819)	7,119
	Total	$15,615	$2,231,080	($12,089)	($1,888,247)	($122,504)	($6,610)	($229,334)	$12,089

Net Assets .... $2,234,606   Fund balance after closing   ($2,234,606)

(a) Investment Income Transfer

The transfer of investment income from one fund to another is very common. Typically, investment income earned on an endowment fund is deposited by the custodian bank in an endowment fund income cash account. Then, from time to time the bookkeeper will transfer portions of this cash to the unrestricted general fund and if any of the income is restricted to a specified use, to the fund for specified purposes. Here are the journal entries that would be made if the endowment fund earned $250 of income, $200 of which is unrestricted and $50 is restricted for a specified purpose:

On endowment fund books:

Debit No. 501 (cash) $250
    Credit No. 557 (investment income) $250
        To record receipt of investment income.
Debit No. 557 (investment income) $250
    Credit No. 541 (payable to unrestricted general fund) $200
    Credit No. 543 (payable to fund for specified purposes) 50
        To record transfer of investment income to unrestricted
        general fund and fund for specified purposes.

On unrestricted general fund books:

Debit No. 145 (receivable from endowment fund) $200
    Credit No. 157 (investment income) $200
        To record transfer of investment income from endowment
        fund.

On fund for specified purposes books:

Debit No. 345 (receivable from endowment fund) $50
    Credit No. 357 (investment income) $50
        To record transfer of investment income from endowment
        fund.

In due course, when the cash is actually transferred from the endowment fund, the entry on the various books would be a debit or credit to cash and a corresponding debit or credit to the interfund payable or receivable account.

(b) Interfund Borrowings

Another frequent interfund transaction is the temporary borrowing of cash by one fund from another fund. Here are the entries to record the unrestricted general fund's borrowing of $10,000 from the unrestricted investment fund.

On unrestricted general fund books:

Debit No. 101 (Cash) $10,000
    Credit No. 142 (payable to unrestricted investment fund) $10,000
        To record interfund loan from the unrestricted investment
        fund.

On unrestricted investment fund books:

Debit No. 241 (receivable from unrestricted general fund) . . $10,000
    Credit No. 201 (cash) $10,000
        To record interfund loan to the unrestricted general fund.

When this loan is paid off, the entries would be reversed.

(c) Expenses Paid by One Fund for Another

The unrestricted general fund may pay expenses which are chargeable to another fund. A common example is payment of expenses out of the unrestricted general fund which are to be charged to the fund for specified purposes.

In the following example the unrestricted general fund buys $200 worth of library books, $75 of which can be charged to the fund for specified purposes. Here are the appropriate entries: On unrestricted general fund books:

Debit No. 143 (receivable from fund for specified purposes) . . $ 75
Debit No. 174 (library books) 125
    Credit No. 130 (accounts payable) $200
        To record amount of library books purchased by unre-
        stricted general fund, part of which is to be paid for by
        fund for specified purposes.

On fund for specified purposes books:

Debit No. 374 (library books) $75
    Credit No. 341 (payable to unrestricted general fund) $75
        To record purchase of library books by the unrestricted
        general fund, out of the fund for specified purposes.

(d)   Contributions Transferred to Unrestricted Investment Fund

All contributions not restricted by donors must be shown in the unrestricted general fund. However, if the board wishes, it can always make transfers out of the unrestricted general fund into the unrestricted investment fund. The contribution must be reported first as income in the unrestricted general fund, so any transfer is effectively a transfer of a portion of the net assets. Here are the entries that would be made to record a gift of $750 and the subsequent transfer to the unrestricted investment fund:

On unrestricted general fund books:

Debit No. 101 (cash) $750
   Credit No. 155 (contributions) $750
      To record receipt of an unrestricted contribution from
      Linda Jean Baker.

Debit No. 146 (unrestricted general fund net assets) $750
   Credit No. 142 (payable to unrestricted investment fund) $750
      To record transfer to unrestricted investment fund of portion
      of unrestricted general net assets arising from gift of
      Linda Jean Baker.

On unrestricted investment fund books:

Debit No. 241 (receivable from unrestricted general fund) .. $750
   Credit No. 246 (unrestricted investment fund net assets) $750
      To record transfer from unrestricted general fund of portion
      of unrestricted general fund net assets arising from gift of
      Linda Jean Baker.

Note that in the unrestricted general fund the transfer was out of the net assets account and not out of the contributions received account. The gift of $750 must be reported as part of unrestricted general fund income, and accordingly the transfer cannot come from the contribution account. Second, note that in the unrestricted investment fund the $750 receipt was shown not as a contribution but, again, as a net asset transfer. This is the important thing to remember about transfers. They don't create income; all they do is transfer portions of the net assets or net worth from one fund to another. Transfers are discussed at length in Chapter 5.

(e) Current Restricted Funds Expended through the Unrestricted General Fund

A related type of transaction between funds takes place with those organizations following the accounting principle of placing all restricted contributions in a current restricted fund (the name often given to the fund for specified purposes) and then transferring to the unrestricted general fund such portion of these restricted contributions as is actually expended by the unrestricted general fund. This is now the method required by SFAS No. 117 for handling restricted contributions for current purposes.[2] Basically the entries to effect this transfer are quite straightforward. Assume $600 is received in the current year but only $500 is expended for the restricted purpose.

On fund for specified purposes books:

Debit No. 301 (cash) $600
    Credit No. 355 (contributions) $600
        To record receipt of $600 restricted contributions.
Debit No. 355 (contributions) $500
    Credit No. 341 (interfund payable) $500
        To record transfer to the unrestricted general fund of a
        portion of restricted contributions for current operations
        that were expended during the year.

(f) Allocation of Unrestricted Fund Balances

Allocations, or as they are often known, "appropriations," of part of the unrestricted general fund balance are occasionally made by the board. While the use of allocations is not recommended because they are seldom understood by the reader, some organizations still use this bookkeeping technique to segregate portions of the unrestricted general fund net assets for future projects. This is an acceptable practice only if the rules outlined in Chapter 5 are followed. When the rules are followed, the entry that would be made to effect an allocation would be:

Debit No. 146 (unrestricted general net assets) $1,000
    Credit No. 147 (unrestricted net assets
    balance—allocated) $1,000
        To record an allocation of the unrestricted general
        net assets for Project A.

---

[2] See Chapter 10 for a complete discussion of alternative reporting practices for current restricted contributions, in addition, the application of this principle to hospitals is discussed in Chapter 16.

Note that this entry merely transfers a portion of the unrestricted general fund net assets to another unrestricted general fund net asset account. No income or expense is involved. At a future date when the expenditure is made for Project A, it will be charged to an expense account, and not to the allocated portion of the unrestricted general fund net assets. At that time, an entry will be made reversing the entry above.

33.4 TRIAL BALANCE

One final word of caution is in order. The usual way in which posting errors are caught is through the use of a trial balance. If the debits and the credits aren't equal, the bookkeeper is alerted to look for an error. The most likely posting error a bookkeeper will make, when fund accounting is involved, is to enter a transaction involving two funds in only one of the two funds. The use of a trial balance, however, will not catch this type of error since the debits and credits may be equal but a complete entry in one of the funds has been omitted (both debit and credit).

(a) Balancing Interfund Transactions

It is easy to prevent this from going undetected. What is required is a balancing of the interfund receivables and payables. If they balance out to zero, then the bookkeeper knows that both sides of all interfund transactions have been recorded. This balancing is easy to do with the chart of accounts provided in Exhibit 33–1 because all of the interorganization accounts are classified in one series of account numbers. Usually all that is required is running an adding machine tape of the aggregate debit and credit balances of the interfund accounts to be sure they net out to zero; if they don't, then the bookkeeper can compare, account by account, the corresponding contra (opposite) account in the other fund. Thus account 142 should be the same amount as 241 except one will be a debit and the other a credit. In this way, it is easy to pinpoint differences.

33.5 CONCLUSION

Fund accounting is not difficult from a bookkeeping standpoint but it requires careful organization and a good chart of accounts. It also requires care to ensure that both sides of interfund transactions are recorded. Other than that, fund accounting follows the same principles used by non-fund accounting organizations.

Fund accounting can be applied to either cash or accrual basis organizations. The principal problem with fund accounting is not the bookkeeping, but the problem of presentation. This is where fund accounting frequently falls down. If the suggestions and recommendations that have been made throughout this book are heeded, the treasurer will be able to put together financial statements that are straightforward and clear to the unknowledgeable reader; in short, that will easily pass the "non-accountant" test.

C H A P T E R 34

Automating the
Accounting Records

At some point, the not-for-profit organization may consider implementing its first automated accounting system or upgrading its existing system.[1] If the organization does not have experience with selecting, implementing, or using an automated accounting system, this can seem like a daunting task. If the automated system is not carefully selected and implemented, the results will be less than satisfactory and could cause much wasted time, money, and frustration. However, if the system is well-implemented, it could improve the quality and timeliness of financial and accounting information and help support organizational objectives.

---

[1] See section on Automated Bookkeeping Systems in Chapter 32. As discussed in Chapter 32, automated bookkeeping systems (referred to in this chapter as automated accounting systems) do not differ in concept from the manual systems illustrated throughout this book. Rather, mechanical aspects of the process are partly or wholly performed by automation instead of by human bookkeepers.

This chapter provides an overview of the major issues to consider when selecting and implementing an automated accounting system. It highlights some of the not-for-profit specific features to be aware of when selecting automated accounting software. Some common pitfalls to successful accounting system automation are discussed. Unless someone in the organization is skilled in selecting and implementing accounting software, it would be advisable to obtain outside assistance to guide you through this process.

34.1   WHEN TO CONSIDER AUTOMATING OR UPGRADING

There are a number of indicators that suggest that it is time for an organization to consider automating or upgrading its accounting systems. Some examples of indicators include the following:

- *Size and Organizational Structure of the Not-for-Profit.* The organization has many departments/cost centers, many funds[2] and/or restricted grants,[3] several tiers to its organization, or is growing rapidly.
- *Complexity of the Transactions.* The organization has complicated allocations, uses encumbrance accounting,[4] or full accrual accounting[5] that has become difficult to manage in the manual or existing automated system.
- *Transaction Volumes.* The number of transactions processed is making it very difficult to keep up on a timely basis or is requiring excessive staff time. Generally more than 50 transactions in a particular accounting function per month warrants automation.
- *Reporting Requirements.* If there is a multiple tier reporting structure, if project or activity level reporting are desired, or if significant manual effort or rekeying is currently required to produce financial statements and special reports.

The organization should not feel compelled to automate everything or to automate everything at once. A careful assessment of the automation requirements should be performed before any commitment is made to purchase accounting software or hardware.

---

[2] Funds are discussed in Chapter 4.
[3] Restricted grants are discussed in Chapter 10.
[4] Encumbrance accounting is discussed in Chapter 15.
[5] Same as full accrual basis bookkeeping, discussed in Chapter 32.

34.2   WHAT TO AUTOMATE

Once the decision to automate has been made, the next step is to consider what the accounting system will be expected to do and the extent of automation desired. This section highlights some of the benefits and misconceptions regarding automated accounting systems and lists some of the more common accounting software modules used by not-for-profit organizations.

(a)   What Accounting Software Will and Will Not Do

Compared with service bureaus[6] or manual bookkeeping systems, an automated accounting system can:

- Provide better internal control[7]
- Provide better and more timely access to data
- Allow greater data security
- Improve clerical productivity
- Reduce some administrative costs
- Stabilize cost as volume increases
- Improve professional quality, and
- Integrate[8] with other software to perform decision analysis.

There are things an automated accounting system won't do: it won't make accounting decisions or tell you how to record transactions, improve poor judgment, or generate reports for data that were not properly organized and recorded. For these reasons, it is important that a professional accountant provide assistance in selecting and implementing[9] the

---

[6] A service bureau is an organization that uses its equipment and software to process data for other organizations for a fee. This chapter assumes an organization is considering obtaining its own equipment and automated software. However, many of the concepts presented in this chapter can also be applied in selecting a service bureau.

[7] Internal control is discussed in Chapter 23.

[8] Automated systems are considered to be integrated when information entered into one system is shared by or passed automatically to another system. The primary objective of "integrated" systems is to eliminate duplication of data entry and data redundancy. Unfortunately, various software vendors' claims that their software modules are "integrated" must be reviewed with healthy skepticism.

[9] Implementation is the series of tasks and steps required to initially set up a new automated system. The system is not ready to use the moment it is loaded on the computer. There are many decisions that must be made, options within the software package selected, chart of accounts and reports designed and developed, and initial accounting data entered in order to tailor the package to the organization. Major implementation tasks are discussed later in this chapter.

automated system. Once properly implemented, the system can be operated for the most part by a less experienced bookkeeper.

An automated accounting system will not replace a bookkeeper; what it can do is help an organization make more effective use of their accounting staff. Another major benefit of an automated system is the ability to generate more meaningful management reports. Once the system automates repetitive tasks, people are able to turn their attention to more challenging and satisfying work.

(b)   Typical Accounting Software Modules for Not-for-Profits

Before deciding what to automate, there should be a basic understanding of the types of accounting software modules[10] generally available and used by not-for-profit organizations. All the major manual books and records discussed in the preceding chapters have an equivalent within the automated accounting software modules available on the market today. An exception generally relates to an operational area that is unique to a particular organization. If an organization has such an area that it wishes to automate, a custom-made system may need to be developed for its use. This chapter does not address customized accounting systems issues.

The following lists some of the typical types of packaged[11] general accounting and specialized not-for-profit software modules.

General Accounting Modules

- *General Ledger*—just as in a manual records system, this is where all transactions from the other systems (subsidiary ledgers) are summarized and where transactions not posted through the subsidiary ledgers are entered. Typically, the general ledger system also has some budgeting capability. Some vendors offer a separate software module for more sophisticated budget planning and forecasting. The general ledger system also provides report-writing capabilities for generating the financial statements and management reports. In some cases, however, an

---

[10] "Accounting software modules" refers to the different units of software that an organization would need to purchase to set up its automated accounting system. With some exceptions, most accounting software vendors sell their software by module. Unfortunately, there are no industry-wide standards regarding the accounting functions found in each module. Some vendors, for example, will sell a separate module each for general ledger, for budgeting, and for financial reporting; another vendor might include all three functions in one module. Understanding the differences among the software vendors is an area where professional assistance would be helpful.

[11] "Packaged" refers to software that has been developed for broad general usage, unadapted to any particular organization, and sold to a mass market. Contrast this with "custom" software that is specifically developed for an organization.

additional report-writer software module may also be required for complex reporting.

The general ledger is usually the first system an organization will automate.

- *Project Accounting*—maintains a detailed subledger to accumulate the costs and revenues associated with individual projects or activities. This would be required, for example, if an organization wishes to keep more detailed records related to a project or a restricted grant than would normally be recorded in the general ledger. Some general ledger systems, especially those intended for not-for-profit organizations, have capabilities to handle project accounting.

- *Accounts Payable*—vendor information, payment terms, invoice and employee expense reimbursement data are entered in the accounts payable module to facilitate automated check-writing and accrual entries for unpaid invoices. The benefit of an accounts payable system is better management of the timing of paying invoices, which can result in improved cash management. The accounts payable system also creates automatic accrual entries for the unpaid invoices, and provides an improved history of payments by vendor. In addition to the general ledger, most organizations will implement an automated accounts payable system.

- *Purchasing*—sometimes part of the accounts payable system and sometimes separate, this module is used to record purchase requisitions and create purchase orders. The purchase order is then passed to the accounts payable system where it is later matched (either manually or automatically) with the vendor invoice and possibly a receiving document. The need for a purchasing system will depend on the purchasing controls and policies of the organization (i.e., whether purchase orders are required) and the volume and nature of purchasing activity. It is not necessary to have a purchasing system in order to have an accounts payable system. The decision factor is the volume of transactions and internal control requirements surrounding purchases.

- *Inventory*—if an organization has a significant number of items that it holds for sale or use, an inventory system may be helpful. This system records the amount of items on hand, including items on backorder and purchase orders. The inventory system will often interface[12] with the purchasing system. The inventory system

---

[12] "Interface" is the automated passing of information created or entered in one accounting module to another accounting module, eliminating the need to re-enter data. The most common form of

may also have an order entry capability, or be interfaced with a separate order entry/billing system.

- *Accounts Receivable*—customer information, credit terms, and billing data are entered in the accounts receivable module to manage the aging of accounts receivable and recording credits and collections. Unless the organization regularly bills individuals for amounts due to the organization, this module may not be required. Many not-for-profits, especially those relying on revenue from donations, grants, and fund-raising, will not need an accounts receivable system. There are other specialized revenue-related systems that may be better suited to the organization, such as a membership system, subscription system, meetings/conventions/events system, and donor/pledges/fund raising system (see below).

- *Payroll*—used to record employee salary information, time worked, vacation and leave taken, generate payroll checks, and calculate the allocation of personnel costs to projects. Many organizations (including large commercial organizations) have found it cost-effective to have payroll processed by a service bureau rather than to perform the task in-house. This is primarily due to the complexity and frequency of change in federal, state, and local withholding and other payroll tax rules and rates. A service bureau also assists in the tax filings.

- *Fixed Assets*—used to record the capital assets (generally furniture and equipment) and calculate depreciation. This is among the least frequently used automated accounting modules for smaller not-for-profit organizations. Many smaller organizations can adequately handle fixed assets records either manually or using an electronic spreadsheet package. The extent of fixed assets records required will in part be dictated by local property tax laws or by government grant requirements.

Specialized Modules for Not-for-Profit Organizations

There are a number of specialized software packages that are used by not-for-profit organizations to support their organizational objectives and

---

automated interface is from the subledgers (such as accounts payable and accounts receivable) to the general ledger to post activity balances to the accounts. In more advanced interfaces, such as between an inventory system and a purchasing system, transactions are originated by the software. For example, an inventory system may automatically generate a purchase order when an item in inventory falls to a certain predetermined level. In the other direction, a purchasing system might send information to the inventory system when certain items are placed on order.

revenue-generating activities. Most of these are primarily informational databases with strong query[13] and report-writing capabilities that are tailored for the organization through the use of user-defined codes. These packages frequently have a mail merge capability to extract selected information to be used with word processing software for mass mailings. These packages, while not primarily financial transaction oriented, often include a cash receipts capability that could be interfaced with the general ledger module. The following are examples of some types of specialized not-for-profit software modules.

- *Meeting/Convention/Event Software*—helps the not-for-profit plan and execute all aspects of meetings and special events. This would include event budgeting, scheduling and logistics, recording event registration and payment information for the event, as well as generating attendance statistics and mailings lists. Similar software can handle ticket sales for concerts and exhibits.

- *Donors/Pledges/Fund-Raising Software*—helps track solicitations and follow-up of prospective and successful donor, pledge, and fund-raising activities. Some include databases of donor profiles that can be used for targeted mailings. These would include a history of donations that, if combined with a cash receipts capability, could be interfaced with the general ledger.

- *Membership Software*—used to record member profiles and generate membership dues invoices, and can include an extensive array of other supporting capabilities for the membership organization. It may include a cash receipts module that would interface with the general ledger, or with the accounts payable system for dues refunds. Similar, but more complex, software is used by colleges for student records and by hospitals for patient records.

This is not an all-inclusive list of possible automated accounting modules. There are many additional packaged software modules available to address most common business and accounting needs of an organization. A qualified business and accounting software consultant[14] can

---

[13] Query is the capability to automatically search the information in the system for data meeting user-specified search criteria. Some systems have the ability to quickly query the data and present the results on the computer screen without the need to generate a report. This is a very useful feature and a tremendous benefit of automating.

[14] A few words about selecting a software consultant. Before you know exactly which software package is best for your organization, be careful about working with a consultant who markets a specific product and whose independence could be questioned. For the requirements and selection phases, the most objective advice will come from a consultant who will not profit from the sale of a specific piece of hardware or software. Once the software package has been selected, then it may be appropriate to identify a consultant who sells and implements a specific vendor's hardware and software.

help you determine whether it is likely that a packaged system already exists to meet a particular need.

34.3   SELECTING THE RIGHT SOFTWARE

After the decision has been made to automate, and there is a general idea of the functions that would benefit from automation, the next step is to more closely analyze the specific accounting system requirements of the organization. This effort should result in a comprehensive list of requirements that the organization will use to evaluate and select the most suitable accounting software. The possibilities are too numerous to include here, especially because there are many accounting packages on the market and thousands of not-for-profit organizations, each with a wide range of capabilities and needs. The best advice for this process is to obtain assistance from a qualified professional who can help you determine the requirements and select a well-suited package.

(a)   Differences between Commercial and Not-for-Profit Accounting Software Functions

For many not-for-profit organizations, almost any commercial accounting package may serve its purposes. However, there are some software features that differentiate commercial accounting software from those suitable for certain not-for-profit organizations. The reader should be aware of these differences that impact his or her organization. This is one area that must receive special attention in selecting the right package for the organization.[15]

The following are some areas where commercial and not-for-profit accounting software capabilities might differ:

- *Fund Accounting*—If the organization has many different funds, the selected software must be able to maintain a balanced set of books and report on each fund separately and also consolidated. This may not be easy for some software that is not specifically designed with fund accounting in mind. There are "fund accounting" systems on the market that simplify meeting this requirement.

- *Grants Accounting*—If the organization must keep track of restricted grants and must report its accounting back to the grantor,

---

[15] Don't just look for these features in the accounting software. Make sure the ease of use is also evaluated. Many packages can be made to accomplish almost anything. It's *how* it accomplishes the functions that can make the difference between a mediocre and great package.

there are a few system capabilities to look for. Similar to fund accounting, the system must be able to separately report on each grant. An additional complexity is the ability to report on the grant from its inception to date. This could mean being able to accumulate the grant expense history across fiscal year-ends. Therefore, the system must be able to generate reports for multiple years and for user-defined periods of time. Some commercial accounting systems do not handle multiple year reporting very well. There are accounting systems on the market that specialize in "grants accounting."

- *Encumbrance Accounting*—The ability to control budgets by· keeping track of purchase commitments, plus invoices, less credits and closed purchase orders is very complicated and is among the more difficult not-for-profit requirements to satisfy with commercial accounting software. This capability is generally found in specialized accounting packages designed for the government or for universities.

- *Financial Reporting*—Many not-for-profits have more complex financial report presentation requirements than commercial businesses. Not-for-profits often require the ability to present functional financial statements as well as to report by account classification. Some commercial accounting packages cannot handle this type of matrix reporting[16] (with accounts listed down the page and functions or funds across the top). Others may offer an additional report-writing module to provide this ability. It is important to verify that the software will be able to generate the types of reports required by the organization. This matrix reporting ability is provided by many specialized not-for-profit accounting packages.

(b) Steps to Selecting the Right Accounting Software

There are some general steps that should be followed in selecting the accounting software that is best suited for the organization. There are hundreds of accounting packages to choose from and no two provide exactly the same features and capabilities. Similarly, no two organizations have exactly the same requirements. Without having a system custom-developed for the organization, which could be cost prohibitive, there rarely will be a "perfect" match. However, by following the steps

---

[16] The basic report-writer of many commercial accounting packages simply lists the accounts or account categories down the page (in the rows), and the columns across the page represent periods of time and/or budget versus actual amounts.

suggested below you will increase the odds of selecting the best match without requiring much, if any, modification to the software.

The following are the typical steps to software selection:

1. *Determine the requirements that must be met by the software.*
   —include those who are to produce and use the information which is to be processed in the requirements determination process
   —concentrate on critical and unusual requirements
   —consider system-generated calculations
   —define all significant reporting requirements
   —consider nature and sources of transactions
   —consider required interfaces among modules and with other systems
   —consider any limitations on computer hardware[17] or costs
   —prioritize requirements by importance

2. *Identify likely packages for detailed review.*
   —use requirements list to screen potential vendors for suitability
   —focus on critical and unusual requirements
   —eliminate obviously unsuitable packages based on requirements and/or cost
   —narrow the list to two or three vendors

3. *Perform a detailed evaluation of the finalist vendors.*
   —prepare a detailed list of questions to ask each vendor
   —arrange to have the vendor provide a detailed demonstration of the accounting modules being considered
   —evaluate functionality and ease of use
   —obtain examples of reports produced by the system
   —obtain examples of documentation and manuals provided by the vendor
   —obtain financial information and business history of the vendor (especially if not well-known)
   —obtain at least three references from each vendor, preferably similar organizations

---

[17] The reader will note that this chapter has been focusing on the functional aspects of the accounting software and not on the potential computer hardware requirements. This is intentional because the more important decision should be selecting the right software, which will in turn determine the hardware requirements. However, if there are limitations on the hardware that will be used by the organization, this information must be considered as a requirement for the software.

4. *Contact vendor references.*

   Develop questions to ask references, including the following:

   —perception of software strengths and weaknesses

   —software problems encountered and limitations

   —ease of use, ease of implementation

   —report-writing capabilities and ease

   —modifications made to the software

   —availability and adequacy of vendor training and documentation

   —vendor support and responsiveness (e.g., local presence, telephone assistance, response time to inquiries)

   —satisfaction with software performance

5. *Obtain and compare cost information.*

   Consider all potential costs and compare each candidate vendor:

   —computer equipment requirements

   —accounting modules

   —other software (e.g., additional software required to operate the vendor's accounting software)

   —cost for installation, modifications, data conversion, training, other additional costs to implement the system[18, 19]

   —on-going maintenance costs (annual expenses for both hardware and software)

6. *Make a selection.*

   —be willing to compromise

   —consider alternatives for missing requirements

   —select the software vendor with the best overall match

   —base final decision on value, not just lowest cost

---

[18] There is a difference between "installing" the system and "implementing" the system that many first-time computer users are not familiar with. The accounting software is "installed" when it is loaded on the computer; being installed does not make it ready for use. "Implementation" is the series of tasks and steps required to initially set up a new automated system. There are many decisions that must be made, options within the software package selected, chart of accounts and reports designed and developed, and initial accounting data entered in order to tailor the package to the organization. Major implementation tasks are discussed later in this chapter.

[19] Make sure there is a very clear understanding regarding the services the software vendor, third-party dealer, and software consultant will provide and for what cost. Many vendors only sell their software through a third-party dealer, and if this is the case, the third-party dealer will most likely charge an hourly rate or monthly fee for any services. Based on the understanding of the services provided by the software vendor or third-party dealer, you will have a better idea of where additional assistance from an independent consultant will be required.

It is tempting to bypass some or all of these steps and select accounting software based on a single recommendation or on hearsay regarding a package's reputation. Automated accounting software represents a major investment for many organizations; being too hasty in its selection can be a costly mistake.

34.4 IMPLEMENTING THE NEW SYSTEM

Critical factors to ensure a successful implementation are to have a detailed plan, timetable, and staff resources to complete the necessary tasks. Don't underestimate the time, effort, and hidden costs required to implement the system. The timing of the implementation is also important. If the accounting staff are under stress keeping up with the current system, consider the additional stress of implementing and learning a new system at the same time. Some organizations will engage consultants to help implement the system and/or hire temporary staff to help keep up with the old system during the implementation period.

An important starting point is to train the users in the new system. The best software will not work well if the users do not know how to operate it. The primary system users (who should have been involved in the automation process from the beginning) should receive training early in the implementation and be involved in the implementation tasks.

Depending on the sophistication and complexity of the selected package, the following tasks would typically be included in a general ledger and accounts payable system implementation. (Similar tasks would be required for other automated accounting modules.)

- Site preparation for hardware and software installation
- Order required forms and supplies (e.g., custom checks)
- Definition of data system security and software backup procedures
- Definition of the chart of accounts and subaccounts
- General ledger reporting definitions
- Definition of general ledger journal types and other coding structures
- Accounts payable vendor master file definition
- Loading and configuration of the application system software
- Loading initial tables
- Loading chart of accounts
- Customization of interfaces

- Conversion of data:
  —plan approach, cut-off dates, and crosswalks of data from old to new system
  —conversion data entry (e.g., beginning balances, open invoices)
  —conversion data reconciliation
- System administrator training (hardware and software trouble-shooting)
- User application training
- Financial report formatting and customization
- Preparation of procedures and custom documentation
- Parallel processing period using both the old and new system and comparing results
- Developing month-end closing, historical data archiving, year-end closing guidelines.

One of the most critical implementation tasks for a new accounting system is the chart of accounts definition. The chart of accounts should include cost centers, project accounts, the organization structure, and anything requiring reports. A properly designed chart of accounts (discussed in Chapter 33) will take all reporting requirements into consideration, will result in the ability to generate meaningful reports, and will reduce the effort in producing financial statements. There may be system restrictions both on how the chart of accounts can be established and on how the software report-writer will work with the chart of accounts. Therefore, it is advisable to obtain professional assistance from your external accountant or a qualified accounting software consultant when you first set up the chart of accounts for the new system.

34.5   COMMON PITFALLS TO SUCCESSFUL AUTOMATION

Sometimes the pressure to automate outweighs the need to spend the time and resources required to properly implement the system. The following are some of the most common pitfalls that could jeopardize the success of automating the accounting records.

- *Not defining requirements, or selecting the software for the wrong reason.* After the software is purchased and you discover your mistake, it cannot be returned. Don't purchase software without having a reasonable basis for its selection. Also, don't purchase a system that is too complex for your organization. Be aware that with increased system flexibility and functionality comes greater complexity. More highly skilled staff are required to deal with the more complex systems.

- *Purchasing the hardware and operating system[20] before making the software selection.* The users' requirements should determine the software selection; the selected software should determine the hardware and operating system requirements. Unless the already installed hardware and operating system happens to be widely used, the choice of accounting software may be severely limited. Also, hardware upgrades may be required sooner and at a greater cost than if the hardware decision had been delayed and coordinated with the software selection.

- *Purchasing a software package and then heavily modifying it.* A heavily modified software package poses several problems. First, the software vendor will not support it, or if it does support it the cost will be greater than for an unmodified version. Second, modifying the package increases the risk that the software will not function as well as desired and could introduce unforeseen problems in other parts of the software. Third, the organization will need to make sure there are qualified staff (internal or external) who can support the modified system. If extensive modifications seem to be necessary, either consider alternative processing methods, or consider having a system custom-developed.

- *Inadequate user training and cross-training.* If the users do not have adequate training, the result could be improper use of the system and unreliable financial data. In addition to training the primary system user, make sure there is at least one back-up person trained in the system in case the primary user leaves or is away.

- *Trying to automate too much at once.* There are no requirements that all accounting modules must be implemented at the same time. Also, it may not be cost-effective or prudent to automate all accounting functions. Remember that implementing a new system adds unscheduled work to the day-to-day operations of your organization. The systems should be implemented at a pace you can deal with to reduce errors.

- *Inadequate procedures and documentation.* The new automated system may come with user manuals that describe how to use the

---

[20] Operating system is the collection of programs that control a computer's internal functions. A specific type of hardware might be able to run different operating systems (for example, a microcomputer might be able to run DOS, OS/2, or UNIX operating systems), but a software package might be written to work only with a specific operating system.

system. What the software vendor won't provide, however, are procedures for incorporating the system into your manual procedures to fit your organization. Supplementary procedures, forms, and checklists will need to be developed to tailor the system to your organization.

- *Poorly designed chart of accounts and reports.* This cannot be stressed enough. A well-designed chart of accounts makes a major difference in the performance of an automated accounting system. The chart of accounts is the backbone to the reporting capabilities of the system. If the chart of accounts is not designed to capture the data to the level of detail required, no report-writer in the world can produce the reports desired. If the organization believes that its current automated system needs replacing, it should first analyze the chart of accounts. Often "poor" systems can be salvaged through redesigning the chart of accounts and reports.

- *Poor back-up and recovery procedures.* The system may be successfully implemented, and everything working fine, when all of a sudden a hardware problem or electrical failure causes the system to lose its data. Procedures need to be in place to make sure the automated programs and data are backed up frequently and stored in a safe, off-site location. This is important to make sure your organization does not lose important data should something happen to the computer or your office space.

34.6 CONCLUSION

Very small organizations may outgrow a checkbook system and move on to a manual double entry ledger system. As time goes on and the organization grows in size and complexity, the manual system may become too cumbersome and automating the accounting records is considered. There are many issues to consider and decisions to make before automating the accounting records. Through careful requirements definition, evaluation of the software alternatives, and implementation, the automation can be a success. However, a not-for-profit organization should not feel compelled to automate all of its accounting functions or to automate everything at once. A well-planned approach to automation will help the organization maximize its resources.

Use of Rulings and Underscorings

One of the areas that causes confusion to the average reader of a financial statement is the number of rulings or underscores on a financial statement. What do they mean? When is something underscored? The rules are straightforward although somewhat complicated in application:

1. A figure is underscored when you want to indicate that you are adding all figures above the line to come to a total or subtotal which will be shown immediately below the line:

$$
\begin{array}{r}
1,139 \\
1,849 \\
\underline{590} \\
3,578
\end{array}
$$

The line here means that everything above the line adds down to the figure below the line (3,578).

2. A single row of figures is underscored where you want to indicate that this single row of figures is not going to be added into the figures immediately below the line. Notice that this occurs only when there is a single row of figures, and not several rows:

$$
\begin{array}{r}
\underline{1,139} \\
1,849 \\
\underline{590} \\
2,439
\end{array}
$$

The 1,139 is not added into the figures below because there is only the single row above the line.

3. A double underscore is used to indicate that absolutely nothing more is carried below this point in this column:

$$
\begin{array}{r}
1,849 \\
\underline{590} \\
\underline{\underline{2,439}} \\
\\
23 \\
\underline{161} \\
\overline{184}
\end{array}
$$

4. If there are several sets of underscored figures which are subtotals, and you want to add all these subtotals together, the figure directly above the final total will be underscored and the final total will be double underscored:

$$
\begin{array}{r}
\underline{1,139} \\
\\
1,849 \\
\underline{590} \\
\\
\underline{2,439} \\
\underline{\underline{3,578}}
\end{array}
$$

Here is an example showing all the possibilities:

Cash in bank	$ 1,000
Cash in petty cash	100
	1,100
Accounts receivable-trade	133,000
Accounts receivable-other	23,000
	156,000
Total current assets	157,100
Fixed assets:	
Land	25,000
Building	116,000
Less accumulated depreciation	(65,000)
	76,000
Total assets	$233,100

The statements should be designed to avoid subtotals as much as possible to reduce possible reader confusion. Two columns can be used to help avoid confusion. Here is the above statement in a two column approach:

Cash in bank	$ 1,000	
Cash in petty cash	100	$ 1,100
Accounts receivable:		
Trade	133,000	
Other	23,000	156,000
Total current assets		157,100
Fixed assets:		
Land	25,000	
Building	116,000	
Less accumulated depreciation	(65,000)	76,000
Total assets		$233,100

As with most other reporting problems, care must be taken to minimize reader confusion. If the treasurer constantly keeps this in mind, the
more complicated presentations can often be presented in a straightforward fashion that will increase reader comprehension without unduly
cutting back on details.

A P P E N D I X   B

Accounting and Disclosure Checklist for Not-for-Profit Organizations*

The following checklist is intended for use in connection with financial statements of not-for-profit organizations covered by the following AICPA documents:

- Industry Audit Guides:
  - —Audits of Colleges and Universities
  - —Audits of Voluntary Health and Welfare Organizations ("VHW")
- Statement of Position No. 78-10, Accounting Principles and Reporting Practices for Certain Nonprofit Organizations ("SOP") (included in the Audit and Accounting Guide, Audits of Certain Nonprofit Organizations). (It is not designed to cover organizations which follow the State and Local Government or the Health Care Providers audit guides.)

This checklist is *not* an audit program, and does not include all matters included in authoritative literature; rather it highlights matters relating to accounting principles, and reporting practices (such as financial statement format and disclosures) which are unique to not-for-profit organizations or call for special attention in the not-for-profit environment.

---

* Note: This version of this checklist reflects the requirements of Statements of Financial Accounting Standards Nos. 116 and 117. It should be used by organizations that have adopted the new FASB statements. Organizations that have not yet adopted the new FASB statements should follow the version of the checklist found at Appendix B of the 1994 Cumulative Supplement to the fourth edition of this book.

As with all accounting and reporting principles, materiality should be considered when using the checklist.

The above audit guides and SOP differ in some of their requirements. These differences are noted in relevant items on the checklist. The absence of a reference to a particular document or type of organization indicates that the requirements of the three AICPA documents are the same in that area. When SFAS No. 116 or No. 117 have superseded a provision of an audit guide or SOP, the checklist refers to the requirement in SFAS No. 116 or No. 117.

SOP 78-10 is not "effective" (as of November 1994) and, hence, compliance with its provisions is not mandatory. Therefore, a "no" answer to a question relating to the SOP does not necessarily mean that the auditor's opinion must take exception to the item. (In the case of an accounting change, or initial adoption of an accounting principle, the requirements of SAS No. 69 must be considered, however.) In addition, it should be noted that the AICPA is preparing a new audit guide which will supersede the SOP (as well as the two guides listed above); this guide is presently planned for issuance in 1995.

	Yes	No	N/A

General

1. Are all required financial statements presented, including statements of:
   (a) Functional Expenses (for VHW organizations only: SFAS No. 117, par. 26) ___ ___ ___
   (b) Cash Flows (SFAS No. 117, par. 29–30; SFAS No. 95) ___ ___ ___

2. Does it appear that the financial statement format (columnar vs. layered) is preferable for the organization? (No particular format is mandatory, however.) ___ ___ ___

3. Does the accounting policies footnote include descriptions of significant accounting policies, including particularly those relating to the classes of net assets (funds), restricted revenue, pledges (unconditional promises to give), contributions made, contributed services and materials, functional allocation of expenses, membership dues, related organizations, bequests, museum collections, valuation of investments, capital gains/losses, long-lived assets, and a measure of operations, as appropriate? ___ ___ ___

4. If any accounting changes have occurred, are they in conformity with SFAS No. 116 and No. 117 and APB No. 20? ___ ___ ___

	Yes	No	N/A

5. If the basis of accounting is other than GAAP, has SAS No. 62 been complied with? ___ ___ ___

6. Where affiliated or related organizations exist:
   (a) if they meet the criteria for inclusion in the financial statements of the reporting entity, are these organizations included? (SOP No. 94-3) ___ ___ ___
   (b) if they do not meet the criteria for inclusion, is the relationship disclosed? (SFAS No. 57) ___ ___ ___

7. With respect to disclosure of related party transactions, has consideration been given to transactions with chapters, foundations, student organizations, auxiliaries, guilds, circles, lodges, fund-raising organizations, trusts, and other related entities (including board and committee members and staff, and other organizations with which such persons are affiliated)? ___ ___ ___
   (a) Are trusts for the benefit of the reporting organization, but not under its control, disclosed? ___ ___ ___

8. If the financial statements cover less than the entire organization (e.g. a fund, department, branch, grant, etc.) do the statements, footnotes, and the auditor's report clearly indicate what is included, what is not included, and relationships between them? ___ ___ ___

9. If the organization has chosen to present an intermediate measure of operations, have the requirements of SFAS No. 117 par. 23 been complied with, and is the classification of items as operating and non-operating appropriate? ___ ___ ___

10. Is the change in net assets clearly shown, in total and for each class? ___ ___ ___

11. Have the requirements of SFAS No. 117 par. 12, regarding information about liquidity been complied with? ___ ___ ___
    (a) If a classified balance sheet is presented, are current items appropriately categorized? (SOP par. 23–24; ARB No. 43, Chapter 3A) ___ ___ ___

Classes of net assets

12. Are all legally unrestricted income and net assets (including quasi-endowment and other board-designated amounts) reported in the same income statement? ___ ___ ___

	Yes	No	N/A

(a) If unrestricted amounts are shown in more than one column (not preferable), are the totals thereof clearly shown? ____ ____ ____

13. Are all funds of the organization reported in the financial statements? ____ ____ ____

14. Where a multi-columnar format is used for the balance sheet, are total assets, liabilities, and net assets presented? (SFAS No. 117, par. 10) ____ ____ ____

15. If only a total column is presented for the preceding year and if a two-year opinion is to be issued, are all required disclosures made with respect to the preceding year? (See also SAS No. 58, footnote 27) ____ ____ ____

16. Do temporarily and permanently restricted net assets include only amounts restricted by outside donors, and are all restricted net assets clearly disclosed? ____ ____ ____

17. If the organization has chosen to present restricted contributions whose restrictions are met in the same period as unrestricted revenue, has this policy been followed consistently for all such contributions, and is the policy disclosed? (SFAS No. 116, par. 14) ____ ____ ____

18. Are all intra-class transfers (e.g., the establishment of a quasi-endowment fund within the unrestricted class) shown in such a manner that they are clearly not revenue or expense of either subclass? ____ ____ ____

19. Are interclass receivables and payables clearly disclosed (if a multiclass balance sheet is presented, or if the criteria in SOP par. 119 are met)? (Also see SFAS No. 117, footnote 8 to par. 85) ____ ____ ____
    (a) If repayment of borrowings appears in doubt, are they recorded as transfers? (SOP par. 118, College p. 10) ____ ____ ____

Assets

20. Are unconditional promises to give (pledges receivable), including any required allowance for estimated uncollectible amounts, properly recorded as assets? ____ ____ ____
    (a) Have the provisions of APB 21, with respect to discounting been appropriately applied? (SFAS No. 116, par. 20) ____ ____ ____
        i. Is accretion of the discount recorded as contributions, not interest? (SFAS No. 116, par. 20, second sentence) ____ ____ ____

	Yes	No	N/A

(b) Were the auditors able to perform appropriate confirmation procedures or, if not, is their report appropriately modified? (VHW pp. 18–19) ___ ___ ___

21. Has appropriate disclosure of the following been made:
 (a) maturity schedule of unconditional promises to give? (SFAS No. 116, par. 24a) ___ ___ ___
 (b) allowance for estimated uncollectible pledges receivable? (SFAS No. 116, par. 24b) ___ ___ ___
 (c) conditional promises to give? (SFAS No. 116, par. 25) ___ ___ ___
 (d) any concentrations of credit risk? (SFAS No. 105, par. 20) ___ ___ ___

22. Are bequests receivable recorded, when they qualify as unconditional promises to give? ___ ___ ___

23. Are investments appropriately valued?
 (a) VHW: Cost or market? (p. 6) ___ ___ ___
 (b) College: Cost or market? (p. 8) ___ ___ ___
 (c) SOP: (par. 79)
  i. Stocks at market, or lower of cost or market? ___ ___ ___
  ii. Bonds at market, or lower of cost or market, or amortized cost (if to be held to maturity)? ___ ___ ___
  iii. Other investments at fair value, or lower of cost or fair value? ___ ___ ___

24. When investments are carried at cost, is current market value disclosed? (SFAS No. 107) ___ ___ ___
 (a) When investments are carried at market, is cost disclosed? (VHW) ___ ___ ___

25. When investments from more than one fund are managed in a pooled account, are transactions in the account recorded using the market value method (even though the underlying accounting records may be kept on some other basis)? ___ ___ ___

26. Are fixed assets capitalized? (Optional for museum collections—see 26a.) ___ ___ ___
 (a) If collection items are not capitalized, have the requirements of SFAS No. 116 par. 11–13 (with regard to meeting the criteria for non-capitalization, method of recording accessions and deaccessions, and required footnote disclosures) been met? ___ ___ ___

27. If the organization has adopted a policy that the restriction on donated fixed assets expires ratably over the life of the assets, has this policy been followed consistently for all such assets? (SFAS No. 116, par. 16) ___ ___ ___

	Yes	No	N/A

28. Are long-lived tangible assets depreciated? (SFAS No. 93) (Optional for individual works of art and historical treasures, if the criteria in paragraph 6 of SFAS No. 93 are met.) _____ _____ _____
    (a) If a college presents a separate plant fund, is depreciation reported only in that fund? (pp. 9–10) _____ _____ _____

29. Are the nature and the cost or contributed value of current-period accessions, and the nature of and proceeds from deaccessions of museum collections disclosed? (SOP par. 114) _____ _____ _____

Liabilities and Net Assets (see also Revenue Recognition)

30. Are the following disclosed:
    (a) the status of the organization under applicable income tax laws? _____ _____ _____
    (b) any contingent tax liabilities? _____ _____ _____
    (c) any contingent liabilities under government grants or contracts? _____ _____ _____

31. Do the financial statements, footnotes and other printed material included in the annual report contain no language which might reflect adversely on the organization's tax status (such as language which might cause the IRS to assert that the organization: is a private foundation (if it is not), is subject to tax on unrelated business income, is engaged in activities which might jeopardize its tax-exempt status, or is subject to any penalty taxes)? _____ _____ _____

32. If the organization makes contributions to others, is a liability for unpaid unconditional pledges (including future installments of multi-year pledges) recorded as an expense and a liability at the time the recipient is entitled to the contribution? (SFAS No. 116, par. 18; SOP par. 101) _____ _____ _____

33. Are compensated absences, including sabbatical leave, properly accounted for? (SFAS No. 43) _____ _____ _____

34. Are encumbrances and other commitments not meeting the criteria of SFAS No. 5 *not* recorded as liabilities? _____ _____ _____

35. If net assets have been appropriated, is the financial statement presentation such that it is clear that such appropriations are *not* expenses or liabilities, but are part of net assets? _____ _____ _____

	Yes	No	N/A

Revenue Recognition

Contributions received:

36. Have receipts which are in substance purchases of goods or services, and transfers of assets in which the reporting entity acts as an agent, trustee, or intermediary, rather than a donor or donee, been excluded from application of the requirements of SFAS No. 116? (SFAS No. 116, par. 3, 4) ___ ___ ___

37. Has the contribution element of bargain sales and purchases been appropriately recorded? (SFAS No. 116, par. 3, last sentence) ___ ___ ___

38. Non-cash donations (including materials, facilities, and services):
    (a) Have donated securities, land, buildings, use of facilities or utilities, materials and supplies, and intangible assets been recorded where appropriate? (SFAS No. 116, par. 5) ___ ___ ___
    (b) Have contributed services which meet the criteria in SFAS No. 116 par. 9 been recorded, and others not recorded? ___ ___ ___
    (c) Have the disclosures regarding contributed services required by SFAS No. 116 par. 10 been made? ___ ___ ___

39. Are all gifts, grants, unconditional pledges and other contributions, whether or not restricted by a donor for a particular purpose or for a particular time period, recorded as revenue when received? (SFAS No. 116, par. 8) ___ ___ ___
    (a) Are they reported in the class of net assets appropriate to any donor restrictions? ___ ___ ___
    (b) Are pledges due in future periods reported as restricted support, unless clear donor intentions indicate otherwise? (SFAS No. 116, par. 15) ___ ___ ___

Other revenue:

40. Gross amounts of revenue and expenses:
    (a) If investment revenues are reported net of related expenses, is the amount of expenses disclosed? (SFAS No. 117, par. 24) ___ ___ ___
    (b) "Special" fund-raising events: (similar logic applies to sales/cost of sales)
        i.   If direct expenses benefitting participants are netted against revenues, does the event meet

the definition of peripheral or incidental transactions? (SFAS No. 117, par. 138; SFAC 6,
par. 82-89)   ____ ____ ____

    ii.   If special events do not qualify as peripheral or
incidental transactions, are both gross revenue
and gross expenses from the events reported
in the statement of activity? (SFAS No. 117,
par. 24, 25, 138; see also SOP par. 93, VHW
p. 42) (Note: it is permissible to present expenses which directly benefit participants as
a deduction, on the face of the statement im-
mediately following the revenue.)   ____ ____ ____

(c)   Are all other revenues and expenses presented
gross? (SFAS No. 117, par. 24)   ____ ____ ____

41. Are membership dues (including "life membership"
dues) recognized as revenue ratably over the periods
during which members are entitled to services? (SOP
par. 84)   ____ ____ ____

42. Is investment income recorded directly in the fund
appropriate to the nature of any restriction on the
income?   ____ ____ ____

43. Are realized and unrealized capital gains recorded in the
unrestricted class of net assets, unless there are explicit
donor stipulations or applicable law which require other-
wise? (SFAS No. 117, par. 22)   ____ ____ ____

(a)   Is the organization's determination of the amount of
capital gains which must be retained permanently,
appropriate under relevant law?   ____ ____ ____

44. Are total capital gains (realized and unrealized) and
investment income disclosed? (SOP par. 83, College
p. 9)   ____ ____ ____

Expenses

45. Are expenses reported on a functional basis, either on
the face of the statement or in a note? (SFAS No. 117,
par. 26)   ____ ____ ____

46. Are all expenses reported in the unrestricted class?
(SFAS No. 117, par. 20)   ____ ____ ____

47. Have expenses which apply to more than one function
been appropriately allocated? (SOP No. 87-2)   ____ ____ ____

	Yes	No	N/A

48. Have all applicable expenses, including a portion of management salaries, depreciation, and other occupancy expenses been included with fundraising expenses? ___ ___ ___

49. Where an organization remits a portion of its receipts to an affiliate, is this amount properly reported? (VHW p. 29, SOP par. 90) ___ ___ ___

50. If expenses have been incurred for purposes for which both unrestricted and temporarily restricted net assets are available, has the organization appropriately reclassified temporarily restricted net assets to unrestricted net assets in accordance with SFAS No. 116 par. 17, third sentence? ___ ___ ___

Adoption of SFAS No. 116 and No. 117

51. Has the organization appropriately reclassified its funds into classes for financial statement purposes? (See Chapter 13 of this book) ___ ___ ___

52. If the organization intends to adopt SFAS No. 116 and No. 117 as of the one-year delayed effective date for small organizations, does it meet the size criteria in SFAS No. 116 par. 28 and SFAS No. 117 par. 31? ___ ___ ___

Implementation of
SFAS No. 116 and No. 117

Many matters related to implementation of these new standards are discussed in various chapters throughout this book. This appendix lists, in convenient reference format, various matters which organizations must consider prior to implementation. ("We," in these lists refers to the organization implementing the standards.)

DECISIONS TO BE MADE

These are all free-choice decisions permitted by the two statements. Organizations may choose either option.

- Restricted contributions:

  Do we wish to report restricted contributions whose restrictions are met in the same accounting period as that in which they are received as restricted or as unrestricted support (SFAS No. 116—Contributions ¶ 14—third sentence).

  Do we wish to adopt a policy which implies that on gifts of long-lived assets there exists a time restriction which expires over the useful life of the donated assets? (Contributions ¶ 16)

- Basic financial statement format:

  What titles do we wish to use for the balance sheet and for the statement of activity? (No particular titles are required or precluded by SFAS No. 117.)

  Do we wish to present additional detail in the statement of financial position of assets and liabilities by class or some other subdivision? (SFAS No. 117—Display ¶ 156—next-to-last sentence.)

Which of the sample formats for the Statement of Activities do we wish to follow? (Display ¶ 157 and the examples which follow)

Do we wish to present a measure of "operations?" (Display ¶¶ 23, 163–167) (See Appendix 14–B for further guidance.)

Do we wish to prepare the statement of cash flows using the direct or the indirect method? (SFAS No. 95, "Statement of Cash Flows," ¶¶ 27–28)

Do we wish to present comparative financial data for prior year(s)? (Display ¶ 70)

- Classification of expenses:

On the face of the statement of activities, do we wish to categorize expenses by functional or by natural classifications? (Display ¶ 26—second and third lines)

If we are not required to disclose expenses in natural categories, do we wish to make such disclosure voluntarily? (Display ¶ 26—last sentence)

If expenses have not previously been categorized by function, what categories (beyond the basic categories of program, management, fundraising, membership-development) do we wish to present? (Display ¶¶ 26–28)

- Do we wish to disclose the fair value of contributed services received but not recognized as revenues? (Contributions ¶ 10—last sentence)

- Collection items:

If our organization has assets which meet the definition of collection items at Contributions ¶ 11, do we wish to capitalize these assets or not?

If we have not previously capitalized but now wish to capitalize these items, do we wish to do so retroactively, or only prospectively? (Contributions ¶ 12)

If we choose to capitalize these items retroactively, how do we wish to determine their value for this purpose? (Contributions, footnote 4)

- Do we wish to present nonmonetary information, as discussed in Display footnote 6?

- Adoption date: (Contributions ¶ 28; Display ¶ 31)

Do we wish to adopt the standards earlier than the required adoption date?

If we qualify as a "small" organization (total assets less than $5 million and annual expenses less than $1 million), do we wish to delay adoption until the later permitted date?

Do we wish to adopt the contributions standard retroactively or prospectively?

If we choose to adopt the contributions standard retroactively, do we wish to adopt ¶ 17 (relating to recognition of expiration of restrictions) prospectively? (¶ 30)

- Do we wish to retain our present fund *accounting* system and convert our financial data to the new class structure by worksheets prior to preparing the financial statements, or do we wish to convert our entire accounting system to reflect the three-class structure discussed at SFAS No. 117 ¶ 13 and Appendix D?

EXTENT OF APPLICABILITY TO TRANSACTIONS ENGAGED IN BY OUR ORGANIZATION

This list identifies accounting and reporting areas for further consideration.

- Scope of Contributions statement:

  Do we receive "contributions" which are in substance purchases of goods or services? (SFAS No. 116—Contributions ¶ 3)—See Appendix 10–B for further guidance.

  Do we receive or make "contributions" for which we are merely acting as an agent, trustee, or intermediary, rather than as donor or donee? (Contributions ¶ 4)—See Appendix 9–A for further guidance.

  To what extent do we engage in transactions which are at least partly bargain sales/purchases, and thus have a contribution element inherent in them? (Contributions ¶ 3—last sentence)

- Promises to give:

  Which of our pledges/promises-to-give meet the criteria for recognition in Contributions ¶¶ 5–7, 22, 23?—See also Appendix 10–E for further guidance.

  Which of our pledges/promises-to-give are considered conditional, for purposes of the disclosure required by ¶ 25? (Contributions ¶¶ 6, 7, 22, 23)—See also Appendix 10–F for further guidance.

- Contributed services of volunteers:

  Which of our contributed services are considered to require specialized skills? (Contributions ¶ 9)—See also Appendix 10–C for further guidance.

  Would the organization typically need to purchase the services if not provided by donation? (Contributions ¶ 9)—See also Appendix 10–D for further guidance.

- Do we have any assets which are "collection items" (works of art, historical treasures, and similar assets) which meet the criteria for non-recognition in Contributions ¶ 11?

- Capital gains on endowment assets: (Display ¶ 22)

  To what extent do the laws of the political jurisdictions to which we are subject require capital gains on donor-restricted net assets to be retained in a restricted fund, or permit such gains to be used for general purposes at the discretion of the organization's governing board?

  To what extent have donors of endowment assets explicitly stipulated that capital gains on such assets are restricted?

  If, based on the answers to the two preceding questions, it is determined that some amounts of capital gains previously recorded as restricted are in fact unrestricted under SFAS No. 117, what is the amount which must be reclassified?

- To what extent do we incur expenses that are for purposes directly attributable to and reimbursed by specific external sources of revenue as discussed in Contributions ¶ 17?

- If we have elected retroactive adoption of ¶ 17 of SFAS No. 116, what is the amount which must be reclassified from restricted to unrestricted net assets?

OTHER MATTERS

- Change the term "fund balance" to "net assets" on the balance sheet.
- If we previously have been netting amounts of revenues and expenses which do not meet the criteria for netting in ¶¶ 24–25 of SFAS No. 117, gross those amounts back up.
- Prepare a statement of cash flows in accordance with SFAS No. 95, if not previously done.
- Categorize expenses by function, if not previously done.

Bibliography

Adams, J. B., Bossio, R. J., and Rohan, P., *Accounting for Contributed Services: Survey of Preparers and Users of Financial Statements of Not-for-Profit Organizations*, Financial Accounting Standards Board, Norwalk, CT, 1989.

American Institute of Certified Public Accountants, New York:

Accounting Standards Division, "Accounting for Joint Costs of Informational Materials and Activities of Not-for-Profit Organizations that Include a Fund-Raising Appeal," Statement of Position No. 87-2, 1987. (In process of revision)

Accounting Standards Division, "The Application of the Requirements of Accounting Research Bulletins, Opinions of the Accounting Principles Board, and Statements and Interpretations of the Financial Accounting Standards Board to Not-for-Profit Organizations," Statement of Position No. 94-2, 1994.

Accounting Standards Division, "Reporting of Related Entities by Not-for-Profit Organizations," Statement of Position No. 94-3, 1994.

Auditing Standards Division, "Compliance Auditing Applicable to Governmental Entities and Other Recipients of Governmental Financial Assistance," Statement on Auditing Standards No. 68, 1991. (In process of revision)

Committee on College and University Accounting and Auditing, "Audits of Colleges and Universities, Including Statement of Position Issued by the Accounting Standards Division," Industry Audit Guide, 2nd ed., 1975. (In process of revision)

Committee on Not-for-Profit Organizations, "Audits of Not-for-Profit Organizations Receiving Federal Awards," Statement of Position No. 92-9, 1992.

Committee on Not-for-Profit Organizations, "Audit Guide for Not-for-Profit Organizations," to be published in 1995.

Committee on Voluntary Health and Welfare Organizations, "Audits of Voluntary Health and Welfare Organizations," Industry Audit Guide, 2nd ed., 1988. (In process of revision)

Health Care Committee, "Audits of Providers of Health Care Services, Including Statement of Position Issued by the Accounting Standards Division," Industry Audit Guide, 1990. (In process of revision)

Subcommittee on Nonprofit Organizations, "Audits of Certain Nonprofit Organizations," including "Accounting Principles and Reporting Practices for Certain Nonprofit Organizations," Statement of Position No. 78-10, 2nd ed., 1988. (In process of revision)

Anthony, R. N., *Financial Accounting in Nonbusiness Organizations: An Exploratory Study of Conceptual Issues*, Financial Accounting Standards Board, Norwalk, CT, 1978.

Anthony, R. N., and Young, D. W., *Management Control in Nonprofit Organizations*, Richard D. Irwin, Homewood, IL, 3rd ed., 1984.

Blazek, J., *Tax Planning and Compliance for Tax-Exempt Organizations: Forms, Checklists, Procedures*, John Wiley & Sons, New York, 2nd ed., 1993.

Cary, W. L., and Bright, C. B., *The Law and the Lore of Endowment Funds—Report to the Ford Foundation*, New York, 1969.

Daughtrey, W. H., Jr., and Gross, M. J., Jr., *Museum Accounting Handbook*, American Association of Museums, Washington, DC, 1978.

Financial Accounting Standards Board, Norwalk, CT:

Statements of Financial Accounting Concepts:

No. 4, "Objectives of Financial Reporting by Nonbusiness Organizations," 1980;

No. 6, "Elements of Financial Statements," 1985.

Statements of Financial Accounting Standards:

No. 93, "Recognition of Depreciation by Not-for-Profit Organizations," Norwalk, CT, 1987 (amended by No. 99, "Deferral of the Effective Date of Recognition of Depreciation by Not-for-Profit Organizations," 1988).

No. 95, "Statement of Cash Flows," 1987.

No. 116, "Accounting for Contributions Received and Contributions Made," 1993.

No. 117, "Financial Statements of Not-for-Profit Organizations," 1993.

Evangelical Joint Accounting Committee, "Accounting and Financial Reporting Guide for Christian Ministries," Christian Management Association, Diamond Bar, CA, 1987. (Revised edition to be published in 1995.)

Henke, E. O., *Introduction to Nonprofit Organization Accounting*, Kent Publishing Co., Boston, MA, 1980.

Holck, M., Jr., and Holck, M., Sr., *Complete Handbook of Church Accounting*, Prentice-Hall, Englewood Cliffs, NJ, 1978.

Holder, W. W., *The Not-for-Profit Organization Reporting Entity*, Philanthropy Monthly Press, New Milford, CT, 1986.

Hopkins, B. R., *A Legal Guide to Starting and Managing A Nonprofit Organization*, New York, John Wiley & Sons, 2nd ed., 1993.

Hopkins, B. R., *The Law of Tax-Exempt Organizations*, New York, John Wiley & Sons, 6th ed., 1992.

Hopkins, B. R., *The Law of Fund-Raising*, New York, John Wiley & Sons, 1991.

Hummel, J., *Starting and Running a Nonprofit Organization*, Minneapolis: University of Minnesota Press, 1980.

Larkin, R. F., "Accounting," Chapter 31 of *The Nonprofit Management Handbook— Operating Policies and Procedures*, New York, John Wiley & Sons, 1993; and 1994 Supplement.

Larkin, R. F., "Accounting Issues Relating to Fundraising," Chapter 2 of *Financial Practices for Effective Fundraising*, San Francisco, Jossey-Bass, Inc., 1994.

National Association of College and University Business Officers, *Financial Accounting and Reporting Manual for Higher Education*, Washington, DC, 1990. (In process of revision)

National Association of Independent Schools, *Business Management for Independent Schools*, 3rd ed., Boston: Author, 1987. (In process of revision)

National Health Council, National Assembly for Social Policy and Development, Inc., and United Way of America, *Standards of Accounting and Financial Reporting for Voluntary Health and Welfare Organizations*, 3rd ed., NHC, NASPD, and UWA, New York, 1988. (In process of revision)

Nelson, C. A., and Turk, F. J., *Financial Management for the Arts: A Guidebook for Arts Organizations*, Associated Councils of the Arts, New York, 1975.

Price Waterhouse, New York:

> *The Audit Committee, the Board of Trustees of Not-for-Profit Organizations and the Independent Accountant*, 1992.
>
> *Effective Internal Accounting Control for Nonprofit Organizations*, 1988.
>
> *Not-for-Profit Organizations' Implementation Guide for SFAS Statements 116 and 117*, 1993.
>
> *Position Paper on College and University Reporting*, 1975.
>
> *1982 Survey of Financial Reporting and Accounting Practices of Private Foundations*, 1982.

Ramanathan, K. V., *Management Control in Nonprofit Organizations*, John Wiley & Sons, New York, 1982.

United States Department of Health and Human Services, "Guidelines for Audits of Federal Awards to Nonprofit Organizations," DHHS, Washington, 1989.

United States General Accounting Office, "Government Auditing Standards," GAO, Washington, DC, 1994 Revision.

United States Office of Management and Budget Circulars, OMB, Washington:

> No. A-21, "Cost Principles for Educational Institutions," 1979. (In process of revision)
>
> No. A-110, "Uniform Administrative Requirements for Grants and Agreements with Institutions of Higher Education, Hospitals, and Other Nonprofit Organizations," 1993.

No. A-122, "Cost Principles for Nonprofit Organizations," 1980. (In process of revision)

No. A-128, "Audits of State and Local Governments," 1985. (In process of revision)

No. A-133, "Audits of Institutions of Higher Education and Other Non-profit Institutions," 1990. (In process of revision)

United States President's Council on Integrity & Efficiency, "Questions and Answers on OMB Circular A-133," Position Statement No. 6, PCIE, Washington, 1992.

United Way of America, Alexandria, Va.:

Accounting and Financial Reporting: A Guide for United Ways and Not-For Profit Human Service Organizations, 2nd ed., 1989.

Budgeting: A Guide for United Ways and Not-for-Profit Human Service Organizations, 1975.

UWASIS-II—United Way of America Services Identification Systems, Rev. Ed., 1976.

Wacht, R. F., *Financial Management in Nonprofit Organizations,* Georgia State University, Atlanta, GA, 1984.

Warshauer, W., Jr., and Larkin, R. F., "Not-for-Profit Organizations," Chapter 25 of the *Accountants' Handbook,* 7th ed., John Wiley & Sons, New York, 1990; and 1994 Cumulative Supplement (Larkin, R. F.).

Index